Roger Bacon's
Philosophy of Nature

ROGER BACON'S PHILOSOPHY OF NATURE

A Critical Edition, with English Translation,
Introduction, and Notes,
of *De multiplicatione specierum*
and *De speculis comburentibus*

═══

BY

DAVID C. LINDBERG

CLARENDON PRESS · OXFORD
1983

Oxford University Press, Walton Street, Oxford OX2 6DP
London Glasgow New York Toronto
Delhi Bombay Calcutta Madras Karachi
Kuala Lumpur Singapore Hong Kong Tokyo
Nairobi Dar es Salaam Cape Town
Melbourne Auckland
and associated companies in
Beirut Berlin Ibadan Mexico City Nicosia

Published in the United States by
Oxford University Press, New York

OXFORD *is a trade mark of Oxford University Press*

© *David C. Lindberg 1983*

British Library Cataloguing in Publication Data

Bacon, Roger
  Roger Bacon's philosophy of nature.
  1. Philosophy of nature
  I. Title   II. Lindberg, David C.
  113'.8   BD581

  ISBN 0–19–858164–5

Library of Congress Cataloging in Publication Data

Bacon, Roger, 1220?–1294?.
  Roger Bacon's philosophy of nature.

  Bibliography: p.
  Includes index.
  *1. Light—Early works to 1800.   2. Philosophy of
nature—Early works to 1800.   3. Bacon, Roger,
1220?–1292?   I. Lindberg, David C.   II. Bacon,
Roger, 1220?–1292?   De multiplicatione specierum.
De speculis comburentibus.   English & Latin.
1983   III. Title.*
  QC353.B313   1983   500   82–8159
  ISBN 0–19–858164–5   AACR2

Typeset by Joshua Associates, Oxford
Printed in Great Britain
at the University Press, Oxford
by Eric Buckley
Printer to the University

To
Greta, Christin, and Erik
who share my love for
the Oxford that nurtured Roger Bacon

Preface

ROGER BACON'S scientific achievement has been much discussed, but little understood. Generations of scholars, beginning with Emile Charles in the middle of the nineteenth century, tended to view Bacon as a man ahead of his time, a modern experimental scientist born out of season, and to credit him with major scientific discoveries and revolutionary methodological innovations. A reaction was inevitably provoked, and it became fashionable for a time to belittle Bacon's achievement. A more balanced picture has now begun to emerge, and it has become apparent (as we should have guessed) that Bacon was fully a man of the thirteenth century—a significant, perhaps brilliant, certainly influential, representative of many of its intellectual currents. He wrote on grammar, logic, astronomy, astrology, alchemy, medicine, moral philosophy, metaphysics, perception, the relationship between philosophy and theology, and a variety of physical topics. He praised the study of foreign languages and the pursuit of mathematical and experimental science. He was a pioneer in the assimilation of the philosophical and scientific works newly translated from Greek and Arabic, and a major disseminator of Greek and Arabic natural philosophy and mathematical science. He was, in many respects, a microcosm of thirteenth-century science and natural philosophy.

Central to Bacon's philosophy of nature was the doctrine that all natural causation occurs by a process of radiation—of which the radiation of light is a visible instance and, therefore, the paradigm case. Bacon thus believed that an investigation of the behaviour of light would lead to an understanding of nature's inner workings. Since the propagation of light is susceptible of geometrical analysis, it follows that mathematics has a place at the very centre of natural philosophy. In the prologue to the revised version of *De multiplicatione specierum*, after acknowledging that the science of optics is directed, strictly speaking, only toward sight, he adds:

Nevertheless, the principles and universal bases defined by authors of [works on] vision and aspects can and ought to be applied to the other senses—and not only to the senses, but to all the matter of the world altered by the species and powers of all agents whatsoever. And therefore the entire action of nature and the generation of natural things take their bases and principles from the aforementioned optical authors. (Appendix, α. 88–94)

This doctrine, which I shall refer to as the 'physics of light', appears

to have its roots in Neoplatonic philosophy, having been inspired
by a passage in Plotinus (d. 270), the founder of Neoplatonism. It
was further developed by the Muslim philosopher al-Kindī (d. c.873)
and the Christian scholar and churchman Robert Grosseteste (d. 1253).
It reached its fullest development in Bacon's *De multiplicatione
specierum*. The physics of light retained a following of at least
modest proportions until the end of the sixteenth century, John Dee
being its best known late representative.

What Bacon meant by 'species', when he spoke of its multiplication, is the virtue or likeness of any natural power, propagated from
that power in all directions through suitable media. For example,
the species or likeness of heat is multiplied or propagated in all
directions from a hot body to warm the surroundings and produce
a variety of other effects. *De multiplicatione specierum* is Bacon's
effort to deal systematically and rigorously with all the details and
implications of this process. In it, he inquires what kinds of entities
produce species; he considers their mode of generation and corruption; he explores the physics and mathematics of propagation; he
investigates the effects on recipients; and he examines the mixing
of species and their mode of existence in the medium. No other
medieval treatise explores these matters as thoroughly as *De
multiplicatione specierum*.

If *De multiplicatione specierum* develops a philosophy of natural
causation on an optical model, *De speculis comburentibus* contributes
to the optical model. *De speculis comburentibus* uses the last proposition of Euclid's *De speculis* (on burning mirrors) as an excuse for an
extended analysis of the modes of propagation of light—probably
the most original and rigorous mathematical analysis of the problem
in all of medieval Christendom.

This volume contains a new critical edition of these two treatises,
replacing the older, defective editions of Bridges (1897) and Combach
(1614). It also presents the first English translation of each treatise.
Translation is sometimes regarded as clerical work, the more-or-less
mechanical rendering of a treatise from one language into another
for the benefit of those who lack proper linguistic training. But in
fact every translation is an interpretation; and therefore, in translating Bacon, I am not merely compensating for somebody's linguistic
deficiencies, but offering a full and complete interpretation of two
Baconian treatises—an interpretation that takes into account every
word that he put into them. I do not, of course, claim infallibility
for my interpretations. Although I have attempted to remain faithful
to Bacon's every meaning, there is no possibility of translating
treatises as long and difficult as the two contained in this volume

without failing, on occasion, to understand precisely the author's intention. My translations should, therefore, be considered a contribution to Baconian scholarship on these two treatises, but surely not the final word.

Many friends and colleagues have helped me to achieve the level of understanding exhibited herein, and to them I express my deepest thanks. Alistair C. Crombie, Richard C. Dales, Girard J. Etzkorn, Edward Grant, John P. Hieronimus, Kent Kraft, Fannie J. LeMoine, Bruce MacLaren, Michael S. Mahoney, A. Mark Smith, Eleonore Stump, Katherine Tachau, Victor E. Thoren, G. J. Toomer, Sabetai Unguru, and William A. Wallace have all responded patiently to my queries and helped me to see what Bacon meant. Leonard E. Boyle offered invaluable aid by dating all of the manuscripts for me and providing descriptions of the scribal hands. Rennie Schoepflin and Jole Shackelford read proof and tracked down many of Bacon's citations. Lucinda Alwa, my relentless graduate assistant, checked the translation in its entirety, improved its flow, and challenged my interpretation of scores of passages; I am especially indebted to her. Lori Grant worked her usual magic at the typewriter. And my colleagues and students in the Department of the History of Science at the University of Wisconsin offered encouragement and inspiration.

I wish to thank a number of institutions for financial support: The John Simon Guggenheim Memorial Foundation for a year of fellowship support, 1977-8; the National Endowment for the Humanities for summer support under its translation grant program; the National Science Foundation for a summer research grant; and the Graduate School of the University of Wisconsin for both summer and academic-year support. Without their financial assistance, this edition and translation would not exist. I am grateful also to the many libraries that have generously allowed me access to their manuscript collections. Finally, I wish to thank Alistair Crombie and the Fellows of Trinity College, and William Urry and the Fellows of St. Edmund Hall, for offering me sanctuary during a year in Oxford, 1977-8.

D.C.L.

Contents

Abbreviations

References are usually given in full in the notes. The following sources, however, have been cited often enough to merit abbreviation.

Alhazen, *De aspectibus* Alhazen, *De aspectibus*, in *Opticae thesaurus Alhazeni Arabis libri septem* . . . , ed. Friedrich Risner (Basel, 1572).

Al-Kindī, *De aspectibus* Al-Kindī, *De aspectibus*, edd. Axel Anthon Björnbo and Sebastian Vogl, in 'Alkindi, Tideus und Pseudo-Euklid. Drei optische Werke', *Abhandlungen zur Geschichte der mathematischen Wissenschaften*, 26. 3 (1912), 3–41.

BGPM *Beiträge zur Geschichte der Philosophie des Mittelalters*, or *Beiträge zur Geschichte der Philosophie und Theologie des Mittelalters*.

Crowley Theodore Crowley, O.F.M., *Roger Bacon: The Problem of the Soul in His Philosophical Commentaries* (Louvain/Dublin, 1950).

DMS Roger Bacon, *De multiplicatione specierum* (the present edition and translation).

DSB *Dictionary of Scientific Biography*. 16 volumes (New York, 1970–80).

DSC Roger Bacon, *De speculis comburentibus* (the present edition and translation).

Easton Stewart Easton, *Roger Bacon and His Search for a Universal Science* (Oxford, 1952).

Elements (Heath) Euclid, *The Elements*, trans. Sir Thomas Heath, 2nd edn. 3 volumes (Cambridge, 1926).

Grant, *Source Book* Edward Grant (ed.), *A Source Book in Medieval Science* (Cambridge, Mass., 1974).

Lindberg, *Pecham and Optics* David C. Lindberg, *John Pecham and the Science of Optics: Perspectiva communis* (Madison, Wis., 1970).

Lindberg, *Science in the Middle Ages* David C. Lindberg (ed.), *Science in the Middle Ages* (Chicago, 1978).

Lindberg, *Theories of Vision* David C. Lindberg, *Theories of Vision from al-Kindi to Kepler* (Chicago, 1976).

Nascimento Carlos Arthur Ribeiro do Nascimento, 'Une théorie des opérations naturelles fondée sur l'optique; le *De multiplicatione specierum* de Roger Bacon'. Ph.D. dissertation, Université de Montréal, 1975.

OHI Roger Bacon, *Opera hactenus inedita*, edd. Robert Steele and Ferdinand M. Delorme. 16 fascicules (Oxford, 1905–40).

Opera (Brewer) Roger Bacon, *Opera quaedam hactenus inedita*, ed. J. S. Brewer (London, 1859).

Opus maius (Bridges) Roger Bacon, *The Opus Majus of Roger Bacon*, ed. John Henry Bridges. 3 volumes (London, 1900).

Pseudo-Euclid, Pseudo-Euclid, *De speculis*, edd. Axel Anthon Björnbo
   De speculis and Sebastian Vogl, in 'Alkindi, Tideus und Pseudo-Euklid. Drei optische Werke', *Abhandlungen zur Geschichte der mathematischen Wissenschaften*, 26.3 (1912), 97–106.

Ptolemy, *Optica* *L'Optique de Claude Ptolémée dans la version latine d'après l'arabe de l'émir Eugène de Sicile*, ed. Albert Lejeune (Louvain, 1956).

RBE *Roger Bacon Essays*, ed. A. G. Little (Oxford, 1914).

Introduction

ROGER BACON'S LIFE AND WORKS

LITTLE is known about Roger Bacon's life.[1] The only evidence
bearing, and that indirectly, on his date of birth is a passage from
the *Opus tertium* (written about 1267) in which Bacon reports:
'I have laboured diligently in sciences and languages, and forty
years have passed since I first learned the alphabet. I have always
been studious, and for all but two of those forty years I have been
in studio.'[2] To arrive at an estimate of Bacon's date of birth, we must
connect this forty-year period, on the one hand, to events in Bacon's
life and, on the other, to the calendar. This might seem a simple
matter, but considerable diversity of opinion has resulted, turning
on the interpretation of the phrases 'learned the alphabet' and *in
studio*. Most of Bacon's biographers have taken *in studio* to mean
'in a university' and, consequently, have identified the beginning
of the forty-year period with the beginning of Bacon's university
education; counting backwards from 1267, when the passage under
consideration was written, they have fixed the date of Bacon's
university matriculation as 1227 and of his birth as approximately
1214.[3] According to this line of argument, Bacon's reference to
learning the alphabet, which surely did not occur in a university,
is to be taken figuratively.

But this calculation has not gone unchallenged. Charles Jourdain
raised two objections.[4] First, Jourdain took literally the phrase 'learned
the alphabet' and argued, on that basis, that the forty-year period
must be counted not from Bacon's entry into the university, but
from the beginning of his primary education—not from age 13,
but from approximately age 7. Second, while thus of necessity
broadening the meaning of the phrase *in studio* at one end to include

---

[1] On Bacon's life, see Crowley, pp. 17–78; Easton; A. G. Little, 'Introduction on Roger
Bacon's Life and Works', *RBE*, pp. 1–31; Lynn Thorndike, *A History of Magic and Experi-
mental Science*, ii (New York, 1923), 610–30; *Opus maius* (Bridges), i, pp. xxi–xxxvi;
Émile Charles, *Roger Bacon, sa vie, ses ouvrages, ses doctrines* (Paris, 1861), 1–96; Charles
Jourdain, *Excursions historiques et philosophiques à travers le moyen âge* (Paris, 1888),
131–45; Charles Borromée Vandewalle, O.F.M., *Roger Bacon dans l'histoire de la philologie*
(Paris, 1929), 129–77.

[2] *Opera* (Brewer), p. 65

[3] Little, 'Introduction', p. 1; Easton, pp. 10–11; Vandewalle, *Roger Bacon*, p. 129. It
was typical to matriculate in the university at about age 13.

[4] Jourdain, *Excursions historiques*, p. 132.

primary schooling, Jourdain narrowed it at the other to exclude the period after Bacon ceased university lecturing to become a friar. That is, he argued that the forty-year period does not end in 1267, when Bacon wrote the passage in question, but in 1257 (or thereabout) when Bacon retired from the lecture hall. Bacon must then have received his first education in 1217 and been born about 1210. If Jourdain's position violates the natural sense of the second clause of the first sentence ('forty years have passed since I first learned the alphabet'), this is apparently the price of interpreting the remainder of the passage strictly.

There is, however, an alternative that does no violence to any part of the passage. The phrase *in studio* can apply, without any stretching of its meaning, both to Bacon's primary education and to his private studies as a friar. There is no warrant for restricting its meaning to the university or to schools in general, for the primary meaning of the term *studium* is simply 'study'. We can thus take the whole of the passage from the *Opus tertium* at face value, without any forcing. The forty-year period can be judged to begin with Bacon's earliest schooling and to end with the writing of the passage in 1267. This would place the beginning of Bacon's schooling about 1227 and his birth about 1220.[5] Of course, on any of these interpretations we are working with rough estimates and round numbers; and we are aiming not for certainties, but for probabilities.

There is no dependable evidence regarding the place of Bacon's birth. If the late traditions in favour of Ilchester in Somerset or Bisley in Gloucestershire rest on anything solid, it is no longer available.[6] Bacon's family, one of many so named,[7] was economically well off: Bacon reports that he was able to spend more than two thousand pounds on books, tables, instruments, and other necessities of his scholarly labours.[8] However, support of Henry III against Simon de Montfort and the barons apparently brought the family to financial ruin and exile, so that Bacon's request for funds in 1266 could not be met.[9] Bacon refers to brothers, one of whom was a scholar.[10]

The details of Bacon's education are as doubtful as those of his birth. The only thing we know for certain is that Bacon's works are sprinkled with references to Oxonian and Parisian masters, some of

[5] I owe this basic framework to Crowley, pp. 17–18, though Crowley does not develop it exactly as I do. Cf. A. C. Crombie and J. D. North, 'Bacon, Roger', *DSB* i. 377.

[6] See *Opera* (Brewer), p. lxxxv n. 1.

[7] Jourdain, *Excursions historiques*, pp. 134–6.

[8] Ibid. 59; Crombie and North, 'Bacon', p. 377.

[9] *Opera* (Brewer), p. 16; Crowley, p. 19.

[10] *Opera* (Brewer), pp. 13, 16; F. A. Gasquet, 'An Unpublished Fragment of a Work by Roger Bacon', *English Historical Review*, 12 (1897), 500.

whom Bacon claims to have seen with his own eyes—from which it can be safely concluded that his academic career was pursued at the Universities of Oxford and Paris. The assumption is generally made that he matriculated first at Oxford, earning the M.A. either there or after transferring to Paris; the date of this degree would be about 1240.[11] It is reasonable to suppose that, if he was not already there, Bacon went to Paris in the early 1240s. The only firm evidence on the subject is Bacon's report that he had seen Alexander of Hales, who died in 1245; Bacon must therefore have reached Paris before that date.[12]

It was doubtless during the 1240s that Bacon began to lecture in the faculty of arts at Paris. Bacon's lectures covered Aristotle's *Metaphysics, Physics, De sensu et sensato*; probably *De generatione et corruptione, De animalibus*, and *De anima*; and perhaps *De caelo et mundo*; also the pseudo-Aristotelian *De causis* and *De plantis*.[13] That Bacon's second set of questions on the *Physics* was written in Paris is confirmed by a remark contained therein: '. . . if I could touch the Seine with my palm. . . .'[14] Bacon later recounts, moreover, that his Spanish students (surely the place can only be Paris, where there was a substantial contingent of Spaniards) laughed at him during one of his lectures on *De plantis* for mistaking a Spanish for an Arabic word.[15] It thus appears that Bacon was one of the early lecturers on Aristotle's *libri naturales* at Paris after the bans of 1210, 1215, and 1231.[16] While there is no evidence to suggest that Bacon ever lectured on Aristotle in Oxford, neither can it be proved that all of the Aristotelian lectures were presented in Paris. It should be noted, however, that many of the Aristotelian questions and commentaries are preserved together in Amiens MS 406 (late thirteenth century), and it is likely that all of these reflect teaching efforts in a single place; since one of these treatises contains the reference to the Seine, that place would have to be Paris.[17]

[11] The evidence for this date is simply that a scholar typically earned the M.A. at age 20 or a little later.

[12] Crowley, p. 25.

[13] On Bacon's Aristotelian commentaries, see Delorme's introduction to *OHI* xiii, pp. xxvii–xxxi; Easton, pp. 59–61. Certain of the commentaries have been published in *OHI*, vii–viii, x–xiii.

[14] *OHI* xiii. 226; Crowley, p. 26.

[15] *Compendium studii philosophie*, in *Opera* (Brewer), p. 468; Crowley, pp. 25–6.

[16] On Aristotelianism at Paris, see Fernand Van Steenberghen, *Aristotle in the West*, trans. Leonard Johnston (Louvain, 1955). Van Steenberghen argues (pp. 109–10) that the new freedom to lecture on Aristotle was associated with the death in 1241 of Pope Gregory IX, who had promulgated the ban of 1231. However, Bacon asserts twice that Aristotle's *libri naturales* were lectured on from about 1237; see *Compendium studii theologiae*, ed. Hastings Rashdall (Aberdeen, 1911), 33; *Communia naturalium*, in *OHI* ii. 12.

[17] On the Amiens MS, see *OHI* xiii, pp. xxiii ff.; Crowley, pp. 72–4.

It has been generally conceded that about 1247 (or perhaps as late as 1250) Bacon gave up his membership in the arts faculty at Paris and returned to Oxford. There are several pieces of evidence, none of them conclusive. Bacon refers on several occasions to the teaching of Adam Marsh in ways that suggest (but surely do not prove) classroom encounter; since Adam's lectures at Oxford (on theology) were probably confined to the years 1247–50, it has been argued that Bacon must have been present during that period.[18] Moreover, Bacon claims to have seen Thomas of Wales, Lector to the Franciscans in Oxford from 1240 to 1247, who left Oxford in 1247 to take a bishopric in Wales.[19] Finally, Bacon remarked in 1267 that for twenty years he had 'laboured specifically in the pursuit of wisdom, abandoning the opinions of the vulgar', and that during this period he had spent two thousand pounds on the purchase of books and instruments, on learning languages, 'cultivating the friendship of the wise', and training assistants.[20] The beginning of this twenty-year period was clearly a major turning point in Bacon's life; it involved (if we can judge from his later writings) an escape from the confines of the Aristotelian tradition and a dramatic broadening of his outlook in the direction of Robert Grosseteste's philosophy and the contents of various Arabic sources; in short, it was the beginning of Bacon's campaign on behalf of mathematics and 'experimental science'. Now such a major intellectual transformation, it has been argued, must have been accompanied by career changes and, in all probability, by a change of locale. Since Grosseteste's philosophy looms large in the new Baconian outlook, what could be more likely than that Bacon should at this time have pulled up stakes in Paris and returned to Oxford, where Grosseteste's influence could be more easily absorbed and his books more easily obtained?[21] These lines of argument, though far from demonstrative, do indeed possess a certain probability. However, one small difficulty with which they must contend is the fact that Bacon was in Paris

[18] Crowley, pp. 27–8. Bacon's remarks are found in *Opera* (Brewer), p. 186.

[19] Crowley, pp. 28–9; *Opus maius* (Bridges), ii. 73; iii. 88. It is quite possible, of course, that Bacon saw Thomas on some other occasion or in some other place. In addition to the encounters with Adam Marsh and Thomas of Wales, it is argued by Easton (p. 88) that Bacon almost certainly heard Richard of Cornwall lecture on the *Sentences* in Oxford about 1250. However, I find Easton's argument totally unconvincing; Bacon's remarks about Richard provide no basis for determining whether or not Bacon was present during Richard's lectures (*Compendium studii theologiae*, ed. Rashdall, pp. 52–3); moreover, it is highly unlikely that Bacon (who was not yet a friar) would have attended theological lectures by the Franciscan Lector. On Bacon's knowledge of Richard, cf. D. E. Sharp, *Franciscan Philosophy at Oxford in the Thirteenth Century* (Oxford, 1930), 115.

[20] *Opera* (Brewer), p. 59. The passage is fully translated in Crombie and North, 'Bacon', p. 377.

[21] Crowley, pp. 29–32; Easton, p. 87; Crombie and North, 'Bacon', p. 377.

in 1251; this we know from his claim to have observed with his own eyes the uprising of the Pastoreaux rebels.[22] It may be, of course, that Bacon moved to Oxford between 1247 and 1250 and returned to Paris in 1251, but it is also possible that he remained in Paris until 1251 or after.

In any case, we know that at some point Bacon returned to Oxford. In a gloss on the pseudo-Aristotelian *Secretum secretorum* he notes that in Oxford he has just discovered four defective copies of this treatise, whereas in Paris he had access to complete ones.[23] It is probable that he supported himself in Oxford with his own funds, for it was doubtless during this period that he engaged in the reading and experimentation that cost him two thousand pounds. Is it possible that he was lecturing in the faculty of arts or studying theology during this period? There is no evidence that bears directly on the question, though Crowley has argued forcefully that Bacon must at some point have 'crossed the threshold of the theological schools', probably in Oxford.[24] There can be no doubt, in any case, that Bacon never became a master of theology.

Some have argued that at this time Bacon became Grosseteste's disciple, perhaps even his assistant.[25] However, two facts militate against such a conclusion. First, Grosseteste became Bishop of Lincoln in 1235, a post he held until his death in 1253. Not only does this mean that he was physically removed from Oxford, and by a considerable distance, but his episcopal duties must have precluded heavy involvement in natural philosophy.[26] Second, although Bacon makes frequent claims to have known or seen various eminent contemporaries, and although he repeatedly eulogizes Grosseteste, he makes no claim even to have met the latter; and, as Easton points out, it would have been very uncharacteristic of Bacon not to capitalize on such an event had it occurred.[27] Bacon surely felt Grosseteste's influence, but (it seems certain) only through the written word.[28]

[22] Crowley, p. 25; *Opus maius* (Bridges), i. 401-2.   [23] *OHI* v. 39.

[24] Crowley, pp. 26-7. Easton, pp. 19-21, argues that Bacon was abysmally ignorant of the methods and content of theology—that his knowledge was that of an outsider—but stops short of denying that Bacon might have studied theology briefly.

[25] Crowley, p. 31; A. G. Little, *Studies in English Franciscan History* (Manchester, 1917), p. 197.

[26] This can be maintained even if Grosseteste wrote a treatise on astrological prognostication in 1249 (see ibid.). Richard C. Dales argues ('Robert Grosseteste's Scientific Works', *Isis*, 52 [1961], 381-402) that virtually all of Grosseteste's scientific works were completed by 1235; for a similar opinion, see A. C. Crombie, *Robert Grosseteste and the Origins of Experimental Science 1100-1700* (Oxford, 1953), 45-52.

[27] Easton, pp. 89-91.

[28] It is probable that Grosseteste left his library to the Franciscans at Oxford, and this has often been identified as the likely mechanism for their transmission to Bacon; on the

Bacon was not yet a member of the Franciscan Order. Since entry into the Order would require a vow of poverty, it seems that Bacon must have spent his two thousand pounds while still a secular. This would have required a substantial period of time, and we may safely conclude that he did not become a friar before the mid 1250s.[29] In view of Bacon's future difficulties in the Order, including possible imprisonment, it would be interesting to know why he decided to join it; however, he offers not a hint. We may speculate that he was looking for relief from the burden of teaching, so that he might continue his scholarly labours without interruption; that he was impressed by the scholarly achievements of other friars and convinced that the Franciscans, owing to Grosseteste's influence, would be favourably inclined towards his studies of mathematical science, and perhaps even bestow on him the status he had not achieved as a secular; or that the Franciscan ideal of holiness offered a path to the perfection of life that Bacon considered indispensable for proper philosophizing.[30] Bacon's true reasons may have been all of these or none of these; all we can conclude with reasonable certainty is that Bacon was persuaded that, in some way, membership in the Order would promote his studies and his grand designs for the reform of Christendom.

It cannot be ascertained when or where Bacon joined the Order, though 1257 is widely held to be the likely date,[31] and Oxford seems the likely place.[32] The evidence favouring a date of 1257 is another passage in the *Opus tertium* in which Bacon refers to ten years of 'exile' from the fame that he had previously acquired in his studies.[33]

disposition of Grosseteste's library, see R. W. Hunt, 'The Library of Robert Grosseteste', in *Robert Grosseteste, Scholar and Bishop*, ed. D. A. Callus (Oxford, 1955), 130–2. However, this theory has the disadvantage of delaying Grosseteste's influence on Bacon until after the former's death in 1253 and probably until after the latter's entry into the Franciscan Order in the mid or late 1250s; and it is clear from Bacon's Aristotelian commentaries (*De sensu* in particular) that he had a lively interest in, and impressive knowledge of, optics and the multiplication of species (the subjects on which Grosseteste's influence is held to have been strongest) before that time. We must therefore conclude either that Grosseteste's works had some circulation before his death and outside the Franciscan Order, or that Bacon's interest in these subjects was awakened by other authors.

[29] Crowley, p. 32, guesses 1257.

[30] These and other possibilities are discussed by Easton, pp. 118–26; Jeremiah M. G. Hackett, 'The Attitude of Roger Bacon to the *Scientia* of Albertus Magnus', in *Albertus Magnus and the Sciences: Commemorative Essays 1980*, ed. James A. Weisheipl, O.P. (Toronto, 1980), 61. Easton conclusively demonstrates Bacon's belief in the intimate relationship between morality and true knowledge, and argues persuasively that the quest for holiness would have led Bacon to join an order.

[31] Jourdain, *Excursions historiques*, p. 142; Crowley, pp. 32–4; Crombie and North, 'Bacon', p. 378. Cf. the introduction to *Opus maius* (Bridges), i, p. xxvii.

[32] Easton, p. 121. This conclusion also seems implicit in Crowley's account, pp. 32–3.

[33] *Opera* (Brewer), p. 7; Crowley, p. 33.

If, as seems reasonable, we identify this exile with Bacon's entry into the Order, the date of 1257 emerges. The arguments in favour of Oxford are the absence of a hypothesis to explain his return to Paris (where we find him a little later) other than the command of his superiors, from which it follows that he was probably already a friar when he returned; and that the Franciscans for whom Bacon had the greatest admiration, who might have influenced him to join the Order, were English.

How did Bacon fare as a Franciscan? He may have undergone a period of extended illness, for in a letter to the Pope, written in 1267, he refers to ten years of infirmity, which kept him from study.[34] However, in the *Opus tertium*, written about the same time, Bacon presents a somewhat different view of this decade:

It is well known that nobody laboured as diligently [as I] in so many sciences and languages; and men thought it remarkable, when I had another status, that I was alive, owing to excessive labours. And yet I was as studious after as before; but I did not work as hard, since it was unnecessary owing to the exercise of wisdom.[35]

The former status to which Bacon refers is undoubtedly that of secular, and Bacon here claims to have been as studious, though not to have worked as hard, after acquiring his new status as before.[36] Everything we know about this period of Bacon's life comes from excuses offered to explain to the Pope why he had put so little on paper, and we must surely take these excuses with a grain of salt. Nevertheless, it seems clear that Bacon continued his studies, though perhaps with some reduction in pace. Whether Bacon's superiors and brothers supported or obstructed his studies is not quite clear, though, in his complaints to the Pope, Bacon paints a picture of unmitigated gloom. He accuses his superiors of keeping him occupied with other duties and of attacking him with 'unspeakable violence';[37] he reports that 'my superiors and brothers, disciplining me with hunger, kept me under close guard and would not permit anyone to come to me, fearing that my writings would be divulged to others than to the chief pontiff and themselves.'[38] But these complaints are applicable, strictly speaking, only to the mid 1260s, when Bacon was writing for the Pope, and it is not clear to what extent they can be extrapolated to an earlier period. Easton makes the extrapolation and argues that Bacon was the object of growing disapproval,

---

[34] Gasquet, 'Unpublished Fragment', p. 500; cf. Crowley, p. 33.
[35] *Opera* (Brewer), p. 65.
[36] See Crowley, p. 33.
[37] Crowley, p. 70; *Opera* (Brewer), p. 15; Easton, p. 134.
[38] *Opera* (Brewer), p. xciv; the translation is that of Easton, p. 134.

which led ultimately to his transfer to Paris for closer watching.[39]

Whether this was indeed the reason for Bacon's transfer we shall probably never know; but we do find him in Paris before 1265, making overtures to Cardinal Guy de Foulques, whose patronage he wished to secure.[40] The Cardinal, failing to understand that Bacon was requesting support so that he might *begin* scholarly labours and produce writings of great importance, responded by asking Bacon to send the writings that he assumed to be already completed. Bacon, of course, had nothing to send. It was now apparent that Foulques was not going to finance his venture—that if Bacon were to proceed, as surely he must, he would have to do it on his own. He had a pressing need for funds; his scholarly efforts would require the purchase of books and equipment, the labour of copyists, and collaboration with other scholars.[41] He endeavoured, probably at this time, to raise money from family and friends, but with meagre results.[42] It is impossible to guess how far Bacon progressed in producing the requested works; some biographers have him making rapid progress despite the lack of money, while others suggest that he nearly stopped working altogether.[43] In any case, Bacon's circumstances were dramatically altered in February 1265, when Guy de Foulques was elected Pope as Clement IV; the man who had already shown interest in Bacon's projects was now in a much better position to support them. Attempting to make the best of this stroke of fortune, Bacon made a new approach, sending the Pope a letter through an English envoy, William Bonecor. The Pope replied in a letter of June 1266, directing Bacon to send the work previously requested and also to 'reveal to us your remedies for the critical problems to which you have recently called our attention, and this as quickly and secretly as possible'.[44] Surely it was a great honour to be directed by the Pope to propose remedies for the ills of Christendom; but again the Pope had done nothing to facilitate Bacon's labours.

[39] Easton, pp. 134-5. Why Bacon could be watched more closely in Paris than in Oxford is not made clear.

[40] Foulques was Cardinal only until February 1265. That Bacon was in Paris during this period is evident from the *Opus tertium*; see *Opera* (Brewer), pp. 13, 15, 61. On Bacon's relations with Foulques, see Crowley, pp. 34-42; Easton, pp. 144-66.

[41] Crowley, pp. 38-41; *Opera* (Brewer), pp. 16-17.

[42] Crowley, pp. 39-41. Easton, p. 160, reports that Bacon eventually managed to raise sixty pounds.

[43] Thorndike, *History of Magic*, ii. 622-4, thinks that Bacon had completed, or practically so, the *Opus maius* by the time the second mandate came in 1266. Crowley, p. 36, thinks that Bacon did nothing. Easton, pp. 145, 149, 158-9, whose view I share, urges that Bacon must have made some limited progress, despite his difficulties.

[44] The letter is printed in *Opus maius* (Bridges), i. 1-2 n. 1; a slightly different text is given in *Opera* (Brewer), p. 1.

If Bacon was not already in trouble with his superiors and brothers, he must surely have become so after this second mandate. Bacon, of course, plunged ahead to produce what he could, and clearly, when one considers the quantity of books and parchment required, this could not be done without the knowledge of his brothers in the Parisian convent. The problem was that the activity in which he was engaged was in direct violation of the rules of the Order. In 1260, in response to the furore caused by the publication of an apocalyptic book, *Introduction to the Eternal Gospel*, by the Franciscan Gerard of San Borgo, the Chapter of Narbonne, presided over by Bonaventura, imposed strict censorship on the Order.[45] Gerard had carried to a heretical extreme the apocalyptic views of Joachim of Fiore, and to prevent repetitions of this, the Constitutions of Narbonne forbade the issuance of books outside the Order, and even their composition, without the licence of the Minister-General of the Franciscan Order. Moreover, it was decreed: 'Let the Provincial Minister not dare to have or keep any books without the licence of the Minister-General, or let any brothers have or keep them without the permission of the Provincial Ministers.'[46] Finally, direct communication with the Papal court on any matter was strictly forbidden. It was in recognition of this that the Pope's mandate enjoined secrecy on Bacon's part. Against the background of these prohibitions, we can see Bacon working feverishly to produce what were obviously very large books. If he revealed to his superiors that his work was mandated by the Pope himself, that might have secured for him the right to continue, but it would surely have exacerbated the tensions.

But there was probably more than this to Bacon's troubles in the Order. Not only was he violating rules by writing anything; but the content of his writings, if revealed to his brothers (and it is difficult to see how this could have been prevented), would have brought him under suspicion. One thing was his bitter attack on theologians of the Order: 'boy theologians', he called them, who had studied theology without first studying the arts, who propagated errors because of their ignorance of the branches of knowledge of which they spoke, who 'were masters before they were disciples'; his contemporary, Richard of Cornwall, he called 'the worst and most stupid author of those errors . . . , the most renowned, who had the greatest reputation in that stupid crowd.'[47] Such an outpouring of wrath was not likely to endear Bacon to his brothers. But there was more than this to be concerned about. Bacon's views on astrology were in strong opposition to those of the Minister-General of the

---

[45] On this episode in Franciscan history, see Easton, pp. 139–43.
[46] Ibid. 143.   [47] Ibid. 30, 219.

Order, Bonaventura. Whereas Bonaventura was deeply sceptical about the possibility of accurate predictions in human affairs, Bacon, while stopping well short of determinism, went to an extreme in defending the general accuracy of astrological predictions and their utility for the church.[48] But more dangerous even than his views on astrology were Bacon's apocalyptic leanings. Although it has been demonstrated that Bacon's apocalyptic views differed significantly from those of Joachim of Fiore, Bacon does recommend Joachim's works and would easily have been identified with the 'spirituals' of the Franciscan Order.[49] Indeed, Bacon's proposed reforms were directed in part towards neutralizing the power of the Antichrist (soon to appear) by supplying Christendom with the same mathematical and scientific knowledge that the Antichrist would employ.[50] Bacon had thus identified himself with the radical elements in the Order and opened himself to the same discipline to which they were subject.[51]

The actual writing of the works for the Pope has been the object of much discussion, which I shall not attempt to recapitulate. I subscribe to the view of Crowley and Easton that Bacon set out to compose a comprehensive statement of his philosophy—a *scriptum principale*—but that after working on the project for a few months he realized that there was no hope of completing it and therefore abandoned it in the following January, after the feast of Epiphany.[52] If the *scriptum principale* was too ambitious a project, Bacon determined to write the next best thing, a *scriptura preambula*, a *persuasio*, in which he offered the Pope at least a summary of his ideas and a foretaste of things to come. It is likely that this *persuasio* was

[48] *Opus maius* (Bridges), i. 238–69; Theodore O. Wedel, *The Mediaeval Attitude Toward Astrology* (New Haven, 1920), 71–5. Crowley, pp. 53–60, links Bacon's troubles in the Order with his astrological views; Thorndike, *History of Magic*, ii. 674–7, and Easton, pp. 137–8, are sceptical of such a connection. It is possible that one should also bring Bacon's views on magic into the picture; see A. G. Molland, 'Roger Bacon as Magician', *Traditio*, 30 (1974), 445–60.

[49] E. Randolph Daniel, 'Roger Bacon and the *De seminibus scripturarum*', *Mediaeval Studies*, 34 (1972), 426–7; *Opus maius* (Bridges), i. 269; Easton, pp. 126–37. Easton treats this matter exceedingly well.

[50] *Opus maius* (Bridges), i. 402; Daniel, 'Roger Bacon and *De seminibus*', pp. 464–5.

[51] Such discipline could be severe indeed. In 1257, both Gerard of San Borgo (whose book had stirred up such a furore in 1254) and John of Parma (who had been Minister-General of the Franciscan Order) were condemned to life imprisonment for their Joachitic sympathies; see John Moorman, *A History of the Franciscan Order from its Origins to the Year 1517* (Oxford, 1968), 145–6. John of Parma escaped this fate through higher intervention. That Bacon would continue to propagate apocalyptic teachings after John of Parma's condemnation testifies either to his courage and strength of conviction or to his foolhardiness.

[52] Crowley, pp. 41–2; Easton, pp. 160–1. Bacon's own statement regarding his efforts before Epiphany is in Gasquet, 'Unpublished Fragment', p. 501; for Bacon's use of the expression *scriptum principale* see ibid. 503.

patched together from writings on various subjects that Bacon had
prepared in the past, with new sections where they were required
for continuity;[53] this is the work that came to be known as the
Opus maius. The *Opus minus* was written about the same time, as
a supplement to the *Opus maius*, and the two works were dispatched,
late in 1267 or early in 1268, to the Papal curia by the hand of
Bacon's student, John. The *Opus tertium* was written slightly later
and was probably never sent.[54] It can be established that *De multiplicatione specierum* was sent to the Pope, in addition to the *Opus
maius* and *Opus minus*.[55] Extant documents reveal nothing of the
Papal reaction to Bacon's works; it can be demonstrated, however,
that they arrived safely, since the Polish mathematician Witelo,
who was attached to the curia, demonstrates knowledge of their
content.[56]

Bacon lived for at least twenty-five years after dispatching his
works to the Pope, but we know virtually nothing of his activities
during this period. He may have been working on the *Communia
mathematica* and *Communia naturalium* in the late 1260s and early
1270s, and the *Compendium studii philosophie* can be dated to
1272.[57] A chronicle written a century later (about 1370) reports
that 'at the advice of many friars, the [minister] General, friar
Jerome [of Ascoli], condemned the teaching of friar Roger Bacon
. . . , master of sacred theology, as containing certain suspected
novelties, on account of which this Roger was imprisoned.'[58] In the
absence of corroborating evidence, one hesitates to put great faith
in a document written a hundred years after the event; and one's
scepticism is strengthened when it is noted that the document
identifies Bacon as 'master of sacred theology', which he surely
was not. Nevertheless, it has frequently been argued that there must

[53] Easton, p. 111, proposes a rough chronology of the preparatory works. In the *Opus
tertium*, *Opera* (Brewer), p. 13, Bacon notes explicitly that he had written 'certain chapters
on various subjects at the insistence of friends'. Again, in the fragment published by Gasquet
('Unpublished Fragment', p. 500), he says, 'I had sometimes compiled in cursory fashion
certain chapters, now on one science and now on another, at the request of friends.'

[54] For a somewhat speculative, but intelligent, reconstruction of the composition of the
works for the Pope, see Easton, pp. 157–66. Part of the *Opus tertium*, at least, can be
definitely dated to 1267; see *Opera* (Brewer), p. 278.   [55] See below, p. xxvii.

[56] See my 'Lines of Influence in Thirteenth-Century Optics: Bacon, Witelo, and Pecham',
Speculum, 46 (1971), 72–5. On science (including optics) at the Papal court, see also
Agostino Paravicini Bagliani, 'Witelo et la science optique à la cour pontificale de Viterbe
(1277)', *Mélanges de l'école française de Rome (moyen âge-temps modernes)*, 87 (1975),
425–53.

[57] Easton, pp. 111, 158, 186; Crowley, pp. 64–5. Easton argues that the *Communia
mathematica* and *Communia naturalium* were begun before the works for the Pope, but
completed later.

[58] This is from the *Chronica XXIV Generalium Ordinis Minorum*. The text is reprinted
in Crowley, p. 67.

have been something behind this account, and it may well be that Bacon was condemned and imprisoned; this, at any rate, is the consensus of Bacon's recent biographers.[59] On the basis of Jerome's career, Crowley dates the event to the period 1277-9.[60] As for the reasons, they may have been associated with the condemnations of 1277, with Bacon's radical leanings, or with some event of which we are unaware. Of the length of this imprisonment, if indeed it occurred, there is no reliable evidence.[61] We encounter Bacon for the last time in 1292, writing again—this time the *Compendium studii theologie*.[62] This treatise is known only in fragments and may have been left unfinished. It is reasonable to assume that Bacon died in 1292 or soon thereafter.[63]

THE WRITING OF *DE MULTIPLICATIONE SPECIERUM* AND *DE SPECULIS COMBURENTIBUS*

Authorship. Although Bacon's authorship of the two works edited in this volume has never been challenged, let us nevertheless briefly examine the evidence. I am aware of twenty-four manuscript copies of *De multiplicatione specierum*, including fragments. Thirteen of these identify Bacon as author in a contemporary hand, two in a later hand.[1] Of the three earliest manuscripts, datable to the period 1280-1300, only *L* gives Bacon as author in a contemporary hand; *M* does so in a later hand. No manuscript assigns authorship to anybody else. At least fifteen of the twenty-four copies appear in codices containing other Baconian treatises, frequently the *Perspectiva* (part V of the *Opus maius*).[2]

This manuscript evidence is sufficient to establish the probability of Bacon's authorship. However, there is impressive confirmation in Bacon's other works (specifically the *Opus maius, Opus tertium*, and *Communia naturalium*), where he refers to a treatise variously entitled: *Tractatus de speciebus, Tractatus specierum, Tractatus specierum rerum activarum, Tractatus de generatione et multi-*

---

[59] Crowley, pp. 67-72; Easton, pp. 192-202; Crombie and North, 'Bacon', p. 378; Little, 'Introduction', pp. 26-7. For a sceptical opinion, see Thorndike, *History of Magic*, ii. 628-9; or Vandewalle, *Roger Bacon*, pp. 143-55.

[60] Crowley, pp. 67-8.

[61] For discussion of a late claim that Bacon was released from prison about 1290 by Raymund Gaufredi, a new Minister-General who had left-wing leanings, see Easton, pp. 201-2; Crowley, pp. 71-2.

[62] 1292 is given as the current year in Rashdall's edition, p. 34.

[63] The date is given as 1292 by John Rous; see *Opera* (Brewer), p. lxxxv.

[1] Manuscripts identifying Bacon as author in a contemporary hand are nos. 3, 4, 8, 9, 11-14, 17-20, and 24 (see the list of manuscripts, p. lxxv ff.). In no. 13, only the initials R. B. are given. MSS 7 and 23 identify Bacon as author in a later hand.

[2] MSS 2-7, 9-14, 17, 20, and 23.

plicatione et corruptione et actione specierum, and *Tractatus de radiis*. Bacon claims authorship of the work in question, and his descriptions of its content correspond perfectly to that of *De multiplicatione specierum*.[3] Of particular significance are the remarks in the *Opus tertium*, where Bacon relates that the *Tractatus de speciebus* or *Tractatus de radiis* was transmitted to the Pope in at least three different forms:

Moreover, it is necessary to consider diligently the treatise *De speciebus et virtutibus agentium*, which I sent to you [Pope Clement IV] in two forms and have begun, but have been unable to complete, in a third form.[4]

And since theologians inquire into many things concerning light—what it is and its multiplication and action—[it should be recognized that] nothing worthwhile can be known in these matters without the power of geometry, as is also revealed in the treatise *De radiis*, which I sent to you separately from the *Opus maius*.[5]

However, a ray does not pass through [a medium], but is generated out of the potentiality of the matter [of the medium], as I have proved in the treatise *De radiis*, which John conveyed [to you] in addition to the principal works.[6]

. . . and to be considered simultaneously with it [part V of the *Opus maius*] is a large portion of the fourth part of the whole work, namely, where I have decided concerning the multiplication of species and the power of agents. . . . But I am sending you a more complete treatise concerning this multiplication, as I make mention below.[7]

The content here assigned to *De speciebus* or *De radiis* is precisely that of *De multiplicatione specierum*—the multiplication and action of light and the generation of species out of the potentiality of matter. Moreover, Bacon refers to multiple versions of the treatise sent to the Pope (at least three), and indeed *De multiplicatione specierum* is extant in a multiplicity of versions and forms—two versions, properly speaking, and at least four additional discussions of the same subject matter.[8] Also, Bacon's comparison, in the final quotation, between 'the fourth part of the whole work' (that is, part IV of the *Opus maius*) and 'a more complete treatise concerning this multiplication', perfectly describes the relationship between part IV of the *Opus maius* and *De multiplicatione specierum*.

Finally, if the foregoing argument should leave any doubters, theoretical similarities between the content of *De multiplicatione specierum* and Bacon's other works are such that if we had no

---

[3] *Communia naturalium*, in *OHI* ii. 38, 103, 104; iii. 203, 204, 272, 274, 289; *Un fragment inédit de l'Opus tertium de Roger Bacon*, ed. Pierre Duhem (Quarrachi, 1909), p. 90; *Opus tertium*, in *Opera* (Brewer), pp. 38, 99, 227, 230; *Opus maius* (Bridges), ii. 39–40.   [4] *Opera* (Brewer), p. 99.

[5] Ibid. 227.   [6] Ibid. 230.

[7] Ibid. 38.

[8] See below. See also my discussion of these matters in 'Lines of Influence', pp. 69–71.

evidence but this, we could confidently assign *De multiplicatione specierum* to Bacon. There is a unity of doctrine on the nature and propagation of species, the place of mathematics in natural science, and a host of details that unmistakably identifies *De multiplicatione specierum* as his.

There is less evidence regarding Bacon's authorship of *De speculis comburentibus*, but what there is seems sufficient. Among the four extant manuscripts, only *W* assigns the treatise to Bacon; however, in *E* and *R* it follows Bacon's *Perspectiva*. Stylistically and doctrinally, it bears the stamp of Bacon's authorship. Finally, we know that it was available to John Pecham, whose theory of radiation through apertures it heavily influenced, and it must therefore have been composed no later than the mid 1270s; this date, combined with a consideration of the treatise's content, leaves no candidate besides Bacon.[9]

Titles. I have chosen to employ the customary titles of the two works edited in this volume. But, it may be inquired, are they Bacon's titles? In answering this question, we must keep in mind that medieval titles were not the 'names' of books, fixed permanently, like the name of a person; rather, they were descriptive phrases which had only to meet the criterion of accurately characterizing the contents of the book. Since a book could be accurately characterized by more than one phrase, medieval books frequently had more than one title. Thus, in the quotation above, Bacon refers to the same book as *De radiis* and as *De speciebus et virtutibus agentium*; and elsewhere he refers to this book as *Tractatus de generatione et multiplicatione et corruptione et actione specierum*. At some point early in its history, either as a short form of the latter title or as the result of an independent effort to characterize the contents of the treatise, it received the name *De multiplicatione specierum*. But what title do the manuscripts employ? The earliest manuscript, *L*, entitles the work *De multiplicatione specierum*; ten additional manuscripts also employ this title.[10] Five manuscripts employ the title *De speciebus*, one the title *De generatione specierum*, and one the title *De generatione specierum et multiplicatione et actione et corruptione eorum*.[11] The printed editions of 1733 and 1897 employ the title *De multiplicatione specierum*, and I see no reason for making a change.

Only two manuscripts of *De speculis comburentibus* entitle the

---

[9] I have discussed Bacon's authorship of *DSC* in 'A Reconsideration of Roger Bacon's Theory of Pinhole Images', *Archive for History of Exact Sciences*, 6 (1970), 214.

[10] MSS 4, 11–12, 14, 17–20, 23, and 24. In MS 23 this title is in a recent hand.

[11] *De speciebus* in MSS 8–10, 13, and 19. *De generatione specierum* in MS 7. *De generatione specierum et multiplicatione et actione et corruptione eorum* in MS 9.

work: MS *E* (in a recent hand) assigns the title *Tractatus de speculis ustoriis*, and MS *W* employs the title *De multiplicatione lucis*. Combach employed the title *Tractatus de speculis* in his printed edition of 1614. Little entitled the work *De speculis comburentibus* in his bibliography of 1914, and this title has now become customary.[12] The treatise is about both burning mirrors and the multiplication of light—a proposition concerning the former giving rise to an analysis of the latter—and one might appropriately choose any of the titles given above. There was a time when I leaned towards *De multiplicatione lucis*. However, I have since been swayed by a remark in part VI of the treatise, where Bacon says that 'our concern is with the gathering of reflected light at a single point, which cannot occur without [mirrors of] the proper shapes. . . .'[13] This seems to be a programmatic statement, suggesting that Bacon conceived the central purpose of the treatise to be the solution of a problem about burning mirrors. I have therefore decided to retain Little's title.

   Versions of De multiplicatione specierum. Bacon dealt with the subject matter of *De multiplicatione specierum* repeatedly. One finds major statements of his view in the following works: *Communia naturalium*, book i;[14] *Opus maius*, part IV;[15] *De multiplicatione specierum*, extant in two versions, both edited in this volume; and two manuscripts (London, British Library, MS 7.F.VIII, fols. 3^r-12^r; and Rome, Biblioteca Angelica, MS 1017 [R.6.32], fols. 76^r-92^r), containing different texts, each claiming to be part of the *Compendium studii theologie*, Bacon's final work. In addition, the *Opus tertium* and *Opus maius*, part V, touch briefly on the multiplication and action of species;[16] and *De speculis comburentibus* explores in depth the geometry of multiplication. What becomes apparent is that Bacon regarded the doctrine of species as central to his natural philosophy and therefore brought it into every work in which it could conceivably fit.

   Some years ago, when cataloguing Bacon's optical manuscripts, I followed A. G. Little in classifying the London and Rome manuscripts (claiming to be part of the *Compendium studii theologie*) as versions of *De multiplicatione specierum*.[17] Since that time, I have examined these manuscripts more closely, and although it is clear that they treat the same subject matter as *De multiplicatione specierum*,

[12] *RBE*, pp. 394-5.   [13] VI. 5-6.   [14] *OHI* ii. 14-19.

   [15] *Opus maius* (Bridges), i. 110-30. Bacon's point in this discussion is the utility of mathematics.

   [16] *Opera* (Brewer), i. 107-17; *Opus maius* (Bridges), ii. 1-166, *passim*.

   [17] David C. Lindberg, *A Catalogue of Medieval and Renaissance Optical Manuscripts* (Toronto, 1975), 37-9. For Little's classification, see *RBE*, p. 388.

I do not think they are close enough to it in wording and structure to be considered alternative versions. They are really not much closer to it than several of Bacon's other discussions of the same topic, and I am of the opinion that we should accept their own claim to be part of the *Compendium studii theologie*.[18] We are thus left with two versions of *De multiplicatione specierum*. The more widely circulated of the two is extant in seventeen manuscripts (if we exclude from consideration the three fragments). The other version, which contains substantial additions (including a prologue) amounting to approximately 6,000 words, and many minor alterations and deletions, is found in two manuscripts (*S* and *A*).[19] Two additional manuscripts (*M* and *P*) contain the prologue, but none of the other additions and alterations. The additions are generally intended to clarify doubtful matters, and one must therefore judge the version containing them to be the revision, and the other the original, of the treatise.[20]

The prologue found in the revised version has some interesting features, which require further discussion. Here are the facts: the prologue appears not only in manuscripts *S* and *A*, which contain the other revisions, but also in manuscripts *M* and *P*; it is referred to at one point in the body of the unrevised text (that is, by all manuscripts, including those that possess no prologue);[21] and it promises a chapter on the multiplication of influence between spiritual substances, which appears in no manuscript of the treatise.[22] Any number of speculative hypotheses might be devised to explain these data. However, the prudent approach, I believe, is simply to acknowledge that Bacon did not engage in an orderly process of writing and revision—that he was constantly producing and circulating drafts—and therefore that it cannot be determined precisely

---

[18] Note that existing portions of the *Compendium studii theologiae* (ed. Rashdall, pp. 35–6) announce that species and virtues will be treated later in the work.

[19] Twenty-three of the additions consist of twenty words or more; the longest of them comes to more than 2,000 words. These twenty-three longer additions are assembled in the appendix to this volume; the remainder are recorded in the apparatus criticus.

[20] In at least two cases, the additional material found in the revised version is so plainly false or foolish that we cannot consider Bacon to be its source; see the variant readings for I. 4. 207, and II. 3. 187. These additions, at least, must have been contributed by some later glossator; and if that is so, then we surely cannot discount the possibility that the same may be true of some of the revisions that make sense. It appears to me, nevertheless, that most of the additions are Baconian in character and should, until evidence to the contrary is presented, be judged his own work. There is a certain amount of repetition and rearrangement of sections in the revised version—changes that seem to make little sense and probably represent corruption of the manuscript tradition, rather than intentional revision. For example, manuscripts *S* and *A* place II. 9–10 between parts IV and V.

[21] III. 3. 55. This is an unmistakable reference to the prologue; see the Appendix, α. 62–70.

[22] Appendix, α. 46. On this promised chapter, see Nascimento, pp. 19–21.

how the manuscript tradition came to assume its present form. The prologue may have been written before, along with, or after the remainder of the treatise; and it may have been added to, or become detached from, the rest of the text in any of countless ways. The crucial fact is that it circulated mainly with the revised version, and I will therefore treat it editorially as part of the revised version.

There have been strenuous efforts to determine the links between *De multiplicatione specierum* and other works in the Baconian corpus. These efforts have focused on statements in the body of the text and the prologue to the revised version, which portray it as part of a larger work.[23] From remarks in the prologue, Nascimento has argued that Bacon conceived *De multiplicatione specierum* as the second of at least three parts of a larger treatise—the first part dealing with 'the common principles of natural things' and the third part with geometrical optics.[24] And in the body of the text Bacon refers several times to 'the fourth part of this treatise' in ways that force one to conclude that he has in mind an anterior part of some larger treatise, to which *De multiplicatione specierum* also belonged.[25] Nascimento and others have made intelligent efforts to identify the larger treatise or treatises of which *De multiplicatione specierum* might have been an intended part, offering such proposals as Bacon's *Metaphysics*, his projected *scriptum principale*, and his *Compendium studii theologie*. However, Bacon's tendency to re-use the same material over and over again, incorporating earlier compositions in new compendia, and to refer to intended works as existing realities, introduces so large a measure of uncertainty and confusion as to place a firm answer out of reach. Perhaps at one time or another he intended to incorporate *De multiplicatione specierum*, or at least its subject matter, in all of the above; this speculation, it seems to me, is at least as good as any other.

Dates of Composition. Bacon appears to have been preoccupied with the doctrine of species for a large part of his scholarly career, writing and rewriting his thoughts on the subject. His commentary on Aristotle's *De sensu et sensato*, which may date from his years of teaching in Paris, and which is certainly an early work, makes frequent reference to the multiplication of species, even if it contains

[23] The best and most extensive analysis is by Nascimento, pp. 19-38. See also *Opus maius* (Bridges), ii. 408 n. 1; i. pp. iv-v; *RBE*, p. 386; Ferdinand M. Delorme, 'Le prologue de Roger Bacon à son traité De influentiis agentium', *Antonianum*, 18 (1943), 82-3.

[24] Nascimento, pp. 21-3. Also the Appendix to this volume, α. 2-5, 21, 75-6.

[25] For the argument, see Nascimento, pp. 27-30. There are eight such references; see II. 1. 8; II. 3. 11, 18, 22; V. 1. 90-1; V. 2. 18-19, 28-9, 36. Notice that these references do not correspond to the subject matter found in Part IV of *DMS* (though some could apply to Part IV of the *Opus maius*) and that two of the references in Part II of *DMS* are in the past tense, apparently referring to something already written.

no fully worked-out doctrine on the subject.[26] And, as we have
seen, Bacon intended to include a section on the multiplication of
species in his final work, the *Compendium studii theologie*, written
forty or fifty years later. This persistence of interest and effort
makes it almost impossible to attach a precise date to any of Bacon's
writings on the subject. It is possible, however, to establish some
broad limits.

In the *Opus tertium*, written about 1267, Bacon reminds the
Pope that he had been sent a treatise on species in two different
forms. One of these was probably part IV of the *Opus maius*; the
other was almost certainly *De multiplicatione specierum*, if not in
exactly the form in which it has come down to us, then in a form
very close to this. We are thus able to establish 1267 as the *terminus
ante quem* for composition of the treatise. Perhaps we can move
this forward several years, before the first mandate, by noting that
De multiplicatione specierum bears no signs of having been written
for a patron. Establishment of the *terminus post quem* is much more
difficult. *De multiplicatione specierum* contains an explicit reference
to the *Communia naturalium*, at least part of which (usually thought
to be Book i, parts I and II) must therefore precede *De multiplicatione specierum*.[27] Unfortunately, there is no way of attaching
a firm date to the *Communia naturalium*; all that can be said is that
it represents the early stages of the broadening of Bacon's outlook,
the usual guess placing it in the early 1260s.[28] A final piece of
evidence is a remark in the *Opus tertium*, in which Bacon reports
to the Pope that he had 'laboured for ten years on these things'
(the multiplication of species), but had begun to put materials into
a writing (*scriptum*) only after receiving the Pope's mandate.[29] However, this passage raises as many questions as it answers. For example,
does the ten-year period end with the writing of this passage (1267),
or with the reception of the mandate, or at some other point? And
which mandate does Bacon have in mind? Was 'putting materials
into a writing' simply a matter of assembling already composed
pieces into a work of larger scope, or did the pieces themselves
need to be written? I am inclined to think that Bacon intended the
ten-year period to end either in 1267 or with the reception of the
first mandate and that *De multiplicatione specierum* had at least

[26] *OHI* xiv, esp. chaps. 3, 8–9, 13, 15, 21–4; Nascimento, p. 148. This treatise is not
included in the Amiens manuscript, which contains many of Bacon's Parisian lectures. On
its dating, see Easton, pp. 59, 232–5; *OHI* xiv, p. v.

[27] Below, I. 2. 172. *DMS* also seems to contain a number of references to the content
of the *Communia naturalium*; see Nascimento, pp. 26–7.

[28] See Easton, pp. 111–12, for a rough estimate.

[29] *Opera* (Brewer), p. 38.

been drafted before the mandate arrived, but no certainty is possible. In the final analysis, I think we must be content to affirm the likelihood that Bacon wrote *De multiplicatione specierum* in the late 1250s or the early 1260s, the probabilities perhaps favouring the latter.[30] The revised version might have been produced at any time thereafter, possibly over an extended period of time.

We have even less to go on in the case of *De speculis comburentibus*. It seems likely that Bacon wrote it during the time of his most intense preoccupation with optics. It is difficult to discern development in Bacon's optical thought—perhaps because of his tendency to be always revising, so that a change of mind or a new idea was quickly incorporated in all the relevant works—and therefore I am unable to arrange the optical works in chronological order.[31] The availability of *De speculis comburentibus* to John Pecham by the time he wrote the *Perspectiva communis* requires it to have been composed no later than the mid 1270s. I would hazard the guess that, like *De multiplicatione specierum*, it dates from the late 1250s or early 1260s, more likely the latter than the former.[32]

Sources. Bacon was very widely read, and therefore was familiar with most of the standard philosophical sources, including Augustine and other patristic writers, Boethius, Pseudo-Dionysius, twelfth-century authors, the newly translated works of Aristotle, Avicenna, Averroes, and other Greek and Arabic authors, and the major works of the first half of the thirteenth century. However, Bacon tended to cite his sources, and it may therefore be useful to list the sources explicitly acknowledged in *De multiplicatione specierum* and *De speculis comburentibus*, as well as those whose influence on these works can be inferred.[33]

In the prologue to the revised version of *De multiplicatione specierum*, Bacon lists the principal authors on geometry and geometrical optics, whose opinions on the influence of agents must be considered: Ptolemy, *De aspectibus* (or *Optica*); Alhazen, *De aspectibus* (or *Perspectiva*) and *De speculis comburentibus*;[34] al-Kindī, *De aspectibus*; Tideus, *De aspectibus*; Euclid, *Elements, De speculis*, and *De aspectibus*;[35] an anonymous *De*

---

[30] Easton, p. 111, suggests a date of about 1262.

[31] There are, however, some indications that *DMS* preceded the *Perspectiva*; see Nascimento, pp. 24–6.

[32] On the dating of Pecham's *Perspectiva communis*, see Lindberg, *Pecham and Optics*, pp. 14–18; Lindberg, 'Lines of Influence', pp. 80–2.

[33] I am indebted to Nascimento, pp. 45–75, for his careful study of the sources of *DMS*.

[34] Bacon was not aware that Alhazen was the author of *De speculis comburentibus*.

[35] Euclid's *Optica* was translated into Latin three times, twice from the Arabic and once from the Greek. One of the translations from the Arabic was entitled *De aspectibus*, the other *De radiis visualibus* or *Liber de fallacia visus*; the translation from the Greek went by

speculis;[36] Theodosius, *De speris*; and Apollonius, *De pyramidibus*.[37] In addition, Bacon cites the *Liber de crepusculis* of Abhomadi Malfegeyr in the body of *De multiplicatione specierum*.[38] Outside of geometrical optics, but still in the realm of mathematical science, Bacon cites Ptolemy's *Almagest* and a *De dispositione spere* that he attributes to Ptolemy,[39] and also the astronomers Thābit ibn Qurra and Albategni.[40] Bacon himself stresses the special importance of Alhazen and Ptolemy, noting in the prologue that 'Ptolemy . . . is principally to be imitated', and later in the work that 'Alhazen . . . is the most trustworthy of authors and has never deceived us in his science' and that 'the great wisdom of these two philosophers, [revealed] in their books, assures us that they do not speak falsely'.[41] It is apparent, as one looks closely at the content of *De multiplicatione specierum*, that Bacon took his knowledge of the principles and laws of optics chiefly from Alhazen and Ptolemy.

In the philosophical realm, Bacon cites nine different works of Aristotle, six of Avicenna, and six of Averroes.[42] From these he drew the basic principles of his Neoplatonized Aristotelianism. He also cites Seneca, Pliny's *Natural History*, Cicero's *De quaestionibus*, Boethius' *Consolation of Philosophy* and *De hebdomadibus*, al-Kindī's *De gradibus*, Porphyry, and al-Fārābī. Finally, he cites the Neoplatonic *Liber de causis*, from which he appears to have drawn several significant principles.[43] One can of course fill out the picture of Bacon's debt to the past by reference to his other writings. But there are several other sources, not cited in *De multiplicatione specierum*, which I nonetheless believe influenced its content. One

the title *De visu*. See Lindberg, *Catalogue of Optical Manuscripts*, pp. 46–54; Wilfred R. Theisen, '*Liber de visu*: The Greco-Latin Translation of Euclid's *Optics*', *Mediaeval Studies*, 41 (1979), 51–4. In the prologue to the revised version, Bacon refers to the Arabo-Latin version, *De aspectibus*; in the body of the work, he cites the Graeco-Latin translation, *De visu* (II. 10. 9, 104–5). On Bacon's familiarity also with the enunciations drawn from the third version, *De radiis visualibus*, see Nascimento, pp. 205–7 n. 207.

[36] Undoubtedly the Arabic Pseudo-Euclidean compilation circulating under the title *De speculis* (see Lindberg, *Catalogue of Optical Manuscripts*, no. 80).

[37] Below, Appendix, α. 65–75. The *De pyramidibus* of Apollonius is presumably the fragment of his *Conic Sections* translated by Gerard of Cremona; see Marshall Clagett, *Archimedes in the Middle Ages*, iv (Philadelphia, 1980), 3–13.

[38] II. 10. 74.

[39] I. 4. 138; VI. 4. 51. An alternative title for the latter work (*Introductorius in Almagesti*) is given in Bacon's *Secretum Secretorum*, in *OHI*, v. 9. On the likelihood that this is in reality the *Liber introductorius Ptolomei ad artem sphericam* of Geminus, see Nascimento, p. 198 n. 179.

[40] Bacon cites these and other astronomical sources also in his *Compotus*, in *OHI* vi, *passim*.

[41] Appendix α. 65–6; IV. 1. 90–2; III. 3. 52–4.

[42] These data are assembled by Nascimento, pp. 69–71, 310–14.

[43] *Liber de causis* is cited in III. 2. 32; V. 1. 54; VI. 4. 27.

of these is al-Kindī's *De radiis*, which teaches the universal radiation of force, a doctrine of physical causation that helped to shape
Bacon's theory of the multiplication of species.[44] Although *De radiis*
is not explicitly cited in *De multiplicatione specierum*, we know
from Bacon's *De sensu* that he was familiar with it, and we may
therefore confidently affirm his dependence on it.[45] From Avicebron
Bacon took a number of important doctrines.[46] And finally, Bacon's
dependence on Grosseteste is undeniable; not only are the doctrinal
similarities too striking to be explained in any other way, but Bacon
occasionally makes veiled references to Grosseteste's optical works
and, indeed, quotes or paraphrases them on several occasions.[47]

Bacon cites only five sources in *De speculis comburentibus*:
Euclid's *Elements, De speculis*, and *Liber de visu*; Ptolemy's *Almagest*; and Alhazen's *De speculis comburentibus* (though without
knowing the identity of its author). It is apparent, however, that
for the writing of this treatise Bacon relied on more or less the same
authors as for *De multiplicatione specierum*.

HISTORICAL BACKGROUND TO BACON'S DOCTRINE
OF THE MULTIPLICATION OF SPECIES

Light metaphors were commonplace in early Greek literature and
philosophy. One finds them, for example, in Homer, Aeschylus,
Pindar, Parmenides, and Heraclitus.[1] But light metaphors were most
fully and effectively put to metaphysical use by Plato.[2] Perhaps the
outstanding instance is Plato's argument in the *Republic* that just
as we cannot see corporeal things unless they are illuminated by

---

[44] See below, pp. xliv–xlvi, liv.

[45] *OHI* xiv. 29. Nascimento points out, pp. 55–6, that the naturalistic determinism of
De radiis is sufficiently extreme to explain why Bacon would be reluctant to cite it, thereby
seeming to endorse its entire content. For a further affirmation of the influence of *De radiis*
on Bacon, see A. G. Molland, 'Roger Bacon: Magic and the Multiplication of Species',
forthcoming in *Paideia*.

[46] See below, pp. xlvi–xlviii, liv.

[47] For doctrinal similarities, see below, pp. xlix–lv. Bacon gives what is virtually a list
of Grosseteste's optical works in *Opus maius* (Bridges), i. 108. On quotations and paraphrases, see Nascimento, pp. 62–3; *DMS* II. 1 n. 5; II. 3 n. 9; II. 8 n. 2.

[1] Rudolf Bultmann, 'Zur Geschichte der Lichtsymbolik im Altertum', *Philologus*, 97
(1948), 1–36; James A. Notopoulos, 'The Symbolism of the Sun and Light in the Republic
of Plato', *Classical Philology*, 39 (1944), 163–72, 223–40; Dorothy Tarrant, 'Greek Metaphors of Light', *Classical Quarterly*, 54 (1960), 181–7.

[2] On Greek light metaphysics, see (in addition to the sources cited in the previous note)
Dieter Bremer, 'Hinweise zum griechischen Ursprung und zur europäischen Geschichte
der Lichtmetaphysik', *Archiv für Begriffsgeschichte*, 17 (1973), 7–22; Clemens Baeumker,
Witelo, ein Philosoph und Naturforscher des XIII. Jahrhunderts (BGPM 3. 2) (Münster, 1908),
pp. 357–79. For additional sources, see the excellent bibliography in Dieter Bremer, 'Licht
als universales Darstellungsmedium: Materialen und Bibliographie', *Archiv für Begriffsgeschichte*, 18 (1974), 185–206.

the sun, so we cannot have knowledge of intelligible things unless they are irradiated by the form of the good:

> It was the Sun, then, that I meant when I spoke of that offspring which the Good has created in the visible world, to stand there in the same relation to vision and visible things as that which the Good itself bears in the intelligible world to intelligence and to intelligible objects.
> How is that? You must explain further.
> You know what happens when the colours of things are no longer irradiated by the daylight, but only by the fainter luminaries of the night; when you look at them, the eyes are dim and seem almost blind, as if there were no unclouded vision in them. But when you look at things on which the Sun is shining, the same eyes see distinctly and it becomes evident that they do not contain the power of vision.
> Certainly.
> Apply this comparison, then, to the soul. When its gaze is fixed upon an object irradiated by truth and reality, the soul gains understanding and knowledge and is manifestly in possession of intelligence. But when it looks towards that twilight world of things that come into existence and pass away, its sight is dim and it has only opinions and beliefs which shift to and fro, and now it seems like a thing that has no intelligence. . . . This, then, which gives to the objects of knowledge their truth and to him who knows them his power of knowing, is the Form or essential nature of Goodness. It is the cause of knowledge and truth. . . .[3]

We see here an epistemological use of light, which was to be very influential: knowledge of the eternal verities is explained by analogy with solar radiation and corporeal vision. But Plato goes further and argues that the objects of knowledge owe their very existence to the Good, just as visible things owe their existence to the sun:

> . . . I want to follow up our analogy still further. You will agree that the Sun not only makes the things we see visible, but also brings them into existence and gives them growth and nourishment. . . . And so with the objects of knowledge: these derive from the Good not only their power of being known, but their very being and reality. . . .[4]

Being, as well as knowing, is thus explained by analogy with the behaviour of light. We shall see the development of both ideas in the Neoplatonic tradition.

If Plato was a major source of inspiration for the Western tradition of light metaphysics, another was the Bible. Old Testament writers made plentiful use of light-imagery. The Psalmist, for example, refers to the light of God's countenance and describes God as 'clothed with honour and majesty' and covered 'with light as with a garment'.[5] And the prophet Isaiah remarks that 'the Lord will be your ever-

---

[3] *Republic*, vi. 508 b–e, trans. Francis M. Cornford (London, 1941), 219–20.
[4] Ibid. 220.
[5] Psalms 44: 3 and 104: 2, Revised Standard Version.

lasting light'.[6] In the New Testament, we read in I John 1: 5 that 'God is light and in him is no darkness at all.'[7] But the most celebrated passage is from the Gospel of John:

In the beginning was the Word, and the Word was with God, and the Word was God. He was in the beginning with God; all things were made through him, and without him was not anything made that was made. In him was life, and the life was the light of men. The light shines in the darkness and the darkness has not overcome it. There was a man sent from God, whose name was John. He came for testimony, to bear witness to the light, that all might believe through him. He was not the light, but came to bear witness to the light. The true light that enlightens every man was coming into the world.[8]

With the use of light-imagery thus sanctioned and exemplified by Plato and the Bible, it is easy to understand its pervasiveness among late antique writers and the early church fathers. Philo of Alexandria (d. AD 45) took Platonic themes and transferred them into a monotheistic framework. In his treatise *On Dreams Being Sent from God*, he wrote:

. . . God is the first light, 'For the Lord is my light and my Saviour,' is the language of the Psalms; and not only the light, but he is also the archetypal pattern of every other light, or rather he is more ancient and more sublime than even the archetypal model, though he is spoken of as the model; for the real model was his own most perfect word, the light. . . .[9]

And in Philo's *On the Cherubim*, we read:

They do not know that He [God] surveys the unseen even before the seen, for He Himself is His own light. For the eye of the Absolutely Existent needs no other light to effect perception, but He Himself is the archetypal essence of which myriads of rays are the effluence, none visible to sense, all to the mind.[10]

More significant than Philo in terms of influence was Plotinus (d. 270), the founder of Neoplatonic philosophy. Plotinus developed a hierarchy of being, which progresses downwards from the transcendent, self-sufficient One through *nous* and soul to the visible universe. The relationship between the One, the ground of all being, and the remainder of reality Plotinus portrayed through the metaphor of

[6] Isaiah 60: 19–20, Revised Standard Version.

[7] Quoted from the Revised Standard Version.

[8] 1: 1–9, quoted from the Revised Standard Version. For other influential Biblical passages, see Genesis 1: 3; Job 12: 22, 25; Psalm 27: 1; Isaiah 9: 2; John 3: 19; Philippians 2: 15; and Colossians 1: 12. This list, however, barely scratches the surface. See also Johannes Hempel, 'Die Lichtsymbolik im alten Testament', *Studium Generale*, 13 (1960), 352–68.

[9] i. 13, *The Works of Philo Judaeus*, trans. C. D. Yonge, ii (London, 1854), 308.

[10] xxviii. 97, *Philo with an English Translation*, trans. F. H. Colson and G. H. Whitaker, ii (London, 1929), 67. Philo's work is filled with light metaphors. See, for example, *De virtutibus*, xxx. 164; *De opificio mundi*, xvii. 53 and xviii. 55. On Philo, see also Baeumker, *Witelo*, pp. 362–4.

radiation or emanation. Lesser being, he argued, proceeds from the One through the overflowing of its essence, just as rays of light proceed from the sun.[11] In his fifth *Ennead*, Plotinus inquires how the unitary and self-sufficient One could be the source of multiplicity:

. . . from such a unity as we have declared The One to be, how does anything at all come into substantial existence, any multiplicity, dyad, or number? Why has the Primal [the One] not remained self-gathered so that there be none of this profusion of the manifold which we observe in existence and yet are compelled to trace to that absolute unity? . . . Everything moving has necessarily an object towards which it advances; but since the Supreme [the One] can have no such object, we may not ascribe motion to it: anything that comes into being after it can be produced only as a consequence of its unfailing self-intention. . . . Given this immobility of the Supreme, it can neither have yielded assent nor uttered decree nor stirred in any way towards the existence of a secondary. What happened, then? What are we to conceive as rising in the neighbourhood of that immobility?

Plotinus answers:

It must be a circumradiation—produced from the Supreme but from the Supreme unaltering—and may be compared to the brilliant light encircling the sun and ceaselessly generated from that unchanging substance. All existences, as long as they retain their character, produce—about themselves, from their essence, in virtue of the power which must be in them—some necessary, outward-facing hypostasis continuously attached to them and representing in image the engendering archetypes: thus fire gives out its heat; snow is cold not merely to itself; fragrant substances are a notable instance; for, as long as they last, something is diffused from them and perceived wherever they are present. Again, all that is fully achieved engenders: therefore the eternally achieved engenders eternally an eternal being.[12]

The significance of this argument in Plotinian philosophy, of course, is that it explains (or attempts to explain) how a self-contained and self-sufficient ground of being can give rise to other beings. Its significance for the tradition of light metaphysics, on the other hand, is that Plotinus has portrayed the origin of both the invisible

[11] On Plotinus' doctrine of emanation, see A. H. Armstrong, *The Architecture of the Intelligible Universe in the Philosophy of Plotinus* (Cambridge, 1940), chap. 4. See also Armstrong, 'Plotinus', in *The Cambridge History of Later Greek and Early Medieval Philosophy*, ed. A. H. Armstrong (Cambridge, 1970); Werner Beierwaltes, 'Die Metaphysik des Lichtes in der Philosophie Plotins', *Zeitschrift für philosophische Forschung*, 15 (1961), 334–62; Emile Bréhier, *The Philosophy of Plotinus*, trans. Joseph Thomas (Chicago, 1958), chap. 4.

[12] *The Enneads*, v. 1. 6, trans. Stephen MacKenna, 2nd edn. rev. by B. S. Page (London, 1956), 373–4. I have obliterated MacKenna's paragraphing. Similar ideas are expressed in *Enneads*, v. 3. 12, pp. 394–5: 'The only reasonable explanation of act flowing from it [the One] lies in the analogy of light from a sun. The entire intellectual order may be figured as a kind of light with the One in repose at its summit as its King: but this manifestation is not cast out from it: we may think rather, of the One as a light before the light, as eternal irradiation resting upon the Intellectual Realm.'

and visible worlds through the metaphor of radiation and, in the course of the argument, has maintained that everything that exists produces an image or likeness of itself, which it directs into its surroundings. The argument was designed for metaphysical purposes, to show how all being can proceed ultimately from the One, but in the end it had significant fall-out in the physical realm, affirming that all things radiate likenesses of themselves. This physical use of the doctrine of emanation is ancestor to Bacon's doctrine of the multiplication of species.

Light metaphors are ubiquitous in Plotinus' *Enneads*,[13] but only one other passage demands our attention. In the first *Ennead*, Plotinus remarks that light or fire is the form of matter:

> And the simple beauty of colour comes about by shape and the mastery of the darkness in matter by the presence of light which is incorporeal and formative power and form. This is why fire itself is more beautiful than all other bodies, because it has the rank of form in relation to the other elements.[14]

This, as Armstrong has noted,[15] seems highly Stoic in character; but what is important from our standpoint is that Plotinus has adopted a position that would reappear in Grosseteste's identification of light with first corporeal form.[16]

Among the fathers of the Christian church, Basil of Caesarea (St. Basil, d. 379) discussed light at some length in his *Hexaemeron*. For the most part this discussion involved literal exegesis of the creation story in Genesis—the creation of light and darkness and the celestial luminaries.[17] However, on several occasions Basil allegorized, as when he discussed the divine beauty:

> If the sun, subject to corruption, is so beautiful, so grand . . . ; if its grandeur is in such perfect harmony with and due proportion to the universe; if, by the beauty of its nature, it shines like a brilliant eye in the middle of the creation; if finally, one cannot tire of contemplating it, what will be the beauty of the Sun of Righteousness? If the blind man suffers from not seeing the material sun, what a deprivation is it for the sinner not to enjoy the true light![18]

St. Augustine (d. 430) went much further than Basil, developing a synthesis of Christianity and Neoplatonism in which light was a central element. In an important study, François-Joseph Thonnard

---

[13] The following list of passages is merely a sampling: iii. 8. 5, iii. 8. 11, iv. 3. 11, iv. 5. 6–7, v. 5. 7, v. 6. 4, vi. 7. 41, vi. 9. 4.

[14] i. 6. 3, from *Plotinus with an English Translation*, trans. A. H. Armstrong, i (London, 1966), 241. For a far more florid translation see *Enneads*, trans. MacKenna, p. 58.

[15] *Architecture of the Intelligible Universe*, pp. 54–5.

[16] Below, pp. li–lii.

[17] *Homilies* II and VI: see the translation in *A Select Library of Nicene and Post-Nicene Fathers of the Christian Church* (2nd ser.), edd. Philip Schaff and Henry Wace, viii (New York, 1895), 60–5, 82–4, 87–8.

[18] Ibid. 82. See also the benediction at the close of *Homily* II, p. 65.

has identified ten different senses in which Augustine used the term
'light': external physical light, the light issuing from the observer's
eye to produce vision, the interior psychological light responsible
for the soul's sensitive and intellectual powers, the intellectual light
of divine illumination, the substantial light by which angels and
spirits are created, the supernatural light of faith, the theological
light of reason co-operating with faith, the mystical light of the gifts
of the Holy Spirit, the uncreated light of divine truth, and the
'light of the Word in the mystery of the trinity'.[19] We need not
concern ourselves with the details of this scheme; what is important
is to understand the pervasive use of light metaphors in Augustine's
philosophy to describe the realities, not only of the created universe,
but also of the Creator and His relationship to creatures.

Let us consider just a few examples. Augustine repeatedly refers
to God as light—the 'uncreated light', the 'intelligible light', the 'in-
accessible light', the 'light that enlightens', the 'truth and the light',
and the 'light of lights'.[20] In *De trinitate* he states that 'the Father
. . . is light, the Son is light, and the Holy Spirit is light, but together
they are not three lights but one light.'[21] Moreover, the relationships
among the members of the Trinity are revealed by a consideration
of light:

For the Word of the Father is the Son, which is also called His Wisdom. What
is, therefore, remarkable about Him being sent, not because He is unequal to
the Father, but because He is 'a certain pure emanation of the glory of the
almighty God'? But there, that which emanates and that from which it emanates
are of one and the same substance. For it does not issue as water from an opening in the ground or a rock, but as light from light. . . . For what is the brightness of light if not light itself? And consequently, it is co-eternal with the light
of which it is the light.[22]

Nor, Augustine maintains, is it a figure of speech to apply the term
'light' to members of the Trinity: 'Christ is called "light" not in the
same way as he is called "a stone", for he is called the latter figuratively but the former properly.'[23] Augustine's point is that God is
the archetypal light, and all other lights are the offspring or the
imitations. The uncreated light is light in the proper sense of the
term; all other lights are so by participation.

[19] François-Joseph Thonnard, 'La notion de lumière en philosophie augustinienne',
Recherches Augustiniennes, 2 (1962), 125–75.
   [20] *Contra adversarium legis et prophetarum*, i. 7. 10, in J.-P. Migne, *Patrologia latina*,
xlii (Paris, 1843), 609; *City of God*, x. 2; *De trinitate*, ii, pref.; ii. 2; vii. 3; viii. 2.
   [21] *De trinitate*, viii. 3, trans. Stephen McKenna (Washington, 1963), 228–9.
   [22] Ibid. iv. 20, pp. 164–5.
   [23] *De Genesi ad litteram*, iv. 28. 45, in Migne, *Patrologia latina*, xxxiv (Paris, 1841),
315; quoted by Thonnard, 'La notion de lumière', p. 131.

This is the core of Augustine's doctrine, but he also introduces an important epistemological strand into his philosophy of light. Augustine often identifies truth and light, echoing John 14: 6. He notes that 'everything that is manifest is light.'[24] He borrows and Christianizes the Platonic claim that the form of the Good irradiates intelligible things so that they may be known:

> . . . the intellectual mind is so formed as to see those things which, according to the disposition of the Creator, are subjoined to intelligible things in the natural order, in a sort of incorporeal light of its own kind, as the eye of the flesh sees the things that lie about it in this corporeal light, of which light it is made to be receptive and to which it is adapted.[25]

This is the doctrine of divine illumination, one of the hallmarks of the Augustinian tradition. For a grasp of intelligible things, the mind must be irradiated with divine light.[26]

The ancient and patristic sources that we have been considering gave rise to a rich medieval tradition of using light-motifs for theological, metaphysical, and epistemological purposes.[27] One of the major figures of this medieval tradition was Pseudo-Dionysius, an anonymous Greek author (perhaps a Syrian monk) of the late fifth century, whose amalgamation of Neoplatonic philosophy and Christian theology, clothed in light metaphors, was to be enormously influential in the West after its translation in the ninth century.[28] Others were William of Auvergne (d. 1249), distinguished Parisian theologian and bishop, and Bonaventura (d. 1274), Minister-General

[24] *De sermone Domini in Monte*, ii. 13. 46, in Migne, *Patrologia latina*, xxxiv. 1289; quoted in Thonnard, 'La notion de lumière', p. 149.

[25] *De trinitate*, xii. 15, trans. McKenna, p. 366.

[26] On Augustine's theory of divine illumination (including controversies over the exact function of illumination, into which we need not go), see R. A. Markus, 'Augustine: Reason and Illumination', in *The Cambridge History of Later Greek and Early Medieval Philosophy*, ed. A. H. Armstrong (Cambridge, 1970), 362-73; Étienne Gilson, *The Christian Philosophy of Saint Augustine*, trans. L. M. Lynch (New York, 1960), 77-96.

[27] On this subject, see Klaus Hedwig, *Sphaera Lucis: Studien zur Intelligibilität des Seienden im Kontext der mittelalterlichen Lichtspekulation (BGPM, NS 18)* (Münster, 1980); Hedwig, 'Forschungsübersicht: Arbeiten zur scholastischen Lichtspekulation. Allegorie-Metaphysik-Optik', *Philosophisches Jahrbuch*, 84 (1977), 102-26; Josef Koch, 'Über die Lichtsymbolik im Bereich der Philosophie und der Mystik des Mittelalters', *Studium Generale*, 13 (1960), 653-70; Baeumker, *Witelo*, pp. 372-422; Graziella Federici Vescovini, *Studi sulla prospettiva medievale* (Turin, 1965), 19-32.

[28] The influence of Pseudo-Dionysius is explained, in part, by his twofold identification as Dionysius the Areopagite, convert of the Apostle Paul, and St.-Denis, who had converted France to Christianity. On the use of light metaphors by Pseudo-Dionysius, see Otto Von Simson, *The Gothic Cathedral: Origins of Gothic Architecture and the Medieval Concept of Order* (New York, 1956), 52-5; Baeumker, *Witelo*, pp. 377-9. For the works of Pseudo-Dionysius, see *Dionysius the Areopagite On the Divine Names and the Mystical Theology*, trans. C. E. Rolt (New York, 1920); *The Works of Dionysius the Areopagite*, trans. John Parker, 2 volumes (London, 1897-9).

of Bacon's own order.[29] But this is not the place to undertake a detailed examination of all of the ramifications of the philosophy of light. Moreover, several aspects of this tradition had little influence on Bacon, or at least made no appearance in *De multiplicatione specierum* or *De speculis comburentibus*.[30] We must concentrate our attention, instead, on that aspect of the medieval philosophy of light that would be seized by Bacon and made a pillar of his new science—namely, the Plotinian doctrine of emanation, particularly in its less metaphysical, more physical, form.

The works of Plotinus were unknown during the Middle Ages, and his influence on Bacon and Bacon's contemporaries was therefore indirect. One of the main channels was Augustine, in whose light metaphysics we have already seen the products of Plotinian influence. Plotinus also came to the West through an abridgement of the second half of his *Enneads*, known as *The Theology of Aristotle*, which (although it was never translated into Latin) profoundly shaped Arabic philosophy and thus found expression in books that would be translated into Latin and read by Bacon and his contemporaries;[31] and through Proclus, whose *Elements of Theology* served as the basis for a treatise (whether first composed in Greek or Arabic cannot be ascertained) that was eventually translated from Arabic to Latin as *Liber de causis*.[32]

Proclus (d. 485) was a Neoplatonic systematizer in whose *Elements of Theology* we find a full exposition of Plotinian philosophy,

[29] On William of Auvergne, see Albrecht Quentin, *Naturkenntnisse und Naturanschauungen bei Wilhelm von Auvergne* (*Arbor scientiarum: Beiträge zur Wissenschaftsgeschichte* (Ser. A, 5) (Hildesheim, 1976), 2–4 and *passim*. On Bonaventura, see *St. Bonaventure's De reductione artium ad theologiam: A Commentary with an Introduction and Translation*, by Sister Emma Therese Healy (*Works of St. Bonaventure*, edd. Philotheus Boehner and M. Frances Laughlin, i) (St. Bonaventure, N.Y., 1955), *passim*; Jakob Fellermeier, 'Die Illuminationstheorie bei Augustinus und Bonaventura und die aprioristische Begründung der Erkenntnis durch Kant', *Philosophisches Jahrbuch*, 60 (1950), 296–305; Étienne Gilson, *La philosophie de Saint Bonaventure*, 3rd edn. (Paris, 1953), 221–35.

[30] For example, Bacon's works exhibit little in the way of a theology of light, except for an occasional tendency to put the phenomena of light to work analogically for purposes of moral and theological instruction; see Lindberg, *Theories of Vision*, p. 99. Bacon was certainly influenced by Augustine's theory of divine illumination, but nothing of this appears in *DMS* or *DSC*.

[31] On the Arabic tradition of the *Enneads*, see ʿAbdurraḥmān Badawi, *La transmission de la philosophie grecque au monde arabe* (Paris, 1968), 46–59. For a brief summary of *The Theology of Aristotle*, see Majid Fakhry, *A History of Islamic Philosophy* (New York, 1970), 33–9.

[32] E. R. Dodds notes that the *Liber de causis* 'is not a translation, a paraphrase, or even a systematic abridgement of Proclus' work, and much even of the substance has been modified to suit the requirements of a different theology' (*The Elements of Theology*, ed. and trans. E. R. Dodds, 2nd edn. [Oxford, 1963], p. xliii; see also pp. xxix–xxx). For an analysis of the Arabic tradition of the *Liber de causis*, see Badawi, *La transmission de la philosophie*, 60–73, Georges C. Anawati, *Études de philosophie musulmane* (Paris, 1974), 117–54. For brief summaries of the *Liber de causis*, see B. Hauréau, *De la philosophie*

including the procession of beings from the One. Although light metaphors are rarely used in this work,[33] Proclus faithfully spells out the Plotinian doctrine of the relationship between the One and its offspring. Indeed, he argues at length that the relationship between the One and *nous* is imitated in the relationship between any being and its immediate inferior. For example:

Every producing cause is productive of secondary existences because of its completeness and superfluity of potency.

For if it had produced not because of its completeness, but by reason of a defect of potency, it could not have maintained unmoved its own station: since that which through defect or weakness bestows existence upon another furnishes the substance of that other by a conversion and alteration of its own nature. But every producer remains as it is, and its consequent proceeds from it without change in its steadfastness. Full and complete, then, it brings to existence the secondary principles without movement and without loss, itself being what it is, neither transmuted into the secondaries nor suffering any diminution. For the product is not a parcelling-out of the producer: that is not a character[istic] even of physical generation or generative causes. Nor is it a transformation: the producer is not the matter of what proceeds from it, for it remains as it is, and its product is a fresh existence beside it. Thus the engenderer is established beyond alteration or diminution, multiplying itself in virtue of its generative potency and furnishing from itself secondary substances.[34]

Proclus also maintains that the effect will resemble (although it will not be identical to) its cause, and that cause is always superior to effect, so that a series of causes and effects constitutes a hierarchy of being, proceeding from perfection to imperfection.[35]

scolastique, i (Paris, 1850), 384–90; Fakhry, *Islamic Philosophy*, pp. 39–44. Badawi (p. 72) thinks the *Liber de causis* was first composed in Greek; Dodds (p. xxx) thinks it was first composed in Arabic.

[33] But see *Elements of Theology*, ed. and trans. Dodds, prop. 98, p. 87, where Proclus writes: 'we mean by "cause" that which fills all things naturally capable of participating [in] it, which is the source of all secondary existences and by the fecund outpouring of its irradiations is present to them all.' See also the Latin *Liber de causis*, prop. 5, in *Die pseudo-aristotelische Schrift Ueber das reine Gute, bekannt unter dem Namen Liber de causis*, ed. Otto Bardenhewer (Freiburg i. B., 1882), 168–9: 'Quod est quoniam causa prima non cessat inluminare causatum suum, et ipsa non inluminatur a lumine alio, quoniam ipsa est lumen purum supra quod non est lumen.' These examples, however, are exceptional. Note also Proclus' discussion of Plato's analogy of the sun in another work, *Platonic Theology*, which remained in Greek until the Renaissance: *Theologie platonicienne*, edd. H. D. Saffrey and L. G. Westerink, ii (Paris, 1974), 43–51.

[34] *Elements of Theology*, ed. and trans. Dodds, prop. 27, pp. 31–3. Note that Bacon wrote a set of questions on the *Liber de causis*, which make clear his indebtedness to Proclus; see Bacon, *OHI* xii. 1–158. Special note should be taken of passages such as the following (p. 40), in which Bacon follows Proclus on the virtue issuing from the One: '. . . set natura lucis est diffundere se extra se et facere se extra se per sui multiplicationem, ergo prima causa maxime habet facere se extra se et multiplicare se extra se, cum maxime habeat naturam lucis.' Bacon goes on to reject this particular argument and insist that the first cause does not emit virtue, but creates it *ex nihilo* in its vicinity.

[35] *Elements of Theology*, ed. and trans. Dodds, prop. 7, p. 9; props. 28–9, pp. 33–5; props. 36–7, pp. 39–41.

One of the important Islamic beneficiaries of the Neoplatonic tradition of Plotinus and Proclus was the philosopher al-Kindī (d. *c*.873). That al-Kindī had first-hand knowledge of the work of Plotinus is evident from his attempts to correct Nā'imah al-Ḥimṣī's translation of *The Theology of Aristotle*.[36] Al-Kindī apparently also knew Plato's *Republic*, for he wrote an *Epistle on the Elucidation of the Numbers Mentioned by Plato in the Republic*, and it is possible that he also knew the *Timaeus* and the *Laws*, translated into Arabic during his lifetime.[37] Neoplatonic metaphysics pervades al-Kindī's work: being is arranged into a hierarchy of perfection, the One is portrayed as the totally self-contained and unmoved first cause, and soul is explained as an emanation from the divine being analogous to the radiation of light from the sun.[38]

But the treatise of al-Kindī that is of greatest interest to us is a work on astrology, known in its Latin translation as *De radiis* or *Theorica artium magicarum*; this work appears to have deeply influenced Bacon, and we must therefore examine its contents with care.[39] Al-Kindī begins with the fundamental astrological claim that 'the world of the elements and everything composed of them depends on the disposition of the stars'; and the reason for this, he argues, is that they send their rays into the world.[40] The radiation varies with the nature of the star, its position in the 'world machine', the precise mode of radiation (rays issuing from the centre of a star are stronger), and the combinations of rays from different stars, so that 'in every different place there is a different tenor of rays derived from the total harmony of the stars'.[41] The motions of the stars and planets must also be taken into account, as well as the condition of the recipient matter. 'Therefore, the diversity of things in the world of the elements . . . proceeds principally from two causes, namely, from the diversity of the matter and the varied action of the stellar rays.'[42] 'All things', al-Kindī insists, 'come into being and exist through rays.'[43]

This much is fairly standard astrological fare. But al-Kindī presses further, probably under the influence of Plotinus, to argue that it is not only stars that radiate force, but that 'everything in this world,

---

[36] 'Abdurraḥmān Badawi, *Histoire de la philosophie en Islam*, ii (Paris, 1972), 386, 400. For a useful survey of al-Kindī's philosophy, see ibid. ii, 385–477; Fakhry, *Islamic Philosophy*, pp. 82–112.

[37] Badawi, *Histoire*, ii. 399.　　　　　　　　　[38] Ibid. ii. 417–18, 427.

[39] The Latin text has been carefully edited and briefly analysed by M.-Th. d'Alverny and F. Hudry, 'Al-Kindi, De radiis', *Archives d'histoire doctrinale et littéraire du moyen âge*, 41 (1974), 139–260. For brief summaries of its contents, see also Vescovini, *Studi sulla prospettiva medievale*, 44–7; Lynn Thorndike, *History of Magic*, i. 642–6.

[40] *De radiis*, ed. d'Alverny and Hudry, p. 218.

[41] Ibid. 219–20.　　　　　　[42] Ibid. 221.　　　　　　[43] Ibid. 220.

whether substance or accident, produces rays in the manner of stars.'[44] These rays proceed in all directions, 'so that every place in the world contains rays from everything that has actual existence',[45] and thereby each thing in the sublunary world acts on all other things.[46] Al-Kindī devotes the remainder of his treatise to examples and applications of this doctrine. He argues that rays of fire transmit heat, while the earth's rays transmit cold; medicines, taken internally or externally, diffuse their rays through the body; bodies in collision send forth rays that convey sound; magnets attract iron through their radiation; even images in the mind radiate; and desire, hope, and fear affect the rays issuing from a person, thereby influencing the things on which the rays fall. Entering the realm of magic and the supernatural, al-Kindī deals at great length with the rays produced by words, thus explaining the efficacy of incantations and prayers; through the power of words scorpions are expelled from their places, the weather is affected, lightning is produced, water is deprived of the ability to receive heavy objects, and various other wonders are produced.[47] Finally, al-Kindī discusses the rays issuing from images and figures and explains the efficacy of ritual sacrifice. Certain features of De radiis (its determinism and its analysis of prayer) were obviously heretical and had little long-term influence in the West; its more lasting contribution was to teach certain medieval scholars, including Grosseteste and Bacon, that every creature in the universe is a source of radiation and the universe itself a vast network of forces. This would be the central doctrine of Bacon's De multiplicatione specierum.

One other fact must be noted. Al-Kindī wrote another book, De aspectibus, in which he investigated the mathematics and physics of radiation.[48] Although nothing in either De radiis or De aspectibus justifies viewing them as a matched pair, it does seem certain that al-Kindī considered the mathematical and physical analysis of De aspectibus applicable to the rays of De radiis.[49] Moreover, it is reasonably certain that Bacon knew both treatises, knew both to

[44] Ibid. 224. [45] Ibid.
[46] Ibid. 228. Al-Kindī does point out, however, that this is the vulgar understanding of the matter and that in fact ('secundum exquisitam veritatem') this is merely an expression of celestial harmony and that 'only celestial harmony produces all things'. Radiation, then, is merely a matter of 'concomitance'.
[47] Ibid. 233–50. Bacon touches on some of these same matters in Opera (Brewer), pp. 96, 528–31.
[48] Analysed in Lindberg, Theories of Vision, chap. 2.
[49] This means that al-Kindī made rays more corporeal than Plotinus would have permitted defining them as modifications of the accidents of the medium. For al-Kindī's view, see ibid. 24–6, 30–1. For Plotinus', see Armstrong, Architecture of the Intelligible Universe, pp. 55–7; R. T. Wallis, Neoplatonism (London, 1972), 61–2; Enneads, ii. 1. 7, iv. 5. 6–7.

be the work of al-Kindī, and therefore viewed them as two aspects of a single philosophical effort. Surely, then, what Bacon discovered in al-Kindī was a mathematical and physical analysis of the doctrine of the universal radiation of force or influence; that Bacon's own efforts were in precisely this same direction must be the result, at least in part, of al-Kindī's example.

Neoplatonic philosophy flourished in Islam—and with it the doctrine of emanation, which one historian has referred to as 'the cornerstone of almost the whole of Arab philosophical thought'.[50] One finds emanationism, for example, in the metaphysics of two of Islam's most influential philosophers, al-Fārābī and Avicenna.[51] However, if we look for the doctrine of emanation in sources that were eventually translated into Latin and in forms that might have influenced Bacon's *De multiplicatione specierum*, another work stands out—the *Fons vitae* of the Spanish Jew (who wrote in Arabic) Avicebron (d. *c*.1058).

Central to Avicebron's philosophy is the doctrine of universal hylomorphism, namely, that all substances (except God) are composites of form and matter; in the case of spiritual substances, this form and this matter are themselves spiritual. Equally important is Avicebron's doctrine of the plurality of forms, according to which God created a universal being consisting of universal form and universal matter; although the latter has only potential existence, it achieves actuality as forms are added to it to produce the various beings in the universe; there is in each actual being, then, a multiplicity of forms, which determine its particular character and its place in the scale of being.[52]

These are important ideas, which were to be extremely influential among thirteenth-century Franciscans. But what must concern us most is Avicebron's teaching on the subject of emanation. Book iii of the *Fons vitae* begins with a demonstration (indeed, a series of demonstrations) of the necessity of simple substances (separated intelligences) intermediate between the divine first cause and the

[50] Fakhry, *Islamic Philosophy*, p. 33.

[51] Badawi, *Histoire*, ii. 538–45, 648–55; Parviz Morewedge, 'The Logic of Emanationism and Ṣūfism in the Philosophy of Ibn Sīnā (Avicenna)', *Journal of the American Oriental Society*, 91 (1971), 467–76; 92 (1972), 1–18. Al-Fārābī's use of the emanation doctrine is in his *The Model State*, which was never translated into Latin. Avicenna's emanationism is expressed in various works, including the *Shifā*, parts of which were rendered into Latin in the twelfth century.

[52] The addition of forms takes one down the scale of being, away from unity and towards multiplicity. On Avicebron, see S. Munk, *Mélanges de philosophie juive et arabe* (Paris, 1859), 3–306 (which includes a French translation of the Hebrew epitome of the *Fons vitae* by Shem Tob Falaquera, d. 1290); Isaac Husik, *A History of Mediaeval Jewish Philosophy* (New York, 1916), 59–79; Étienne Gilson, *History of Christian Philosophy in the Middle Ages* (New York, 1955), 226–9.

corporeal substance that supports the Aristotelian categories of being—essentially a discussion of the procession of all beings from the One.[53] Having established the existence of these intermediate substances, Avicebron inquires into the action of one substance on another. This action, he argues, is 'a thing giving its form to another thing when both are suited to it.'[54] But why, the pupil in Avicebron's dialogue asks, does such action occur?

> MASTER: . . . this occurs through the sublime universal cause, because the power that is the author of all things and moves all things by itself operates as long as it finds something to receive its action. Hence it is necessary that the universal form, made by this power, should also act by itself. It is therefore a maker and an agent. Similarly it is also necessary that the first universal matter should receive the action by itself. . . . And it is consequently necessary that all forms should be active and all matters passive. . . .
>
> PUPIL: Why is the universal form said to act necessarily?
>
> MASTER: Because the First Author, sublime and holy, dispenses the abundance that he has with him, for all that exists flows from him. And since the First Author is the dispenser of the form that is with him, he does not prevent it from flowing out; he is therefore the source that maintains, envelops, and comprehends everything that is. Hence it is necessary that all substances should obey his action and imitate him in giving their forms and bestowing their energies, as long as they find a matter ready to receive them. . . . In short, the first emanation that embraces all substances makes it necessary that the substances emanate into others. And in this regard take an example from the sun that does not emanate by itself and does not communicate its rays except for the reason that it falls under the first emanation and obeys it.[55]

All substances emanate their forms in imitation of the First Author. This emanation, Avicebron argues, does not involve flow of the substance's essence, but simply of its force (*vis*) or ray (*radius*).[56] He maintains that these forces or rays (even when they issue from body) are spiritual.[57] And he insists that whatever 'emanates from something is the image of the thing from which it emanates'.[58]

Avicebron's chief concern is with emanation from simple substances, and within that context he argues repeatedly that emanation is from superior to inferior: 'so every simple substance extends

[53] *Avencebrolis (Ibn Gebirol) Fons vitae*, ed. Clemens Baeumker (*BGPM* i. 2–4) (Münster, 1895), iii. 1–12, pp. 73–104.

[54] Ibid. iii. 13, p. 106.

[55] Ibid. iii. 13, pp. 106–8. I quote here from Wedeck's English translation in *The Fountain of Life (Fons vitae)*, specially abridged edition, trans. Harry E. Wedeck (New York, 1962), 35–6.

[56] *Fons vitae*, ed. Baeumker, iii. 15, p. 110; iii. 52, p. 196.

[57] Ibid. iii. 15, p. 110. However, in iii. 16 Avicebron concedes that 'this action is not corporeal absolutely nor spiritual absolutely, but is intermediary between the two extremes' (trans. Wedeck, p. 40).

[58] *Fons vitae*, ed. Baeumker, iii. 24, p. 136. The translation is Wedeck's, p. 63. Cf. iii. 53, p. 198.

its ray and its light and spreads them on that which is inferior.'[59]
Again:

If the corporeal substance receives the forms, that are supported in it, from
another substance different from itself, it is necessary that this substance should
be superior to it. Now the simple substance is superior to the compound substance. Therefore the corporeal substance receives the forms that it has from the
simple substance.[60]

It is clear from these quotations that the action Avicebron has in
mind is in the metaphysical, rather than the physical, realm; emanation accounts for the beings of things, not for their physical inter-
actions. Consequently, we must distinguish Avicebron's teaching
from al-Kindī's doctrine of the universal radiation of force—although
in at least one passage Avicebron expressed himself in terms that
could be taken for al-Kindī's view: 'the forces of all things that
exist are infused and penetrate through everything.'[61]

Despite certain troublesome doctrines, Neoplatonism proved
highly attractive to many Western thinkers, and in the thirteenth
century its influence became widespread.[62] Augustine's works, with
their Neoplatonic undercurrent, had of course been available from
the time he wrote them. The works of Pseudo-Dionysius were translated into Latin on several occasions: in the ninth century by Hilduin
and again by John Scotus Eriugena, in the thirteenth century by
Robert Grosseteste. Portions of Avicenna's Shifā, in which Neoplatonic emanationism appears, were translated by Dominicus
Gundissalinus (with the assistance of Avendauth and perhaps others)
between 1151 and 1166. This same Gundissalinus, along with a
different collaborator, Johannes, also translated Avicebron's Fons
vitae. The Liber de causis was translated into Latin by Gerard of
Cremona before 1187. And al-Kindī's De radiis was rendered into
Latin by an anonymous translator late in the twelfth century or
early in the thirteenth. Of course, Neoplatonic works were not the
only ones translated. By the beginning of the thirteenth century,
most of Aristotle had become available. And in addition, scores
of treatises on technical subjects had been translated, including

---

[59] Fons vitae, ed. Baeumker, iii. 52, p. 196.

[60] Ibid. iii. 17, pp. 117–18; translated by Wedeck, pp. 45–6.

[61] Fons vitae, ed. Baeumker, iii. 16, p. 114. Avicebron does not state that these forces
act on everything through which they penetrate, and as far as physical action is concerned,
I am not prepared to judge what his view might have been.

[62] Among the troublesome doctrines were Neoplatonism's tendency toward pantheism
and determinism and its denial of ex nihilo creation. The solution to such difficulties, of
course, was to be somewhat selective in one's choice of Neoplatonic doctrines and to down-
play troublesome elements. Thus one could retain an emanationist metaphysics while
repudiating its pantheistic and deterministic implications, and one could, of course,
continue to put light metaphors to theological and epistemological use.

geometrical optics—Euclid's *Optica* (*De visu* or *De aspectibus*) and *Catoptrica* (*De speculis*), Ptolemy's *Optica* or *De aspectibus*, al-Kindī's *De aspectibus*, and the *De aspectibus* or *Perspectiva* of Alhazen.[63] The materials were thus available for constructing a Neoplatonized Aristotelianism, with as much geometrical optics built in as the emanationist metaphysics would bear.[64]

One of the first in the West to feel the effects of these traditions was Robert Grosseteste (*c*.1168–1253), influential Oxford lecturer and shaper of English Franciscan thought. It is certain that Grosseteste knew Augustine's works and much of the Aristotelian corpus; Pseudo-Dionysius, of course; Basil's *Hexaemeron*; *Liber de causis*; probably Avicenna's *Metaphysics* and Avicebron's *Fons vitae*; Euclid's *De speculis*; probably Euclid's *De visu* and al-Kindī's *De aspectibus* and *De radiis*.[65] Grosseteste espouses a Platonic or Neoplatonic position at many points in his philosophy: he believes in a hierarchically arranged scale of being and the emergence of multiplicity out of unity; he accepts the nobility of light, arguing that it is 'more exalted ... than all corporeal things';[66] he adopts the Augustinian position on the illumination of the intellect and the relationship between soul and body; and he holds to the plurality of forms.[67] Grosseteste also develops a broad philosophy of light, Neoplatonic in inspiration, consisting of at least the following strands: 1. an epistemology of light, in which it is argued that intelligible things can be grasped only if illuminated by a spiritual light; 2. a metaphysics or cosmogony of light; 3. a physics of light; and 4. a theology of light, which employs light metaphors to express theological truths.[68] Let us consider more closely the second and third of these strands.

[63] For a general discussion of the translations, see David C. Lindberg, 'The Transmission of Greek and Arabic Learning to the West', in Lindberg, *Science in the Middle Ages*, pp. 52–90. For additional detail on translations referred to above, see Moritz Steinschneider, *Die europäischen Übersetzungen aus dem Arabischen bis Mitte des 17. Jahrhunderts* (Graz, 1956), 16–17; M.-Th. d'Alverny, 'Notes sur les traductions médiévales d'Avicenne', *Archives d'histoire doctrinale et littéraire du moyen âge*, 19 (1952), 337–58; d'Alverny and Hudry, 'Al-Kindi, De radiis', pp. 169–72; M. L. W. Laistner, *Thought and Letters in Western Europe, A.D. 500–900*, rev. edn. (London, 1957), 246–7. On the optical translations, see Lindberg, *Theories of Vision*, pp. 209–11.

[64] References to Neoplatonism in medieval Christendom from the thirteenth century onward always denote Neoplatonized Aristotelianism.

[65] See Daniel A. Callus, 'Robert Grosseteste as Scholar', in *Robert Grosseteste, Scholar and Bishop*, ed. Callus (Oxford, 1955), 23; Hunt, 'The Library of Robert Grosseteste', ibid. 121–45; Lindberg, *Theories of Vision*, pp. 94–5. I judge it probable that Grosseteste knew al-Kindī's *De radiis* purely on the basis of similarities in content.

[66] *On Light*, trans. Clare C. Riedl (Milwaukee, 1942), 10.

[67] On Grosseteste's philosophy, see Ludwig Baur, *Die Philosophie des Robert Grosseteste* (*BGPM* 18. 4–6) (Münster, 1917), especially pp. 170–288; Sharp, *Franciscan Philosophy*, pp. 9–46.

[68] Grosseteste's philosophy of light is examined in Lindberg, *Theories of Vision*, pp. 95–9; Crombie, *Grosseteste*, chap. 6; Baur, *Philosophie des Grosseteste*, pp. 76–84.

Grosseteste wrote no metaphysical *summa*, but from scattered remarks in his many short tracts it would seem clear that he adopted much of Neoplatonic emanationist metaphysics. For example, in *De ordine emanandi causatorum a Deo* he remarks that 'the Father is the cause of the Son, and the Son emanates from the Father'. Why, then, 'if the Son is co-eternal with the Father, since he emanates from the Father, are not created beings co-eternal with God, since they emanate from God . . .?'—a question that Grosseteste proceeds to answer in the remainder of the treatise.[69] In *De luce*, he points out that 'the first corporeal form is . . . more exalted and of a nobler and more excellent essence than all the forms that come after it. It bears, also, a closer resemblance to the forms that exist apart from matter.'[70] And later in the same treatise, Grosseteste argues that

every higher body, in virtue of the light which proceeds from it, is the form and perfection of the body that comes after it. And just as unity is potentially every number that comes after it, so the first body through the multiplication of its light, is every body that comes after it.[71]

It is apparent, then, that Grosseteste was willing to affirm the derivation of the whole of reality ultimately from the divine being by a succession of emanations. But for a Christian theologian there are tensions between the idea of emanation (which, strictly interpreted, derives inferior being from the super-abundant and overflowing essence of the supreme being) and the doctrine of *ex nihilo* creation. Grosseteste attempts to reduce these tensions (or perhaps simply to overlook them) in *De luce* by developing an account of the origin of the corporeal universe in terms of light, which largely bypasses metaphysical issues. That is, *De luce* offers a cosmogony rather than a metaphysics; it concentrates on temporal origins rather than being; by looking exclusively at the lower (corporeal) portion of the scale of being, it avoids examining the relationship of that portion to the regions above it; instead, it describes the generation of corporeal things through the action of a point of created light (created, of course, *ex nihilo*),[72] without explaining how this creative act fits into the overall pattern of emanation. In short, Grosseteste makes a novel attempt to bring the creation story in *Genesis* into

---

[69] *Die philosophischen Werke des Robert Grosseteste*, ed. Ludwig Baur (*BGPM* 9) (Münster, 1912), 147. The term that I have translated 'emanates' is *procedit*; it is clear from the title of the treatise that emanation is intended. Moreover, *procedere* is the term employed by Augustine to denote the emanation of the Son and the Holy Spirit from the Father (interchangeably with *manare*); see *De trinitate*, iv. 20, in J.-P. Migne, *Patrologia Latina*, xlii (Paris, 1843), 906–8.

[70] *On Light*, trans. Riedl, p. 10; Latin text in *Phil. Werke*, ed. Baur, p. 52.

[71] *On Light*, trans. Riedl, p. 15; *Phil. Werke*, ed. Baur, p. 56.

[72] The term employed by Grosseteste (*creare*) makes his intention perfectly clear— and, in any case, it could not be otherwise for a Christian theologian of Grosseteste's stature.

relation with Plotinian light metaphysics, without really facing the difficulties that must attend a serious attempt at reconciliation.[73]

One of the cornerstones of Grosseteste's doctrine is the idea that the first corporeal form—that which, when imposed on first matter, gives rise to the substratum of corporeal things—is light.[74] Light, as the form of corporeity, is both 'of a nobler and more excellent essence than all the forms that come after it' and their source.[75] Now in the beginning of time God created a point of light and imposed it on first matter. But both the point of light and the matter (in itself) are devoid of extension. However, it is the nature of a point of light to diffuse itself instantaneously in all directions; and as it does so, it draws first matter with it (since the two are inseparable), giving rise to a great sphere of simple body:

The first corporeal form which some call corporeity is in my opinion light. For light of its very nature diffuses itself in every direction in such a way that a point of light will produce instantaneously a sphere of light of any size whatsoever, unless some opaque body stands in the way. Now the extension of matter in three dimensions is a necessary concomitant of corporeity, and this despite the fact that both corporeity and matter are in themselves simple substances lacking all dimension. But a form that is in itself simple and without dimension could not introduce dimension in every direction into matter, which is likewise simple and without dimension, except by multiplying itself and diffusing itself instantaneously in every direction and thus extending matter in its own diffusion. For the form cannot desert matter, because it is inseparable from it, and matter itself cannot be deprived of form. . . . Thus light, which is the first form created in first matter, multiplied itself by its very nature an infinite number of times on all sides and spread itself out uniformly in every direction. In this way it proceeded in the beginning of time to extend matter which it could not leave behind, by drawing it out along with itself into a mass the size of the material universe.[76]

Multiplication is infinite not in extent or duration (the sphere of simple body is certainly finite, and the process is instantaneous), but in the number of self-replications required for the point of light to generate a sphere equal in size to the corporeal universe. An infinitesimal multiplied infinitely, Grosseteste believes, must yield a finite quantity.[77]

---

[73] I do not mean to imply that Grosseteste was fully aware of the tensions and engaged in subterfuge to escape them. It appears to me, rather, that he was committed to the truth of both doctrines, that he was (at most) dimly aware of their fundamental incompatibility, and that he was groping his way through difficult territory as honestly and skilfully as he could.

[74] *On Light*, trans. Riedl, pp. 10–11; *Phil. Werke*, ed. Baur, pp. 51–2. Grosseteste is here describing the corporeal analogue of Avicebron's universal form and universal matter, which combine to produce a universal being; see above, p. xlvi. On light as first corporeal form, see also Plotinus, above, p. xxxix.

[75] *On Light*, trans. Riedl, p. 10; *Phil. Werke*, ed. Baur, p. 52.

[76] *On Light*, trans. Riedl, pp. 10–11; *Phil. Werke*, ed. Baur, pp. 51–2.

[77] *On Light*, trans. Riedl, pp. 11–13; *Phil. Werke*, ed. Baur, pp. 52–4.

As the process of multiplication continues, the simple corporeal substance produced becomes ever more rarefied, until finally it reaches the maximum of rarefaction (which is the complete fulfilment of its potentiality).[78] The outermost sphere thus generated, consisting of nothing but fully actualized first matter and first form, is the firmament, which defines the outer limits of the corporeal universe. The firmament, in turn, diffuses its light inward towards the centre of the universe, producing additional rarefaction in upper regions and leaving lower regions more condensed. Through this process, which we need not examine in detail, nine celestial spheres and four elemental spheres are produced.[79] Grosseteste has thus formulated at least the outlines of a cosmogony of light.

Grosseteste's physics of light is far less developed than his cosmogony of light; indeed, he merely touches on the physics of light in a few paragraphs of *De lineis, angulis, et figuris*. He introduces the topic by stating that 'we must now consider universal action in so far as it partakes of the nature of sublunary things'.[80] He proceeds then to repeat the essentials of al-Kindī's claim that everything in the sublunary world acts on its surroundings through radiation:

A natural agent [*any* natural agent, as we shall see] multiplies its power from itself to the recipient, whether it acts on sense or on matter. This power is sometimes called species, sometimes a likeness, and it is the same thing whatever it may be called; and the agent sends the same power into sense and into matter, or into its own contrary, as heat sends the same thing into the sense of touch and into a cold body. . . . But the effects are diversified by the diversity of the recipient, for when this power is received by the senses, it produces an effect that is somehow spiritual and noble; on the other hand, when it is received by matter, it produces a material effect. Thus the sun produces different effects in different recipients by the same power, for it cakes mud and melts ice.[81]

This is virtually Grosseteste's entire statement on the subject. He does, however, extend al-Kindī's view in an important respect. Al-Kindī argued that everything sends forth rays to influence other things; Grosseteste appears to make the stronger claim that all physical causation can be reduced to such radiation. Grosseteste does not state this directly and unambiguously, but there are certain passages from which it can be inferred. Just before the long passage quoted above, Grosseteste writes: 'Now, all causes of natural effects must be expressed by means of lines, angles, and figures, for otherwise it is impossible to grasp their explanation.'[82] And after presenting

---

[78] *On Light*, trans. Riedl, p. 13; *Phil. Werke*, ed. Baur, p. 54. Grosseteste does not explain why there is a maximum of rarefaction or how it is defined.

[79] *On Light*, trans. Riedl, pp. 13–15; *Phil. Werke*, ed. Baur, pp. 54–7.

[80] My translation, from Grant, *Source Book*, p. 385; *Phil. Werke*, ed. Baur, p. 60.

[81] Grant, *Source Book*, pp. 385–6; *Phil. Werke*, ed. Baur, p. 60.

[82] Grant, *Source Book*, p. 385; *Phil. Werke*, ed. Baur, p. 60.

the geometrical rules governing the propagation of rays, he adds:

These rules, foundations, and fundamentals having been given by the power of geometry, the diligent investigator of natural things can in this manner specify the causes of all natural effects. And he can do this in no other way, as has already been shown in general, since every natural action is varied in strength and weakness according to variation of lines, angles, and figures.[83]

If all natural effects are expressible in terms of lines, angles, and figures, this is because all natural effects are caused by the radiation of force.[84]

Thus Grosseteste follows and extends al-Kindī's venture into the physics of light. He also follows al-Kindī in developing, at some length, the associated geometrical optics—the rules of rectilinear propagation, reflection, and refraction of light.[85]

BACON'S DOCTRINE OF THE MULTIPLICATION OF SPECIES

We are now in a position to appreciate the nature of Bacon's achievement in *De multiplicatione specierum*. Let us be clear at the outset that this work does not foreshadow the science of subsequent ages—the undulatory theory of light, the idea of experimental physics, or any other modern scientific development; rather, it represents an intelligent and creative response to a variety of ancient traditions. Bacon did not possess a seventeenth-century or twentieth-century mind, but a very good thirteenth-century one; and there is no possibility of understanding his achievement unless we view it in medieval context.[1]

---

[83] *Phil. Werke*, ed. Baur, pp. 65–6. This passage is from *De natura locorum*, which is frequently joined to *De lineis* in manuscripts and which can be considered a continuation of it. For further discussion of the significance of this passage, see David C. Lindberg, 'On the Applicability of Mathematics to Nature: Roger Bacon and His Predecessors', *British Journal for the History of Science*, 13 (1982), 10–14.

[84] In the article cited in the preceding note, I have argued that one should not take literally Grosseteste's claim that all of natural philosophy is reducible to mathematics. It does not follow that we must discount Grosseteste's claim that all causation is reducible to the radiation of force. That is, one can reduce causation to the radiation of force without conceding that the radiation of force is totally reducible to mathematics.

[85] Grant, *Source Book*, pp. 386–90. These matters are analysed in Crombie, *Grosseteste*, pp. 116–27; and Bruce S. Eastwood, 'Grosseteste's "Quantitative" Law of Refraction: A Chapter in the History of Non-Experimental Science', *Journal of the History of Ideas*, 28 (1967), 403–14.

[1] Bacon's friends, by portraying him as a man ahead of his time, able to foresee or anticipate later scientific developments, have done him a disservice; for this *ersatz* reputation has been an obstacle to an appreciation of Bacon's genuine achievements. See, for example, Bridges' introduction and notes to his edition of Bacon's *Opus maius* and *De multiplicatione specierum*; Charles Singer, 'The Dark Ages and the Dawn', in *Science and Civilization*, ed. F. S. Marvin (London, 1923), 139–43. That such judgements are not a thing of the distant past is evident from Joseph Kupfer's 'The Father of Empiricism: Roger not Francis', *Vivarium*, 12 (1974), 52–62.

Bacon was, first of all, an Aristotelian. Like every scholar of his age, Bacon took the basic framework and categories of his thought from Aristotle; the broad outlines of his logic, metaphysics, cosmology, and physics all came from the Aristotelian tradition. But Bacon's Aristotelianism was heavily Neoplatonized—and, of course, modified according to the necessities of Christian theology. Among the doctrines that Bacon took from the Neoplatonic tradition were the divine illumination of the intellect, universal hylomorphism, the plurality of forms (properly qualified), and the separability of the soul.[2] But Bacon deals with none of these matters in De multiplicatione specierum; nor does he touch upon the doctrine of emanation or develop a metaphysics or cosmogony of light. Rather, he simply lifts Grosseteste's physics of light (itself an outgrowth of al-Kindī's universal radiation of force) out of its metaphysical and cosmogonical context and develops it into a comprehensive doctrine of physical causation. What had been little more than the germ of an idea in al-Kindī and Grosseteste receives systematic development from Bacon.

There is no mystery about the sources of Bacon's philosophy. He knew the entire Aristotelian corpus, and himself lectured on a number of Aristotelian books at the University of Paris. He doubtless knew his Augustine well; commented on the Liber de causis; and was influenced by Avicebron's Fons vitae, directly and perhaps also through Dominicus Gundissalinus.[3] He was the chief early disseminator of Greek and Arabic optics in the West and had a thorough mastery of all the principal texts.[4] Grosseteste's influence is everywhere evident in his works. And finally, there can be no doubt that Bacon was influenced by the doctrine of the universal radiation of force taught by al-Kindī in De radiis.[5]

Before examining Bacon's physics of light, we must briefly consider the term 'species', by which he denotes the effect of an agent. The primitive meaning of the term, Michaud-Quantin has pointed out, was that of aspect, form, or exterior appearance.[6] During the Middle Ages various shifts and refinements occurred. As early as Augustine, we see the term put to use for psychological purposes,

[2] For an excellent analysis of various aspects of Bacon's philosophy see Crowley, chaps. 2–4. On the plurality of forms see pp. 106–15.

[3] On Avicebron's influence, see ibid., pp. 82, 90, 98–9. Bacon cites Avicebron's Fons vitae in his Questions on Aristotle's Physics, his Questions on the Metaphysics, and his Questions on De causis; see OHI viii. 46, 64; xi. 68; and xii. 88, 118.

[4] On Bacon's optical knowledge, see Lindberg, Theories of Vision, pp. 107–16.

[5] See the section above on sources.

[6] Pierre Michaud-Quantin, 'Les champs sémantiques de species. Tradition latine et traductions du grec', in Études sur le vocabulaire philosophique du moyen âge (Rome, 1970), 113.

to denote the image or likeness of a perceived object in the senses and the intellect—the agent by which a thing is perceived. Augustine argues in *De trinitate* that a corporeal object gives rise to an incorporeal likeness, a species, in both the external and the internal senses:

In this arrangement, therefore, when we begin with the species of the body, and finally arrive at the species which is formed in the gaze of thought, four species are found; they are born, as it were, step by step, one from the other: the second from the first, the third from the second, and the fourth from the third. For the species of the body, which is perceived, produces the species which arises in the sense of the percipient; this latter gives rise to the species in the memory; finally, the species in the memory produces the species which arises in the gaze of thought.[7]

The species, too, of the man is known to us in ourselves, and is likewise presented to the senses of the body from without in other men: to the eyes when it is seen; to the ears when it is heard; to the touch when it is held and touched; it also has its own image in our mind, incorporeal it is true, but yet similar to the body.[8]

This sense of the term remained current throughout the Middle Ages and appears constantly in scholastic theories of perception.

But with Grosseteste and Bacon, there is a significant broadening of the term's meaning. No longer does 'species' apply merely to the perceptual realm; now it denotes the likeness of any object, emanating from the object, whether or not a percipient being is present to receive it. Indeed, the term 'likeness' is no longer an adequate translation; the species is, of course, the similitude of the object from which it emanates, but it is more than that; it is the force or power by which any object acts on its surroundings. In short, the term has been appropriated by Grosseteste and Bacon to denote al-Kindī's universal force, radiating from everything in the world to produce effects. Grosseteste does not dwell on the matter at length, but remarks (in a passage already quoted in part):

A natural agent multiplies its power from itself to the recipient, whether it acts on sense or on matter. This power is sometimes called species, sometimes a likeness, and it is the same thing whatever it may be called; and the agent sends the same power into matter, or into its own contrary, as heat sends the same thing into the sense of touch and into a cold body. For it does not act by deliberation and choice, and therefore it acts in a single manner whatever it encounters, whether sense or something insensitive. . . .[9]

Bacon develops the idea much more extensively in the first chapter of his *De multiplicatione specierum*. 'Species', he says, 'is meant to designate the first effect of any naturally-acting thing.'[10] This first effect has different names in different contexts:

---

[7] *De trinitate*, xi. 9, trans. McKenna, p. 337; for context see the remainder of book xi.
[8] Ibid. xiii. 1, p. 373.   [9] Grant, *Source Book*, pp. 385–6.   [10] I. 1. 27–9.

It is called 'similitude' and 'image' with respect to the thing generating it, to which it is similar and which it imitates. It is called 'species' with respect to sense and intellect. . . . It is called 'idol' with respect to mirrors. . . . It is called 'phantasm' and 'simulacrum' in the apparitions of dreams. . . . It is called 'form' by Alhazen. . . . It is called 'intention' by the multitude of naturalists because of the weakness of its being in comparison to that of the thing itself. . . . It is called 'virtue' with respect to generation and corruption. . . . It is called 'impression' because it resembles impressions. . . . It is called 'passion' because the medium and sense, in receiving species, undergo a transmutation in their substance. . . .[11]

In certain optical contexts it is also called 'shadow of the philosophers'. But in all of these cases, it is the same thing differently named—and the name Bacon will prefer throughout this treatise is 'species'. A species, then,

is the first effect of an agent; for all judge that through species [all] other effects are produced. Thus the wise and the foolish disagree about many things in their knowledge of species, but they agree in this, that the agent sends forth a species into the matter of the recipient, so that, through the species first produced, it can bring forth out of the potentiality of the matter [of the recipient] the complete effect that it intends. And therefore, there is no doubt that the species is the first effect.[12]

It is apparent that Bacon attributes all natural causation to the multiplication of species.

The remainder of *De multiplicatione specierum* is given over to elucidating the process here summarized—determining what things produce species, how they produce species, how species are multiplied through a medium (both physically and mathematically), how species are received, and how they are weakened and corrupted. This is a complete physical and mathematical analysis of the radiation of force—and, thus, of natural causation. Let us survey the main points of Bacon's analysis.

First of all, the species resembles the agent—in nature, definition, specific essence, and operation. This must be so, since an 'agent directs its efforts to making the recipient similar to itself, because the recipient . . . is always potentially what the agent is in actuality', as Bacon establishes by quoting Aristotle.[13] Before receiving action, a recipient is dissimilar to the agent, but upon receiving the action becomes like the agent, as one can see by noting that fire produces fire in a recipient that was not fiery to begin with. But this will occur only if the species, the first effect of the agent and the

[11] I. 1. 42–69.
[12] I. 1. 75–81. See also the Appendix, α. 88–94 (quoted in the Preface, p. vii); *Compendium studii theologiae*, ed. Rashdall, pp. 35–6.
[13] I. 1. 83–5.

mediating instrument by which it acts on the recipient, is similar
to the agent. Thus the species of colour is colour, and the species
of light is light.[14] But here an objection arises. It may be true that
the species of light is light, but surely the species of man cannot be
called 'man'. Bacon explains that the species differs from the agent
as the incomplete from the complete; the species resembles the agent
in all respects except that its being is incomplete. It does, however,
possess the same specific nature, even if we choose in certain cases
(as man and his species) not to employ the same name.[15]

The species is not only like the agent, it is also univocal. That is,
there are not various first effects, but only one; secondary and
tertiary effects, on the other hand, may be numerous and equivocal.
Thus the first effect of light (*lux*) is always the same thing, namely,
light (*lumen*).[16] However, there may be diverse secondary (or yet
lower order) effects, including heat, putrefaction, and death.[17]
Diversity, then, in the lower orders of effect cannot result from the
agent or its species, but must arise from diversity in the recipients.[18]

What things produce species? Obviously the proper sensibles do,
since it is through their species that the proper sensibles are perceived.[19] Substance too produces species, albeit species that are
perceived only by the cogitative and estimative powers and not by
the external senses; it is thus that when a sheep first encounters
a wolf, even if it has never encountered one before, it perceives
the danger and flees.[20] The species of substance, Bacon argues,
'is not only the species of its form, but also of its matter and of the
entire composite', thus denying the claim of those who believe
that only form is active.[21] The senses and sense organs also produce
species, as we know from the fact that one man can see the eye of

---

[14] I. 1. 138.

[15] I. 1. 147-73. On the similarity of an emanation to its source, see Avicebron, *Fons
vitae*, iii. 53, ed. Baeumker, pp. 197-9.

[16] This distinction between *lux* (the luminosity of a luminous source) and *lumen* (its
species) is not always observed by Bacon. Indeed, he says specifically that he will usually
employ the terms interchangeably (I. 1. 36-7). On this distinction, see Lindberg, *Science
in the Middle Ages*, pp. 356-7.

[17] I. 1. 174-9.

[18] I. 1. 273-318. This point had been amply made before Bacon: see Grosseteste's *De
lineis*, in Grant, *Source Book*, p. 386; Husik, *History of Mediaeval Jewish Philosophy*,
pp. 66-7 (on Avicebron).

[19] The proper sensibles are the objects that the senses are particularly suited to perceive
and concerning which they cannot err—colour for sight, sound for hearing, flavour for
taste, odour for smell, and the tangible qualities for touch; see Aristotle, *De anima*, ii. 6.
On the question of the species of sound, Bacon seems ambivalent, for he both affirms and
denies the existence of such species; see I. 2. 3-29.

[20] I. 2. 30-92.

[21] I. 2. 138-9. Bacon later (line 217) affirms that 'matter [by its own proper nature]
in no way produces species'.

another; and, at least in the case of vision, the species issuing from
the organ participates in perception not only *of* that organ, but also
by that organ.[22] The common sensibles (size, shape, number, motion,
and the like) and other corporeal things belonging to the categories
(such as relation, position, and time), Bacon argues, do not produce
species.[23] Finally, both singulars and universals produce species. However, just as the universal exists only in the singular, so the species
of the universal will be present only in the species of the singular:

> And since singular men produce their species in the medium and sense and the
> intellect, so universal man simultaneously produces his species in the singular
> species; so that as universal man is one specific whole nature, wholly in each
> singular man, so the universal species is in its way one specific nature, and all
> of it is wholly in each singular species; for it cannot exist in any other way. . . .[24]

Bacon concludes this chapter by calling attention to what might be
called a 'principle of homogeneity': the species of a substance is
substance, of an accident is accident, of a composite is composite,
of a simple is simple, of matter is matter, of a form is form, of
a universal is universal, and of a singular is singular. Moreover, the
relationship of accident to substance, form to matter, and universal
to singular is replicated in the relationship of the species of accident
to the species of substance, the species of form to the species of
matter, and the species of the universal to the species of the
singular.[25]

Having established what things generate species, we must now
inquire how they generate species. In I. 3 Bacon considers five
possibilities and systematically demolishes all but the final one.
First, nothing flows out of the agent as from an odoriferous substance. If such an emission were to occur, it would be either of
substance or of accident, and either of these would entail corruption
of the agent. Since incorruptibles, such as spiritual and celestial
substances, produce species, the emission theory is clearly false.[26]
Second, the agent does not create species *ex nihilo*. This conclusion
required no defence, and Bacon offered none, since it would have
been obvious to all medieval readers that only God can create *ex
nihilo*. Third, the agent does not obtain a species somewhere outside
itself and deposit it in the recipient, for such an idea is 'ridiculous'.
Bacon thus rules out three modes of generation according to which
'the agent dispatches something to the recipient, which flows into
it'.[27] In all of these, something enters the recipient from outside,

---

[22] I. 2. 180–210. Bacon displays considerable confusion on this point; for a brief analysis,
see Lindberg, *Theories of Vision*, pp. 114–15.

[23] I. 2. 220–349.   [24] I. 2. 357–63.   [25] I. 2. 378–90.

[34] I. 3. 4–19. Bacon is here attacking the doctrine of the atomists.

[27] I. 3. 23.

and Bacon will tolerate no such scheme. Only two possibilities remain. According to one of them, the agent makes an 'impression' on the recipient, as a seal makes an impression in wax. This, however, is impossible, since impressions are surface phenomena, whereas natural actions occur 'in the interior of the recipient';[28] moreover, through species we perceive the agents that generate the species, while impressions reveal to us only the impressed recipients. (Bacon does admit, however, that 'impression' in the broader sense, according to which every alteration of a recipient by an agent is an impression, may be applied to the generation of species.)[29]

Only one possible mode of generation remains. Species must be generated by a 'bringing forth out of the active potentiality of the recipient matter'.[30] The agent does not deposit a species in the recipient, but elicits a species out of the recipient's potentiality—not, however, its passive potentiality (the aptitude of matter for receiving forms), but its active potentiality (the predisposition of matter towards a particular form, comparable to Augustine's *ratio seminalis*).[31] But there is an objection, Bacon says, which has deceived many. The agent and recipient must, of course, be conjoined in order for action to take place. But if the species is elicited from the interior of the recipient and the agent is conjoined only to the exterior of the recipient, there would of necessity be an additional virtue sent by the agent into the interior of the recipient to elicit the species; and this additional virtue cannot, of course, be generated out of the potentiality of the recipient, but must be given to it by the agent. Thus the true instrument of the agent for producing its effects would be a virtue or species 'not brought forth out of the potentiality of matter, but . . . given and infused . . .; and it is produced only by the agent, in order to alter the interior of the recipient, and through it the effect is brought forth out of the potentiality of the matter.'[32] Bacon attacks this objection with a variety of arguments—one of them being an effort to turn the objection against itself: if the agent cannot act directly on the interior of the recipient without the aid of this auxiliary virtue, then it cannot produce the auxiliary virtue in the interior of the recipient without yet another intermediary: the result of this argument, one can see, will be an infinite series of auxiliary virtues, which gets us nowhere. In any case, it is clear to Bacon that no intermediary

[28] I. 3. 33.
[29] I. 3. 33–43. For this usage, see Lindberg, *Theories of Vision*, pp. 114–16.
[30] I. 3. 52.
[31] On the active and passive potentiality of matter (a characteristic Franciscan doctrine), see Sharp, *Franciscan Philosophy*, pp. 14–15, 122–3.
[32] I. 3. 82–6.

between agent and the interior of the recipient is required 'because
natural action does not require this.' Rather,

the active substance of the agent, touching the substance of the recipient without intermediary, can alter, by its active virtue and power, the first part of the
recipient that it touches. And this action flows into the interior of that part,
since that part is not a surface, but a body, however small it may be; nor can
it be perceived or understood without its depth—and therefore without depth
it can be neither touched nor altered.[33]

When an agent acts on some part of a recipient, it alters that part in
its interior, as well as its surface. 'For since the agent touches the
recipient, and not only the bare surface, but the substance [of
the recipient] through the mediation of the surface . . . , I say that
the agent sufficiently touches the interior of the first part.'[34]

An important question raised by this discussion is whether agents
and recipients behave as wholes or as parts, and, if the latter, how we
are to conceive of the production and reception of species. Bacon
offers six conclusions to clarify the matter. First, there is no
minimum size for an agent; since, according to Aristotle, all
recipients are also agents, and a thing cannot be too small to receive
action, it follows that a thing cannot be too small to act.[35] Second,
the recipient is acted upon not only by the surface of the agent with
which it is in contact, but by the entire depth of the agent. That is,
the agent acts as a whole: 'Nor is there distinction of parts in action,
so that one [part of the agent] would produce one part [of the
action] and another would produce another part, . . . but the whole
agent produces the whole action.'[36] Third, the depth of action on
a recipient is of some determined quantity, which is not a function
of the agent's strength. Weak and strong agents will reach to the
same depth of the recipient, as the sun and moon illuminate the
same amount of space (in a given time): 'If a certain power could
alter or generate a certain form, then twice the power could produce
double the effect in the same subject, but not through twice the
space.'[37] It would seem to follow that there is some universal (though
apparently unknown) depth of action. Fourth, a portion of the
affected part of the recipient cannot be 'a sufficient subject of
action' as long as it remains part of the whole.[38] Fifth, one half of
the agent does not alter one half of the recipient, and the other

[33] I. 3. 149–56.   [34] I. 3. 159–62.
[35] This is only one of several arguments presented in I. 4. 13–91.
[36] I. 4. 113–15.
[37] I. 4. 148–50. Bacon later compromises this claim, arguing that there is an upper limit
on an agent's depth of action, but no lower limit; see IV. 2. 50–2; also the Introduction,
below, p. lxix.
[38] I. 4. 151–63.

half of the agent the other half of the recipient. Rather, the agent acts
as a whole on the recipient to the appropriate depth. Finally, it cannot
be that the first half of the first part of the recipient is altered and then,
in turn, alters the second half of the first part; for, according to such
a scheme, 'there would be no size limit as far as action is concerned,
and half of the first half could be altered, and so on to infinity'.[39]
It would then be impossible for an action ever to be accomplished,
since before any portion of the agent could be altered, its half would
need to be altered. Moreover, the second half of the first part of the
recipient would not, in any case, be altered by the first half of that
first part, but by the agent itself: 'Nature . . . grants to the principal
agent the task of altering the second half and denies this task to the
first half, and thus the action of the agent itself does not end until
it completes its action by alteration of both halves.'[40] What this
sixth point amounts to is a demonstration of the absurdity that
would result if agents did not act to a fixed and determined depth.

To this point, most of the discussion has concerned agents and
recipients in the terrestrial region. Bacon now inquires into action
among celestial bodies and between celestial and terrestrial things.
He argues, first, that terrestrial things are influenced by the species
of celestial things, because they belong to the same genus and must,
therefore, share the same matter; we know, moreover, that terrestrial
things are illuminated by celestial bodies and that generation and
corruption in the terrestrial realm are caused principally by the
motion of the sun.[41] Furthermore, celestial bodies can be influenced
by other celestial bodies. The obvious case in point is the illumination of the moon and stars by solar light. To the objection that the
generation of species in the moon constitutes change in the heavens,
Bacon replies that the generation of the species of the sun in the
moon is the realization of a natural disposition and the satisfaction
of an appetite, which is permissible.[42] Finally, terrestrial things are
able to act on celestial things. This may seem to be a troublesome
claim, but it is proved by the fact that we can view things in the
heavens, and vision requires the multiplication of species from the
observer's eye to the observed object; moreover, if an observer
were located in the lunar sphere, he would be able to see terrestrial
things by means of their species, multiplied to the heavens. There
are, of course, various objections to be met: change in the heavens
is appropriate, Bacon argues, if its function is assimilation of celestial
nature to terrestrial nature 'for the sake of well-being and greater
unity of the universe and to meet the needs of sense, especially

[39] I. 4. 176-8.
[41] I. 5. 6-24.
[40] I. 4. 200-3.
[42] I. 5. 29-48.

sight'; as for the acknowledged fact that an inferior cannot act on its superior, Bacon points out that

in so far as the heaven has aptitude and potentiality and a certain appetite with respect to the virtues of terrestrial things that it lacks, so that it would be assimilated to them for the sake of greater uniformity in the universe, in this respect it is less noble than a terrestrial thing, however base, that has such a species perfectly and in actuality. Nor does this detract from the nobility of celestial substance, since it does not contribute to its ignobility, but to its splendour, being directed towards complete harmony and well-being and perfection among the parts of the universe. . . .[43]

Effects may be complete or incomplete. Complete effects are those in which the agent so prevails over the recipient as to destroy the latter's specific nature and replace that specific nature with an effect similar to itself in name and definition. The completion of an effect requires two things: that the agent be more powerful than the recipient, and that the agent and recipient share the same matter.[44] Which agents, then, are able to produce complete effects? Among substances (spiritual, celestial, and corporeal), only the four elements—and especially fire, which is 'more noble and therefore more active [than the other elements]; and it would convert all non-celestial bodies into itself and act to infinity if it were to meet [only] combustible matter. . . .'[45] Fire is strong enough to produce complete species or effects even in mixed bodies; the remaining elements can complete their effects only in other elements, as when water converts air into itself and vice versa. But mixed bodies (both animate and inanimate) and spiritual and celestial substances are nobler than the elements; consequently, they have more active virtue and should be better able than the elements to produce complete effects; why do they not do so? Because God so ordains, for the sake of maintaining the order of the universe. If spiritual substances could complete their species or effects, all things would become spiritual; if celestial substances could complete their effects, all noncelestial substance would be destroyed. Therefore, 'by divine ordination and a universal law of nature', mixed bodies and spiritual and celestial substances are permitted to produce species, but are deprived of the ability to produce complete effects similar to themselves in name and definition.[46] The same is true of other noble agents in relation to ignoble recipients. In short, the ability to generate complete effects is restricted to four substances—the elements, and especially fire. As for accidents, the four tangible qualities (warmth, coldness, dryness, and humidity) can produce

[43] I. 5. 77–89.   [44] I. 6. 4–7, 78–97.   [45] I. 6. 32–40.
[46] I. 6. 56–173; the quoted phrase is in line 119.

complete effects, as can light in suitable bodies, but nothing else.[47]

All of the analysis thus far has been applicable only to the production of an agent's first effect (its species) in an immediately adjacent recipient—or, as Bacon puts it, in the first part of the recipient. It is necessary now to enlarge the analysis and consider the multiplication of species—that is, the transmission of species through a larger recipient or medium by successive replication. The agent produces its species in the first part of the medium, according to the rules outlined above. The species in the first part then gives rise to a new species in the second part, and the species in the second part generates yet another species in the third part, and so on. Note that it is not the agent that generates the second species in the second part of the medium (for it is not in contact with that part of the medium), but the species in the first part. Note, moreover, that the parts of the medium involved in this process of multiplication are of equal size; as we proceed outward from the agent, the species are of diminishing virtue, but that means that they produce alterations weaker in quality, but equal in quantity.[48] Bacon summarizes the process in his *Opus maius*:

But a species is not body, nor is it moved as a whole from one place to another; but that which is produced [by an agent] in the first part of the air [or other medium] is not separated from that part, since form cannot be separated from the matter in which it is unless it should be mind; rather, it produces a likeness to itself in the second part of the air, and so on. Therefore, there is no change of place, but a generation multiplied through the different parts of the medium; nor is it body which is generated there, but a corporeal form that does not have dimensions of itself but is produced according to the dimensions of the air; and it is not produced by a flow from the luminous body, but by a drawing forth out of the potentiality of the matter of the air.[49]

There in a nutshell is Bacon's doctrine on the physics of the propagation of force.

But Bacon is also interested in the mathematics of this propagation—like al-Kindī and Grosseteste—and in part II of *De multiplicatione specierum* he undertakes a comprehensive analysis of the mathematical laws of radiation. All of his material comes from the standard Greek and Arabic sources (which he read in Latin translation) on geometrical optics—for although it is the propagation of force in general with which he is concerned, light is his paradigm case.[50] Bacon's starting point is the spherical radiation of light or

---

[47] I. 6. 189–219. On complete effects, see also IV. 2. 93–119.

[48] II. 1. 11–24.

[49] *Opus maius* (Bridges), pt. V. 1, dist. 9, chap. 4, vol. ii. 71–2; translation reprinted, with minor variations, from Grant, *Source Book*, p. 394.

[50] Bacon explains that 'the multiplication of light is more apparent to us than the multiplication of other things, and therefore we transfer the [terminology of the] multiplica-

force from every least part of the agent—or, more properly, from the first part of the recipient affected by each least part of the agent.[51] Thus infinitely[52] many rays issue in all unobstructed directions from every point or part of the agent, or from the part of the recipient immediately adjacent to it. These rays proceed along straight lines as long as they are in homogeneous inanimate media, and they have width corresponding to the width of the part of the agent (or the first part of the recipient) that produces them.

But not all media are homogeneous or inanimate, and therefore Bacon must describe the other possibilities. There are five lines, he says, along which multiplication can occur.[53] First, there is direct radiation in a straight line. Second, if radiation passes obliquely from a medium of one transparency to a medium of another, the rays are refracted in such a way as to be closer to the perpendicular in the medium of greater density or less transparency. Bacon notes, however, that if the ray falls perpendicularly on the interface between the two media, it proceeds without refraction. Moreover, it is possible to have two different media, with distinct surfaces, which nevertheless have the same transparency, as the spheres of air and fire or the various celestial orbs.[54] Third, a species traversing one medium may encounter a second medium so dense as to prevent altogether the passage of species. Under such circumstances, the species, 'seizing the occasion from the [presence of] the dense body, returns by its own power in the direction from which it came';[55] it does this in such a way as to make equal angles with the incident ray. The fourth line is what Bacon calls the 'twisting path'. In an animated

tion of light to the others' (II. 1. 58–60). See also the prologue to the revised version, Appendix, α. 88–94, quoted in the Preface, p. vii.

[51] II. 1. 25–32. A 'least part' of the agent is small, but finite, though for convenience Bacon often refers to it as a point. Note that Bacon is willing to entertain a division of the agent into parts, in apparent contradiction of his earlier claim that agents act as wholes. However, it should be noted that the earlier argument pertained to division of the agent in depth, whereas the present claim has to do with division in a lateral sense. There can be little doubt (in view of the doctrine of punctiform analysis of the visible object, which Bacon knew from al-Kindī and Alhazen and fully accepted in his visual theory) that Bacon subscribed to the view that when one observes a wall, each least part of the surface radiates force independently of other least parts of the surface, but that the radiation from each of these least parts represent the entire depth or thickness of the wall. See Lindberg, *Theories of Vision*, pp. 29–30, 73–4, 109; *Opus maius* (Bridges), pt. V. 1, dist. 6, chap. 1, vol. ii. 35; below, II. 9. 6–40; V. 3. 4–18.

[52] Bacon carefully qualifies his use of this term in II. 1. 37–40.

[53] II. 2. For a similar account, see *Opus maius* (Bridges), pt. IV. 2, chap. 2, vol. i. 111–17, partly translated in Grant, *Source Book*, pp. 393–4. Modes of multiplication are also examined in detail in *DSC*.

[54] II. 2. 36–43; II. 4. 9–30. On refraction, see also *DMS*, II. 3–5; *Opus maius* (Bridges), pt. V. 3, dist. 2, vol. ii. 146–59 (partly translated in Grant, *Source Book*, pp. 426–30).

[55] II. 2. 87–8. On reflection, see also *DMS*, II. 5–7; *Opus maius* (Bridges), pt. V. 3, dist. 1, vol. ii. 130–46; *DSC, passim.*

medium, such as the fluid filling the optic nerve, light is not bound by the law of rectilinear propagation, but is 'directed according to the requirements of the soul's operations; and since the operations of the soul with regard to species occur in the twisting nerves, the species follows the twisting of the nerve . . . '.[56] Finally, the fifth line is that of accidental multiplication. From each point within a beam of primary radiation (proceeding from the agent along straight, reflected, or refracted lines) rays of weaker secondary radiation issue in all directions. Such species, he says, are the species of species, and through them one sees not the original agent, but only the principal species of the original agent. To illustrate, Bacon points out that solar radiation falling through an open window directly illuminates (that is, by its principal species) a spot in the house; however, parts of the house outside this directly illuminated region do not remain completely dark, for they are the recipients of accidental or secondary radiation proceeding from each point of the primary beam.[57]

Having set forth the fundamental principles of propagation, Bacon proceeds (in II. 3-10) to supply additional detail and deal with specific problems. He takes a mathematical look at incidence on curved surfaces—spherical, pyramidal, columnar, oval, annular, and lenticular—and extends the principles of refraction to such surfaces. He develops a rather elaborate physical theory to explain why species adopt a path closer to the perpendicular in the denser medium, arguing that a species must 'choose' a direction in the second medium which will most nearly preserve the strength it possessed in the first medium.[58] Bacon presents a mathematical analysis of the burning sphere. He considers refraction of stellar rays as they pass from the celestial to the terrestrial region, and argues (following Ptolemy and Alhazen) that every star is observed outside its true place. He discusses bodies, such as water, that reflect and refract simultaneously, considers the unformity of surface that produces clear mirror images, and argues that reflection does not involve the impression of an image in the mirror. Bacon returns to the mathematics of reflection to explore reflection at equal angles in concave and convex mirrors, and to analyse hemispherical, oval, and annular burning mirrors. Finally, he considers the figures in which multiplication occurs, especially spherical

[56] II. 2. 101-4. For an analysis of Alhazen's views (which Bacon is following), see Lindberg, *Theories of Vision*, pp. 80-4.

[57] II. 2. 116-41.

[58] II. 3. 81-168. For an analysis of Bacon's views on the physical causes of refraction, see David C. Lindberg, 'The Cause of Refraction in Medieval Optics', *British Journal for the History of Science*, 4 (1968-9), 23-38.

and conical, and deals briefly with the problem of radiation through apertures.[59]

The mode of existence of species in media has already been touched upon, but Bacon undertakes a fuller analysis in part III. He argues, first of all, that species are not bodies *per se*, because they do not have dimensions or corporeal natures distinct from those of the media in which they are situated. We know this, for example, because when species are generated in a medium, the sides of the medium are not forced outward. Rather, the medium is the material cause, out of the potentiality of which species are generated.[60] But what about the species of corporeal substance? Will this not occupy place of itself, like the agent that produced it? Bacon replies that the species of corporeal substance has exceedingly incomplete being, and therefore the medium prevails over it and endows it with dimensionality. As for the ability of a species to change its place in the medium, like a moving body, Bacon contends that it is not numerically the same species situated in successive parts of the medium. If the species remains in its place, although the medium moves (as light in moving air), the species 'is corrupted when the part of the air in which it was moves from that place; and a new species is not generated until another part of the air occupies that place. . . .'[61] Bacon considers the reflection of species and the formation of shadows and finds that they do not refute his position. However, in antiquity, it was especially the species of light that had been considered body—by the atomists and those who associated light with fire.[62] Bacon refutes this opinion by appealing to the authority of Aristotle.

If species are not bodies, are they corporeal or spiritual in nature? Definitely the former, as Bacon establishes in a series of arguments. Everything in the universe is corporeal except soul, intelligence, and the first cause. The species of a corporeal agent is similar to its agent in name and definition and must therefore be corporeal. No agent is less noble than the thing generated, as would be the case if a corporeal agent produced a spiritual species. But if the species is corporeal in essence, is it possible that it is spiritual in its mode of existence in the medium? No, since the mode of existence must be in agreement with the essence having that mode of existence; moreover, the reception of anything (including a species) must be according to the mode of existence of the recipient, and the recipient in the case under consideration is corporeal; furthermore, the causes of the

---

[59] A number of these matters are treated more fully in *DSC*.

[60] III. 1. 3–46.   [61] III. 1. 98–100.

[62] See Lindberg, *Theories of Vision*, pp. 2–6.

being of species are corporeal (the agent and the matter from the potentiality of which it is generated), and it must therefore possess corporeal being. Any other conclusion Bacon labels 'madness'.[63] If Aristotle, Avicenna, and Averroes have seemed to maintain the contrary, this is through mistranslation and faulty interpretation of their works. For example, if Averroes, in his *De sensu et sensato* and commentary on Aristotle's *De anima*, seems to endow the species of a corporeal thing with spiritual being in the medium, 'this should be understood entirely to refer to insensible being, to which some vulgar [scholar] or the translator applied the name "spiritual" because of the similarity between spiritual things and insensibles'.[64]

One of the *raisons d'être* of the doctrine that species have spiritual existence in the medium had been its ability to explain how beams of radiation could intersect (and therefore occupy the same space at the same time) without losing their identity. For example, the lines of sight of two observers can cross without any interference or confusion of the observers' visual perceptions.[65] But since it has now been established that species have corporeal existence in the medium and that mixing therefore occurs, Bacon must find some way of explaining this apparent lack of interference. He admits that when the species of different colours (say, white and black) come to one point of the medium, a true compounding occurs, and a single mixed species is produced, which proceeds to the observer's eye.[66] How, then, is it possible for the observer to have independent perceptions of the original colours rather than a single perception of their compound? Bacon replies that

from the first place of mixing in the medium, one of those species comes [directly] from the perceived thing itself, falling perpendicularly on the eye and the pupil, while the other comes [to the eye] along an accidental line; and the latter comes perpendicularly to the eye not from the perceived object, but only from the place of mixing.[67]

Therefore, the stronger species conceals the weaker ('the visual power is occupied with the species that alters it more strongly and dismisses the other'),[68] and the observer perceives only the colour lying directly behind the place of mixing. In short, one of the species comes by its principal line, the other by an accidental line, and the former is strong enough to conceal the latter. This is not, of course, a satisfactory solution of the problem, for Bacon explains the absence of confusion and interference when species mix by the simple

---

[63] III. 2. 3–81.
[64] III. 2. 91–3. Avicebron had also maintained the spirituality of species; see above, p. xlvii.
[65] On this doctrine, see Lindberg, *Science in the Middle Ages*, pp. 357–8.
[66] III. 3. 20–9. [67] III. 3. 70–3. [68] III. 3. 75–6.

expedient of treating the species as though no mixing had occurred.

Three related topics remain—the strength of action, weakening, and corruption of species. Bacon treats these matters briefly in parts IV–VI. All media, however rare, he argues, offer some resistance to the passage of species. This is so because all action produces rarefaction and condensation in the medium; and the dense naturally resists rarefaction, while the rare naturally resists condensation.[69] To the argument that only contraries resist and that some species have no contrary, Bacon replies that although there is no absolute contrary to celestial virtue, there is a contrary to the rarefaction that it produces. To the argument that species perfect and fulfill matter and therefore should not be resisted by it, Bacon replies that matter 'experiences a certain modest transmutation' on account of species, and this transmutation leads to rarefaction or condensation, which matter must resist.[70]

But, surprising though it may seem to one educated in modern physics, resistance in the medium does not of itself explain the weakening of species. Bacon associates weakening of species not with resistance, but with increasing resistance, and uniformity of strength not with the absence of resistance, but with uniformity of resistance; indeed, he goes so far as to argue that a species propagated through a medium in which the resistance is progressively reduced can actually gain strength.[71] Obviously, then, one cause (there are two) of the weakening of a species is progressively greater resistance in the medium; this explains the weakening of celestial radiation as it descends, since density increases as one proceeds from the heavens to the earth. The second cause is accidental multiplication or dispersion, which draws off some of a species' power. The two causes may, of course, work together; but they may also work in opposition, as when strengthening as a consequence of the progressive reduction of resistance in the medium is countered by weakening as a result of dispersion.

Could a species proceed to infinity if it should continuously encounter matter receptive of it? Yes, but in actuality no such matter exists, and therefore in actuality the propagation of a species is always finite. However, in apparent opposition to this conclusion is Aristotle's statement that 'if the whole power can perform some operation, then the part can perform part of the operation';[72] for it would seem to follow that the last of a series of species could

---

[69] IV. 1. 6–14.
[70] IV. 1. 21–39. See also VI. 1. 10–27.
[71] IV. 1. 97–124.
[72] IV. 2. 46–7, citing Aristotle, *Physics*, vii. 5, $250^{a}1-^{b}9$.

always produce a further species, and that the species would therefore proceed to infinity. Bacon proposes two possible solutions. The
first (which he says resolves the matter for some people) requires
him to back down on an earlier claim. When he stated earlier that
the depth of action of an agent is of some fixed value ('that a species
is generated in a certain determined space'), this was not meant to
impose a lower limit on the depth of an agent's action, but only
an upper limit.[73] Therefore, the species occupying the penultimate
part of the space produces its likeness in the final part of the space,
but not in the whole of the final part, and in particular not up to
the extreme boundary. Therefore 'this multiplication counts for
nothing', and multiplication of the species comes to an end.[74] The
second solution is based on the premise that there is a ratio (equal
to or greater than one) between the strength of the species in the
prior part of a space and the strength of the species in the posterior
part of that space. It follows that any species (here the final species
in the series) is suited to alter something according to that ratio.
But it is not necessary, Bacon argues, that this something be part
of the same medium that has been altered up to this point; it may
rather be a medium of greater subtlety and alterability, and it is
impossible for such a medium to extend infinitely.[75]

Bacon also explains the corruption and termination of species
in another way. It is true, he admits, that the medium or recipient
may have potentiality and appetite with respect to some species
generated in it; however, it has even greater potentiality and appetite
towards things of its own specific nature. Consequently, there is
no power in the medium that would tend to preserve a species not
of the medium's own specific nature, and the power of preservation
must come from the species' own strength or from an outside agent.
Thus if the medium is left to itself, it 'perfects itself according to
things proper to it' and 'returns completely to its own nature',[76]
thereby corrupting the species.

Does it follow, then, that a species must disappear in the absence
of the agent that generated it? No; this would occur only if species
were body or a flux from body and thus 'continuous with the substance of the agent'.[77] The species is corrupted not by removal of
the generating agent, but by the weakness of its being and the
medium's assertion of its own nature. But if the medium is the
heaven, where there are no contraries, how can the medium's own

---

[73] IV. 2. 43–68. The earlier claim (I. 4. 16 ff.) was that weak and strong agents reach
to the same depth of the recipient, a claim now clearly compromised.

[74] IV. 2. 55–6.   [75] IV. 2. 69–82.

[76] VI. 1. 42, 46.   [77] VI. 2. 8.

nature assert itself against the species? Bacon replies that in the heavens there are no contraries as regards the four tangible qualities (warmth, cold, humidity, and dryness), but that contrariety between rare and dense, light and dark is present there. If it should be pointed out that the virtues of the father are present in his semen and remain during the generation of progeny, even in the absence of the father, and therefore similarly in other cases, it is replied that the father and mother (the agent and the recipient) are of the same specific nature, and 'therefore the species and virtue of the father received in the mother are preserved by the presence of the mother, which suffices in place of the father owing to the identity of specific nature.'[78] In other cases where the species remains in the absence of the agent, this is because a more complete effect is produced and the recipient has greater density, which contributes to the preservation of species.[79]

When the generating agent is present for a period of time, does the first species remain as long as the agent is present, or is it continually corrupted and replaced by another species? The answer is that species are quickly generated and quickly corrupted. We know this by the authority of the perspectivists, especially Alhazen, but it can also be established by argumentation. Burning glasses and burning mirrors are able to produce combustion by assembling species in one place. However, combustion would be far stronger than it is if the first species coming from the sun were to endure and be 'augmented by continuous [additional] multiplications until sunset'.[80] Also, if this process of continuous augmentation were to occur, species in a rare medium would be far stronger and better able to preserve themselves than in fact they are.

Bacon deals with a miscellany of other matters in these final three parts of De multiplicatione specierum. He argues that the multiplication of species is not instantaneous, but occupies time.[81] He argues that when the same agent returns to act a second time on the same recipient, it produces a species numerically distinct from the previous species.[82] And he undertakes a brief mathematical analysis of strength of action, concluding that action is strongest along straight lines perpendicularly incident on the recipient; that

[78] VI. 2. 30-2.

[79] VI. 2. 32-50; VI. 4. 39-48, 64-76.

[80] VI. 4. 16-17.

[81] IV. 3. Bacon deals with the topic somewhat more fully in Opus maius (Bridges), pt. V. 1, dist. 9, chap. 3, vol. ii. 68-71. Bacon's arguments are analysed in David C. Lindberg, 'Medieval Latin Theories of the Speed of Light', in Roemer et la vitesse de la lumière (Centre national de recherche scientifique, Collection d'histoire des sciences, 3) (Paris, 1978), 53-6.

[82] VI. 3.

refracted lines are, in general, stronger than reflected lines; that, among refracted lines, those are weaker which diverge more from the perpendicular to the surface of the body; and that action through shorter pyramids, other things being equal, is stronger than action through longer pyramids.[83]

THE CONTENT OF *DE SPECULIS COMBURENTIBUS*

De speculis comburentibus and *De multiplicatione specierum* have an obvious relationship, inasmuch as both deal with optical matters —*De multiplicatione specierum* by developing a philosophy of natural causation on an optical model, *De speculis comburentibus* by investigating the modes of propagation of light and applying them to the analysis of the burning mirror. It could be reasonably argued that *De speculis comburentibus* submits to microscopic scrutiny a small piece of the subject matter of *De multiplicatione specierum*.[1] But there are also important differences between the two treatises. *De multiplicatione specierum* is one of Bacon's most successful and interesting attempts to carry through a sustained analysis of a broad physical (or philosophical) topic; to be sure, it contains a good stiff dose of mathematics, but this is no more than a quarter of the total, and it does not intrude on the predominant physical concerns. *De speculis comburentibus*, on the other hand, is clearly Bacon's best and most sophisticated treatment of a narrow mathematical question; indeed, it contains possibly the most incisive and original piece of geometrical optics produced in the West during the entire Middle Ages.[2]

The starting point for *De speculis comburentibus* is the last proposition of *De speculis*, the medieval Latin translation of the Euclidean *Catoptrica*.[3] In this proposition, the author presented two demonstrations regarding the modes of radiation between the sun and a spherical burning mirror. According to one of them, light is multiplied from one point on the surface of the sun to all points on the surface of the mirror; according to the other, light passes from every point on the surface of the sun through the centre of curvature of the mirror, falls perpendicularly on the mirror, and is

---

[83] V. 1–3.

[1] The portion of *DMS* scrutinized in *DSC* is II. 7–10 (less than ten per cent of the whole).

[2] There have been only two studies of *DSC*: J. Würschmidt, 'Roger Bacons Art des wissenschaftlichen Arbeitens, dargestellt nach seiner Schrift *De speculis*', *RBE*, pp. 229–39; David C. Lindberg, 'A Reconsideration of Roger Bacon's Theory of Pinhole Images', *Archive for History of Exact Sciences*, 6 (1970), 214–23.

[3] On this work see *DSC*, I. n. 1.

reflected back on itself (see figs. 40 and 41, pp. 276-7). Bacon repeats these demonstrations quite competently and then raises four questions: whether light is multiplied according to the first of the demonstrated modes; whether multiplication also occurs according to any other mode; which of these modes is strongest and most important; and whether combustion in a burning mirror is caused principally by multiplication in the first mode or by some other mode.[4] Bacon thus uses a proposition regarding burning mirrors as the occasion for an exhaustive analysis of the modes of propagation of light.

Bacon answers his four questions as follows. Multiplication does indeed occur according to the first of the demonstrated modes—from a single point on the sun to all points of the mirror. Indeed, light comes from that point of the sun to all points of the medium to which straight lines can be drawn. We know this because we can see that point of the sun from any point in the medium. However, this argument is applicable not merely to some particular point on the surface of the sun, but to all points on the sun; therefore, radiation comes to the whole surface of the mirror and all points of the medium from every point on the surface of the sun. But among the rays thus defined, there is a subset of particular importance. To each point of the mirror comes a ray which, if extended backwards, would pass through the centre of the sun. This is the strongest ray coming to that point of the mirror, both because it is the shortest and because it represents an agent of greater depth than any other ray (the whole diameter of the sun).[5] From all of this, Bacon argues, it is clear that there is a mode of radiation 'more basic and more efficacious' than the first of the demonstrated modes—namely, radiation from the entire surface of the sun to a single point of the mirror or medium.[6] According to this mode, each point of the mirror receives not just one ray, as in the first demonstrated mode, but an infinity of rays, including the aforementioned strongest ray. Therefore, the final proposition of De speculis (which provided the occasion for this treatise) is defective because it fails to take account of the infinity of rays actually reaching the point of combustion of a burning mirror.

This much occupies the first two parts of the treatise. In parts III and IV, Bacon seeks confirmation of his analysis in observable phenomena. He argues from data on lunar eclipses that the earth's

---

[4] Parts I-II. Note that the breakdown of DSC into sections is my doing rather than Bacon's.

[5] II. 57-93. On the entire depth of the agent as source of action, see above, pp. lx-lxi; DMS, I. 4. 102-15.

[6] II. 94-124.

shadow must converge to an apex on the side opposite the sun and that this demonstrates the truth of his analysis of the modes of propagation. He considers radiation passing through apertures and argues that if radiation issued from only one point of the luminous source, the radiation (after passing through the aperture) would always be of the same shape as the aperture, whereas in fact it assumes the shape of the luminous source; from this we can conclude that multiplication occurs from the entire surface of the source. Finally, Bacon claims that if a convex spherical mirror is placed opposite the sun, it can be 'clearly perceived by the eye' that an infinity of rays is reflected from each of its points—which means, of course, that each point receives radiation from the entire surface of the sun.[7] Bacon concludes, therefore, that from the sun cones issue in all directions, with vertices at all points of the medium and lateral surfaces tangent to the body of the sun; the axis of each cone is its strongest ray, the outermost rays are the weakest, and everything between is of intermediate strength (see fig. 50, p. 301). An important feature of the mode of radiation thus described is that it embodies all other modes of radiation; that is, it includes all rays actually proceeding from the luminous source.

Perhaps it seems that Bacon is belabouring the obvious. But it must be vigorously maintained that what is obvious to us need not have been obvious in the thirteenth century. Nobody in the West and no Greek or Arabic source available in the West had ever probed the modes of propagation as thoroughly as this, and it was by no means obvious, until Bacon made it obvious, precisely how light is propagated. For example, how could one know whether a luminous source radiated as a whole or as a collection of parts? Was it really self-evident that the radiation from the sun should be considered a collection of cones with the solar surface as base and every point of the medium as vertex, rather than a collection (say) of cylinders with the sun as base? In considering these questions, we must keep in mind that although Bacon's analysis was mathematical in character, it was intended to provide an accurate description of a physical process involving corporeal things. That is, Bacon was not interested merely in exploring various mathematical conventions that might be descriptive of the effects of radiation; he was searching for a description of the way in which physical radiation was truly multiplied. It was not a question of whether multiplication of light could be represented by means of an infinity of cones, but whether multiplication really took place in that manner.

In part V Bacon returns to the problem of radiation through

[7] IV. 23-33.

apertures, now attempting a detailed analysis. The question is how the roundness of radiation that has passed through angular apertures is consistent with the modes of propagation that Bacon has established in the preceding parts. I have given Bacon's argument a close analysis elsewhere[8] and will therefore discuss the matter no further here, except to stress two points. First, Bacon's purpose in discussing radiation through apertures was not because of its relevance to the *camera obscura* or the functioning of the human eye, but strictly as a test case for his theory of propagation. He makes this clear when he says that 'if the true and complete cause of [the shape of] this radiation incident through apertures were known, it would lead the knowledgeable person to great understanding of the multiplication of solar light and the actions that result from it'.[9] Secondly, nowhere in his analysis does Bacon relax his commitment to the rectilinear propagation of light.

Having now established the principles of propagation to his satisfaction, Bacon returns in parts VI–VIII to burning mirrors. In part VI he argues that a cone falling on a plane mirror returns either on itself or on another cone with the same vertex and, as its axis, the reflection of the axis of the incident cone. The same thing, he then argues, must be true of all other mirrors. He calculates the angle at the vertex of the cone of solar radiation falling on a burning mirror and from this calculates the diameter of the reflected cone at the focus or point of combustion.

Bacon begins part VII by noting that henceforth he will discuss only the axes of the cones of incident radiation, since the rest of the cone follows the axis. He argues that although the axes of the cones of solar radiation incident on a plane mirror are sensibly parallel, they in fact diverge slightly before reflection and therefore diverge after reflection. The same is true of convex spherical mirrors, only more so. However, solar axes incident on a concave spherical mirror are made to converge and collect together near the point of combustion. Solar axes incident on one circle about the central axis of the mirror all converge to a single point; solar axes incident on another circle about the central axis of the mirror converge to another point, and so on. The furthest of these points of convergence (associated with solar axes incident on the smallest possible circle) is no further from the mirror than half its radius of curvature. Bacon has nicely located the focal point of the mirror and identified the phenomena that we associate with spherical aberration.

Finally, in part VIII, Bacon describes how to fabricate a rough

[8] 'Reconsideration of Bacon's Theory', pp. 214–23.
[9] V. 150–2.

approximation of a paraboloidal burning mirror. He knows that such a mirror will bring all solar axes to a single point of focus, but he presents no mathematical analysis, and he admits that he does not know how to calculate the exact location of the point of combustion.[10]

MANUSCRIPTS AND EDITIONS

De multiplicatione specierum. The twenty-four known extant manuscripts of this treatise are listed immediately below. The first ten, given with sigla and descriptions, are those employed in this edition. These ten are arranged alphabetically by siglum in two groups of five. Manuscripts 1–5 have been transcribed in full, and all significant variants are given in the apparatus criticus. Manuscripts 6–10 have been employed where additional manuscript testimony was required.

1. *B* = Brugge, Stadsbibliotheek, MS 490, ff. 1^v–21(20)^v.

The hand is textual gothic, written in the Rhineland between 1350 and 1400.[1] Parchment; double column; no figures. Spaces are frequently left for omitted words, which were apparently illegible in the exemplar from which this manuscript was copied. Described by A. de Poorter, *Catalogue des manuscrits de la Bibliothèque Publique de la Ville de Bruges* (*Catalogue général des manuscrits des bibliothèques de Belique,* ii) (Paris/Gembloux, 1934), pp. 560–1.

2. *F* = Florence, Biblioteca Medicea Laurenziana, MS Plut. 29 cod. 41, ff. 30^r–55^v.

Written *c.*1300 in the Rhineland in a notular text hand. Parchment; double column; figures. Part VI is lacking from the manuscript. Follows Bacon's *Perspectiva.* Described in A. M. Bandinus, *Catalogus codicum latinorum Bibliothecae Mediceae Laurentianae,* ii (Florence, 1775), col. 58.

3. *L* = London, British Library, MS Royal 7.F.VIII, ff. 13^r–46^v.

This is the earliest extant manuscript, written in Oxford between 1280 and 1300 in three different hands, the first two (ff. 13^r–19^v and 20^r–44^r) textual cursive, the third (ff. 44^v–46^v) formed textual. Vellum; figures. There are many marginal and interlinear corrections in a later hand. Preceded by a Baconian text on the multiplication of species claiming to be part of the *Compendium studii theologie;*[2] followed by Bacon's *Perspectiva.* Described by George F. Warner

---

[10] A surprising admission; see *DSC*, VIII. n. 9.

[1] I owe the date, the provenance, and the description of the hand—here and in all of the remaining manuscript descriptions—to Fr. Leonard E. Boyle.

[2] See above, pp. xxix–xxx.

and Julius P. Gilson, *Catalogue of Western Manuscripts in the Old Royal and King's Collections*, i (London, 1921), pp. 202–3.

4. *O* = Oxford, Bodleian Library, MS Digby 235, pp. 305–388.

Written in a very clear English secretary hand about 1425. Parchment; double column; figures. The remainder of the codex contains Bacon's *Opus maius*; *De multiplicatione specierum* is inserted immediately after part V (the *Perspectiva*). Described by G. D. Macray, *Catalogi codicum manuscriptorum Bibliothecae Bodleianae*, ix (Oxford, 1883), cols. 244–5.

5. *S* = Salamanca, Biblioteca Universitaria, MS 2662, ff. 213^r–235^r.

A Parisian textual gothic hand of about 1350. Parchment; double column; figures. Ends at V. 3. 35 (*longioris*). Other Baconian works are contained in the same codex. This manuscript contains the revised version of *De multiplicatione specierum*. Described by Guy Beaujouan, *Manuscrits scientifiques médiévaux de l'Université de Salamanque* (Bordeaux, 1962), pp. 174–8.

6. *A* = London, British Library, MS Add. 8786, ff. 20^v–46^r.

Written, probably at Oxford, between 1300 and 1350, in Anglicana formata. Vellum; double column; figures. This manuscript suffers from considerable fading and is not everywhere legible.[3] This is another copy of the revised version and would, on that account, have been transcribed in its entirety had it been legible throughout. Contains extensive marginal corrections in a later hand. Other Baconian works are found in the same codex. Described by Robert Steele in *OHI* xiv, pp. xi–xii.

7. *M* = Milan, Biblioteca Ambrosiana, MS R 47 sup., ff. 1^r–42^v.

An Italian rotund gothic hand, written about 1300 in Lombardy. Parchment; figures. This copy contains the prologue of the revised version, but no other revisions. The codex also contains Bacon's *Perspectiva*. Described in Astrik L. Gabriel, *A Summary Catalogue of Microfilms of One Thousand Scientific Manuscripts in the Ambrosiana Library, Milan* (Notre Dame, 1968), pp. 333–4.

8. *N* = Florence, Biblioteca Nazionale, MS Conv. soppr. J.IV.29, ff. 2^r–47^r.

The hand is Italian bastardina, written about 1450. Parchment; no figures. Ends at VI. 4. 40 (*luna*). Formerly belonged to the Dominican convent of San Marco in Florence. Described by Axel Anthon Björnbo, 'Die mathematischen S. Marcohandschriften in Florenz', *Bibliotheca Mathematica* (Ser. 3), 12 (1911–12), pp. 214–15.

---

[3] This is true even when viewed under ultraviolet light.

9. *P* = Paris, Bibliothèque Nationale, Fonds Latin, MS 2598, ff. 21^r-56^v.

A careless Italian cursive humanist hand, written between 1450 and 1500. Paper; few figures. Followed (in a different hand) by Bacon's *Perspectiva*. Contains the prologue of the revised version, but no other revisions. Described in Bibliothèque Nationale, *Catalogue général des manuscrits latins*, ii (Paris, 1940), pp. 539-40.

10. *V* = Venice, Biblioteca Nazionale Marciana, MS Lat. VI.133 (Valentinelli, XI.10), ff. 1^r-21^r.

Written in an Italian notular text hand, about 1350. Parchment; double column; figures. Followed by Bacon's *Perspectiva*. Described by J. Valentinelli, *Bibliotheca Manuscripta ad S. Marci Venetiarum*, iv (Venice, 1871), pp. 222-3.

There are fourteen additional manuscripts of *De multiplicatione specierum*, which have not been used in the preparation of this edition:

11. Cambridge, Magdalene College Library, MS Pepsyan 1207, ff. 61^v-74^r. 15th cent. A highly abridged version.

12. Cambridge, Trinity College Library, MS 0.5.13 (1294), pp. 557-647. 17th cent.

13. Douai, Bibliothèque Municipale, MS 691, ff. 52$^{'r}$-60$^{'v}$, 61^r-68^v. 17th Cent. Incomplete.

14. Dublin, Trinity College Library, MS D.2.2 (381), ff. 154^r-190^r. 16th cent. A copy of *O*.

15. Erfurt, Wissenschaftliche Bibliothek, MS Ampl. Q.234, ff. 115^r-122^v. 14th cent. Fragment.

16. Florence, Biblioteca Medicea Laurenziana, MS Ashburnham 957, ff. 1^r-70^v. 15th-16th cent.

17. London, British Library, MS Sloane 2156, ff. 42^r-71^v. 1428.

18. Oxford, Bodleian Library, MS Savile 18, ff. 89(88)^r-105^v, 165^v-168^r. 15th cent.

19. Oxford, University College Library, MS 48, ff. 65(62)^r-118(112)^v. 17th cent.

20. Paris, Bibliothèque Mazarine, MS 3488, pp. 239-303. 1690.

21. Paris, Bibliothèque Nationale, Fonds Latin, MS 16621, ff. 1^r-24^v. 14th cent. Incomplete.

22. Vatican City, Biblioteca Apostolica Vaticana, MS Ottob. Lat. 1870, ff. 1^r-48^r. 15th cent. Incomplete.

23. Vienna, Österreichische Nationalbibliothek, MS 5311, ff. 101^r–106^r. 14th–15th cent. Fragment.

24. Winchester, Winchester College Fellows Library, MS 39, ff. 47^r–85^v. 15th cent.

This is the third time *De multiplicatione specierum* has been edited. The first edition was by Samuel Jebb, a physician, published in 1733 as part of the *Opus maius*.[4] Jebb based his edition on a collation of MS *L* and the Dublin MS. Jebb's edition was reissued, with corrections, in Venice in 1750. The second edition was by John Henry Bridges, published along with the *Opus maius* (but not as part of it) in 1897.[5] Bridges based his edition on MS *O* and the Dublin MS, only to discover too late that the latter was a copy of the former; he also consulted MS *L* and the Sloane MS in the British Library.[6] Despite Bridges' critical stance towards Jebb,[7] I believe it can be demonstrated that Bridges relied quite heavily on Jebb's edition, for he often took from Jebb a reading found in none of the manuscripts on which his own edition was based. This first attempt of Bridges was seriously deficient, and he therefore brought out a new printing in 1900 with a supplementary volume in which the worst errors were corrected.[8] This corrected edition was again printed in 1964.[9] My edition, though it will of course not be totally free of error, corrects or improves upon Bridges' final text in perhaps a thousand readings, many of them minor, but some of considerable importance. In addition, I supply a much larger list of variant readings, as well as the text of the revised version.[10] No translation of *De multiplicatione specierum* has hitherto been made.

The manuscript tradition of *De multiplicatione specierum* is quite complex, and it is apparent that the multiple affiliations could be captured only in a stemma too complicated to be useful. Nevertheless, three main groups of manuscripts can be identified. If, for this purpose, we ignore the three seventeenth-century manuscripts, the three fragmentary copies, and the Vatican manuscript, which

---

[4] *Fratris Rogeri Bacon, Ordinis Minorum, Opus Maius ad Clementum quartum*, ed. Samuel Jebb (London, 1733).

[5] *The Opus Majus of Roger Bacon*, 2 volumes (Oxford: Oxford University Press, 1897).

[6] See Bridges' introduction, *Opus maius*, i, pp. xiv–xvi.

[7] Ibid., pp. xii–xiii.

[8] *The Opus Majus of Roger Bacon*, ed. John Henry Bridges, 3 volumes (London: Williams and Norgate, 1900). For the corrected text, J. A. Herbert of the British Museum collated Bridges' original text with MS *O*.

[9] By Minerva, GmbH, Frankfurt am Main.

[10] Variant readings, even in the manuscripts collated by Bridges, are far more significant than he acknowledges. Also, his variant readings are sometimes erroneous. And on occasion he amends the text without indication.

came to my attention too late for a personal examination, the remaining manuscripts can be grouped as follows: the largest group (I) consists of *B, F, L, N, V,* 16, 17, 18, and 21; a second group (II) consists of *O,* 14, and 24; and the third group (III) of *A, M, P,* and *S,* which contain all or part of the revised version. Within group I, the affiliations are complex and shifting; consequently, I have chosen to collate five of the nine manuscripts in this group: *B, F,* and *L* in their entirety, *N* and *V* when difficult choices required additional evidence. Group II is simplicity itself: all three copies contain virtually identical texts; 14 is a copy of *O,* 24 may also be a copy of *O;* from this group, I have therefore chosen to collate only MS *O.*[11] Finally, from group III, containing the revised version, I have collated *S* in its entirety; I have collated *A* wherever the text of *S* differs from that of groups I or II, including all major revisions contained in the Appendix; and I have collated *M* and *P* for the prologue, the only major revision they contain.

De speculis comburentibus. There are four known manuscripts of this treatise. The first three have been collated for the present edition:

1. *E* = Oxford, Bodleian Library, MS Bodley 874, pp. 71–87.
   Written in Anglicana bookhand between 1350 and 1400. Parchment; figures. Follows Bacon's *Perspectiva.* Described in Falconer Madan, *A Summary Catalogue of Western Manuscripts in the Bodleian Library,* ii, pt. 1 (Oxford, 1922), p. 551.

2. *R* = Florence, Biblioteca Riccardiana, MS 885 ff. 200^r–212^r.
   An Italian notular text hand, written about 1350. Parchment; figures. Follows Bacon's *Perspectiva.* In the margin of f. 209^r is part of an anonymous *Notule de speculis,* which appears also in MS Bodley 874, pp. 95–6, and which Combach published along with *De speculis comburentibus* in 1614.[12] Described by J. Lamius, *Catalogus codicum manuscriptorum qui in Bibliotheca Riccardiana Florentina adservantur* (Livorno, 1756), p. 343 (under MS L.II).

3. *W* = Vienna, Österreichische Nationalbibliothek, MS 5311, ff. 108^r–113^v.
   Written in the Rhineland about 1350 in a notular text hand. Paper; figures. The codex also contains other Baconian works. Described in *Tabulae codicum manuscriptorum praeter graecos et orientales in Bibliotheca Palatina Vindobonensi asservatorum,* iv (Vienna, 1870), pp. 98–9.

---

[11] MSS 12 and 13 (from the 17th century) also appear to belong to this group.
[12] On this treatise see my *Catalogue of Optical Manuscripts,* no. 33.

The fourth manuscript was not employed in the preparation of this edition:

4. Oxford, Bodleian Library, MS Ashmole 440, ff. 1^r-23^v. 16th cent. Incomplete.

There are few significant differences among the three manuscripts collated for this edition. However, when one of them stands alone, it is usually *W*. *De speculis comburentibus* has been published once, in 1614, along with Bacon's *Perspectiva*;[13] it has never before been translated.

EDITORIAL PROCEDURES

Critical Apparatus. All significant variations of the primary manuscripts (*B, F, L, O,* and *S* for *De multiplicatione specierum*, and *E, R,* and *W* for *De speculis comburentibus*) are recorded in the apparatus. Among variations not considered significant are the substitution of certain exact synonyms one for another (*ergo/igitur, quod/quia, nichil/nil, sive/seu*, and so forth); insertion or elimination of *est, et*, and the prepositions *de, in, ex*, and *ab*, where the meaning is not at stake; obvious orthographic mistakes or variations; minor grammatical errors; trivial strokes or letters deleted by the scribe himself or a corrector; and words or brief phrases that are mistakenly repeated. In short, I have recorded only those variations that affect the meaning of the text. Among the secondary manuscripts of *De multiplicatione specierum* (*A, M, N, P,* and *V*), I record all significant variations of *A* and *M* for the prologue of the revised version, of *A* for the remainder of the revisions contained in the Appendix; I supply additional variant readings for any of the five when this serves a purpose.

The critical apparatus is designed along traditional lines. The textual word or phrase whose variants are to be communicated (the key word) precedes the colon; in complicated cases, it is sometimes accompanied before the colon by the sigla of those manuscripts (or some of those manuscripts) in which it is found. Following the colon I record the variations, each accompanied by the siglum of· the manuscript containing it. The key word is omitted when sufficiently similar to the first variant for its omission to produce no ambiguity. An unmodified siglum indicates the scribal hand without correction; a siglum followed by a prime (′) indicates the original scribal hand before correction; and a siglum to which a superscript 'c' (^{c}) has been added signifies the hand of a corrector. When the

[13] *Rogerii Bacconis Perspectiva*, ed. I. Combach (Frankfurt, 1614), 168-204.

key word reappears in one of the variants, it is usually abbreviated
Two examples will illustrate the pattern:

  45 species: s. rerum *O* lucis *F*

signifies that 'species' (the preferred reading) in line 45 is replaced in
in MS *O* by the phrase 'species rerum' and in MS *F* by the word 'lucis'.

  27 sive² *SAL*ᶜ : sed *BFL'* om. *O*

signifies that the second 'sive' in line 27 (the preferred reading) is
found in MSS *S, A,* and *L* (after correction); MSS *B, F,* and *L* (before
correction) substitute 'sed' for 'sive', while *O* simply omits the word.

  The following abbreviations and symbols are employed in the
apparatus criticus:

  add. = addidit
  corr. = correxit
  del. = delevit
  interl. = interlineariter
  mg. = in margine
  obs. = obscuravit
  om. = omisit
  rep. = repetivit
  scr. = scripsit
  (*?*) signifies a doubtful reading.

  Translation. Unlike some of my colleagues in the translation enter-
prise, I do not give high priority to incorporating the syntax of the
original Latin in my translation. This practice is frequently justified
on the grounds that one thus captures the 'flavour of the original'—
a claim of which I am profoundly sceptical. I consider two other
criteria to be far more important: 1. that the English translation
capture the exact sense of the Latin text (one translates meanings,
not sentence structure); and 2. that the English translation read
smoothly. If one can meet both criteria and also retain the original
syntax, there is no harm (and there may be some small benefit) in
doing so, but often one cannot. In short, I have permitted myself
to be 'free' with the Latin syntax, but not with its meaning.[1]

  Lengthy additions. Greek letters indicate the locations of major
additions to the text found in MSS *A* and *S*. (The first, a lengthy
prologue, is found also in MSS *M* and *P.*) Such passages are printed,
without translation, in the Appendix.

---

[1] The one structural feature of the Latin text that I have frequently attempted to
convey in my translation is redundancy. For example, the following sentence from II. 10.
89–91 would win no prize for parsimony: 'Consequently, when there is a multiplication
from the sun and stars to the earth and other smaller spheres, more than half the earth must
receive the species of the sun and stars, which are larger than the earth.' The final clause
could be elminated with no loss of content, but my doing so would impose on Bacon an
economy of style that is not his.

De multiplicatione specierum

PARS I

CAPITULUM 1

Primum igitur capitulum circa influentiam agentis habet tres veritates
5 seu conclusiones. Prima est quid sit secundum nomen et secundum
essentiam. Recolendum est igitur quod in tertia parte huius operis
tactum est quod essentia, substantia, natura, potestas, potentia,
virtus, vis significant eandem rem, sed differunt sola comparatione.
Nam essentia dicitur secundum se considerata, substantia respectu
10 accidentis, alia respectu operationis eliciende. Sed natura dicit
aptitudinem operandi, cetera ulteriorem inclinationem. Sed potentia
et potestas sunt idem, et communiter sumuntur respectu operationis
complete vel incomplete. Virtus vero et vis sunt idem, sed dicunt
solum complementum operationis. Et hic loquor de potentia que
15 elicit actionem, non de illa que expedit. Nam hec est in secunda
specie qualitatis, que vero elicit est in omnibus activis; et hec sunt
substantie et sensibilia propria, nisi sit instantia in sono, sicut inferius
exponetur.

Aliter sumitur virtus pro effectu primo virtutis iam dicte propter
20 similitudinem eius ad hanc virtutem, et in essentia et in operatione,
quia similis est ei diffinitione et in essentia specifica; et per consequens est similis in operatione, quia illa que sunt similis essentie
habent similes operationes. Et hec virtus secunda habet multa
nomina, vocatur enim similitudo agentis et ymago et species et
25 ydolum et simulacrum et fantasma et forma et intentio et passio
et impressio et umbra philosophorum apud auctores de aspectibus.

Species autem non sumitur hic pro quinto universali apud Porphir-
ium, sed transumitur hoc nomen ad designandum primum effectum
cuiuslibet agentis naturaliter. (β) Et, ut in exemplo pateat hec
30 species, dicimus lumen solis in aere esse speciem lucis solaris que
est in corpore suo; et lumen forte cadens per fenestram vel foramen

4 *ante* primum *add. D* incipit tractatus Rogeri Baconis de multiplicatione specierum /
influentiam L^C: in fluentam L' 5-6 prima . . . essentiam: prima est ut sciatur
quid sit influentia ista secundum nomen et causam suam specificam et suam essentiam *SA*
6-7 operis . . . est: operationis est declaratum videlicet *S* operis determinatum est videlicet *A*
8 significant . . . rem: idem significant in re *A* / comparatione: c. ut expositum est *SA*
9 *post* secundum *add.* L^C nomen / substantia: s. dicitur *O*   10 alia *FL*: aut *BO*
nec *S* natura *A*   12 et[2]: sed *O* / operationis: comparationis *F*   13 dicunt *S*[C]:
differunt *S'*   14 solum: *om. F* / operationis: comparationis *B* / hic: sic *F* /
loquimur *SA*   15 actionem: operationem *SA* / de illa: *om. SA* / secunda: *mg.* L^C
16 hec: hee *O*   18 exponitur *S*   19 aliter: a. autem *SA*   21 diffinitione:
in d. *O* nomine et d. *SA* / in: ita in *A*   22 operatione *ONHV*: opere *AFLS obs. B* /

$$(\alpha)^1$$

PART I

CHAPTER 1

Now the first chapter concerning the influence of an agent has three truths or conclusions. The first conclusion considers what this influence is according to name and essence.[2] Accordingly, it should be recalled that in the third part of this work it was mentioned that essence, substance, nature, power, potency, virtue, and force signify the same thing, but differ only in relation.[3] For 'essence' is considered with respect to itself, 'substance' with respect to accident, the others in reference to the eliciting of an action.[4] But 'nature' means an aptitude for acting, apart from any further inclination. 'Potency' and 'power' mean the same thing, and they are commonly applied to either a complete or an incomplete operation. 'Virtue' and 'force' also mean the same thing, but they are applied only to that which completes an operation. And I speak here concerning a potency that elicits an action, rather than that which accomplishes an action.[5] For the latter is in the second species of quality,[6] while that which elicits [an action] belongs to [the class of] all active things; and these are substances and the proper sensibles, unless there is an exception in sound, as we shall explain below.[7]

'Virtue' is taken in another way, as the first effect of the aforementioned virtue, because of its similarity to this [other] virtue in both essence and operation, since it is similar to it in definition and specific essence; and consequently it is similar to it in operation, since things of similar essence have similar operations. And this second virtue has many names, for it is called 'the similitude of the agent', 'image', 'species', 'idol',[8] 'simulacrum', 'phantasm', 'form', 'intention', 'passion', 'impression', and 'shadow of the philosophers' by authors of works on vision.

By 'species' we do not here mean Porphyry's fifth universal;[9] rather this name is meant to designate the first effect of any naturally-acting thing. (β) And to explain this meaning of 'species' with an example, we say that the *lumen* of the sun in the air is the species of the solar *lux* in the body of the sun;[10] and *lumen* falling, perchance, through a window or an aperture is sufficiently

post quia *scr. et del. S* similis   25 simulacrum: s. et simulacra *B* / fantasma: *om. SA* fantasia *F*   26 impressio: *om. SA* / *post* aspectibus *add. SA* quorum vocabulorum ratio data est in tertia parte huius operis (operationis *S*)   27 hic: *om. A*   28 designandum: designationem *S* significandum *A*   29 cuiuslibet . . . naturaliter: *om. SA* / ut: *om. S*   30 solum *S*   31 lumen: hoc *B* / foramine *F*

nobis satis est visibile, et est species lucis stelle. Et Avicenna dicit
tertio *De anima* quod lux est qualitas corporis lucentis, ut ignis
vel stelle; lumen vero est illud quod est multiplicatum et generatum
35 ab illa luce, quod fit in aere et in ceteris corporibus raris, que vocantur media quia mediantibus illis multiplicantur species. Sed tamen
usualiter accipimus lucem pro lumine et econtrario. Et quando per
medium vitri aut cristalli aut panni fortiter colorati transit radius,
apparet nobis in obscuro iuxta radium color similis colori illius
40 corporis bene colorati; et ille color in opaco dicitur similitudo et
species coloris in corpore fortiter colorato per quod transit radius.
   Dicitur autem similitudo et ymago respectu generantis eam, cui
assimilatur et quod imitatur. Dicitur autem species respectu sensus
et intellectus secundum usum Aristotelis et naturalium, quia dicit
45 secundo *De anima* quod sensus universaliter suscipit species sensibilium, et in tertio dicit quod intellectus est locus specierum. Dicitur
vero ydolum respectu speculorum, sic enim multum utimur. Dicitur
fantasma et simulacrum in apparitionibus sompniorum, quia iste
species penetrant sensus usque ad partes anime interiores et apparent
50 in sompnis tanquam res quarum sunt, quia eis assimilantur;   et
anima non est ita potens iudicare in sompnis sicut in vigilia, et ideo
decipitur, estimans species esse ipsas res quarum sunt propter similitudinem. Forma quidem vocatur in usu Alhacen, auctoris *Perspective*
vulgate. Intentio vocatur in usu vulgi naturalium propter debilitatem
55 sui esse respectu rei, dicentis quod non est vere res sed magis intentio
rei, id est similitudo. Umbra philosophorum vocatur, quia non est
bene sensibilis nisi in casu duplici dicto, scilicet de radio cadente
per fenestram et de specie fortiter colorati; et dicitur esse philosophorum quia soli potenter philosophantes cognoscunt istius umbre
60 naturam et operationem, ut ex hoc tractatu clarescet. Dicitur vero
virtus respectu generationis et corruptionis, unde dicimus solem
facere virtutem suam in materiam mundi pro generatione et corruptione faciendis; et sic de omni agente dicimus quod facit virtutem
suam in patiens. Impressio vocatur quia est similis impressionibus;

33 tertio: secundo *SA*   35 quod fit: que sit *O*   36 mediantibus: medium
S / species: *om. SA* / *post* species *scr. et del. L* lucis stelle / sed: licet *S*   37 pro:
per *F*   39 radium: *om. SA* / illis *S* ipsius *A*   42 respectu: idem *B*
43 imitatur: univocatur *S*   44 qui *F* / dicitur *SA*   45 species: s. rerum *O*
s. respectu *F*   46 dicitur *SA*   47 vero: autem *F*   48 fantasia *F* / simulacra
S / apparitionibus: apostolibus(?) *S*   49 et apparent: ut appareant *B*   50 assimilatur *S* assimilat *A*   52 sunt: s. species *SA*   53 formarum *S* / Halacen *F*
53–4 forma . . . vulgate: *mg. L*^C   54 intentio *L*^C: intensio *L'*   55 respectu: om. *S* /
dicentes *F*   56 rei: *om. F* / id est: *om. S* / quia: eo quod *BN*   58 specie: *om. F*
60 ex: in *A om. S*   61 unde: ut *O*   62 suam: *om. O* / materiam *FOSA*: materia
BLN / mundie *B*   63 et: *scr. et del. L* de / agenti *S*   64 in *L*^C: et *L'*

visible to us, and it is the species of the *lux* of a star. And Avicenna says in *De anima*, book iii, that *lux* is a quality of a luminous body, such as fire or a star; but *lumen* is that which is multiplied and generated from that *lux* and which is produced in air and other rare bodies, which are called media because species are multiplied by their mediation.[11] Nevertheless, we usually employ *lux* and *lumen* interchangeably. And when a ray passes through a medium of strongly-coloured glass or crystal or cloth, there appears to us in the dark, in the vicinity of the ray, a colour similar to the colour of that strongly-coloured body; and this colour in an opaque substance [that intercepts it] is called the 'similitude and species' of the colour in the strongly-coloured [transparent] body through which the ray passes.

Moreover, [the aforementioned second virtue] is called 'similitude' and 'image' with respect to the thing generating it, to which it is similar and which it imitates. It is called 'species' with respect to sense and intellect, according to the use of Aristotle and the naturalists, for Aristotle says in *De anima*, book ii, that sense universally receives the species of sensible things, and in book iii he says that the seat of species is the intellect.[12] It is called 'idol' with respect to mirrors—for thus we frequently employ the term. It is called 'phantasm' and 'simulacrum' in the apparitions of dreams, since these species penetrate sense as far as the interior parts of the soul and appear in dreams as if they were the things of which they are [in fact only] apparitions, since the apparitions resemble the things; and the soul is not able to judge as well during dreams as when awake, and therefore it is deceived, judging the species to be the things themselves of which they are species, on account of the resemblance. It is called 'form' by Alhazen, author of the widely known *Perspectiva*.[13] It is called 'intention' by the multitude of naturalists because of the weakness of its being in comparison to that of the thing itself, for they say that it is not truly a thing, but rather the intention, that is, the similitude, of a thing. It is called 'shadow of the philosophers', since it is not clearly sensible except in the two instances mentioned, namely, of a ray falling through a window and of a strongly-coloured species;[14] and the expression 'of the philosophers' is employed because only skilful philosophers know the nature and operation of this shadow, as this treatise will make clear. It is called 'virtue' with respect to generation and corruption, and therefore we say that the sun extends its virtue into the matter of the world for producing generation and corruption; and thus we say that every agent produces its virtue in a recipient.[15] It is called 'impression' because it resembles impressions;

65 unde Aristoteles secundo *De anima* comparat generationem speciei
impressioni facte ab anulo et sigillo in cera, licet non sit simile
per omnia, sicut postea scietur. Vocatur autem passio quia medium
et sensus in recipiendo speciem patiuntur transmutationem in sua
substantia, que transmutatio tamen est in perfectionem et salutem,
70 nisi fiat plus quam sola species, ut postea melius exponetur.

Investigandum est igitur quid sit secundum suam essentiam; et
quoniam intentio est ostendere quod hec species sit similis agenti
et generanti eam in essentia et diffinitione, ideo primum oportet
duci in medium quod omnes habent confiteri, scilicet quod species
75 est primus effectus agentis; per hanc enim omnes estimant effectus
ceteros produci. Unde sapientes et insipientes circa multa in specierum cognitione differunt; communicant tamen in hoc quod agens
influit speciem in materiam patientis quatinus, per eam primo
.factam, possit educere de potentia materie effectum completum
80 quem intendit. Et ideo nulli dubium est quin species sit primus
effectus. Quod vero iste primus effectus cuiuslibet agentis naturaliter
similis sit ei in essentia specifica et natura et operatione manifestum
est ex dicendis, quia agens intendit assimilare sibi patiens, eo quod
patiens, ut vult Aristoteles *Libro de generatione*, universaliter est in
85 potentia tale quale est agens in actu, sicut ibidem dicit. Et in principio est de se dissimile agenti ante actionem, et per actionem fit
simile, ut dicit; et agens statim quando operatur in patiens assimilat
illud ei et facit illud patiens esse tale quale est ipsum agens in actu,
sicut Aristoteles dicit. Et ideo si ignis est agens facit ignem; si calor
90 calorem; si lux lucem; et sic de omnibus. Sed plus potest in primum
effectum et immediatum quam in secundum et mediatum; ergo
illum maxime assimilabit. Propter quod oportet ponere quod virtus
seu species facta ab agente sit consimilis agenti natura et diffinitione
et in essentia specifica et operatione. Item omnis diversitas ad idempti-
95 tatem reducitur; et dualitas ab unitate descendit et non econtrario.
Et ideo primus effectus agentis non potest esse diversus ab eo in
essentia specifica, ut postea nascatur consimilis et uniformis; nam sic
diversitas esset principium unitatis, quod est contra naturam. (γ)

65 secundo *BN*: tertio *FLOSA*   68 speciem: *om. F* | transmutatione *B*   69 trans-
mutatio *L*[C]: transmutationem *L'*   70 quam: quod *F* | melius: *om. SA*   71 *ante*
essentiam *scr. et del. F* substantiam   73 in essentia: nomine *SA* | prius *SA*   75 agentis
. . . effectus[2]: *om. S* | omnes *L*[C]: omnis *L'*   76 ceteros: omnes alios *A* | unde: u.
scilicet *L* | circa multa *B*[C]: certa *B'* m. diversificati *S*   77 differunt *BON*: *om. FLSA*
78 in: et *L* | materiam: natura *O* | patientis: *om. F* | primo: p. sunt autem *L*   79 fac-
tam: *mg. OL* | completum: *om. B*   80 nulli: *om. F*   82 similis *O*: simile *BFLSA* |
et natura: *om. O*   85 in actu *SAO* (*mg. O*): *om. FLBN* | sicut . . . dicit: *om. SA* |
ibidem *OBN*: idem *FL* | et: *om. S*   86 agenti . . . actionem[1]: *om. SA* | fit: facit *SA*
87 ut: sicut idem *SA* | *post* operatur *scr. et del. L* potentia tale quale est agens   88 ei:
sibi *SA*   89 sicut . . . dicit: *om. SA* | ideo: *om. F*   90 lux: *interl. L*[C]   91 in:

thus Aristotle, in *De anima*, book ii, compares the generation of a species to the impression made in wax by a signet ring or seal,[16] although the two are not similar in all respects, as will be shown later. It is called 'passion' because the medium and sense, in receiving species, undergo[17] a transmutation in their substance; however, this transmutation is towards perfection and well-being, unless there should be more than a solitary species, as will be better expounded later.[18]

Therefore, we must investigate the essence of a species; and since our intention is to show that this species is similar in essence and definition to the agent and the thing generating it, we must first set forth what all must acknowledge, namely, that a species is the first effect of an agent; for all judge that through species [all] other effects are produced. Thus the wise and the foolish disagree about many things in their knowledge of species, but they agree in this, that the agent sends forth a species into the matter of the recipient, so that, through the species first produced, it can bring forth out of the potentiality of the matter [of the recipient] the complete effect that it intends. And therefore, there is no doubt that the species is the first effect. But that this first effect of any natural agent is similar to the agent in specific essence, in nature, and in operation is evident from things to be said below; for the agent directs its efforts to making the recipient similar to itself, because the recipient, as Aristotle intends in *De generatione*, is always potentially what the agent is in actuality, as he there asserts.[19] And at first, before the action, the recipient is of itself dissimilar to the agent, and through the action it becomes similar, as Aristotle says; and when the agent acts on the recipient, it at once assimilates the latter to itself and makes the recipient to be such as the agent is in actuality, as Aristotle says. And therefore, if fire is the agent, it produces fire; if heat, heat; if light, light; and so for all things. But this can occur better in the first and immediate effect than in the secondary and mediated; therefore, the former, especially, will be made to resemble the agent. Hence, it must be posited that the virtue or species produced by an agent is similar to the agent in nature, definition, specific essence, and operation. Likewise, every diversity can be traced back to identity; and duality descends from unity and not vice versa. And therefore, the first effect of an agent cannot differ from it in specific essence while subsequently giving rise to a [further] effect similar [to the agent] and uniform [with it]; for thus diversity would be the source of unity, which is contrary to nature. (γ)

ita *F om. S*   92 ponere: *om. F*   93 fit *L* / natura: nomine *SA om. L* / *ante* diffinitione *mg. add. L* et ideo species cum sit primus effectus agentis erit similis in natura / diffinitione: dispositione *F*   94 *ante* item *add. B* prima responsio / idem *S*   95 et[1]: etiam *F*

Item effectus lucis sunt hii, scilicet species eius et lux generata
100 in medio, calor, putrefactio, mors, sic enim in re corrumpenda
ordinantur. Sed nos videmus quod tertius gradus effectus magis
distat ab agente in natura quam secundus; quare secundus magis
quam primus, vel erunt idem in essentia et numero. Et hoc est quod
intendimus. Unde species lucis est lux, licet primo incompleta et
105 postea complenda in quibus potest compleri, ut in luna et stellis,
que sunt retentiva lucis.

Item species ignis, si non est similis natura et essentia et diffinitione igni, ut sit in eadem specie specialissima cum igne, tunc non
erit in aliquo predicamento, quod est impossibile, quia in predica-
110 mentis accidentium esse non potest, quia non contingit hoc assignari
in quo predicamento esset. Neque in tantum posset primus effectus
elongari ab agente ut transeat in aliud predicamentum, nullus enim
potest dicere quod species albedinis et lucis transit in aliud predicamentum. Et ideo nec species ignis, precipue cum per hanc speciem
115 dicatur ignis generari, nullum enim accidens est principium generandi
substantiam; sed nec potest esse aque vel aeris; nec in aliqua specie
specialissima substantie, nec subalterna, ut patet. Quare oportet
quod sit in eadem specie cum igne. Nec contingit dici quod est
medium inter substantiam et accidens, quia methaphysicus probat
120 quod inter ea non potest esse medium. Atque non potest dici quod
reducatur ad speciem ignis specialissimam, et sit in eodem genere
et in eadem specie specialissima solum per reductionem, quia
quelibet res habet aliquam essentiam et naturam, per quam
necessario est substantia determinate vel accidens; et ideo secun-
125 dum se collocabitur et per se in aliqua rerum manerie, et hoc est
in aliquo predicamentorum et in aliquo genere et in aliqua specie
specialissima.

Item per Ptolomeum secundo *De opticis* sive *De aspectibus* declaratur quod a colore et luce advenit medio et visui coloratio et
130 illuminatio. Sed coloratio non est nisi per esse coloris, nec illuminatio
nisi per esse lucis. Et videmus hoc per experimentum; nam radius
solaris cadens per fenestram est nobis visibilis, et immutat visum
per se et primo; nec est color, et ideo est lux vera, solum enim

---

99 *ante* item *add.* B tertia responsio / sunt: *mg.* F / hii: *om.* S / scilicet: *om.* SA / et:
om. SA   100 in medio: est de potentia materie S   101 ordinatur F   103 *post*
primus *add.* S *et scr. et del.* A nec potest diversitas esse principium et causa ydemptitatis
nec precedere naturaliter / est quod: *om.* L   105 postea: p. potestas S / completa
OF / compleri: compelli(?) S   106 que: et S ut A   107 diffinitione: dispositione F   108 ut: *om.* S   109 erit: esset S   111 neque: sed *nec* B / in tantum
posset: i. t. possit L enim potest i. t. S potest t. A   112 *ante* aliud *scr. et del.* L eodem /
post predicamentum *scr. et del.* L et ideo nec species   113 et lucis: *om.* S   114 cum:
tamen F   115 ignis generari: i. generare ignem S / principuum B   116 esse
aque: de natura a. e. SA   118 contingit: convenit O   120 quod[1]: et L   123 per

Moreover, the effects of light are these, namely, its species and light generated in the medium, heat, putrefaction, and death; for this order is followed when a thing is corrupted. But we see that the third degree of an effect is further from the nature of the agent than is the second; and therefore the second is further than the first, if they are not essentially and numerically the same.[20] And this is what we intend. Accordingly, the species of light is light, although at first incomplete and afterwards completed in things in which this is possible, as in the moon and stars, which can retain light.

Likewise, if the species of fire is not similar to fire in nature, essence, and definition (so as to belong to the same lowest species as fire), then it will not belong to any category—which is impossible —since it cannot be in the categories of accidents, because there is no way of telling to which category [of accidents] it should be assigned.[21] Nor could the first effect be so removed from its agent as to pass into another category, for nobody can say that the species of whiteness or light passes into another category. And therefore the species of fire cannot do so, especially since fire is said to be generated by means of this species, for no accident is the source from which substance is generated; nor can [the species of fire] be of [the same nature as] water or air; nor can it belong to some lowest species of substance, or a subordinate species, as is evident.[22] Therefore it must be in the same species as fire. Nor does anybody claim that there is something between substance and accident, since the metaphysician proves that there can be no such intermediate thing. And therefore it cannot be said that [the species or similitude of fire] is reduced to a lowest species of fire,[23] so that it would be in the same genus and the same lowest species only by reduction, for everything has a certain essence and nature, by virtue of which it is necessarily a determined substance or an accident; and therefore of itself it is classified as some kind of thing, belonging to a certain category and a certain genus and a certain lowest species.

Also, in Ptolemy's *De opticis* or *De aspectibus*, book ii, it is declared that colouring and illumination come to the medium and the eye from colour and light.[24] But there can be no colouring except through the being of colour, nor illumination except through the being of light. And we learn this by observation; for a solar ray falling through a window is visible to us, and it alters sight primarily and by itself; and since this is not colour, it must be true light, for

quam *VN*: que *BFLOSA*   124–5 secundum se: *om. SA*   125 collocabatur *B* | per: *om. S* | in: et erit pars in *SA*   126 predicamento *S*   128 *ante* item *add. B* quarto | item: et hoc patet *S* | secundo *OLS*: tertio *F* quinto *N* libro *B* | declaratur: nisi declaravit *S* 131 nisi: *om. L* | videmus: inde *S*   133 nec: et non *SA* | est²: *om. SA* | solis *O*

lux et color nata sunt immutare visum per se et primo. Similiter
135 quando aspicimus radios penetrantes vitra bene colorata, videmus in
opaco iuxta vitrum colorem sensibiliter, qui visum per se immutat et
sensibiliter; et tamen scimus quod est species et similitudo coloris
vitri. Quapropter species coloris est color, et species lucis est lux,
et sic de omnibus. Ergo species communicat cum suo agente in
140 natura et diffinitione. Et ideo dicit Aristoteles in secundo *De anima*
quod susceptivum coloris et soni et omnis sensibilis est non colora-
tum et absonum et carens naturis sensibilium de se, ut medium et
organa sentiendi—volens per hoc quod medium et sensus recipiant
colorem et sonum ut recipiant species illorum, et sic de aliis specie-
145 bus sensibilium. Et ideo species de qua hic loquimur est similis agenti
in natura specifica et diffinitione.
        Si igitur contra hoc obiciatur quod tunc species solis erit sol et
species hominis erit homo, et sic de omnibus rebus, quod omnino
absurdum est, dicendum quod ista nomina homo et sol et asinus et
150 planta et huiusmodi imponuntur rebus in esse completo, et ideo non
dicuntur de illis que habent esse incompletum, quamvis sint eiusdem
essentie; ut embrio in ventre matris non dicitur homo et maxime
ante receptionem anime intellective. Et tamen postquam essentia
animalis transmutatur et promovetur ut fiat species humana, oportet
155 quod illud renovatum ultra essentiam generis antequam anima
rationalis infundatur sit de natura hominis, quia natum est recipere
animam rationalem et non animam asini nec aliam. Non igitur
dicimus quod illud sit homo, et tamen est in specie hominis, sed
secundum esse incompletum. Similiter vero dicimus de specie
160 hominis, que est similitudo eius facta in aere ab eo, non enim est
homo, quia habet esse incompletissimum quod potest inveniri in
specie hominis et longe incompletius quam embrio ante receptionem
anime rationalis; quia embrio compleri potest in hominem, species
vero nequaquam. Et considerandum est quod quedam possunt facere
165 fortes species, ut calor et lux et color et quedam talia, ut exponetur
postea. Sed res quanto sunt nobiliores, ut celestia et homo et
huiusmodi, tanto incompletiorem faciunt speciem, cuius causa
dabitur inferius; et ideo species coloris et lucis et caloris magis

134 visum: *om. F*   135 vitra *FLO*: inter *B* intra *SA*   136 vitrum: intra *SA* /
sensibiliter: *om. O*   137–8 et[2] . . . species[2]: *mg. L*[C] (*post* species *add.* lucis et cetera)
138 quapropter: quare ipsa *SA*   140 natura: nomine *SA* / in diffinitione *O* / secundo
L[C]: libro *L'*   142–3 medium[1,2]: mundus *S*   143 respiciant *S*   144 colorem
. . . ut: *om. L* / ut: cum *BS* / recipiat *F*   148 est *L* esset *S* / rebus: quod *S* / quod:
et *B* / *post* quod *scr. et del. S* sic   149 dicendum: decendum est *L* d. est *B*
151 sunt *F*   153–4 essentia animalis: essentialiter *S*   154 transmutatur: *mg. L*[C]
transumatur(?) *L'*   155 illud: sic *O*   156 sit: sic *S*   159 vero: non *FN*
160 que: quod *SA* / eo *F*[C]: eis *F'*   161 qui *S* / incompletissimum *FLO*: incompletum
BSN / invenire *S*   162 quem *F* / *post* embrio *add. O* quem embrio   163 *post*

only light and colour are suited to alter sight primarily and by themselves. Similarly, when we observe rays penetrating strongly-coloured glass, we sensibly observe the colour in an opaque body near the glass, and the colour sensibly and by itself alters vision; and yet we know that what alters vision is the species and similitude of the colour of the glass. Therefore, the species of colour is colour, and the species of light is light, and similarly for all things. Thus a species agrees with its agent in nature and definition. And therefore Aristotle says in *De anima*, book ii, that the recipient of colour and sound and every sensible, such as the medium or the sense organs, is of itself uncoloured and soundless and lacking the nature of sensibles[25]— meaning by this that the medium and sense receive colour and sound as they receive the species of colour and sound, and similarly for the other species of sensible things. And therefore the species of which we here speak is similar to the agent in specific nature and in definition.

If, against this, it is objected that the species of the sun would then be sun and the species of man would then be man, and similarly for all things (which would be utterly absurd), we reply that the names 'man', 'sun', 'ass', 'plant', and the like are imposed for things that have complete being and not for things that have incomplete being, even though both are of the same essence; thus the embryo in the mother's womb is not called 'man', especially before it receives the rational soul. Nevertheless, after the animal essence is transmuted and pushed onward to the point where it becomes a human species, it is necessary for that which develops beyond the essence of the genus, before infusion of the rational soul, to possess the nature of man, since it is suited to receive a rational soul and not the soul of an ass or anything else. Therefore, we do not say that it is man, and yet it does belong to the same species as man according to incomplete being. We say the same thing concerning the species of man (that is, man's similitude produced by man in the air),[26] for it is not man, since it has the most incomplete being that can be found in the species of man, far more incomplete than that of the embryo before the reception of the rational soul; for the embryo can achieve the perfection of man, whereas the species of man cannot. And it must be recognized that some things, such as heat, light, colour, and the like, can give rise to strong species, as will be explained below.[27] But the nobler things are (such as celestial bodies and man and the like), the more incomplete are their species, the cause of which will be given below;[28] and therefore the species of colour, light, and heat are more

quia *add.* OL' est   165 calor . . . color: color et lux O / alia S   166 res L^C
168 et caloris: *om.* SA

170 potest dici lux et calor vel color quam species solis vel hominis dicatur homo vel sol. Semper tamen erit eiusdem nature specifice, sed sub esse incompletissimo et impossibili ad complementum, propter quod non recipit nomen quod esse completiori est impositum.

175 Ex quo sequitur secunda veritas: quod impossibile est quod sit effectus similis agenti in essentia nisi unus; et hic vocatur primus, et vocatur univocus, et eius generatio dicitur univoca. Alii possunt esse plures, et vocantur equivoci, et generatio eorum dicitur equivoca, ut calor et putrefactio et mors sunt effectus plures lucis, 180 sed equivoci non univoci. Solum enim lumen in medio vel lux in corpore stelle producta per lumen solis dicitur effectus univocus lucis solaris. Sed in principio, dum est effectus incompletus, nominatur species et virtus et nominibus predictis; et hoc est dum patiens manet in natura sua specifica, assimilatum tamen agenti per speciem illam et virtutem, ut ligna cum in principio igniuntur 185 habent speciem et virtutem ignis dum adhuc ligna manent in sua natura specifica, licet assimilentur igni per speciem receptam. Cum autem agens invalescit super patiens, ut tollat naturam specificam patientis et corrumpat eam, ut inducat completum effectum suum in materiam convenientem ei et patienti, ut accidit in rebus generabili-190 bus et corruptibilibus, tunc cessat effectus vocari species et virtus et ceteris nominibus dictis, et vocatur nomine ipsius agentis. Ut cum ignis invalescit super ligna et corrumpit naturam specificam ligneam, inducens completam ignis essentiam, tunc quod generatum est vocatur ignis et non species nec virtus, sive fiat carbo vel flamma; et ideo 195 species ignis et ignis completus non differunt nisi sicut incompletum et completum. Et propter hoc, unus effectus et idem numero est qui primo vocatur species, dum habet esse incompletum, et deinde sortitur plenum nomen agentis et generantis quando completur in esse et destructa est natura totalis specifica patientis. Sed hoc 200 est intelligendum in istis rebus inferioribus corruptibilibus.

In rebus vero incorruptibilibus potest bene species aliqua compleri in effectum completum sine destructione patientis, quia patiens natum est ad huiusmodi effectum de natura sua, ut stelle et luna nate sunt habere lucem perfectam quantum exigit earum natura,

169 vel¹: et *S* / vel²: et *S*   170 erit: esset *S*   171 sed: si *S* / esse: omne(?) *B* / completum *S*   172-3 est *OL*: esse *SA om. BF* / incompositum *B*   174 *ante* ex *mg. add. O* secunda conclusio / secunda: *mg. L*   175 vocatur: est *SA* 176 univoca *L^C*: equivoca *L'*   177 vocantur: vocteis(?) *B* / dicitur: vocatur *SA* 179 non: nisi *S* / solis *SA*   180 lumen: *mg. L^C* lucis *L'*   181 dum: tantum *S* 182 dum: tantum *S*   183 assimilata *S*   186 natura: *om. S*   188 efficium *O* 189 materiam: naturam *O* / in rebus: *om. O*   189-90 ut . . . corruptibilibus: *om. SA* 190 et³: *interl. L^C*   192 convalescit *S* / naturam: materiam *F*   194 sive *SA*: sed *BF om. OL* / fiat *L'*: sed fit *L^C*   199 est *L^C*: non *L'* / sed *L^C*   200 inferi-

appropriately called 'colour', 'light', and 'heat' than is the species of the sun or man called 'sun' or 'man'. Nevertheless, the species will always be of the same specific nature, but under being that is very incomplete and incapable of being completed, and therefore it does not receive the name that is applied to the more complete being.

From this follows a second truth: that there can be only one effect having an essence similar to that of the agent; and this is called 'the first effect' and a 'univocal effect', and its generation is said to be univocal. There can be many other effects, and they are called 'equivocal effects', and their generation is said to be equivocal; thus heat, putrefaction, and death are several effects of light, and they are not univocal, but equivocal. For only *lumen* in the medium, or *lux* in the body of a star produced by the *lumen* of the sun, is called a univocal effect of the solar *lux*. But at first, while it is an incomplete effect, it is called 'species' and 'virtue' and the afore-mentioned names;[29] and this is while the recipient maintains its specific nature, although it is made to resemble the agent through that species and virtue; thus wood, when first ignited, receives the species and virtue of fire while still retaining its own specific nature as wood, although it is made to resemble fire through the received species. However, when the agent prevails over the recipient, so as to corrupt and destroy the specific nature of the recipient, and thus to introduce into the matter its own complete effect, agreeing both with it and with the recipient, as occurs in generable and corruptible things, then the effect ceases to be called 'species' and 'virtue' and the other names mentioned above and is called by the name of the agent itself. Thus when fire prevails over wood and corrupts the specific nature of the wood, introducing the complete essence of fire, then what is generated is called 'fire' and not 'species' or 'virtue', whether charcoal or flame results; and therefore complete fire and the species of fire differ only as the complete and the incomplete. Therefore, it is numerically one and the same effect that is first called 'species', while it has incomplete being, and then, when its being is complete and the total specific nature of the recipient has been destroyed, receives the full name of the agent and source. And it is to be understood that this is true of corruptible terrestrial[30] things.

In incorruptible things[31] a certain species can easily be developed into a complete effect without destruction of the recipient, since the recipient is naturally adapted to such an effect, as the stars and moon are suited to possess perfect light in the quantity required by their

205 licet sol plus habeat de luce. Et tunc in principio fit species lucis usque ad lunam et stellas et postea completur in eis, sicut fuit a prima creatione et sicut post eclipses stellarum accidit. Nam primo debiliter habent lucem, tanquam similitudinem et speciem, et postea claram et completam; cuius signum est quod luna etiam in eclipsi

210 rubea est, quia non nisi extra umbram recipit lumen, sed in umbra habet speciem lucis debilem que venit a luce transeunte extra per latera et fines umbre, sicut postea magis explanabitur. Verumptamen sciendum quod species solis, que est de natura eius specifica, non potest compleri in luna et stellis, licet in eis fiat, quia tunc oporteret

215 lunam et stellas fieri solem, quod est impossibile; lux enim est qualitas communis soli et stellis et igni, licet magis sit in sole; et ideo potest species lucis compleri in luna et stellis, et non species substantie solis, quia sol et luna et stelle differunt in substantia specifica, sicut ex posterioribus manifestum erit. Et lux non est

220 de eorum substantia, sed est accidens commune eis et igni, licet aliqui solebant dicere lucem esse formam substantialem solis et stellarum; sed hoc est falsum. (δ)

Et hec nunc dicta, manifestantur per hoc, quod si sint duo effectus omnino similes agenti et omnino diversi numero, ita quod

225 non sint sicut unus effectus, qui primo est incompletus, et postea ille idem numero compleatur, tunc cum agens agat in eandem partem patientis erunt in eadem parte patientis due forme eiusdem speciei, ponentes in numerum. Sed hoc non est possibile, quia forma appropriat et numerat sibi materiam propriam in qua est; et tunc essent

230 duo ignes in eadem parte ligni igniti, quod fieri non potest, propter dictam rationem. Et iterum quia alter esset otiosus, una enim illarum formarum sufficeret perficere materiam in qua est, ergo reliqua superfluit. Sed natura nichil facit superflue nec otiosum nisi ex errore, ut in monstris et peccatis nature, quod hic non habet locum.

235 Sciendum tamen quod licet species sit similis nomine et diffinitione generanti eam, ut species ignis in aere et ligno, tamen magis proprie et intelligibilius dicitur quod aer et lignum assimiletur igni per speciem quam quod ibi sit individuum ignis; propter hoc quod

209 etiam: e. quando est *O om. S*   210 nisi *BN*: est *SA om. FLO* / recipit: non r. *O* / lumen: lucem *O*   211 habet: recipit *S* / qui *S* / a luce *L*[C]: ad lucem *L'* 212 explanabitur: manifestabitur *S* intendit *A*   213 que est: *om. B*   214 stellis: illis *S* / eis: hiis *L* / *post* fiat *mg. add. O* lux / quia: ne q. *B*   215 quod: et *B* 218 differunt: dicuntur *S* differenter(?) *A*   219 erit: est *S*   220 earum *B* / sed: sicut *S* / ei *S*   221 soleant *B*   224 similes: *om. F* / *post* numero *scr. et del. L* compleatur tunc cum agens   225 non: nec *O om. S* / sunt *L* / completus *B* 226 cum: tamen *B*   227 erant *B*   229-30 essent . . . eadem *L*[C]: esset duo igne in eodem *L'*   231 *post* quia *mg. add. L* sequeretur quod   232 sufficeret *L*[C]: sufficunt *L'*   233 facit: *om. F*   234 nature *L*[C]: vere *L'* / non: nisi *S*   237 et[2] *BSN*: vel *FLO* / lignum: l. sit *S* / assimilatus *S*   238 speciem *L*[C]: specie *L'* / quam:

nature, although the sun has more light. And thus the species of light first reaches the moon and the stars and is afterwards perfected in them, as it was at the first creation and as occurs after stellar eclipses. For at first they have weak light, as though a similitude and species, and afterward clear and perfect light. The evidence for this is that the moon is red when eclipsed, since it receives light only when it is outside the shadow; however, while it is within the shadow it has a weak species of light coming from the light[32] that passes outside, along the sides and edges of the shadow, as will be explained more fully later.[33] Nevertheless, it must be known that the species of the sun, which is of the same specific nature as the sun, cannot be perfected in the moon and stars (although it comes to be in them), since that would require the moon and stars to become the sun, which is impossible; for light is a common quality of the sun and stars and fire, although the sun has more of it [than do the others]; and therefore the species of light can be perfected in the moon and stars, while the species of the substance of the sun cannot, since the sun, moon, and stars differ in specific substance, as will be evident below.[34] And light does not share in their substance; but it is an accident common to them and to fire, although some people are accustomed to claim that light is the substantial form of the sun and stars; but this is false. (δ)

Having now asserted these things, we demonstrate them as follows: if there are two effects altogether similar to the agent, but altogether distinct numerically—that is to say, not one effect, which at first is incomplete and afterwards (remaining the same in number) is completed —then (to put the matter numerically) when the agent acts on one part of the recipient there will be in that part of the recipient two forms belonging to the same species. But this is not possible, since form appropriates to itself and numbers the particular matter in which it is; and then [if there could be such numerically distinct effects], there would be two fires in the same part of burning wood, which, for the reason given, cannot be. And again, since the second form would be useless, because one form would suffice to perfect the matter in which it is, it follows that the additional one is superfluous. But nature does nothing superfluously or uselessly except through error, as in monsters and mistakes of nature, which will not be treated here.

However, it should be recognized that although a species is similar in name and definition to that which generates it, as the species of fire in air or wood, nevertheless it is more properly and intelligibly said that air and wood are assimilated to fire through the species than that an individual of fire is present there; for an

q. habet q. *S* ∣ quod¹: *om. F* ∣ ibi: illud *mg. O* ∣ sit: fit *FO* ∣ propter hoc: eo *S* 238-9 ignis ... individuum: *om. F*

individuum aeris vel ligni est ibi actu existens in sua natura specifica,
240 et ideo non sunt ibi duo individua (ponentia in numerum), scilicet
unum aeris et aliud ignis, sed unum absolute, scilicet aeris, quod
habet esse completum; et ideo prevalet in hac parte, ut fiat ab eo
denominatio individuitatis. Et tamen hoc individuum aeris est igni
assimilatum in natura igneitatis, per speciem ignis presentem in eo;
245 unde hoc individuum dicitur aer ignitus, nec enim est tantum aer,
nec tantum ignis, nec principaliter ignis, sed principaliter aer ignitus
tantum; et ideo quod ibi est de igne est individuum ignis incompletum, et in alio completiori existens, quod principalius est et
quod magis nominatur. Et ideo multo minus dicemus quod in aere
250 est individuum hominis vel solis vel alterius rei nobilis; sed dicemus
quod aer est assimilatus homini vel soli per speciem, que tamen
est eiusdem nature specifice in qua est homo vel sol, et infra eam
collocatur, licet secundum esse incompletissimum, quod etiam
impossibile est compleri, ut docebitur post. Et propter istud esse
255 incompletissimum dicitur individuum aeris assimilatum soli, non individuum solis cum individuo aeris, nam a completo fit denominatio.
  Si vero contra hanc veritatem et priorem adhuc dicatur quod
Aristoteles dicit *Libro de sensu et sensato* quod color non habet
esse nisi in mixto, et similiter odor et sapor et huiusmodi, et ideo
260 in aere et in simplicibus elementis et corporibus non potest esse
color aliquis, dicendum est quod color secundum esse completum
non potest ibi esse nec odor nec sapor nec huiusmodi, sed tamen
secundum esse incompletum. Et iterum concedendum est quod aer
et cetera simplicia, quantum recipiunt de esse coloris et huiusmodi
265 passionum que sunt naturaliter in mixtis, tantum recipiunt de esse
mixtionis; agens enim quod potest alterare aerem ad colorem potest
alterare ad mixtionem, scilicet ut in aere simplici species cuiuslibet
mixti fiat secundum quod requiritur ad species passionum, que fiunt
in aere ab illis passionibus, cuiusmodi sunt color et odor et huius-
270 modi. Nam aer est in potentia ad mixtum, et potest mixtum completum fieri de eo, et ideo multo fortius potest alterari ad esse mixti
quantum species mixti requirit.

    239-40 actu . . . ibi: *rep.* O   240 et ideo: quapropter quod S | non: enim L |
ponentia: *mg.* L^C potentia L'   241 unum^2 S^C: ad u. S'   242 ut fiat: *om.* S
243 et: est LA et est O | tamen: *om.* O | hoc: *om.* FSA | est: *scr. et del.* L *om.* OF
aeris S | igni: i. agenti SA   245 hoc . . . aer^2: dicitur ignitus non tamen est tantum
hoc individuum aeri S | dicitur: proprie(?) d. A | *post* ignitus *scr. et del.* A et non quod
sit sicut(?) ignis et aer ponentes(?) in(?) | nec: non A   246 sed: *mg.* F^C nec F'
247 tantum FO: *mg.* L^C et ideo quod ideo L' tamen BS   248 incompletiori O |
existens: *mg.* L^C ex ientes L'   249 quod^1: *om.* F | nominatus F nominatum O
249-72 et . . . requirit: *om.* SA (*A's omission begins with* ignitus *in l.* 246)   250 dici-
mus L   252 in: *mg.* L^C | infra: in forma O | eam L^C: cum L' eadem O   253 quod:
quam B   253-4 incompletissimum . . . esse: *mg.* L^C   254 *ante* compleri *scr. et del.*

individual of air or wood actually exists there in its specific nature, and therefore two individuals are not present there (speaking numerically), namely, one of air and another of fire, but one absolutely, namely, of air, which has complete being; and therefore the latter prevails in this place and gives its name to the individual. Yet this individual of air is assimilated to fire (in its fiery nature) through the species of fire present in it; and therefore this individual is called 'ignited air', for it is not only air and not only fire and not principally fire, but principally air, only ignited; and therefore such fire as is there is an incomplete individual of fire, existing in another more complete [substance], which predominates and more justly supplies the name. And therefore [with] much less [justification] would we say that an individual of man or of the sun or of some other noble thing is present in air; rather, we will say that air is assimilated to man or the sun through a species, which nevertheless has the same specific nature as man or the sun and is classified under it, although according to being that is very incomplete and incapable of completion, as will be taught below.[35] And through this very incomplete being the individual of air is said to be assimilated to the sun; but there is no assimilation between an individual of air and an individual of sun, for the name comes from the complete being.

But if, against this truth and the previous one, it is stated that Aristotle says in *De sensu et sensato* that colour exists only in a mixed body,[36] and similarly odour, flavour, and the like, and therefore that there can be no colour in air or in [other] simple elements and bodies, it is replied that colour, odour, flavour, and the like cannot exist in air and simple bodies according to complete being, but according to incomplete being. And again it can be conceded that in so far as air and other simple bodies receive the being of colour and effects of this kind, which exist naturally in mixed bodies, to that extent they receive the being of a mixture; for an agent that can alter the air to [the state of] colour can alter it to [the state of] being mixed, so that in simple air the species of whatever mixture you wish would come into being as required by the species produced in the air by such effects as colour, odour, and the like. For air is in potentiality to mixture, and a completed mixture can come into being from it, and therefore much more easily can it be altered to the being of a mixture in the degree required by the species of the mixture.

L^c ut | docebatur L^c | post *BFN*: postea *O* prius L^c | istud *FN*: istum BL^c illud *O*
256 solis: *ex* solum *corr. L* | cum: *mg.* L^c 257 adhuc: *ex* ad hunc *corr. L*
258 calor *B*   259 nisi: *mg. O* | et . . . odor: *om. F*   264 huius *L*   265 tantum:
tamen *B* | de: *om. L* | esse: *mg.* L^c 266 *ante* aerem *scr. et del. F* speciem
268 requiritur: requa(?) *L*   269 cuiusmodi sunt: *om. B* cuius s. *L*   270 et . . .
mixtum: *om. O*

Tertio sciendum est quod agens naturaliter facit eundem effectum primum, ut speciem, in quodcunque agat, ita quod uniformiter agit
275 a parte sua; quia solum agens quod agit secundum libertatem voluntatis et per deliberationem potest agere difformiter a parte sua. Sed agens naturale non habet voluntatem nec deliberationem, et ideo uniformiter agit. Etiam si agens habens voluntatem, ut homo, agat per modum nature in generando speciem, adhuc aget uniformiter et
280 uno modo a parte sua, quia et natura et modus nature se habent uno modo; et propter hoc, quodcunque patiens ei occurrat, semper facit eundem effectum primum. Et ideo sive agat in sensum, sive in contrarium, sive in materiam ei proportionalem que non sit contraria, oportet quod solam faciat speciem incompletam vel completam, ita
285 quod non facit alium effectum primum. Quapropter calidum, sive agat in sensum tactus sive in frigidum ei contrarium, semper facit speciem calidi solam quantum ad effectum primum. Et si sol operetur in ista inferiora que non sunt ei contraria, similiter faciet solam speciem, quantumcunque sint diversa ad invicem et contraria. Similiter si
290 res agat in intellectum, faciet speciem suam solam, sicut in sensum et ideo sicut in contrarium. Sed de hoc, scilicet quomodo in universali et in particulari fiat species in diversis patientibus, tam spiritualibus quam corporalibus, patebit inferius. Nunc autem solum hic tango de patientibus propter respectum agentis ad illa in faciendo
295 eundem effectum primum in quodcunque fiat actio.

Et quia sic est quod agens naturale agit a parte sua uno modo, et omne agens quod est agens naturaliter et per modum nature, ideo cum calidum diversas operationes facit in frigidum et in tactum, hoc erit propter diversitatem recipientium, sicut sol per eandem virtutem
300 dissolvit ceram et constringit lutum. Et ex hoc evacuatur error eorum qui estimant quod agens aliud immittit in sensum et aliud in contrarium, volentes quod fiat species in sensum et non in contrarium sed alia virtus, dicentes quod calidum corrumpit frigidum sed non corrumpit sensum dummodo non excedat. Aristoteles enim dicit in
305 secundo *De anima* quod actio in contrarium est in corruptionem, sed actio in sensum est in salutem et perfectionem; et delectatur sensus in specie sensibili, sed contrarium semper leditur et corrumpitur in parte vel in toto. Et licet in sensu sit aliqua passio et lesio ex

274 ut: et *F* / ita quod: ita que *S̄*   275 a: *ex* in *corr. F* / voluntatis: et voluntatem *B*   276 deformiter *B* / sed: *om. O*   277–8 nec . . . agit: *mg. L^C*
278 etiam . . . voluntatem: *om. L* / etiam: et *BS* / agat: si a. *L*   280 modus: motus *O*   281 occurrit *F*   282 sensu *O*   284 faciet *B* / speciem: rationem *S*
285 faciat *S* / calidum: capitulum *SL' om. L^C*   286 in[1]: et *L* / frigidum *O^C*: f. mentum *O'*   287 calidi solam *BN*: *om. FLOS*   288 faciat *L* facit *O*   289 sunt *L* / ad . . . et: et ad invicem *S*   291 hoc *L^C*: hec *L'*   295 in: *ex* etiam *corr. F*
296 et[1]: *om. B* / naturaliter *L*   297 quod est agens: *om. F* / ideo: et i. *F*
300 ceram: essentiam *L* causam *S*   302 fiant *S*   303 corrumpit . . . sed: *om. O*

It is to be known, in the third place, that an agent naturally produces the same first effect (that is, species) in whatever it acts upon, because for its part it acts uniformly; for only an agent that possesses free will and acts by deliberation can, for its part, act difformly. But a natural agent possesses neither will nor the ability to deliberate, and therefore it acts uniformly. Also, if an agent possessing will, such as man, should act in a natural mode in generating species, to that extent it will act uniformly and (so far as it is concerned) in one way, since nature and a natural mode have the same mode [of action]; and therefore, whatever recipient it meets, it always produces the same first effect. Therefore, whether it acts on sense, on its contrary, or on matter proportioned (and not contrary) to it, it can produce only a species, whether complete or incomplete, because it produces no other first effect. Thus heat, whether it acts on the sense of touch or on a cold thing contrary to it, always produces only the species of warmth as its first effect. And if the sun should act on terrestrial things that are not its contraries, it will similarly produce only a species, no matter how different from, and contrary to, each other these terrestrial things are. Likewise, if a thing acts on the intellect, it will produce only its species, just as when it acts on sense or on its contrary.[37] But how, in general and in particular, species are produced in various recipients, both spiritual and corporeal, will be revealed below.[38] Here, though, I deal with recipients only from the standpoint of the agent producing in them the same first effect, no matter what recipient it acts upon.

And since indeed a natural agent, for its part, acts in one way, and this for every agent that acts by nature or in a natural mode, therefore, when warmth produces different effects in a cold body and in the sense of touch, this must be the result of diversity in the recipients, just as sun by the same virtue melts wax and hardens mud. And from this we can refute the error of those who judge that the agent sends one thing into sense and another into its contrary, meaning that a species is produced in sense while some other virtue is produced in the agent's contrary; for they say that warmth corrupts cold but, provided it is not excessive, does not corrupt sense. For Aristotle says in *De anima*, book ii, that the action [of an agent] on its contrary corrupts, while action on sense is beneficial and perfects; and sense delights in a sensible species, while the contrary is always injured and corrupted in part or in whole.[39] And although in sense there is some suffering and injury owing [even] to

304 dicit: *om. B*   306 sensus: *om. F*   306–7 est . . . sensibili: *mg. L^C*   307 sed:
scilicet *S* / corrumpitur: corpora *S*   306 toto: loco t. *S* / sensu: passu *B* / sit: *om. FL* /
et²: vel *S*

sensibili quantumcunque proportionali, secundum auctores aspec-
310 tuum, et precipue per Alhacen primo *De aspectibus*, tamen simul
cum hoc est delectatio vincens illam passionem et lesionem, quod
non est in contrario. Et ideo posuerunt aliud recipi in sensum et aliud
in contrarium, quod impossibile est per predictam. Et hoc confirma-
tur per Aristotelem in septimo *Physicorum*, ubi dicit quod 'quale
315 naturale alterat et alteratur in eo quod sensibile'; sed in eo quod
sensibile non facit nisi illud quod natum est sensum immutare, et
hoc est species; ergo in eo quod omne agens naturale agit naturaliter
non facit nisi speciem.

PARS I
CAPITULUM 2

Deinde considerandum est secundum principale circa influentiam
corporalem, scilicet que res agant et faciant huiusmodi species; et
5 habet octo veritates. Et planum est de sensibilibus propriis quod
agunt species, quia immutant sensum, et universaliter sensus recipit
species sensibilium, ut Aristoteles dicit. Et in hoc omnes auctores
et magistri concordant, nisi de sono. Non enim video quomodo sonus
faciat speciem aliquam; sed aliter tamen fit sufficienter per tremorem
10 partium rei percusse, quia in prima parte rei percusse generatur
sonus non nisi per tremorem partium et egressum continuum a situ
naturali. Nam rarefiunt partes consequenter et ordinate egrediuntur
a situ naturali per violentiam percussionis, ex quo egressu causatur
tremor qui facit primum sonum tanquam effectum equivocum. Et
15 consimilis tremor fit in secunda parte rei percusse per primam partem
trementem; nam ad tremorem prime tremit secunda, et ad tremorem
secunde tremit tertia, et sic ultra. Et ideo nascitur ex secundo
tremore secundus sonus qui est similis primo sono nomine et diffinitione; et ideo eius similitudo et species debilior est primo, quia

309 quantumcunque: *mg. L*^{C} quamcunque *L'* | secundum: sed *B*   310 per: *om. O*
secundum *S* | Alhacen: Halacen *F* Alphacen *B* (*these forms of the name typify MSS F and*
B; henceforth they will not be noted as variants) | simul: naturalis *O*   311 hec *S*
313 per: *mg. L*^{C} predicta *BS*   314 septimo: libro *L*   316 immutare: *ex* immutat
corr. L   317 naturale: *om. F*   318 species *B*
2 capitulum secundum *O* distinctio secunda in quam consideratur que res possit facere
species habens (*post* habens *scr. et del. L*^{C} scilicet) capitula primum est quod sonus multi-
plicat speciem et similiter ödor *L*   3 deinde: quarto *S* | principalem *S*   4 cor-
poralis *S* | scilicet: sed *L* | faciat *F* | huius *S*   6 agent *O* | in muteant *B*
7 sensibilium: *om. O* | ut . . . dicit: *om. S* | dicit *L*^{C}: *om. L'*   8 de: in *BL*
10 partium: *om. F* | *post* percusse *add. SA* nam rarefiunt (rarefiunt et *S*) partes communiter
et ordinate egrediuntur a situ naturali per violentiam percussionis ex quo (qua *A*) egressu

a sensible proportioned as closely as you please [to the sense organ], according to the authors of books on optics, and especially Alhazen in *De aspectibus*, book i,[40] nevertheless there is simultaneously a pleasure that prevails over the suffering and injury, which is not [so] in the contrary. And therefore, [the holders of the erroneous opinion] supposed that one thing is received by sense and another thing by the contrary; but this is impossible, according to the aforesaid. And our view is confirmed by Aristotle in *Physics*, book vii, where he says that 'whatever the natural agent, alteration and being altered occur in sensible things';[41] but the agent produces in sensible things only that effect which is suited to alter sense, and this is a species; therefore, in the natural action of every natural agent, only a species is produced.

PART I

CHAPTER 2

We now take up the second principal question concerning corporeal influence, namely, what things act and produce such species; and it contains eight verities. [First,] it is clear that the proper sensibles produce species, since they alter sense, and universally sense receives the species of sensible things, as Aristotle says.[1] And all authors and masters agree on this, except in the case of sound. For I do not see how sound could produce a species; rather, sound is sufficiently explained by the vibration of the parts of the thing struck, since sound is generated in the first part of the thing struck simply by the vibration of parts and their repeated displacement from their natural places. For the parts are successively rarefied and displaced in an orderly fashion from their natural places by the force of percussion, and this displacement causes the vibration that produces the first sound as an equivocal effect. And the first vibrating part produces a similar vibration in the second part of the struck object; for the second part vibrates according to the vibration of the first part, and the third vibrates according to the vibration of the second, and so on. And therefore, from the second vibration arises a second sound similar in name and definition to the first sound; and therefore its similitude and species is weaker than [that of] the first, since the

causatur tremor qui facit primum sonum tanquam effectum equivocum et consimilis tremor (effectus *A*) fit in parte secunda rei percusse per primam partem trementem nam ad tremorem prime tremit (tremuit *S*) secunda et ad tremorem secunde tremit (tremuit *S*) tertia et sic ultra / quia: q. ergo *SA* / rei percusse: percussa *A*   11 continuum: etiam c. *O* 12 consequenter *L*^C: consequentur *L'*   12–13 nam . . . naturali: *om. O*   12–14 nam . . . equivocum: *om. SA*   13 percussionis *L*^C: percussionibus *L'*   14 equivocum: *om. F*   15–17 per . . . ultra: *om. SA*   16 tremit *L*^C: tremat *L'* / secunda: octava *L*   17 ex: de *O*   18 secunda *B* / consimilis *F*   19 eius: est *L* / debilior *L*^C: debiliorem *L'*   19–20 quia . . . primo: *om. BO*

20 tremor secundus debilior est primo, eo quod fit a virtute violenter
movente, et omnis motus violentus debilitatur et deficit in fine;
quapropter soni generatio semper debilitatur sicut in aliis speciebus
et virtutibus. Quare igitur sonus omnis ex tremore causatur immediate
et non est res fixa nec permanens. Ideo non videtur michi quod
25 aliquis sonus ex alio generetur, et ideo alium habent soni modum
quam qualitates alie sensibiles. Sed in omnibus est simile preterquam
in causa generationis soni et modo generandi. Unde secundus sonus
est species primi et tertius secundi et sic ulterius; sed non fit secundus a primo nec tertius a secundo propter causam dictam.
30   Secundo est magna dubitatio de substantiis et maior ignorantia.
Quod vero substantia agat similiter speciem manifestum est per hoc,
quod substantia nobilior est accidente quasi in infinitum; quapropter
poterit effectum sibi similem producere longe magis quam accidens, et
hunc effectum vocamus speciem. Item substantia generatur, ut ignis
35 et alie multe. Sed nullum generans est vilius generato. Quare non
generabitur natura substantialis ignis ab accidente; ergo a substantia.
Sed quod in fine generationis dicitur ignis vocatur species in principio
cipio et dum habet esse incompletum. Ergo substantia generat suam
speciem in principio, sicut accidens.
40   Item accidens non generatur in aliquo nisi prius natura generetur
suum subiectum proprium, propter quod Aristoteles dicit septimo
Methaphysice quod prius est aggregatum quam accidens, absolute consideratum. Et Averroys vult quod omne accidens alicui subiecto per
accidens est accidens per se alterius subiecti, aut iretur in infinitum.
45 Et illud subiectum proprium cadit in diffinitione accidentis sicut
Aristoteles determinat septimo *Methaphysice*, et in tertio dicit quod
eadem sunt principia essendi et cognoscendi. Quapropter accidens
non potest esse sine suo subiecto proprio. Et ideo si caliditas ignis
renovetur in aqua per actionem ignis in eam, oportet quod natura
50 substantialis ignis, que est subiectum proprium caliditatis ignis
ibi renovetur prius natura, quoniam subiectum est prius natura

---

20 fit: sit *BL* / a: ex *F*   23 quare: quia *S* / igitur: cum *O* / immediate *L*^C:
immedietatur *L'*   25 aliquis: aliis *O* / generatur *O* / et ideo: sed *S* / modum:
medium *L*   27 modi *S* / sonus: *om. O*   28 non: *om. L*   30 secundo est:
hec solebat esse *S* sed solebat esse *A*   31 vero: non *S*   32 nobilior: *om. F* / in:
om. L   33 similes *S* / producitur *L*   34 generatur ut ignis: i. g. *S*   37 in²:
a *O*   38 completum *S*   40 generatur: generantur *F* / alio *L* / nisi: *mg. L*^C
nichil *L'*   42 consideratum *OAN*: considerandum *BFL* considerando *S*   43 *post*
consideratum *mg. add. O*^C ergo cum subiectum proprium caloris est pars illius aggregati et
hoc est substantia ignis fiet ibi species substantie ignis sicut species caloris / *ante* Averroys
scr. et del. F accidens / vult: inter *S*   44 in: *om. F* / *post* infinitum *mg. add. O*^C
ergo calor ignis fit in aqua vel in alio cum calor sit accidens per accidens aque erit accidens
per se alicuius alterius per cuius generationem in ipsa aqua regenerabitur calor in ea ergo
substantia ignis ibi fiet sive species substantie eius similis substantie caloris   45 et illud:

second vibration is weaker than the first, because it is produced by a violently moving virtue, and every violent motion weakens and finally dies away; consequently, the generation of sound is always weakened, as are other species and virtues.[2] Thus all sound is caused immediately by vibration and is not a fixed and permanent thing. Therefore, it does not seem to me that one sound is generated by another, and consequently sounds have a mode [of generation] different from that of other sensible qualities.[3] But sound is similar to other sensible qualities in every respect except cause and mode of generation. Thus [we can properly affirm that] the second sound is the species of the first sound, and the third of the second, and so on; but the second does not arise from the first, nor the third from the second, for the stated reason.

Second, there is great doubt and greater ignorance regarding substances. That substance also produces a species is evident from this, that substance is almost infinitely more noble than accident, and therefore it will be able to produce an effect similar to itself far more easily than will accident; and we call this effect 'species'. Also, substance comes into being through a process of generation, fire and many other things being examples. But no source of generation is inferior to the thing it generates. Thus the substantial nature of fire cannot be generated from accident, and therefore it must be generated from substance. But that which at the end of the process of generation is called 'fire', at the beginning (and while its being is incomplete) is called 'species'. Therefore, substance generates its species at the beginning, as does accident.

Also, accident is not generated in anything unless its proper subject is first generated by nature, on which account Aristotle says in *Metaphysics*, book vii, that (absolutely considered) the composite being is prior to its accident.[4] And Averroes asserts that every accident of a certain subject *per accidens* is an accident of some other subject *per se*, for otherwise there would be an infinite regress.[5] And this 'proper subject' falls within the definition of accident as Aristotle presents it in *Metaphysics*, book vii;[6] and in book iii he says that the principles of being and of knowing are the same.[7] Consequently, accident cannot exist without its proper subject. And therefore, if the warmth of fire should be generated in water through the action of fire on it, the substantial nature of fire, which is the proper subject of the warmth of fire, must first be generated there by nature, since in the order of nature the subject is prior

item *O* / subiectum: secundum *B*   46 dicitur *S*   48 suo: *om. S*   49 renovetur *LONA*: removetur *F* renovet *B* innovetur *S* / eam: eadem *L* ea *B*   51 ibi *LSA*: *om.* *BFO* / renovetur: removetur *F* innovetur *S* / quoniam . . . natura: *om. L*

suo accidente, licet sint simul tempore. Sed illam caliditatem generatam in aqua vel alio quocunque vocamus speciem caliditatis.
Ergo similiter illa natura substantialis ibidem generata vocabitur
55 species substantie. Item sicut se habet substantia ad accidens, sic
species accidentis ad speciem substantie; ergo sicut accidens non
potest esse sine substantia, sic nec species accidentis sine specie
substantie.

Ex quibus sequitur necessario quod falsa est positio eorum qui
60 dicunt speciem tantum fieri ab accidentibus. Et si textus Aristotelis
perverse translatus et ideo male expositus adducatur in contrarium,
solvendum est secundum virtutem rationum predictarum. Si enim
allegetur illud septimi *Physicorum*, 'quale alterat et alteratur in eo
quod sensibile et fiat vis in hoc', planum est quod alteratio est in
65 faciendo speciem sensibilem; quare alteratio est penes accidens. Sed
ad hoc non artatur generatio que fit a forma substantiali; et ideo licet
accidens, per quod est alteratio, faciat speciem sensibilem, non
propter hoc oportet quod forma substantialis faciat speciem sensibilem, sed aliam speciem quam sensibilem, saltem a sensu communi
70 et particulari. Et ad litteram, Aristoteles in illo capitulo tractat motum
alterationis, ut manifestum est in textu, quoniam vult ostendere
quod alterans et alteratum sunt simul et nichil ipsorum medium.

Potest etiam aliter dici magis realiter quod etsi illud verbum
extendatur ad omne agens naturale, quod substantia facit speciem
75 sensibilem, non tamen a sensibus exterioribus quinque nec a sensu
communi. Sed tamen haberi potest a cogitatione et estimatione
quibus ovis sentit speciem complexionis lupi inficientem et ledentem
organum estimative; et ideo fugit lupum primo aspectu, licet numquam
prius viderit eum. Et hec est species substantie nocive et inimice ipsi
80 ovi; et econtrario species substantie amice et convenientis alterius
ovis comfortat organum estimative, et ideo non fugit una ovis aliam.
Unde bene potest anima sensitiva percipere substantiam per speciem
suam, ut nunc dictum est, licet pauci considerent hoc, cum velit
vulgus naturalium quod substantialis forma non immutet sensum. Et

52 *post* caliditatem *scr. et del.* L ergo similiter illa natura substantialis   53 vocamur
B   54 vocabitur *LON*: vocatur F vocabatur BS   55 sic: sicut L   56 *post*
speciem *scr. et del.* B gratie   59 que L   61 perverse: male F valde male O
62 secundum: per S / virtutem rationum: veritatem positionum F   63 septimo F
64 hoc: eo F   65 quare: quia B quoniam SA / penes: *om.* B   66 artatur: alteratur F   67 est: e. accidens F   67–8 non . . . sensibilem: *mg.* O   68 propter:
tamen p. S   69 a S^C: ad S' / sensum S   70 modum O   71 ostendere:
eandem L   72 medium: est m. O   73 potest . . . aliter: *mg.* L^C obs. L'   74 extendatur: exceditur S extenditur A   75 a^1: aliud L / quinque: *obs.* L   76 haberi:
om. SA sentiri *mg.* O / potest *BON*: *om.* FLSA / a: bene a SA quasi O *om.* F / et estimatione: *mg.* O   77 lupi inficientem: lupum facientem B   78 lupum: *om.* B
79 prius: *om.* FO   82 potest: dicit L / percipe F   83 nunc: *om.* O / cum: causa L
84 forma: solis(?) B / immutat O immitet S

to its accident, even though in the temporal order they are simultaneous. But the warmth generated in water or anything else is called 'the species of warmth'. Therefore, similarly, the substantial nature generated in the same place will be called 'the species of substance'. Also, as substance is to accident, so is the species of substance to the species of accident; therefore, just as there can be no accident without substance, so there can be no species of accident without the species of substance.

It follows necessarily from this that those who maintain that a species is produced only by accidents are wrong. And if the text of Aristotle, incorrectly translated and therefore badly expounded, is used to prove the contrary, the question must be resolved by the force of the aforementioned arguments. For if one should appeal to the passage from *Physics*, book vii, that 'whatever [the natural agent], alteration and being altered occur in sensible things, and force is produced in them',[8] it is clear that this alteration occurs in the production of sensible species, and therefore the alteration concerns accident. But the generation produced by a substantial form is not restricted in this way; and therefore, although accident, through which the alteration occurs, produces a sensible species, it does not follow that substantial form produces a sensible species, but rather a species that is insensible, at least by the specific senses and the common sense.[9] And as for the letter of the text, in that chapter Aristotle is treating the motion of alteration, as the text makes clear, wishing to show that the agent of alteration and the thing altered exist simultaneously and with no intermediary between them.[10]

We can express the matter differently and more concretely: although the claim that substance produces a sensible species can be extended to every natural agent, nevertheless this species is not sensible by the five exterior senses or by the common sense. However, it can be received by the power of cogitation and estimation, by which a sheep perceives the species of the complexion of a wolf when that species pervades and distresses the organ of its estimative power;[11] and therefore it flees the wolf at first glance, even if it has never seen a wolf before. And this species is that of a substance injurious and hostile to the sheep; and conversely, the species of the friendly and harmonious substance of another sheep soothes the organ of the estimative power, and therefore one sheep does not flee another. Thus the sensitive soul can easily perceive a substance through its species, as we have now asserted, although few people recognize this, since the common student of nature prefers that substantial form not alter sense. And the

85 sic loquimur communiter; sed hoc intelligendum est de sensibus
exterioribus et sensu communi, qui retinent nomen sensus, non enim
estimationem et cogitationem vocamus sensus, licet sint partes anime
sensitive. Quinque enim sensus particulares et sensus communis, et
si volumus adiungere eis ymaginationem, quod bene possumus facere,
90 ut patuit in precedentibus et magis tangetur posterius, non compre-
hendunt nisi accidentia, quamvis per eos transeant species formarum
substantialium. Sed horum plenior certificatio patebit suo loco.

Si etiam dicatur illud Aristotelis *De sensu et sensato*, quod ignis
secundum quod ignis non agit nec patitur, sed secundum quod con-
95 trarium, dicendum est quod hec et huiusmodi auctoritates intelliguntur ad litteram de alteratione et generatione sensibili et manifesta
sensui particulari et communi. Hanc enim naturalis philosophus considerat, quia principaliter considerat ea que sunt ad sensum, secundum
quod dicit Aristoteles pluries quod considerat materiam sensibilem et
100 ea que sensus sunt. Et ideo hec potest esse una causa Aristotelis
quare inter virtutes anime sensitive nichil tangit de estimativa et
cogitativa, que naturam sensibilem vulgariter excedunt; sensibilia
enim vulgato nomine dicuntur que apprehenduntur a sensibus parti-
cularibus et communi, et ideo non cogit illa auctoritas nec aliqua
105 consimilis.

Potest etiam veraciter dici quod substantie est aliquid contrarium, ut exponetur; et est contrarietas inter formas substantiales
elementorum et substantias eorum. Et tamen non agunt ad invicem
transmutando se et mutuo corrumpendo secundum quod eorum
110 substantiales nature considerantur in se; non prout contrarietatem
habent, sed in quantum contrarie sunt. Et hoc est quod Aristoteles
dicit, quod ignis et terra non agunt secundum quod ignis et terra, sed
in quantum contraria. Non tamen intelligit hic de sola contrarietate
inter accidentia elementorum, licet de illa magis exemplificat quia
115 sensibilior est, sed de contrarietate formarum substantialium eorum,
propter quod fit fallatia consequentis in cavillatione. Et licet
Aristoteles dicat logice quod substantie nichil est contrarium, tamen
patet quod uno modo est contrarietas aliquarum formarum circa idem

86 retinent: *om. B | nomen: naturam O | post* sensus *mg. add. O* et nomen
89 volumus *BFON*: volimus *L* velimus *SA* / eis: *om. L*   90 in . . . posterius: ex primo
capitulo et ex sequentibus patebit *SA*   91 eas *S*   92 substantialium: sensibilium *S* /
plenior: purior *O* / patebit: p. inferius *S*   94 secundum[1] . . . ignis: *om. S* / quod[2]:
om. S   95 auctoritates *F*C: auctores *F'*   95–6 intelligimur *B* intelligimus *F*
98 secundum: sed *B*   99 pluries: per p. *S* / materiam: naturam *O*   100 ideo:
om. O   101 quare: *mg. L*C quidem(?) *L'*   102 vulgaliter *L*   103–4 a . . . auctoritas: *mg. L*C *om. L'*   106 potest: et p. *O* preter *L*   107 *post* ut *mg. add. O*C
inferius   108 tamen: inde *L' om. L*C   109 eorum: *mg. L*   110 prout: secundum quod *F*   111 habent *L'*: *del. L*C / *post* sunt *add. O* agunt se corrumpendo
secundum eorum substantiales formas   112 secundum: sed *B*   113 hic *F*C: hoc

latter is commonly asserted; but it must be understood that this is true only of the exterior senses and the common sense, which retain the name 'sense', for we do not call estimation and cogitation 'senses', although they are parts of the sensitive soul. For the five specific senses and the common sense (and if we wish, we can easily add the imagination, as was evident above and will be touched upon more fully below)[12] perceive only accidents, although the species of substantial forms pass through them. But these things will be more fully demonstrated in the proper place.

If the statement of Aristotle in *De sensu et sensato* is put forward, that fire acts and receives action not by virtue of being fire, but by virtue of being a contrary,[13] it is replied that Aristotle and similar authorities are literally understood to be talking about alteration and generation that are sensible and manifest to a particular sense and the common sense. For this is what natural philosophers suppose, since they consider principally things that are sensible—for, as Aristotle says several times, he considers sensible matter and things that pertain to sense. And this could be one reason why Aristotle, when treating the powers of the sensitive soul, says nothing of the estimative and cogitative faculties, which [are] commonly [thought to] go beyond sensible nature; for sensibles, commonly speaking, are the things apprehended by specific senses and the common sense, and therefore neither Aristotle nor any other authority links [the estimative and cogitative faculties with the other powers of the sensitive soul].

It can also be truly said that substance has some contrary, as will be explained; and this is a contrariety between the substantial forms of the elements and between their substances. Nevertheless, they do not act in such a way as to transmute and corrupt each other in so far as their substantial natures are considered in themselves; [that is, they are mutually corruptive and transmutative] not in so far as they have contrariety, but in so far as they are contraries. And this is what Aristotle says, namely, that fire and earth do not act [on each other] by virtue of being fire and earth, but by virtue of their being contraries.[14] However, we do not mean to speak here only of contrariety between the accidents of the elements, although contrariety is better illustrated there because there it is more sensible, but also of contrariety between their substantial forms; from this, in sophistical argumentation, has arisen the fallacy of affirming the consequent.[15] And although Aristotle may say logically that substance has no contrary,[16] nevertheless it is evident that in one way there is contrariety of certain forms pertaining to the same

OF' / solum *S*   114 exemplificant *L* exemplificet *S*   116 fit: sit *L* / et: quia *SA*

subiectum actualiter constitutum in esse specifico, ut albedinis et
120 nigredinis circa Sortem, et calidi et frigidi circa lignum. Et huiusmodi contrarietas non est in substantia, sed maxime aut solum
in qualitate. Et de hac loquitur in *Predicamentis* suis logice et ad
instructionem grossam, et similiter in quinto *Physicorum.* Sed aliter
dicit in fine *De generatione* substantiam esse contrariam substantie;
125 et in primo *Physicorum* secundum quod contrarietas est duarum
formarum circa subiectum ens in potentia, quod est res alicuius generis,
non alicuius speciei, ut forma gravis et levis circa idem genus, cuius
essentia est eadem materia communis gravi et levi, in qua communicant et circa quam se mutuo transmutant et expellunt—cum de terra
130 fit ignis et econtrario, et quodlibet elementum de alio, et mixtum de
elemento et econtrario, vel unum mixtum de alio, propter commune
genus et materiam, circa quam variantur et diversificantur et contrariantur—ut contrarietas exigitur in substantia. Et ideo forma
substantialis ignis facit suam speciem substantialem in corpus terre
135 vel ligni vel alterius et corrumpit formam substantialem terre vel
ligni, tanquam sibi contrariam ea contrarietate que in substantiis
reperitur et requiritur.

Tertio considerandum est quod species substantie non est tantum
ipsius forme, sed materie et totius compositi; eo quod Aristoteles
140 vult primo *De anima* quod omnes operationes sunt ipsius coniuncti
et compositi. Etiam nititur ostendere quod intelligere est ipsius
compositi. Unde homo intelligit, licet per animam; et magis proprie
et verius sic dicitur quam quod anima intelligat in homine. Quapropter
generatio speciei erit ipsius compositi, et ideo species est similitudo
145 totius compositi. Preterea forma propria esse non potest nisi in
materia propria; quapropter si innovatur in ligno vel quocunque
alio forma ignis, oportet quod ibi innovetur materia eius. Et hoc
patet per predicta, quoniam si accidens non potest innovari nisi cum
subiecto suo proprio, propter quod oportet poni speciem subiecti
150 generari in materia in qua species accidentis sui proprii, et essen-
tialior est comparatio forme ad materiam quam accidentis ad
subiectum, necesse est quod ubi generatur forma vel species forme
quod ibi generetur materia seu species materie; et ideo species

124 dicunt *F*   125 secundum: *om. O* sed *B*   126 alicuius: *om. O*   132 et
materiam: ut materia *FO*   133 ut: et talis *SA* | ideo: *mg. L*   135 substantialem:
om. F substantiale *B*   135–6 vel² . . . ligni: *om. O*   136 substantiis: hiis *S*
138 tertio: sexto *S*   139 sed *BLNV*: seu *O* nec *F* et *SA* | et *BN*: sed *FLOA* si *S*
140 vult: ulter *B* | operationes: orationes *F*   141 etiam: et *S* et eo iam *B* scientia *L* |
intelligentie *B* | *post* est *mg. add. O* magis proprie   143 sic: sit *L* sicut *S*
145 preterea *FO*: p. quod *N* propterea *LA* propterea quod *B* propterea ea *S*   146 in-
novatur: *mg. Lᶜ* novatur *L'* | quocunque: *mg. Lᶜ om. L'*   148 innovari: *mg. Lᶜ*
invocari *L'*   149 propter quod: p. hoc *L* quod non *O* | subiecti: *om. S*   150 quam
B | accidentis: *mg. corr. L ex* accidens | et: *om. O*   151 comparatio: composita *S*

subject as it is actually constituted in specific being, as whiteness and blackness in Socrates,[17] and warmth and cold in wood. And contrariety of this kind is not found in substance, but principally or only in quality. And concerning this Aristotle speaks logically and for the purpose of general instruction in his *Categories*, and similarly in *Physics*, book v.[18] But he speaks differently at the end of *De generatione*, asserting that substance is contrary to substance.[19] And in *Physics*, book i,[20] he asserts that because there is contrariety between two forms as related to a subject existing in potentiality, itself a thing of some genus but not of a particular species, as the forms of heavy and light are related to the same genus, the essence of which is the matter common to both the heavy and the light, in which they share and with respect to which they transmute and expel one another—since from earth comes fire and vice versa, and each element comes from each of the others, and a mixture comes from an element and vice versa, or one mixture from another, because of the common genus and matter with respect to which they are varied and diversified and made contrary—as a consequence there must be contrariety in substance. And therefore the substantial form of fire produces its substantial species in the body of the earth or of wood or of something else and corrupts the substantial form of the earth or wood—inasmuch as [the latter is] contrary to it by virtue of the contrariety found and required in substances.

Third, it should be recognized that the species of a substance is not only the species of its form, but also of its matter and of the entire composite; for Aristotle says in *De anima*, book i, that all operations are operations of conjoined and composite things;[21] he also endeavours to show that understanding is a property of composite things. Thus man understands, but through his soul; and this is a better and truer way of expressing it than to say that the soul in man understands. Therefore, the composite produces a species, and the species is the similitude of the entire composite. Besides, there can be no proper form except in proper matter; consequently, if the form of fire is generated in wood or anything else, its matter must [also] be generated there. And this is evident from the foregoing, for if accident cannot be generated except with its proper subject (on which account it is necessary to posit that the species of the subject is generated in the matter in which the species of the accident proper to it is generated, and the relationship of form to matter is more essential than the relationship of accident to subject),[22] it is necessary that where form or the species of form is generated, there matter or the species of matter is also generated; and therefore a

152 ubi: nisi *F* / forma: *ex* formalis *corr. L*

composita generatur. Ad hoc idem est quod Aristoteles in septimo
155 *Methaphysice* probat et determinat, quod forma tantum non generatur,
sed compositum novum ex materia nova et forma nova. Cum ergo
effectus generantis univocus sit unus et idem, qui primo vocatur species
et postea sortitur nomen generantis, oportet quod species sit composita; et hoc est omnino necessarium. Ex quo sequitur quod error
160 est eorum qui ponunt speciem esse similitudinem forme et non
materie nec compositi; nec habent auctoritatem nec rationem appar-
entem per se, sed solam consuetudinem falsitatis.

Si dicatur quod tunc materia faciat speciem, quod falsum est, quia
eius non est agere sed recipere tantum et pati, dico quod compositum
165 per formam facit sibi similem in quantum est compositum; et ideo per
unam et eandem actionem compositi per formam oritur in patiente
species totius compositi, et ideo non solum forme sed materie, primo
tamen et principaliter compositi. Si dicatur quod nullum agens finite
potentie potest in totum compositum, quia hec est creatio, nam
170 materia semper supponitur in actione nature, dicendum est quod
materia que est subiectum generationis supponitur, sed materia specifica renovatur sicut forma, ut prius in *Communibus naturalium*
demonstratum est. Et sicut est in generatione completa, quod materia
specifica completa et forma specifica completa et compositum speci-
175 ficum completum generantur, sic est hic in generatione incompleta,
que est generatio speciei, quod materia incompleta et forma incompleta et compositum incompletum fiunt secundum quod esse specierum requirit. Et ideo fit hic species materie sicut forme; et propter
hoc species composita generatur.
180 Quarto potest verificari quod omnis substantia corporalis potest
facere speciem, et non est calumpnia nisi in uno casu, ut in sensu.
Quoniam tamen accidentia et substantie viliores quolibet sensu faciunt
speciem, necesse est quod sensus faciat. Et hoc patet considerando
particulariter in singulis. De visu enim patet hoc, quia homo videt
185 oculum alterius sine speculo et per speculum, et oculum proprium per
speculum; sed nichil videtur sine specie, et hoc nullus negare potest

154 idem: *ex* dicendum *mg. corr.* L   156 ex: et S / et forma nova: *om.* O
157 sit: *ex* sed *mg. corr.* L   158 fortitur S   159 ex: ergo ex S   162 per: pro S
163 si . . . tunc: non tamen dico quod S / quod[2] . . . est: *om.* S   164 recipere . . . pati:
p. quoniam et r. F / *ante* dico *add.* OFSL' (*del.* L[C]) sed / compositam F   165 per[1]:
mg. O / simile B similitudinem S   168 dicat S   169 hec: de hac L   170 supposita F   171 que: *om.* FO / generationi B / supposita F   171–2 specifica:
ex specificata *corr.* L   172 renovamur L / ut: sicut S   173 demonstratum:
detractum(?) B / sicut: sic S   174 et[1] . . . completa[2]: *mg.* O   175 generatur F /
sic: sit L / hic: *om.* S   176–7 que . . . incompleta [2]: *mg.* O   176 quod: et F
177 incompletum: *om.* S / fuit F / secundum quod: s. F sicut O   177–8 specierum:
specificum B   179 hoc: *mg.* O *om.* F hos B / compositi F / generatur L[C]: geniatur
L' generatus F   180 quarto: septimo S   181 sensu: uno s. FO   182 accidentia

composite species is generated. In support of the same conclusion, Aristotle determines and proves in *Metaphysics*, book vii, that not only is form generated, but also a new composite from new matter and new form.[23] Therefore, since the univocal effect of a source of generation is one and the same thing, first called 'species' and afterwards designated by the name of the thing that generated it, the species must be composite; and this is altogether necessary. It follows that the error belongs to those who suppose that a species is the similitude of form but not of matter or of a composite; and of themselves they possess neither authority nor [any] evident rationale, but only the habit of falsity.

If it should be said that in that case matter would produce species, which cannot be, since matter does not act but only receives and undergoes action, I reply that a composite, through its form, produces something similar to itself in so far as it is composite; and therefore by one and the same action of the composite, through its form, the species of the entire composite is generated in the recipient—and thus not only the species of the form, but also of the matter, though first and principally the species of the composite. If it should be said that no agent of finite power can [produce] the whole composite, since this would be an act of creation, for matter is always assumed in an action of nature, one may reply that what is assumed is matter that is subject to generation, whereas specific matter is renewed along with the form, as has been demonstrated previously in the *Communia naturalium*.[24] And just as is the case in complete generation, where complete specific matter and complete specific form and a complete specific composite are generated, so it is here in incomplete generation (that is, the generation of a species), where incomplete matter and incomplete form and an incomplete composite come into being as the being of the species requires. And therefore here the species of matter, as well as the species of form, comes into being; and thus a composite species is generated.

Fourth, it can be verified that every corporeal substance can produce a species, and this is indisputable except in one case, that of sense. However, since accidents and substances, which are inferior to any sense, produce a species, sense must do so also. And this is shown by considering specific senses individually. It is evident in the case of vision, since a man sees the eye of another man with or without a mirror, and he sees his own eye with a mirror;[25] but nothing is seen without species, and this nobody can deny

et: *om. B*   184 quia: quod *BS* / videt: *om. F*   185 alterius: *mg. L^C om. L'*
185–6 et² . . . speculum: *om. S*   186 sed: licet *S*

absolute. Sed multi negaverunt aliquid fieri ab oculo propter actum videndi complendum, ponentes quod visio compleatur solum intus recipiendo et non extramittendo, nec quod aliquid fluat ab oculo
190 quod operetur et faciat actionem videndi. Quod autem hoc sit falsum patet per Aristotelem nono *De animalibus* expresse et per Tideum *De aspectibus* manifeste et per Ptolomeum in *Libro aspectuum* multipliciter. Et hec verificari debent in sequentibus; et solventur omnia que Alhacen et Avicenna et Averroys videntur in contrarium ful-
195 minare, et ostendetur quod non est contra eos hec veritas; et hoc fiet quando erit sermo in particulari de agentibus et patientibus.

Similiter instrumenta tactus, gustus, olfactus, auditus, cum sint corpora sensibilia naturalia, possunt per suos colores et odores et sapores et quatuor qualitates tangibiles facere species, sicut res
200 alie, et sensum immutare quantum est de se. Et multo magis erunt activa specierum in quantum sunt animata, quia sic sunt nobiliora et ideo magis activa. Quapropter faciunt species, et hoc negari non potest absolute. Sed an hee species facte ab eis cooperentur ad actus sentiendi dubium esset aliquibus, non tamen illis qui bene examinant
205 veritatem; quia proculdubio faciunt species a se ut compleantur et certificentur sue operationes per illas species circa sensibilia, ut expresse potest probari per Aristotelem et Avicennam in *Libris de animalibus* et multis modis. Sed hec inferius habent certificari; nunc in tantum sufficiat quod sensus universaliter faciat speciem, sicut
210 alia agentia corporalia.

Deinde considerandum est de aliis a predictis an faciant species, non enim est ita notum de ceteris rebus corporalibus, et que sunt passiones corporum an faciunt vel non. Quia vero Aristoteles dicit quarto *Metheororum* quod materia est in sola potentia passiva, et in
215 *Libro de generatione* quod materie debetur pati et forme agere, et omnes abhorrent dicere materiam aliquo modo agere, potest dici quod materia nullo modo facit speciem; sed per actionem compositi et forme generatur species materie specifice, sicut et forme et compositi, ut tactum est prius.

220 Alia autem corporalia que maxime accedunt ad ista accidentia sunt sensibilia communia, quia per se sunt sensibilia, ut Aristoteles dicit;

187 fieri: *om. F*   189 recipiendo: suscipiendo *S* / fluat *N*: fiat *FLOS* faciat *B* 189-90 nec . . . videndi: *mg. L*   190 faciat: f. ad *BS* faciet ad *L*   191 nono: et econtrario *B* 19 *S* / nono de animalibus: n. methaphysice *mg. O* / expresse: et commentatorem e. *O*   192 Ptolomeum: *om. B*   194 videantur *L* videatur *O* / falminare *F* fabulare *O*   195 hoc fiet: *mg. L^C* f. *L'*   198 corporalia *B*   199 quatuor: secundum *S*   200 se: *om. O* / multo: *om. O* / magis: malus(?) *O* / erunt: erit *F* sunt *B* erint *mg. L'*   202 activa: *mg. L* / hec *O*   203 an: si *B* / facte: *mg. O* / comparentur *S* / ad actus: *rep. F*   204 sensiendi *O* / non: *om. F* / tamen: *om. O*   207-8 de animalibus: *mg. L*   212 rebus: *om. S*   213 faciant *BS*   215 debentur *S* 216 materiam: naturam *O* / quod: q. et si *S* q. si *A*   217 nullo: de sua natura propria

absolutely. But many have denied that something issues from the eye
to complete the act of sight, positing that vision is completed only
by intromission and not by extramission, and denying that something flowing from the eye operates and produces the act of sight.[26]
However, that this opinion is false is demonstrated expressly by
Aristotle in *De animalibus*, book ix,[27] manifestly by Tideus in *De
aspectibus*,[28] and multifariously by Ptolemy in *De aspectibus*.[29] And
these things will be proved below; and all of the lightning bolts that
Alhazen, Avicenna, and Averroes seem to hurl against them will be
fended off, and it will be shown that the truth [of extramission] is
not opposed to their position; and all of this will take place in
specific sections concerning agents and recipients.[30]

Similarly, the organs of touch, taste, smell, and hearing, since they
are sensible natural bodies, can produce species through their
colours, odours, flavours, and four tangible qualities, just as other
things do; and these organs can, according to. their capacities, alter
sense. And in so far as they are animate, the more active will they be
in producing species, since animate things are nobler and therefore
more active. Therefore, they produce species, and an absolute denial
of this is impossible. But whether the species produced by them
assist in the act of perceiving is doubted by some, but not by those
who examine the truth carefully; for undoubtedly they send forth
species in order that their operations with respect to sensibles may be
completed and certified through those species, as can be expressly
proved from Aristotle and Avicenna in their *Libri de animalibus*
and in many [other] ways.[31] But these things must be proved below;
here it suffices merely that sense universally produces a species, as
do other corporeal agents.

It must next be considered whether things other than those
treated above produce species (for this is not as well known concerning other corporeal things), and whether or not the passions[32] of
bodies produce species.[33] But since Aristotle says in his *Meteorology*,
book iv, that matter is only in passive potency,[34] and in *De generatione* that it is fitting for matter to receive and for form to act,[35]
and everybody abhors saying that matter acts in any way, it can be
said that matter [by its own proper nature][36] in no way produces
species; but the species of specific matter, and also the species of the
form and of the composite, are generated through action of the composite and the form, as was mentioned above.[37]

The other corporeal things that most closely approach these accidents are the common sensibles, since they are sensible *per se*, as

n. *S* de sua propria natura nullam *A* / faciat *SA* / sed: tamen *SA*   218 species: *mg.*
L^C *om. L'*   219 est prius: *om. F*   221 communia: contraria *F*

que sunt magnitudo, figura, numerus, motus, et huiusmodi usque
ad viginti, cum eis que reducuntur ad illa, sicut habitum est prius.
De hiis vero dicit Ptolomeus in secundo *De aspectibus* quod non
225 faciunt passionem in visum similem eis nomine et diffinitione; sed
solum lux et color hanc faciunt, que passio nominatur ab eo coloratio
et illuminatio; alia autem sensibilia comprehenduntur per aliam viam,
ut determinat. Et hoc idem vult Alhacen secundo *Aspectuum*; et expresse determinat hoc quarto *Aspectuum*, dicens quod nichil venit a
230 corporibus nisi species lucis et coloris. Et uterque determinat hanc
viam aliam, propter quam visus solus non sufficit ad iudicandum veritatem horum; nec ei attribuitur iudicium de aliis, sed alii virtuti anime
mediante visu vel tactu vel alio. Unde Alhacen dicit quod virtus distinctiva et ratiocinativa hec iudicant mediante sensu particulari. Et
235 Tideus *De aspectibus* hiis concordat, volens quod situm et figuram et
magnitudinem et huiusmodi non posset visus cognoscere nisi species
visus fieret ad rem ipsam, quoniam species istorum sensibilium communium non fiunt a rebus secundum eum. Et istud patet per hoc,
quod nos percipimus visum pati a forti luce et colore, ita quod quando
240 aspeximus fortem lucem vel colorem et convertamus nos postea ad
alia visibilia debilioris lucis et coloris, non statim percipimus illa
alia visibilia propter impressionem adhuc remanentem a forti colore
vel luce; sed cum paulatim evanescit, augmentatur visio et apprehensio
rerum illarum. Sed hoc non accidit nobis in videndo forte densum vel
245 rarum vel asperum vel lene vel magnitudinem vel corporeitatem vel
figuram vel huiusmodi, quando postea aspicimus alia visibilia; et per
hoc scimus quod sensus non patitur ab hiis sicut a sensibilibus
propriis.
Item si non esset densum a parte post ipsius perspicui, non
250 perciperemus ipsum perspicuum; similiter nec densum nisi quia inter
nos et ipsum est perspicuum. Nec corpus et figuram et cetera percipimus nisi quando percipimus densum; sed hec tamen sine denso et
densum sine perspicuo habent esse naturale et vere esse. Quare si ex
natura sua activa facerent speciem in visum, tunc videremus aerem et

223 *post* que *scr. et del.* L non   /   prius: in primo capitulo *SA ex* primis *corr.* L
224 Ptolomeus: *om.* S / secundo: s. libro O   226 nominantur S   229 a: *ex* in
corr. L   230–1 hanc . . . aliam: *om.* S   231 solum O / iudicandum: videndum
S   232 horum . . . anime: *mg.* L / aliis sed: *mg.* O / alii virtuti: aliis virtutibus O
a. virtute S   233 medietate *OS* / vel²: et B   234 rationativa *BO*   235 hiis:
om. F / figuras B   236 potest O   237–8 communium *SAN*: contrarium *BFLO*
238 per hoc: *om.* B   239 quando: *om.* S   240 aspeximus *FLO*: aspexerimus *BS*
conspexerimus N   241–2 debilioris . . . visibilia: *mg.* L^C *om.* L'   244 illarum:
mg. L^C aliarum L' / non: enim L   245 vel¹: *om.* F / vel⁴: *om.* S   246 postea:
alia p. S / alia: sensibilia S   249–50 a . . . densum: *rep.* O   250 perciperemus:
percipiemus O / perspicuum: *om.* FO / inter: *om.* F   251 figuram: *ex* signum *corr.*
L   252 nisi . . . densum: *mg.* L^C *om.* L' / hec: hoc F *om.* O / tamen: t. perspicuum O
253 *ante* habent *scr. et del.* F non / quare: quasi S / si: sit L

Aristotle says; and these are size, shape, number, motion, and the like, up to twenty in number, with others that are reduced to them, as was shown above.[38] But concerning these Ptolemy says in *De aspectibus*, book ii, that they do not produce effects in vision similar to themselves in name and definition; for only light and colour do this, and their effects are named by him 'colouring' and 'illumination'; and he argues that the other sensibles are grasped by another means.[39] And Alhazen intends the same thing in *De aspectibus*, book ii; and he specifically determines this in *De aspectibus*, book iv, saying that nothing comes from bodies except the species of light and colour.[40] And both authors determine this in another way, namely, that sight alone does not suffice for judging the truth of these things [the common sensibles]; nor is judgement concerning other [sensibles] attributed to sight, but to another power of the soul by the mediation of sight or touch or some other sense. Thus Alhazen says that the discriminative and ratiocinative power judges these things, with the mediation of a particular sense.[41] And Tideus in *De aspectibus* agrees, wishing to affirm that sight cannot grasp position, shape, size, and the like unless the species of the visual power[42] comes to the thing itself, since according to him things do not send forth species of these common sensibles.[43] And this is also evident from the fact that we notice that sight is affected by strong light and colour, so that when we have looked at a bright light or colour and afterwards shift our gaze to other visible things of weaker light and colour, we do not immediately perceive these other things because of the impression still remaining from the bright colour or light; but when this impression gradually dissipates, sight and the apprehension of these [dimmer] things are strengthened.[44] But this does not occur when we observe, for example, something that is dense or rare or rough or smooth, or when we observe size, corporeity, shape, or the like, and afterwards look at other visible objects; and from this we know that sense is not influenced by these in the same way as by the proper sensibles.

Also, we would not perceive a transparent body if there were not a dense body behind it; similarly, we would not perceive the dense body if between us and it there were not a transparent body. And we do not perceive body and shape and the rest [of the common sensibles] except when we perceive a dense thing; nevertheless, these [common sensibles, including transparency] have natural and true being without the dense, and the dense without the transparent. Therefore, if by their active nature they should produce a species in the eye, then we would see air and the sphere of

255 speram ignis et speras celestes extra loca planetarum, cum in omnibus
hiis sint quantitas et figura et magnitudo et corporalitas et per-
spicuitas et huiusmodi; et tunc sine huiusmodi perspicuis videmus
densum si densum de se natum esset facere speciem. Sed visus non
iudicat de denso nisi mediante perspicuo ad quod terminatur.

260 Ceterum, quantitas debetur materie, quia est passio materie, et
ideo non debet esse activa, sicut nec materia, que est substantia et
eius subiectum proprium; quare nec passiones quantitatis, que sunt
rectum, curvum, figura, superficies, et forma corporis, nec huiusmodi.
Et iterum susceptivum soni est absonum, et coloris similiter et aliorum
265 immutantium medium et sensum. Sed sensus et medium habent
quantitates et figuras et huiusmodi. Item multa horum reperiuntur in
subiecto generationis, et ideo precedunt generationem et sequuntur
corruptionem, et sunt in rebus ingenerabilibus et incorruptibilibus,
et in omnibus corporibus omnia aut plura. Propter quod oportet quod
270 horum saltem multorum non sit generatio nec corruptio; augmentatio enim vel diminutio posset in hiis esse, sed quod de novo gene-
rentur et corrumpantur totaliter non accidit in omnibus. Sed
immutatio speciei est per generationem et eius annichilatio per
corruptionem totaliter. Quapropter non sunt generativa speciei hec
275 que sic reperiuntur circa subiectum nature et materiam naturalem.

Sed eadem ratio est sensibilis in omnibus istis que vocantur
sensibilia communia, eadem ratio dico generalis, propter quod si
aliqua non sunt nata facere speciem, nec alia. Et cum contra hoc
videatur esse quod ista sunt sensibilia per se, sicut propria, propter
280 quod videretur quod speciem agerent et immutarent plures sensus sicut
sensibile proprium immutat unum sensum, dicendum quod non ob
hoc dicuntur sensibilia per se nec propria nec communia, sed quia
virtus distinctiva, que est cogitativa, cuius esse est in media cellula
cerebri, iudicat de hiis sensibilibus, tam propriis quam communibus,
285 mediante sensu communi et particulari, qui solum de partibus anime
sensitive vocantur a vulgo nomine sensus, et quia de sensibilibus per
accidens eadem cogitativa iudicat mediante estimatione et memoria et

255 *ante* speram *scr. et del.* F speciem / planetarum: philosopharum *B*   256 sint:
fuit *L* sicut *S* / quantitas: *mg.* L^C quatinus *L'* magnitudo *S om. B*   256–7 perspicuitate
B   258 densum²: *om. B* / esse *L*   259 medietate *LO*   260 ceteram *F* /
debemus *L* / quia: que *L* / materie: modo *S*   261 debet: dicitur *F* / nec: *om. L*
262 quare: quasi *S*   263 superficies *FON*: superficiei *BLS*   264 absolum *B* /
aliori *L*   265 medium¹: medietatem *S*   267 sequuntur *FO*: sequitur *L* secuntur
BS   268 sunt: est *L* / ingenerabilibus *BSN*: generabilibus *FLO* / corruptibilibus *F*
269 autem *L*   272 corrumpantur *ex* corrumpentur *corr. S* / non: n. est *B* / accidens *BL*
274 sunt: fiunt *O*   275 materie *L*   276 vocamur *L*   278 cum: tamen *O*
279 videatur: *mg.* F^C videntur *F'* videtur *O* / sint *B*   280 species *S* / immutaret *O*
immutaretur *L*   281 dicendum: d. est *BL* / ab *L*   283 cogitationem(?) *F* /
post cellula *scr. et del.* F capitis   284 cerebra *OF* / sensibus *S* / communibus: *mg. L*

fire and the celestial spheres (besides the regions of the planets), since all of these have quantity, shape, magnitude, corporeity, transparency, and the like; and then without such [intervening] transparent bodies we would see a dense body if the dense body were suited of itself to produce a species.[45] But [in fact] sight is unable to judge concerning a dense body at which it is terminated, except by the mediation of a transparent body.

Moreover, quantity is associated with matter, since it is property of matter, and therefore it should not be active, just as matter (which is a substance and the proper subject of quantity) is not active; therefore, neither are the modifications of quantity—straight, curved, shape, surface, and the form of a body—nor other such things. And again, it is the soundless that is receptive of sound, and similarly for colour and other things that alter the medium and sense.[46] But sense and the medium have quantities and shapes and the like. Also, many of these things[47] are found in the subject of generation, and therefore they precede generation and follow corruption, and they are in ungenerable and incorruptible things, and all or several of them are in all bodies. From which it follows that there is neither generation nor corruption of at least many of these; for augmentation or diminution could occur in them, but generation *de novo* and total corruption do not occur in all of them. But the transmutation of a species is entirely by generation and its annihilation entirely by corruption. Therefore, species are not generated by these things, which are thus encountered in the subject of nature and natural matter.

But the same argument is applicable to all of the common sensibles—that is, the same general argument, according to which if some are not suited to produce a species, then neither are the others. And since against this would seem to be the fact that the common sensibles are sensibles *per se*, just as the proper sensibles are, and therefore ought to produce a species and alter several senses, as a proper sensible alters a single sense, it is replied that neither proper sensibles nor common sensibles are called 'sensibles *per se*' for this reason, but rather because the discriminative (that is, the cogitative) faculty, which exists in the middle cell of the brain, judges concerning these sensibles, proper as well as common, by means of the common sense and the particular senses (the latter of which alone, of the parts of the sensitive soul, are called 'senses' in ordinary usage), and because the same cogitative power judges concerning sensibles *per accidens* by means of the estimative power and the memory

non mediante sensu communi et particulari; propter quod sensibilia communia et propria vocantur per se sensibilia quia mediante sensu et
290 non estimatione comprehenduntur. Horum autem intellectus planior patet non solum ex precedentibus, sed dependet ex subsequentibus; et ideo quod hic minus planum est requiratur a locis aliis propriis.

Quod autem posset dici quod nichil videtur nisi densum; et densum etiam sine colore et luce innata potest videri, ut in terra et aqua
295 et forte in celo octavo vel nono secundum diversitatem opinionum de illis, ut inferius patebit; propter quod densum videtur esse maxime sensibile et visibile, et ideo quod speciem faceret in sensum. Dicendum est quod hoc non valet, non enim est maxime visibile propter hoc quod nichil sine eo videtur, quia occasio magis est quam causa, et
300 quia per aliud comprehenditur, sicut perspicuum interiacens; et ideo non est ex sua natura absoluta ut videatur, sed dependet a perspicuo. Propter quod non debet facere speciem ut de se immutet. Nec requiritur eius perceptio ad hoc ut percipiantur color et lux; sed sufficit visui quod color et lux sint in denso aliquali, scilicet, ut terminetur
305 visus, non enim terminatur nisi per densum. Ad esse ergo coloris et lucis exigitur densitas, ut visus terminetur ad colorem et lucem. Sed tunc ex natura sua propria faciente speciem videntur, et prius quam percipiatur densum, quoniam densum nec comprehenditur solo sensu, sed per cogitationem, nec per se, sed per collationem ad per-
310 spicuum et mediante eo, sicut patet ex libris aspectuum.

Quod vero dicit Alhacen, secundo *De aspectibus*, quod in concavo nervi communis duorum oculorum et in parte membri sentientis, id est, anterioris glacialis, que est anterior pars pupille, figuratur circumferentia rei vise. Sed circumferentia reducitur ad sensibilia communia,
315 ut patet ex eodem libro. Quapropter videretur quod quantitas et figura et huiusmodi faciant impressionem et speciem in organo, et ideo prius in aere. Ad hoc dicendum est quod illud intelligendum est sicut loquitur de magnitudine rei vise quando dicit quod ordinatur et describitur in superficie membri sentientis; hoc enim non est quia
320 magnitudo faciat suam speciem, sed quia a tota rei magnitudine venit

288 particulari: in p. *S*   289 mediante: *ex* meditante *corr. L*   289–90 et non: cum *B*   291 patet: *mg. L* / precedentibus: p. in parte *S*   293 videatur *S* 295 opinioni *S*   296 ut: sicut *S* / maxime: *ex* magis *mg. corr. F*   298 hoc[1]: *om. L* / est[2] . . . visibile: *om. F*   299 occasio: o. actio *B*   300 perspicuum: per p. *S* 301 absolute *S* / videatur: non v. *O* / dependet: *ex* dependeat *corr. L*   302–3 requirit *S* 303 percipiatur *S*   304 sint: *mg. L*[C] *om. L'* / aliqualis *L*   305 terminatur: *mg. L*[C] *obs. L'*   307 speciei *S* / et *L*[C]: quod(?) *L' scr. et del. O*   308 quam *ONV*: tanquam *BLF* antequam *SA* / nec: non *O*   309 sed[2]: nec *O* / per[3]: *om. L* / collocationem *FL* 310 et: sed *O*   311 *ante* quod[1] *mg. add. L*[C] quomodo   312 parte: superficie *B* 313 pupille: *om. B*   314 sed: *om. B* / reducitur: autem r. *B* redditur *S*   318 vise *OSA*: *om. L* in se *F* in re *B*   320 suam: *om. S* / re *F*

rather than the common sense and the particular senses;[48] thus common sensibles and proper sensibles are called 'sensibles *per se*' because they are apprehended by means of sense rather than through the estimative faculty. However, clearer understanding of these things depends not only on the foregoing, but also on that which follows; and therefore let what is not perfectly clear here be looked into in other suitable places.[49]

But it could be said that only dense substances are visible; and the dense, even if it lacks intrinsic colour and light, can be seen, as in earth and water and perhaps the eighth or ninth heaven, according to differing opinions, as will be evident below;[50] and so it seems that what is principally sensible and visible is that which possesses density, and therefore that the dense produces a species in sense. We reply that this [argument] is invalid, for density is not [to be judged] the principal visible thing from the fact that anything lacking it is invisible, since density is more the occasion for vision than the cause of vision, and since the visible object is perceived as a result of something else, that is, intervening transparency; and therefore a dense substance is not seen as a result of its absolute nature, for its visibility depends on the transparent medium. Consequently, it need not produce a species in order of itself to alter [the observer's visual power]. Nor need it be perceived in order for colour and light to be perceived; but for vision of light and colour it is sufficient that they be in a dense substance of some sort, so that sight will be terminated, for sight is terminated only by a dense body. Therefore, the existence of colour and light requires density, so that sight will be terminated at the colour and light. And light and colour are seen as a result of their own nature producing a species; and they are perceived before density is perceived, since the latter is grasped neither by sense alone (but through cogitation) nor *per se* (but through juxtaposition with a transparent substance and by its mediation), as is evident from books on optics.[51]

But Alhazen says, in *De aspectibus*, book ii, that the circumference of the visible object is represented by a figure in the hollow of the common nerve[52] of the two eyes and in part of the sentient organ (that is, the anterior glacial humour, which is the anterior part of the pupil).[53] But this circumference is reduced to the common sensibles, as is evident from the same book.[54] Therefore, it would seem that size and shape and such things produce an impression and a species in the organ [of sight], and consequently first in the air. We reply that this claim is to be understood exactly as the claim that the magnitude of a visible object is arranged and represented on the surface of the sentient organ; for it is not the case that magnitude produces a species, but that from the entire magnitude and the

species coloris et lucis et a tota superficie; et tunc species coloris
venientes a singulis partibus rei vise non confunduntur in una parte
pupille, sed distiguuntur et ordinantur in superficie pupille in
quantitate sensibili, secundum numerum partium in re visa, ut visus
325 distincte comprehendat totum colorem vel lucem rei vise. Sic igitur
describitur in pupilla magnitudo rei vise, id est, color totius magnitudinis vel lux, ita quod solum sit ibi species coloris et lucis ordinata
in pupilla, et non ipsius magnitudinis. Propter quod similis intellectus est de figuratione circumferentie rei et descriptione eius
330 in membro sentiente et nervo communi, scilicet, quod color vel
lux ipsius circumferentie totius facit speciem suam, que figuratur
et ordinatur in organo et medio, sed non ipsa circumferentia; hic
enim est auctoris intellectus de omnibus talibus.

Quod autem dictum est quod species materie renovatur sicut forme;
335 tunc proprietatum materie species debent similiter renovari cum suo
subiecto; sed quantitas est proprietas materie. Dicendum est quod
species materie prime non renovatur, sed specifice, et illius proprietates renovantur. Sed hee non sunt corporeitas et figura et huiusmodi
communia, quoniam sunt proprietates materie prime. Si igitur ista
340 sensibilia communia non faciant species, multo fortius nec alie res
predicamentales corporales, ut relatio, situs, quando, et huiusmodi.
Sensibilia autem per accidens dicuntur respectu sensuum particularium
et communis, qui autonomatice vocantur sensus. Sed tamen multa
eorum sunt sensibilia per se ab estimativa, ut prius dictum est de sub-
345 stantiis. Sed sensibilia per accidens alia a substantiis, sicut filius et
pater et cetere res predicamentales a substantiis et sensibilibus
propriis et communibus, non sunt activa specierum, postquam sensibilia per se multa non possunt facere species, cum tamen sunt magis
activa quam talia sensibilia per accidens.

350 Post hec autem ergo expedit considerari quod, sicut rerum quedam sunt universales quedam singulares, sic species fiunt ab hiis et
illis; et ideo, sicut species singularium sunt singulares, sic universalium universales. Et cum universale non sit nisi in singularibus,
sicut ostensum est in methaphysicis propter contentiones multorum,

322 vise: in se B / confunduntur L': confundentur L^C confunditur B   325 calorem
S   326 describimur L   327 et: vel O   329 post rei scr. et del. F vise
331 ipsius: om. B / suam: om. B   335 tunc: autem S   336 sed . . . materie: om. S /
est²: om. L   337 specifice: ex specie corr. L   338 ante corporeitas scr. et del. F
proprieta / figura: ex figurata corr. L   339 communia: om. S / si: om. L / igitur: om.
B / ista: substantia S   340 fortius: minus F   343 vocantur FO: vocatur BLSN
dicitur A   344 dictum: tactum S   345 sed: et O   346 sensibus S
347 active S   348 tamen: non S   348–9 per . . . sensibilia: mg. L^C om. L'
350 hoc B / autem: om. O / ergo: octavo FN xi S / considerare O / rerum: ex res corr. L
352 sicut: om. F / sic: sicut F   354 sicut: ut S / methaphysicis: mathematicis O alio
scilicet in m. loco S alio scilicet m. A

entire surface of the object come the species of colour and light; and the species of colour coming from individual parts of the visible object are not mixed in one part of the pupil, but are kept separate and are arranged on the surface of the pupil in [a figure of] perceptible magnitude, according to the number of parts in the object, so that sight may distinctly perceive the entire colour or light of the visible object.[55] In this way is the magnitude of the visible object represented on the pupil—that is, the colour or light of the whole magnitude, so that only the species of colour and light are [actually] arranged on the pupil, and not the species of magnitude itself. The arrangement and representation of the circumference of the visible object in the sentient organ and the common nerve are to be understood in the same way, namely, that the colour or light of the whole circumference produces its species, and this species, rather than the circumference itself, is arranged and gives rise to a figure in the organ and the medium; for this is the understanding of the author[56] concerning all such things.

However, it is objected that the species of matter is generated,[57] just as the species of form; therefore, the species of the properties of matter should be similarly generated with their subject; but quantity is a property of matter, [and therefore the species of quantity ought to be generated]. To this it is replied that the species of prime matter is not generated, but [only] of specific matter, and it is [therefore the species of] the properties of the latter that are generated. But these properties do not include corporeity, shape, and such common sensibles, which are properties of prime matter. Therefore, if these common sensibles do not produce species, much more clearly do other corporeal things belonging to the categories not produce species, such as relation, position, time, and the like. Now sensibles *per accidens* are so called with respect to the particular senses and the common sense, which are called 'senses' antonomastically.[58] Nevertheless, many of the [sensibles *per accidens*] are sensible *per se* by the estimative faculty—the same claim made above concerning substances.[59] But sensibles *per accidens* other than substances, such as son and father and things belonging to the categories other than substances and proper and common sensibles, do not produce species, since many sensibles *per se* cannot produce species, although they are more active than such sensibles *per accidens*.

After these things, it is useful to consider that, just as some things are universals and others singulars, so species are produced by the one and by the other; and therefore, as the species of singulars are singulars, so the species of universals are universals. And since a universal exists only in singulars, as has been shown in metaphysics by the arguments of many people, and a singular

355 nec singulare potest carere suo universali, erit proportio speciei
universalis ad speciem singularem sicut rei universalis ad rem
singularem quarum sunt hee species. Et ideo cum singularia hominis
faciunt suas species in medio et in sensu et intellectu, sic homo
universalis simul facit suam speciem in speciebus singularibus; ita
360 quod sicut homo universalis est una natura specifica in quolibet
singulari tota et totaliter, sic species universalis est una natura
specifica suo modo, et tota et totaliter est in qualibet specie
singulari, sine quibus impossibile est quod sit, sicut nec universale
sine singulari nec econtrario. Et propter hoc iteratur in medio et
365 sensu et intellectu species universalis quando venit cum specie
cuiuslibet singularis; et sic figitur in anima fortius quam species
alicuius singularis. Et hoc determinat Alhacen evidenter in libro
secundo.

   Ex hiis igitur sequitur correlarium, quod sive in medio sive in
370 sensu sive in intellectu sint species universales, oportet quod
ibidem sint species singulares eis respondentes. Et ideo non intelligo
quod in intellectu aliquo creato sint tantum species universales fixe
sine singularibus speciebus, ut per applicationem multarum talium
universalium specierum, quarum res universales sint in aliquo indi-
375 viduo alicuius speciei, fiat cognitio de tali re singulari, quamquam et
ipsa applicatio non est michi intelligibilis. Sed de hiis tractabitur alias
suis locis.

   Ex dictis in hoc capitulo patet quod cum queritur universaliter
de omni specie in medio, an sit substantia vel accidens, nulla est
380 questio, et similiter an species sit quidam compositum vel simplex,
et an universale vel singulare. Nam species substantie est substantia,
et species accidentis est accidens, et species compositi est composita,
et species simplicis est simplex, ut materie species est materia, et
forme est forma, et species rei universalis est universalis, et rei
385 singularis est singularis; quia breviter dicendum quod sicut se
habet accidens ad substantiam et forma ad materiam et universale ad
singulare, scilicet, quod nullum istorum est sine suo compari, sic
se habet species accidentis ad speciem substantie et species materie
ad speciem forme et species rei universalis ad speciem rei singularis,
390 quod nullum earum est sine sua socia.

  358 faciant S / et²: id est B 359 simul: om. FO 361 post totaliter scr. et del.
O sic universalis est una natura specifica suo modo et tota et totaliter 362 est: et O
363 sit: fit F sic L 363–4 sine . . . singulari: om. O 364 sine: ex sit corr. L
369 correlarium FO: correlarie BLS / sive¹: sint S 370 in: interl. L^C om. L'FO
371 sint: ex sunt corr. L 372 creato: tanto B 373 per applicationem: mg. L^C
propter dicationem L' 374 sunt L 375 fiat: mg. L 376 michi: nisi S
377 suis locis: ex suas lociis corr. L 378 universaliter: om. B 379 vel: om. L /
nulla: quod n. S 380 similiter: om. B / quidam BL: quiddam F quoddam ON om. SA /

cannot lack its universal, therefore the species of the universal will be in the same relation to the species of the singular as the universal source of species is to the singular source of species. And since singular men produce their species in the medium and sense and the intellect, so universal man simultaneously produces his species in the singular species; so that as universal man is one specific whole nature, wholly in each singular man, so the universal species is in its way one specific nature, and all of it is wholly in each singular species; for it cannot exist in any other way, just as the universal cannot exist without the singular and vice versa. And therefore the universal species is repeated in the medium and sense and the intellect when it comes with the species of each singular; and thus it is fixed in the soul more powerfully than is the species of any singular. And Alhazen determines this clearly in his second book.[60]

From these things a corollary follows: that whether universal species are in the medium or sense or the intellect, singular species corresponding to them must be in the same place. And therefore I do not hold that any created intellect has fixed in it only universal species (without singular species), so that through the application of many such universal species (of which the corresponding universal things exist in some individual of a certain species) there could be cognition of such an individual—indeed, the application [of many universal species] is unintelligible to me. But these matters will be treated elsewhere in their proper places.[61]

From what has been said in this chapter, it is evident that when it is inquired universally concerning every species in the medium, whether it is substance or accident, the answer is obvious, and likewise whether a species is simple or a certain composite, and whether it is universal or singular. For the species of substance is substance, the species of accident is accident, the species of a composite is composite, and the species of a simple is simple, just as the species of matter is matter, of a form is form, of a universal is universal, and of a singular is singular; for it is to be said, in brief, that as accident is to substance and form to matter and universal to singular, namely, that none of these is without its companion, so is the species of accident to the species of substance and the species of matter to the species of form and the species of a universal to the species of a singular, because none of these is without its companion.

vel: et *F*   381 species: *om. S*   382 composita: compositum *O*   383 est[1]: *mg. L*[C] ex *L'* | ut: et *S* .   384 forme: species f. *S* | rei[1]: *om. L* | universalis[1]: *om. S* 386 habent *L* | substantiam: subiectum *L* | ad[2]: ad a *L* | materiam: numerum *B* | ad[3]: ad in *L*   387 sic: sed *L*   389 et: *om. B* | rei[1]: *om. O*   390 quod: ita q. *O* | eorum *F* | est . . . socia: *om. S*

PARS I
CAPITULUM 3

Habito de agente, consequenter considerandum est de modo agendi, quod est tertium hic principale. Et habet tres conclusiones, quarum 5 prima est quod non potest species exire nec emitti ab ipso agente, quia accidens non permittat subiectum nec pars substantialis sine corruptione substantie totius. Sed maxime activa, ut substantie spirituales et celestia, non sunt corruptibilia. Quare species nullo modo exibit ab agente, cum omne quod est in eo sit substantia vel accidens; nec 10 contingit ponere medium, ut prius declaratum est. Quapropter male loquitur vulgus et improprie quando dicit quod agens emittit a se speciem, exemplificans in odorabili, quod aliquid emittit, ut in musco since accensione vel in thure accenso. Sed dicendum quod odorabile in quantum activum est speciei non emittit aliquid, sed in quantum 15 patitur per calidum intra resolvens aut extra. Et ideo agens naturale in quantum agens non emittit aliquid, sed in quantum patitur et destruitur. Ceterum actio non est in deperditionem et corruptionem agentis, sed perfectionem, quia tunc unumquodque perfectum est cum sibi simile facere potest, secundum Aristotelem secundo *De anima*. 20   Deinde manifestum est quod agens non creat speciem ex nichilo; neque accipit eam alicubi extra se et extra patiens, ut eam reponat in patiente, hoc enim ridiculosum esset. Quapropter improprie et male dicitur quod agens immittit aliquid in patiens et quod influit, nam tunc ab extra ingrederetur aliquid in ipsum patiens; quod 25 non potest esse, quia tunc vel exiret ab agente, vel agens inveniret illud extra se et patiens, vel crearet illud de nichilo, quorum quodlibet est falsum. Et ideo oportet unam duarum viarum eligi, scilicet, quod per viam impressionis fiat species, aut quod per naturalem immutationem et eductionem de potentia materie patientis. 30   Sed via impressionis non est possibilis, quoniam impressio non fit nisi in superficie, ut sigilli in cera, per elevationem quarundam partium superficiei et depressionem aliarum; sed actio naturalis est in profundo patientis. Item per species rerum sentimus res ipsas; sed per impressiones que fiunt in cera et huiusmodi, non sentimus

---

2 capitulum tertium *O mg. L*^C   6 permittat *BFO*: permutat *LSAN* | sine: nisi *L*
9 ab: de *B*   10 declaratum: *mg. L*^C declinatum *L'*   11 loquitur: *om. S* |
dicitur *F*   11-12 a . . . emittit: *mg. L*^C *om. L'*   13 vel: et *F* | accensio *S*
15 resolventes *B*   19 secundo: *mg. L*^C *om. L'*   21 et: vel *FO*   22 enim:
ex habens *corr. L*   22-7 improprie . . . oportet: *om. S*   23 aliquid: ad *B*
24-6 quod . . . patiens: *mg. O*   26 illud[1]: aliud *B* | de: a *L'* ex *L*^C
27 viarum: *om. S* | scilicet: secundum *F*   28 quod[1]: *om. F* per q. *L*   30 via:
per viam *mg. L*^C *om. L'*   31 fit: sit *O* / in[1]: de *B*   32 aliarum: ab Aristotele *S*
33 *post* item *mg. add. L*^C per impressiones sive   34 per: *om. S*

PART I
CHAPTER 3

Having treated the agent, we must now consider its mode of action, which is the third principal subject of this treatise. And [this chapter] has three conclusions, the first of which is that a species cannot exit from or be emitted by the agent itself, since neither accident nor a piece of substance can depart from a subject without corruption of the whole substance.[1] But things that are of the greatest activity, such as spiritual and celestial substances, are incorruptible. Therefore, a species will in no way be emitted by an agent, since everything in the agent is either substance or accident; nor do we posit an intermediary [between substance and accident], as was declared above.[2] Therefore, the vulgar express themselves badly and improperly when they say that an agent emits a species from itself, offering as an example odoriferous substances (such as burning frankincense or musk that is not burning), which send forth something. But it is replied that an odoriferous substance does not emit anything owing to its being a source of species, but owing to its being affected by heat, which decomposes it internally or externally. And therefore, a natural agent does not emit anything by virtue of being an agent, but by virtue of being acted upon and destroyed. Moreover, acting does not destroy and corrupt an agent, but perfects it, since, according to Aristotle in *De anima*, book ii, a thing is perfect when it is able to produce a like thing.[3]

Next it is shown that an agent does not create a species *ex nihilo*; nor does it receive a species from outside itself and the recipient and deposit it in the recipient, for that would be ridiculous. Therefore, it is badly and improperly said that the agent dispatches something to the recipient, which flows into it, for in that case something would enter the recipient from outside; but this cannot occur, since either this something would be emitted by the agent, or the agent would find it outside itself and the recipient, or the agent would create it *ex nihilo*—none of which is possible. And therefore we must choose one of two alternatives, namely, that a species comes into existence either through an impression or through a natural alteration and bringing forth out of the potentiality of the matter of the recipient.[4]

That this should occur by means of an impression is impossible, since an impression is produced only in a surface (as the impression made by a seal in wax) by elevation of certain parts of the surface and depression of others; but a natural action occurs in the interior of the recipient. Also, through the species of things we perceive the things themselves, whereas through impressions in wax and the like

35 res imprimentes. Ergo non est consimilis actio hinc et inde, ex quo
sequitur quod improprie dicitur quod speciei generatio est per viam
impressionis, secundum quod utimur hoc nomine prout est impressio
in sigillo et huiusmodi. Sic enim ad litteram intelligit vulgus species
imprimi ab agentibus, sed non est ita. Si tamen largius accipiatur
40 impressio, prout signat communiter omnem transmutationem patientis
per actionem agentis, sicut aliquando inveniuntur auctoritates accipi
apud ipsos auctores vel apud interpretes, tunc posset dici quod per
impressionem fieret species. Et sic convenit quodammodo cum impressione, primo modo dicta, licet non omnino, quia continet eam,
45 sicut universale suum particulare; hec enim impressio est communiter,
sive fiat actio in superficie sive in profundo. Et sic usus est Aristoteles,
cum dixit secundo *De anima* quod sensus suscipit species sensibilium
sicut cera anuli; quodammodo enim est similitudo, sed non plena;
et sic multe auctoritates inveniuntur, que hoc modo habent solvi.

50   Cum igitur nullo predictorum modorum fiat generatio speciei,
manifestum est quod quinto modo oportet fieri, scilicet per veram
immutationem et eductionem de potentia activa materie patientis, non
enim est aliquis alius modus excogitabilis preter dictos; et hec est
conclusio tertia. Et non solum per hunc locum a divisione patet hoc;
55 sed necessarium est hoc, quoniam effectus naturaliter facti dicuntur
generari secundum Aristotelem de potentia materie activa, ut
omnes fatentur sine contradictione. Sed species est effectus agentis
naturalis et naturaliter productus est; quare ipsa species debet de
potentia materie generari. Item potentie receptive respondet dator
60 forme, et hic est Creator; quare si in materia esset potentia solum
receptiva specierum, tunc poneremus in rebus naturalibus datorem
formarum, contra Aristotelis doctrinam. Ergo non fiet species in
potentia receptiva, sed de potentia activa, materie naturalis seu
patientis. Et iterum patet ex dictis quod hec virtus est eadem cum
65 effectu completo, illa enim fit ipse effectus completus quando agens
invalescit; et ideo idem erit modus producendi effectum istum
incompletum et completum. Quare si completus effectus educitur

35 ex quo: unde *S* / 38 in sigillo: sigillatio *O* / 38 enim: eius *S* / 39 tamen:
non *S* / accipiatur: sumatur *A* / 40 *post* impressio *add. SA* ut habitum est in prima
parte huius tractatus / 41 inveniunt *B* / 42 apud[1]: *mg. L*C arua aupud *L'* / 43 sic:
cum *F* / 44 modo: *om. S* / 48 *post* cera *mg. add. O* speciem / 48-9 quodammodo
. . . solvi: quod modo habent similitudinem *O* / 49 dissolvi *S* / 50 speciei: *om. B*
51 manifestam *B* / quinto: hoc *O* / 52 patientis: *mg. L*C patiens *L'* / 53 predictos *O*
54 tertia: 19a vel 3 *S* / 57 fateretur *S* / 60 in: *om. S* / solis *S* / 62 species: *mg.*
*L*C *om. L'* / 63 de: *mg. O* / 67 quare: quia *S* / educeretur *S*

we do not perceive the impressing objects. Therefore, in neither respect is the action similar, and therefore it is improper to say that a species is generated by means of an impression—if by this word we mean the sort of impression made by a seal or its like. For the vulgar literally believe that species are impressed by agents in this way, but it is not so. Nevertheless, if 'impression' is taken in a broader sense,[5] according to which it commonly designates every alteration of a recipient by the action of an agent (just as 'authorities' is sometimes taken to mean the works of the authors themselves, sometimes the works of their interpreters), then it can be said that a species comes into existence by means of an impression. And thus to a degree it resembles an impression (in the first way mentioned above), but not altogether, since [the idea of] a species contains [but is not equivalent to the idea of] an impression, as a universal contains its particular; for it is commonly [called] an 'impression', whether the action is produced in the surface or in the interior. And thus Aristotle used the term when he said in *De anima*, book ii, that sense receives the species of sensible things as wax receives a seal;[6] for in a way there is similitude [between the two processes], but not fully; and many authorities are seen [to use the term] thus, and they are to be understood in this way.[7]

Since the generation of a species occurs in none of the afore-mentioned [four] ways, it is apparent that it must occur in a fifth way, namely, by a true alteration and bringing forth out of the active potentiality of the recipient matter, for no mode beyond the said [five] can be devised; and this is the third conclusion. And this is evident not only by the foregoing argument from division;[8] but it is necessary, since effects that are naturally produced are said by Aristotle to be generated out of the active potentiality of matter, and all acknowledge this without contradiction. But a species is the effect of a natural agent and is naturally produced; therefore, the species must be generated out of the potentiality of matter. Also, to passive potentiality there corresponds a giver of form, and this is the Creator; therefore if in matter there were only a [passive] potentiality receptive of species, we would [need to] posit in natural things a giver of forms, contrary to the teaching of Aristotle.[9] Therefore, a species does not come into existence in the passive potentiality, but out of the active potentiality, of natural or recipient matter.[10] Again, it is evident from what has been said that this virtue is the same as the complete effect, for it becomes a complete effect when the agent becomes stronger; and therefore the mode of producing this effect, whether complete or incomplete, will be the same. Therefore, if a complete effect is brought forth out

de potentia materie, oportet quod prius educatur effectus incompletus de eadem potentia.

70 Sed contra hoc quedam obiectio decipit multos. Arguitur enim quod
agens et patiens simul sunt; et nichil est ipsorum medium, secundum
quod Aristoteles probat septimo *Physicorum* et determinat nono
Methaphysice et *Libro de generatione.* Precipua enim conditio agendi
est quod coniungatur agens cum patiente sine medio, et aliter non
75 transmutabit ipsum. Sed coniunctio duplex intelligitur, scilicet vel
secundum substantiam vel secundum virtutem, ut dicunt; sed agens
non potest esse simul secundum suam substantiam cum profundo
patientis; quare oportet quod sit simul secundum virtutem, ut generet
effectum suum per eductionem eius de profundo patientis. Et ideo
80 dicit multitudo quod virtutis est datio et infusio in profundum patientis, ut de potentia eius educatur effectus, et quod non debeat virtutis
generatio fieri de potentia illa. Et ideo ponitur quod virtus seu species
non educitur de potentia materie, sed quod datur et infunditur, et
quod est aliud ab effectu intento finaliter; et solum fit ab agente, ut
85 transmutetur profundum patientis, et per illam educatur effectus
de potentia materie. Unde instrumentum est agentis ad effectum
producendum principalem. Et aliter, ut dicunt, non posset agens
producere effectum quem intendit, ut ignis ignem seu formam ignis;
nec homo hominem, nec aliquod agens produceret effectum ei similem
90 nomine et diffinitione. (ε) Et sic cogimur redire ad predicta circa
pluralitatem effectuum univocorum. Sed cum illa suo loco non poter-
unt contradici—quin, sequatur quod species est ipse effectus agentis
primus et univocus, complendus per operationem completam, ut tunc
recipiat nomen et diffinitionem agentis, sicut prius ostensum est,
95 nec potest esse nisi unus talis effectus—manifestum est has cavilla-
tiones vanas esse.

Et iterum contingit argui contra generationem virtutis quam ipsi
fingunt aliam ab effectu principali, sicut contra generationem effectus principalis, scilicet quomodo faciat agens eam in profundo
100 patientis, cum substantia agentis non sit infra illud profundum.
Quapropter fictio istius virtutis preter effectum principalem non
evadet hanc obiectionem, quia qua ratione agens non potest generare

70 multos: *ex* multis modis *corr. F*   71 sint *F*   72 determinans *F*   75 vel:
ut *B*   76 *post* virtutem *add. O* sol enim est simul   76-7 vel . . . substantiam:
om. F / ut . . . substantiam: *om. O*   78 *post* patientis *add. O* non secundum suam substantiam   78-9 quare . . . patientis: *mg. rep.* L^C 79 eius: e. est *L* / *post* patientis
scr. et del. L ut de potentia   79-80 et . . . patientis: *om. F*   80 et infusio: *mg.* L^C *om.*
L' / profundo *S*   81-2 eius . . . ponitur: *mg.* L^C *om. L'*   82 quod virtus: *mg. rep.* L^C
83 infunditur: in profunditur *S ex* funditur *corr. L*   84 solis *S*   85 et: et ut *BS*
86 instrumentum: *om. B*   87 principalem: *om. B*   88 quod *B*   90 predicta
circa: predictam *O*   91 illo *B*   95 nisi: *om. S*   97-8 virtutis . . . generationem:
om. L   99 agens: *om. F* / profundum *B*   100 patientis: p. de eius potentia *S* /

of the potentiality of matter, an incomplete effect must first be brought forth out of the same potentiality.

But many are deceived by a certain objection to this. For it is argued that agent and recipient are joined to one another;[11] and there is no intermediary between them, as Aristotle proves in *Physics*, book vii, and determines in *Metaphysics*, book ix, and *De generatione*.[12] For the principal condition of acting is that the agent and recipient be conjoined without intermediary, for otherwise the former does not alter the latter. But conjunction can be understood in two ways, namely according to substance or according to virtue, as they say; but the agent cannot be joined to the interior of the recipient according to substance; therefore, it must be joined to it according to virtue, in such a way as to generate its effect by bringing it forth from the interior of the recipient. Consequently, the multitude says that this is the giving and infusing of virtue into the interior of the recipient, in order to bring forth the effect out of its potentiality, and that the virtue [itself] must not be generated out of that potentiality. And therefore it is supposed that virtue or species is not brought forth out of the potentiality of matter, but that it is given and infused and that it is different from the effect finally intended; and it is produced only by the agent, in order to alter the interior of the recipient, and through it the effect is brought forth out of the potentiality of the matter. Thus it is the instrument of the agent for producing its principal effect. And they say that in no other way could an agent produce its intended effect, as fire produces fire or the form of fire; nor could man produce man; nor would any agent produce an effect similar to itself in name and definition. (ε) Thus we are forced to return to what we said above concerning the plurality of univocal effects.[13] But since that could not be refuted in its place—rather, the argument shows that a species is the first and univocal effect of the agent, destined to be completed by means of a complete operation, so that it then receives the name and definition of the agent, as was shown above (nor can there be more than one such effect)—it is evident that these quibbles are groundless.[14]

And again, we can argue against the generation of this virtue, which they invent as an additional entity beyond the principal effect, in the same way as against the [direct] generation of the principal effect, namely, [by inquiring] how the agent would produce it in the interior of the recipient, since the substance of the agent cannot be within that interior. Thus the fiction of this [additional] virtue beyond the principal effect does not evade the objection, since, from the reason that explains why the agent cannot generate

sit: fit *L*   101-3 non ... principalem: *om. L*

effectum principalem in fundo patientis sine tertio ab eis, eo quod
non sit secundum se in illo fundo, et hoc tertium est virtus, sequitur
105 quod nec generabit virtutem in profundo illo sine aliquo tertio,
cum ipsum agens dum generat virtutem hanc non sit in profundo
patientis; et sic ibitur in infinitum. Et ideo propter evasionem istius
obiectionis non debet fingi talis infusio virtutis preter effectum
principalem. Contra igitur sic arguentes est argumentum eorum sicut
110 contra eos quos impugnant; et ideo male arguunt.

Item species accidentis, ut caloris vel alterius, est forma accidentalis ipsius patientis; et species forme substantialis ignis fit
forma substantialis patientis quando ignitur, quia calor et species
caloris sunt eiusdem essentie specifice; et universaliter species cum
115 eo cuius est, ut prius ostensum est. Et ideo, sicut calor est forma
eius in quo est, sic species caloris, et sic de aliis. Sed nulla forma
alterat materiam cuius est actus nisi anima tantum, quia anima
non solum est actus sed motor sui corporis. Unde forma ignis non
alterat materiam ignis, sed materiam aeris vel alterius. Ergo non
120 potest species facta in prima parte patientis alterare illam partem
ad alium effectum producendum in ea, sed partem secundam; et illa
que fit in secunda alterabit tertiam, et sic ulterius.

Preterea, in confirmationem istius sententie, quero ab eis qui sic
dicunt quo devenit hec virtus postquam effectus principalis generatus
125 est; ut postquam ignis generavit ignem ex alia materia, vel homo
hominem, vel quodlibet aliud iuxta speciem suam, quid accidit de hac
virtute? Si enim non est educta de potentia materie, tunc non corrumpetur in eam; ergo si corrumpitur, corrumpetur in nichil; quare fuit
producta ex nichilo; ergo fuit creata, quod est impossibile. Si
130 dicatur quod non corrumpitur sed manet in generato, sequitur inconveniens, quoniam cum generabitur, oportet quod sit corruptibilis,
omne enim generabile est corruptibile; et probabitur post quod
omnino sit corruptibilis et quod corrumpitur. Et si umquam corrumpatur, vel statim vel tarde, non corrumpetur in potentiam materie,
135 sed in nichil, ut dictum est; et tunc fuit facta de nichilo et creata,

103 in fundo *BL*: *om. F* in profundo *OS*   104 fundo *BLF*: profundo *OS*
106 ipsam *L* / dum: tantum *S* / non: *om. F*   107 istius *FS*: ipsius *O* illius *BL*
108 obiectionis: *mg. F* / infusio: *om. FO* / virtus *O*   110 impugnat *FS* / *post* arguunt
add. S prima utrum impressiones agentium fiant tote ab eis an pars post partem ut lux
generata a sole aut species ab aliquo agente quia iste vult quod pars post partem ita quod
agens non agat totam impressionem mediante sed primam partem tantum et illa aliam
111 ut: vel *F*   112 forme: *rep. F* / ignis: *rep. S* / fit: est *S*   113 gignitur *S*
115 est[1]: e. species *B*   117 *ante* materiam *mg. add. L*[C] suam propriam   118 solum:
tantum s. *B* / corporis: *ex* cordis *corr. L*   121 illa: ita *O*   122 fit: sit *F*
123 preterea: *om. S*   124 hic *S*   128 corrumpitur: corrumpatur *O*   129 ex:
de *BL*   131 quoniam: *om. S* / corruptibile *S*   132 probabitur *LS*: probatur *BF*
132–3 omne . . . corruptibilis: *om. O*   133 et[1] . . . corrumpitur: *mg. L*[C] *om. L'* /
corrumpitur: corrumpetur *BL* / umquam *A*: numquam *FOS* non quam *BL* aliquando *N*

its principal effect in the interior of the recipient (that the agent is not itself in the interior) without some third entity (the virtue) different from the agent and the recipient, it follows that the agent cannot generate this virtue in the interior without some third entity, since the agent, while generating this virtue, is not in the interior of the recipient; and so forth to infinity. And therefore, for the purpose of evading this objection there is no point in inventing such an infusion of virtue in addition to the principal effect. Therefore, those who argue in this fashion are as much the victims of their own argument as are those whom they attack; and therefore they argue badly.

Also, the species of an accident, such as heat or some other accident, is an accidental form of the recipient; and the species of the substantial form of fire becomes the substantial form of the recipient when the latter is ignited, since heat and the species of heat have the same specific essence; and this is universally true of a species and that of which it is species, as was shown above.[15] And therefore, as heat is the form of that in which it subsists, so is the species of heat, and similarly for other things. But no form except the soul alters the matter of which it is the actuality—for the soul is not only the actuality, but also the motor, of its body. Therefore, the form of fire does not alter the matter of fire, but the matter of air or another element. Consequently, a species produced in the first part of the recipient cannot alter that part in order to produce some other effect in it, but [rather] the second part; and that which is produced in the second part will alter the third, and so on.

In order to confirm this view, I inquire of my opponents where [their additional] virtue goes after the principal effect has been generated: thus, after fire has generated fire out of some other matter, or man has generated man, or anything else has generated something by its species, what happens to this virtue? For if the virtue is not brought forth out of the potentiality of the matter, it will not be corrupted into it; therefore, if it is corrupted, it will be corrupted into nothingness; it must, then, have been produced from nothing; consequently, it was created, which is impossible. If it should be said that the virtue is not corrupted but remains in the generated effect, a difficulty follows, for since it is generated it must be corruptible, because everything generable is [also] corruptible; and it will be proved later that it is altogether corruptible and that it is [in fact] corrupted.[16] And if it should ever be corrupted, either instantaneously or slowly, it would not be corrupted into the potentiality of matter, but into nothingness, as was said; and if that is the case, it must have been made from nothing (that is, created),

134 non: vel *S*   135 et[1]: sed *S* / de: ex *S*   135-6 ut . . . nichil: *mg. L^C om. L'*

quod est impossibile. Nec cadit creatura in nichil, propter hoc quod a
Creatore continue manutenetur, derogaretur enim infinitati bonitatis
et sapientie et potentie Creatoris. Item res agens per naturam et
sine deliberatione agit uno modo; ergo agens eodem modo aget in
140 faciendo speciem et effectum quodcunque, quantum est a parte sua.
Cum igitur a parte materie recipientis non est diversitas, quia etiam
uniformis est, manifestum est speciem fieri ab agente sicut alium
effectum, et ita de potentia materie.

Quapropter cum hec omnia inconvenientia sequantur ex hoc, quod
145 dicitur quod species non de potentia materie generatur, oportet quod
sic fiat eius generatio. (ʒ) Et ad obiectionem communem responden-
dum, scilicet, quod agens non debet esse in profundo patientis, neque
secundum substantiam suam neque aliter, ut de potentia profundi
educatur aliquid, hoc enim non requirit actio naturalis. Nec Aristoteles
150 hoc determinat, sed solum quod inter agens et patiens nichil sit
medium; tunc enim substantia agentis activa tangens sine medio
substantiam patientis potest ex virtute et potentia sua activa trans-
mutare primam partem patientis quam tangit. Et redundat actio
in profundum illius partis, quia illa pars non est superficies, sed
155 corpus quantumcunque sit parva; nec sine profunditate sua potest
accipi nec intelligi, et ideo nec tangi nec alterari. Sed illa pars, licet
quantitatem habeat et sit maximum quod potest secundum naturam
recipere actionem agentis, tamen valde modicum est et insensibile.
Postquam enim agens tangit patiens, et non solum superficiem nudam,
160 sed substantiam mediante superficie (et hec substantia corpus est,
quantumcunque sit parva, et ideo habens profundum), dico quod agens
tangit profundum prime partis quantum sufficit. Nec oportet quod
sit in illo profundo neque secundum substantiam neque aliter. Et sic
fit tota actio nature et generatio effectuum naturalium; nec plus
165 requiritur secundum verum iudicium, quamvis false ymaginationi
nichil sufficiat.

Et iam patet quod obiectio vana est que dicit speciem non esse
formam aeris, quia est motor et facit calorem in eo, dicendum est

136 cadit creatura: radicata *B*   137 derogatur *B* derogaret *O* | *post* bonitatis *scr. et*
del. F eius   138–43 item . . . materie: *om. SA*   139 uno . . . aget: uniformiter
ergo agens eodem modo agit *mg. O*   140 quodcunque *O*ʹ: quod *O*ᶜ | quantum: *om. O*
141 etiam: *om. O*   142 uniformis: *ex* uniformitas *corr. B*   144 cum: *om. O* |
sequuntur *O* sequatur *A*   145 dicitur: *om. F* dicit *O* | quod¹: *om. F* | oportet: sed *O*
146 obiectionem: *mg. L*ᶜ obiectem(?) *L*ʹ electionem *B* | communem: *om. F*   146–7 re-
spondendum: dicendum *SA*   148 suam: *om. F*   149 educat *S*   150 determinat: declarat *O*   151 substantia: *ex* substantiam *corr. L*   156 nec²: non *S*
157 et sit maximum: tamen est minimum *SA*   158 tamen . . . insensibile: *om. SA*
159 patiens: *ex* patientis *corr. L*   160 mediante: *ex* medietatem *corr. L* | hec sub-
stantia: hoc *B* | corpus: *ex* corporum *corr. F* | est: sit *O*   162 *post* partis *add. SA*
minime (et minime *S*) secundum naturam   163 *ante* substantiam *scr. et del. L*
subiectum / alter *S*   165 verum: vetus *F*   166 *post* sufficiat *add. S* in hac parte

which is impossible. Nor does a created being perish into nothingness, for it is continually maintained by the Creator, since its perishing would detract from the infinite goodness, wisdom, and power of the Creator. Also, a thing that acts by nature and without deliberation acts in a single way; therefore, an agent will (for its part) act in the same way whether it produces a species or some other effect. Consequently, since there is no diversity on the part of the recipient matter, because it too is uniform, it is evident that a species is produced by an agent in the same way as any other effect, that is, out of the potentiality of the matter.

Therefore, since all of these difficulties follow from denying that a species is generated out of the potentiality of matter, its generation must occur in this way. (ʓ) And to the common objection, it should be replied that the agent need not be in the interior of the recipient, according to its substance or in any other way, in order for something to be brought forth out of the potentiality of the interior, because natural action does not require this. Nor does Aristotle so determine, but only that between agent and recipient there is no intermediary; for thus the active substance of the agent, touching the substance of the recipient without intermediary, can alter, by its active virtue and power, the first part of the recipient that it touches. And this action flows into the interior of that part, since the part is not a surface, but a body, however small it may be;[17] nor can it be perceived or understood without its depth—and therefore without depth it can be neither touched nor altered. But that [first small part], although it possesses quantity and might [even] be the largest part naturally capable of receiving action from an agent, is nevertheless exceedingly small and insensible. For since the agent touches the recipient, and not only the bare surface, but the substance [of the recipient] through the mediation of the surface (and this substance is body, however small it may be, and therefore possesses depth), I say that the agent sufficiently touches the interior of the first part. And it is unnecessary for it to be in that interior, either according to substance or in any other way. And the entire action of nature and the generation of natural effects occur in this way; nor is more required according to true judgement, although for a deceitful imagination nothing suffices.

And it is now evident that there is no justification for objecting that a species cannot be the form of air because it is a mover[18] and

qualiter fit intelligendum hoc minimum et indivisibile in passione et actione naturali patebit inferius prima in confirmatione *et add. A* in hac parte qualiter autem sit intelligendum(?) minimum et indivisibile in actione nature et passione patebit inferius   167 vana: una *B* / dicunt *S* / non: *om. S*   168 et: est *S* / est²: *om. S*

enim quod non est motor eius cuius est forma sed alterius. Unde
170 species in prima parte aeris non inducit calorem in ea, sed in secunda
parte facit calorem, et sic ulterius, ut tactum est in obiectione veridica
facienda in hiis terminis: 'Si dicatur quod species fortis et sensibilis
fit a vitro bene colorato quando radius solis fortis penetrat huiusmodi vitrum, sed non posset tam vehemens color produci ita cito de
175 potentia materie, et precipue aeris, quod est corpus simplex; quapropter videtur quod alius modus sit gignendi speciem quam de potentia materie; dicendum est quod non est alius modus, ut probatum est.'
Et ad hanc cavillationem dicendum est quod in duobus peccat. Unum
est quod supponit colorem fortem esse generatum a vitro, sicut ap-
180 paret. Non enim est ita fortis sicut videtur, nam quando radius debilis
solis transit per huiusmodi vitrum, non apparet color talis; et ideo
magis est in apparentia quam in existentia coloris veri; et est sola
species, et ideo potest produci de potentia materie, precipue alicuius
mixti. Nam quando iterum supponit hec cavillatio quod primo fiet in
185 aere, dicendum est quod species vitri prius fit in aere quam in opaco
mixto, sed debilior longe fit in aere propter simplicitatem corporis;
et quando venit ad corpus mixtum, quod magis aptum est ad colorem,
potest species in aere existens educere de potentia materie speciem
pleniorem, sicut virtus magnetis defertur in aere usque ad ferrum,
190 sed fortior est in ferro quam in aere propter aptitudinem ferri
maiorem. In mixto tamen opaco, concedendum est hoc, quod species
sola est, licet appareat habere multum de colore. Huius autem
apparentie causa duplex est: una est multitudo lucis penetrantis
vitrum, nam in debili luce non apparet sic, lux enim nata est de-
195 tegere colores et facere eos apparere; alia causa est debilitas coloris
opaci respectu fortis coloris vitri et speciei eius respectu speciei
coloris vitri. Et ideo non solum color vitri apparet sensui fortis
et bene sensibilis respectu coloris opaci, sed species coloris vitri
potest sensui apparere licet species coloris opaci non appareat. Dico
200 igitur quod huiusmodi apparitio est species, et non est ita vivus
color sicut apparet; et habet satis parum de esse, ut bene possit

169 eius: est e. *L* | cuius: *mg. L*^{C}*O om. L' spatium vacuum habet B* | est^2: *mg. O*
170 eo *F*   172 si: *ex* sit *corr. F* | fortis: f. coloris *B*   173 fit: sit *LA* | quando:
quod *F*   174 sed: tamen *S* | possit *LS*   176 sit: est *S*   177 non: *om. O* | ut:
prout *B* | probatum: pretactum *SA*   178 hanc: *om. SA*   179 calorem *S* | esse
generatum: *mg. L*^{C} *om. L'* | generatum a: generaliter ex *S* g. ex *A*   180 non: et *B* |
enim: tamen *FO*   181 transit: *om. S* | calor *S* | ideo: *mg. L*^{C} *obs. L'*   182 veri:
vitri *B*   183 potentie *F* | materie: *om. F*   184 primo *L* | fiet *BAN*: fiat *LS* fieret
FO   185 fit: sit *B ex* fuit *corr. S* | quam: quod *F*   186 fit in aere: *om. B*
187 et: sed *O* | quod: quia *O*   188 potest: prima *S* | educunt *S*   189 defertur:
differtur *L*^{C} differtur *L'*   190 est: e. usque *S*   191 maiorem: manentem *O* | tamen:
tam *L* | hic *L*   192 habere: *om. O* | huius: huiusmodi *F*   194 vitrum: *om. O*
195 coloris: *om. S*   196 respectu^2: r. fortis *OSA*   199 licet: cum *O*   200 est
ita: in *S*   201 sic *S* | de: *om. S*

produces heat in the air; for it is replied that it is the mover not of
the thing of which it is the form, but of something else. Therefore,
the species in the first part of the air induces heat not in it, but in the
second part, and so forth; this was mentioned when a reasonable
objection was made in the following terms:[19] 'If it is noted that a
strong and sensible species is produced by strongly coloured glass
when such glass is penetrated by a strong solar ray, but that such an
intense colour cannot be produced that quickly out of the potentiality of the matter (especially in the case of air, which is a simple
body), and therefore that the generation of a species apparently
occurs in some other way than out of the potentiality of the matter,
it is replied that there is no other way, as has been proved.' I reply
to this cavilling that it errs in two respects. One is that it assumes
that the glass [indeed] generates intense colour, as it appears to do.
However, the colour is not as intense as it seems, for when a weak
solar ray passes through the same glass, such [intense] colour does
not appear; and therefore this colour is more apparent than real;
and it is merely a species, and therefore it can be produced out of
the potentiality of matter, especially that of a mixed body. Again,
when this cavil supposes that the species will first be produced
in air, we grant that the species of the glass is produced in air before
it is produced in an opaque mixed body, but it is produced far
more weakly in air because of the simplicity of the body of air;
and when it reaches a mixed body more suited to colour, the species
existing in air can call forth a stronger species out of the potentiality
of the matter [of the mixed body], just as magnetic virtue is conveyed to iron by air, but is stronger in the iron than in the air because the iron is better suited [to receive it]. However, it must be
conceded that in an opaque mixed body there is only a species,
although it appears to possess much colour. There are two causes
of this appearance: one is the quantity of light penetrating the
glass, for in a weak light the strength of colour is not apparent,
since light is naturally suited to reveal colours and to make them
appear; the other cause is the weak colour of the opaque body
by comparison with the strong colour of the glass and the weakness
of its species by comparison with the species of the colour of the
glass. And therefore, not only does the colour of the glass appear
strong and easily sensible by comparison with the colour of the
opaque body, but the species of the colour of the glass can appear to
sense even though the species of the colour of the opaque body does
not. Therefore, I maintain that what appears in such cases is a
species, and the colour is not as strong as it seems to be; and it has
little enough being so that it can easily be brought forth out of the

educi de potentia materie opaci. Item ponamus quod habeat tantum
de esse sicut apparet, quid prohibet ipsum de potentia saltem corporis
mixti educi, quia corpora mixta nata sunt colorari? Nos enim videmus
205 multos effectus nature completos subito quasi fieri, ut una candela
accenditur ab alia, et combustibilia statim igniuntur cum igni appli-
centur; quare similiter potest esse hic.

PARS I
CAPITULUM 4

Sed nunc ad ista plenius intelligenda oportet annecti capitulum
quartum, quod habet sex conclusiones. Prima est quod ad agens in hac
5 influentia non exigitur quantitas determinata. Secunda est quod totum
agens secundum lineam profunditatis sue agit secundum se totum in
patiens, et non aliqua sola pars signanda. Tertia est quod omne agens
attingit aliquam partem patientis quam potest alterare, et non plus.
Quarta quod minus quam illud non potest esse subiectum sufficiens
10 actionis, ut est in suo toto. Quinta est quod medietas agentis non
alterat unam medietatem et altera medietas aliam. Sexta quod
medietas prime partis patientis alterata non potest secundam alterare.
Prima igitur est quod ad agens in hac influentia non exigitur
quantitas determinata, ita quod in minori non possit agere. Nam tunc
15 in rebus inanimatis oporteret ponere virtutem augmentativam, sicut
in animatis, ut per aliquod corporale adveniens convertendum in rem
inanimatam virtus illa augmentativa duceret illam rem ad debitam
quantitatem in qua possit operari, sicut accidit de animatis pro
actione generandi secundum propagationem; hec enim est necessitas
20 quare in rebus animatis est augmentatio. Sed istud locum non habet
in rebus inanimatis; quare ad actionem earum non requiritur quantitas
determinata; et hec est actio speciei, que similiter est communis
rebus animatis, quia in actione ista omnia agunt eodem modo.
Item Aristoteles vult tertio *Physicorum* quod omne agens physice

202 item: et *FO* / habeat *FON* habet *LS* hanc *B*   203 quis *B*   204 nota *S* /
colorari: *ex* colorarem *corr. L* / enim: autem *S*   205 completo *B* completes *S* / quasi:
quali *L*   206 accendetur *B* accendatur *O*   206–7 applicatur *S*   207 simile *S*
2 capitulum quartum *LO*   3 nunc: ut *S*   4 quantum *B* / ad: *om. F*
5 totus *S*   7 patens *L* / aliqua: est a. *S* / designanda *B*   8 attingit: assignit(?) *L*
9 minus: *mg. L*^C unus *L'*   10 medietas agentis: *om. S* / *post* non *scr. et del. S* est
10–11 agentis . . . aliam: *mg. L*^C *om. L'*   11 *post* sexta *add. S* medietas (*et del.*
medietas) est   11–12 quod medietas: *om. O*   12 patientis: *om. S*   13 primo
B / igitur: i. secundo(?) *S* / ad: *om. B*   14 determinata: d. agentis *S* / possunt *B*
14–22 nam . . . hec: *om. SA' mg. A*^C   15 oportet *L*   16 aliquid *B*

potentiality of the matter of the opaque body. Moreover, if we should suppose that it has as much being as it seems to have, what would prevent it nevertheless from being brought forth out of the potentiality of a mixed body, since mixed bodies are naturally suited to being coloured? For we observe that many complete natural effects are produced almost instantaneously, as when one candle is ignited by another; and combustible things are ignited immediately when touched by fire; and therefore it can be the same in the present case.

PART I
CHAPTER 4

So that these things may be better understood, it is necessary to add a fourth chapter having six conclusions. The first conclusion is that the agent responsible for this influence need not have a determined [minimum] size. The second is that the entire depth of the agent, rather than some single designated part, acts as a whole on the recipient. The third is that every agent reaches to some part of the recipient that it can alter, and no further. The fourth is that a portion of that [affected part] cannot be a sufficient subject of action, as the whole of it can. The fifth is that one half of the agent does not alter one half of the recipient and the other half of the agent the other half of the recipient. The sixth is that if [the first] half of the first part of the recipient is altered, it cannot [in turn] alter the second [half of the first part].

The first conclusion, then, is that the agent responsible for this influence need not have a determined [minimum] size, so that if smaller it could not act. For then it would be necessary to posit a faculty of growth in inanimate beings, as in animate beings, so that when corporeal substance is being turned into an inanimate thing the faculty of growth would bring the thing to such size as enables it to act, as occurs in animate beings for the action of procreation;[1] for growth in animate beings can be explained only in this way. But this has no place in inanimate things, and therefore no determined quantity is required for their action; and the action to which we refer is that of a species, which is also common to animate beings, since in this respect all things behave in the same way.

Also, Aristotle intends in the *Physics*, book iii, that every agent is

17 animatam *F* / illa: *om. L*   18 *ante* possit *scr. et del. O* non / possint *B* / per *B*
19 secundum: sed *B* / necessitas: *mg. L*^{C} *obs. L'*   20-1 animatis . . . rebus: *om. B*
21 animatis *F* / quare: *om. B*   22 est^2 . . . communis: quia actio speciei est communis *A'*
quia actio speciei que similiter est communis *mg. A*^{C} 23 animatis: a. et inanimatis *SA*
24-5 agens . . . omne: *om. B*

25 patitur et transmutatur insimul dum agit, et quod omne patiens
physice agit; et in *Libro de generatione* primo vult idem. Sed in
quacunque quantitate parva ponatur aliquid, illud potest alterari et
corrumpi per agens forte; ergo simul aget, ut corrumpens patiatur
et alteretur. Nec contingit dicere quod patitur in hoc quod illud
30 corrumpendum resistit per naturam contrarietatis, licet non alteret
ipsum corrumpens. Nam sic celum pateretur ab ipsis inferioribus; et
computaretur inter agentia physice, eo quod sue virtuti resistit
materia elementaris, aliter enim non fieret motus nec actio in tempore.
Cum enim lux solis debet generare calorem in aere frigido, necesse
35 est quod frigiditas aeris resistat luci sicut resistit igni; sed non
alterat lucem sicut ignem. Cum ergo celum non agat physice nec
patiatur per Aristotelem, et ut omnes volunt, tunc cum dicitur quod
agens physice patitur et quod patiens physice agit, hoc non est solum
in resistendo, sed in hoc, quod patiens transmutat et alterat ipsum
40 agens.

Item Averroys dicit super secundum *Methaphysice* quod nulla
substantia est otiosa in fundamento nature, et ideo oportet quod
substantia sub quacunque quantitate possit suam facere operationem.
Item per Aristotelem septimo *Physicorum*, ubi dicit quod si aliqua
45 virtus alterat aliquod mobile in aliquo tempore, tunc medietas virtutis
mobile ei proportionale alterabit tantum et in tanto tempore. Si allegetur illud in primo *Physicorum* de carne minima, dicendum est quod
non loquitur nisi de minimo secundum sensum, non secundum
naturam et simpliciter; nam hoc sufficit sue demonstrationi contra
50 Anaxagoram, qui posuit omnia esse in quolibet (ut in aqua esse ignem
et carnem et os et cetera omnia, sed denominatur magis aqua, quia
secundum sensum excedit alia et habundat). Veritas igitur est quod
divisio carnis stat secundum sensum ut minor accipi non possit sensibilis, et sic de quacunque re. Deveniatur igitur ad carnem minimam
55 secundum sensum, et tamen hec erit secundum quantitatem divisibilem
et secundum substantiam, licet sensum non possit immutare aliqua
pars eius. Accipiatur igitur aliqua pars, ut medietas sit; ita hec pars non

25 et transmutatur: *om.* F / insimul: *om.* A   25–6 patitur . . . physice: *om.* S /
et² . . . agit: *mg.* O   26 agit: *om.* F   27 illud: aliud S   28 similis F / aget:
agens L   29 contingit: convenit O / quod¹: quia L / patiatur S / in: *ex* et *corr.* L
32 virtuti: virtutit B *ex* virtute *corr.* L   33 materie S   34 lucem F / debet: oportet
FL / calorem: colorem F *om.* S   36 nec: per S   37 per: nec S   38 hoc: sed
h. S   39 resistendo: *ex* rescestendo *corr.* L   41 Averroym O   42 ideo: *om.* O
43 sub: *om.* S / suam: *om.* S   45 aliquod: aliquid B / aliquo: alio L / virtutis: virtus L
46 *post* alterabit *scr. et del.* S aliquod mobile   46–7 allegetur: *ex* allegeretur *corr.* L
47 in primo: primi S / dicendum est: dicitur S   48 nisi: ibi S / sensum: s. et O s. sed S /
non²: *mg.* O *om.* S   49 et simpliciter: *om.* O   50 esse²: *om.* S   51 os: *ex* eos
corr. L / omnia: *om.* S / aqua: a quo O / quia: *om.* O   52 excedit: *ex* extendit *corr.* L
53 ut: et O / minor: numquam S / possit: p. secundum substantiam vel S   54 sic: si
B *om.* L / quamcunque L / devenietur O   55 hec: *om.* SA   56 et: *om.* S /

the recipient of physical influence and is altered physically even
while it acts, and that every recipient acts physically; and he intends
the same thing in *De generatione*, book i.[2] But however small a thing
is supposed to be, it can be altered and corrupted by a strong agent;
therefore, this recipient [however small] will simultaneously act, so
that the corrupting agent becomes the recipient of action and is
altered. Nor can it be said that the corrupting agent is a recipient by
virtue of the fact that the thing being corrupted resists through the
nature of contrariety, without altering the corrupting agent itself.
For if this were the case, the heaven would be affected by terrestrial
things; and it would be counted among the physical agents, because
elemental matter is resistant to its power, for otherwise motion and
action [involving heaven and earth] would not require time.[3] Thus,
since one function of the light of the sun is to generate heat in cold
air, the coldness of the air must resist light just as it resists fire; but it
does not alter light as it alters fire. Therefore, since, according to
Aristotle, the heaven neither acts physically nor is the recipient of
physical action,[4] as all agree, then when it is said that the agent
receives physical action and that the recipient acts physically, this is
not simply a matter of resisting; rather, the recipient transforms
and alters the agent.[5]

Also, Averroes says, [when commenting] on *Metaphysics*, book ii,
that in the foundations of nature no substance is inactive,[6] and
therefore substance of any quantity must be able to carry out its
operation. The same thing is gathered from Aristotle's *Physics*, book
vii, where he says that if some power moves a certain movable body
in a certain time, then half the power will move a body half as great[7]
equally far in the same time. If the remark [of Aristotle] in *Physics*,
book i, concerning the minimum of flesh[8] is advanced [in this connec-
tion], we reply that this remark concerns the minimum in terms of
sensibility rather than the minimum without qualification or according to nature, for that meets the needs of his demonstration against
Anaxagoras, who supposed that all things are present in everything
(so that in water there is fire and flesh and bone and all other things,
but it is more justly called 'water' because according to sense water
predominates and is more abundant).[9] Therefore, the truth is that
the division of flesh proceeds according to sense until a smaller part
cannot be judged sensible—and so it is for everything else. Therefore,
one comes to the sensible minimum of flesh, and yet this will have
divisible quantity[10] and will exist as substance even though no part of
it can transform sense.[11] Thus, take some part of it, such as half; this

substantiam: *mg.* F^c sensum F' / sensum: secundum s. *S*   57 accipitur *S* / ita: illa *O*
itaque *B* / hic *S*

habet naturam carnis sensibilem. Ergo caro non dicetur magis quam aliud, quia res quelibet denominatur a superhabundanti secundum
60 sensum, ut posuit Anaxagoras. Quapropter non erit caro secundum rectam denominationem carnis, sed neque aliquid aliud, quia nichil aliud sensibiliter in eo potest denominari. Nam maxime videtur hoc de carne; quare nec erunt omnia in eo, nec erit principium materiale in quo sint omnia, nec aliquid erit. Et sic destruitur positio Anaxagore, qui
65 posuit omnia esse in quolibet, quod denominetur a superhabundanti secundum sensum. Sic habet intelligi pertractatio rationis Aristotelis in illo loco; et dictum Commentatoris ibidem habet sic exponi.

Quod allegatur ex fine *Libri de sensu et sensato* nichil est, nam ibi loquitur de actione in sensum, ut patet ex conditione libri, quia
70 loquitur de sensibilibus agentibus in sensum. Et bene concedendum est quod aliquod sensibile potest esse tam parve quantitatis quod non immutabit sensum, et tamen alterabit aerem et sensum, sed sensus non percipiet. Et sensus perceptionem dicimus eius immutationem. (η)

Quod vero Averroys vult secundo *Celi et mundi* et alibi, quod terra
75 vel aliud non habet speciem vel actionem terre nisi in quantitate debita, potest hoc intelligi (θ) quantum ad actionem non impeditam, vel quantum ad actionem sensibilem in sensibili tempore. Nam ad hoc quod lapis debeat medium penetrare, ut resistentia medii non impediat ipsum, et ut faciat actionem divisionis et descensus in tempore
80 sensibili sensibilem, oportet quod quantitatem habeat sufficientem, nec in omni quantitate potest hoc facere; et sic de aliis rebus intelligendum est. Nam proculdubio non exigit grave quantitatem determinatam. Nam sit A grave illud, et cum sit quantum sint B et C partes eius. A igitur est gravius quam B, quia per additionem ipsius
85 C additur ad gravitatem; ergo B est grave; ergo A totum non fuit minimum grave. Et sic in infinitum, ut Aristoteles tertio *Physicorum* vult quod divisio magnitudinis naturalis vadit in infinitum, quia ibi loquitur de rebus naturalibus; ergo non solum quantitas, sed quantitas naturalis. Quapropter natura sensibilis, que est naturalis,

58 naturam: virtutem *O* / sensibile *B* / dicitur *O*   59 res: pars *FO* / quilibet *L*
60 est *S*   61 aliquid: aliquod *S*   62 sensibilem *S* / maxime: magis *S* / videtur
BSAN: videretur *LFO*   63 quare: quia *F* / nec[1]: non *O* / erunt: *mg. L*[C] esset *L'* / erit:
om. F   64 sunt *L* / aliquid erit: adest *S* / positio: opinio *S*   65 quod: sed *SA* /
denominetur *BFLN*: denominari *SA* denominatur *O*   66 Aristotelis: materialis *B*
67 commentatoris: consequenter *S* / habet sic exponi: *om. SA*   68 et: *om. S* / sensato:
om. BS / nam: quia *S*   69 sensu *S*   72–3 non ... sensus: *om. F*   73 immutationem: unitionem *S*   74 Averroim *O* / terra: circa *S*   75 vel actionem: nec a. *B*
om. SA   77 quantum: quo *L*   78 debiat *L* / debeat ... penetrare: penetret medium
A preventet medium *S*   79 ut: non *O* / actionem: divisionem vel a. *S* operationem *A* /
divisionis: *ex dictionis corr. L*   81 in: in causam *L*   83 sint: sicut *BS* / C: est *S*
84 ipsius: et i. *B*   84–5 partes ... C: *mg. L*[C] *om. L'*   85 additur: *rep. F* /
ad: in *SA* / ergo[1]: licet e. *B om. SA* / est: *om. SA ex* cum *corr. L* / A: *om. A* / totum:
om. SA / fit *O*   87 vult: ubi dicit *SA* / vult ... infinitum: *om. B*   89 sensibilis:

part then does not have the sensible nature of flesh. Therefore, there is no more reason to call it 'flesh' than to call it anything else, since everything is named from the sensibly predominant ingredient, as Anaxagoras asserts. Thus it will not be flesh according to the proper meaning of the term; but neither will it be anything else, since nothing else in it can be sensibly named. Now this is especially apparent in the case of flesh; therefore, neither will all things be in it, nor will there be in it a material principle in which all things reside, nor will there be anything. And thus we destroy the position of Anaxagoras, who supposed that all things are present in each thing and who named the thing from its predominant ingredient according to sense. Thus should we understand Aristotle's argument in that place; and the statement of the Commentator in the same place is similarly explained.

What is asserted on the basis of the end of *De sensu et sensato* is not a problem, for what [Aristotle] speaks of there is action on sense, as is evident from the nature of the book, since it concerns sensibles acting on sense.[12] And it should be readily conceded that a sensible can be so small as not to transform sense—even though it will alter air and sense, but without being perceived. For what we call sense perception is the transformation of sense. (η)

But the opinion that Averroes puts forth in [his commentary on] *De caelo et mundo*, book ii, and elsewhere, that the earth or something else does not exhibit the species or action of earth [or of that other thing] unless it is of suitable size,[13] ought to be understood (θ) in reference to unimpeded action or sensible action in a sensible time. That is, in order for a rock to penetrate a medium and the resistance of the medium not to prevent this, and so that the rock will perform a sensible action of division [of the medium] and descent in a sensible time, it is necessary for the rock to have sufficient size, for it is not possible for a rock of just any size to do this; and it should be understood that other things behave similarly. For it is undeniable that a heavy body does not require a determined [minimum] size [in order to be heavy]. For example, let A be the heavy body, and since it possesses extension, let B and C be its parts. Accordingly, A is heavier than B, since [the gravity of] C is added to the gravity of B [to produce the gravity of A]; therefore B is a heavy body, and consequently the entire body A was not the smallest heavy body. And so the process continues to infinity, just as Aristotle, in *Physics*, book iii, intends that the division of natural magnitude continues to infinity, since he is there speaking of natural things;[14] therefore, not only [is] quantity [infinitely divisible], but natural quantity.[15] Consequently, sensible nature, which is natural,

mg. L^C universalis *L'B* / est: et *L*

90 est divisibilis in infinitum; et ideo agens sensibile naturale non
determinat sibi quantitatem.

Secunda conclusio est quod totum agens secundum lineam profunditatis sue agit secundum se totum in patiens, et non aliqua sola
pars signanda que tangit patiens, nam tunc reliqua pars esset otiosa.
95 Item tunc parvum corpus sicut magnum equalem faceret operationem.
Et loquor de magnitudine secundum profundum; et ideo si medietas
solis secundum profundum amoveretur, tunc ageret tam nobilem
actionem sicut nunc; et sic de quolibet agente, quod est impossibile.
Si dicatur quod una pars secundum profundum tangit patiens et alie
100 non, et agens et patiens debent esse simul sine medio, ut Aristoteles
dicit, dicendum quod totum secundum profunditatem acceptum tangit
patiens in sua superficie sicut aliqua pars illius profundi. Et sicut
interior pars cuiuslibet partis date distat a superficie patientis per
corpus illius partis interiacens, et tamen ipsa pars dicitur suffi-
105 cienter coniungi patienti respectu actionis, sic similiter erit de toto
quod sufficienter coniungitur cum patiente per tactum sue superficiei sine medio, licet extremum totius alterum distet a patiente
per corpus superiacens totius. Unde non requiritur alia approximatio nisi quod agens coniungatur in sua superficie cum superficie
110 patientis, quantumcunque alia extremitas agentis distet. Si dicatur
quod si pars posterior agentis agat speciem, tunc faciet eam in partem
priorem, et ideo alterabit se ipsum prius quam patiens, dicendum
est quod pars hic non agit per se, nec est distinctio partium in
actione, ut una faciat unam partem et alia aliam, sicut obiectio
115 precedit, sed totum facit totam actionem. (ι)

Tertia conclusio est quod omne agens attingit aliquam partem
patientis quam potest alterare, ita quod plus non alteret (κ). Nam
agens non proicit nec infundit aliquid in patiens, ut prius probatum
est, sed ipsum per sui contactum transmutat. Sed agens non transmutat
120 superficiem; quare oportet quod aliquam partem substantie patientis
alteret, que pars est corpus necessario, licet non actu divisum a toto.
Sed quia approximatio requiritur ad actionem tanquam necessaria

90 natura *A*   92 *post* quod *scr. et del.* *S* quantitatem   93 patens *L* / non:
n. est *SA* / sola: *om.* *SA*   94 que: q. non *SA* / tangat *SA* / patens *L* / reliqua: alia *S*
aliqua *A*   95 parvum: parum *L*^{C} puerum(?) *L'*   97 profunditatem *B* / amovetur *S*
98 sicut: sic *L* / sic: ita *SA*   99 si: item si *SA* / secundum: *om.* *SA* parva secundum *O* /
patientis *SA*   100 debet *F*   100–1 ut ... dicit: *om. O*   102 superficie: profunditate s. *S* profunditate et s. *A* / aliqua: alia *O*   103 cuiuslibet: istius *S* / a: in *L* /
post patientis *add.* *S* sicut alia pars illius profundi et sicut interior pars partis illius date
distat a superficie   104 tamen: inde *O ex* t. tantum *corr. L* / ipsa: illa *SA*
105–6 patienti ... coniungitur: *om. SA*   106 coniungatur *B*   108 superiacens
BFO: interiacens *LSAN* / requiritur: *mg.* *L*^{C} reliqua *L'*   109 coniungatur: *om. S*
110 quamcunque *L* / agendis *S*   111 si: *om. OS* / agit *S* / faceret *L*   112 se:
tamen se *S* / prius: in *S*   113 *post* agit *scr. et del.* *S* speciem tunc faciet eam partem /
distinctio: distantia *S*   114 ut: ita quod *C* / alia: a. faciat *S*   115 totum: tota *FO*

is divisible to infinity; and therefore a sensible natural agent is not of determined size.

The second conclusion is that the entire depth of the agent acts as a whole on the recipient, rather than some single designated part that touches the recipient, for if the latter were the case the remainder of the agent would be inactive. Also, then small and large bodies would perform equal operations. And I speak of magnitude according to depth; and therefore, [under the assumption that activity is confined to a part of the agent,] if half the depth of the sun were removed, it would produce as noble an action as it now does; and similarly for any agent, which is impossible. If it should be argued that one part of the agent [differentiated from the others] according to depth affects the recipient, and the others[16] not, and that the agent and recipient must be joined without intermediary, as Aristotle says, we reply that the recipient is affected in its [depth and][17] surface just as well by the entire given depth [of the agent] as by some part of it. And just as the interior of each given part [of the agent] is separated from the surface of the recipient by the intervening substance of that part, and yet the part itself [as a whole] is said to be sufficiently joined to the recipient with respect to action, so it is with the entire agent, which is sufficiently joined to the recipient if its surface touches the recipient without intermediary, although the far extreme of the entire agent is separated from the recipient by the intervening body of the agent. Therefore, the agent need come no closer to the recipient than for their surfaces to be in contact, however far removed the other extremity of the agent may be. If it should be objected that if the posterior part of the agent were to produce a species, then it would produce it in the prior part, and therefore it would alter itself before it alters the recipient, we reply that in the present case the [posterior] part does not act *per se*, nor is there distinction of parts in action, so that one [part of the agent] would produce one part [of the action] and another would produce another part, as the objection implies, but the whole agent produces the whole action. (*ι*)

The third conclusion is that every agent reaches to some part of the recipient that it can alter, in such a way that the alteration extends no further (*κ*). For the agent does not thrust or infuse something into the recipient, as was proved above,[18] but alters it by contact with it. But the agent does not alter the surface; therefore, it must alter some part of the substance of the recipient; and this part is necessarily body, although it is not actually separated from the whole. But since proximity is required as a necessary condition

116 contingit *O*   118 non: nunc *L*   120 substantie: *mg. L*^C *om. L'*
121 necessario: vitro *B*   122 necessaria: vitri *B*

conditio, ideo oportet quod partis alterande extremitas remotior ab
agente sit remota, ad minus quod fieri potest per naturam. Et ideo
125 non erit hec pars cuiuscunque quantitatis sed determinate, ita quod
plus alterari non poterit. (λ)

Ceterum nos videmus quod sol et luna eque cito immutant quantitatem eandem medii, et candela et ignis locum obscurum eundem
eque cito illustrant, licet unum intensius et magis quam aliud; et sic de
130 omnibus agentibus. Quare oportet quod quantitas determinetur. Si
dicatur quod hoc est secundum sensum, sed aliter est secundum
naturam actionis, dicendum est quod tunc sensibilis excellentia unius
agentis super aliud, ut in centupla vel maiori, faceret sensibilem differentiam secundum quantitatem. Et ita sol longe plus quam centies
135 posset alterare tantam quantitatem spatii plus quam luna, quia sol est
centies maior quam tota terra et fere septuagesies, et luna non est
nisi una de 39 partibus terre vel circiter hoc, sicut Ptolomeus docet
in *Almagesti*. Sed non accidit soli quod in eodem tempore centies
plus de spatio illustret quam luna.

140 Si dicatur quod si aliqua virtus movet aliquod mobile per aliquod
spatium, tunc duplum illius virtutis potest movere idem mobile per
duplum illius spatii, secundum Aristotelem septimo *Physicorum*, concedendum est hoc in motu locali naturali gravium et levium, non in
violento, nam homo debilis proiciet ita longe unum folium sicut fortis.
145 Sed nec in alteratione concedendum est, quia alteratio non respicit
quantitatem per se, sed formam, quam oportet intendi vel remitti
in eadem quantitate; et similiter generatio et corruptio. Unde concedendum est quod si aliqua virtus posset alterare vel generare
aliquam formam, tunc dupla virtus potest facere duplum illius in
150 eodem subiecto, sed non in duplo spatio.

Deinde queratur quarto an minus quam illud potest esse sufficiens
subiectum actionis. Et dicendum quod non, ut est in toto; sed si
dividatur a toto, tunc potest esse subiectum sufficiens. Ad hoc enim
quod aliquid patiatur ab alio non requiritur in rebus generabilibus
155 nisi quod contrarietas sit et quod approximentur. Et si celum est

123 conditio: condicto(?) *BL* | *post* ideo *scr. et del. S* partis   124 minus: m. quam
poterit secundum *S* | quod: quantum *O* | potest: non p. *L* | ideo: *om. S*   125 cuius-
cunque: cuiuslibet *O*   127 ceterum: *mg. L^C* causam *L'* | *ante* cito *scr. et del.* L in
127–78 ceterum . . . infinitum: *om. S mg. A*   129 quam: quod *F* | aliud: *mg. L^C om. L'*
130 quod: *interl. L^C om. L'*   133 centuplo *F*   135 alterare: illustrare *O*
137 una de 39: de 39 *F* 139[1a] de *O* | circiter: circum *O* | hoc: *interl. L^C om. L'* | Ptolomeus:
mg. L^C polus *L'*   138 Almalesti *L* | accidit: *ex* accedit *corr. L*   139 de: *interl.*
L^C om. L'   140 aliquod[1] . . . per: *rep. F* | per: pro *O*   142 secundum . . . Physi-
corum: *mg. L^C om. L'*   142–3 conceditur *B*   143 est: cum *L om. B* | hoc: *om. F* |
naturali: *ex* naturale *corr. L*   145 quia *L^C*: quod *L'* eo quod *B*   146 quam *BN*:
quod *FO* que *L* | oportet: debet *FO*   148–9 alterare . . . potest: *mg. O*   149 ali-
quam: aliam *F*   150 in: *om. L*   152 est *BLN*: *om. FO*   152–3 sed . . . toto:

of action, [it should be noted that] the extremity of the part to be altered that is farthest from the agent must be separated [from it], at least in the order of nature.[19] Therefore, this part [that receives the action] cannot be of any quantity you please, but must be of a determined quantity, so that no larger part can be altered. (λ)

Moreover, we see that the sun and moon alter the same quantity of the medium with equal speed; and a candle and a fire illuminate the same dark place with equal swiftness, although one is stronger and more intense than the other; and this is true of all agents. Therefore, the quantity [of the recipient altered by the agent] must be determined. If it should be claimed that this is true as far as sense can discern, but that according to the [true] nature of action it is otherwise, we reply that in that case the sensible superiority of one agent over another (for example, a hundredfold or more) would produce a sensible difference in the quantity [of the recipient altered in a given time]. And thus the sun could alter far more than one hundred times as much space as the moon could alter [in the same time], since the sun is approximately 170 times as large as the entire earth while the moon is only a thirty-ninth part of the earth or thereabouts, as Ptolemy teaches in the *Almagest*.[20] However, the sun does not illuminate one hundred times as much space as the moon in the same time.

If it should be argued that if a certain power moves a certain mobile through a certain space [in a given time], then twice the power can move the same mobile through twice the space [in the same time], according to Aristotle in *Physics*, book vii,[21] this is conceded in natural local motion of heavy and light bodies, though not in violent local motion, since a weak man can throw a leaf as far as a strong man can. But the same concession is not to be applied to alteration,[22] since alteration does not pertain to quantity *per se*, but to form, which must be intensified or remitted in the same quantity—and similarly for generation and corruption. Therefore, what must be conceded is that if a certain power could alter or generate a certain form, then twice the power could produce double the effect in the same subject, but not through twice the space.

In the fourth place, it is inquired whether a portion of that [affected part] can be a sufficient subject of action. We reply that it cannot be as long as it is part of the whole; however, if it is separated from the whole, then it can be a sufficient subject. For in order that one thing be acted on by another, it is required in general only that there be contrariety and that they be in proximity. And if the agent

mg. L^c *om. L'*   154 patitur *L* / requiruntur *O*   155 *post* quod² *scr. et del. L*
contrarietas

agens, non requiritur nisi materia obediens et approximatio; sed hec duo sunt hic. Si dicatur quod contraria nata sunt fieri circa idem, et ideo si determinatur hic quantitas patientis in magnitudine, similiter in parvitate, dicendum est quod non, quia approximatio non salvatur in omni extensione magnitudinis, sed salvatur in omni divisione quantitatis. Et ideo non sequitur, nec oportet, quod contraria semper ferantur circa idem quando unum inest determinate propter aliquam causam, ut est hic.

Deinde quinto an medietas agit in medietatem vel totum agit in medietatem. Et dicendum est quod totum, quia prima pars non ageret in primam partem, sed secunda, quia secunda ei coniungitur; nec in secundam, quia secunda pars agentis magis ei appropinquat. Item si prima pars agentis ageret in partem primam et secunda in secundam, tunc magis ageret secunda in primam quam in secundam, quia ei coniungitur. Si obiciatur de septimo *Physicorum* quod si tota virtus agit totam actionem, ergo medietas medietatem, dicendum est quod iam patuit prius quod actio totius est indivisa dum partes sunt in toto; sed si totum individeretur et patiens similiter, sequeretur hec regula.

Deinde sexto, an medietas alterata potest reliquam alterare. Dicendum quod non, quia tunc non esset quantitas determinata in magnitudine ad actionem, et tunc medietas medietatis prime alteraretur, et sic in infinitum. Si igitur obiciatur quod dum medietas illius partis remanet in toto, oportet quod agens illam medietatem primo alteret quam alteretur secunda et antequam alteretur totum, per secundam conclusionem septimi *Physicorum* (que est quod nullum mobile primo movetur, sed aliqua pars eius, quia parte quiescente quiescit totum), et ideo pars primo movetur; sed species in illa prima medietate est completa in actu suo; ergo non erit otiosa; quare alterabit medietatem secundam, et sufficiet ad hoc; ergo agens principale non alterabit medietatem secundam, et precipue cum medietas prima est magis coniuncta cum medietate secunda quam agens principale; dicendum est quod tunc eadem est obiectio de illa medietate prima,

156 requiretur *L*   157 quod: *om. O rep. L*   158 hec *F* / magnitudinem *L* 159 quia: qui *L*   160 omni[1]: *om. F* / extentione *B* continuatione *O*   161 non: nec *F* / contraria: *om. F*   167 item: ita *L*   167-8 secunda . . . secundam: *mg. O* 168 ageret: *om. F*   169 *ante* secunda *scr. et del. F* prima in secundam / secunda: *mg.* *L*[c] *om.* *L'*   170 quod: et *L* / tota: *om. F*   171 totam: in t. *B*   172 prius: primum *B* / est: *om. B* / dum: cum *F* / in: etiam in *O*   173 *post* toto *scr. et del. F* etiam / divideretur *O* / patiens: pars *O* / similiter: s. quod *L* / sequeretur: *ex* consequeretur *corr. L*   175 *post* potest *scr. et del.(?) F* totum   177 medietas: *mg. O*   178 in: *om. L* / si: sed *L* / dum: *mg. O*   179 medietatem: *ex* remedietatem *corr. L* 180 tota *FO*   182 sed: si *L*   183 quiescit: q. et *FO* / ideo: tunc *S*   184 est: erit *O ex* et *corr. L*   185 *post* et *add. O* precipue cum medietas / sufficeret *O* 187 principale: *om. S*   188 tunc: *om. SA* / est[2]: *om. B*   188-9 prima . . . medietatem: *om. O*

is a heaven, only proximity and compliant matter are required, and both are present. If it should be argued that it is the nature of contraries to come into being in the same subject, and therefore that if the upper limit of the recipient's quantity is determined, so also is the lower limit, this is denied, since not every increase in quantity preserves proximity, although every division of quantity does. And therefore, it does not follow, nor is it necessary, that contraries are always borne by the same subject when one of them is present in a determined manner for some reason, as it is here.

Fifth, [it is inquired] whether half [of the agent] acts on half [of the recipient] or whether the whole acts on the half. And it is answered that the whole [acts on the half], because the first part [of the recipient] would be acted upon, not by the first part [of the agent], but by the second, since the second part [of the agent] and the first part [of the recipient] are conjoined; nor could the second [part of the recipient be acted upon by the first part of the agent], since the second part of the agent is closer. Also, if the first part of the agent should act on the first part [of the recipient] and the second [part of the agent] on the second [part of the recipient], then the second [part of the agent] would act on the first [part of the recipient] more than on the second, since those two are conjoined. If it should be objected, on the basis of *Physics*, book vii, that if the whole power produces the whole action, then half the power must produce half the action, we reply, as we made clear above, that the action of the whole is undivided as long as the parts remain in the whole; but if the agent and recipient were divided into parts, this rule would hold.

Sixth, [it is inquired] whether, if half [of the first part of the recipient] should be altered, it could [in turn] alter the remainder. We reply that it could not, since otherwise there would be no size limit as far as action is concerned, and half of the first half could be altered, and so on to infinity. If it should be objected to this that while the [first] half of that part remains within the whole, the agent must alter that half before the second half and before the whole, by the second conclusion of *Physics*, book vii (that no mobile is at first moved, but some part of it, since when the part is at rest the whole is at rest),[23] from which it follows that the part is moved first; and [moreover] that the species in that first half is perfect in its actuality and will therefore not be inactive; and, therefore, that it will alter the second half, and that it is sufficient for this; and, consequently, that the principal agent will not alter the second half, especially since the first half is more closely joined to the second half than is the principal agent; [to this] it is replied that the same objection would apply to

nam habet medietatem de qua eodem modo potest argui, et sic ulterius
190 in infinitum, quod est impossibile. Et sic sequetur quod non contingit
dare aliquam partem determinatam in quam possit agens datum, quia
quelibet habet medietatem, quam solam medietatem primam alterabit
agens principale secundum has rationes. Et, ideo hee obiectiones
nulle sunt, quia redarguunt ipsum qui eas proponit.

195   Preterea solvendum est aliter, videlicet quod licet agens primo
alterat medietatem primam quam secunda alteretur, tamen illam
secundam alterabit agens, et non medietas prima, quia agens potest in
eam et habet maiorem virtutem quam medietas prima iam alterata; et
ideo potentius et melius potest medietatem secundam alterare quam
200 prima medietas. Et natura facit quod melius est et perfectius, propter
quod concedit principali agenti ut alteret secundam medietatem et
denegat hoc prime medietati, ita ut non terminetur actio ipsius agentis
donec compleat suam actionem per alterationem utriusque medietatis.
Sed si obiciatur illud Aristotelis in septimo *Physicorum* in fine, quod
205 si aliqua virtus alteret aliquod mobile in aliquo tempore, tunc medietas
virtutis alterabit medietatem mobilis secundum equalem alterationem
in toto eo tempore, dicendum est quod hec intelligenda sunt si mobile
dividatur actualiter, sed dum totum est integrum non terminabitur
actio antequam totum alteretur. Si dicatur quod idem manens idem
210 natum est facere idem, ergo idem manens idem natum est pati idem et
eodem modo, quare sive sit in toto medietas sive separata poterit
esse subiectum passionis in quo terminetur actio agentis; et dicendum
est quod non sequitur, quia in toto est pars in potentia non in actu,
et simul cum hoc dicendum est quod totum potest in totum, et ideo
215 natura non abscindit suam actionem usquequo compleatur in tota
parte patientis in quam natum est agens suam actionem complere; et
etiam dicendum quod agens principale potest melius et perfectius
alterare secundam medietatem quam eandem alteret prima medietas,
ut dictum est. (μ)

189 qua *OSA*: quo *BFL* / *post* ulterius *scr. et del.* S quod est   190 sequetur:
sequeretur *F ex* sequitur *corr.* L   191 quam possit: qua posset S   192 quelibet:
quilibet *L* q. pars *SA*   193 hee: esse *L*   194 quia *FOA*: que *BL om.* S / ipsum
LSA: ipsos *FO* ipsas *B* / proponunt *O*   195 propterea *B* / solvendum: sciendum S /
videlicet: *om. SA*   196 alterat: alteret S / alteretur: alteratur L / tamen: tantum F /
post tamen *scr. et del.* S secundum   197 prima: *ex* primam *corr.* L   197–8 prima
... medietas: *rep.* S   198 iam: *mg.* L^C *obs.* L'   200 prima: potest S   201 principale *F* principium S   202 denegat: deneretur S / hoc: *om.* F / prime: *om.* S / *post*
medietati *scr. et del.* L et denegat hoc in prime medietati   204 sed: *om. SA* / obiciatur
BLN: obicitur *FOSA* / quod: *om. SA*   205 aliqua *OAN*: alia *BLS om.* F / alterat *O* /
post tempore *add. SA* eadem virtus alterabit medietatem secundum duplum intensionis
(intentionis *A*) in eodem tempore et iterum   206 mobile *OS*   207 eo: *om. SA* /
post tempore *add. SA* et iterum totum alterabit medietatem in medietate temporis secundum medietatem alterationis sicut patebit in motu locali / si: sed L   208 determina-
bitur L   210 idem[1]: *om.* S / idem[2] natum: *om.* S   211 eodem: eo *B* / medietatis S

the first half [of the recipient], for it has a half, concerning which one can argue in the same way, and so on to infinity, which is impossible. And it would then follow that there is no determined part on which a given agent could act, since every part can be divided into halves, and according to this argument the principal agent would alter only the first of these halves. Therefore, these objections are of no force, since they are self-refuting.

Besides, the question is to be answered in another way, namely, [by pointing out] that although the agent alters the first half [of the recipient] before the second half is altered, nevertheless this second half will be altered by the agent rather than by the first half, since the agent can act on it and possesses more power than the already-altered first half; and therefore it can alter the second half better and more powerfully than can the first half. And nature does what is better and more perfect, and therefore it grants to the principal agent the task of altering the second half and denies this task to the first half, and thus the action of the agent itself does not end until it completes its action by alteration of both halves. But if what Aristotle says at the end of *Physics*, book vii, should be raised as an objection, namely, that if a certain power alters a certain mobile in a certain time,[24] half the power will produce an equal alteration in half the mobile in the same whole time,[25] we reply that these things apply if the mobile is actually divided, but while the whole is intact the action will not be terminated until the whole is altered. If it should be argued that what remains the same is naturally suited to do the same thing[26] and, therefore, that a thing that remains the same is suited to receive the same effect in the same way, and thus whether the half is separated or remains as part of the whole it can be a recipient in which the action of the agent is terminated; to this it is replied that the conclusion does not follow, since the part is in the whole potentially but not actually, and also that the whole [agent] can [act] on the whole [recipient], and therefore that nature does not terminate its action until this action is completed in the entire portion of the recipient in which the agent is suited to complete its action; and it is also replied that the principal agent can better and more perfectly alter the second half [of the recipient] than can the first half [of the recipient], as has been said. (μ)

212 esse: omne *B*   214 et[1] ... totum[2]: *om. SA* / simul *BLN*: similiter *FO*
215 abscondit *B* / usquequo *FO*: usquoque *LSN* usque quod *A* usque *B*   216 qua *L*
218 prima: post *L om. S*

Pars I
Capitulum 5

Nunc considerandum est quintum principale circa influentiam agentis in patiens, et consistit in hiis que exiguntur a parte patientis; et
5 sunt hic conclusiones tres. Prima est de inferioribus respectu celestium. Et quod a superioribus possint pati inferiora patet, quia communicant in materia, eo quod illa que communicant in genere communicant in materia, ut dicitur quinto *Methaphysice*. Et ideo, licet non communicent in tantum ut sit mutua generatio et corruptio
10 completa inter inferiora et celestia, hoc enim negatur *Libro de generatione* et alibi, tamen postquam in genere communicant oportet quod in materia communicent, secundum quod Aristoteles dicit. Et ideo manifestavit hoc in prioribus quod essentia generis proximi est materiale principium in naturalibus respectu duarum specierum, et
15 individuum generis respectu duorum individuorum illarum specierum. Congruentia autem est ad hoc, quoniam quanto magis partes universi assimilentur tanto maior est salus earum et utilitas. Et ideo cum inferiora non possunt assimilari per naturas completas celorum, congruit ut saltem per species receptas. Necessitas autem concludit
20 hoc idem per generationem rerum et corruptionem, cuius causa principalis est duplex: allatio solis sub obliquo circulo. Sed sol non est per substantiam in inferioribus, et ideo per virtutem; et sic de aliis corporibus celestibus. Et per experientiam patet illud de luce diffusa a celestibus per omnia inferiora. Et ideo cum obicitur
25 quod natura celestis non est generabilis nec corruptibilis, propter quod non generabitur in materia elementari, dicendum est quod hoc est verum sub esse completo; sed sub esse speciei non est inconveniens, immo necessarium.

Sed secundo sciendum est quod celestia possunt recipere species
30 ab aliis celestibus, ut luna et stelle recipiunt virtutem et speciem solis, ita quod lux solis veniens ad superficiem lune vel stelle cuiuslibet educit ibi, per naturalem immutationem, lucem de potentia

2 capitulum quintum *O mg. L*   3 quintum: 4 *S*   4 exigunt *S*   5 hic *FO*: hec *SA* huiusmodi *BN om. L*   6 a . . . possint: ab eis possunt *S*   7 eo: et *BL* 7-8 eo . . . materia: *om. O*   9 in: in materia *O* / sint *S* / et: sed *O*   11 genere: generatione *S*   12 *post* communicent *add. S* secundum quod in materia communicent 13 ideo: ratio *FS* i. hoc *O* / manifestabit *S* manifestantur *L* / hoc: hec *F* hic *A om. OS* / in prioribus: *mg. L^C* in pluribus *L'* suo loco *S* prius *A* / essentia: ratio *A*   15 illorum *B* 16 partes: *mg. F^C om. F'*   17 assimilentur *BFL*: assimilantur *OSAN* / maior: *mg. L^C*. magis *L'* / ideo: *om. F*   18 naturas: *mg. L^C* natus(?) *L'* / *post* completas *interl. add. O* nature   19 autem: etiam *S*   21 allatio: ablatio *BF* / solis: solum *S* / obliquo: aliquo *BF*   21-2 circulo . . . sic: *mg. L^C om. L'*   22 in: et *L^C* / sic: fit *L^C* 24 et ideo: quapropter *SA* / cum: tamen *mg. L^C obs. L'* quod *SA* / obici *SA*   25 quod . . . corruptibilis: possit (posset *A*) de natura celesti quod est in generalis (generabilis *A*)

PART I

CHAPTER 5

We must now consider the fifth principal [subject] concerning the influence of an agent on a recipient, and it consists of the requirements on the part of the recipient, about which there are three conclusions. The first concerns terrestrial things in relation to celestial. Now it is evident that lower things can be influenced by higher things, since they share the same matter, because things of the same genus have the same matter, as *Metaphysics*, book v, states.[1] And therefore, although celestial and terrestrial things are not linked to the point where there is complete mutual generation and corruption between them, for this is denied in *De generatione* and elsewhere,[2] nevertheless because they belong to the same genus they must share the same matter, as Aristotle says. Accordingly, it was manifest above that in natural things the material principle with respect to two species is the essence of the proximate genus; the material principle with respect to two individuals of those species is the individual of the genus.[3] Now the purpose of this conformity is that the more the parts of the universe are like one another, the greater are their well-being and utility. And therefore, although terrestrial things cannot resemble the heavens in their complete natures, they agree at least to the point [of being linked] through the reception of species. Moreover, the same conclusion follows necessarily from the generation and corruption of things, the principal cause of which is twofold: the motion of the sun and the obliquity of its circular path.[4] But the sun does not exist in terrestrial bodies according to substance, and therefore it is in them according to virtue; and the same is true of the other celestial bodies. And this is evident from experience of light diffused through all terrestrial things from celestial bodies. Consequently, when it is objected that celestial nature is not generable or corruptible, and therefore that it will not be generated in elemental matter, we reply that this is true as regards complete being; however, as regards the being of species it is not unsuitable, but necessary, [for celestial nature to be generated in elemental matter].

Second, it should be recognized that celestial bodies can receive species from other celestial bodies, as the moon and stars receive the virtue and species of the sun,[5] so that the light of the sun coming to the surface of the moon or any star brings light into being there, by natural alteration, out of the potentiality of the matter.

SA / nec: et *O*   25-6 propter . . . elementari: *om. A*   26 materia: natura *F* /
dicendum: solvendum *SA*   29 sed: *om. O* sed 16 et *S*   30 et¹: *om. BS*
31 solis²: *om. F*

materie. Et hoc dicit Commentator super secundum *Celi et mundi*; et arguit ad hoc per equalitatem angulorum incidentie et reflexionis,
35 ut patebit inferius. Et Aristoteles ipse dicit octo *Methaphysice* quod non omne alterabile est generabile, propter celestia, et hoc est quod alteratio lucis est in celestibus. Et ideo dicit Aristoteles secundo *Metheororum* quod sol illuminat omnes stellas. Si igitur obiciatur quod Aristoteles vult primo *Celi et mundi* quod natura celi
40 sit incorruptibilis, nec sit alterabilis, nec passibilis, dicendum est quod alteratio est duplex secundum Aristotelem secundo *De anima*: uno modo, ut eius utar eloquio, 'in habitus naturam et perfectionem'; et hec est alteratio que est per species et virtutes, seu fiat in sensum seu in aliud. Et cum hoc non fiat sine quadam generatione,
45 concedenda est hec generatio speciei que est in perfectionem appetitus celestis nature, et non in corruptionem nisi ipsius defectus et cuiusdam imperfectionis quam habent luna et stelle respectu solis precipue. Alia est alteratio seu transmutatio que est cum completa generatione nove forme in patiente et cum completa ablatione et
50 corruptione nature specifice patientis; et huiusmodi transmutatio vel alteratio non est in celestibus, et hec non est in speciebus. Et si dicatur quod potentia in celestibus est completa per actum et appetitus materie est terminatus, dicendum est quod respectu nove forme que tolleret formam presentem in corpore celi per veram et
55 completam corruptionem nature specifice celestis est appetitus terminatus, et non respectu speciei et virtutis lucis et huiusmodi, que simul stant cum natura specifica lune et stellarum. Unde appetitus quidam est in luna et stellis incompletus de se, et perficitur per speciem et virtutem solis, et similiter per species cuiuslibet alterius
60 stelle, quelibet enim in aliam facit suam speciem.

Sciendum quod non solum contingit fieri speciem in celestibus ab alio celesti, sed ab inferioribus. Est enim ad hoc passibilitas et congruentia, sicut dictum est de actione celestium in inferiora; sed absoluta necessitas non est propter celestia in se, sed in quantum
65 sunt partes universi assimulande aliis per receptionem specierum et in quantum sunt medium in sensu. Si enim oculus esset in orbe lune,

34 equalitatem: *ex* equalitates *corr. S* | angulorum: *ex* angelorum *corr. L*   35 inferius: i. suo loco *S* | octo: 4 *S*   37 quod: quia *FO* q. dicit ibi Averroys quod *SA*   38 secundo: *interl.* L^C *om. L'* primo *S* | Metheororum: Methaphysice *S* | solis *L*   39 obicitur *S* | primo: in p. *L* in *F*   40 *ante* alterabilis *scr. et del.* F mutabilis   42 ut: *om. L* | et: *om. S*   43 per: *mg.* L^C *om. L'*   44 hec *O*   45 *post* concedenda *scr. et del. L* sed   46 et[1]: et tamen *B* | ipsius: *om. O*   47 habent: *mg.* L^C habet *L'*   49 generatione . . . completa: *om. L*   50 patienti *F*   56 lucis et: *tr. B*   58 quidem *O* | completus *F*   60 alia *O* | suam speciem: *mg. O*   62 alio: aliquo *O* | inferioribus: i. est *B* | hec *L* | passibilitas: *mg.* L^C possibilitas *BFLOSAN*   63 *ante* congruentia *scr. et del. L* in | in: et *B*   64 in[2]: neque(?) *L*   65 assimulandem *O*   66 enim *LSA*: autem *BFO* | *post* oculus *add. SA* et (*obs. A*) maxime (*obs. A*) significatur

And this is what the Commentator says [in his commentary] on *De caelo et mundo*, book ii;[6] and he argues for it by the equality of the angles of incidence and reflection, as will be evident below.[7] And Aristotle himself says in *Metaphysics*, book viii, that not every alterable thing is also generable, celestial things being a case in point, for the alteration associated with light occurs in the heavens.[8] And therefore Aristotle says in *Meteorology*, book ii, that the sun illuminates all the stars.[9] If it should be objected that in *De caelo et mundo*, book i, Aristotle wishes to maintain that celestial nature is neither corruptible nor alterable nor susceptible to influence,[10] we reply that according to Aristotle in *De anima*, book ii, alteration is of two kinds:[11] one (to employ his eloquent words) is alteration 'towards perfection and [the realization of] natural disposition', and this is the alteration that results from species and virtues, whether in sense or in something else; and since this [alteration] could not occur without a certain generation, we concede this generation of a species that is directed towards fulfilment of the appetite of celestial nature and involves no corruption except of its defect and of a certain imperfection that the moon and stars have principally with respect to the sun. The other is the alteration or transmutation that occurs with the complete generation of a new form in the recipient, accompanied by the complete corruption and elimination of the recipient's specific nature; and such transmutation or alteration does not occur in the heavens, nor is it found in species. And if it should be said that in the heavens potentiality is completed by actuality, while the [natural] appetite of [celestial] matter is satisfied, we reply that appetite is satisfied [only] through a new form, which [were it to arise] would destroy the present form in the celestial body by a true and complete corruption of the specific nature of the heaven, and not through the species and virtue of light and the like, which exist along with the specific nature of the moon and stars. Thus in the moon and stars there is a certain appetite, of itself unfulfilled, but satisfied through the species and virtue of the sun, and also through the species of every other star, for each produces its species in the others.

[Third,] it should be understood that a species is produced in celestial bodies not only by other celestial bodies, but also by terrestrial things. And it is for this purpose that there is conformity and susceptibility to influence [between heavens and earth], as we said [above] concerning the action of celestial bodies on terrestrial;[12] but there is no absolute necessity in so far as celestial bodies are considered in and of themselves, but in so far as they are parts of the universe, assimilated to the others by reception of species, and in so far as they function as media in sensation. For if the eye were situated in the lunar

posset videre multa in speris elementorum posita; sed non videt nisi per species. Et cum species visus nostri exigitur ad actionem videndi, ut prius tactum est et tenendum secundum auctores et probatur post,
70 tunc in videndo stellas oportet quod visus nostri species generetur in celo, sicut in speris elementorum. Et ideo quicquid hic obiceretur de intransmutabilitate celi, et quod non est generabile nec corruptibile, dicendum quod hoc solum est intelligendum de transmutatione et generatione et corruptione que tollunt naturam specificam patientis
75 et renovant formam aliam specificam in esse completo. Sed bene est hic alteratio que est per generationem speciei qua celestis natura assimuletur inferiori, propter maiorem conformitatem universi et salutem, et propter necessitatem sensus et maxime visus, cuius species venit ad stellas et ad quem species stellarum veniunt ad visum.
80 Si vero obiciatur quod omne agens est nobilius patiente, ut Aristoteles dicit tertio *De anima*, dicendum quod hoc est verum in quantum huiusmodi, quoniam in quantum celum habet aptitudinem et potentiam et appetitum quendam respectu virtutum rerum inferiorum quibus caret, ut assimuletur eis propter maiorem proportionem
85 universi, in hoc est minus nobile quam res inferior quantumcunque vilis que talem speciem habet in actu et completam. Nec derogatur in hoc nobilitati celestis substantie, quia non est hoc ad eius ignobilitatem, sed ad decorem, ut completa sit concordia partium universi et salus et perfectio, quatinus conveniant ad invicem
90 quantum possibile est.
Si obiceretur ex decimo *Methaphysice* quod corruptibile et incorruptibile non communicant in genere, et hoc non possit exponi de genere predicabili, ut patet cum sint in eodem predicamento, necesse est exponi de eodem genere ˙subiecto, quia genus dicitur
95 equivoce ad subiectum et ad illud quod de pluribus differentibus specie predicatur in eo quod quid; quare videretur quod in eodem subiecto celesti non erit natura corruptibilis cum incorruptibili, precipue cum corpus celeste sit simplex; aliud enim est de homine, qui est composite nature multipliciter, in quo est aliquid corrupti-
100 bile et aliud incorruptibile. Sed dicendum est quod corruptibile et incorruptibile completa in esse nature non possunt esse in eodem

67 in: per *O* / speris: *mg. L*^C specis *L'* speras *O*   69 et²: est *O* / secundum: sed *S* / probabitur *S* / post: *om. F*   71 hic: *om. O*   74 et corruptione: *om. FO* 75 completo: *ex* completam *corr. L*   78 et²: sed *L*   79 ad quem *B*: ad quod *F* ad quam *LSAN* quoniam *O*   80 obicitur *S* / nobilius: *mg. L*^C nobilis *L'*   81–2 in quantum: *mg. L*^C im(*!*) quam *L'*   83 quedam *L* / virtutum rerum: *om. F* / rerum: *mg. L*^C obs. *L'*   85 minus: unus *S* / quam: quia *B*   86 que: *om. B* 88 decorem: eius d. *S*   91 si: sed *F* / decimo: 2 *F*   91–2 et incorruptibile: *mg. L*^C *om. L'*   92 exponi: *om. B*   93 patet: *interl. L*^C *om. L'*   94–6 genere . . . eodem: *mg. L*^C *om. L'*   96 videretur *BLS*: videtur *FOAN*   98 aliud: aliquid *L* 99 qui: que *B* / multiplex *SA*   100 et . . . incorruptibile: *om. O* et aliquid i. *FA*

sphere, it could see many things placed in the elemental spheres; but it sees only by means of species. And since the species of our eye[13] is required for the act of sight (as was mentioned above, as authorities hold, and as we prove below),[14] when we see the stars the species of our eye must be generated in the heaven, just as in the elemental spheres. Therefore, whatever objections should be here presented, based on the unchangeability of the heaven, or the fact that it is neither generable nor corruptible, we reply that they apply only to such transmutation, generation, and corruption as destroy the specific nature of the recipient and generate another specific form with complete being. However, that alteration is quite appropriate which consists in the generation of a species by which celestial nature is assimilated to terrestrial, for the sake of well-being and greater unity of the universe and to meet the needs of sense, especially sight, the species of which comes to the stars and to which the species of the stars come in order to produce vision.

If it should be objected that the agent is always nobler than the recipient, as Aristotle says in *De anima*, book iii,[15] we reply that it is true to this extent: that in so far as the heaven has aptitude and potentiality and a certain appetite with respect to the virtues of terrestrial things that it lacks, so that it would be assimilated to them for the sake of greater uniformity[16] in the universe, in this respect it is less noble than a terrestrial thing, however base, that has such a species perfectly and in actuality. Nor does this detract from the nobility of celestial substance, since it does not contribute to its ignobility, but to its splendour, being directed towards complete harmony and well-being and perfection among the parts of the universe, in order that they may conform to one another in so far as possible.

If it should be objected, by *Metaphysics,* book x, that the corruptible and incorruptible do not belong to the same genus,[17] and this cannot be said of genus [taken as] a predicable, as is evident, since they are in the same category, [and therefore] it must be said concerning one and the same genus [taken as] a subject, since 'genus' is applied equivocally to a subject and to [a predicable, namely,] that which is predicated of many things differing in kind in respect to what they are; and consequently it would seem that corruptible and incorruptible nature cannot be together in the same celestial subject, especially since celestial substance is simple; for it is otherwise with man, who has a composite nature in many different ways, in whom there is something corruptible and something incorruptible; [to this objection] we reply that the corruptible and incorruptible cannot have complete natural being in the same simple body, although

simplici; possunt tamen esse dummodo unum sit in esse specifico naturali completum et aliud sit assimulatio eius ad aliquod alterum, hoc enim est possibile et valde conveniens et quodammodo necessarium.

105 Si dicatur illud Aristotelis primo *Metheororum*, quod celum non recipit peregrinas impressiones, et has vocat alterationes formarum elementarium, dicendum est quod non sunt peregrine propter esse speciei renovande de qua hic loquimur, sed solum propter completum esse huiusmodi formarum et transmutationum que accidunt per cor-

110 ruptionem patientis in parte vel in toto et per lesionem sue substantie specifice; et huiusmodi transmutationes non fiunt in celestibus. Si obiciatur quod cum celum agat in hec inferiora et possit ab eis pati per generationem speciei, tunc erit agens physice, cuius contrarium vult tertio *Physicorum* et *Libro de generatione* et alibi

115 pluries, dicendum est quod passio que est in generatione speciei non inducit actionem physicam, sed ista que est per corruptionem essentie patientis, que non est in celestibus. Quod autem dicit Avicenna tertio *De anima*, quod absurdum est dicere quod celi patiantur a nostro visu; dicendum quod ipse prius immediate tetigit quo-

120 modo intellexit hanc passionem, loquens contra eos qui posuerunt aerem et celum in tantum pati a visu et alterari ut aer et celum essent instrumentum sentiendi visibile et deferendi seu reddendi visui eius speciem, et quod a visu fieret aliquid corporale protensum in medio usque ad rem visam; et non loquitur contra hoc quod celum sit sicut

125 medium in visu, recipiens speciem visus et visibilis, hoc enim necessarium est.

PARS I

CAPITULUM 6

Nunc considerandum est sextum principale circa influentiam agentis in patiens. Et in hoc consistit, ut sciatur que agentia corporalia

5 possunt complere suas species in patientibus extrinsecis, que ab

---

103 aliquid *L* aliquem *S*   104 impossibile *S*   105 non: *om. B*
106 vocatur *S*   107 elementarium: celestium *F*   109 transmutationes *O*
110 in parte: *mg. B* / vel: et *S* / sue substantie: *mg. L*ᶜ sue subiecte *L*′ in parte substantie sue
SA   112 si: sed *L* / obicitur *S* / cum: *om. S* / hec: ista *SA*   114 vult: v. Aristoteles
F   115 speciei: ipsa *S*   116 inducit: dicit *B*   117 essentie: *om. S*

they can be [in the same simple body] provided one of them has complete specific natural being and the other represents the assimilation [of the simple body] to something else, for this is possible and very suitable and in a certain way necessary.

If Aristotle's assertion in *Meteorology*, book i, is brought forward, namely, that the heaven does not receive alien impressions, and these he calls 'alterations of the elemental forms',[18] it is replied that one cannot judge an impression to be alien owing to [its possession of] the being of a generated species (concerning which we speak here), but only in so far as [it has] the complete being of forms and transmutations involving the corruption of the recipient in part or in whole and harm to its specific substance; and such transmutations do not occur in the heavens. If it should be objected that since the heaven acts on terrestrial things and can be acted upon by them through the generation of a species, therefore it must be a physical agent, the contrary of which is asserted in *Physics*, book iii, and *De generatione* and many other places,[19] we reply that physical action is not involved in the reception of influence that occurs in the generation of a species, but [only] in that which occurs in the corruption of the essence of the recipient; and the latter is not found in the heavens. However, Avicenna says in *De anima*, book iii, that it is absurd to claim that the heavens are affected by our sight.[20] But we reply that he himself, immediately before that, showed how he conceived this effect [on the heavens], speaking against those who supposed that air and the heaven were so affected and altered by sight as to become the instrument for perceiving the visible object and conveying or returning its species to sight, and that from sight there issues some corporeal substance extended through the medium to the visible object; and he does not speak against the heaven serving as a medium for sight, receiving the species of the eye and the visible object, for this is necessary.

PART I

CHAPTER 6

We must now consider the sixth principal [subject] concerning the influence of an agent on a recipient. And it consists of this, that it should be known which corporeal agents can complete their species in extrinsic recipients touched by them, in such a way that

119 immedietate *L*   119–20 quomodo: *mg. L*^{C} *om. L'*   120 intelligat *B*
intelligit *O*   123 corporale: *om. S* / pertensum *O* processum *S*   124 loquimur *L*
125 recipiet *L*   125–6 hoc . . . est: *om. O*

   2 capitulum sextum *O*   3 nunc: sectio octava *S* / sextum: 5 *S*   4 patientis *S*
5 complere: *mg. L*^{C} corporale *L'*

eis tanguntur, ut tollant naturam specificam patientis et faciant
effectus completos similes eis nomine et diffinitione. Et scimus
quod de complemento universi sunt generabilia et corruptibilia; si
enim omnia essent ingenerabilia et incorruptibilia, non essent nisi
10 spere elementorum et celestia et substantie spirituales; et ita omnia
alia deessent mundo, quod inconveniens esset. Sed cum mundus
sit sperice figure propter rationes proprias que postea inducende
sunt suo loco, nunc una est necessaria ad presens, videlicet quod
sperice figure esse debet ut undique a partibus spere confluant
15 virtutes celorum in centrum huius spere, quod est locus generationis;
et hec est terra, que est locus mixtionis et generationis et corruptionis. Et ideo superiora, ut celestia, sunt ingenerabilia et incorruptibilia secundum ordinem universi, et quia continuant
generationem et corruptionem in hiis inferioribus. Quando vero
20 oportet quod moveantur propter generationem et corruptionem, quia
motus adducit generans, id est stellam, sicut Aristoteles dicit in
fine *De generatione*, et exemplificat in obliquo circulo solis in quo
movetur per accessum et recessum respectu climatum et regionum, ideo
oportet dari motores continuos motuum celestium. Sed cum hic motus
25 non sit naturalis, eo quod non est a contrario in contrarium, propter
uniformitatem orientis et occidentis et ceterarum partium celi in
quibus non est contrarietas, oportet quod hii motus sint voluntarii
et ideo a substantiis habentibus voluntatem et rationem, cuiusmodi
sunt intelligentie. Propter quod oportet quod intelligentie moveant
30 orbes et stellas; et quia omne movens nobilius est moto, oportet
quod huiusmodi motores sint incorruptibiles et ingenerabiles.

Quamvis et rationes alie sint ad hoc idem et cetera nunc tacta,
sed transeo per ea que sunt propria ad id quod intendo, scilicet ad
videndum que agentia possunt complere effectus et que non. Et patet
35 quod quatuor elementa possunt hoc facere, Aristoteles enim dicit
Libro metheororum quod aqua multotiens convertit aerem in se et
econtrario; et quodlibet potest fieri ex quolibet, ut vult *Libro de
generatione*. Et maxime ignis hoc facit, quia magis est nobile et ideo
magis activum; et omnia corpora non celestia in se converteret et
40 ageret in infinitum, si ei materia combustibilis apponeretur, secundum

6 *ante* tanguntur *scr. et del.* F patiuntur / tangimur *BL*   7 completes *S*
8 de: *interl.* L^C *om.* L' 9 ingenerabilia . . . essent: *om.* *S*   11 quod: *om.* L /
esset: *om.* L est *S*   13 videlicet: scilicet *F*   14 spere: *om.* F sperice *O*
14–15 confluant . . . huius: *om.* F   15 centrum: *mg.* L^C cenceus L' centro *B* /
huiusmodi *S*   16 hoc *F*   18 universi: *mg.* L^C in diversi L' 19 quando *FLN*:
ideo *O* quandoque *B* quoniam *SA* / vero: non *O*   22 exemplificat: *mg.* L^C exificat L' /
obliquo: aliquo *F*   23 climatum: thūartū *B*   26 uniformitatem: *mg.* L^C
infinitatem L' / ceterarum: *mg.* L^C ceterum L' 28 et[2]: vel L / rationem cuiusmodi:
potentiam eius *F*   29 intelligentie[1]: intelligende *F*   30 oportet: *new hand begins in L*
32 hoc: *om.* FO   33 per: ad *O*   38 ideo: *om.* F   39 corporalia *O* /

they destroy the specific nature of the recipient and produce complete effects similar to themselves in name and definition. And we know that for a complete [and perfect] universe there must be generables and corruptibles; for if all things were ungenerable and incorruptible, there would be nothing except the spheres of the elements, the celestial spheres, and spiritual substances; and everything else would be missing from the world, which would be unsuitable. Now, although the specific reasons for the sphericity of the world will be introduced below in their proper place,[1] one of these reasons is relevant here, namely, that it must be of spherical shape so that from all parts of this sphere celestial powers can assemble in its centre, which is the place of generation; and this is the earth, which is the region of mixing and generation and corruption. And therefore superior, that is, celestial, things are ungenerable and incorruptible in accordance with the order of the universe. [They can] also [be shown to be ungenerable and incorruptible] on the grounds that they unceasingly cause generation and corruption in terrestrial substances. For, since generation and corruption require motion of the heavens, because a star becomes a source of generation on account of its motion, as Aristotle says at the end of *De generatione* (and he illustrates with the oblique circle along which the sun is moved, advancing and retreating with respect to the climes and regions),[2] therefore there must be continuous movers producing [these] celestial motions. But since such a motion is not caused by nature, because it does not proceed from a thing to its contrary, owing to the uniformity of east and west and the other parts of the heaven, in which there is no contrariety, these motions must be voluntary and therefore [result] from substances having will and reason; and intelligences are substances of this kind. Therefore, the spheres and stars must be moved by intelligences; and since every mover is nobler than the thing it moves, such movers must be incorruptible and ungenerable.

Although there are other arguments bearing on the same matter and others here touched upon, I pass to those things germane to my purposes, namely, to seeing which agents can complete their effects and which cannot. And it is evident that the four elements can, for Aristotle says in his *Meteorology* that water often converts air into itself and vice versa; and any [of the elements] can come into being from any other, as *De generatione* urges.[3] And fire especially does this, since it is more noble and therefore more active [than the other elements]; and it would convert all noncelestial bodies into itself and act to infinity if it were to meet [only] combustible matter, according

convertet *B* convertent *S*   40 aget *B* / si: sed *F* / apponitur *S*

quod vult Aristoteles secundo *De anima*, licet hoc verbum habeat suam expositionem, ut tangetur post. Unde non solum effectum suum complet in elementis, sed in mixtis omnibus. Alia vero elementa non tantum possunt facere, sunt enim longe debilioris operationis, et
45 multas operationes debiles et insensibiles faciunt. Et hee sole substantie corporales possunt suas species complere in effectus suos, factas scilicet in patientibus extra eas. Unde nec mixta inanimata nec animata generata ex putrefactione nec propagata nec celestia faciunt nisi species suas in rebus mundi eis propinquatis extra se.
50 Hoc dico propter plantas et matres in animalibus, que in semine deciso perficiunt species in effectus completos cum adiutorio virtutis celi et motorum in celestibus. Sed tamen nec plante nec matres facientes suas species in corporibus extra se complent eas, velut ignis speciem factam in ligno ei propinquato extra se complet in
55 effectum plenum similem ei nomine et diffinitione.

Sed gravissima dubitatio est in hac parte, eo quod nobiliora sunt omnia mixta inanimata et animata et celestia quam elementa; et ideo habent plus de virtute activa, et ideo in materia mundi magis videntur posse complere suas species. Nec est impedimentum per hoc, quod
60 solet dici quod non est aptitudo a parte materie mundi ad tam nobiles formas complendas, ut celestium et hominum et huiusmodi propagatorum; quoniam si queratur, cum elementum agit in mixtum vel in aliud elementum, que est aptitudo a parte materie naturalis, non potest dici nisi quia illa materia apta nata est et habet aptitudinem
65 naturalem ad species diversas et communis eis. Et hec secundum veritatem est essentia alicuius generis proximi que est in potentia ad species contrarias et apta nata ad utramque, ut substantia corporea non celestis est in potentia ad elementum et mixtum. Et res significata per hanc circumlocutionem est subiectum et materia in transmutatione
70 mixti in elementum et econtrario. Et quando elementum est fortius mixto, corrumpit naturam specificam mixti usque ad radicem communem ei et mixto, id est ad essentiam illius generis, de cuius potentia producitur natura specifica elementi; et econtrario, cum mixtum vel aliud agens sufficiens ad generationem mixti, sicut celum, potest
75 invalescere super elementum, tollit naturam specificam elementi,

41 secundo: libro *L*   47 factos *O* / eos *O*   49 propinquas *F* propinquis *O*
50 matres: vires *O* / in²: et *S*   52 motor *BL*   53–4 eas . . . complet: *mg. O*
54 propinquato *BLSN*: appropinquato *FOA*   56 gravissimum *O* / dubium *O* dubere *L*
57 et animata: *om. B* / et²: *om. O*   58 *post* materia *add. B* elementata et ideo habent
plus de virtute et ideo in materia   59 posse: *interl.* *L*^{C} *om. L'* / nec est: *ex* aerem *corr. L*
60 materie: *mg. F*^{C} *om. F'* / ad: et *S*   61 celestium: corporum c. *O* est c. *B*
62 quoniam: quantum *S*   62–3 agit . . . naturalis: *mg. O*   64 nisi: *mg. O om. F* /
et: ut *B*   65 communis eis: est c. *S*   67 utrumque *S*   68 ad: *om. B*
75 elementi: causari(?) *L*   75–6 specificam . . . naturam: *mg. O*

to Aristotle's intention in *De anima*, book ii—although this passage requires interpretation, as will be shown below.[4] Therefore, fire completes its effect not only in the elements, but also in all mixed bodies. The other elements cannot achieve as much, for they are much weaker in their action and produce many weak and insensible actions. And only these corporeal substances are able to bring their species to completion[5] in their effects—that is, species produced in recipients outside themselves. Thus neither inanimate mixed bodies, nor animate bodies generated by putrefaction or by procreation, nor celestial bodies produce anything but their species in things of the world outside themselves and in their vicinity.[6] I say ['outside themselves' in order to make the matter clear] with regard to plants and mother animals, which bring [their] species to perfection in complete effects [inside themselves] in a determined seed, with the assistance of celestial virtue and celestial movers. However, neither plants nor mother animals, in producing their species in bodies outside themselves, bring those species to completion as fire completes the species that it produces in wood (outside itself and in its vicinity) in a full effect similar to itself in name and definition.

But there is a most serious doubt regarding this matter, for all mixed inanimate and animate and all celestial bodies are nobler than the elements; and therefore they have more active virtue and seem better able to complete their species in the matter of the world. Nor is this doubt countered by the common assertion that there is no aptitude in the matter of the world whereby such noble forms could be completed, as there is in the heavens and man and other procreated beings; for if it is inquired, when an element acts on a mixed body or another element, what is the aptitude on the part of natural matter, nothing can be said except that this matter is naturally suited and has a natural aptitude to different species and is common to them. And in truth, this [matter] is the essence of a proximate genus that is in potentiality to contrary species and naturally suited to both, as noncelestial corporeal substance is in potentiality to both an element and a mixed body. And what we mean by this circumlocution is the subject and matter in the transmutation of a mixed body into an element and vice versa. And when the element is stronger than the mixed body, it corrupts the specific nature of the mixed body down to their common root, that is, to the essence of that genus, out of the potentiality of which the specific nature of the element is produced; and conversely, when a mixed body or another agent able to generate a mixed body, such as the heaven, can prevail over the element, it destroys its specific nature,

et de radice communi et ex eius potentia producit naturam specificam mixti.

Stat igitur ratio generationis effectus completi in duobus, scilicet quod agens habeat potentiam maiorem quam patiens ut vincat, 80 et quod materia sit communis agenti et patienti, que materia est essentia alicuius generis proximi quod est commune duabus speciebus, scilicet agenti et patienti. Et in generatione individuorum est individuum generis respectu duorum individuorum diversarum specierum (sicut enim se habet genus ad species, sic individuum generis ad 85 individua specierum) loco principii materialis apti ad utrumque. Hec uberius patuerunt in precedentibus; sed nunc sufficit ad hoc quod volo ut concedatur sine contradictione quod victoria alterius speciei agentis posite sub genere et potentia generis proximi sufficiunt ad generationem et corruptionem effectuum completorum. Cum igitur 90 celum sit maioris potentie ad agendum quam ignis et quam aliquod corpus inferius, et communicat in genere proximo cum corpore non celesti (communicant enim in primo genere subalterno), et celum est nobilius et magis activum, invenietur hic tota ratio complendi effectus; et sic ulterius de homine et omnibus mixtis, que sunt nobiliora ele-95 mentis et ideo magis generativa specierum suarum complendarum in effectus, cum inveniatur materia seu essentia generis proximi communis duabus speciebus quibuscunque datis.

Quapropter sequetur quod in illis et in omnibus agentibus est aptitudo ut compleant suos effectus quantum est a parte agentium et 100 patientium et materie communis eis. Sed tamen, licet sit aptitudo dicta, non tamen est potestas nec possibilitas ad hos effectus complendos propter multas rationes; non enim omne quod habet aptitudinem habet possibilitatem, ut cecus aptus natus est ad videndum, non tamen potest videre nec potentiam videndi habet per naturam. 105 In proposito vero est sola aptitudo et tamen ante privationem; unde non est ablata potentia per inductionem privationis, ut in ceco, sed excluditur potentia et similiter actus propter mundi necessitatem. Cum enim non sit quasi proportio virtutis active in corpore respectu substantie spiritualis, et similiter in corpore non celesti respectu 110 substantie celestis, si complerentur species substantiarum spiritualium, omnia fierent spiritualia; et si complerentur species substantiarum celestium, tollerentur omnes nature corporales inferiores, et fierent

76 ex: *om.* FSA   78 stat *LSAN*: constat *FO* fiat *B*   81-2 alicuius . . . patienti: *mg. O*   82 genere *O*   85 individuum *F*   87 ut: quod *L*   88 generatione *S* 91 communicant *O* communicet *S* / proximo: *om. S*   92 communicat *L*   93 invenitur *O* / totum *O*   104 non: nec *S*   105 *ante* tamen *mg. add. O* non 107 mundi *O'*: videndi *mg. O^C*   109 substantie . . . respectu: *mg. O*   110 substantie: *om. S*   112 tollentur *O* / corporalis *S*

and out of the common root and its potentiality it produces the specific nature of the mixed body.

Therefore, it remains that the reason for the generation of a complete effect is twofold—namely, that the agent has greater power than the recipient in order to prevail over it, and that there is matter common to agent and recipient (which matter is the essence of some proximate genus common to the two species, that is, to the agent and recipient). And in the generation of individuals, the individual of the genus is related to two individuals of different species [falling under that same genus] as a material principle suited to both (for as genus is to species, so is the individual of the genus to the individuals of the species). These things are more fully treated above,[7] but it suffices for my purposes that it be conceded without contradiction that the generation and corruption of complete effects are sufficiently provided for by the domination of an agent of one species [over a recipient of another species] placed under one genus, and by the potentiality of the proximate genus. Therefore, since the heaven has greater power to act than does fire or some terrestrial body, and it belongs to the same proximate genus as noncelestial body (for they belong to the same first subalternated genus), and the heaven is nobler and more active, we find here the whole reason for completion of the effect. And the same is true of man and all mixed bodies, which are nobler than the elements and therefore more generative of species that are brought to completion in effects, when matter or the essence of the proximate genus common to any two given species is present.

It follows, therefore, that those and all other agents have the aptitude to complete their effects, in so far as it depends on the agents and the recipients and the matter common to them. Nevertheless, although the said aptitude exists, there are many reasons why the power and the possibility of completing their effects may be lacking; for not everything that has the aptitude has the possibility, as a blind man has the natural aptitude for seeing, but cannot see and does not, by nature, have the power to see. But in the case before us there is aptitude alone, even before[8] privation; therefore, the power [of generating complete effects] is not removed through the introduction of privation, as in the blind; rather, the power and also the actuality are excluded owing to the necessities of the world. For since corporeal matter has nowhere near the active virtue of spiritual substance[9] (and the same relationship holds between noncelestial body and celestial substance), if the species of spiritual substances should be completed, all things would become spiritual; and if the species of celestial substances were completed, all terrestrial corporeal natures would be destroyed, and there would be

solum substantie celestes; et ideo destrueretur ordo universi et
mundi. Propter quod, licet ex lege nature particularis aptitudo sit
115 a parte substantie spiritualis active et a parte substantie celestis
active et a parte materie communis substantie spirituali et corporali,
et similiter communis substantie celesti et non celesti, ut fierent
substantiarum spiritualium et celestium effectus completi, tamen
ex ordinatione divina et ex lege nature universalis, de qua facit
120 Avicenna mentionem sexto *Methaphysice*, abscinditur potentia et
excluditur actus, ita quod non possunt substantie spirituales nec
substantie celestes facere nisi suas species et nullo modo complere
effectus eis similes nomine et diffinitione, quia tunc fierent omnia
spiritualia et celestia, et destruerentur res multe que sunt de com-
125 plemento universi, non solum secundum statum presentis cursus,
sed simpliciter. Hoc dico quia multa finaliter auferentur omnino a
numero rerum, que tamen nunc sunt necessaria in mundo propter
hominem, propter quem facta sunt cetera. Et tamen nichilominus ex
natura particulari ipsius substantie spiritualis et celi est quod sit
130 aptitudo a parte sua, ut produceret effectum completum; et aptitudo
est a parte materie mundi, que est communis spirituali et corporali
atque celesti et non celesti. Nec obstat quod tunc aliqua spiritualia
et celestia essent generata et alia creata, quoniam si Creator crearet
modo unum hominem et alius generaretur per propagationem,
135 modus hic diversus exeundi in esse non diversificaret speciem; prima
enim individua animalium et plantarum non fuerunt generata, sed vel
creata vel plasmata. Et substantie spirituales et celestes generate
non essent corruptibiles, sed incorruptibiles sicut alie, quia nulla
virtus activa creata haberet posse super earum corruptionem, nec
140 umquam deficerent in se. Propter quod sermo ille, quod omne
generabile est corruptibile artandus est ad ea que actualiter nunc in
mundo subsunt generationi, non ad omnia que apta nata sunt generari,
que, quia solum aptitudinem habent et non potentiam nec actum, ideo
non computantur inter generabilia de quibus loquimur in hoc mundo.
145   Eodem modo est per omnia de aliis nobilibus agentibus comparatis
ad ignobiliora, ut de hominibus respectu aliarum rerum generabilium et
corruptibilium. Si enim species hominum complerentur in patientibus

114 mundi: mundus iste *S*   115 spiritualis: *mg. O* / et: et similiter *S*
115-16 substantie² . . . parte: *om. F*   116 corporali *OSA*: corpori *BLFN*
117 et²: *om. S*   118 et celestium: *mg. O*   119 universalis de: dicit *S*
124 et²: ut *B*   126 quia: eo quod *B* quod *SA* / auferuntur *S*   127 nunc: non *FO* /
in: *om. O*   131 mundi: *om. O*   132 atque: *om. S* / et non celesti: *om. O* /
quem *S*   133 aliqua *S* / crearet: caret *S*   134 generetur *S* / per: propter *BO* /
135 non: n. dum *FO*   136 fuerunt: sunt *F*   136-8 generata . . . essent:
mg. O   137 generande(?) *S*   140 quod¹: *om. O* / quod²: *om. A*
140-1 quod¹ . . . ad: *om. S*   141 nunc: numerus *L*   142 subsistunt *F*
143 solam *O*   144 loquitur *FO*   146 ignobilia *B* / hominibus: omnibus *F*

only celestial substances; and therefore the order of the universe and the world would be destroyed. Therefore, although by a law of particular nature there is aptitude on the part of active spiritual substance, active celestial substance, the matter common to spiritual and corporeal substance, and also the matter common to celestial and noncelestial substance, through which there could be complete effects of spiritual and celestial substances, nevertheless by divine ordination and a universal law of nature, concerning which Avicenna writes in *Metaphysics*, book vi, the power is withheld and the actuality excluded, so that spiritual and celestial substances can do no more than produce their species, and they can in no way complete effects similar to themselves in name and definition, since then all things would become spiritual and celestial, and many things that contribute to the perfection of the universe would be destroyed, not only according to their position in the present course [of nature], but absolutely. (I say 'absolutely' because in the end many things [in the present order of nature] will be completely eliminated from the number of [existing] things, which are nevertheless now required in the world on account of man, for whose sake the other [non-eliminable] things were [also] made.)[10] Nevertheless, owing to the particular nature of spiritual substance and the heaven, there is an aptitude on their part to produce a complete effect; and there is also aptitude on the part of the matter of the world, which is common to spiritual and corporeal and to celestial and noncelestial things. Nor can it be objected that then some spiritual and celestial beings would be generated and others created [and, therefore, that some would be corruptible and others incorruptible], for if the Creator were to create only one man and generate the rest through procreation, this different mode of coming into being would not diversify the species; for the first individual animal or plant was not generated, but either created or fashioned. And generated spiritual and celestial substances would not be corruptible, but incorruptible like the others,[11] since no active created virtue would be able to corrupt them, nor would they ever fail of themselves. Therefore, the statement that every generable is corruptible should be restricted to things in the world that are actually now subject to generation, for it does not apply to all things that have a natural aptitude for generation, which, since they have only aptitude and not potentiality or actuality, are not counted among the generable things in this world, concerning which we speak.

It is the same in every way for other noble agents in relation to ignoble recipients, such as men in relation to other generable and corruptible things. For if the species of men were completed in

147 *ante* enim *scr. et del.* F autem

extrinsecis, tunc cetera res destruerentur et delerentur de mundo,
quod fieri non debet ex lege nature universalis, licet ex natura
150 particulari humana sit aptitudo ad huiusmodi effectus complendos
propter nobilitatem eius respectu aliarum rerum generabilium. Et
quia aptitudo materie communis invenitur, sed utilitas totius mundi
prefertur, et etiam hominis propria, quia sine aliis rebus vivere et
esse non posset, propter quod non respondet huic aptitudini potentia
155 nec actus. Et ideo artata est generatio hominis ad modum propagandi,
non solum propter alias res, sed propter ipsos homines ne multipli-
carentur plus quam oporteret. Insuper ipsa mors singulorum secundum
statum presentis vite necessaria est ex lege nature universalis, ut
dicit Avicenna secundo *Physicorum*, licet natura particularis istius
160 vel illius non intendat corruptionem, sed vitam et salutem.

Et eodem modo est de aliis rebus mixtis omnibus ad patientia
viliora semper comparatis, quod ex lege nature universalis intendentis
bonum commune ablata est potentia et actus similiter complendi
species in effectus completos, licet ex natura particulari sit ibi
165 aptitudo. Propter quod artata est generatio effectus completi in
paucissimis, scilicet in elementis et precipue in igne. Nec accidit
inconveniens de hoc, quia ignis qui est aliis nobilior in sua spera
non facit nisi speciem in alia corpora mundi, eo quod locus
salvat locatum; et est simile de eo respectu aliorum sicut de
170 celestibus respectu inferiorum. Alius autem ignis hic inferius
generatus non generatur nisi determinata quantitate secundum usum
hominum, et reprimitur eius actio et cavetur, nisi quando ex stultitia
humana multiplicat se ultra modum in nocumentum rerum aliarum.

Et eadem ratio est de speris aliorum elementorum quantum ad
175 puritatem naturarum suarum. Ut continent se mutuo, nobilius non
corrumpit vilius, sed per suam virtutem salvat, sicut locus salvat locatum, ut Averroys determinat secundo *De anima*, quamvis ex hoc quod
miscentur ad invicem, et in quantum per virtutes celorum alterantur,
contrahunt naturam activam et corruptivam mutuo et possunt sic
180 facere effectus completos; ut dictum est quod aqua convertit aliquando
aerem in se et econtrario. Et huiusmodi elementorum transmutatio

150 *post* aptitudo *scr. et del.* S eius   151 alium B   154 potest S
155 actus: aptus S   160 intendit O / corruptioni F   161 patienda(!) B
162 quod: quia SA / nature: *om.* F   167 quia: quod O / aliis O: in a. BFLSN in
illis A   171 determinata: de animata F a terminata BN   172 nisi: n. quia F /
stultius S   174 ad: aliquid O   175 continent se: continentur O   176 sicut . . .
salvat: *om.* F   177 ut: et B / Averoim O   178 per: *om.* FO   179 *ante* activam
scr. et del. (?) S alterius

extrinsic recipients, then other things [these extrinsic recipients] would be destroyed and eliminated from the world, which according to the law of universal nature ought not to occur, although according to particular human nature there is aptitude for the completion of such effects owing to man's nobility in relation to other generable things. And although the aptitude of common matter is present, the utility of the whole world is given priority—and also the utility proper to man, since he could not live or be without other things— and therefore there is neither the potentiality nor the actuality to correspond to this aptitude. Consequently, the generation of mankind is restricted to the mode of procreation, not only for the sake of other things, but for the sake of man himself, in order that men not be multiplied beyond necessity. In addition, the death of individuals (with respect to the present life) is necessary according to the law of universal nature, as Avicenna says in *Physics*, book ii,[12] although the particular nature of this or that individual is not directed towards corruption, but towards life and health.

And it is the same for all other mixed bodies compared, in each case, to less noble recipients, because by the law of universal nature, intending the common good, the power and the actuality of bringing the species to completion in complete effects are lacking, although according to particular nature the aptitude is present. Therefore, the ability to generate a complete effect is restricted to very few things, namely, the elements, especially fire. Nor is this rendered absurd by the fact that fire, which is nobler than the other elements,[13] when it is in its own sphere merely extends its species into the other bodies of the world, because place preserves the thing located there; and its relationship to [those] other things is like the relationship of the heavens to terrestrial things. However, other fire generated here in lower regions is generated only in a determined quantity according to mankind's needs, and its action is curbed and held in check, except when by human foolishness it is multiplied beyond due measure to the point of harming other things.

And the same argument applies to the spheres of the other elements, in so far as their natures are pure. So that they may mutually contain one another, the nobler does not corrupt the more ignoble, but preserves it through its virtue, just as place preserves the thing located there, as Averroes determines in [his commentary on] *De anima*, book ii,[14] although from the fact that they are mixed one with another, and in so far as they are altered by celestial virtues, they mutually unite their active and corruptive natures and can thus produce complete effects; thus it was said that water sometimes converts air into itself and vice versa.[15] And such transmutation of the

maxime accidit in elementis, scilicet ut sunt in mixto, aut in confinio sperarum suarum, ubi etiam quodammodo miscentur et confunduntur nature eorum ad invicem, sicut patet ex *Libro metheororum* et *De* 185 *generatione*. Similiter etiam alterantur ad invicem in simplicitate sua propter mixti necessariam generationem, quorum tunc alteratio magis est per virtutem celi quam per unum elementum in sua spera transmutans illud.

Et cum dictum est que substantie possunt complere species et que 190 non, sciendum est in accidentibus. Et certum est quod quatuor qualitates tangibiles, scilicet caliditas, frigiditas, siccitas, et humiditas, possunt suas species complere in patientibus aliquibus, et maxime caliditas, quia magis est nobilis et magis activa et magis mundo necessaria. Similiter et lux potest in aliquibus corporibus aptis 195 complere suum effectum, ut lux solis complet effectum in corpore planetarum et stellarum et nubibus, ita quod, sufficienter generata in eis, potest facere ad inferiora suam speciem et virtutem efficaciter. Et in flamma et carbone similiter, unus enim fumus inflammatus illuminat alium et res multas; et similiter carbo illumi- 200 natus alias res illuminat ei iunctas, ut compleatur species lucis in eis. Color autem non sic potest quamvis aliquis color fortis faciat sensibilem speciem que bene apparet, precipue in obscuro iuxta radium lucis, sicut contingit de coloribus fortibus vitrorum quando per ea radius transit solaris sensibiliter. Sed hoc expositum est prius.

205   Odor vero non complet speciem, quia illud quod relinquitur extra odorabile fortiter immutans sensum est fumus subtilis resolutus per calidum extra vel intra; et non est species nec effectus completus odoris, sed corpus quoddam in esse specifico odorabilis constitutum, quod dividit partes medii et optinet locum inter latera continentis. 210 Sapor vero non facit extra se nisi speciem, nec complet eam, licet magna sit immutatio gustus per saporem, quia sapor non immutat bene nisi propter humiditatem salivalem cui commiscetur et per quam saporabile resolvitur, ut fortius immutet. Sonus vero non facit effectum completum, cum nec videatur facere speciem, ut tactum est 215 prius. Et cum hee qualitates sensibiles non omnes faciunt effectum completum, multo magis nec alie qualitates in prima specie, secunda,

182 maxime: in aere *O* / in³: *om. FO* / confinio: infimis *S*   183 etiam: et *S* / quodammodo: quod modo *O* / confundunt *S*   184 sicut: sic *S*   185 alterantur *OSA*: alterentur *FN* alterarentur *BL*   186 necessariam: necessaria in *B* / quarum *B* 188 illud: aliud *S*   191 tangibiles: *om. B*   193 mundo: *om. S*   195 ut: et *B* / solis: *om. O*   196 sufficienter: *om. O*   198 et²: a *S*   200 iunctas: necessitas *B*   201 color: *ex* calor *corr. F* / autem: enim *S* / sic: *rep. S*   202 radium: rubium *B*   205 illud: id *FL*   208 *post* odoris *scr. et del. O* sed odoris 210 nisi: *om. O*   212 per: *ex* post *corr. S*   213 immutat *L*   214 nec: non *S* 215 *post* prius *scr. et del. O* et cum hee qualitates sensibiles non omnes faciunt effectum completum cum nec videatur facere speciem ut tactum est prius

elements occurs especially when the elements are in a mixed body, or at the boundaries of their spheres (where they are also mixed to some degree and their natures are intermingled), as is evident from the *Meteorology* and *De generatione*.[16] Similarly, they are transmuted into one another in their simplicity by the necessary generation of a mixed body, this transmutation then occurring more through celestial virtue than through one element in its sphere transmuting another.

Since we have determined which substances can produce complete species and which cannot, we must now consider the same thing for accidents. And it is certain that the four tangible qualities, namely, warmth, coldness, dryness, and humidity, can complete their species in certain recipients, and especially warmth, since it is nobler and more active and more necessary to the world [than the others]. Similarly, light can complete its effect in certain suitable bodies, as the light of the sun completes its effect in the bodies of the planets, stars, and clouds, so that, having been sufficiently generated in them, it can efficaciously produce its species and virtue in terrestrial things. The same is true of flame and burning charcoal, for burning smoke illuminates other smoke and many other things; and similarly illuminated[17] charcoal illuminates other things joined to it, so that the species of light is completed in them. Colour, however, cannot do this, although certain strong colours produce sensible species that appear clearly, especially in a dark place in the vicinity of a ray of light, as happens with the intense colours of glass when a solar ray sensibly passes through them. But this was discussed above.[18]

However, odour does not complete its species, since that which is released outside an odoriferous body to alter sense strongly is a subtle smoky exhalation, released by internal or external heat; and it is not a species or a complete effect of odour, but a certain body, so constituted in specific being as to be odoriferous, which divides the parts of the medium and obtains a place between the sides of the containing parts.[19] Flavour produces only a species outside itself, and it does not complete this species, despite there being a strong altera-tion of taste by flavour, since flavour is able to alter taste well only through the moisture of the saliva with which it is mixed and by virtue of which the things possessing flavour are dissolved and thereby enabled to alter [taste] more strongly. Sound does not pro-duce a complete effect, since we have seen above that it does not produce a species.[20] And since not all of these sensible qualities [those in the third species of quality] produce complete effects, it is all the more obvious that the other qualities in the first, second,

et quarta, quoniam aut non agunt aut minus active sunt in res extra,
et multo minus res alie predicamentales. Et ideo sola quatuor tangi-
bilia et lux videntur posse complere suos effectus extra se.

220   Et sic terminatur prima pars istius tractatus, que est de generatione
speciei.

PARS II
CAPITULUM 1

Nunc dicendum est de secundo principali, scilicet de multiplicatione
ipsa ab agente et a loco primo sue generationis secundum omne genus
5 lineationis et anguli et figure in quibus natura delectatur operari.
Et hec multiplicatio est actio univoca agentis et speciei, ut lux
generat lucem et lux generata generat aliam, et sic ulterius. Sed
in quarto principali est consideratio de actione equivoca, que est
ut lux generat calorem et huiusmodi. (*v*) Et hec multiplicatio habet
10 veritates multas, que in capitulis decem congregantur.

Et prima est quod prima pars patientis transmutata et habens
speciem in actu transmutat partem secundam, et secunda tertiam, et
sic ulterius. Et hoc vult Aristoteles secundo *De sompno et vigilia*
et septimo *Physicorum* et primo *De generatione*. Et oportet hoc,
15 quoniam agens non coniungitur secunde parti patientis nec aliis, et
eas non transmutat. Et prima pars iam habens speciem in actu habet
unde possit secundam alterare, propter quod alterabit eam.

Secundo sciendum quod oportet partes has esse equales et eiusdem
quantitatis, sicut in motu locali idem mobile semper transit partes
20 equales spatii. Et causa est quia oportet hic approximationem in
omnibus esse equalem, nam super approximationem fundatur actio
naturalis. Si dicatur quod pars prima habet minus de virtute quam
agens, ergo minus alterabit, dicendum quod non in quantitate, sed
in qualitate.

25   Preterea considerandum quod ab eodem puncto, seu a parte agentis
minima secundum latitudinem et longitudinem sive a parte prima
patientis, quod magis proprie dicitur, multiplicantur species radiose
quasi infinite, quia qua ratione ille punctus lucis vel alterius

217 aut[1]: autem *B* | aut[2]: *om. S*   218 sola: *om. F* | quatuor: *ex* decem *corr. L*
219 videntur: nostra(?) *B* videretur *S*   220 istius: huiusmodi *S*
1 pars secunda *O* pars secunda huius tractatus *L*   2 capitulum primum *O*
3 secunda *B* sexto *S*   4 ipsa: *mg. F*   5 lineationis: *om. B* | delectatur: *om. S*
6 actio: *om. B* | ut: et *L*   8 in quarto: quarti *B* in octo *SA* | principalis *B*
9 multiplicatio: conclusio *B* | habet: *om. S*   10 que: *om. S*   11 quod: quia *B*
12 partem: speciem *O om. F*   14 generatione: g. et corruptione *O* | oportet: o. quod *O*
15 quoniam: *om. B* | coniungit *S*   20 quia: quod *O*   23–4 sed in qualitate: *mg. O*
25–6 agentis . . . parte: *mg. O*   26 primi *BL*   27 multiplicatur *S* | species: *om. F*

and fourth species do not do so,[21] since either they do not act [at all] or they are less active in things external to themselves; and much less should things in the other categories [produce complete effects]. And therefore, [of the accidents,] only the four tangible qualities and light seem to be able to complete their effects outside themselves.

Thus ends the first part of this treatise, which is concerned with the generation of species.

PART II
CHAPTER 1

We must now discuss the second principal subject, namely, multiplication itself from the agent and from the place of initial generation, according to every kind of line, angle, and figure in which nature is pleased to operate. And this multiplication is a univocal action of the agent and [its] species, so that light generates light, and generated light generates further light, and so on. But in the fourth[1] principal part [of this treatise] we consider equivocal action, according to which light generates heat and the like. (*v*) And there are many truths regarding this multiplication, gathered in ten chapters.

Now the first truth is that the first part of the recipient, having been transmuted and possessing species in actuality, transmutes the second part, the second part transmutes the third, and so on. This is what Aristotle intends in *De somno et vigilia*, book ii, in *Physics*, book vii, and in *De generatione*, book i.[2] And it is necessarily true, since the agent is not joined to the second part of the recipient or to other parts, and [therefore] it does not alter them. And the first part [of the recipient], since it already has a species in actuality, has what it requires to alter the second; and therefore it does alter it.

Secondly, it should be known that these parts [of the recipient] must be equal and of the same size, just as in local motion a given mobile always occupies equal parts of space. And the reason in the present case is that there must always be equal proximity, since natural action is founded on proximity.[3] If it should be argued that the first part [of the recipient] has less virtue than the agent and therefore will produce a smaller alteration, we reply that its virtue is less in quality, but not in quantity.

In addition, it should be recognized that from a single point, whether a least part (according to length and breadth) of the agent or, more properly, the first part of the recipient [affected by that least part of the agent], there is a virtually infinite[4] multiplication of species in radiant fashion; for the explanation of multiplication in

28-9 ille . . . ratione: *mg. O*

multiplicabit se in partem unam, eadem ratione in partem alteram;
30 aut igitur secundum omnem aut secundum nullam; sed non secundum
nullam; ergo secundum omnem differentiam positionis, sursum,
deorsum, ante, retro, et secundum omnes diametros. Item ubicunque
ponitur oculus secundum omnes diametros, fit visio illius partis si non
sit obstaculum; sed oculus non videt nisi per speciem venientem; ergo
35 oportet quod ad omnem partem veniant species radiose ab eodem
puncto; nec est aliquid hic in contrarium quod probabiliter posset dici.
Et tamen non pono infinita in actu, sumendo infinitum absolute, sed
sub sensu Aristotelis secundo *De generatione*, scilicet non tot quin
plura, quia non tot radii signandi sunt et fiendi ab eodem puncto,
40 quin plures possunt signari. Nec tamen fit huiusmodi species radiosa
a parte agentis quod exeat ab ea sed, ut dictum est, quod fiat de
potentia patientis, a virtute tamen et potentia activa partis ipsius
agentis. Et non solum est de parte verum quod sic fiunt infiniti
radii in omnem partem in qua non sit impedimentum, sed de quo-
45 cunque agente est ita, quod agens est tanquam punctus communis, a
quo linee in omnem partem fiunt infinite, super quas multiplicantur
species radiose. Et tamen magis proprie dicitur quod prima pars
patientis est tanquam huiusmodi punctus, quia in veritate prima origo
speciei est totaliter in prima parte patientis; et ab ea diffunditur ubique
50 in omnem partem et secundum omnes differentias positionis et omnes
diametros. Unde pars prima patientis est tanquam centrum commune
ad infinitas lineas et radios; sed est terminus omnium intra ad quem
continuantur, pars vero agentis est centrum et terminus ad quem
contiguantur. Et quia huiusmodi multiplicatio, cuiuscunque sit,
55 est similis radiis multiplicatis a stella, ideo universaliter omnem
multiplicationem vocamus radiosam, et radios dicimus fieri sive
sint lucis sive coloris sive alterius. Et alia ratio est huiusmodi
nominationis, quia scilicet magis manifesta nobis est multiplicatio
lucis quam aliorum, et ideo transumimus multiplicationem lucis
60 ad alias.
   Sed animadvertendum est, de istis lineis super quas est multiplicatio, quoniam oportet quod sint recte quantum est ex natura
multiplicationis usquequo recipiant impedimentum reflexionis et

   29 alteram: aliam *S*   30 sed non: si enim *B*   30–1 sed . . . nullam: *mg. O*
35 ad: *om. S*   36 in: *om. FS* / contrarium: *om. S*   37 infinita: in *B* / infinitum:
infinita *S*   38 secundo: *om. B* / quin: an *S*   39 significandi *B* / sunt et: sunt
sumendi scilicet *S* scilicet sumendi et *A*   40 quinto *F* / possint *F*   41 quod[1]:
ita q. *S* / ab ea: *mg. O* / quod[2]: ut *O*   42 a: pro *S* / et: in *S* / ipsius: *ex* ipsis *corr. L*
43 parte: p. lucis *B* / verum: sui *S*   44 sit: fit *FO*   47 tamen: non *S*   47–8 pars
. . . origo: *mg. L*[C]origo *L'* (*post* origo *mg. add. L*[C] et cetera)   48 patientis: *om. B*
49 transfunditur *OS*   51 est: non e. *S*   52 sed: et *O* / intra: *om. OF* / *ante* ad[2]
scr. et del. F necessario / quem: quoniam *S*   53 terminus: est extra *S* t. extra *A*

one direction from that or some other point of light would also
apply to multiplication in other directions; therefore the point would
multiply itself either in all directions or in none; not the latter, and
therefore in all different directions: up, down, in front, behind, and
along all diameters. Also, wherever the eye is placed, along any
diameter, it observes that [radiating] part if there is no obstacle; but
the eye sees only if a species comes to it, and therefore radiant
species must proceed from a given point [of the observed object] in
all directions; nor is there anything to the contrary that could be
said here with any probability.[5] However, I do not posit an actual
infinite, taking 'infinity' absolutely, but in Aristotle's sense in *De
generatione*, book ii,[6] that is, not as so many that there are no more,
since it is impossible for so many rays to be produced by or drawn
from a given point that no more can be drawn. But such a radiant
species does not come into being from a part of the agent by exiting
from it—rather, as was said, [by generation] out of the potentiality
of the recipient, though owing to the virtue and active power of the
part of the agent. And it is true that infinitely many rays proceed
thus in all unobstructed directions not only from a part [of the
agent], but any [whole] agent can be considered the common point
from which infinitely many lines proceed in all directions and along
which species are multiplied as rays.[7] However, it is more proper to
say that the first part of the recipient is such a point, since in truth
the first origin of a species is entirely in the first part of the recipient;
and from it species are diffused everywhere, in all directions, according to all differences of position, and along all diameters. Thus the
first part of the recipient serves as a centre common to an infinity
of lines and rays; it is the inward terminus of all the rays, with which
they are *continuous*, whereas the part of the agent is the centre and
terminus with which they are *contiguous*. And since such multiplication (of whatever kind) is similar to the rays multiplied from a star,
we call every multiplication 'radiant', and we say that 'rays' are produced whether they are of light or colour or something else. And
there is another reason for these names, namely, that the multiplication of light is more apparent to us than the multiplication of other
things, and therefore we transfer the [terminology of the] multiplication of light to the others.

   But it should be recognized that the lines along which multiplication occurs must be straight, in so far as the nature of multiplication
determines, until they meet impediments that cause reflection and

54 sit: sic *L om. B*   55 stellis *S*   57 huius *FA*   58 nominationis: vocationis
SA   59 lucis … multiplicationem: *mg. O*   61 sed: s. septem *S*   62 ex: a *O*
de *S*   63 et: aut *O*

fractionis aut mutentur propter anime necessitatem, ut patebit
65 inferius. Et post impedimentum, non cessant multiplicationes, quin
vadant super rectas lineas quantum est de se. Quod autem multiplicatio
ex natura sua appetat fieri secundum rectas lineas auctores aspectuum,
precipue Ptolomeus et Alhacen, determinant; et per experimenta
docent ad sensum quomodo multiplicatio in omnibus rebus inanimatis
70 currit per lineas rectas donec per obstaculum redeat et faciat angulum,
aut per corpus secundum alterius raritatis, quod est magis vel minus
rarum, occurrens aliud a primo, in quod secundum corpus multiplicatio
cadens non perpendiculariter facit angulum, ut patebit satis inferius.
Et Iacobus Alkindi in *Libro de aspectibus* dicit hoc manifestum esse
75 ex rectitudine finium umbrarum corporum et ex luminibus per fenes-
tras ingredientibus. Unde hoc ita manifestum est ex huiusmodi communibus considerationibus quod non est necesse querere experimenta
secreta nisi propter pulcritudinem operationum nature.

Sed sciendum quod huiusmodi linee super quas est multiplicatio
80 non sunt habentes solam longitudinem inter duo puncta extensam, sed
earum quelibet est habens latitudinem et profunditatem, sicut auctores
aspectuum determinant. Alhacen in quarto libro hoc ostendit, quod
omnis radius qui venit a parte corporis habet necessario latitudinem
et profunditatem, sicut longitudinem. Et similiter Iacobus Alkindi
85 dicit quod impressio similis est cum eo a quo fit; imprimens autem
corpus est habens tres dimensiones, quare radius habet corporalem
proprietatem. Et addit quod radius non est secundum lineas rectas
inter quas sunt intervalla, sed multiplicatio est continua; quare
non carebit latitudine. Et tertio dicit quod illud quod caret latitudine
90 et profunditate et longitudine non sentitur visu; radius igitur non
videtur, quod falsum est. Et scimus quod radius non potest transire
nisi per aliquam partem medii; sed quelibet pars medii est habens
trinam dimensionem.

Sed oportet hic descendere ulterius ad omnes modos linearum
95 super quas est multiplicatio possibilis, quoniam licet natura appetat
operari super lineas rectas, tamen quando impeditur aliquando vel
alias propter necessitatem aliquam mutat incessum speciei et facit
eam decurrere super lineas non rectas. Et quibus modis hoc fiat
intendo nunc declarare.

67 fieri: tantum *S*   68 precipue: *interl.* L^C *om.* *L'* | Ptolomeus: philosophus *F* |
determinat *B*   71 secundum: scilicet *O* | raritatis: diafanitatis *SA* | vel *FO*: et *BLN*
71-2 quod . . . rarum: *om. SA*   73 facit: frangitur et f. *SA*   74 Alkindi: *om. B* |
hoc: *scr. et del.* *F* | esse: est *O* est e. *F*   76 ex: quod *F*   76-7 communibus:
omnibus *O*   77 querere: *ex* communicare *corr.* *L*   78 secreta: secta *B* | nisi . . .
nature: *om.* *L* | propter: per *O*   82 ostendit: *ex* causa *corr.* *L*   83 qui: vel linea
que *SA* | a: ex *SA*   85 ea *S*   86-7 quare . . . proprietatem: *mg.* *O*   87 et . . .
quod: quare *O*   88 quare: que *B*   89 illud quod: res que *O*   90 visui *F*

refraction or are altered for the sake of the soul's needs, as will be evident below.[8] And the multiplications do not cease at these impediments, but continue along straight lines in so far as it is up to them. Now, that multiplication desires by nature to occur along straight lines is determined by the authors of works on optics, especially Ptolemy and Alhazen;[9] and they show by sensible experiments how multiplication runs along straight lines in all inanimate substances until it is turned back by an obstacle and forms an angle—or else by a second medium of different rarity (more or less rare), in which an obliquely incident multiplication passing from the first medium to the second forms an angle [with the line of multiplication in the first medium], as will be sufficiently evident below.[10] And Jacob Alkindi says in *De aspectibus* that this is manifest from the rectilinear boundaries of the shadows cast by bodies and from light entering [a dark room] through windows.[11] And since this is so plainly evident from common observations of this sort, we need not seek esoteric experiments, unless for the sake of [appreciating] the beauty of nature's operations.

It is to be understood that the lines along which multiplication occurs do not consist of length alone, extended between two points, but all of them have width and depth [as well], as the authors of books on optics determine. Alhazen demonstrates in his fourth book that every ray coming from a part of a body necessarily has width and depth, as well as length.[12] Similarly, Jacob Alkindi says that an impression is similar to that which produces it;[13] now, the impressing body has three dimensions, and therefore the ray has [this same] corporeal property. And he adds that rays do not consist of straight lines between which are intervals, but that multiplication is continuous, and therefore it does not lack width.[14] And, in the third place, he says that whatever lacks width, depth, and length is not perceived by sight;[15] therefore a ray [if it were to lack width and depth] would be unseen, which it is not. And we know that a ray must pass through some part of the medium; but every part of the medium has three dimensions.

We must now consider all kinds of lines along which multiplication is possible, since, although nature prefers to act along straight lines, when the rectilinear path is impeded (or some other necessity presents itself) nature alters the path of a species and makes it travel along nonrectilinear paths. And I now intend to describe the modes in which this occurs.

PARS II
CAPITULUM 2

Secundum vero quinque modos linearum potest fieri hec multiplicatio. Prima est protensa ab agente in continuum et directum, et vocatur
5 recta, super quam currit generatio speciei quousque medium, hoc est corpus, in quo multiplicatur est uniforme, scilicet unius raritatis, ut est aer vel aqua vel aliud, et non recipit obstaculum, nec sit medium animatum, ut in humoribus contentis in nervis sensuum, et principalem habeat multiplicationem non accidentalem; quia hiis
10 modis quatuor currit multiplicatio speciei super lineam habentem angulum (ξ).

Dyaphanum enim et dyaphonum, perspicuum, et pervium, transparens, translucens, et lucidum (luce transeunte, non fixa), et rarum: hec omnia idem significant secundum rem, sed differunt secundum
15 considerationes aliquas. Nam rarum dicit dispositionem corporis absolute, secundum quod partes eius remote iacent, ut est aer et aqua et huiusmodi. Alia dicuntur per comparationem ad sensum vel sensibile secundum quod species eorum potest transire, ut patet in aqua et aere et spera ignis et orbibus planetarum extra corpus earum; nam
20 visus penetrat hec omnia, et species rerum penetrant ipsa. Et dyaphanum idem est quod duplicis apparitionis, scilicet in superficie et profundo; nam phano Grece idem est quod apparitio Latine, et dya idem est quod duo. Et phonos est sonus; unde dyaphonum quasi duplicis sonoritatis, tam scilicet in imo quam in summo. Lucidum vero
25 dicitur dupliciter: vel illud quod habet lumen innatum, sicut ignis, carbo, flamma, et stella, vel quod de se non lucet, sed est medium in luce per quod transit, ut aer vel aqua et ignis in sua spera et orbes planetarum. Unde Aristoteles dicit secundo *De anima* quod color est motivus visus secundum actum lucidi, id est medii illuminati, ut
30 aeris vel alterius. Et in primo *Metheororum* dicit quod ignis est lucidus in spera sua; sed tamen non habet lucem fixam sed transeuntem, quia non habet lucem fixam nisi in carbone et flamma. Densum vero opponitur omnibus istis, sed primo et per se contrariatur raro,

2 capitulum secundum *mg. O*   3 linearum: *mg. F*   4 est: cum *S*   5 super: supra *O* / quousque: *ex* quoque *corr. O* / medium: *om. O*   5–6 hoc est corpus: *om. SA* hoc c. *O*   6 est: *om. L* / scilicet: et *A* / raritatis: diafanitatis *SA*   7 *post* aliud *scr. et del. L* tis(!) in nervis sensuum / nec: ut *F*   8 animatum: *mg. O* / ut: in *S* / humoribus: honoribus *B* humoris *F* / nervis: *om. B*   9 habebit *S* / accidentale *B* accidentalem ut tangetur *SA*   12 enim: *om. SA* / pervium: parvum *B*   13 luce: et l. *L* 14 signant *O*   15 alias *S*   16 absolutam *S om. B* / remote *O*: propinque *FLSA* propinqua *B* propinque non *N*   18 patet: *om. O*   19 corpora *FO* / earum *SA*: eorum *BFLO*   22 phanos *S* / apparitio *OSN*: apparet *F* appareo *BLA*   23 phanos *O* phones *S* / dyaphanum *FO*   25 lumen innatum: lucem innatam *F*   26 quod: que *B* / non: *om. B* / lucet: habet lucem *S* / sed: ut *S*   27 per: *om. B* / aer vel aqua:

PART II
CHAPTER 2

Now this multiplication can occur along five kinds of line. The first is the line extended continuously and directly from the agent, and it is called the 'direct' line; and the generation of a species proceeds along this line provided the medium (that is, the body) in which it is multiplied is uniform (that is, of a single rarity), as air or water or some other substance, and no obstacle is encountered, and there is no animated medium (such as the humours contained in the nerves of the sense organs), and we have [only] the principal multiplication without the accidental;[1] for if any of these four conditions is not met, the species is multiplied along a bent line (ξ).[2]

Now 'diaphanous' (or 'diaphonous'), 'perspicuous', 'pervious', 'transparent', 'translucent', 'lucid' (in the sense of light in transit rather than fixed), and 'rare'—all these terms have the same meaning as far as the thing [itself] is concerned, but differ according to certain [other] considerations. For 'rare' designates the disposition of body absolutely, according as its parts are widely separated[3] from each other, as in air and water and the like. The other terms are employed in relation to sense or sensible objects, according as their species are able to pass through [the medium so designated], as we observe in water, air, the sphere of fire, and the planetary spheres apart from the bodies of the planets; for sight penetrates all of these, as do the species of [visible] things. And 'dyaphanum' means 'double in appearance', that is, in the surface and in the interior; for 'phano' in Greek has the same meaning as 'appearance' in Latin, and 'dya' means 'two'.[4] But 'phonos' means 'sound', and therefore 'dyaphonum' means something like 'dual in sound', that is, in both the lowest and the highest.[5] 'Lucid' is applied in two ways: either to that which has innate light, as fire, charcoal, flame, and a star, or to that which does not itself shine but which serves as a medium for light and through which light passes, as air and water and fire (in its sphere) and the planetary orbs. Thus Aristotle says in *De anima*, book ii, that colour moves sight, according to the actuality of 'the lucid',[6] that is, of an illuminated medium, as air or some other substance. And in *Meteorology*, book i, he says that fire is 'lucid' in its sphere;[7] however, this is not a case of fixed light, but of light in transit, since fixed light exists only in coals and flame. Now the dense is opposed to all of these, but primarily and of itself it is the opposite of rarity, since the dense

aqua vel aer vel aqua *O* / et[1]: vel *S*   28 unde: *mg. O* / Aristoteles: anima *S*
29 visus: *mg. O*   31 habet: *mg. F*

quia densum est quod habet partes propinque iacentes; et mediante
35 raro opponitur aliis.

Si etiam medium sit duplex in natura et specie, et tamen conveniat
in dyaphanitate ordinata, ut accidit in confinio aeris et ignis, adhuc
est incessus rectus. Unde omnes radii qui transeunt a spera ignis
in speram aeris tenent incessum rectum et non faciunt angulum,
40 sicut inferius explanabitur suo loco. Et sic est de corporibus celestibus, nam orbes celestes, licet sint diversi in natura et specie, tamen
conveniunt in dyaphanitate, ut non impediatur incessus rectus quoad
iudicium sensus nostri. Si etiam sint media diverse dyaphanitatis
sensibiliter, ut est celum et ignis, similiter aer et aqua, tunc si species
45 venit perpendiculariter super ea, adhuc fit incessus rectus, nec
fit angulus. Unde omnes radii qui cadunt perpendiculariter super
corpora mundi, hoc est in centrum mundi, tenent incessum rectum in
illis corporibus. Sed quando species non cadit perpendiculariter
super corpus secundum diverse dyaphanitatis a primo, tunc mutatur
50 incessus, nec fit rectus in corpore secundo secundum incessum quem
habuit in primo; sed in ingressu speciei in corpus secundum, incipit
declinare ab incessu recto ad dextram vel sinistram, et facit angulum.

Et hoc est proprie fractio speciei et incessus fractus, secundum quod
moderni utuntur. Sed tamen auctores aspectuum vocant reflexionem,
55 et ab eis vocatur species reflexa et radius reflexus. Sed quia aliter
utimur reflexione, et similiter ipsi auctores, et magis proprie, sicut
postea scietur, ideo imputandum est vitio translationis, que non
distinxit in Latino equivocationem et dubietatem alterius lingue. Et
ideo apud Ptolomeum et Alhacen et ceteros valde cavendum est quod
60 sciatur quando accipitur reflexio pro fractione et quando non, et
maxime primo libro et secundo et septimo Alhacen, ubi multum
accipitur reflexio pro fractione, et similiter apud libros Ptolomei ei
conformes.

Sed quoniam fractio non plene intelligitur sine incessu recto et
65 perpendiculari ducenda a loco fractionis in corpus secundum, ideo
ponam exemplum, ubi traham perpendicularem et incessum rectum et
fractionem in aere et aqua. Quando enim species descendit ab aere in

---

36 *ante* si *add.* B sciendum etiam quod durum et solidum hic sunt idem et non densum
nam cristallus est dura et solida sed non est densa sed rara vitrum similiter et multa que
pervia sunt visui / si: si vero *FO*   37 adhuc: ad hoc *L*   38 incensus *B* / qui: *ex* que
mg. corr. F   39 incessunt *B*   40 *post* loco *add.* SA per eorum demonstrationem
41 tamen: *om.* L   42 rectus: *om.* F / quoad: quod *B*   42-3 quoad . . . nostri:
om. S secundum iudicium sensus n. *A*   43 etiam: autem *O*   45 eam *SA* / fit: sit *B*
46 fit: adhuc f. *S*   47 rectum: per r. *S*   51 in[1]: et *S* / recipit *B*   52 dextrum
vel sinistrum *F* / angulum: *om.* F *mg.* O   53 hec *O*   54 tamen: *om.* F /
ante reflexionem *mg. add.* O fractionem   55 eis: aliis *S*   58 et[1]: vel *SA*
59 Ptolomeum: *ex* fit hominum *corr.* L / quod: ut *B om.* F   60 sciatur: *om.* F non
s. *S* / accipit *B*   61 Alhacen: *om.* FO   62 Ptolomei: philosophi *F* / eis *S*

is that which has its parts close together; and it is opposed to the others through its opposition to rarity.

If a medium should be binary in nature and kind, and yet [its two parts] agree in their [divinely] ordained transparency,[8] as at the interface between [the spheres of] air and fire, the path [of radiation] is nevertheless rectilinear. Therefore, all rays that pass from the sphere of fire to the sphere of air maintain a rectilinear path and do not for form an angle, as will be explained below in its place.[9] And this is also true of celestial bodies, for the celestial orbs, though different in nature and kind, nevertheless agree in transparency, so that rectilinear propagation is not impeded as far as sense can judge. Also, if there should be media of sensibly different transparencies, as heaven and fire or air and water, then if a species falls on them[10] perpendicularly, propagation is still rectilinear and no angle is formed. Therefore, all rays that fall perpendicularly on the bodies of the world (that is, fall towards the centre of the world) retain their rectilinearity in those bodies. But when a species falls obliquely on a second body whose transparency differs from that of the first, then its course is altered, and the straight line in the second body does not have the same direction as in the first body; but upon entering the second body, the species begins to deviate from the direct path, to the right or the left, and forms an angle.

This is properly speaking the 'refraction' of a species and a 'refracted path', according to the usage of modern authors. However, the authors of books on optics speak of it as 'reflection' and a 'reflected species' and a 'reflected ray'. But since we use 'reflection' in another sense, as do these authors themselves (and more properly, as will be shown later),[11] we therefore blame imperfect translations, which failed to distinguish in Latin the equivocations and ambiguities of the other language. And so in the works of Ptolemy and Alhazen and others, one must take great care to discern when 'reflection' is used to mean 'refraction' and when not, and especially in the first, second, and seventh books of Alhazen, where 'reflection' is often used for 'refraction', and also in the books of Ptolemy, which follow the same pattern.[12]

Now since refraction cannot be fully understood without [knowledge of the meaning of] 'the direct path' and 'the perpendicular extended into the second body from the point of refraction', I therefore present an example, in which I draw a perpendicular and the direct path and [the line of] refraction between air and water. For when a species descends obliquely from air into water, it must be

65 ducenda: ducendo est (*del.* est) *O*   66–7 ubi . . . fractionem: de hoc *SA*   67 aqua *BLAN:* aquam *FOS*

aqua non perpendiculariter, oportet quod frangatur, et cadet fractio
inter incessum rectum et perpendicularem ducendam a loco fractionis
70 (o). In spericis vero corporibus perpendicularis cadit in centrum
spere. Et quia facta est mentio de fractione in corporibus mundi
spericis, ideo nunc subiungam exemplum in eis, et inferius in planis
et secundum omnes modos spericorum, ubi in particulari dicetur de
natura fractionis. Sit igitur agens A [fig. 1], ut avis in aere vel nubes
75 vel aliud; et medium subtilius sit aer, et densius sit aqua. A igitur
facit perpendiculariter et non perpendiculariter suam speciem per
medium aeris et aque. Quando vero illa species venit non perpendiculariter ad superficiem aque, invenit medium densius; et ideo oportet
quod mutet incessum suum rectum, et declinet ab eo, et faciat angu-
80 lum; et transibit usque D, relinquens incessum, que vadit ad B, quia

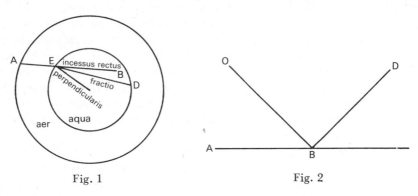

Fig. 1   Fig. 2

frangitur inter incessum rectum et perpendicularem ducendam a loco
fractionis, qui est E. Quomodo vero multis aliis modis fiat fractio
patebit inferius; sufficit enim nunc ut videatur in universali qualiter
frangitur radius per angulum declinando ab incessu recto.
85   Si vero corpus secundum non differt in dyaphanitate a primo, sed
omnino est densum ita quod potest impedire transitum speciei, tunc
species sumens occasionem a denso redit in partem alteram ex propria
virtute; ut cum non possit se multiplicare in densum corpus, multiplicat se in primo corpore, faciens angulum; et dicitur species reflexa
90 proprie et in communi usu apud omnes. Nec tamen repellitur per
violentiam, sed solum sumit occasionem a denso impediente transitum,
et vadit per aliam viam ut possibile est ei. Sic sit AB [fig. 2] densum

68 cadat *S*   69 perpendicularem *OAN*: perpendiculariter *BFLS* / ducenda *S*
70 cadit: *om. S* / centrum *OSA*: centra *BFL*   72 exemplum in: etiam *S*   74 sit: sic
B / aere: a est *S*   75 A: *om. B*   76 perpendiculariter[1,2]: perpendiculos *S*   77 illa:
om. S   77–8 perpendiculat *S*   78 ideo oportet: imo *S*   79 suum: *om. B* / et[2]:
ut *B* / faciet *F*   80 D: ad D *O* / delinquens *B* / incessum *V*[c]: densum *BLOSAN* quem
densum *F* / ad: a *S*   82 que *F* / E: C *B* / fiat: fit *FO*   83 universaliter *B*
85 in: a *S*   86 densum . . . tunc: *om. S*   87 sumens: sumit *S om. F*   88 se:

refracted, and the refracted ray falls between the direct path and the perpendicular drawn from the point of refraction (o). Now, in spherical bodies, the perpendicular is drawn to the centre of the sphere. And since mention has been made of refraction in the spherical bodies of the world, I here attach an example of this, and below I shall give examples of plane surfaces and all kinds of spherical surfaces, where the nature of refraction will be discussed in detail. Therefore, let A [fig. 1] be the agent (a bird or cloud or something else) in air; and let air be the subtler medium and water the denser. A produces its species both perpendicularly and nonperpendicularly through the media of air and water. When the species falls non-perpendicularly on the surface of the water, it meets a denser medium, and therefore it must alter its rectilinear course and deviate

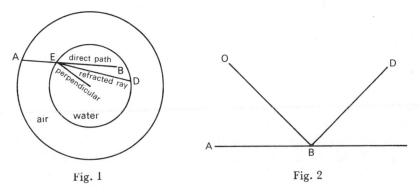

Fig. 1   Fig. 2

from it and form an angle; thus it will pass to D, abandoning its line of approach (which goes to B), since it is refracted between the direct path and the perpendicular drawn from the point of refraction, E. But how the many other modes of refraction occur will be evident below; it suffices at present to see in general how the ray is refracted through an angle by deviating from its direct line of approach.

However, if the second body does not differ in transparency from the first, but is entirely dense, so that it can prevent the passage of a species, then the species, seizing the occasion from [the presence of] the dense body, returns by its own power in the direction from which it came; thus, since it could not multiply itself in the dense body, it multiplies itself in the original medium, forming an angle; and it is properly (and in the common usage of everybody) called a 'reflected species'. However, it is not forcibly repelled, but merely seizes the occasion from the dense body blocking its path and proceeds along another path open to it. Thus let AB [fig. 2] be the dense

et O agens. Species igitur veniens ad AB non potest transire, et ideo
constituit angulum et redit per lineam BD. Prima vero species, que
95 est OB, vocatur species vel radius incidentie, quia incidit ad densum,
et alia pars vocatur reflexa vel conversa; et tamen tota multiplicatio
vocatur reflexa vel conversa, et denominatur pars a toto.

Quarta linea est tortuosa super quam venit species aliquando.
Et hoc non est in medio inanimato; impossibile enim est quod agens
100 in medium inanimatum faciat speciem tortuose, sed recte, ut prius
ostensum est. Sed in medio animato per virtutem anime, dirigitur
species secundum exigentiam operationum anime; et quia operationes
anime circa species fiunt in nervis tortuosis, sequitur species
tortuositatem nervi propter necessitatem operationum anime. Unde
105 species tangibilium currunt per fila nervorum tortuosa ab ipsa cute
corporis per vias flexuosas usque ad instrumentum tactus, quod
radicatur iuxta cor. Et similiter est de specie gustus, quod currit
per nervum lingue continuatum flexuose usque ad prope cor, quia
organa radicalia istarum duarum virtutum sunt prope cor, ut
110 Aristoteles dicit *Libro de animalibus.* Similiter species omnium sensibilium vadunt ad cor, quia ibi est radicaliter virtus sensitiva, sicut
Aristoteles et Avicenna determinant. Sed nervi sic a sensibus usque
ad cor extensi habent multas flexuositates, et ideo species incedit
per lineam tortuosam. Et hoc Alhacen determinat in pluribus locis
115 in libro suo.

Quinta autem linea super quam vadit species differt ab omnibus
predictis, quia scilicet non venit ab agente, sed ab aliqua dictarum
linearum quatuor; et ideo non venit a re faciente speciem, sed a
specie. Unde species super eam decurrens est species speciei, sicut
120 lux in angulo domus venit a radio solari cadente per fenestram. Nam
radius ille venit a sole super lineam rectam, fractam, vel reflexam;
et ideo est multiplicatio principalis. Sed lux ista que a radio venit
ad partes alias domus est multiplicatio accidentalis. Et quod omnino
alia sit multiplicatio hec a predictis non solum patet per dictam,
125 sed per hoc quod oculus per eam non videbit agens principale,
sed eius speciem principalem, rectam vel fractam vel reflexam,
quoniam oculus in angulo domus non videt solem, sed radium

93 veniens: v. ab O *O*   94–5 que est: *om. O*   95 OB: O *F* / OB . . . species: *mg. O*
96–7 et² . . . conversa: *om. SA*   100 in: et *B* / faciat: *om. F*   104 operationum
BSA: operum *FLO*   106 flexuosas: *ex* reflexuosas *corr. O* / tactus: totius *FO*
107 quod: quia *B*   111 radicaliter: radicabiliter *B ex* radicabiliter *corr. L*   112 sic:
sunt *S*   120 radio: stellis r. *F*   122 radio: medio *S*   124 dictam:
predictam *O*   125 per eam: postea *S*

body and O the agent. A species coming to AB cannot pass through, and therefore it forms an angle and returns by line BD. The first species, OB, is called the 'incident' species or ray, since it is incident on the dense body, and the other part is called the 'reflected' or 'converted' species or ray; nevertheless, the entire multiplication is also called 'reflected' or 'converted', for the part is named from the whole.

The fourth line along which a species sometimes comes is the twisting path.[13] And this does not occur in an inanimate medium; for an agent cannot produce a species along a twisting path in an inanimate medium, but only in a straight line, as was shown above.[14] But in a medium animated by the power of the soul, a species is directed according to the requirements of the soul's operations; and since the operations of the soul with regard to species occur in the twisting nerves, the species follows the twisting of the nerve because of the necessity of the operations of the soul. Thus the species of tangible things run through the twisting threads of the nerves from the skin of the body through winding paths to the instrument of touch, which has its seat near the heart. And it is the same for the species of taste, which runs through the nerve of the tongue extending circuitously to a place near the heart; for the basic organs of these two faculties are near the heart, as Aristotle says in *De animalibus*.[15] Similarly, the species of all sensible things go to the heart, since there the sensitive power has its seat, as Aristotle and Avicenna determine.[16] But the nerves thus extended from the senses to the heart have many bends, and therefore a species proceeds along a twisting path. And Alhazen determines this in many parts of his book.[17]

The fifth line along which a species proceeds differs from all the aforementioned, since it does not come from the agent [itself], but from any of the four aforementioned lines; and therefore it comes not from the object that produces the species, but from the species. Thus the species travelling along this line is the species of a species, just as the light in the corner of a house comes [not directly from the sun, but] from the solar ray entering through the window. For the latter ray comes from the sun along a rectilinear, refracted, or reflected path; and therefore it is the principal multiplication. But the light that comes from the [principal] ray to other parts of the house is an accidental multiplication. And that this multiplication is altogether different from the aforementioned multiplications is evident not only from the foregoing, but also from the fact that the eye cannot see the principal agent by means of it, but only the principal species of the agent (rectilinear, refracted, or reflected)—for an eye situated in a corner of the house does not see the sun, but the ray

cadentem per foramen vel fenestram vel aliam aperturam; quod si
ponatur ad radium principalem, videbit solem. Et Plinius dicit secundo
130 *Naturalium*, et scitur per experientiam, quod oculus existens in
profundo putei videret stellas fixas de die, quia radii solis principales non cadunt in puteum, sed accidentales tantum, et ideo non
impeditur oculus in contuitione stellarum per radios principales
earum cadentes in puteum. Sed existens in superficie putei, recipit
135 impedimentum per radios principales solis, qui sunt fortiores longe
quam radii principales stellarum, propter quod occultantur a visu,
quia maior lux abscondit minorem. Que etiam multiplicatio accidentalis specierum celestium et aliarum rerum plurium magis est
necessaria hominibus et ceteris animalibus et multis rebus quam
140 multiplicatio principalis, quia ille res non possunt continue sustinere
species principales.

PARS II

CAPITULUM 3

Et quatinus hec plenius cognoscantur, oportet nos descendere in
particulari ad has lineas propter actionem specierum in hoc mundo,
5 de qua dicetur inferius, quia nisi sciatur varietas multiplicationis
non potest sciri diversitas actionis. Notum est autem satis quod
species veniens super lineam rectam potest dici cadere ad lineam vel
ad superficiem. Si ad lineam, tunc cadit vel ad rectam vel ad convexam
vel concavam vel tortuosam. Si ad rectam, vel cadit ad angulos rectos
10 vel obliquos. Si ad convexam, tunc vel cadit ad angulos obtusos
equales, si per centrum transeat, ut in quarta parte huius tractatus
ostensum est; vel ad unum obtusum et alium acutum, si non vadat per
centrum. Si ad concavam, tunc potest cadere ad equales quorum uterque est acutorum maximus, qui sunt anguli semicirculi, si per centrum
15 transeat; vel ad obliquos inequales, qui sunt anguli portionum
maioris et minoris. Si vero super tortuosam, tunc vel cadit super
partem rectam vel concavam vel convexam, et variatur multiplicatio
sicut prius. Et hec omnia patent ex quarta parte, et diversificant

129 dicit: docet in *F*   131 videt *FO*   133 contuitione: *om. B*
134–5 earum . . . principales: *mg. O*   136 quam: quod *B* / principales: *om. S*
137 etiam: *om. O*   140 ille: alie *S*
    2 capitulum tertium *mg. O* tertium capitulum habens duas conclusiones *mg. L*   5 in-
ferius: *om. F*   8 vel[1]: *om. L* / ad[4]: *om. S*   10 si: sed *B*   11 vel equales *S* /
quatuor *BS* / huiusmodi *S*   12 acutum: rectum (*corr. ex* obtusum) *O ex* vacutum

entering through a hole or window or other aperture, whereas if it is exposed to the principal ray, it will see the sun. And Pliny says in his *Natural History*, book ii, and it is also known from experience, that an eye located at the bottom of a well can see the fixed stars during the day, since the principal rays of the sun do not enter the well, but only the accidental rays, and therefore the eye is not prevented from seeing the stars by means of their principal rays, which do enter the well.[18] However, an eye situated at the top of the well is hindered by the principal solar rays, which are far stronger than the principal stellar rays, and therefore the latter are hidden from sight, since a greater light conceals a lesser. Also, this accidental multiplication of the species of celestial and many other things is of greater necessity to mankind and other animals and many things than is the principal multiplication, since these things cannot continuously endure the principal species.[19]

PART II
CHAPTER 3

So that these matters will be better understood, we must deal in more detail with these lines [of propagation, which are of interest] because of the action of species in this world, concerning which we will speak below; for unless the varieties of multiplication are known, the diversity of action cannot be understood. It is sufficiently understood that a species proceeding along a straight line is said to be incident on a line or a surface. If incident on a line, this line must be straight, concave, convex,[1] or twisting. If it is straight, the species is incident either at right angles or at oblique angles. If the line is convex, the species is incident either at equal obtuse angles (if it is directed towards the centre [of curvature], as we have shown in the fourth part of this treatise),[2] or at an obtuse angle and an acute angle (if it is not directed towards the centre). If the line is concave, the species can be incident at equal angles, each of which is the maximum acute angle, that is, the angle of a semicircle[3] (if the species is directed towards the centre), or at unequal oblique angles, which are angles of portions of a [circle, one] larger and [one] smaller [than a semicircle].[4] But if the line is twisting, then the species falls on either a straight or a concave or a convex part, and multiplication varies as above. All these things are evident from the fourth part [of this treatise], and they

corr. *S* / vadat: cadat *O*　　　　15 ab obliquo *B* / equales *B* inquales inquales(!) *S* / que *F*

actionem speciei in hoc mundo, ut patebit. Et similiter multiplicatio
20 cadens ad lineas dictas vel est perpendicularis vel non, secundum
quas multum variatur actio nature; que autem sint perpendiculares et
que non ad singulas lineas dictas patuit ex quarta parte et patebit
postea quantum necesse est.

Si vero dicatur species recta venire ad superficiem vel corpus
25 (quod idem est, cum non cadat super corpus nisi quia super aliquam
superficiem), tunc cadit super superficiem planam vel concavam vel
convexam; in quibus multum diversificatur actio naturalis, et maxime
secundum quod concava et convexa dividuntur in sperica, pyramidalia, et columnaria, et ovalia, et anulosa, et lenticularia. Hec enim
30 specialiter diversificant actionem specierum venientium ad ea, propter
diversitatem suarum superficierum, ad quas cadunt species perpendiculariter et non perpendiculariter, secundum diversas positiones et
modos varios iuxta proprietatem singularum superficierum dictorum
corporum. Nec est notabilis diversitas nisi in dictis corporibus reci-
35 pientibus species agentium, quoniam corpora que habent superficies
concavas vel convexas in quibus est notabilis varietas actionis
naturalis sunt sperica vel pyramidalia vel columnaria vel ovalia
vel anulosa vel lenticularia; cetera habent planas superficies.

Similiter oportet secundo sciri quod diversificatur multiplicatio
40 super lineas fractas; et fractio est duobus modis. Quando igitur
medium secundum est densius, tunc fractio speciei est in superficie
corporis secundi inter incessum rectum et perpendicularem ducendam
a loco fractionis in corpus secundum; et declinat ab incessu recto
in profundum corporis secundi, dividens angulum qui est inter in-
45 cessum rectum et perpendicularem ducendam a loco fractionis in
corpus secundum. Non tamen dividit illum angulum semper in duas
partes equales, licet hoc senserunt aliqui, quoniam secundum diversitatem densitatis medii secundi accidit maior recessus et minor
fractionis ab incessu recto, secundum quod Ptolomeus in quinto
50 *Aspectuum* et Alhacen in septimo determinant quantitates angulorum
fractionis multipliciter diversificari. Nam quanto corpus secundum est

19 in: ita *F*   20 perpendiculariter *O*   21 que: quod *B*   22 que: eque *B* |
non: *om. S* | patuit: patet *FO*   23 necessarium *FO*   25 vadat *S* | super²: per
mg. O | aliam *F*   25–6 aliquam ... cadit: *mg. O*   26 super: s. aliquam *O*
28 dividunt *S*   29 ovaria *S* | et anulosa: *om. O*   30 specialiter: s. corpora *S*
31 cadit *B*   32 positiones: rationes *F*   34 notabilis: vocabilis *B*   35 corpus *BL*
36 notabilis: vocabilis *B* | varietas: diversitas vel v. *O*   37 ovaria *B*   38 cetera:
nam c. *O* c. autem *S*   39 secundo sciri: *om. B*   42 incessum: casum *B*   43 et:
quod et *O*   44 dividens: dicens *B*   46–7 duas partes: *ex* duos rectos *corr. F*

diversify the action of a species in this world, as will be evident.
Similarly, multiplication incident on the said lines is either perpendicular or oblique, and according to this the action of nature
is greatly varied; however, which multiplications are perpendicular
and which nonperpendicular to the aforementioned lines was
evident in the fourth part and will be explained below in so far as
necessary.

But if it should be said that a rectilinear species comes to a surface
or body (which is the same thing, since it cannot be incident on a
body without being incident on some surface), then it falls on a
plane, concave, or convex surface; and natural action is greatly varied
among these, owing especially to the fact that concave and convex
are divided into spherical, pyramidal,[5] columnar,[6] oval, annular,[7] and
lenticular. For these especially diversify the action of the species
coming to them, owing to the diversity of their surfaces, on which
species are incident perpendicularly and nonperpendicularly, according to different orientations and various modes, as a function of the
properties of the individual surfaces of the said bodies. Nor is there
noticeable diversity except in the reception by the said bodies of the
species of agents, since the bodies having concave or convex surfaces
in which there is noticeable variety of natural action are spherical,
pyramidal, columnar, oval, annular, or lenticular; for the others have
plane surfaces.

It must be recognized, secondly, that multiplication is diversified
along refracted lines; and refraction occurs in two ways. When the
second medium is denser [than the first], refraction of the species
at the surface of the second substance takes place between the
direct path and the perpendicular extended into the second substance from the point of refraction;[8] thus it deviates from the direct
path into the depth of the second body and divides the angle
between the direct path and the perpendicular extended into the
second body from the point of refraction. Nevertheless, it does
not always divide that angle into two equal parts, although some
have thought it does,[9] since more or less deviation of the refracted
ray from the direct path occurs as a result of different densities of
the second medium, according to the manifold differences in the
angles of refraction determined by Ptolemy in *De aspectibus*, book v,
and Alhazen in book vii.[10] For the denser the second body, the more

47 hoc senserunt: senserint *S*   49 Ptolomeus: philosophus *BF*   51 secundum:
om. *F*

densius, tanto minus recedit fractio ab incessu recto, propter resistentiam medii densioris, densitas enim resistit radio, ut Alhacen dicit.
Quando vero corpus secundum est subtilius, tunc fit fractio speciei
55 in superficie corporis secundi ultra incessum rectum per recessum a
perpendiculari ducenda a loco fractionis; id est, quod inter fractionem
et perpendicularem illam cadat incessus rectus. Et variatur fractionis
et anguli quantitas secundum quod corpus subtilius est minus et
magis subtile.
60   Figurabo igitur in planis et spericis quomodo intelligantur radii
fracti et non fracti. Et primo in planis; et loquor de corpore secundo
plane superficiei, quia de eius figura est tota vis. Si ergo corpus
secundum sit plane superficiei, tunc radius veniens perpendiculariter
non frangitur, ut dictum est; sed omnes non perpendiculares frangun-
65 tur. Si igitur corpus secundum (quod est planum) est densius, tunc
fractio est, ut dictum est, inter incessum rectum et inter perpendicularem ducendam a loco fractionis in illud corpus secundum, hoc modo
[fig. 3]. Si vero corpus secundum est subtilius, tunc incessus rectus fit
inter fractionem et perpendicularem ducendam a loco fractionis, verbi
70 gratia [fig. 4]. Si vero corpus secundum quod sit spericum est densius
priori, tunc fiet fractio in superficie eius inter incessum rectum et

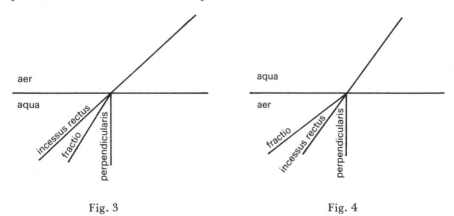

Fig. 3   Fig. 4

52 recedet *S*   53 *ante* resistit: *scr. et del. S* recessit   54 speciei: *mg. F*
55 per recessum: *om. F*   57 cadit *O* / fractionis: recessus f. *FOA* (recessus *mg. A*)
57-8 et²... quod: *spatium vacuum S*   60 intelliguntur *O*   63 radius: rarius *B*
64-5 franguntur: non f. *F*   65 plenum *F* / densus *B*   67 dicendam *B* /

the refracted species deviates from the direct path, on account of the resistance of the denser medium, for density resists the ray, as Alhazen says.[11] But when the second body is subtler [than the first], refraction of the species at the surface of the second body is beyond the direct path, by recession from the perpendicular drawn at the point of refraction; that is, the direct path falls between the refracted ray and the perpendicular. And the amount of refraction and the size of the angle vary as the subtler [second] body is more or less subtle.

Therefore, I will illustrate with diagrams the manner in which rays are understood to be refracted or unrefracted at plane and spherical surfaces. First, in plane surfaces; and I speak [here] concerning a second substance of plane surface, since the whole power [of refraction] depends on its shape. Therefore, if the second substance should have a plane surface, a ray incident on it perpendicularly is not refracted, as has been said; but all nonperpendicular rays are refracted. And if the second substance (which is plane) is denser, then, as has been said, the ray is refracted between the direct path and the perpendicular extended into the second substance from the point of refraction, in this manner [fig. 3]. But if the second substance is subtler, the direct path falls between the refracted ray and the perpendicular drawn from the point of refraction, as in the [following] example [fig. 4]. If, however, the second substance should be spherical and denser than the first, refraction would occur at its surface between the direct path and the

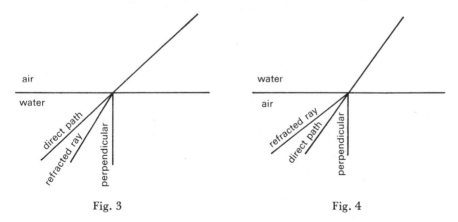

Fig. 3   Fig. 4

in . . . corpus: *om.* F   68 corpus: *om.* F / rectus: totius F   69–70 verba gratia:
mg. F

perpendicularem in centrum eius ducendam, hoc modo [fig. 5]. Si vero
corpus secundum sit subtilius, tunc incessus rectus fit inter perpendicularem ducendam a loco fractionis et inter ipsam fractionem, ut
75 patet in hac figura [fig. 6]. Et in hanc duplicem fractionem Ptolomeus

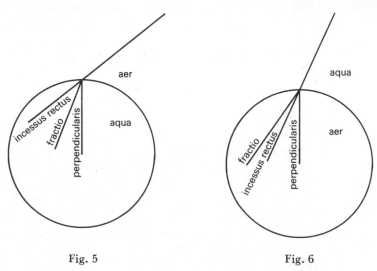

Fig. 5   Fig. 6

quinto *De aspectibus* et Alhacen septimo et omnes concordant; nec
potest aliter esse. Atque probant hoc per instrumenta, que docent
figurari ad hoc, ut videatur sensibiliter quomodo frangantur radii
non perpendiculares. Similiter probant has fractiones per causas et
80 experimenta.

Causam autem huius fractionis assignant per hoc, quod casus
speciei perpendicularis fortis est, sicut patet in lapide cadente
deorsum, si non obliquetur eius casus, ut si aliquis impediverit casum
perpendicularem et fecerit lapidem deviare ab incessu perpendiculari,
85 manifestum est sensui quod debilem faciet penetrationem. Unde homo
cadens perpendiculariter ab alto moritur ex casu; quod si aliquis
pellat eum ab incessu recto dum cadit, quatinus declinet ab incessu
perpendiculari, salvatur. Similiter ensis vel securis vel aliud natum
scindere, si aptetur a manu percutientis perpendiculariter super
90 lignum, penetrat et dividit illud; si oblique, tunc vel non scindet

72 ducenda *B* / post ducendam *mg. add. O* a loco fractionis   73 fit: sit *B*
74 ipsam: suam *O* / ut: *om. B* sic *SA*   75 patet . . . figura: *om. SA* hic *FO* / fractionem:
rep. S   76 nec: non *S*   77 potest: patet *B* / probatum *S* / instrumenta: infinita *F*
78 figurari: signari *S* / quomodo: quando *O* / frangantur *BFL*: franguntur *OSAN*   80 per
experimenta *S*   82 speciei: superficiei *F*   83 impediverit *FLSA*: impedierit *BON*
85 faciat *O*   86 perpendiculariter: perpendicularem p. *F* / ex: a *S* / aliquis: quis *S*

perpendicular leading to its centre, in this manner [fig. 5]. But if the second substance should be subtler, the direct path falls between the refracted ray and the perpendicular drawn from the point of refraction, as is evident in this figure [fig. 6]. And Ptolemy, in *De*

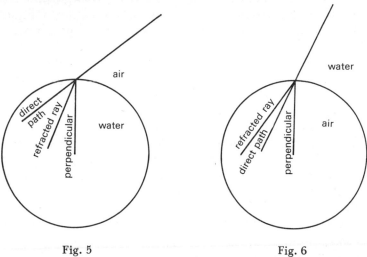

Fig. 5   Fig. 6

aspectibus, book v, and Alhazen, in book vii, and all [other authors] agree regarding this dual refraction;[12] nor can it be otherwise. And they prove this by means of instruments, which they show how to construct for this purpose, so that one can sensibly observe how non-perpendicular rays are refracted.[13] Likewise, they examine these refractions through [their] causes and through experiments.

However, they assign the cause of this refraction as follows.[14] Since the descent of a perpendicular species is strong, as is evident in a falling stone, provided its descent is not diverted from the vertical, if something should impede perpendicular descent and make the stone deviate from a perpendicular course, it is manifest to sense that its ability to penetrate is weakened.[15] Wherefore a man falling vertically from a high place is killed by the fall; but if something should divert him from his direct path as he descends, he is spared in so far as he diverges from perpendicular incidence. Similarly, if a sword or axe or some other instrument designed to cut is applied to a rod perpendicularly by the hand of the one wielding the instrument, it penetrates and divides the rod; [however,] if the instrument is applied obliquely, either it does not cut [at all]

vel minus longe quam quando fuit perpendicularis. Quod si corpus recipiens rem cadentem perpendiculariter resistet omnino, tunc res cadens perpendiculariter rediret propter incessus fortitudinem in eandem viam per quam incessit, sicut de pila iactata ad parietem vel
95 ad aliud resistens omnino. Et pila cadens ex obliquo laberetur ex altera parte incessus perpendicularis secundum casum obliquum, ut patet ad sensum; et non rediret in viam qua venit propter casus debilitatem. Experimenta de hiis sunt infinita.

Sed dyaphanum non omnino resistit speciei, ut redeat, hoc enim
100 facit solum corpus densum a quo fit reflexio. Quapropter species veniens super dyaphanum quodcunque pertransit in illud, sive cadat oblique sive perpendiculariter. Sed cum perpendicularis sit fortior et species obliqua debilior, non possunt eandem legem retinere in corpore dyaphano. Sed non est alia via quam incessus rectus vel
105 declinatus. Et incessus rectus fortior est; quapropter ille debetur speciei perpendiculari, ut recte incedat in secundo corpore sicut in primo; et declinatus speciei oblique competere necesse est. Et ideo perpendicularis species non declinat; nec frangitur, quia declinatio est fractio; sed obliqua frangetur in superficie secundi corporis
110 propter hoc, quod dyaphanum resistit ei magis quam perpendiculari propter debilitatem eius et fortitudinem perpendicularis; omne enim dyaphanum habet aliquid grossitiei, unde potest aliquantulum resistere et impedire transitum speciei. Determinata enim est, ut dicit Alhacen in septimo, natura dyaphanitatis in rebus naturalibus, ut non vadat
115 in infinitum, sed stet ad aliquam grossitiem etiam in celesti corpore. Propter quod tam perpendicularis quam obliqua species impedietur aliquantulum, sed magis species obliqua. Non enim aufertur perpendiculari rectitudo incessus propter eius fortitudinem, sed tamen successio maior causatur in suo transitu propter grossitiem medii qualemcunque.
120 Si enim esset vacuum medium sine omni grossitie naturali, et posset transire lux in eo seu etiam quodcunque corpus, fieret ibi successio que esset causata a parte medii solum propter prius et posterius ipsius spatii, et non propter medii grossitiem resistentem. Sed in medio naturali pleno, quod habet aliquam grossitiem naturalem, opor-
125 tet quod ratione grossitiei, que non omnino cedit nec omnino resistit,

91 perpendiculariter *S* iacta *corr. O.*): iacta *BFL* laberetur: labetur *O* haberetur *SA* lariter *S om. O* / obliquum: *om. S* propterea *O*   101 quocunque *BS*   102 cum: tamen *O* / perpendicularis: perpendiculariter *F* / sit: fit *F* species *O*   106 rectus *O*   107 declinatur *BL* 108 reclinat *B*   109 *post* corporis *add. SA* et non incedit recte in eo sicut in primo 110 quod: quia *S*   115 etiam: et *L om. F*   116 propter: *om. F* / tam *L*^C: cano(?) *L'* / obliqua *L*^C: aliqua *L'* / impedietur *LOSA*: impediretur *F* impediatur *B*   117 species: *om. F* / aufertur: impeditur *S a. a O*   119 propter: per *B*   121 fieret: *om. O*

94 per . . . incessit: in quid incepit *S* / iactata *SANO* (*ex* 95 ex^1: *om. O* omnino *scr. et del. F* / oblique *FO* / 96 altera: alia *FO* / perpendicularis: perpendiculariter *F* / 97 in: ad *B*   100 inflexio *S* / quapropter:

or it cuts much less than when perpendicular. But if the body that receives an object incident perpendicularly should resist it altogether, the incident object would return along the same path by which it approached because of the strength of its approach, as a ball thrown against a wall or something else that altogether resists [penetration]. And a ball incident obliquely would deviate towards the other side of the perpendicular in accordance with the obliquity of its incidence, as is evident to sense; and, because of the weakness of its incidence, it would not return along the path by which it approached. Experiences of these things are without number.

But a transparent substance does not altogether resist [penetration by] a species, causing it to return, for only a dense substance, which produces reflection, does that. Wherefore, a species incident on any transparent substance penetrates it, whether incident obliquely or perpendicularly. But since a perpendicular species is stronger and an oblique species weaker, both cannot behave according to the same law in the transparent body. But there is no path except a direct and a bent course. Now, since the direct course is the stronger, it characterizes a perpendicular species, allowing the latter to proceed along the same straight line in the second body as in the first; and a bent path is necessarily possessed by an oblique species. Therefore, a perpendicular species does not bend; nor is it refracted, since refraction is bending; but an oblique species is refracted at the surface of the second body, since it is more strongly resisted by the transparent body than is the perpendicular species, owing to the weakness of the oblique species and the strength of the perpendicular species; for every transparent body possesses some coarseness, by which it is able to resist somewhat and to impede the passage of a species. As Alhazen says in book vii, transparency in natural things is limited so that it does not proceed to infinity, and there is some coarseness even in celestial substance.[16] Consequently, both perpendicular and oblique species are somewhat impeded, but oblique species more so. For, on account of its strength, the perpendicular is not diverted from a rectilinear path, although greater succession[17] is introduced into its traversal [of the medium] by any coarseness whatever of the medium. Indeed, if there were a void without any natural coarseness, and if light or any body whatsoever could pass through it, there would be [some] succession caused by this void medium simply as a result of the prior and posterior [character] of space itself, and not because of [any] resisting coarseness of the medium.[18] But in a natural plenum, which has some natural coarseness, it is necessary that the resistance arising from the coarseness (which neither altogether yields

122 que: *om. O* | medii: *ex* media *corr. F*   124 grossitiem naturalem: *mg. O*

sed partim sic et sic, causabitur successio nova propter illam resistentiam. Et ideo dyaphanum, per suam grossitiem, resistit speciei oblique
et perpendiculari et inducit successionem in utraque; et in hoc communicant. Sed ulterius, propter debilitatem speciei oblique, impedit
130 eam plus et denegat viam incessus recti quam prius habuit in corpore
altero.

Causa vero quare a corpore subtiliori veniens in corpus grossius
frangatur versus partem perpendicularis ducende a loco fractionis,
inter scilicet incessum rectum et illam perpendicularem, est quia
135 sicut incessus perpendicularis fortior est, sic omnis incessus ei
magis vicinus est fortior remotiori, ut ratio dictat et asserunt
auctores. Et ideo cum multum velocius ferebatur species in corpore
subtiliori quam possit in corpore secundo densiori propter magnam
resistentiam grossitiei corporis talis, virtus naturalis generans ipsam
140 speciem appetit faciliorem transitum et eligit illum; et hic est versus
perpendicularem. Quapropter sic debet frangi inter incessum rectum
et perpendicularem ducendam a loco fractionis.

Et cum contrariorum contrarie sunt cause et contrariarum causarum
contrarii effectus, tunc oportet quod cum species veniat a densiori
145 in subtilius quod declinet a perpendiculari, ut incessus rectus cadat
inter lineam fractionis et perpendicularem ducendam. Cum enim in
corpore denso priori magnam resistentiam habeat, propter grossitiem
excellentem super grossitiem secundi corporis, cuius grossities est
subtilitas magna, ut de facili agat species veniens in ipsum, non
150 oportet quod querat faciolorem transitum, scilicet versus perpendicularem, quia omnis transitus est ei facilis respectu difficultatis quam
habuit in priori corpore. Et ideo potest ire in partem diversam
a perpendiculari, et necessario debet hanc partem eligere, quia
quantum potest uniformiter agit et uno modo. Et ideo invita transit
155 ad contrarietatem dispositionis sue vehementem. Propter quod, cum
in primo corpore habuerit magnam difficultatem transitus seu modicam facilitatem, ideo ex uniformitate sua, quam intendit semper quantum potest, non debet eligere contrarietatem excellentem, scilicet ut
ad partem facilimi transitus, scilicet versus perpendicularem, declinet;
160 sed continuet quodammodo, ut potest et debet, difficultatem transitus
seu minorem facilitatem; et hoc est transeundo ultra incessum rectum

126 partem *F* / propter: per *O*   128 in utraque: utramque *B*   130 quem *L*
132 veniens: species v. *O*   134 scilicet: *om. F*   140 elecit *FO*   141 perpendicularem: *ex* perpendicularitatem *corr. L* / rectum *OS*: *om. BFL*   143 sint *S*
146 perpendicularem: lineam p. *O* / cum enim: *ex* sensum *corr. L*   147 habeat:
licet *F*   152 ire: ut *B* / diversam: densum *S*   154 quantum: natura q. *B* natura in
q. *S* / potest: p. debet *S* / agere *S* / ideo: *om. O*   156 habuerit *LFO*: habuit *BSN*
157 facultatem *O* / quantum: quam *O*   158 scilicet: sed *O*   160 continue *B*
161 seu ... facilitatem: *om. O* / minorem: interiorem m. *B*

nor altogether resists, but partly the one and partly the other) should produce a new succession. Therefore, by its coarseness a transparent substance impedes both an oblique and a perpendicular species and introduces succession into both; and an oblique and a perpendicular species have this in common. But beyond this, an oblique species, because of its weakness, is impeded more by a transparent substance and is not allowed to continue in a straight line along the same path as it formerly had in the other substance.[19]

Now, the reason why [a species] passing from a subtler into a coarser substance is refracted towards the perpendicular drawn from the point of refraction (that is, between the direct path and the perpendicular) is that just as the perpendicular course is strongest, so every course close to the perpendicular is stronger than any course more remote from the perpendicular, as reason dictates and authors assert.[20] Accordingly, since the species [in the case under discussion] was moved much more swiftly in the more subtle substance than was possible in the denser substance because of the great resistance offered by the coarseness of the latter, the natural virtue generating the species desires the easier passage and chooses it;[21] and this is towards the perpendicular. Therefore, it must be refracted between the direct path and the perpendicular drawn from the point of refraction.

And since contraries are causes of contraries and the effects of contrary causes are contrary, it is necessary that when a species passes from a denser substance into a subtler substance, it bends away from the perpendicular, so that the direct path falls between the line of refraction and the perpendicular. For since there is great resistance in the first (dense) body (because its coarseness surpasses the coarseness of the second body, which is very subtle, so that a species entering it acts with ease), it is unnecessary for the species to seek an easier course (that is, towards the perpendicular), since every path is easy for it by comparison with the difficulty it encountered in the first body. Therefore, the species is able to assume a direction away from the perpendicular, and it must necessarily choose this direction, since in so far as possible it acts uniformly and in one mode.[22] And therefore it passes reluctantly towards that which is strongly contrary to its disposition. Accordingly, since in the first body it had great difficulty or [only] moderate ease of passage, for the sake of uniformity (which it always maintains in so far as possible), it ought not choose the superior of the [two] contraries, according to which it would deviate towards the direction of easiest passage (that is, towards the perpendicular); but to a certain degree, as much as it can and ought, it will maintain [its] difficulty or diminished ease of passage; and this occurs as the species deviates

per elongationem a perpendiculari, cum ei sufficiat ille transitus
et poterit eum adimplere; sicut quando species venit a subtiliori in
grossius continuat in grossiori facilitatem transitus in corpore
165 secundo, ut eius incessus in utroque corpore sit proportionalis
quantum potest et uniformis; quamquam et simul cum hoc grossities
superflua corporis secundi excitat virtutem generativam speciei, ut
ad partem facilioris transitus declinet.

Et quod per causam manifestatum est de duplici fractione, possumus
170 multipliciter verificare per effectum et experientiam. Nam si quis
cristallum spericum vel corpus urinalis rotundum plenum aqua teneat
in radiis fortibus solis, stans contra radios venientes per fenestram,
inveniet punctum in aere inter ipsum et urinale cui puncto, si
combustibile apponatur quod de facili comburatur, accendetur et
175 inflammabitur, quod impossibile est fieri nisi ponamus duplicem
fractionem predictam. Nam radius solaris exiens a puncto solis per
centrum urinalis non frangitur, quia est perpendicularis super urinale
et aquam et aerem eo quod per eorum centrum transeat, idem enim est
centrum omnium istorum trium, quia idem est centrum continentis et
180 contenti. Omnes autem radii qui exeunt ab eodem puncto solis a quo
dicta perpendicularis exivit franguntur necessario super corpus
urinalis, quia cadunt ad angulos obliquos et quoniam corpus urinalis
est densius aere; ideo fractio vadit inter incessum rectum et perpendicularem ductam a loco fractionis in centrum urinalis. Et quando
185 transit extra ad aerem, tunc, cum occurrit corpus subtilius, cadit
incessus rectus inter fractionem et perpendicularem ducendam a loco
fractionis, ut possit radius fractus cadere super perpendicularem
primam que venit a sole sine fractione. Et cum radii infiniti exeunt ab
eodem puncto solis, et unus solum est perpendicularis super urinale,
190 omnes alii franguntur et concurrunt in punctum unum super perpendicularem que cum eis exit a sole; et hic punctus est locus combustionis, quia in eo congregantur radii infiniti, et congregatio lucis
facit combustionem, que congregatio non fieret nisi per duplicem

162 a: et *B*   163 poterit: *ex* poteris *corr. L*   166 quantum: *om. S* | hoc: h.
ergo *B*   168 faciliorem *O*   169 manifestatum: manifestum *FO ex* manifestum
corr. S | de: *om. FL*   170 experientiam: per e. *BS*   171 urinale *O* | rotundum:
iocundum *B* totum de *S*   172 stans: factas *F*   174 comburitur *O*   175 fieri:
om. S   176 fractionem: f. radiorum *S*   177 super: sunt *B*   178 aquam et
aerem: aqua et aere *B*   179 quia: quod *B*   180 radii: alii r. *S*   181 exurit(?)
B   183 ideo: ista *O* | fractio: si actio *L*   185 cum: *om. O* | et cadit *O*
187 *post* ut *add. S* in centrum urinalis et *scr. et del. A* centrum urinalis   188 que:
quando *O* | cum: tamen *S* | exeant *S*   189 unum *BL* | solum: solus *S* | supra *O*

from the direct path in the direction away from the perpendicular, since such a course suffices for it and is able to fulfil it.
Similarly, when a species passes from a subtler into a coarser
substance, it maintains its ease of traversal in the second substance, so that its passage through the two substances is, in so
far as possible, proportional and uniform; at the same time, the
greater coarseness of the second substance excites the generative
power of the species, so that it bends towards the direction of
easier traversal.

And what has been made clear concerning the two modes of
refraction through [an analysis of their] cause, we can verify
multifariously through its effect, by experience. For if somebody
should hold a sphere of crystal or a round urinal full of water
up to strong solar rays, while he stands on the opposite [side of
the sphere or urinal from] the rays entering through the window,
he will find a point in the air between himself and the urinal
where, if something easily combustible is placed, it is ignited and
set on fire; and this is impossible unless we assume the aforementioned dual refraction. For a solar ray issuing from a point
of the sun through the centre of the urinal is not refracted, since
it is perpendicular to the urinal, the [contained] water, and the
[surrounding] air because it passes through the centre—for all
three of these share a common centre, since the centres of the
container and the contained are identical. However, all [other] rays
that issue from the same point of the sun as the aforementioned
perpendicular are necessarily refracted at the urinal, since they are
incident at oblique angles and the urinal is denser than air; therefore, the refracted ray passes between the direct path and the perpendicular drawn from the point of refraction to the centre of the
urinal. When it passes outside into the air, then, since it encounters
a subtler substance, the direct path falls between the refracted ray
and the perpendicular drawn from the point of refraction; thus the
refracted ray can intersect the original perpendicular [ray], which
comes from the sun [and through the urinal] without refraction.
And since infinitely many rays issue from the same point of the
sun, and there is only one perpendicular to the urinal [from that
point of the sun], all other rays are refracted and intersect at one
point on the perpendicular that issues with them from the sun;
this point is the place of combustion, since an infinity of rays
is gathered there, and the gathering of light produces combustion, and this gathering cannot occur except by the dual

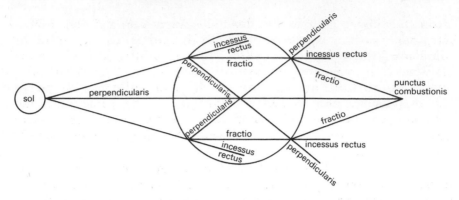

Fig. 7

fractionem, sicut patet in figura [fig. 7]. Et sicut super perpendicu-
195 larem principalem concurrunt in punctum unum duo radii per
duplicem fractionem, sic intelligendum est de omnibus radiis exeuntibus ab eodem puncto solis, qui sunt nobis infiniti.

PARS II
CAPITULUM 4

Postquam autem manifesta est varietas hec in fractionibus specierum
et virtutum agentium multiplicatarum, oportet considerare in quibus
5 corporibus mundi principalibus possibile est fieri hanc fractionem,
ut videatur in quibus frangantur virtutes celorum et in quibus non;
per hoc enim certificabitur postea diversitas actionis stellarum in
omnia inferiora.

Et primo sciendum quod in corpore celesti non fit aliqua fractio
10 sensibilis nec de qua curandum est, propter uniformitatem celestis
perspicui; fractio enim non est nisi quando occurrit corpus secundum
alterius dyaphanitatis. Sed orbes celestes sunt eiusdem dyaphanitatis,
aut simpliciter aut quoad sensum nostrum; propter quod radii stellarum fixarum non reputantur frangi in speris planetarum, nec radii
15 planetarum superiorum in speris inferiorum, quamvis sint orbes con-
tigui et diversarum superficierum; ad fractionem enim, ut satis tactum
est secundum documenta auctorum, exigitur quod corpus secundum
sit alterius dyaphanitatis a primo, et hoc sensibiliter si iudicium

194 figura: f. ista subscripta *F* f. ista substrata *O*
  2 capitulum quartum *O*   3 veritas *FS* / speciebus *BL*   6 virtutes celorum:
ille v. elementorum *S*   7 *post* enim *scr. et del.* *S* lux ita   9 fit: sit *B*
10 curandum: mirandum *B*   12 sed . . . dyaphanitatis: *mg. O*   14 fixarum:

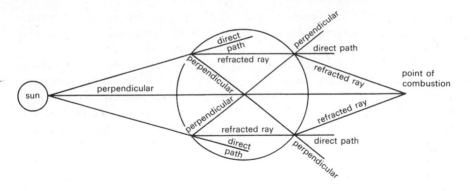

Fig. 7

refraction, as is evident in the figure [fig. 7]. And exactly as two rays converge at one point of the principal perpendicular by a double refraction, so it is to be understood concerning all rays issuing from the same point of the sun, which are (for practical purposes) infinite in number.[23]

PART II

CHAPTER 4

Since this variety in the refraction of species and the propagated virtues of agents has been explained, it is necessary to consider in which principal bodies of the world this refraction can occur, so that we can see in which of them celestial virtues are refracted and in which not; for by this means we will later certify the diversity of stellar action on all terrestrial things.

And first it should be known that there is no sensible refraction nor any refraction worthy of concern in celestial substance, because of the uniformity of celestial transparency; for refraction occurs only when a second substance of different transparency is encountered. But the celestial spheres are all of the same transparency (either without qualification or as far as sense can discern); and therefore the rays of the fixed stars are judged not to be refracted in the planetary spheres, nor the rays of superior planets in the spheres of inferior planets, although the spheres are contiguous and possess distinct surfaces; because refraction, as we have sufficiently explained according to the teachings of [optical] authors,[1] requires the transparency of the second substance to be different from that of the first, and sensibly so if our discernment [of the refraction]

om. F   15 superiorum *S*   16 specierum *B*   18 a primo: *om. S*

nostrum debeat esse hoc ut curetur. Unde non invenitur per instru-
20 menta diversitas sensibilis que causaretur ex fractione in celo; nec
auctores hoc perceperunt, sed supponunt non esse.

Sed in superficie ignis franguntur omnes radii non perpendiculares.
Et hoc vult Ptolomeus quinque *Aspectuum* et Alhacen in septem, et
demonstrant hoc per considerationes instrumentorum. Et propter
25 pulcritudinem harum veritatum et probationis, volo recitare verba
multa dictorum philosophorum quatinus evidentius et certius appareant que dicenda sunt. Celum autem vocat ethera, in quo dicit sidera
collocari; et corpus contiguatum etheri vocat aerem, sub aere compre-
hendens speram ignis propter rationem dicendam inferius. Et similiter
30 Alhacen non curat de diversitate ignis et aeris, ut patebit. Dicit
igitur Ptolomeus: 'Possibile est nobis dinoscere quod in loco contigua-
tionis aeris ad etherem fit flexio radii,' id est fractio. 'Invenimus
enim res que oriuntur et occidunt magis declinantes ad septentrionem
cum fuerint prope orizonta, et metite fuerint per instrumenta quo
35 mensurantur sidera. Cum enim fuerint orientes vel occidentes, circuli
utique equedistantes equinoctiali, qui describuntur super illas, propinquiores sunt septentrioni quam circuli qui describuntur super
illas cum fuerint in medio celi; et quanto magis appropinquant orizonti
habent maiorem declinationem ad septentrionem. Siderum vero
40 semper apparentium distantia a septentrionali polo erit minor cum
fuerint in meridionali linea versus orizontem; et cum fuerint in linea
meridionali in loco qui est propinquior puncto qui est super caput
nostrum, fit in ipso loco circulus equedistans equinoctiali maior, in
priori autem loco minor. Quod accidit propter flexionem radii que
45 fit a superficie que determinat inter aerem et etherem, que debet esse
sperica, et centrum eius est centrum commune universis elementis,
quod est centrum terre.' Igitur videtur stella describere minorem
circulum de equedistantibus equinoctiali quando est in orizonte quam
quando plus ascendit, ita quod quanto magis ascendit versus cenith
50 capitis tanto maiorem equedistantem videatur describere; que equedistans erit maior necessario propter maiorem distantiam a polo, ut
patet ad sensum in spera, quoniam portio circuli meridionalis seu cuiuslibet coluri maior erit inter polum et equedistantem quam describit
stella cum fertur per cenith capitis quam quando est in orizonte.

19 ut: *om.* F   19–20 unde . . . causaretur: *mg.* O   21 percipiunt O
22 *post* ignis *scr. et del.* S non   24 considerationes: demonstrationes S   25 pul-
chritudinum B | velo B | recitare: *ex* recitatur *corr.* F   26 citius B   27 dicenda
L': dicta L^C | vocant O | considera B   28 vocant O   29 dicenda B   30 *ante*
non *scr. et del.* F dicit   31 igitur: *om.* B   32 ad: et ad F | fit FO: sit BLSAN |
flexio: reflexio FO | *post* fractio *add.* SA propter diversitatem istorum corporum ex hiis
que apparent *et add.* O linee   34 orizonta: orizonte F orizontem S | mente B | quo:
quibus O   35 considera B   36 equedistantes: distante F   36–8 propin-
quiores . . . illas: *om.* S   38 celi: circuli S | orizonti: orienti S   40 semper: super S

is at issue. Thus, [even] with instruments, no sensible diversity is found that could be caused by celestial refraction; nor have authors perceived any, and they assume that it does not exist.

But all nonperpendicular rays are refracted at the surface of [the sphere of] fire. And Ptolemy intends this in *De aspectibus*, book v, and also Alhazen in book vii, and they demonstrate it by the use of instruments.[2] And because of the beauty of these truths and their proof, I wish to quote many words from the aforementioned philosophers, so that what is to be said will appear more clearly and with greater certainty. The heaven [Ptolemy] calls 'ether', and he says the stars are situated in it; and the substance adjoining the ether he calls 'air', including under this term the sphere of fire, for reasons discussed below.[3] Likewise, Alhazen is not concerned about the difference between fire and air, as will be evident. Thus Ptolemy says: 'We can discern that where air and ether adjoin rays are bent,' that is, refracted.[4] 'For we find that celestial bodies that rise and set incline more towards the north when near the horizon,[5] and this can be measured by means of the instruments used for stellar measurements. For circles that are exactly parallel to the equator, drawn through these stars when they are rising or setting, are closer to the north than circles drawn through them when they are in midsky; and as they approach the horizon they incline towards the north.[6] And stars that are always visible[7] will be less distant from the north pole when situated on a meridian near the horizon; and when they are on a meridian nearer the zenith, a greater circle parallel to the equator can be drawn through them than through their former location [on the horizon]. This occurs because of the bending of the ray at the interface between air and ether, which must be spherical, and its centre is the common centre of all the elements and of the earth.'[8] Therefore, a star is observed to describe a smaller circle parallel to the equator when on the horizon than when higher in the sky; thus the more it ascends towards the zenith the greater the circle it is seen to describe; and this circle will necessarily be larger because of its greater distance from the pole, as can be seen in a sphere, since the portion of a meridian circle or any colure[9] between the pole and the circle described by the star is greater when the star is carried through the zenith than when it is on the horizon.

41 fuerint[1] *S* / cum: c. enim *B* / fuerint[2] *mg. A*   41-2 versus . . . meridionali: *om. S*
mg. A   43 fit: sic *L* / circulo *S*   44 minor: fit m. *S* / flexionem *BL*
reflexionem *OS* fixionem *F* / radii: *ex* radiorum *corr. F* / que: qui *F*   45 determinant
BF terminat (*corr. ex* determinat) *O*   46 est centrum: *om. O*   47 *post* terre
add. SA hec sunt verba Ptolomei / *ante* igitur *add. BSA* cum   48 orizontem *B*
oriente *S*   49 quanto: quando *S ex* multo *corr. F*   53 inter: minus *B* / describitur *S*
54 per: super *S* / capitis: *om. B* c. et prope *S* / quando est: longius et *S* / orizonte: o. capitis *B*

55   Et cum hoc sit verum, tunc de necessitate sequitur quod stella non videatur semper in loco suo vero, nec per lineas rectas, quoniam si per lineas rectas et in suo loco vero semper videretur, tunc eandem distantiam a polo habere iudicaretur in orizonte et alibi, quia in eadem nocte et semper videretur ferri in eodem circulo equedistante.
60 Nisi quod in maximo tempore aliter apparet secundum quod Thebit et multi probationum magistri firmaverunt, scilicet capita Arietis et Libre zodiaci mobilis in circulis brevibus circa capita Arietis et Libre zodiaci immobilis circumferri, aut totum zodiacum mobilem moveri motu accessionis et recessionis secundum latitudinem, ascen-
65 dendo et descendendo, ut sapientes Indi posuerunt, aut propter aliquem alium motum quem magistri probationum excogitaverunt esse possibilem in celo stellato, sive sit inventus adhuc sive non, secundum quod unus eorum, Albategni, dicit possibile est aliquem motum in celo latere omnem philosophum. Cum igitur non videatur stella
70 secundum lineas rectas, propter diversam distantiam a polo, quam habere non potest secundum veritatem, oportet quod videatur reflexe vel secundum lineam fractam; sed non est ibi reflexio, cum non sit ibi densum; ergo oportet quod per lineam fractam videatur.
       Et Alhacen exponit Ptolomeum in hac parte, sicut in aliis, dicens
75 quod si 'aliquis voluerit hoc experiri, accipiat instrumentum de armillis et ponat illud in loco eminenti et in quo poterit apparere orizon orientalis. Et ponat instrumentum armillarum suo modo proprio, scilicet quod ponat armillam que est in loco circuli meridionalis in superficie circuli meridiei, et polus eius sit altior terra secundum
80 altitudinem poli mundi super orizonta loci in quo ponitur instrumen-tum. Et in nocte preservet aliquam stellam fixarum magnarum que transit per cenith capitis illius loci aut prope; et preservet eam in ortu suo ab oriente. Stella autem orta, revolvat armillam que revolvitur in circuitu poli equinoctialis donec fiat equedistans equinoctiali,
85 et certificetur locus stelle ex armilla, et sic habebit longitudinem stelle a polo mundi. Et deinde preservet stellam usquequo perveniat ad circulum meridiei, et moveat armillam quam primo moverat donec fiat equedistans equinoctiali; et sic habebit longitudinem stelle a polo mundi cum stella fuerit in vertice capitis. Hoc autem facto,

55 tunc: *om. O* / de necessitate: demonstrative *F*   56 nec: non *B*
56–7 quoniam . . . et: si enim *O* et *S*   57 videretur *LSA*: videtur *O* videntur *BF* /
ante tunc *mg. add. O* et per lineas rectas   58 habere: h. videret *S*   59 eadem
. . . in: *om. B* / fere *O*   60 Thebit *LAO (mg. O)*: patebit *F* debebat *S*   61 multi:
ex multe *corr. F*   62 et zodiaci *S*   63 mobile *F*   64 motu: *om. F*
65 Indi *LO*: mundi *SA* vidi *B* niri(?) *F*   67 adhuc: ad hoc *L*   68 *ante*
Albategni *scr. et del. S* dicit / Albateni: *om. B* Albateni *S*   69 latere: *om. S* / per
philosophum *S*   70 lineas rectas: linea (*corr. ex* lineas) recta sed *S*   72 *ante*
fractam *scr. et del. F* rectam / sed: si *L* / reflexio: r. possibilis *LS*   72–3 sed
. . . fractam: *om. B*   73 ibi: *om. S* / per: *om. S* / linea fracta *S*   74 exponit
Ptolomeum: philosophum *F*   80 orizontam *B*   81 aliquam *FOA*: aliam *BLSN* /

Since this is true, it follows necessarily that a star is not always seen in its true place, nor by straight lines, since if it were always seen by straight lines and in its true place, it would be judged to have the same distance from the pole on the horizon and elsewhere; for during a given night, and [indeed] always, it would appear to be carried on the same circle parallel [to the equator]. However, it happens otherwise over a very long period of time, as Thabit and many masters of demonstration establish;[10] [for they show] that the heads of Aries and Libra in the movable zodiac rotate in small circles about the heads of Aries and Libra in the stationary zodiac, or that the entire movable zodiac is moved with a to-and-fro motion in latitude, ascending and descending, as the wise men of India have proposed, or with some other motion that the masters of demonstration have thought possible in the stellar heaven, whether invented for this purpose or not—for one of them, Albategni, says that it is possible for some motion in the heaven to be concealed from all philosophers.[11] Therefore, since a star is not seen by means of straight lines, as the variable distance from the pole (which it cannot have in truth) demonstrates, it must be seen either by reflection or by refraction; but no reflection occurs there, since no dense body is present; therefore, it must be seen by a refracted line.

And in this matter, as in others, Alhazen explains Ptolemy, saying that if 'somebody should wish to experience this, he should take an armillary sphere and put it in a high place in such a way that the eastern horizon can be seen. And he should give the armillary sphere its proper arrangement; that is, he should place the ring that represents the meridian circle in the plane of the meridian circle, with its pole above the earth according to the altitude of the pole of the world above the horizon of the place where the instrument is located. And at night he should observe[12] one of the great fixed stars that passes through or near the zenith of that place; and he should observe it as it rises, beginning in the east. However, as the star ascends he must turn the ring that moves in a circuit about the pole of the equator until it becomes parallel to the equator, and he certifies the place of the star with the ring, and thus he will have the longitude of the star from the pole of the world. Then he should observe the star until it reaches the meridian circle, and he should move the ring that he first moved, until it becomes parallel to the equator; and thus he will have the longitude of the star from the pole of the world when the star is directly overhead. When this has been done,

stellarum *SA*   82 eam: illam *S*   83 autem: enim *S*   85 et¹: ut *B* / stelle:
iste *B*   86 usquoque *B*   87 armilla *O* / primus *B* prius *S*   89 autem: *om.*
O / factio *B*

90 inveniet remotionem stelle a polo mundi apud ascensionem (id est, ortum) minorem remotione eius a polo mundi in hora existentie eius in verticatione capitis. Ex quo patet quod visus comprehendit stellas reflexe (id est, fracte), non recte; stella enim fixa semper movetur per eundem circulum de circulis equedistantibus equatori diei, et
95 numquam exit ab ipso, ita quod appareat, nisi in longissimo tempore. Et si stella comprehenderetur recte, tunc linee radiales extenderentur a visu recte ad stellas, et extenderentur forme stellarum per lineas radiales recte quousque pervenirent ad visum; et si forma extenderetur a stella ad visum recte, tunc visus comprehenderet eam in suo loco,
100 et sic inveniret distantiam stelle fixe a polo mundi in eadem nocte eandem. Sed distantia stelle mutatur in eadem nocte a polo mundi; ergo visus non recte comprehendit stellam. In celo autem non est corpus densum tersum, neque in aere, a quo possunt forme converti; et cum visus comprehendit stellam et non recte neque secundum con-
105 versionem, ergo est secundum reflexionem (id est, fractionem), cum hiis solis tribus modis comprehenduntur res a visu.' Hec sunt verba Alhacen in septimo.

Similiter ostendit illud idem per lunam, quoniam si per computa-tionem, id est, per tabulas et canones, distantia lune a verticatione
110 capitis equetur, et similiter per instrumentum sumatur altitudo lune, invenietur minor distantia lune a verticatione capitis per considera-tionem instrumenti quam per computationem. Ergo lux lune non videtur recte per duo foramina instrumenti per quod sumitur elevatio, tunc enim distantia eius a verticatione capitis esset ista que esset
115 inventa per computationem; sed non est ita. Ergo lux lune non ex-tenditur a celo ad aerem per lineas rectas; quare per reflexionem. Et qua ratione de lumine lune, similiter de lumine aliarum stellarum; et ideo oportet quod species omnium stellarum frangantur. Et sic patet quod fractio debeat esse omnium radiorum celestium in superficie
120 ignis qui non cadunt perpendiculariter super corpus ignis.

Quod autem hec fractio sit, propter transitum speciei a subtiliori in densius, versus perpendicularem declarant per hoc, quod circulus equedistans equinoctiali transiens per stellam quando venit ad circu-lum meridiei et cenith capitis est vere designans locum stelle, et est

92 vertice S / ex OSA : in F om. BLN   93 reflexe id est: reflexa B   96 appre-henderetur O   97 recte: correxi ex recto BFLOSN obs. A / ad: om. B   98 per-veniret S   99 comprehendet O comprehendent B / suo: om. S   101 sed: si B
102 autem: om. S   105 inflexionem S   109 id . . . canones: om. BSN mg. A / et: om. O   110 equatur ON   111 invenitur O   112 quam: quantum S
113 videtur: ostenditur SA ex ostenditur corr. L / elevationem B   114 eius: om. S / esset²: esse S   117 qua ratione: aquationem B / lune: l. eadem S / similiter: s. ratione S s. est A   118 patet: apparet SA   119 post quod add. SA celum est alterius dyafanitatis ab elementis propter quod   120 cadit B   121 sit: fit F

he should find the distance of the star from the pole of the world at an ascension (that is, place)[13] closer to the pole of the world than when it is directly overhead. It is evident from this that sight perceives the stars not by a straight, but by a broken (that is, refracted)[14] ray; for a fixed star is always moved along the same parallel to the equator[15] and never departs from it, as one observes, except over a very great period of time. And if the stars were perceived by rectilinear rays, then radial lines would be extended directly[16] from the eye to the stars, and the forms of the stars would be extended directly, along radial lines, until they reached the eye; and if the form were extended in a straight line from the star to sight, then sight would perceive the star in its true place, and it would then find the distance of the fixed star from the pole of the world throughout a given night to be fixed. But the distance of a star from the pole during a given night varies; therefore, sight does not perceive the star by a rectilinear ray. However, neither in the heavens nor in air is there a polished dense body from which forms could be reflected; and since sight perceives the star neither directly nor by reflection, it must perceive the star by a bent (that is, refracted) ray, since things are perceived by vision only in these three ways.'[17] These are the words of Alhazen in book vii.

Alhazen shows the same thing for the moon,[18] since if the lunar distance from the zenith were determined by computation (that is, by tables and canons),[19] and if with an instrument the altitude of the moon were measured, the lunar distance from the zenith would be found smaller by use of the instrument than by computation. Therefore, the light of the moon passing through the two sighting holes of the instrument with which the elevation is measured does not come in a straight line, for then its distance from the zenith would be the calculated value; but this proves not to be so. Therefore, the light of the moon is not extended from the heaven into the air by straight lines; consequently this light is extended by means of bent lines.[20] And whatever arguments apply to the light of the moon apply similarly to the light of the other stars; and therefore the species of all stars must be refracted. And thus it is evident that all celestial rays that fall obliquely on the sphere of fire must be refracted at the surface of that sphere.

[Ptolemy and Alhazen] reveal that this refraction is towards the perpendicular (as an instance of the passage of a species from a subtler to a denser medium) by the fact that the circle parallel to the equator and passing through the star when it comes to the meridian circle and the zenith truly indicates the location of the star, and the

122 in: ad *S*   123 stellam: fenestram *S*   124 et locum *O*

125 in quo deferebatur stella a principio noctis quousque venerit ad
circulum meridiei; quoniam visus tunc comprehendet stellam recte,
quia linea extensa a visu ad cenith est perpendicularis super corpus
celi et corpus ignis, ut certum est; et uterque hoc dicit, scilicet
Ptolomeus et Alhacen. Cum ergo stella est in verticatione capitis et
130 in circulo maiori, qui secundum veritatem est circulus eius, tunc
species radiosa non frangitur, quia perpendicularis non frangitur;
sed cum appareat in circulis minoribus versus orizontem, erit
necessario fractio, ut prius probatum est; et videbitur stella per
lineas fractas, quia tunc radii cadunt ad angulos obliquos super
135 speras elementorum. Sed quelibet illarum fractarum declinat ad diametrum mundi que exit a puncto fractionis, sicut docent Ptolomeus
et Alhacen figurationibus diversis; et hec diameter est perpendicularis
super concavitatem celi et convexitatem spere ignis. Quapropter
fractio hec est secundum legem incessus a subtiliori in densius, per
140 declinationem ad perpendicularem, ut cadat species fracta inter
incessum rectum et perpendicularem ducendam a loco fractionis, que
est mundi diameter in hac parte.

Secundum autem Ptolomeum et Alhacen oportet scire secundo quod
non fit fractio in superficie aeris, qui proprie dicitur aer, secundum
145 quod distinguimus aerem ab igne; cum non inveniatur aliqua diversitas aspectus nostri causari nisi propter unicam fractionem specierum
venientium a stellis per speram aeris et ignis, quantum est de puritate
nature sue. Hoc dico quia mediantibus nubibus et vaporibus accidit
magna diversitas, quia sol et stelle omnes videntur esse maioris
150 quantitatis in orizonte quam in medio celi propter interpositionem
vaporum existentium in aere inter nos et stellas orientes; in quibus
vaporibus franguntur radii solares preter fractionem quam habuerunt
in superficie ignis, que fractio facit ut videantur maioris quantitatis
in orizonte quam in celi medio (quamvis et alia sit causa huius
155 maioritatis perpetua, sicut Ptolomeus et Alhacen determinant); de
qua fractione per vapores exemplificabitur postea in figura, cum fiet
mentio de actione speciei. Sed dum spera aeris est munda a vaporibus,
non est ibi fractio, ut auctores aspectuum certificant. (π) Secundum
quod dicit Alhacen quod 'aer quanto magis appropinquat celo tanto
160 magis purificatur donec fiat ignis. Subtilitas ergo eius fit ordinate

125 deferebat S   126 comprehenderet B comprehendit O   127 a: om. B
128 ut: om. B / scilicet: om. O   132 circulo S / orizontem: o. et in orizonte FL
136 docet S   137 hic O   138 celi et convexitatem: om. O   140 ad: et B
141 qui B   143 ante secundum mg. add. L secunda conclusio / Alhacen: alba B /
oportet . . . quod: om. S   144 fit: est mg. O   146 aspectus: om. B
147 et: ut F aut O   149 et: om. S / videntur: om. B   150 orizonte: oriente
S / celi: om. S   151 orientis B om. F   153 videatur S   154 orizonte:
oriente OS   155 Alhacen: Hali F   156 vapores: om. F   158 ut: aut B /

star is carried in that circle from the beginning of the night until
it reaches the meridian circle; for at that point sight perceives the
star by a rectilinear ray, since the line extended from the eye to
the zenith is perpendicular to the celestial and fiery spheres, and
this is certain; and both Ptolemy and Alhazen say this.[21] Therefore,
when a star is at the zenith and in the larger circle (which is in
truth its circle), its radiant species is not refracted, because a perpendicular ray is not refracted; but when it appears in the smaller
circles near the horizon, refraction will necessarily occur, as was
proved above; and the star will be seen by refracted lines, since
the rays are obliquely incident on the spheres of the elements.
But each of those refracted lines bends towards the diameter of
the world that issues from the point of refraction, as Ptolemy and
Alhazen teach by various figures; and this diameter is perpendicular to the concavity of the heaven and the convexity of the
sphere of fire.[22] Therefore, this refraction occurs according to
the law that governs passage from the subtler to the denser substance, by bending towards the perpendicular, so that the refracted
species falls between the direct path and the perpendicular (that
is, the diameter of the world in this place) drawn from the point
of refraction.

It must be recognized, secondly, that according to Ptolemy and
Alhazen there is no refraction at the surface of the air (that is, 'air'
properly speaking, which we distinguish from fire); for no diversity
is produced in our sight except that resulting from a single refraction
of species coming from the stars through the sphere of air and
fire, in so far as the nature of this sphere is pure. I add this [qualifi-
cation] because great diversity is produced by clouds and vapours;
[this we know] because the sun and all stars appear larger at the
horizon than in the middle of the sky owing to the interposition
of vapours in the air between us and the rising stars; and there
is refraction of solar rays in these vapours, in addition to their
refraction at the surface [of the sphere] of fire, and this refraction
makes them appear larger on the horizon than in the middle of
the heaven (although another cause of enlargement is also always
operative, as Ptolemy and Alhazen determine); but this refraction
by vapours will be illustrated by a figure later, when we make
mention of the action of a species.[23] But if the sphere of air is free of
vapour there is no refraction, as authors of books on optics attest.
(π) For this reason Alhazen says that 'air becomes purer as it approaches the heaven, until it becomes fire. Therefore, its subtlety

aspectuum: perspectuum *O*   159 quod²: quia *O*   160 purificatur: *ex* rarificatur
corr. F | ordinata *S*

secundum successionem, non in differentia terminata. Forme ergo eorum que sunt in celo, quando extenduntur ad visum, non reflectuntur (id est, non franguntur) apud concavitatem spere ignis, cum non sit ibi superficies concava determinata. Nullum ergo invenitur
165 corpus subtilius aere cum quo extenduntur forme visibilium et reflectuntur apud superficiem eius nisi corpus celeste.' Hoc dicit. Quapropter secundum ipsum et Ptolomeum, non est fractio speciei in superficie spere aeris cum venit species a spera ignis (ρ). Sed in superficie aque est fractio sensibilis, propter manifestam diversitatem dyaphanitatis
170 aeris et aque, cum differentia superficierum.

Sed adhuc tertio sciendum est quod a Tropico Cancri versus polum nostrum fit fractio omnium specierum venientium a planetis, propter hoc quod species ille multiplicantur super lineas que non sunt perpendiculares eo quod non cadunt in centrum mundi, sed tendunt ad
175 orizonta; propter quod oportet quod nulla species directa veniat citra illum tropicum ad loca climatum. Similiter nec ultra Tropicum Capricorni per eandem rationem. Sed nec a stellis que sunt inter tropicos veniunt species directe ultra eos propter consimilem rationem; ab illis tamen stellis fixis que sunt extra tropica possunt venire
180 perpendiculares ad loca climatum, quando scilicet transeunt earum species super lineas cadentes in centrum mundi per loca illa.

PARS II

CAPITULUM 5

Reflexio vero, ut dictum est, est generatio radii in partem contrariam incessus incidentis super corpus densum impediens transitum speciei.
5 Considerandum autem primo quod nullum est tam densum quin species potest transire, quia omnia communicant in materia, et ideo potest fieri transmutatio cuiuslibet per aliud, saltem que est per multiplicationem speciei. Et ideo per medium dolii aurei et enei, species ignis et soni transiret. Et cum Boetius velit tertio *De consolatione*
10 et alibi quod Linceus oculus possit penetrare parietes densos, oportet quod species oculi et visibilium transeant per medium parietis. Sed tamen sunt multa densa que visum hominis impediunt omnino, et alios

163 spere: *mg. F*   164 concava: continua *L* c. sibi *S*   165 quo: ergo *B*
166 celeste: reflecte *O* / *post* dicit *mg. add. O* Alacen   167 Ptolomeum: philosophum *F*
168 aque: aeris *F*   173 super: secundum *S* / sunt: *om. F*   173-4 perpendiculariter
S   174 *ante* cadunt *scr. et del. S* sunt   176 climatum: *ex* terminatum *corr. L*
177 capricorum *L* capricornum *S* / *ante* per *scr. et del. L* per eorum / nec: hec *L* / stellis:
s. fixis *SA*   178 *ante* tropicos *scr. et del. F* tempore / directe: *om. F* / similem *L*
179 *post* stellis *scr. et del. F* spericis / possent *SA*   180 perpendiculariter *S*

increases gradually rather than in discrete steps. Thus the forms of celestial bodies, extended to sight, are not bent (that is, are not refracted)[24] at the inner surface of the sphere of fire, since it has no determined inner surface. Therefore, there is no body subtler than air through which visible forms are extended, and at the surface of which they are bent, except celestial substance.'[25] This Alhazen says. Therefore, according to him and Ptolemy, a species is not refracted at the surface of the sphere of air when it comes from the sphere of fire (ρ). But there is sensible refraction at the surface of water, because of the manifest difference in transparency between air and water and their distinct surfaces.

In the third place, it must be known that all species coming from the planets [and incident] between the tropic of Cancer and our [north] pole are refracted, because those species are multiplied along nonperpendicular lines, since they do not fall to the centre of the world but tend towards the horizon;[26] and therefore no rectilinear species [of the planets] can come north of that tropic to the region of the climes.[27] The same is true of rays incident south of the Tropic of Capricorn, for the same reason. And for a similar reason species cannot come in straight lines [to regions] beyond the tropics from [fixed] stars situated between the tropics; however, from fixed stars located outside the tropic,[28] perpendicular species can come to the region of the climes, that is, when they pass through that region along lines directed towards the centre of the world.

PART II

CHAPTER 5

As we have said, reflection is the generation of a ray in a direction opposite to that of its incidence on a dense body that impedes the passage of the species. However, it must first be understood that nothing is so dense that a species cannot pass through it, since all things share a common matter, and therefore any of them can be transmuted by another—at least with the transmutation that occurs in the multiplication of a species. Thus the species of fire and sound pass through a jar of gold or bronze. And since Boethius maintains in *De consolatione*, book iii, and elsewhere[1] that an eye as keen as that of Lynceus can penetrate dense walls, the species of the eye and visible objects must pass through walls.[2] However, there are many dense substances that altogether prevent human sight (and also the

2 capitulum quintum habens quatuor conclusiones *O mg. L*   3 generatio: g. recta *S*
6 potest: possit *SA* / omnia: illa *S*   8 dolii: dolei *FO*   9 transeunt *O*   10 alibi:
alii *BFOSAN ex* alii *corr. L*   12 hominum *FO*

sensus similiter, ita quod species sensibiles non pertranseunt in
tanta fortitudine ut valeant sensum humanum immutare, licet
15 secundum veritatem transeant, sed insensibiliter nobis.

Sunt etiam aliqua corpora mediocris densitatis a quibus fit reflexio simul et fractio, ut est aqua. Nam videmus pisces et lapides in
ea per fractionem, et videmus solem et lunam per reflexionem, sicut
experientia docet. Unde propter densitatem que sufficit reflexioni
20 aliquali, radii omnes reflectuntur; sed propter mediocritatem
densitatis, que non impedit transitum lucis, franguntur radii in
superficie aque. Et ideo quilibet radius solis cadens super aquam
multiplicat sibi similem tam reflexive quam per viam fractionis; et
ideo debilior est reflexio quam illa que fit a denso perfecte, et
25 debilior fractio quam si corpus secundum esset tam rarum ut nulla
fieret reflexio, sicut est in aere.

Considerandum etiam secundo quod durum et solidum nec faciunt
reflexionem nec fractionem, sed solum densum et rarum. Nam cristallus est dura et solida, et vitrum et huiusmodi multa; et tamen, quia rara
30 sunt, pertransit species visus et rerum visibilium, et fit bona fractio
in eis, quod non contingeret si essent ita densa sicut sunt dura et
solida. Densum enim est quod habet partes propinque iacentes, et
rarum est quod habet partes distanter iacentes. Et ideo vitrum est
rarum, et cristallus et huiusmodi non densum perfecte, licet ali-
35 quantulum, sed sufficienter sunt rara ut permittant species lucis
transire. Durum autem et solidum non dicuntur ex congregatione
partium, sed ex stabilitate et firmitate et fixione, propter naturam
siccitatis ad quam consequitur durities et soliditas, ut Aristoteles
vult secundo *De generatione.*

40 Tertio considerandum est quod densum lene et politum, ut speculum, facit bonam reflexionem et sensibilem propter equalitatem sue
superficiei; partes enim ipsius omnes concordant in una actione, ut
dicit Averroys super secundum *De anima,* capitulo de sono; et ideo
equaliter et concorditer agunt, et integra fit reflexio speciei a superficie
45 speculari. Sed partes corporis asperi, propter eius superficiei in-
equalitatem, non concordant in una actione; propter quod dissipatur
tota species et, amittens suam integritatem, non sufficit representare
rem cuius est; et ideo non videmus per corpora aspera sicut per
specula. Et Ptolomeus dicit secundo *Aspectuum* quod de aspero fit

---

13 similiter: sensibiliter *O*   16 etiam: et *L* autem *SA* / aliqua: alia *O*
19 reflexioni: densitati r. *S*   20 aliquando *SA*   21 impedit: ponit i. *S* / in:
scilicet in *O*   23 reflexione *O*   23–4 per . . . illa: *om. S*   24 perfecto *SA*
25 tam: *om. S*   29 dura: d. res *O*   30 et[1]: *om. S*   31 quod: quia *S*
33 vitrum *L*^C: *om.* L'   35 permittat *S*   38 et soliditas *BON: om. FLSA*
42 partes: per p. *B om. S*   43 Averroim *O* / supra *L om. SA*   44 agunt: *om. SA* /

exercise of the other senses); thus sensible species do not pass through
them with sufficient strength to alter human sight, although in truth
they do pass through them, but insensibly to us.

There are also certain bodies of moderate density, such as water,
in which reflection and refraction occur simultaneously. For by refraction we see fish and stones in it, and by reflection [from its
surface] we see the sun and moon, as experience teaches. Thus, because of density sufficient to produce such a reflection, all rays are
reflected; but, because the density is sufficiently moderate to permit
the passage of light, [all] rays are [also] refracted at the surface of
the water. And therefore every solar ray incident on water multiplies
a ray similar to itself both by reflection and by refraction; consequently, the reflection is weaker than that which would occur from
a perfectly dense body, and the refracted ray is weaker than if the
second body were (like air) so rare that no reflection occurred.

It must be recognized, in the second place, that neither reflection
nor refraction is produced by hardness and solidity, but only by
density and rarity. For crystal is hard and solid, as are glass and many
such substances; and yet, because they are rare, the species of sight
and of visible objects pass through them, and the refracted ray is
strong, which would not be so if they were as dense as they are hard
and solid. For a dense body is that which has its parts close together,
and a rare body is that which has its parts far apart. And therefore
glass is rare; and crystal and the like arc somewhat (but not perfectly) dense, and yet they are sufficiently rare to permit the species
of light to pass through them. However, a substance is not called
'hard' and 'solid' from the closeness of its parts, but from its stability
and firmness and fixity, owing to a dry nature, from which hardness
and solidity derive, as Aristotle says in *De generatione*, book ii.[3]

Third, it should be noted that a smooth, polished, dense body,
such as a mirror, produces a clear, sensible reflection because of
the uniformity of its surface; for all of its parts concur in a single
action, as Averroes says [in his commentary] on *De anima*, book ii,
in the chapter on sound;[4] and therefore they act uniformly and
in unity, and an integral reflection of a species is produced by a
mirror surface. But the parts of a rough body, because of its
irregularity of surface, do not concur in a single action; and therefore
the whole species is dispersed and, losing its integrity, does not
suffice to represent the thing of which it is species; and therefore
we do not see by means of rough bodies, as by mirrors. And Ptolemy
says in *De aspectibus*, book ii, that 'a rough surface produces

integre *SA*   47 suam: totam s. *B*   48 ideo: *om. F* / videtur *O*   49-52 de ...
politum: *om. SA*

50 confusio, eo quod partes eius non sunt ordine consimiles. Et Alhacen
dicit in quarto libro quod ex politis corporibus, non ex asperis, fit
bona reflexio, quoniam corpus politum eicit speciem lucis, sed asperum
non potest, quoniam in corpore aspero sunt pori quos subintrat
species lucis vel alterius.

55   Atque oportet sciri quarto quod determinant auctores perspective
quod reflexio non est intelligenda ut forma seu species veniat a re
et figatur in corpore polito et faciat suam speciem ulterius in sensum;
quoniam tunc si sentiens primo videns illam formam in parte speculi
prima, propter hoc quod forma ibi fixa est, incipiat moveri a situ
60 illius partis adhuc videret se in parte illa speculi, quia forma eius fixa
est, sicut quando sic movetur, videt rem quamcunque fixam in suo
loco. Sed nunc non est ita, eo quod cum videns est in directo secunde
partis vel tertie vel quarte, videt se vel formam non in prima parte,
sed in secunda vel tertia vel quarta vel aliqua alia respectu cuius
65 se habet. Amplius viso corpore aliquo et vidente ab eo situ remoto,
poterit accidere quod non videbit corpus illud in speculo illo, licet
videat totam speculi superficiem; quod quidem non esset si imprime-
retur forma in speculo, cum videatur speculum, et speculum non mutet
locum, et corpus visibile similiter sit immotum, quia forma eius simili-
70 ter inficiet speculum, sicut prius. Amplius viso corpore in speculo et
post elongato, comprehendetur corpus magis intra speculum quam
prius, quod non erit si forma corporis sit in superficie speculi.

Et planum est consideranti quod nulla forma est impressa in speculo
per reflexionem, sed magis contrarium, quoniam reflexio, ut dictum
75 est prius, est virtutis venientis ad superficiem densi generantis se
in partem contrariam et contra incessum incidentem, occasione
sumpta a densitate speculi, que prohibet transitum ipsius virtutis se
multiplicantis. Et ideo non imprimit hec virtus aliquid in speculo,
sed facit suam speciem in aere recedendo a speculo per continuam
80 generationem. Unde tali impressioni facte in speculo repugnat ipsa
proprietas reflexionis. Quod si ex habundanti virtute generativa sui
similis posset illa species veniens ad superficiem speculi non solum
per reflexionem generare se in contrariam partem in aere, sed in
substantia speculi, sicut bene possibile est, tamen illa species sic

50 eo: et B | Alhacen: alba B   52 sed: ex vel corr. S   53 quod S
55 scire FO   56 quod: quia B | intelligenda: illuminanda B | ut: om. B | seu: aut O
57 figuratur BS | sensum: oppositum ut in s. illum in aliud S oppositum ut in s. vel in alio A
58 quoniam tunc: quod stans S | viderit S   59 hoc: mg. O | est: cum O   60 vident
F videretur S | se: om. S mg. A | illa: mg. B^C sua B'   61 videret O | quacunque B
62 secunde: ex prime mg. corr. F   63 vel¹: om. S   65 amplius L | aliquo: a. nec O |
et: etiam O om. S   66 viderit S | licet: om. B   67 si: sed S   68 speculum²
non: om. S   69 immotum: in motum BL in motu S   71 inter F   72 sit:
sic B | speculi: om. B   75 generantis se: generatio S   76 occasione: o. occasio
se B   77 a: ad O | densitatem O   78 aliquid: aliud S   82 simul O | possit O
84 substantia: subiecto S

confusion because its parts are not arranged uniformly'.[5] And Alhazen says in book iv that clear reflection results not from rough bodies, but from polished bodies, since a polished body projects the species of light, whereas a rough one cannot, since in a rough body there are pores into which the species of light or of something else can enter.[6]

Fourth, it must be known that the authors of books on perspective[7] determine that reflection should not be understood as a form or species coming from the object and being fixed in a polished body, which [then] extends its species to the sense organ;[8] for in that case if an observer, who at first sees his form in the first part of the mirror (by virtue of the form being fixed there), should begin to move from in front of that part, he would still see himself there, since his form is fixed there, just as when he moves he sees any fixed thing in its place. But this does not occur, for when the observer is opposite the second or third or fourth part of the mirror, he sees himself or his form not in the first part, but in the second or third or fourth or some other part, opposite which he is located.[9] Furthermore, if a certain body is seen [by reflection] and the observer then alters his position, it can happen that the observer no longer sees that body in the mirror [at all], even though he sees the entire surface of the mirror; but this could not occur if, in the observation of [something in] a mirror, its form were impressed in the mirror, and the visible object and mirror were to remain immobile, since the form of the object would stain the mirror as before.[10] Moreover, if a body is seen in a mirror and is then moved further from the mirror, it appears further behind the mirror than formerly, which would not occur if the form of the body were [fixed] in the surface of the mirror.[11]

It is [therefore] clear from a careful consideration of the matter that no form is impressed in the mirror in the process of reflection, but quite the contrary, since, as was said above, reflection is [a matter] of a virtue coming to the surface of a dense body and taking the occasion, from the fact that the density of the mirror prevents its [forward] multiplication through [the mirror], to generate itself in the opposite direction, against the incident path. And therefore this virtue impresses nothing in the mirror, but produces its species in the air, receding from the mirror by continuous generation. Thus an impression made in the mirror is incompatible with the nature of reflection. But if by an abundance of power tending to generate its like, that species coming to the surface of the mirror could not only generate itself by reflection in the opposite direction through the air, but also in the substance of the mirror (which is clearly possible), nevertheless the species so produced in the [substance

85 in speculo producta nichil faciet ad visionem per reflexionem et per
proprietatem speculi, scilicet ut per eam res visibilis cognoscatur
et videatur, hoc enim impossibile est, et otiosum si esset; impossibile
quidem propter rationes tactas de modo videndi per reflexionem et
secundum proprietatem reflexionis; otiosum autem et vanum quia
90 sufficit reflexio seu forma reflexa, ut perficiat visionem de re visibili
quantum ad hanc visionem exigitur, quoniam visio per reflexionem
denominatur solum a reflexione, sicut et fit solum secundum eius
proprietatem et non per alicuius forme impressionem.

Ceterum magis impediret hec impressio, quia esset sicut macula in
95 speculo. Et ideo si esset bene fortis et sensibilis, sentiretur et non
ipsa res per eam, sicut nec aliquid videmus per maculam in speculo
quantumcunque esset ei aliquid simile, sed ipsam solam maculam;
quoniam si ymago Hercules esset ibi depicta, quantumcunque similis,
non videretur Hercules iuxta positus, sed solum ymago; quare similiter
100 hic sola ymago impressa videretur et non res cuius esset ymago. Cum
tamen dicimus et scimus nos videre ipsam rem per ymaginem suam
medietate speculo, et ideo nichil aliud videmus nisi ipsam rem per
speciem reflexam, sicut nichil nisi rem videmus per speciem venientem
super lineam rectam super speculo. Et ideo sicut res est terminus
105 linee recte per quam fit visus rectus, et dicitur sola videri, et non
aliqua forma vel ymago, sic terminus linee reflexe erit ipsa res, et
illa sola per eam videbitur, et nulla ymago in speculo nec in aere.
Sed tamen fiet eius ymago ab ipsa re usque ad speculum, a quo
redibit ad oculum, ut sic solum compleatur visio per reflexionem.
110   Considerandum ergo in hac parte quod dum superficies speculi sit
una, aut sit multipliciter fracta dummodo partes habeant eundem
situm et equalem sicut ante fractionem, fit una reflexio et apparet
una ymago unius rei. Quando vero partes franguntur et mutant situm,
tunc secundum multitudinem partium est multitudo reflexionum et
115 multitudo ymaginum unius rei. Et quoniam hoc non est propter

85 facit *O*   87 est: fieret *S* | *post* si *mg. add. O* sic   88 propter: per *B*
91 quantum: quam *B*   92 denominatur: determinatur *S*   93 non: tamen *B*
96 in speculo: *om. S*   98 similis *OS* simul *BFL*   99 videntur *B*   100 videntur
B   102 mediante *BL* | ipsam: illam *S*   104 super²: sub *L* sine *S* | sicut: *interl.*
*F*ᶜ *om. F'* | res: *om. B*   105 dicitur: illa d. *S*   106 forma vel: formalis *S* | ipsa:
illa *S*   112 equalem: *om. S* | fractionem: f. et equalem *S*   114 tunc: *om. S* |
multitudinem: multiplicationem *B*

of the] mirror would not effect vision by means of reflection and the [reflecting] property of the mirror (that is, in such a way that the visible object would be seen and discerned through it), for this is impossible, and if it were possible it would be useless. It is impossible for the reasons given concerning the mode of seeing by reflection and according to the nature of reflection. It would be useless and in vain because reflection or a reflected form [understood not to involve an impression in the mirror] suffices to complete the visual perception of the object, in so far as this is a visual perception requiring reflection—for vision by reflection takes its name only from reflection, just as it occurs only according to the nature of reflection and not by the impression of a form.

Indeed, such an impression would more impede [than assist vision], since it would be like a blemish in the mirror. And therefore if it were quite strong and sensible, we would perceive it, rather than the object through it, just as we do not see anything through a blemish in a mirror, however much the blemish resembles the thing, but only the blemish itself; for if the image of Hercules should be depicted in the blemish, however much it resembles him, we would not see him (it being assumed that he is nearby [and so situated as to be visible by reflection]), but only his image; by a similar argument, in the present case, only the impressed image would be seen and not the thing of which it is the image. However, when we know and affirm that we see the thing itself through its image by means of a mirror, we see nothing but the thing itself through a reflected species, just as, through the species incident on the mirror along a straight line, we see nothing but the thing [of which it is the species]. Consequently, just as the terminus of the straight line by which direct vision takes place is the object, and it alone is said to be seen, and not some form or image, so the terminus of a reflected line will be the object itself, and it alone will be seen through the reflected line, and not an image in the mirror or in the air. Nevertheless, its image will be extended from the thing to the mirror, from which it will proceed to the eye, and thus vision will be completed only by reflection.

It should be considered in this part that as long as the surface of the mirror remains one, even if it is broken into many pieces, provided the parts retain the same position and the same uniformity [of surface] as before the mirror was broken, a single object will produce one reflection and one image. But when the broken parts are moved from their positions, then a single object produces a multitude of reflections and a multitude of images according to the multitude of the broken parts. And since this does not occur

solam partium divisionem, sed propter difformitatem situs, ideo
oberrant qui putant ex sola fractione semper ymagines multiplicari,
nam sensus probat contrarium.

PARS II
CAPITULUM 6

Deinde sciendum quod radii quidam cadunt super speculum ad angulos
obliquos, et convertuntur seu redeunt ad obliquos; et quidam cadunt
5 ad angulos rectos, et ad rectos convertuntur. Et dicit auctor *Libri*
de speculis comburentibus: 'Significo, per radium conversum secundum angulos rectos, quod radius conversus continet, cum linea que est
differentia communis inter superficiem duarum linearum rectarum,
que sunt radius conversus, et inter superficiem planam, que est super-
10 ficies speculi aut superficies contingentes specula concava et gibbosa,
duos angulos equales.' Quando igitur cadit radius ad angulos obliquos,
tunc angulus incidentie vocatur ille qui est acutus; et a parte anguli
obtusi fit reflexio secundum quantitatem anguli incidentie, ita quod
illa pars anguli obtusi que separatur per lineam reflexam et linea
15 que est communis differentia, de qua dictum est, est angulus
reflexionis. Et sic linea incidens et linea rediens sunt diverse et in
diversis locis site, in eadem tamen superficie, et constituunt unam
lineam totalem, que ab auctore *Libri de speculis comburentibus*
vocatur radius conversus, quamvis et eius pars una que a superficie
20 speculi oritur vocetur proprie reflexa vel conversa, et alia que a re
venit vocatur proprie incidens. Et dicit Ptolomeus tertio *De aspectibus*
quod talis est positio radii incidentis et reflexi ad angulos obliquos
'quod unusquisque istorum duorum pervenit ad punctum speculi a
quo fit reflexio, et continent cum perpendiculari que ab ipso puncto
25 procedit de speculo equales angulos.' Et hoc vult Alhacen et alii.

116 divisionem: diminutionem *O* / situs: s. partium *S*   ·117 oberrant: errant *S* /
ymaginationes multiplicare *B*   118 nam: et iam *O*
    2 capitulum sextum habens duas conclusiones *O mg. L*   3 sciendum: consider-
andum *O* / super speculum: *mg. O*   3-30 deinde . . . reflexo: *S and A repeat this
material at the end of this chapter; variants are supplied only for the first appearance*
4 ad: ad consimiles *S*   5 rectos[1]: *om. F* / rectos[2]: talis r. *S* / et[2]: ut *O* / libri: l.
aspectuum *F*   6 significo: significando *FO* significit(?) *B* / radium conversum:
angulum c. r. *SA*   6-7 secundum: duos *O*   7 quod: quia *OA* qui *S*
8 rectarum: *om. O*   10 contingens *O* / specula: speculi *S*   13 secundum: per *S*

merely because of the division [of the mirror] into parts, but because of their dislocation, those people err who judge that images are always multiplied merely because of the breaking [of the mirror], for sense proves the contrary.[12]

PART II
CHAPTER 6

Next it must be known that some rays fall on the mirror at oblique angles, and these are reflected or return at oblique angles; and some fall at right angles, and these are reflected at right angles. And the author of *De speculis comburentibus* says: 'By [the expression] "ray reflected according to right angles", I mean that the reflected ray forms equal angles with the line of intersection of the plane containing the two straight lines (constituting the "reflected ray") and the plane surface of the mirror (or the plane tangent to a concave or convex mirror [at the point of reflection]).'[1] Now, when a ray is incident at oblique angles, the acute angle is called the 'angle of incidence'; and reflection occurs in the direction of the obtuse angle, according to [an angle of] the same quantity as the angle of incidence, so that the part of the obtuse angle contained between the reflected line and the line formed by the intersection [of the two planes], concerning which we have spoken, is the 'angle of reflection'. Thus the incident and reflected lines are distinct and situated in different places, although they lie in the same plane, and they form one whole line,which the author of *De speculis comburentibus* calls the 'reflected ray'—although the part that originates at the surface of the mirror is properly called 'reflected' or 'reversed', and the part that comes from the object is properly called 'incident'. And Ptolemy says in *De aspectibus*, book iii, that the position of the incident and reflected rays (when they form oblique angles) is such 'that every pair of them extends to the point of the mirror where reflection occurs, and [there] they form equal angles with the perpendicular proceeding from the mirror at that point'.[2] This is also intended by Alhazen and others.

14 que: *om. O* | *ante* reflexam *scr. et del. S* rectam   15 differentia: omnia *BF* |
est[3]: *om. BS*   16 reflexionis: *om. F* | incidens et linea: *om. S*   18 totalem: *om. S* |
auctore: hac *S*   19-20 superficie speculi: superficies *S*   20 vocetur: et vocatur *S*
23 quod: et *B*   24 cum perpendiculari: perpendicularem *S*   25 equales: *rep. B*

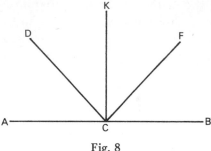

Fig. 8

Ut si speculum sit AB linea [fig. 8] et radius incidens sit DC et reflexio
sit CF et perpendicularis sit KC, tunc angulus DCK et KCF sunt
equales. Quando vero fit reflexio ad angulos rectos, tunc redit radius
in se, et simul loco sunt incidens linea et rediens, et fit radius
30 unus compositus ex incidente et reflexo. Quando vero reflectuntur
ad angulos obliquos, tunc radius incidens et reflexus separantur loco
et distant; sed tamen sunt in eadem superficie.

Deinde considerandum est secundo quod reflexio omnis fit ad
angulos equales, sicut Ptolomeus *De opticis*, hoc est *De aspectibus*, et
35 Alhacen in *Perspectiva* et Iacobus Alkindi *De aspectibus* et omnes auctores concordant; unde experimentum et causa et effectus hoc ostendunt, et docent fieri instrumenta ad hoc experiendum. Et de facili
possumus dicere quod si accipiatur instrumentum columpnare rotundum circiter altitudinem pedis et dimidii, cuius latitudo est semipedalis,
40 concavum interius et sine basi superiori habens basem inferiorem, in
qua constituatur speculum convexum, cuius speculi superficiei subtendatur conus quarte partis circuli de ere vel alio metallo, et illius
quadrantis basis tangat instrumenti concavitatem lateralem habentem
foramina parva rotunda in circuitu, e directo quorum lineentur in
45 lamina dicta protractiones linearum super quas veniant radii ad
speculum et super quas reflectantur, ita quod linea incidens super
speculum et reflexa contineant angulos equales cum superficie speculi,
inter quas perpendicularis cadat a foramine ad superficiem speculi,
quam perpendicularem circumstent linee incidentes et reflexe, vide-
50 bitur ad sensum quomodo natura operatur miro modo, quoniam radius
veniens redebit super lineam continentem angulum equalem angulo

26 AB: a *B* / linea: *scr. et del. O* nam / sit²: *om. O*   27 CF: EF *O* / tunc . . . DCK:
om. B / DCK: DEK *O* DKF *S* / et KCF: et KEF *O om. S*   28 radius: *om.FS*
30 unius *F* / et reflexo *SA*: et rediente *O om. BFLN*   31 et: *om. B* / reflexa *L* / *ante*
loco *scr. et del. F* a / loco: *om. S*   32 tamen: tunc *F*   34 sicut: tunc et *S* /
de²: *om. O*   35 Alhacen: Hali *F*   36 et²: *om. B* / hoc: et h. *F*   40 interius:
om. B   42 conus: corpus c. *F* sonus *B* / quarte *L*ᶜ: quare *L'B*   43 quadrantis:
om. S / lateraliter *S*   44 e: et *BN*   46 reflectantur *FLA*: reflectuntur *OS*

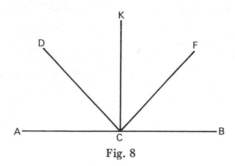

Fig. 8

Thus if line AB [fig. 8] represents the mirror, and if DC is the incident ray, CF the reflected ray, and KC the perpendicular, then angle
DCK and KCF are equal. When reflection occurs at equal angles,[3]
then the ray returns on itself, and the incident and returning line are
in the same place, and there is one ray composed of the incident and
reflected rays. But when they are reflected at oblique angles, the
incident and reflected rays are in different places separated by a
distance; nevertheless, they are in the same plane.

It must be recognized, second, that every reflection occurs at
equal angles, as Ptolemy in *De opticis* (that is, *De aspectibus*),
Alhazen in his *Perspectiva*, Jacob Alkindi in *De aspectibus*, and all
other authors agree;[4] and this is revealed by experiment and by cause
and effect, and the aforementioned authors show how to construct
instruments for establishing this by experience.[5] And to simplify the
matter, we can say that if one takes a cylindrical instrument, about a
foot and a half in height and half a foot in width, hollow inside with
a base below but none above, and on the base a convex mirror is
erected,[6] against the surface of which is placed the vertex of a
quarter of a circle of brass or some other metal, in such a way that
the base of that quadrant touches the concave interior of the lateral
surface of the instrument, in which are small circular apertures, and
directly from these apertures one marks on the said [quadrant-
shaped] sheet [of brass] the lines along which rays come to the
mirror and along which they are reflected, in such a way that the
incident and reflected lines form equal angles with the surface of the
mirror, and between these lines a perpendicular is dropped from an
aperture to the surface of the mirror (and the incident and reflected
lines lie one on each side of the perpendicular), then it will appear
to sense, if the experimenter knows how to apply himself to the
investigation of nature's secrets, how marvellously nature acts,
since the incident ray will return along a line forming an angle equal

flectantur *BN* 48 perpendiculariter *S* 51 angulo: *om. F*

incidentie et non super aliam, si experimentator sciat se aptare ad
secreta nature contuenda; et radius veniens super perpendicularem
redebit in se, ut ad sensum patere potest.

55 Et ratio ad hoc est cum species venit ad speculum, si transiret
in eius profundum, faceret angulos interiores equales exterioribus
super communem differentiam superficiei in qua est radius incidens
et superficiei speculi plani, aut superficiei contingentis speculum
convexum vel concavum, quia omnis linea recta stans super aliam
60 facit angulos rectos vel equales duobus rectis; et ita ex utraque parte
faciet rectos vel equales rectis; sed omnes recti sunt equales, et omnes
duo equales rectis sunt equales coniuncti aliis dubous equalibus
rectis. Quapropter anguli duo interiores A B [fig. 9] sunt equales
angulis duobus exterioribus C et D. Et anguli contrapositi equales
65 sunt; quapropter angulus A et angulus C sunt equales. Sed cum non

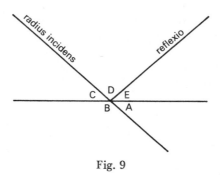

Fig. 9

potest species transire superficiem speculi sensibiliter, ut nunc est
intentio, qualem angulum faceret intra speculum (ut A) talem faciet
in suo reditu citissimo a superficie speculi, qui vocatur angulus
reflexionis, ut est E pars ipsius D, quia eodem modo se habet ad
70 superficiem speculi extra et intra; ergo cum angulus incidentie,
scilicet C, et hic angulus reflexionis, scilicet E, sint equales angulo
interiori, scilicet ipsi A, ut habitum est, erunt equales inter se, ut
patet in figura.

Hoc etiam demonstratur libro Iacobi Alkindi *De aspectibus*, et

52 si: sed *B*   55 ratio: *mg. O*   56 exteriores *S*   57 superficie *F* speciei *S*
59 recta *LOAN*: *om. BFS*   60-1 duobus ... equales[1]: *om. B*   62 aliis: *om. B*
63 interiorum *S* / A B: *om. F* / equales: e. scilicet AB *F*   64 angulis: *om. S* / *post*
D *add. S* totalis enim *et add. A* et totalis / compositi *F*   65 A: exterior incidentie
scilicet C et angulus interior ei contrapositus *SA* / C: id est *S* A *A*   66 ut: et *O*
67 A: est A *L^C om. L'*   69 ut: autem *S* / ipsius: illius *S* / *post* modo *mg. add. O* A /
ad *OL^C*: *om. BFL'S*   69-71 ut ... reflexionis: *rep. S* (*sed vice* ut *habet* qui)

to the angle of incidence, and along no other; and the ray incident along the perpendicular will return on itself, as can be perceived by sense.

And the reason for this is that when a species encounters a mirror, if it were to pass into it, it would form (with the line of intersection of the plane in which the incident ray lies[7] and the plane surface of the mirror, or the plane tangent to a convex or concave mirror [at the point of reflection]) interior angles equal to the exterior angles, since every straight line erected on another straight line forms right angles or angles equalling two right angles; and thus on each side it will form right angles or angles equalling two right angles; but all right angles are equal, and every pair of angles equalling [two] right angles is, in combination, equal to any other pair of angles equalling [two] right angles. Thus the two interior angles A and B [fig. 9] are

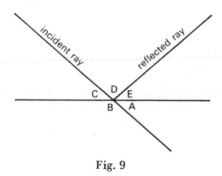

Fig. 9

equal to the two exterior angles C and D.[8] And since vertical angles are equal, angles A and C are equal.[9] But since a species cannot sensibly pass through the surface of a mirror, as we now understand, whatever angle it would have formed within the mirror (as A) it will [in actuality] form in its swift return from the surface of the mirror (and this is called the 'angle of reflection', as, for example, E, which is part of D), since the species retains the same relationship to the surface of the mirror outside and inside; therefore, since the angle of incidence C and the angle of reflection E are equal to the interior angle A, as has been shown, they are equal to each other, as is evident in the figure.

This is also demonstrated in Jacob Alkindi's *De aspectibus*, and

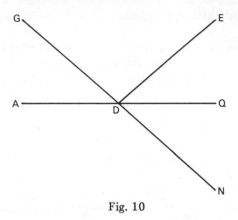

Fig. 10

75 primo in planis speculis sic. Si AQ linea [fig. 10] moveatur super polos
    suos A et Q immobiles, cadet DN linea super DE quando, per motum
    AQ, linea DN veniet ad partem alteram in circuitu; et ideo idem
    angulus constituetur ex DE et DQ ac ex DN et DQ, postquam AQ re-
    volvitur tantum in loco suo et poli eius sunt immobiles. Sed angulus
80 GDA et angulus NDQ sunt equales, quia sunt contrapositi; quare
    GDA et EDQ erunt equales. Et hanc probationem eandem affert
    Euclides ad quintam propositionem sui libri.
        Et hoc probato, ostenditur idem in reflexione a concavis et con-
    vexis. Nam ex nunc probatis patet quod anguli HBN et CBZ [fig. 11]
85 sunt equales; et quia ABN et GBZ sunt anguli contingentie (et ideo
    equales, cum uterque sit omnium acutorum minimus, ut ex *Libro*

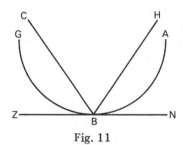

Fig. 11

    75 speculis: *om. F* | sic: scilicet *S* | si: *ex* sit *corr. F*   75–6 polos suos *A*^{C}: *om. A'*
76 A . . . immobiles: *mg. A*^{C} *om. A'* | *post* immobiles *add.* SA revolvet igitur secum GN et
DE et in hac revolutione   77 alteram: aliam *F* | in circuitu: *om. BS*   78 post-
quam: *interl. L*^{C} *om. L'* | AQ: A *F*   79 et: qui est angulus incidentie *S* qui est angulus
incidentie et *A* est *F*   80 NDQ: ADQ *O* NDQ qui est angulus quem faceret species cum

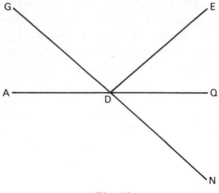

Fig. 10

first in plane mirrors, as follows.[10] If line AQ [fig. 10] is rotated about its immobile poles A and Q, line DN will fall along DE when, by the motion of AQ, it reaches the opposite side of its circuit; and therefore DE and DQ form the same angle as DN and DQ, provided AQ is revolved only in its place with its poles immobile. But angle [of incidence] GDA and angle NDQ are equal, since they are vertical angles; therefore, GDA is equal to [angle of reflection] EDQ. And Euclid offers this same proof in the fifth proposition of his book.[11]

Having proved this, we now show the same thing for reflection from concave and convex mirrors. From things proved above it is evident that angles HBN and CBZ [fig. 11] are equal; and since ABN and GBZ are angles of tangency (and therefore equal, since each is the smallest of all acute angles, as is evident from the

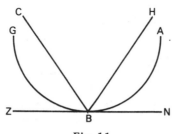

Fig. 11

speculo a parte altera *SA*   81 *post* EDQ *add. SA* qui est angulus reflexionis / erunt:
e. species *S*   82 sui libri: suam l. s. *B* s. l. de speculis *S*   83 ostendit *SA*
84 nam *FLO*: si que *B* et per hoc quia *SA* sic *N* / CBZ: TBA *BL*   85 sunt: super *B* /
GBZ: GA *S* / contingentie: continue *BL* / et ideo: oportet quod sint *SA*

elementorum patet), tunc si illos angulos contingentie auferimus a
totalibus angulis HBN et CBZ, oportet quod HBA et CBG sint
equales, qui sunt anguli reflexionis a concavo speculo, cuius figura
90 hec est. Et si NBD et ZBE anguli contingentie [fig. 12] addantur ad
HBN et CBZ equales, oportet per conceptionem quod HBD et CBE
sint equales; et sic anguli reflexi a superficie convexa erunt equales,
ut patet in figura.

Et hec eadem demonstratur in principio *Libri de speculis* vulgati,
95 quoniam prima propositio dicit: 'In planis speculis et convexis et
concavis, visus in equalibus angulis revertuntur.' Sed de convexis et
concavis probat eodem modo sicut iam probatum est. De planis vero
aliter dicit hoc modo, scilicet quod proportio GK ad KA [fig. 13] est
sicut cathetorum, scilicet BG et DA, hoc enim est in elementis positum.
100 Trianguli ergo BGK et DAK erunt similes per Euclidem; ergo angulus
E est equalis angulo Z, similia enim trigona sunt equiangula, ut ex
elementis patet; cuius figura est hec.

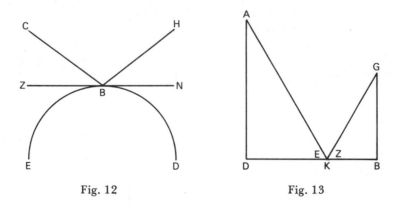

Fig. 12   Fig. 13

Et per effectum similiter potest declarari; quia enim angulus
incidentie et reflexionis sunt equales, non potest visus compleri per
105 reflexionem, ita ut forma impressa in speculo faciat visionem, de qua
impressione tactum est, quoniam propter equalitatem angulorum
incidentie et reflexionis, oportet quod oculus videns per reflexionem
occurrat radio reflexo, quoniam ille radius, propter eius equalitatem
ad angulum incidentie, vadit ad partem determinatam ita quod non

87 tunc: qualiter *S* / contingentie *OS* (*ex* continue *mg. corr. O*): continue *BFL*
88 CBZ: TBZ *BL* / CBG *OS*: TBG *BFL*   90 hic *S*   90 NBD: ABD *F* / anguli: *om.*
S / contingentie *OS*: continue *BFL*   91 CBZ: TBZ *B* / CBE: TBE *BL*   92 sic:
sicut *S om. L*   92 equales[2]: *om. S*   94 demonstratur *OS*: demonstrantur *FL* detra-
huntur *B* / *ante* speculis *scr. et del. F* spera (?) convexa / vulgati *SA*: vulgatis *FLO* vulgaris
N   95 dicitur *B*   97 vero: nec *FO*   98 GK: BK *B*   99 elementis: e

Elements),[12] if these angles of tangency are deducted from the composite angles HBN and CBZ, [the differences] HBA and CBG (the angles of reflection at the concave mirror) must be equal; and here is the figure. And if angles of tangency NBD and ZBE [fig. 12] are added to equal angles HBN and CBZ, it follows by reason that HBD and CBE are equal; and thus the angles of reflection at a convex surface will be equal, as is evident in the figure.

The same thing is demonstrated at the beginning of the common *De speculis*, since in the first proposition the author asserts: 'In plane, convex, and concave mirrors, sight is reflected at equal angles.'[13] His proof of this for convex and concave mirrors is the same as the proof that has already been presented. But concerning plane mirrors he speaks differently, namely, in this manner: that the proportion of GK to KA [fig. 13] equals the proportion of the perpendiculars BG and DA, for this is supposed in the definitions.[14] Therefore, triangles BGK and DAK are similar by Euclid; and there-

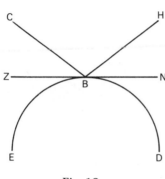

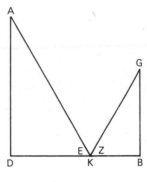

Fig. 12   Fig. 13

fore angle E is equal to angle Z, for similar triangles are equiangular, as is evident from the definitions;[15] and here is the figure.

This is also revealed through an effect. For since the angles of incidence and reflection are equal, sight cannot be completed by reflection conceived as the impression of a form in the mirror (which impression we have discussed above),[16] for because of the equality of the angles of incidence and reflection, the eye that sees by reflection must encounter the reflected ray, which (because of the equality [of its angle] with the angle of incidence) proceeds in a determined direction and no other; and therefore

Euclidis *S*   100 per: *om. B*   101 est: erit *S*   103 per effectum: perfectum *F* /
potest: p. hoc *S*   104 per: *om. B*   105 ita: *om. O*   106 impressione: *ex*
impressionibus *corr. F* / tactam *S*   107 reflexionis: reflexiones *S*

110 ad aliam; et ideo si oculus sit in illa parte videbit, si vero in alia
non videbit, quod dicitur videri per reflexionem. Sed si visio per reflexionem compleretur per impressionem speciei in parte determinata
speculi, non oporteret visum esse in loco determinato nec in termino
reflexionis, quoniam ubicunque poneretur, dummodo videret specu-
115 lum videret illam formam impressam, sicut maculam in parte determinata aut sicut ipsam speculi partem. Et ideo falsa est illa opinio
vulgi que estimat formas seu species imprimi in speculo ad hoc, ut
visus compleatur per reflexionem per illam formam.

Et non solum sic ostenditur per effectum equalitatis angulorum
120 incidentie et reflexionis, sed per alium effectum in caelestibus. Quia
enim talis equalitas est necessaria, ideo lux veniens a luna illuminans
totum emisperium habitationis impossibile est quod sit lux solis
reflexa a superficie lune; si enim esset lux solis reflexa, iret ad partem
determinatam orizontis propter equalitatem angulorum incidentie
125 et reflexionis. Sed non est ita, cum totum quod est supra orizontem
illuminat. Sed de hoc fiet sermo plenior in sequentibus. (σ)

PARS II
CAPITULUM 7

Et ulterius sciendum est quod radii adhuc diversimode reflectuntur a
speculis diversis. Et una notabilis diversitas est ista, scilicet que
5 ponitur in *Libro speculorum comburentium*, et est 'quod radius qui
convertitur a speculo plano ad punctum unum non convertitur nisi ab
uno puncto tantum ipsius speculi; et ille qui convertitur ex speculo
sperico non convertitur nisi a circumferentia unius circulorum qui
cadunt in illa spera.' Sed philosophi aspexerunt in proprietatibus sec-
10 tionum pyramidum, et invenerunt radios cadentes super communem
planitiem superficiei concave corporis ovalis figure aut secundum
figuram anuli converti ad punctum unum eundem. Quoniam propter
equalitatem cuiuslibet anguli reflexi ad angulum incidentie, non possunt duo radii venientes a plano speculo converti ad unum et eundem
15 punctum in superficie in qua radii extenduntur incidentes et reflexi.

112 compleretur: diceretur c. *S*   113 oporteret *BL*: oportet *OS* opereret *F* | *ante*
termino *scr. et del. S* loco   114 videret *L*^C: vident *L*'   115 videret *L*^C: vident *L*'
116 sicut: secundum *O*   117 qui *FO*   119 effectuum *S om. A* | equalitatis *FO*:
equalitas *BL* equalitates *A*   119–21 angulorum . . . equalitas: *mg. O*   120 quia:
quod *B*   122 sit: fit *FL* | solis et *O*   123 a . . . reflexa: *om. S* | iret: nec *BF*
125 quod: *om. B* | super *S*   126 illuminet *S*

if the eye is located along that line it will see, and if along some other line it will not see, the object said to be seen by reflection. However, if vision by reflection were completed by the impression of a species in a determined part of the mirror, it would be unnecessary for the eye to be in a determined place or at the terminus of the reflected ray, since wherever it was located, if it could see the mirror it would [also] see the impressed form, just as it would see a blemish or a part of the mirror itself in a specific place. And therefore the opinion of the vulgar, which holds that forms or species are impressed in the mirror and that vision by reflection is completed through those forms, is false.

This is shown not only through the effect of the equality of angles of incidence and reflection, but also by another effect in the heavens. For since such equality [of angles] is necessary [in every reflection], the light coming from the moon and illuminating the whole inhabited hemisphere [of the earth] cannot be solar light reflected from the surface of the moon; for if this were reflected solar light, it would go to a certain determined part of the horizon because of the equality of the angles of incidence and reflection. But it does not do this, since it illuminates everything above the horizon. However, this will be more fully discussed below.[17] (σ)

PART II
CHAPTER 7

It should be known, furthermore, that rays are reflected from other mirrors even more diversely. And one notable diversity is the following, presented in *De speculis comburentibus*, namely, 'that the ray reflected from a plane mirror to one point is reflected from only one point of the mirror; and rays reflected from a spherical mirror [to one point] are reflected from the circumference of [only] one of the circles on that sphere.'[1] But philosophers have investigated the properties of conic sections, and they have discovered that rays [originating from the same point] incident on a common plane of the concave surface of a body of oval figure,[2] or on a ring, are reflected to a single point. For because of the equality of every angle of reflection to its angle of incidence, two rays [from a common origin] cannot, when they have been reflected from a plane mirror, come to one and the same point in the plane of the incident and reflected rays.[3]

---

2 capitulum septimum habens duas conclusiones *O mg. L*   4 et: sed *B*
6–7 plano . . . speculi: *om. B*   8 unius: illius u. *L*   9 in²: *om. S*   10 communem: omnem *L*   11 corpori *B*   12 figuram: *om. S* / converti: consequenti *L*
13 incidentem *B*   15 incidentes: viciantes *B*

Sed propter figuram speculi concavi aptiorem, omnes radii qui cadunt
in circumferentia unius circuli circa axem transeuntem per centrum
speculi concavi reflecti possunt ad punctum unum ipsius axis; et qui
cadunt in circumferentia alterius circuli describendi circa axem
20 possunt reflecti ad punctum aliud in axe; et sic de omnibus circulis
ymaginandis circa axem; quorum omnium punctus qui est extremitas
axis inferior est polus; quorum circulorum quidam sunt minores, quidam maiores, secundum quod eorum circumferentie magis et minus
accedunt ad axem; et hii circuli sunt intra speram ymaginandi, sicut
25 extra describimus equinoctialem et equedistantes ei. Et radii circumferentie minimi circuli concurrunt in puncto axis superiori et maioris
circumferentie post illam ad punctum inferiorem, ita quod quanto
circulos est minor tanto radii eius reflectuntur altius, et quanto circulus est maior tanto reflectuntur eius radii inferius.
30   Quod ad presens demonstrare volo in sperico speculo dimidiato.
Nam radii infiniti exeunt a centro solis, qui cadunt in superficiem
speculi concavi, quorum unus transit per centrum speculi et per axem
eius et per polos. In isto igitur speculo concavo contingit ymaginari
circulos magnos transeuntes per polos eius infinitos intersecantes
35 se, sicut sunt coluri in spera; quorum omnium diameter est linea que
est axis spere. In quolibet igitur circulorum istorum cadunt radii
infiniti, et aliqui cadunt prope polum axis inferiorem, et aliqui altius;
omnes tamen transeunt per polum superiorem seu per terminum diametri altiorem versus solem. Et postea transeunt ultra in semicirculo
40 cadentes in puncto sue circumferentie, aliqui altius, aliqui inferius,
tanquam linee a termino diametri ducte usque ad diversa puncta in
circumferentia utriusque semicirculi hoc modo [fig. 14]. Sed linee

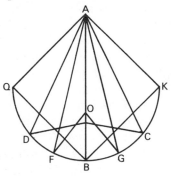

Fig. 14

16 aptiorem O': artiorem *mg.* O^c 17 circumferentiam *FO* / transeunte *B*
18 que *B*   20 de: in *S*   21 ymaginandis: magnitudinis *S*   23 magis: magnum *B*
24 circuli: Herculi *B* / intra: circa *O*   24-5 et . . . ei: *om. S*   25 et[1] *FA*: ut *BL om.*
O / ea *L*   26 superiorum *L*   27 post illam: radii concurrunt *S*   28 alterius *B*
30 quod: quia *L* / demonstrare: determinare *S* / speculo: circulo *O*   34 infinitos: in
puncto *O* quod inter i. *S*   35 omnium: causam *L*   36 igitur: *om. SA* / istorum:

But because of the more suitable shape of a concave mirror, all rays [from a common origin] that fall on the circumference of one circle about the axis passing through the centre of the concave mirror can be reflected to one point on its axis; and those that fall on the circumference of another circle about the axis can be reflected to another point on the axis; and so it is for all circles that can be imagined about the axis. And the lower extremity of the axis is the pole of all such circles; and some of the circles are smaller, some larger, according as their circumference approaches the axis more or less; and these circles are to be imagined [as those] within a sphere, as we have elsewhere described the equator and the circles parallel to it.[4] Now rays [reflected] from the circumference of the smallest circle converge at a higher point of the axis, while rays [reflected] from a larger circumference converge beyond this circumference, at a lower point,[5] so that as the circle is smaller its rays are reflected higher, and as the circle is larger its rays are reflected lower.

I would like now to demonstrate this in a hemispherical mirror. Infinitely many rays issue from the centre of the sun and fall on the surface of the concave mirror; one of these passes through the centre of the mirror, along its axis, and through its poles. In this concave mirror we can imagine an infinity of intersecting great circles passing through its poles, like the colures of the [celestial] sphere; and the diameter of all of these circles is the axis of the sphere.[6] Therefore, infinitely many rays fall on each of these circles, some near the lower pole of the axis, some higher; but all pass through the upper pole or the upper terminus of the diameter, in the direction of the sun.[7] And afterwards they proceed into the semicircle [of the mirror], each

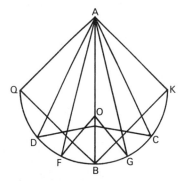

Fig. 14

incident on a point of its circumference, some higher and some lower, so that lines from the end of the diameter are drawn to different points on the circumference of each semicircle in this fashion [fig. 14]. But

mg. A^C om. A'
et aliqui altius   36–7 cadunt . . . aliqui[1]: *om.* S   38 *post* superiorem *scr. et del.* F
41 termino: tertio *B* / ducte: ducit *L*   42 circuli *F* / sed: *om.* O

cadentes propinquius ipsi B faciunt angulum obtusum minorem et angulum acutum maiorem quam linee cadentes remotius. Cum ergo
45 acuti anguli sint anguli incidentie, et ab obtusis fiat reflexio, et anguli incidentie et reflexionis sunt equales, oportet ut radius AG, quando reflectitur, minus distet a via incidentie et maiorem angulum reflexionis relinquat quam radius AC; ergo AG radius reflectetur ad punctum altiorem in diametro AB quam AC radius. Et adhuc AK reflectetur
50 inferius quam AC, hoc enim exigit equalitas angulorum incidentie et reflexionis. Et sic in alio semicirculo AF reflectetur altius quam AD, et AD altius quam AQ. Sed si AG et AF sint equales, ponatur ita, tunc reflectentur ad punctum idem in axe; nam anguli incidentie quos faciunt sunt equales, ergo anguli reflexionis sunt equales. Quare
55 radius GO reflexus nec plus nec minus distabit a loco incidentie quam FO reflexus; et ideo oportet quod ad idem punctum diametri transeant, scilicet ad O. Et similiter AC et AD reflectentur ad idem punctum, posito quod sint equales. Et eodem modo AK et AQ, qui cadunt in terminis diametri et in finibus medietatis spere, qui radii reflectentur
60 ad terminum axis inferiorem; nam cum radius incidentie, scilicet AK vel AQ, attingit quartam circuli habens angulum minoris portionis valde acutum, cui habet equari angulus reflexionis, oportet quod linea reflexa cadat in extremitatem poli spere et axis eius inferiorem; nulla enim alia linea alibi terminata constituet angulum reflexionis
65 equalem angulo incidentie nisi illa, quia nulla constituit portionem equalem portioni quam radius incidentie facit nisi illa, oportet enim quod sit quarta circuli; quare nullus angulus portionis reflexus potest esse equalis angulo incidentie nisi iste quem constituit linea cadens in extremitate axis.
70   Quoniam igitur in hoc coluro seu circulo linee equales, et arcus resecantes equales et que equaliter declinant ab axe, reflectuntur ad idem punctum axis, oportet quod ita sit in omnibus aliis coluris, quasi infinitis, habentibus eandem axem spere pro diametro. Ex quibus manifestum est quod si comparaverimus omnes istos coluros ad invi-
75 cem et sumpserimus lineas equales in omnibus, que de suis coluris arcus resecent equales, que etiam linee equaliter declinent ab axe communi, oportet quod anguli incidentie et reflexionis sint equales ubique.

43 ipsi: ibi S / faciunt: om. B / obtusi B   44 remotius: om. B / ergo: autem S
45 sunt O / ab: om. F   46 reflexiones O reflexi F / AG: ANG L   47 reflectuntur
B   48 reflectitur O   49 AK: AB L   50 quam AC: om. S   51 sic: fit F /
alio: om. B   53 reflectetur B reflectuntur S   55 GO: FGO B AF SA   56 FO:
F S / reflexionis B / transeunt L   57 scilicet ad O: om. S / O: C B / reflectuntur O
58 quales S / et AQ qui: quasi S   59 reflectuntur S   60 AK: IK F AB S
61 vel: et LS / quartum S / minorum B / proportionis S   62 valde: vel S / acutum:
ac B   64 nullam O / determinata S / angulum: alteri a. O   65 portionem: minorem
p. S   66 radius S: angulus BLOAN angulus quia F   66–7 nisi . . . circuli: om. S
68 quod L   69 extremitatem LS   70 quoniam: quando O / igitur: autem S

lines incident closer to B form a smaller obtuse angle and a larger acute angle[8] than lines incident further from B. Therefore, since the acute angles are the angles of incidence, and reflection occurs in the direction of the obtuse angles, and the angles of incidence and reflection are equal, it is necessary that ray AG, when reflected, should be less distant from the incident path and should yield a larger angle of reflection than does ray AC; therefore, ray AG will be reflected to a higher point on diameter AB than will ray AC. And finally, AK will be reflected lower than will AC, for this is required by the equality of the angles of incidence and reflection. Then in the other semi-circle, AF will be reflected higher than AD, and AD higher than AQ. But if AG and AF are equal, as we suppose, then they will be reflected to the same point on the axis; for they form equal angles of incidence, and therefore their angles of reflection are equal. Therefore, reflected ray GO will be neither more nor less distant from the incident path than reflected ray FO; and therefore they must proceed to the same point on the diameter, namely, to O. And similarly AC and AD, assumed to be equal, will be reflected to the same point. Likewise, AK and AQ, which fall on the ends of the diameter and the limits of the hemisphere; and these rays will be reflected to the lower end of the axis; for since the incident ray, AK or AQ, stretches over a quarter of a circle and has [as its angle of incidence] the very acute angle of the smaller portion [of the circle],[9] to which the angle of reflection must be equal, it is necessary for the reflected line to be incident on the lower pole or the lower extremity of the axis of the sphere;[10] for no other line, terminated elsewhere, forms an angle of reflection equal to the angle of incidence, since no other line determines a portion [of a circle] equal to the portion determined by the incident ray, for this must be a quarter of a circle; therefore, no reflected angle of the [smaller] portion [of the circle] can be equal to the angle of incidence except that formed by the line falling to the extremity of the axis.

Therefore, since in this colure or [great] circle equal lines, which intercept equal arcs and are equally inclined with respect to the axis, are reflected to the same point on the axis, the same thing must occur in all other colures (practically infinite in number) having the same axis of the sphere as diameter.[11] From this it is evident that if we should compare all those colures to one another and in all of them took equal lines (which intercept equal arcs in their colures and which incline equally with respect to the common axis), the angles of incidence and reflection would necessarily be everywhere equal.

Et quoniam reflexio hec fit necessario ad axem, tunc omnes ille linee reflectuntur per equalem distantiam ab incidentiis suis et respectu
80 axis; quare oportet quod in idem punctum axis concurrant omnes. Sed si hec vera sunt, tunc cum dicat Theodosius vicesima octava propositione libri sui primi: 'Si a polo alicuius circuli in spera signati recta linea ad spere superficiem producatur que sit equalis linee ab eodem polo super eius circumferentiam descendenti, necesse est eam in
85 eiusdem circuli circumferentia terminari,' oportet quod circumferentia circuli que transit per extremitatem unius istarum linearum transeat per omnes, quoniam omnes sunt equales et equaliter distantes ab axe communi et equales arcus suorum colurorum resecantes. Quapropter patet ultima conclusio, quod omnes radii cadentes in circumferentiam
90 cuiuscunque circuli ymaginati in concavitate speculi sperici circa axem reflectentur ad unum et idem punctum in axe; et qui in alia circumferentia cadent reflectentur ad alium punctum; et qui in tertia ad tertium. Et sunt isti circuli quasi equedistantes in spera, ut equinoctiales et sui compares.
95   Considerandum tamen quod isti circuli non faciunt ad reflexionem, sed accidunt omnino. Non enim in eorum superficiebus iacent radii incidentes et reflexi, sed in coluris dictis coincidunt isti circuli solum in locis reflexionum qui sunt in coluris propter equalem distantiam ab axe in circuitu; et ex hoc oriuntur isti circuli, et
100 possunt intelligi circa axem. Et ideo multi decipiuntur, estimantes quod hii circuli sunt necessarii ad reflexionem, quia omnes radii cadentes in unam circumferentiam reflectuntur ad punctum unum (τ); sed hoc omnino accidentale est, quoniam et si non essent hii circuli, fieret reflexio; sed nobis manifestatur levius per ymaginationem
105 istorum circulorum.

Et hec reflexio probatur per experientiam et effectum. Nam speculo concavo ad solem posito ignis accenditur, ut dicit ultima propositio *De speculis*, scilicet in puncto axis ad quem reflectuntur omnes radii circumferentie unius circuli. Unde si stupa vel aliud combustibile
110 apponatur sole fortiter radiante potest comburi in puncto illo. Sed non omnes radii cadentes in superficie illius speculi concurrunt in punctum unum, nec ad omnem distantiam quam volumus. Et ideo

78 ille: *om. S*   79 reflectentur *S*   80 idem: id *FL* / sed: et *O*   81 tunc: *om. O* / dicit *B*   81-2 propositio *S*   82 signat *B* / recta: *ex* recte *corr. B* 83 spere: *om. S*   84 descendenti *SA*: decedenti *LO* decenti *F* dicte *B* ducto *N* 85 eius *O* / circumferentia[1]: circumferentiam *B*   88 colurorum: oculorum *B* 89 quod: quoniam *B* / *ante* cadentes *scr. et del. S* concludentes   91 reflectuntur *FO* 92 cadunt reflectuntur *FO* / aliud *S* / qui in: quasi *BL*   93 ad: in *O*   94 equinoctialis *OS* / sue *S*   96 non: nunc *F*   97 incidente *B* / reflexi: reflexa *S ex* reflexa *corr. B* / in: *om. O* / coincidunt: c. enim *LS* / isti circuli: *om. S*   98 que *S*   99 ab: in *O* / ex: *mg. O*   101-2 quia . . . unum: *om. SA*   102 flectuntur *B* 103 essent: esset *B* / hii *LSAN*: hic *BFO*   107 accendatur *L*   108 scilicet: *om.*

And since all the reflected lines necessarily meet the axis, they are all reflected through an equal distance from their incident rays and with respect to the axis; it is therefore necessary that all converge to the same point of the axis. But if these things are true, then, since Theodosius says in book i, proposition 28: 'If, from the pole of any circle marked on a sphere, a straight line is drawn to the surface of the sphere, equal in length to another line descending from that pole to the circumference [of the circle], the first line must terminate on the circumference of the same circle,'[12] it follows that the circumference of the circle that passes through the end of one of those lines passes through [the ends of] all, since all are equal and diverge equally from their common axis and intercept equal arcs of their colures. Thus the final conclusion is evident—that all rays incident on the circumference of any circle imagined on the interior of a spherical mirror about the axis will be reflected to one and the same point of the axis; and those incident on another circumference will be reflected to another point; and those incident on a third to a third. And these circles are as parallels on a sphere, such as equators and their like.

It must be recognized, however, that these circles do not produce reflection but are entirely incidental. For the incident and reflected rays do not fall on their surfaces; rather, these circles intersect the said colures only at the points of reflection in the colures, according to the equal distances [of the points of reflection] from the axis [as measured] along the circumference [of the colure]; and this is the origin of these circles, and they can be understood to circle the axis.[13] And therefore many people are deceived, judging these circles to be necessary for reflection, since all rays falling on one circumference are reflected to one point (τ); but this is entirely accidental, since even if there were no such circles, reflection would occur; however, imagining these circles helps us to understand the reflection.

This reflection is also proved by its effect and by experience; for, as the final proposition of *De speculis* says, 'fire is kindled by a concave mirror that faces the sun',[14] namely, at the point of the axis to which all rays from the circumference of one circle are reflected. Therefore, if oakum or some other combustible substance is placed before a bright sun [in the presence of such a mirror], it can be ignited at that point. But not all rays incident on the surface of that mirror converge at one point, nor at whatever distance [from the mirror] we may wish. Therefore,

LO / reflectentur *S*   109 *ante* circumferentie *scr. et del. S* circumstante / stupa vel:
stepalis(?) *S* / aliud: aliquod *F*   112 omnem: communem *S*

philosophi ingeniati sunt specula concava aliarum figurarum quam sint
specula dicta communiter concava, ut fiat congregatio omnium radi-
115 orum cadentium in superficie speculi ad punctum unum in axe; et non
solum fiat ad aliquam determinatam distantiam, sed ad omnem quam
voluerit experimentator perfectus. Et hoc probatur per auctorem *Libri
de speculis comburentibus*, qui dicit: 'Qualiter autem habeam speculum concavum comburentem cuius combustio sit secundum longi-
120 tudinem notam quamcunque voluerimus, ponemus laminam de calibe,
et cetera', quod docet fieri secundum figuram ovi vel anuli. Et ponit ad
hoc demonstrationes suas, ut ex libro eius patent, quas nimis longum
esset enarrare et difficilius explicari quam presens opusculum requirat.

Breviter tamen sciendum quod istud speculum sic debet figurari
125 quatinus omnes anguli cadentes in omnibus circulationibus circa axem
fiant equales, ut si speculum concavum spericum premeretur undique
equaliter donec omnes equedistantes circa polum suum possent recipere terminos linearum que in omnium colurorum singulis punctis
facerent angulos equales, et quatinus in quolibet coluro ymaginato,
130 quorum diameter est axis speculi, radii cadentes tam longe quam prope
respectu axis constituant angulos equales, ut scilicet quos angulos
unus radius faciat in medietate coluri faciat quilibet. Et hoc est impossibile in spera. Sed oportet quod speculum spericum mutet undique
suam figuram parumper, ut laxetur spericitas ex omni parte, quatinus
135 declinet ad ovalem figuram vel anularem ubi coluri et equedistantes
ymaginandi non sint veri circuli. Nam non omnes linee directe a
puncto in medio ad circumferentiam sunt equales, sed sunt sicut
communes sectiones pyramidum rotundarum et superficierum
planarum, quando secantur secundum longitudinem, non secundum
140 latitudinem. Docet etiam Euclides in tertia decima propositione *De
speculis* sic figurari speculum ut congregatio radiorum fiat ante et
retro; et qualiter possit intelligi exponetur inferius.

113 concava: *om. O*   113–14 aliarum . . . dicta: *mg.* (*sed* sint *om.*) *O*
114 communiter: *om. O* | *post* fiat *add.* S *et mg. add.* A^C valida combustio per | congre-
gationem *SA*   114–16 radiorum . . . aliquam: *mg.* (*sed post* radiorum *add.* quasi) *O*
116 *ante* distantiam *scr. et del.* L substantiam   117 et . . . libri: secundum quod
auctor *S*   118 qui: *om.* S | autem: *om.* B | habeamus *O*   119 fit *FO*
120 volueris *F* | ponamus *B*   121 et cetera: *om. FO* | ponit: porat *B*   122 patent
BLO: patet *FSA^C om. A'*   123 explicare *S* | quam: quantum *F* quantum ad *O* |
requiratur *O om. SA*   124–6 sic . . . speculum: *mg.* (*sed* quatinus *obs.*) *O*

philosophers have invented concave mirrors of a different shape from those commonly called 'concave', in which all rays incident on the surface of the mirror converge to one point of the axis; and this convergence occurs not only at a certain determined distance [from the mirror], but at any distance the skilful experimenter chooses. And this is proved by the author of *De speculis comburentibus*, who says: 'To produce a concave burning mirror in which combustion occurs at whatever determined distance [from the mirror] we wish, . . . we take a thin piece of steel, etc.',[15] for he teaches how to construct such a mirror of oval or annular shape.[16] And he presents demonstrations to this end, and these are available in his book, but their exposition is too long and their explanation too difficult for the present small work.

Nevertheless, in brief, it should be known that this mirror must be so shaped that all angles formed [by reflection] on all circles about the axis are equal,[17] as if a spherical concave mirror were equally compressed on all sides until all parallel circles about its pole could receive the ends of lines that form equal angles at individual points of all colures, and so that in each of the imagined colures (the diameter of which is the axis of the mirror) rays falling both near and far from the axis form equal angles; and thus whatever angles one ray forms with half the colure, all form. And this is impossible in a sphere. But the spherical mirror must have its shape altered a little on all sides and depart everywhere from sphericity, until it achieves an oval or annular figure in which the imagined colures and parallels are not true circles.[18] For not all straight lines from the point in the middle [of the colure or parallel] to the circumference are equal, but [the colures] are like the cross-sections of cones cut longitudinally (rather than transversely) by plane surfaces. Also, Euclid, in proposition 13 of *De speculis*, shows how a mirror can be shaped to produce convergence of rays before or behind [the mirror];[19] and how this is to be understood will be explained below.[20]

126 fiant: *ex* fiunt *corr.* L   126-9 ut . . . equales: *om. SA' mg. A*^{C} 128 omnium: modum O   129 coluro: colure *BL'* colunt *mg. L*^{C} 132 radius: angulus S / in medietate: immediate O   134 parumper: *om.* O   135 anularem: *om.* B / ubi: ut B   136 sint: sicut L sic B / vere S / directe: ducte O   139 quando: que O   140 etiam: enim FO / tertia decima: *correxi ex* 33^a O *in* 21^a L 22^a B 15 S secunda A   141 speculum: de speculis F / ut . . . fiat: ut comburat SA / et: quod L   141-2 et . . . inferius: sed hoc maiori considerationem relinquatur SA

PARS II
CAPITULUM 8

Deinde consideranda est multiplicatio secundum figuras. Et patet quod multiplicatio est sperica naturaliter, quoniam agens undique et in
5 omnem partem et secundum omnes diametros facit speciem suam, ut probatum est prius. Quare oportet quod agens sit centrum a quo linee in omnem partem procedant. Sed tales linee sunt semidiametri spere, et non possunt terminari nisi ad superficiem spericam. Item natura facit quod melius est ad salutem rei, et ideo acquirit sibi figuram
10 que magis operatur ad salutem; sed vicinia partium in toto est maxime operativa salutis earum et totius, quia divisio et distractio earum saluti maxime repugnat. Quapropter omnis natura acquirens sibi figuram ex sua potestate debet querere illam que maxime habet viciniam partium in toto, nisi propter causam finalem repugnet; sed hec est sperica,
15 quoniam omnes partes plus vicinantur in ea quam in alia, cum non pellatur in angulos nec latera in quibus distant partes ad invicem. Quapropter lux acquiret sibi figuram spericam, sicut gutte roris pendentes a terminis herbarum spericam sibi figuram acquirunt, quamvis in rebus animatis, propter operationes anime varias, oportet quod
20 figura sit secundum exigentiam operationum anime. Et hoc volunt omnes auctores. Possent autem rationes hic induci de proprietatibus figure sperice, sed quia sunt communes figurationi aliarum rerum multarum et non proprie speciei, nec est necesse modo eas induci; ideo pertranseo, inferius enim circa mundi corpora figuranda considera-
25 bitur ratio istius figure.

Sed in oppositum arguitur quod lux cadens per foramen oblongum vel multiangulum cadit in figuram secundum figurationem foraminis, precipue si sit aliquantulum magnum, quia si sit valde parvum tunc lumen in figura cadit rotunda. Et dicendum est quod licet in distantia
30 parva non acquirat sibi figuram debitam, tamen in sufficienti distantia acquiret; quanto enim foramen est maius tanto in maiori distantia acquirit, quia scilicet maiores dimensiones foraminis multilateri magis a circulo et spera elongantur. Si enim paries in tantum a foramine elongaretur quantum foramen ab agente, ut a sole
35 vel alio, necesse est quod species solis fiat equalis portioni solis

2 capitulum octavum habens unam veritatem principalem et tres incidentales vel annexas *O* mg. *L* (*sed vice* vel *hab. L* seu)   5 speciem: speram *S*   7 precedunt *F* 9 salutem: naturam *B*   10 vicinia: intima *S*   12 maxime: magis *O* / requirens *B* 13 vicinam *FS*   14 finalem: *om. B*   16 pellantur *O*   17 *post* figuram *scr. et del. L* in rebus animatis propter operationes anime varias oportet quod figura sic secundum exigentiam   18 acquirit *S*   19–20 in . . . exigentiam: *mg. L*^C *om. L*' 20 hec *L*   21 possunt *S*   23 non: *om. O* / est: esse *L* / et ideo *B* 24–5 figurandi considerabitum *B*   31 acquirit *O* / magis *S*   32 in maiores *S* 33 circulo et: circulorum *FO*   35 proportioni *S*

PART II
CHAPTER 8

Next we must consider multiplication according to figures. And it is evident that multiplication is naturally spherical, since an agent produces its species everywhere and in all directions and along all diameters, as has been proved above.[1] Thus it is necessary that the agent be a centre from which lines proceed in every direction. But such lines are radii of a sphere, and their terminus must be a spherical surface. Also, nature does that which contributes most to the well-being of a thing, and therefore it acquires for itself the shape that contributes the most to well-being; now, that which contributes most to the well-being of both the parts and the whole is proximity of the parts within the whole, since their well-being is harmed above all by division and separation. Therefore, every nature acquiring a shape by its own power ought especially to seek that which has proximity of parts within the whole, unless some final cause should intervene; and this is the spherical shape, since all parts are more closely situated in it than in any other, because it is not pushed outward into angles and [straight] sides in which the parts are far removed from each other. Therefore, light assumes a spherical figure, just as drops of dew suspended from the tips of plants assume a spherical shape; however, in animated beings, because of the various operations of the soul, the figure must meet the requirements of the soul's operations. And all authors agree on this. Arguments could be presented here concerning the properties of spherical figures, but since these are common to many other things and are not peculiar to species, they need not be presented now; I therefore pass over them, for below, in dealing with the shapes of the bodies of the world, we will consider the reason for this shape.[2]

But in opposition to this it is argued that light passing through an oblong or multi-cornered aperture is incident [on a surface behind the aperture] in a shape conforming to the shape of the aperture, especially if the aperture is rather large, since if it is very small the light is incident in a round figure.[3] And we reply that although light does not acquire its proper [circular] shape in a small distance, nevertheless it acquires this shape in a greater distance; for the larger the aperture the greater the distance required, since a multi-cornered aperture of large dimensions is more elongated from a circle and sphere [than is a small multi-cornered aperture]. If there were a wall as far from the aperture as the aperture is from an agent, such as the sun or something else, the species of the sun would necessarily be equal [in breadth] to the portion of the sun

multiplicanti speciem illam, ut patet per vicesimam quintam et quartam primi *Elementorum*. Anguli enim duorum triangulorum, quorum
unius basis est corda portionis in sole multiplicantis speciem, et
alterius corda speciei cadentis super parietem, sunt equales, quia
40 contraponuntur; et ex ypotesi latera triangulorum illorum sunt equalia;
quare bases sunt equales, que sunt corde portionis solis et sue
speciei, ut patet in figura [fig. 15]. Et ideo patet quod ex elongatione
accidit acquisitio quantitatis et figure que non accidit ex propinquitate distantie. Et similiter videmus quod radii solis vel alterius
45 cadentis in meridie transeuntes per idem foramen faciunt speciem
magis rotundam quam in mane. Unde non oportet quod licet sit

Fig. 15

idem foramen, quod propter hoc sit omnibus modis eadem conditio
speciei, et prope et longe, et in una hora et alia, et ad unum casum
radiorum et alium; non enim ita est, nam in mane cadunt radii ad
50 angulos obliquos et per medium vaporum, propter quas causas debiliores sunt facientes speciem debiliorem; que cause non accidunt in
meridie, et ideo acquirunt sibi figuram rotundam in meridie, quoniam
fortiores sunt. Econtrario accidit quod in meridie sit species minoris
quantitatis quam in mane, quia colligitur in spera quod in alia figura
55 minus rotunda dispergitur.

36 per: *om. O* / vicesimam quintam: 95 *B* 15 *S*   38 multiplicante *O*   44 vel:
om. L   46 mane: aere *S*   49 *ante* nam *scr. et del. S* illa   52 sibi *LA*:
ibi *BFO* similiter *S* quoniam: quia *O*   53 sit: fit *F*   54 mane: aere *S*

multiplying that species, as is evident by [Euclid's] *Elements*, i. 25 and i. 4.[4] For the angles of the two triangles, which have as bases the chord of the portion of the sun multiplying the species and the chord of the species falling on the wall, are equal, since they are vertical angles; and by hypothesis the sides of those triangles are equal; therefore, the bases, which are the chords of the portion of the sun and its species, are equal, as is evident in the figure [fig. 15].[5] Therefore, it is evident that shape and size not acquired at a small distance [beyond the aperture] are acquired as the result of elongation. Similarly, we see that rays from the sun or some other [luminous body] passing through a given aperture produce a more

Fig. 15

rounded species at noon than in the morning. Therefore, although it is the same aperture, it does not follow that the condition of the species must be the same in all ways, both near and far and at all times and for every incidence of rays;[6] for this is not so, since in the morning rays are incident at oblique angles and through vapours, and these weaker causes give rise to a weaker species. But these [weaker] causes are not operative at noon; and therefore rays [more readily] acquire a round figure at noon, since they are stronger [then]. On the other hand, it happens that the species is of smaller size at noon than in the morning, since that which would be dispersed if it were of a less rounded form is drawn together in a sphere.[7]

Quod autem lux ignis ascendit in figura pyramidali, hoc est ratione corporis ascendentis, non ratione lucis, quia figura illa apta est motui sursum, precipue quia partes ignis interiores, propter distantiam a contrario continenti, scilicet aere frigido, sunt efficaciores in ascensu;
60 et ideo in ascendendo expediunt se, et ideo altius attingunt; et alie partes consequuntur per ordinem, secundum quod magis et minus distant a contrario circumstanti; quapropter rotundantur in pyramidem. Sed tamen si ad locum naturalem ignis devenit, non staret in pyramide, sed spericam figuram eligeret, in qua quiesceret naturaliter,
65 nam ignis in spera iacet in concavitate orbis lune sperica. Et sicut dicit Euclides *Libro de speculis* et probat in septima propositione, figura lucis est maior quam foramen; sed hoc est intelligendum in distantia debita, quoniam valde prope foramen non accideret hoc, sed intersectio radiorum cum debita distantia est causa huius.

70 Et considerandum est quod semper est maius lumen et fortius in medio lucis cadentis. Et causa huius est quia ad illud medium pertingunt radii non solum intersecantes se, sed recti; sed ad circumferentiam non attingunt nisi intersecantes, qui sunt causa debilitationis. Quoniam vero in spera possunt omnes figure corporales et regulares
75 intelligi, et in spera possunt omnes circuli circumduci, in quibus omnes figure superficiales regulares possunt similiter inscribi (atque licet proprie inscribi alie non possunt per diffinitionem inscriptionis, tamen valent figurari in spera omnes); quapropter in multiplicatione sperica omnia genera figurationum includuntur, et ideo omnis multi-
80 plicatio speciei secundum quamlibet figuram potest reperiri in multiplicatione sperica, quam facit. Sed quantum ad fortem illuminationem cuiuslibet puncti rei tenebrose, sola figura pyramidalis requiritur naturaliter, et non quelibet, sed illa cuius basis est super os luminosi corporis, et eius conus cadit in partem corporis tene-
85 brosi; nam in hac sola figura salvatur perfecta illuminatio et actio nature, ut exponetur inferius suo loco.

56 autem: vero S / hec B   57 apta: a. nata S   59 efficaciores: edificatiores B
60 ideo[2]: om. S / alterius L   61 consecuntur S   62 rotundatur S
63 stat FO   64–5 naturaliter . . . sperica: om. SA   65 sperica: sperice O
66 probatur FO   67 figura: per figuram S / sed: et F   70 est[2]: om. S / post maius
scr. et del. S et minus   71 illud: id L   72 sed[2] BN: om. FLOS   73 non:
necnon S / que BS / sunt . . . debilitationis: est dilatationis causa S   75 omnes: om. S /
quibus: qualibet S   77 licet: hoc l. F / per: sed S / inscriptionem L om. F
82 pyramidalis: perpendiculariter S   83 cuius: ex que corr. S   83–4 super os:
superficies S   84 eius: cuius S / sonus B / parte S   85 sola: om. F   86 inferius: in F

That the light of fire ascends in a conical figure[8] is because it is an ascending body, not because it is light, since the conical figure is better suited to motion of ascent, especially since [in this case] the interior parts of the fire, owing to their distance from the containing contrary (namely, cold air), are more efficacious in ascending; and therefore they disengage themselves as they ascend, and thus they reach higher; and the other parts follow in order, according as they are more or less distant from the surrounding contrary; and consequently they are rounded into a cone. However, if fire reaches its natural place, it does not remain conical in shape, but chooses a spherical figure, in which it naturally remains, for fire resides in [the form of] a sphere in the spherical concavity of the lunar orb. And, as Euclid says in *De speculis* and proves in proposition 7, the figure of light is larger than the aperture;[9] but it is to be understood that this holds for a suitable distance [from the aperture], since it does not hold very close to the aperture, and its cause is the intersection of rays, along with the required distance.[10]

It must be recognized that light is always greater and stronger in the middle of the incident beam. And the reason for this is that to the middle extend not only intersecting rays, but also direct rays;[11] whereas to the circumference extend only intersecting rays, and the latter account for the weakness [of light at the periphery of the beam]. But since within a sphere all regular solid figures can be imagined and all circles drawn, and within the latter all regular plane figures can be inscribed—and although properly speaking, according to the definition of 'inscription', the other figures cannot be inscribed, nevertheless all of them can be drawn within the sphere—therefore, all kinds of figures are included in spherical multiplication, and consequently every multiplication of species according to any figure whatsoever can be discerned in, and produced by, spherical multiplication.[12] As for the strong illumination of each point of a nonluminous body, nature requires only a pyramidal figure, and not any pyramidal figure you please, but that having its base on the face of the luminous body and its vertex on the [illuminated] part of the nonluminous body; for only in this figure are perfect illumination and the action of nature preserved, as will be explained below in the proper place.[13]

PARS II
CAPITULUM 9

Habito in universali de figuratione specierum, nunc magis in particulari considerandum propter quedam corpora a quibus est prin-
5 cipalis multiplicatio in hoc mundo considerata, ut est in spericis,
cuiusmodi sunt stelle et oculi. Et certum est quod ab una parte agentis
tantum non fit species, nec a duabus solum, sed ab omnibus, quod
certificatur per dicta Iacobi Alkindi *De aspectibus*. Quoniam si ab una
parte, ut ponamus a centro, de quo maxime credebant aliqui, speciem
10 radiosam solum fieri, tunc omnis umbra dilataretur quanto magis
procederet, ut arguit predictus philosophus et patet in figura [fig. 16].

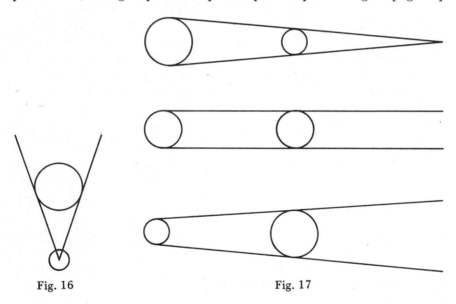

Fig. 16   Fig. 17

Et destruit consequens ex hoc quod umbra coangustatur in pyramidalem figuram quando corpus illuminatum minus est illuminante;
et protenditur in infinitum contenta lineis equedistantibus quando
15 illuminans et illuminatum sunt equalia; et dilatatur solum quando
illuminatum est maius illuminante, sicut patet in figura [fig. 17].
Similiter nec potest fieri a duabus partibus tantum, quoniam si
equedistanter fiat multiplicatio, tunc species lucis seu alterius, et

2 capitulum nonum habens tres veritates *O mg. L*   3 figurationE: multiplicatione et
f. *S*   3–II. 10. 106 habito . . . predictis: *S and A shift this material* (II. 9–10) *to the
end of Pars* IV, *immediately after insertion* (φ)   5 mundo: modo *FO* / considerata:
om. SA   6 cuiusmodi *OSAN*: cuius *BFL*   7 fit: sit *BO* / solum: tantum *S*
8 certificatur: certificatum est *O*   10 dilatantur *B*   11 et: ut *BL*
13 figuram: *om. B* / illuminante: illuminate *L*   14 contantis *L*   15 illuminans:

PART II
CHAPTER 9

Having considered in a general way the shapes of species, we must now consider them in particular, with respect to certain solid figures according to which the principal multiplication in this world is conceived—as spherical multiplication, which characterizes the stars and eyes. And it is certain that a species is not produced by only one part of the agent, or by only two, but by all, and this is proved by the arguments of Jacob Alkindi in *De aspectibus*. For if a radiant species should be produced by only one part, let us say the centre, as some have certainly believed, then every shadow would grow in size as it

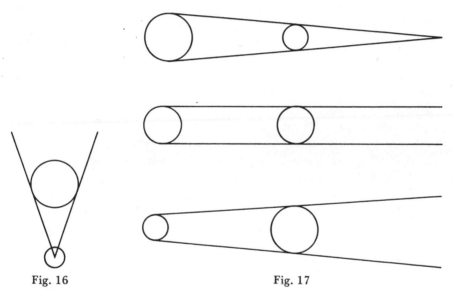

Fig. 16   Fig. 17

proceeds [beyond the umbrageous body], as the aforementioned philosopher argues and as is evident in the figure [fig. 16].[1] But Alkindi destroys the conclusion [of this argument] by the fact that when the illuminated body is smaller than the illuminating body the shadow is narrowed in the form of a pyramid; and when the illuminated and illuminating body are equal, it is infinitely extended between parallel lines; and only when the illuminated body is larger than the illuminating body does the shadow spread out, as is evident in the figure [fig. 17]. Likewise, species cannot be produced by only two parts, since if multiplication were to occur in parallel fashion, then the species of light or something else (and consequently

i. sunt *F*   16 illuminante: illuminate *L*

umbra per consequens, similiter continerentur semper duabus lineis
20 equedistantibus, et neque augmentarentur neque minuerentur, sed
protenderentur in infinitum. Si vero non equedistanter fiat multiplicatio a duabus partibus, tunc cum natura operatur semper uno modo,
oportet quod vel fiat lumen semper dilatando, et umbra semper
dilataretur in infinitum, vel semper contrahendo, et tunc umbra
25 semper contraheret et artaretur; et hec patent ex ratione figurarum
presentium. Et ideo oportet quod sit a pluribus una et duabus, sed
qua ratione a tribus et a quatuor et ab omnibus; propter quod
oportet quod sit ab omnibus et a tota superficie agentis.

Et huius causam preter dicta dat Iacobus in hoc quod agens est
30 consimilis nature in toto et in qualibet parte, ut lucidum et colora-
tum, et sic de aliis sive sit substantia sive accidens, dummodo sit
homogeneum; si vero sit etherogeneum, adhuc componitur ex partibus
homogeneis. Et preter hoc patet ex dictis a principio quod omnis
natura substantialis est activa preter materiam, et ideo quelibet pars
35 substantie facit speciem, licet alique sunt diversarum naturarum. Et
similiter de partibus habentibus diversas formas activas accidentales,
ut diversos colores vel huiusmodi. Quodlibet tamen talium de quibus
habitum est prius quod natum est agere aget speciem, sive tota
superficies agentis habeat alicuius illorum naturam, sive aliqua pars
40 superficiei habeat unum et alia habeat aliud.

Sed tamen secundo considerandum quod radii quibus utuntur astro-
nomi et perspectivi et ceteri qui per foramina instrumentorum consid-
erant radios, oportet quod concurrant in centrum si ymaginentur trahi
in corpus spericum, et sunt perpendiculares super speram. Et quilibet
45 illorum est axis unius pyramidis luminose cuius conus cadit in aliquod
punctum corporis patientis. Et tota illa pyramis denominatur ab illo
radio; unde tota vocatur nomine illius in consideratione philosophantium. Et causa huius est quia fortitudo pyramidis est ab hoc radio,
nam hic radius est brevior omnibus, sicut patet per undeviginti

19 continerentur *OSN*: continentur *BFLA* / semper: sub *F*   21 protenderent *S*
22 cum: *om. B*   23 vel: *om. O scr. et del. F* / umbra: in u. *L* tunc u. *SA* / semper:
om. O   24 vel: ut *B om. F* / contrahendo: concurrendo *S*   25 contraheret *BFL*:
contraheretur *O* concurreret *SAN* / artaretur *FLOA*: artarentur *B* coartaretur *SA* / patent:
ponit *S* / ratione *BLSN*: positione *FOA*   28 oportet quod: *om. F*   29 dicta:
dictam *SA* / dat: ait *B* dicit *S* / Iacobus: Iacobus Alkindi *S*   30 nature: *om. O*
32 etherogeneus *S*   35 licet: sed *O*   37 huius *S*   38 toto *F*   39 superficie *S* / habeat: hanc *S* / aliqua: aliquas *B*   40 habeat[2]: *om. F*   43 ymaginatur
S   44 corpus: centrum *S*   45 illarum *B* / sonus *B* / aliquod: aliud *S*
49 omnibus: o. aliis *S* / undeviginti *SA'*: 29 *A*^C*O* 20 *FL* 19 *B*

shadows) would likewise always be contained within two parallel lines, and they would be neither enlarged nor diminished, but would extend to infinity [between the parallel lines]. But if multiplication should occur from two parts in nonparallel fashion, then since nature always acts uniformly, either light must continually spread out, and then the shadow would continually spread out without end; or it must continually contract, and then the shadow would continually contract and be narrowed; and these things are evident from the present figures. Therefore multiplication must occur from more parts than one or two, and consequently from three and four and [indeed] from all parts; and thus multiplication must occur from all parts and from the whole surface of the agent.

And Jacob [Alkindi] finds the cause of this beyond what has already been said, in the fact that the agent is of similar nature in whole and in each part, as lucid or coloured, and so of other things, whether substance or accident, provided the agent is homogeneous; but even if it should be heterogeneous, it is composed of homogeneous parts.[2] Moreover, it is evident from things said at the beginning that except for matter, every substantial nature is active,[3] and therefore each part of a substance produces a species even if some [of the parts] are of different natures. The same is true of parts having different active accidental forms, as different colours and the like. In any case, a species is produced by everything that was shown above to be suited to act, whether the entire surface of the agent has the nature of one of those things, or one part of the surface is of one nature and another part is of another.

Second, we must consider that the rays employed by astronomers and perspectivists[4] and others who view rays through the apertures of instruments must, if they are imagined to be drawn into a spherical body perpendicularly, converge at its centre. And each of them is the axis of a luminous pyramid[5] with vertex at some point of the recipient body. And the entire pyramid takes its name from that [axial] ray, and therefore philosophers use the name of that ray to denote the entire pyramid. And the reason for this is that the strength of the pyramid derives [especially] from this ray, for it is shorter than all others, as is evident by

50 primi Euclidis, ut in hac figura [fig. 18] patens est; nam facit
angulos rectos cum corda portionis spere, et ideo per undeviginti
latera duorum triangulorum reliqua sunt longiora. Item plus de
virtute activa causat illum radium, quia totum profundum spere
usque ad alteram extremitatem diametri, quod est maius quolibet
55 illorum quod perficit alias lineas pyramidis, ut patet per octavam
tertii *Elementorum* Euclidis, ymaginato circulo AB [fig. 18], qui
transeat per polos spere, cuius unus sit in termino axis pyramidis
qui est E; sequitur enim per octavam tertii quod illa linea intra
circulum que transit per centrum erit omnium longissima. Et sic
60 habebit plus de virtute profundi ipsius agentis; quare axis pyramidis
a maiori virtute causabitur quam alie linee.

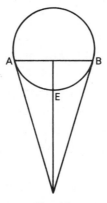

Fig. 18

Et tertio sciendum quod quia hii radii nati sunt concurrere in
centrum, non sunt equedistantes. Unde radii solares sic accepti
philosophice non sunt equedistantes, sicut docet Euclides in libro suo
65 *De speculis* nona propositione, ostendens quod lumen solis quod
venit ad nos non est equedistans, licet appareat. Si tamen obiciatur
quod umbre sunt equedistantes, ergo et radii, dicendum est quod
umbre diversarum rerum, ut hominum vel aliarum rerum obiectarum
recte soli, sunt equedistantes secundum sensum, sed non secundum
70 veritatem. Nam axes umbrarum sicut pyramidum luminosarum

51 undeviginti *SA'*: 29 *A^cOFL* 20 *B*   54 magis *S*   55 eorum *L* | quod:
quia *O* | alias: illas *O*   56 qui: quod *S* q. quod *B*   57 cuius: eius *BL* |
termino: tertio *S*   58 sequitur: constat *B*   60 quare: quia *S*
61 quod *F*   62 quod quia: tr. *B* | quia: *mg. O* | concurrere *FOAN*: contrahere
BLS   65 propositionem *B*   66 *post* non *scr. et del.* *S* venit | obiciatur:
appareat *S*   67–8 sunt . . . umbre: *om. SA*   68 vel: et *B*   69 recto
L | *post* equedistantes *add. SA* sic (*om. S*) et radii dicendum quod umbre sunt eque-

Euclid, i. 19, and from the following figure [fig. 18]; for it forms right angles with the chord of the portion of the sphere [producing it], and therefore, by proposition 19, the remaining sides of the two triangles are longer.[6] Also, this [axial] ray is the product of greater active virtue [than is any other ray], since the entire depth of the sphere to the far end of the diameter [is involved in its production], and this is greater [depth] than any that perfects the other lines of the pyramid. And this is evident by Euclid's *Elements*, iii. 8, if we imagine circle AB [fig. 18] passing through the poles of the sphere, one of which is E, the extremity of the axis of the pyramid; for it follows by proposition iii. 8 that the line within the circle that passes through the centre is longer than any other.[7]

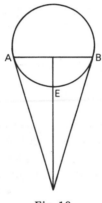

Fig. 18

Thus it will have more of the virtue produced by the depth of the agent, and therefore the axis of the pyramid is the product of greater virtue than is any other line.

Third, it must be known that since these rays are disposed to converge in the centre, they cannot be parallel. Thus solar rays considered parallel in philosophy are not [in fact] parallel, as Euclid teaches in his book *De speculis*, proposition 9, where he shows that the light of the sun that reaches us is not parallel, even if it seems to be.[8] However, if it is objected that shadows are parallel, and therefore also radiation, we reply that the shadows of various things, such as man or other things located directly opposite the sun, are parallel as far as sense can discern, but not in truth. For the axes of shadows proceed to the centre of the sun,[9]

vadunt in centrum solis; quoniam igitur concursus radiorum et umbrarum distat a nobis quasi per infinitam distantiam respectu iudicii sensus nostri, non percipimus concursum, et ideo iudicamus esse equedistantes. Nam soli F G radii [fig. 19] sunt equedistantes
75 ad angulos rectos; et C et D noti sunt non esse equedistantes, quia punctus concursus eorum est notus oculo, qui prope est. Sed A B non bene apparent non esse equedistantes, quia longiores sunt et punctus concursus non apparet. Item H et E longe minus apparebunt non esse equedistantes, quia propinqui sunt equedistantibus et
80 remotius concurrunt; multa enim sunt que secundum sensum nostrum

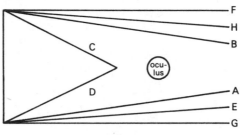

Fig. 19

apparent equedistare propter hoc, quod eorum concursum non percipimus sensu; ut parietes domus videntur secundum sensum esse equedistantes, sed non sunt, cum tendant in centrum mundi, quia omne grave tendit ad centrum. Similiter circuli meridiani diversi
85 videntur esse equedistantes, sed tamen concurrunt in polos mundi; et sic de multis. Sic igitur est hic intelligendum.

PARS II
CAPITULUM 10

Et quoniam bonitas operationum nature est per multiplicationes venientes in figura pyramidali, ut tactum est superius et explicabitur
5 inferius, quarum pyramidum coni cadunt in partes patientium et bases sunt in agentibus, atque corpora sperica, ut stelle, maxime in hoc mundo sunt active, oportet considerari multiplicationem speciei

72 distant *O*   73 non: ideo n. *B* et n. *S* / percipimus: per ipsum *S*   74 equedistantes[1]: equedistans *BL*   75 *post* D *mg. add. O* radii   76 eorum: e. scilicet(?) *S* 77 bene: *om. B* / apparentis *L* apparerent *B* / non[2]: *om. BL*   77-9 longiores . . . quia: *om. S* 78 appareret *B* / item: et *FO* / minus: unus *B*   79 et: cum *SA*   81 hoc: *interl.* *O*[c] *om. O'* / eorum: e. contrarium *S*   82 sensu: sensum *S* / ut: ut propter hoc *B* / esse: nostrum *O*   83 tendant: tendunt et *B*   85 polis *O*   86 hic: hoc *interl. O* /

as do the axes of luminous pyramids; but since the intersection of the rays or shadows is almost infinitely distant from us (as far as sense can discern), we do not perceive the convergence, and therefore we judge them to be parallel. For only rays F and G [fig. 19] are parallel, forming right angles [with the line on which both fall]; and C and D are known not to be parallel, since the eye (which is nearby) knows their point of intersection. However, it is not obvious that A and B converge, since they are longer and their point of intersection is not seen. And it is even less obvious that H and E converge, since they are nearly parallel and intersect at a greater distance [from the

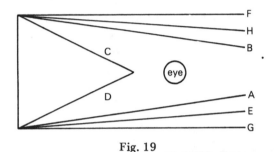

Fig. 19

eye]; for there are many things that sense judges to be parallel because it does not perceive their intersection; thus the walls of a house are sensibly parallel, but are not parallel [in fact], since they extend towards the centre of the world, as do all heavy bodies. Similarly, different meridian circles seem parallel, although they intersect at the poles of the world; and so it is with many other things. And this is what we wish to be understood here.

PART II

CHAPTER 10

And since, as we have mentioned above and will explain below, nature's most excellent operations are through multiplication in pyramidal [or conical] figures, the vertices of which are incident on the parts of the recipient while the bases are on the agents, and since spherical bodies, such as stars, are especially active in this world, we must consider how pyramidal multiplication of a species from

intelligendum: *Here L writes and deletes the text of* II. 10. 31–41 (hiis . . . oculi)—*material that appears again in its proper place*

2 capitulum decimum habens tres veritates *O mg. L*   4 et: *om. BL* et tangetur sive *SA* / explicabitur: exemplificabitur *F*   5 inferius: *om. B*   7 considerari *BFL*: considerare *OSA*

pyramidalem, quomodo habet fieri a talibus spericis. Et patet iam origo
dicendorum per viginti quatuor *De visibus*, que dicit quod de spera
10 cernitur eius medio minus est. Impossibile quidem est quod diametri
sperarum sint bases pyramidum dictarum, quia linee contingentes terminos diametri non possunt concurrere eo quod contineant angulos
rectos super illos terminos, ut patet per viginti quinque tertii Euclidis;
nec possunt linee recte intercidere per eandem. Et linee exeuntes a
15 terminis diametri extra lineas contingentie non possunt concurrere,
quia faciunt angulos maiores rectis, secundum quod cadunt a stellis ad
terram. Et si basis pyramidis cadentis in terram non possit esse diameter
stelle, non poterit multo magis esse corda maioris portionis; quapropter oportet quod sit corda minoris portionis.

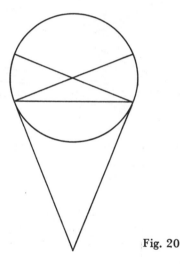

Fig. 20

20   Et quia magna differentia est actionis penes pyramides breviores
et longiores, ut patebit, ideo consideranda est differentia multiplicationis pyramidis longioris et brevioris. Et patet figuranti quod
pyramis brevissima que veniet a tota corda minoris portionis est illa
cuius linee laterales sunt contingentes speram in terminis illius corde;
25 nec tamen contingunt eam propter terminos corde, sed quia illi
termini sunt termini diametrorum duarum, ut patet. Et omnes alie
pyramides sunt longiores, quarum omnium basis una est, scilicet
corda illius portionis, ut patet in figura [fig. 20] per decimam quintam

8 quomodo: quando *L* / tabulis *S* / spericis: s. dictis *O*   8–9 et . . . dicit: *mg. O*c
om. O'   9 per . . . visibus: *om. F* / viginti quatuor: 34am *mg. O*c   9–10 que . . .
est[1]: *om. S*   10 eius: *om. B*   11 spera *F*   12 contineantur *S*   14 nec:
vel non *B* / incidere *O*   15 contingentie *OS*: continue *BFL*   17 possunt *FO* / diameter *N*: diametri *BFLOSA*   18 stelle: intelligere *S*   20 actionis: *ex* actiones
corr. *F*   23 veniet *BFLN*: venit *OSA*   24 *ante* laterales *scr. et del. L* radiales
25 nec . . . corde: *om. S* / nec: n. tamen *BL* n. eam *A* / eam: *om. A* / corde: illius c. *A* /

such spheres takes place. And the first thing to be said is already evident from *De visu*, proposition 24, which says that less than half a sphere is perceived.[1] Thus it is impossible for the diameters of the spheres to be the bases of the said pyramids, since lines tangent [to a sphere] at the ends of the diameter cannot intersect because they form right angles with those ends, as is evident from Euclid, iii. 25;[2] nor can straight lines be interposed [between the tangent and the circumference], by the same proposition. And lines issuing from the ends of the diameter outside the tangents cannot intersect, because they form angles larger than right angles—as when rays fall from the stars to the earth.[3] And if the base of the pyramid [the vertex of which is] incident on the earth cannot be the diameter of the star, there is all the more

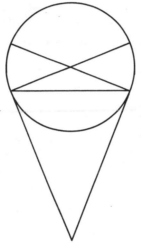

Fig. 20

reason why it cannot be the chord of a portion of the star greater than half; consequently, it must be the chord of a portion less than half.

And since shorter and longer pyramids differ greatly in their action, as will be evident, we must consider the differences in multiplication between a longer and shorter pyramid. And it will be evident, if you draw it, that the shortest pyramid coming from the whole chord of a portion [of a sphere] smaller than half is the one whose sides are tangent to the sphere at the ends of that chord; however, they owe their tangency not to incidence on the ends of the chord, but to incidence on the ends of two diameters, as is evident.[4] And all other pyramids sharing that same base, namely, the chord of that portion [of the sphere], are longer, as is evident in the figure [fig. 20] and by

quia illi: *om.* S   26 termini[1]: tamen S / duarum *BSA′N*: duorum *LFOA*[c] / patet: p. in
corde *L* p. corde *B*   28 decimam quintam: 5[am] *B* 3[am] *L*

tertii *Elementorum*; que pyramis maxime est activa, et quanto
30 longiores tanto minus agunt, ut exponetur et probabitur inferius.

Hiis habitis oportunum est considerari quod licet quelibet pars
agentis nata est multiplicare se sperice, tamen ab aliis partibus et
exterioribus obstaculis recipit impedimenta. Quoniam tamen in
spericis corporibus est impedimentum regulare et naturaliter, et hec
35 corpora maxime multiplicant virtutes in hoc mundo, ut stelle, et
maxime iudicant de hac multiplicatione in omnibus rerum differentiis,
ut oculi, ideo iustum est in hiis videri quantum contingat impedimenti
et quantum non, ut nobis determinetur multiplicatio istorum
corporum nobilium.

40 Et satis convenienter determinat Iacobus Alkindi veritatem huius
rei, dicens quod ab omni puncto corporis sperici convexi, ut oculi
vel stelle, venit species radiosa ad omnia loca medii ad que a quolibet puncto dato in agente corpore contingit duci lineam rectam,
et solum ad illa medii puncta ad que linee recte possunt a puncto
45 agentis sperici et convexi deduci. Quod autem virtus extendatur
radiosa super lineas rectas ad loca medii iam ostensum est secundum
ipsum et alios auctores aspectuum. Sed quod non possit ad alia loca
pertingere species radiosa quam ad illa ad que a puncto agente ducantur
linee recte, hoc ostendit per vicesimam quintam tertii *Elementorum*,
50 ponens exemplum in terminis et figura [fig. 21] sic. Corpus spericum

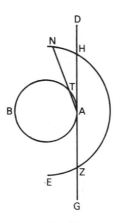

Fig. 21

29 que: quod *B*   30 probatur *L*   31 optimum *SA* / considerare *O om. F* / pars:
om. F   31–106 hiis . . . predictis: *S and A shift this forward to the beginning of Cap.*
10 (*before* et, *in line* 3)   32 est: sit *S* / et: *om. B*   34 et²: etiam *O*
34–5 hec corpora *OSAN*: hoc corpus *BFL*   35 hoc mundo: humido *B* / ut: non *S*
36 in: et in *S*   37 in: etiam *S*   38 quantum: q. est *S*   40 veritate *B*

Elements, iii. 15;[5] and this [shortest] pyramid is the most active, and as the pyramid grows in length it decreases its activity, as will be shown and proved below.[6]

Now that we have presented these things, it is appropriate to point out that although every part of an agent is disposed to multiply [species from] itself spherically, nevertheless other parts and external obstacles may prevent this. But since there is regular and natural hindrance in spherical bodies, and it is chiefly such bodies that both multiply their virtues in this world (as, for example, stars), and judge all the differences of things from such multiplication (as, for example, the eyes), it is therefore fitting that we see to what extent impediments exist (and to what extent not) in these noble bodies, in order to understand fully their multiplication.

And Jacob Alkindi determines the truth of the matter quite suitably, saying that radiant species come from every point of a spherical convex body, such as the eye or a star, to all places in the medium to which, from the given point of the acting body, a straight line can be drawn—and only to those places.[7] That radiant virtue is extended along straight lines to places in the medium has already been shown by him and other optical authors. But that a radiant species cannot reach any places other than those to which straight lines can be drawn from the acting point he shows by *Elements*, iii. 25,[8] employing the following terms and figure [fig. 21]. Let the spherical

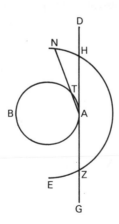

Fig. 21

42 vel: *om B* / veniet *B* / ad¹: non ad *B* / que: quia *S*   42–3 a quolibet: *om. S*
42–4 loca . . . illa: *mg. O^C om. O'*   44 ad¹: ab *B*   46–7 iam . . . loca: *mg. O^C*
om. O'   47 et: et secundum *mg. O^C*   49 vicesimam quintam: 15 *B* XVII (*post*
XVII *scr. et del.* 5) *S*

convexum faciens virtutem et speciem, ut stella vel oculus, sit AB; et
linea contingens ipsum in A puncto sit GD; corpus illuminandum sit
EN; arcus vero illius corporis qui secatur a linea GD sit HZ. Dicit
igitur quod ab A puncto possibile est duci lineas rectas ad omnem
55 punctum in arcu ZH, et patet per petitionem. Sed ad puncta in arcubus EZ et NH non est possibile lineas rectas duci ab A puncto, per
secundam partem vicesime quinte tertii Euclidis; si enim aliqua linea
recta contingat circulum, non est possibile, ut dicit iste Iacobus, ut a
nota super quam contingit circulum producatur linea recta in partem
60 circuli nisi linea circulum secans, sicut est linea AN, que circulum
secat in T puncto. Non est ergo possibile ut protrahatur ab A puncto
linea recta ad notam N, gibbositas namque AT prohibet lineam a
rectitudine; nec ad notam aliquam aliam que sit in arcu HN, et
similiter in arcu EZ, quoniam impossibile est lineam rectam cadere
65 inter lineam contingentie et circumferentiam circuli. Quapropter non
veniet species ab A puncto usque ad loca que sunt in arcubus EZ et
HN, sed solum ad puncta arcus HZ, ut patet in figura. Igitur ex hiis
colligendum est precise quod ad nichil spatii quod est inter lineam
contingentie et corpus spericum potest venire species a puncto in quo
70 linea speram contingit; sed ad omnia illa loca que separantur a corpore
sperico per lineam contingentie possibile est ut veniat species et
virtus corporis agentis, non solum prope, sed longe secundum fortitudinem virtutis ipsius.

Simul cum hoc considerandum est quod dicitur *Libro de crepusculis*;
75 cum due spere sunt equales, tunc illud de utraque quod respicit aliam
est medietas spere; cum vero altera est minor, tunc illud quod ex
minore respicit maiorem est plus medietate minoris, et de maiore
minus medietate illius. Et ex hoc patet cum species venit a maiori
sperico super minus, veniet a minore eius portione; et cum veniet a
80 minori spera super maiorem, veniet a maiori portione spere minoris;
et cum equales sint spere, veniet species a medietate spere utriusque.
Et iuxta hoc manifestum est quantum de superficie patientis recipit
speciem agentis, quoniam cum equalia corpora influunt in se invicem,
species agentis occupat medietatem patientis, et neque plus neque
85 minus; et cum maius et minus in se invicem multiplicant species suas,
tunc species minoris occupabit minus medietate maioris, et species

51 virtutem: et virtute *L* / stella: et s. *B*   52 illuminatum *S om. L*   53 EN:
HN *S* / qui: quod *S* / sit: super puncta *S*   55 et: ut *S*   56 et: vel *S*
57 vicesime quinte: 15 *S*   59 supra *O*   60 linea[1]: l. A *S* / qui *B*   61 secat:
om. F / T: C *BL* / puncto[1]: *om. F*   62 AT: *om. S*   63 aliquam: aliam *S*
64 impossibile: *ex* possibile *corr. O*   66 EZ: EN *F*   69 continue *B* / a: in *B*
70 speram: *mg. O*[c] *om. O'* / sed: et *O*   72 *post* corporis *scr. et del. S* sperici / *ante*
fortitudinem *scr. et del. F* longitudinem   74 simul: similiter *O*   75 illum *S* /

convex body producing virtue and a species (such as a star or the eye) be AB; and let GD be its tangent line at point A, and EN the body to be illuminated, and HZ the arc of the illuminated body cut by line GD. Alkindi says, therefore, that, from point A straight lines can be drawn to every point in arc ZH, and this is evident by supposition. But it is not possible for straight lines to be drawn from point A to points in arcs EZ and HN, by the second part of Euclid, iii. 25; for if a certain straight line is tangent to the circle, it is impossible, as this Jacob says, that from the point of tangency a straight line should be extended to [any other] part of the circle without intersecting the circle, as, for example, line AN, which intersects the circle at point T. Therefore, it is impossible for a straight line to be drawn from point A to point N, for the convexity AT forbids rectilinearity of the line; nor to any other point in arc HN and also arc EZ, since no straight line can fall between the tangent and the circumference of a circle. Therefore, a species will not come from point A to places on arcs EZ and HN, but only to points on arc HZ, as the figure makes clear. Therefore, from these arguments it can be gathered without qualification that a species from the point of tangency can come to no part of the space between a sphere and its tangent line; but the species and virtue of the agent can come to all places outside the tangent line, not only nearby, but also as far as the strength of the virtue permits.

Along with this we must consider what is said in *De crepusculis*: that when two spheres are equal, the part of one that faces the other is a hemisphere; but when one is smaller, the part of the smaller that faces the larger is more than a hemisphere, and the part of the larger that faces the smaller is less than a hemesiphere.[9] And from this it is evident that when a species comes from a larger sphere to a smaller, it comes from less than a hemisphere of the larger; and when it comes from a smaller sphere to a larger, it comes from more than a hemisphere of the smaller; and when the spheres are equal, the species comes from a hemisphere of each. And from this it is [also] evident how much of the surface of a recipient receives species from the agent, since when equal bodies irradiate each other, the species of the agent occupies half the recipient, no more and no less; and when unequal bodies multiply their species to one another, the species of the smaller will occupy less than half of the larger, and the species

recipit *B*   77 recipit *O*   78 alius *S* / maiori: minore *S*   79 minus: unus *B*
veniet¹: venit *O* / veniet²: veniat *O*   80 minori: minore *S*   81 utricunque *S*
82 patiens *S*   83 agentis quoniam: *om. S*   85 suas: *om. S*   86 minoris:
minores *B*

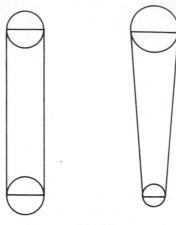

Fig. 22

maioris plus medietate minoris. Et hec omnia patent exemplariter in figura [fig. 22].

Propter quod cum a sole et stellis venit multiplicatio ad terram
90 et cetera minora sperica, oportet quod plus medietate terre recipiat speciem solis et stellarum, que sunt maiores terra. Et similiter est de stellis respectu solis, cuius speciem recipiunt. Et econtrario species corporum convexorum minorum non occupabunt medietatem maiorum spericorum. Quapropter species terre vel totius oculi multi-
95 plicata ad stellas et ad alia maiora eis occupabit de eorum convexitate minus medietate. Quamvis non loquor hic de virtute oculi pyramidali, cuius conus tendit ad centrum visus et basis cadit ad superficiem rei vise, que virtus facit operationem videndi, ut inferius demonstrabitur, sed de specie totius oculi seu a quocunque alio corpore sperico multi-
100 plicata ampliori modo quo potest ad superficiem corporis sperici maioris; de specie enim visus, que deservit operationi videndi, coartata in pyramide visuali cuius conus nititur in centrum visus, certum est quod non potest eius basis occupare medietatem corporis convexi maioris neque equalis neque minoris, sicut dicit viginti quatuor *Libri*
105 *de visu*, propter hoc quod radii istius pyramidis concurrunt in visum, cuius ratio patet satis ex predictis.

87 exemplariter: *om. O*   89 cum: *om. F* | stella *S*   90 recipias *B*
91 terre *S*   92 stella *S*   94 terre vel: *om. S*   95 eis: eo *S* | convexione *L*
96 oculi: *om. F*   98 vise: *om. F*   99 a: de *F om. O*   99–100 multiplicata
BSAN: multiplicato *FLO*   101 operationem *B*   102 conus: totus *B*
104 viginti quatuor: 25 *B* duo *F*   106 cuius: *om. SA* | satis: *om. F*

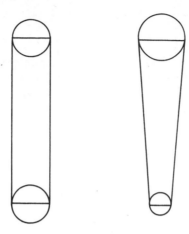

Fig. 22

of the larger more than half of the smaller. And all these things are evident by way of example in the figure [fig. 22].

Consequently, when there is a multiplication from the sun and stars to the earth and other smaller spheres, more than half the earth must receive the species of the sun and stars, which are larger than the earth. And the same is true of the stars with respect to the sun, from which they receive species. And conversely, the species of smaller convex bodies do not occupy half of larger spheres. Therefore, the species of the earth or the entire eye multiplied to the stars, or other things larger than they, will occupy less than half of their convex surfaces. However, I do not speak here about the pyramidal [or conical] virtue of the eye responsible for the operation of sight (as will be demonstrated below),[10] the vertex of which [virtue] extends to the centre of the eye and the base of which falls on the surface of the visible object, but rather about the species of the entire eye or the species multiplied in the fullest possible way from any other spherical body to the surface of a larger spherical body; for concerning the species of sight, which serves for the operation of seeing and is confined to the visual pyramid whose vertex is located at the centre of the eye, it is certain that its base cannot occupy half of a convex body larger than or equal to or smaller than it, as *De visu*, proposition 24, says,[11] because the rays of the pyramid intersect in the eye, and the reason for this is sufficiently evident from the foregoing.

PARS III

CAPITULUM 1

Habito de lineatione et figuratione speciei multiplicate, consequenter considerandum est de modo eius existendi in medio; et habet capitula
5 tria. In primo consideratur an species sit corpus veraciter, sicut multi posuerunt. Quod vero non sit corpus probatur per hoc quod non dividit latera continentis medii, quod est locum in alio occupare, ut omnes sciunt. Et ideo si species esset corpus secundum se, essent duo corpora simul, quod non est possibile. Et Aristoteles dicit tertio
10 *Methaphysice* quod corpora esse simul verificari non potest de naturalibus, nec de mathematicis, nec de spiritualibus corporibus. Et quarto *Physicorum* dicit quod dimensio corporalis data vacuo non potest aliam sustinere secum; et ideo posito vacuo, nullum corpus recipietur in eo, ut ipse vult ibi, quia non cederent dimensiones vacui dimensioni-
15 bus corporis advenientis, eo quod in vacuo nulla est natura qua cedat, cum nec habeat mollitiem nec aliam passionem naturalem; nec sua dimensio stans fixa in loco suo permitteret aliam recipi, ut dicit, quia dimensio vacui habet unde impleat locum. Repletio enim loci est per trinam dimensionem, quam dederunt philosophi vacuo veraciter ut
20 estimaverunt; non enim est repletio vacui per calidum et frigidum, nec aliquam aliam passionem naturalem, sed solum per trinam dimensionem, ut dicit Aristoteles. Ex quibus omnibus patet quod species in medio non faciens dimensionem inter latera eius non potest habere aliam dimensionem a dimensione medii, quia se non possent compati
25 simul.

Item prius tactum est quod generatio naturalis non tollit naturam corporis, quia certum est quod natura presupponit corpus in principio materiali; aliter enim posset de corpore fieri spiritus, ut angelus vel anima, per naturam. Sed hoc est impossibile; ergo natura non
30 aufert a principio materiali in quod agit dimensionem corporis; nec generat novam, cum illa sufficiat. Unde corpus quod est genus secundum nec est generabile nec corruptibile, sed creabatur in elementis, et de elementis remanet in mixtis sine generatione et corruptione, licet augmentetur vel diminuatur, quia augmentum et diminutio sunt

1 incipit tertia pars huius tractatus *O*   2 capitulum primum *O*   3 lineatione et: *om. S*   4–5 capitula tria: quatuor conclusiones principales una est an habeat modum existendi corporalem *S* tria una est an habeat modum existendi corporalem *A*   5 in: et *SA* / consideratur: *om. SA* / species: *om. SA*   6 vero: *om. B* / sit: fit *L*   7 continentis medii: *om. AN*   9 simul: in eodem loco *F* / *post* possibile *add. SA* statim (saltem *A*) in non glorificatis / et: et etiam *SA*   11 mathematicis: methaphysice *SA* 12 in vacuo *B*   13 recipietur *BFLN*: reciperetur *OSA*   17 alia *S*   21 aliquam: aliam *S* / naturalem: *om. S*   23 faciet *S*   24 aliquam *O* / a. dimensione: *om. FO* / possunt *O*   26 iterum *BL* / generato *L*   27 natura: *om. B* / corpus: corpora *L om. S*   28–30 aliter . . . materiali: *om. S*   29 anima: aliam *L*

PART III

CHAPTER 1

Having considered the lines and figures by which a species is multi-plied, we must now consider its mode of existence in the medium; we do this in three chapters. In the first we consider whether a species is truly body, as many have supposed.[1] That it is not body is proved by the fact that it does not force the sides of the containing medium outward, which means that it occupies a place in something else, as everybody knows. Therefore, if a species were itself body, two bodies would be simultaneously [in the same place], which is impossible. And Aristotle says in the *Metaphysics*, book iii, that it cannot be verified that natural bodies or mathematical bodies or spiritual bodies are simultaneously [in the same place].[2] Also in *Physics*, book iv, he says that the corporeal dimensions with which void is endowed cannot sustain any other [dimensions] with them-selves;[3] and therefore, even if a void were posited, it could receive no body into itself, as Aristotle indicates there, since the dimensions of the void would not yield to the dimensions of the intruding body, for in a void there is no nature capable of yielding, since the void has no flexibility or other natural susceptibility; nor would its dimen-sions, remaining fixed in their place, permit the reception of any other dimensions, as Aristotle says, since the dimensions of the void are such as to fill the place. For the occupancy of place is by three dimensions, which philosophers assigned to the void, truthfully, as they judged; for void is not occupied by heat and cold, nor by any other natural quality, but only by three dimensions, as Aristotle says. From all of this it is evident that a species in a medium not produc-ing [added] dimension between the sides of the medium cannot have dimensions distinct from those of the medium, since the medium and [such a] species could not coexist [in the same place] at the same time.

Furthermore, it was mentioned above[4] that natural generation does not destroy corporeal nature, since it is certain that nature presupposes body in the material cause; for otherwise spirit (such as angel or soul) could be naturally generated from body. But this is impossible, and therefore nature does not remove bodily dimensions from the material cause on which it acts; nor does it generate new dimensions, since the former [dimensions] suffice. Therefore, body, which is the second genus,[5] is neither generable nor corruptible, but was created in the elements, and through the elements remains in mixtures without generation and corruption—although it may be augmented or diminished, since augmentation and diminution

32 causabatur *S*   34 quia: *om. B*

35 circa quantitatem, non generatio nec corruptio. Hec sunt magis
verificata in prioribus; sed nunc que dicta sunt sufficient.

Quapropter cum medium sit principium materiale in quo et de
cuius potentia per agens et generans educitur species, non poterit hec
species habere aliam naturam corporalem a medio distinctam. Et hoc
40 certum est per hoc, quod effectus completus similis agenti nomine et
diffinitione non habet novam dimensionem corporalem, sed illam que
fuit medii sive corporis in quo generatur talis effectus completus
quando agens invalescit super ipsum et tollit naturam specificam eius,
de cuius potentia educit illum effectum completum. Quapropter con-
45 cedendum est illud idem de specie, que est effectus incompletus
vadens ad effectum completum nunc dictum.

Quod autem dici posset quod ad minus species substantie corporee,
cum sit idem in essentia, nomine, et diffinitione cum eo cuius est,
erit corpus et habens trinam dimensionem et locum per se occupabit,
50 sicut agens; dicendum est quod habebit hec species quantum potest
de omnibus hiis; sed quia nimis est sub esse incompleto, nec per se
existens, sed in alio quod per illam assimilatur agenti, manens in
natura sua specifica corporali, replens locum precise, quod ideo
prevalet in hac parte, ut ei locus ascribatur et trina dimensio simul,
55 in quo loco et sub trina dimensione claudit secum ex incidenti debilitatem speciei; ideo hec species non meretur dici corpus, saltem cum
medio in quo est (ponens in numerum, in trina dimensione, et loci
determinatione). Sed est una dimensio et unus locus quibus unum
corpus principaliter correspondet, scilicet ipsum medium, assimilatum
60 tamen agenti per speciem eius corporalem incompletam; unde est
corpus in actu distinctum; et ideo est corporale in corpore actualiter
existens.

Quod etiam generaliter pro omni specie videatur posse proferri
quod species incedit per se in medio, licet medium sit immobile et
65 quietum; et ex sua potestate petit loca diversa, non operante aliquid
ipso medio nec iuvante nec movente nec moto; sit ita quod quiescat;
quare erit corpus, cum nichil per se transmutet locum in corpore
quiescente nisi corpus. Dicendum est quod non est idem numero in
prima parte medii et secunda et aliis; nec illud quod est in parte

35 non . . . corruptio: *om. S*   36 sed: *om. S* / sufficiunt *L*   37 quo: q. est *B*
40 completus: c. est *FS* / agenti: *ex* agentis *corr. B*   42 medii sive: *om. S*
43–4 eius de: eiusdem *S*   44 *ante* potentia *scr. et del. S* causa   44–5 concedendum
O^c: considerandum *O'*   47 quod ad minus: *om. S*   51 hiis: *om. O* / nimis: unus *F*
om. B   53 locum: l. suum *F*   54 locum *B*   55 ex: et *B*   56 ideo hec:
non ista *S*   59 assimilatur *S*   61 in² . . . actualiter: in corpore a. alias *mg. O*
62 existens: accidentaliter e. *O*   63 posse: *om. F*   64 immobile: *ex* in medio
mobile *corr. S*   65 quietum: *om. S*   66 iuvante: imutante *B* / nec movente:
om. O / sit ita: sicut *B*   67 est *FO* / per: in *S*   69 est: erit *S*

pertain to quantity, while generation and corruption do not. These things are better demonstrated above; but what we have said is sufficient for present needs.

Therefore, since the medium is the material cause, in which and from the potentiality of which a species is generated by the agent and generator, this species cannot have a corporeal nature distinct from the medium. This is certain, because a complete effect, similar to the agent in name and definition, does not have a new corporeal dimension, but that which belongs to the medium or body in which the complete effect is generated when the agent prevails over it and destroys its specific nature, out of the potentiality of which it brings forth that complete effect. Therefore, the same thing must be conceded concerning a species, which is an incomplete effect becoming the complete effect here mentioned.

However, it could be said that at least the species of corporeal substance, since it is the same in essence, name, and definition as that of which it is the species, will be body and have three dimensions and occupy place of itself, like the agent [that gave rise to it]. [To this argument] we reply that this species will have as much as it can of all these things; but since it possesses exceedingly incomplete being and does not exist of itself, but in something else which, through it, is made to resemble the agent while retaining its own specific corporeal nature and precisely occupying a place—and this something else [the medium] therefore prevails in this region, so that place and three dimensions are ascribed to it, in which place and under [which] three dimensions it incorporates, from the incident [virtue], the weak species—consequently, this species does not deserve to be called 'body', or not, at any rate, in the same sense as the medium in which it exists (that is, numerically, in three dimensions, and by the determination of place). For to one set of dimensions and one place there corresponds principally one body (namely, the medium), although it is assimilated to the agent through the incomplete corporeal species of the latter; thus it is a distinct body in actuality; and therefore the species is a corporeal thing actually existing in body.

Also, in general, for every species it seems possible to show that the species proceeds by itself through the medium, even if the medium is immobile and at rest; and by its own power it moves towards various places, without the medium doing anything or assisting or moving or being moved, for the medium is assumed to be at rest; and therefore species must be body, since nothing except body changes place of itself in a motionless corporeal medium. [To this] we reply that the species is not numerically the same thing in the first and second and other parts of the medium; nor does that which is in the

70 prima exit eam, nec similiter quod est in secunda vadit ad tertiam,
sed quelibet in suo quiescit loco. Et ideo non est aliquid quod moveatur
ibi de loco ad locum, sed est continua generatio nove rei; sicut est de
umbra, que non movetur, sed renovatur diversa et diversa. Nec est
renovatio penes loca primo et per se, sed penes subiecta, quia species
75 est passio medii; nec locus ibi requiritur nisi locus medii.

Si dicatur quod moto aere per ventum vel aliud, ab aere non
movetur species, sed secundum eandem extensionem linee vel spere
continue a suo agente multiplicatur, occupans locum fixum immobilem
secundum se totum, licet renovetur secundum partes medii in eodem
80 loco, ut nunc tactum est; sed si esset indistinctum ab aere et eius
passio, tunc moveretur moto aere, quia moventibus nobis moventur
omnia que in nobis sunt indistincta in dimensionibus; dicendum est
quod hec est fallatia consequentis, a duabus causis ad unam. Quod
enim species sic iaceat in uno incessu immobiliter licet aer moveatur,
85 hoc potest esse aut quia nata est occupare locum per se ut corpus,
et sic non est hic, aut quia propter directionem agentis debentis
facere suam actionem in partem unam, ipsa species, que est passio
medii, tenet incessum unum; sed tamen semper presupponit partem
aeris in qua fit, per quam habeat locum, licet illa pars aeris sit diversa
90 et diversa succedens propter motum quarum partium aeris. Locum immobilem non tenet species ut corpus et per se, sed semper per partem
aeris prius renovatam in tali loco, que pars speciei est subiectum;
et non solum pars aeris renovatur in qua species iacet sicut in subiecto, non in loco, sed ipsa species in partibus renovatis renovatur;
95 nec manet eadem numero, quoniam etsi aer quiesceret, renovaretur
in parte renovata, id est in parte alia et alia. Et ideo cum partes
aeris succedunt in eodem loco, non manet eadem species occupans
locum illum, sed corrumpitur cum pars aeris in qua fuit mutat illum
locum; et non generatur nova antequam alia pars veniat in illum
100 locum; et ideo non habet locum per se, sed per aliud.

Si vero arguatur de reverberatione a corpore, patet ex dictis quod

---

70 eam: secundam S / in: *om.* L   71 movetur S   73 *post* sed *scr. et del.* O non
74 locum S / et: est F / sed: *om.* S   75 medii[1]: *om.* F / nec: non F   76 si: nisi B /
quod: *om.* B / per . . . aere: *om.* S / vel: et B / ab: quod in toto B / aere[2]: *scr. et del.* L /
non: ideo B   77 species: *om.* S / secundum: per S   78 immobilem FOAN:
immobile BLS   79 renovetur FLAN: removetur OS aer removeatur B   80 si:
om. B / indistinctum: indistincta in indistinctam S   81 moto: in m. B / quia: *om.* S /
moventibus: motis F   83 hic BS   85 natum S   88 presupponat B
89 *post* qua *add.* S *et scr. et del.* A fuit vel / fit: sit BSA   90 quarum: quarundam O
quartum S *om.* B   90-2 locum . . . aeris: l. immobilem non tenet species ut corpus sed
semper per partem a. *mg.* O   92 prius: post B   93 sicut: ut S   96 renovata:
determinata S / id . . . alia[2]: *om.* S / id est: et L   97 aeris: *om.* B / remanet B
98-9 sed . . . locum: *om.* S   101 arguitur O

first part of the medium leave that part, nor does that which is in the second part proceed to the third, but each remains in its place. And therefore nothing is moved from place to place, but there is [instead] a continuous generation of a new thing; in the same way, shadow is not moved, but new shadows are [continually] generated.[6] Nor is this generation primarily according to place and *per se*, but according to subject, since a species is an effect in the medium; nor does it require place there, except the place of the medium.

If it should be pointed out that when air is moved by wind or something else, the species is not moved with the air, but continues to be multiplied from its agent according to the same line or sphere, occupying (as a whole) a fixed and immobile place, even though it is generated according to the parts of the medium in that same place, as is here mentioned; but that if the species or the effect in the air were not distinct from the air, then it would be moved with the air, since when we move, everything in us that lacks distinct dimensions [of its own] is also moved; we reply that this is the fallacy of affirming the consequent, reducing two causes to one. For as regards the fact that a species lies immobile along one line while the air is moved, this can occur either because it is suited of itself to occupy place, like body (and this is not the cause in the present case), or because, owing to the command of the agent, which is obligated to produce its action in a given direction, the species itself, which is an effect in the medium, maintains one line of motion; nevertheless, it always presupposes the part of the air in which it comes into being and through which it occupies a place, although that part of the air is constantly changing because of the motion of the parts of the air. A species does not retain a fixed position through itself, as does body, but always through the part of the air first renewed in such a place, which part is the subject of the species; and not only is the part of the air renewed in which the species is situated as in subject (not as in place), but also the species is renewed along with the renewed parts of air; nor does the species remain numerically the same, because even if the air were at rest, the species would [still] be renewed in a renewed part, that is, in one part after another.[7] And therefore, when parts of the air succeed one another in the same place, that place is not occupied by the same species, for the species is corrupted when the part of the air in which it was moves from that place; and a new species is not generated until another part of the air occupies that place, and therefore it does not occupy place through itself, but through something else.

Now if the reflection [of a species] from a body should be presented as an objection, it is evident from what has been said that

non fit ei violentia; sed generat se in partem sibi possibilem cum
prohibetur transire propter densitatem resistentis. Si enim violenter
repercuteretur, ut pila a pariete, oporteret necessario quod esset
105 corpus. Quod si dicatur, cum facit se iterum per reflexionem in alium
locum per suam naturam propriam, medio non pellente nec movente
nec moto nec aliquo alio iuvante nec faciente quod renovet locum,
quod non accidit in umbra, quia ad motum corporis renovatur, videtur
quod per se locum occupare debeat; dicendum est quod locum non
110 querit ut corpus sed subiectum, nec tamen unum numero illud querit
subiectum, sed diversum semper propter hoc quod species in una parte
medii generata potest facere sibi similem in alia; et ideo non est ibi
acquisitio loci ut corpus acquirit, sed est ibi renovatio speciei per
generationem in partibus medii pluribus. Quod vero diversum est hic
115 et in umbra, accidit non ex hoc quod species sit corpus: sed quia
habet virtutem activam qua potest sibi similem producere in parte
medii coniuncta illi in qua est secundum omnes diametros; sed umbra
non est activa, nec sui similis generativa, sed generatur umbra per
aliud et requirit illud aliud, scilicet corpus obiectum, preter medium
120 in quo fit. Sed species solum requirit medium postquam est in medio
iam multiplicata; et potest sibi similem per se facere ex sua potestate
activa.

Multa alie truphe possunt hic obici, que nichil valent; et ideo
transeo determinando quoddam incidens. Inter omnes species, maxime
125 estimatur de luce sive lumine in medio quod sit corpus. Sed hoc esse
non potest, secundum Aristotelem, qui dicit quod lux non est corpus
nec defluxus corporis. Similiter nec tenebra est corpus, sed passio;
quare nec eius oppositum, quod est lumen, ut arguit. Et iterum tertio
dicit quod tunc ab oriente ad occidens translatum non lateret nos,
130 licet in parvo spatio nos posset aliquo modo latere. Et in veritate
lux est in tertia specie qualitatis, cum sit passibilis qualitas inferens
sensui per se passionem; quare non erit corpus. Que vero dicuntur
in contrarium omnia sunt fantasie communes omni speciei, cuiusmodi dicte sunt et consimiles, preter exemplum Aristotelis in *Topicis*,

---

102 fit: sit *B* / ei *LSA*: ex *BFON*   103 prohibetur: probeatur *S*   104 esse *L*
106 nec: non *BF*   107 renovet *SAN*: removet *BFLO*   108 non: nec *B* / corporis:
om. F / videretur *S*   110 nec: non *F* / illum *SA*   111 subiectum: solum *O* /
semper: sed *F* / *post* semper *add. S et scr. et del. A* et ideo non est ibi acquisitio loci corpus
dicitur (*om. S*) habere et presidere locum / propter ... species: *om. B*   112 sibi: *om.
OS* / simile *SA*   113 ibi: *om. S*   114 generationem: *mg. F^C* renovationem *F'* /
pluribus: *mg. F^C om. F'*   116 que *S* quia *O* / simile *F*   117 illa *S*   118 nec ...
umbra: *om. S* / nec: ut *L* / generatur: convertitur *L*   119 aliud[1]: ad *S* / illum *B* / aliud[2]:
a per illud *S*   120 sed: hec *S* / est: quia e. *B*   121 sibi: similiter *S* / similem *BOSN*:
simile *FLA* / ex *SAN*: et *BFLO*   122 activa: a. locum acquirere *B*   123 alie:
autem *S om. F*   124 quoddam: quod *L* / *ante* inter *add. S* qua *et add. A* nam *et mg.
add. O^C* quia / omnes: hos *B* has *N*   126 *post* Aristotelem *add. S* secundo de anima

the species undergoes no violence; rather, when it is prevented from proceeding [straight ahead] by the density of the resisting body, the species generates itself in some [other] direction open to it. For it could be violently driven back, as a ball from a wall, only if it were body. Again, if it should be argued that since a species reproduces itself by reflection in another place through its own nature, the medium neither driving it back, nor moving, nor being moved, and nothing else assisting or doing anything that would alter[8] its place (a description inapplicable to shadow, because the latter is generated according to the motion of a body),[9] it seems that a species must occupy place *per se*; [to this argument] we reply that a species does not require place, as does body, but requires a subject, and that subject need not be numerically one, but can be constantly different, because a species generated in one part of the medium can produce its like in another part of the medium; and therefore, there is no acquisition of place as a body acquires place, but there is a renewing of the species by generation in various parts of the medium. But as for the fact that there is a difference between this and shadow, it does not follow from this that a species is body: for a species has active virtue by which it can produce its like along all diameters in the part of the medium immediately adjacent to it; whereas shadow is not active, nor able to generate its like, but is generated by something else and requires that other thing, namely, the umbrageous body, in addition to the medium in which it comes into being. But a species, once it has been multiplied in the medium, requires only the medium;[10] and by itself, from its active power, it can produce its like.

Many other quibbles can be presented here, but they have no validity; therefore I pass on to the analysis of a certain problem. Among all species, it is especially *lux* or *lumen* in the medium that is judged to be body. But this cannot be, according to Aristotle, who says that light is neither body nor an emanation from body.[11] Similarly, darkness is not body, but an effect [on the medium]; therefore, neither is its contrary, light, as Aristotle argues.[12] And in the third place, he says that then [if light were body] its motion from east to west would not be concealed from us, although over a short distance it could in some way be conccaled from us.[13] Now in truth light is in the third species of quality, since it is a quality that affects sense,[14] bearing an effect to sense by itself; therefore it is not body. And all things that are said to the contrary are fantasies common to every species—such as sayings and the like, and also the example of Aristotle in the *Topics*, where he

128 arguitur S / tertio: *om.* L   129 dico F / ad: in OSA / translatum: eius transitum O
130 nos: non B

135 cum recitat quod ignis est lux, quia species ignis dicit tres: carbonem,
flammam, et lucem. Hoc multipliciter evacuatur per hoc quod ipse-
met dicit: 'quod exempla non ponimus ut vera sint, sed ut sentiant
qui addiscunt.' Et quia omnia exempla sua in *Topicis* sunt positiones
philosophorum, secundum diffinitionem positionis ibidem datam, et
140 ideo fere omnia sunt falsa. Unde hec falsitas venit ex hoc, quod
posuerunt stellas esse ex luce sua calidas et igneas, quia lux calefacit, sicut ipse recitat secundo *Celi et mundi*. Et ideo posuerunt
lucem esse ignem et unam speciem ignis esse lucem stellarum; nec
posuerunt stellam esse nisi lucem congregatam et densatam secundum
145 trinam dimensionem; et ideo posuerunt lucem esse corpus. Sed hec
omnia falsa sunt. Quod autem mitius communiter dicitur ad hanc
auctoritatem quod Aristoteles, cum dicit lucem esse tertiam speciem
ignis, hoc dicitur pro igne secundum se et secundum suam essentiam,
non pro aliquo ignito, cuiusmodi sunt carbo, qui est substantia grossa
150 terrestris ardens, et flamma, qui est fumus terrestris ardens; et ita
sumitur lux concretive, non pro forma, sed pro subiecto sub forma,
scilicet pro substantia et natura lucida, estimando quod ignis de se
luceat et in spera sua. Hoc omnino falsum est, quia certificabitur in
posterioribus quod impossibile est quod ignis de se luceat, nec in
155 spera sua nec alibi quam denso terrestri et aqueo, sicut Averroys
declarat in diversis locis. Et hoc tactum est supra, et patebit inferius.

PARS III

CAPITULUM 2

Secundo considerandum an species agentis corporalis debeat dici res
corporalis vel spiritualis, propter hoc quod multi solebant dicere
5 quod species habet esse spirituale in medio et in sensu. Et patet quod
est vere res corporalis, quia non est anima nec intelligentia nec
prima causa; sed omne aliud ab illis est vere res corporalis. Item
species agentis corporalis est similis ei nomine et diffinitione, ut
in principio ostensum est; sed res spiritualis non est huiusmodi
10 respectu corporis. Item species est eiusdem essentie cum effectu

136 hoc[1]: hoc enim *F*   138 quia: *om. L* | omnia: *om. SA* | sua: eius *FO*
139 physicorum *B*   140 fere: *om. S*   142 ipse: *om. S* | celi et mundi: de celo et
mundo *S*   144 aggregatam *O*   146 mitius: *scr. et del. O* | communiter: *om. F*
147 quod Aristoteles: Aristotelis *O* | tertiam *OSA*: trinam *BFL*   148 dicit *S*
149 cuius *BS*   150 que *S* | famus *L* | ardens[2]: *mg. O*   151 concretive: conscientie
B   152 ignis: i. lucidus *S*   153 *post* quia *add. B* quod *et add. SA* certificatum est

reports that fire is light, since he says there are three species of fire;
[hot] coals, flame, and light.[15] This is rendered invalid multifariously
by what he himself says—[namely,] 'that we present examples not
as truth, but so that those whom we teach might achieve understanding.'[16] And since all of his examples in the *Topics* are positions
of the philosophers, according to the definition of 'position' given
there, nearly all are false. This falsity originated from their supposition that the stars are hot and fiery on account of their light, since
light produces warmth, as Aristotle reports in *De caelo et mundo*,
book ii.[17] As a result, they supposed that light is fire and that the
light of the stars is one species of fire; and they supposed too that a
star is nothing but light gathered together and condensed in three
dimensions; and consequently they supposed that light is body. But
all of these suppositions are false. However, it is commonly and
mildly replied to this view that Aristotle, when he calls light the third
species of fire, says this about fire according to itself and its essence,
but not about something that is ignited, such as charcoal, which is a
burning gross terrestrial substance, and flame, which is burning
terrestrial smoke; and so light is taken specifically, not as form, but
as the subject beneath form, namely, as substance and lucid nature, it
being judged that of itself fire sheds light, even in its own sphere. But
this is completely false, since it will be certified below that fire
cannot emit light of itself, either in its sphere or anywhere except
in the density of the earth and the aqueous sphere, as Averroes
declares in many places.[18] And this is touched on above and will be
evident below.[19]

PART III

CHAPTER 2

Secondly, it must be considered whether the species of a corporeal
agent should be called a corporeal or a spiritual thing, for many
people used to say that a species has spiritual being in the medium
and in sense.[1] But it is evident that in truth it is a corporeal thing,
since it is neither soul nor intelligence nor the first cause; and everything else is truly corporeal. Also, the species of a corporeal agent is
similar to the agent in name and definition, as was shown at the
beginning [of this treatise];[2] but a spiritual thing cannot be so related
to body. Also, a species is of the same essence as a complete effect

alibi hoc (*om. A*) et   153–4 in posterioribus: posterius *SA*   154 lucet *BL*
155 Averroim *O*   156 et²: ut *O* / inferius: i. suo loco *S*
   2 capitulum secundum *O mg. L*   3 an: utrum *O* est an *L*   4 hoc: *om. O*
6 nec intelligentia: intellectiva *S*   8 corporalis: *mg. O* / ei: enim *O*   9 res:
effectus *S*

completo, ut prius probatum est; sed effectus completus corporalis
agentis est vere corporale, ergo et species. Item nullum agens et
generans est ignobilius generato, ut dicitur quarto *Methaphysice* et
tertio *De anima*; si igitur species est res spiritualis, non habebit
15 causam corporalem; ergo nulla species fieret a corporibus, quod
falsum est.

Sed cum hoc necessario concludunt, dicunt quidam quod species
rei corporalis, licet nec sit corpus distinctum a medio nec sit res
spiritualis, sed corporalis secundum suam essentiam, habet tamen esse
20 spirituale in medio; unde habet secundum eos modum existendi spiri-
tualem et non corporalem; et ita habebit esse spirituale, licet sit res
corporalis secundum essentiam; ita quod accipiunt spirituale in
propria significatione alia a corporali. Sed istud stare non potest,
quia universaliter modus existendi proportionatur essentie habenti
25 illum modum, ut videmus in singulis. Et huius causa est quia esse est
propria passio eius cuius est, secundum veritatem et Avicennam, vel
essentialius secundum Averroys et vulgus sequens eum; et ideo si
essentia cui debetur esse est corporalis, et modus existendi erit
corporalis, precipue cum istud esse habeat in re corporali et secundum
30 eius proprietatem. Ex quo contingit iterum arguere quod omne quod
recipitur recipitur per modum recipientis, ut omnes concedunt et
multipliciter dicit auctoritas, scilicet *Libri de causis* et Boetius quinto
De consolatione et alibi. Cum igitur medium corporale recipiens
speciem, sive verius de cuius potentia educitur, ut prius probatum
35 est, habet esse penitus corporale, non poterit hec species habere nisi
esse corporale.

Item essentia nobilior est quam eius essendi modus, ut certum est;
sed spirituale nobilius est corporali; quare modus essendi spiritualis
non debetur rei corporali secundum essentiam. Item spiritus existens
40 in se vel in re spirituali (ponamus absolutus a corpore, ut anima)
non amittit aliquid de dignitate sui modi essendi spirituali, que sue
essentie proportionalis est; ergo nec corporalis essentia existens
in corpore amittet aliquid de esse corporali, que proportionatur sue
essentie. Et iterum quod plus est, spiritus in corpore et unitus sicut
45 forma et perfectio, ut anima rationalis, non amittit suum esse

12 agentis: *om. F* | corporalis *O*   17 cum: tamen *OS* | concludant *FS*   18 nec[1]:
non *F*   21 sit: fit *S*   21-2 et[1] . . . spirituale: *mg. O*   24 universaliter:
naturaliter *S*   25 modum: *om. F*   26 et: dicit *O* | *post* Avicennam *add. S* in
methaphysica et tertio physicorum   27 essentialibus *S* exemplarium *O* | Averroym
O Augustinus *A* | *post* et[1] *add. S* quatuor et decem methaphysice *et add. A* secundum
28-9 est . . . esse: *mg. O*   30 quod[2]: *om. BL*   32 multiplex *FO* | scilicet: id est *O*
34 sive verius: *om. FO*   35 poteris *BL*   35-6 non . . . corporale: *mg. O*
37 iterum *L*   38 sed: s. esse *F*   38-9 quare . . . essentiam: *mg. O*   39 rei:
ei *B* | spiritus: species *S*   40 vel: ut *F* | *post* spirituali *add. O* si *et add. BFL* rei |

[of its agent], as was proved above; but the complete effect of a corporeal agent is truly corporeal, and therefore so too is its species. Also, no agent and source of generation is less noble than the thing generated, as Aristotle says in *Metaphysics*, book iv, and *De anima*, book iii;[3] therefore, if a species is a spiritual thing, it cannot have a corporeal cause; and consequently, no species would be produced by bodies, which is contrary to fact.

But some, since they necessarily reach this conclusion, say that the species of a corporeal thing, although it is not a body distinct from the medium nor a spiritual thing, but is corporeal in essence, nevertheless has spiritual being in the medium; thus, according to them, it has a spiritual, rather than a corporeal, mode of existence; and therefore it has spiritual being even though in essence it is corporeal; and thus they acknowledge that 'spiritual' in its proper meaning is different from 'corporeal'. But this cannot stand, since universally the mode of existence is proportioned to the essence having that mode, as we see in individual cases. And the cause of this is that being is the proper affection of that to which it belongs, according to truth and according to Avicenna, or more essentially according to Averroes and the vulgar who follow him;[4] and therefore if the essence to which it owes its being is corporeal, its mode of existence will also be corporeal, especially since it has that being in a corporeal thing and according to its properties. From which it is further argued that everything that is received is received according to the mode of the recipient, as all concede and many authorities say, for example, *Liber de causis* and Boethius, *De consolatione*, book v, and elsewhere.[5] Therefore, since the corporeal medium receiving a species (or, more accurately, from the potentiality of which the species is brought forth, as we proved above)[6] has entirely corporeal being, this species can have only corporeal being.

Furthermore, essence is nobler than its mode of being, and this is certain; but the spiritual is nobler than the corporeal; therefore, a spiritual mode of being is not suitable for a thing of corporeal essence. Also, spirit existing by itself or in a spiritual thing (let us suppose it to be separated from body, as soul) does not give up any of the spiritual excellence of its mode of being, which is proportional to its essence; therefore, a corporeal essence existing in a body would give up none of its corporeal being, which is proportioned to its essence. And what is more, spirit in body and united with it as its form and perfection (as, for example, the rational soul) does not give

ponatur *O* / anima: angelus et a. *SA*   41 non: nec *B om. F*   42 essentia: *om. S*
43 amittet *F*^C: amittit *F'O*   44 spiritus in corpore: species in c. *S om. B* / et unitus *L*:
et unicus *F* et virtus *S* est u. *A* mutus *B* coniunctus *O*

spirituale, quod debetur sue essentie; immo magis istud esse spirituale
redundat in corpus quam econtrario; et fit homo quasi totus quodammodo spiritualis propter nobilitatem anime spiritualis, cum anima sit
principalior quam corpus quasi sine comparatione. Quapropter cor-
50 porale, cum existit in corporali, longe minus amittet esse quod secundum legem corporalem ei debeatur.

Item esse non habet ipsa species a casu nec fortuna, sed nec a
creatione, ut planum est; nec aliquid creatum est causa sui esse;
quare habebit ex suis causis. Sed cause sue sunt omnino corporales,
55 scilicet generans et materia corporalis de cuius potentia generatur;
quare oportet quod esse speciei sit corporale. Item esse habet secundum rationem trine dimensionis, sed indistincte a medio; ergo habet
esse corporale. Et in idem inconveniens redit quod dicitur a vulgo,
quod species non habet esse materiale, quod materiale vocetur
60 hic corporale, et sic est. Et ideo falsum est istud sicut aliud, scilicet
quod dicitur habere esse spirituale; et magis falsum, quoniam angelus
et anima, licet sint substantie spirituales, tamen habent esse in
materia, quia sunt composite ex vera materia et vera forma, ut nunc
suppono et probabitur inferius; quare multo magis habebit species
65 esse materiale. Item educitur de potentia materie activa; quare esse
materiale habet. Item probatum est prius quod species substantie
corporalis est similitudo totius compositi, et quod non renovatur in
medio esse formale tantum cum species generatur, sed esse materiale
et vera materia sub esse incompleto. Quapropter insania est dicere
70 quod species non habet esse materiale. Item est simile agenti nomine
et diffinitione; ergo habet esse materiale sicut illud. Item est idem
in essentia cum effectu completo, quod habet esse materiale. Item
propter nobilitatem generantis respectu generati, sequeretur quod
aliquid spirituale daret esse spirituale speciei; sed non potest hoc
75 dici.

Quoniam igitur istud non potest salvari aliquo iudicio rationis,
nec etiam habet probabilitatem aliquam, ut patet omni homini volenti
dimittere stultitiam vulgi et sequi rationem, ideo absolute diffinio
quod species rei corporalis est vere corporalis et habet esse vere
80 corporale, ut expositum est precipue ut est in corpore de cuius potentia
educitur. Postea vero inquiretur de speciebus rerum corporalium ut

46 quod . . . spirituale: *om.* B | illud S   50 cum: *mg.* F^C non F' | quod: *om.* B
50–1 *post* secundum *scr. et del.* F esse   51 debetur O   52 esse: est B | a²: id est BL
53 nec: ut F | creatum: tantum L *om.* S   54 habebit: h. esse ON   56 esse¹: ex e. B
57 rationem: *om.* S | sed: licet LSA   58 idem: id B | inconveniens: non conveniens B
59 vocatur O   60 sic est et: *om.* S   62 et anima: *om.* L | substantie: specie B |
in: *om.* L   65 active B ad actum SA   66 prius: *om.* FL   69 *ante* vera *scr. et*
del. F non   74 aliquod FO | spirituale¹: corporale O   79 est . . . et: *mg.* O
81 inquiritur O

up the spiritual being which it owes to its essence; rather, that spiritual being is more apt to overflow into body than the converse; and virtually the whole of a man becomes in a certain way spiritual because of the nobility of his spiritual soul, since the soul is more important (almost beyond comparison) than the body. Therefore, a corporeal thing existing in body is far less apt to give up the being which, according to the law of body, is due it.

Also, species itself does not have being by chance or fortune, but neither by creation, as is clear; nor is a created thing the cause of its own being, but it receives being from its causes. However, its causes are altogether corporeal, namely, that which generates it and the corporeal matter from the potentiality of which it is generated; therefore the being of a species must be corporeal. Also, a species possesses being in three dimensions (although these dimensions are not distinct from the medium); therefore, it has corporeal being. The same absurdity follows from the common opinion that a species does not have material being—'material' and 'corporeal' here being used interchangeably, and properly so. And therefore this is as false as to maintain that a species has spiritual being; or more false, since an angel and soul, although spiritual substances, nevertheless exist in matter, since they are composites of true matter and true form, as I now suppose and as I will prove below;[7] therefore, much more will species have material being. Also, a species is brought forth out of the active potency of matter and so has material being. Moreover, it has been proved above that the species of corporeal substance is the similitude of the whole composite, and that when a species is generated not only is formal being produced in the medium, but also material being and true matter having incomplete being.[8] Therefore, it is madness to say that a species does not have material being. Also, a species is similar to the agent in name and definition; therefore it has material being, as does the agent. Furthermore, it has the same essence as the complete effect [of its agent], and the latter has material being. Also, because of the nobility of the generator with respect to that which it generates, it would follow that a spiritual thing would give spiritual being to species; but this cannot be said.

Thus, since this [opinion] cannot be saved by any rational judgement, nor does it have any probability, as is evident to any man who wishes to dismiss the foolishness of the vulgar and to follow reason, I therefore state unconditionally that the species of a corporeal thing is truly corporeal and has truly corporeal being—as has been maintained chiefly concerning species as it exists in the body from the potentiality of which it is brought forth. Later we will investigate the species of corporeal things as they exist

sunt in anima et intelligentia, et causa prima qualiter se habeant ibi.
Nec est aliquid contra illud nisi mala translatio verborum Averroys
et Avicenne et Aristotelis. Scimus quidem quod innumerabilia sunt
85 ad litteram eorum que sustinere non possumus; nec etiam vulgus
naturalium propter horrorem falsi cupit sustinere; sed oportet inter-
pretari et exponi in melius, cuius cause date sunt a principio. (v)
Et ideo quod translatio imponit Averroys *Libro de sensu et sensato*
et super librum Aristotelis *De anima*, quod species rei corporalis
90 habet esse immateriale et esse spirituale in medio; dicendum est quod
omnino intelligendum est de esse insensibili, ad quod vulgus vel
translator traxit hoc nomen spirituale propter similitudinem rerum
spiritualium ad insensibiles. Nam res spirituales sunt insensibiles,
et ideo convertimus sermonem vulgariter, transumentes hoc nomen
95 insensibile ad spirituale, ut omne quod non habet esse sensibile
nobis dicatur habere esse intelligibile et spirituale; sed sic
spirituale est equivoce acceptum, et remanet veraciter de natura
corporali et secundum esse corporale. Et ideo quod Aristoteles dicit
secundo *De anima*, quod sensus suscipit species sensibilium sine
100 materia, dicendum est quod ipse sumit ibi sine materia, hoc est immateriale pro insensibili, non pro spirituali secundum quod opponitur
corporali. Sed si cavillator dicat species habere esse sensibile, ut
patet de radio cadente per fenestram et de specie colorum fortium,
ut patet cum radius penetrat vitra vel pannos bene coloratos, iam
105 solutum est prius quod hoc in paucis speciebus est, et in illis in
quibus est accidit et per accidens est, ut prius expositum est.

Quod autem contra medicos dicentes substantiam cerebri mollem,
ut recipiat aptas figuras ymaginandi, eo quod res humida de facili
recipit impressiones, Avicenna decem *De animalibus* dicit sub hiis
110 verbis: 'Non videtur michi istud, quia res humida de facili recipit
alterationem, sed non omnem, sed illam que est cum divisione et
receptione figurarum; sed ymaginatio et estimatio non sunt cum motu
corporis vel divisione aliqua in corpore'; propter que verba videtur
quod species non debeat habere esse corporale, et ideo spirituale.
115 Dicitur ad hoc primo quod auctoritas Aristotelis prevalet in hac parte,

82 in: *om. O* | habeant *LSAN*: habent *FO* habeat *B*   83 Averroim *O*
84 quidem: *om. FOA* | quod: q. ad litteram *S*   86 horrorem: errorem *S*
87 cuius . . . principio: *om. SA*   88 Averroim *O*   90 esse²: *om. OS*   92 trahit
L transit *F* | nomen: unde *S om. F*   93 insensibiles¹: sensibiles *B*   94 vulgaliter
OA | transeuntes *S*   95 insensibile *OSAN*: sensibile *BFL* | ad: et in *S*   96 habere:
om. FO | sed: *om. L*   96–7 sed . . . est: *mg. O*   97 veraciter: *om. F*
98 quod: *om. F*   100 ibi: *spatium vacuum B*   101 pro¹: per *F*   103 et . . .
fortium: *mg. O* | colorum: *om. F*   104 vitra *FOAN*: vatra *L* intra *BS*   105 prius
BSAN: primum *FLO* | hoc: *om. S* | *post* hoc *scr. et del. O* est   107 mollem: esse
mollerem *S*   109 decem: 20 *B*   109–10 sub . . . verbis: *om. S*   110 non:
nam *O* | quia: quod *O*   112 ymaginationes et estimationes *S* | sunt: fiunt *S*

in the soul and intellect, and the first cause of their being there.[9] Nor is there evidence to the contrary except as the result of faulty translation of the words of Averroes, Avicenna, and Aristotle. Indeed, we know that there are innumerable statements [in their works] that we cannot take literally; nor even does the ordinary student of nature wish to maintain them because of his aversion to error; but they must be interpreted and better expressed, the reasons for which have been given from the beginning. (*v*) Therefore, when the translation imputes to Averroes, in his *De sensu et sensato* and his [commentary] on Aristotle's *De anima*,[10] that the species of a corporeal thing has immaterial and spiritual being in the medium, it is replied that this should be understood entirely to refer to insensible being, to which some vulgar [scholar] or the translator applied the name 'spiritual' because of the similarity between spiritual things and insensibles. For spiritual things are insensible, and therefore in common usage we interchange the terms, converting the name 'insensible' to 'spiritual', so that everything that lacks being sensible to us is said to have intelligible and spiritual being; but this is to use 'spiritual' equivocally, and [the thing lacking sensible being] remains in truth [an object] of corporeal nature and corporeal being. Therefore, as regards what Aristotle says in *De anima*, book ii,[11] that sense receives the species of sensible things without matter, it is replied that he there uses 'without matter', that is, 'immaterial', to mean 'insensible' rather than 'spiritual' (which [properly speaking] is the opposite of 'corporeal'). But if a quibbler should say that species have sensible being, as is evident in a ray falling through a window and in the species of strong colours, as when a ray passes through strongly coloured glass or cloth, it has already been shown above that this is [true only] of a few species, and in those of which it is true it occurs accidentally, as we explained above.[12]

However, against the physicians who say that the substance of the brain is delicate so as to receive suitable figures from the imagination, because a moist thing easily receives impressions, Avicenna speaks in *De animalibus*, book x, in the following words: 'This does not seem [so] to me, since a moist thing easily receives alteration, though not every kind of alteration, but that which involves division and reception of figures; however, imagination and estimation do not involve motion of body or any division of body';[13] and from these words it seems that species must not have corporeal being and therefore must have spiritual being. To this it is replied, first, that the authority of Aristotle prevails in this matter,

113 videtur *FON*: videntur *BL* videretur *SA*   114 debet *SA* / habere: *om. FL*
115 prevalent *S*

determinans *Libro de memoria et reminiscentia* quod senes habent
debilem memoriam propter nimiam siccitatem organorum, quorum
organa sunt sicut ligna antiqua putrefacta que non bene recipiunt impressiones et figuras; et pueri nichilominus habent malam memoriam
120 eo quod habent organa nimis humida, propter quod non retinent
species et figuras rerum. Deinde dico quod Avicenna est alibi istius
sententie in multis locis, tam in libris medicinalibus quam naturalibus.
Dicit enim in *Libro de anima* primo quod sensus communis recipit
species, sed non retinet, ymaginatio vero retinet, addens quod aliud est
125 retinere aliud vero recipere, ponens exemplum de aqua, que recipit
impressionem sigilli sed non retinet. Sed innumerabilia verba sua ad
hoc possent induci, nec oportet. Et ideo cum non est fatendum quod
ipse tantus philosophus fuerit sibi nec Aristoteli contrarius, dicendum
quod male fuit illud verbum decimi *De animalibus* translatum et peius
130 exponitur, ut concludatur in hoc casu ex hoc esse spirituale ipsius
speciei corporalis, precipue cum sua verba ad litteram nichil tangant
de esse spirituali. Et preter hec omnia, dici potest quod Avicenna
non contradicit proposito in aliquo, quoniam nos loquimur hic de
specie comparata ad solum corpus inanimatum in quo est, et ipse
135 loquitur de specie comparata ad animam et ad corpus animatum precipue ratione anime, de qua comparatione nichil hic loquimur, hec
enim auctoritas habet locum proprium in sequentibus, et ibi dabo
eius intellectum secundum quod videbitur expedire.

PARS III

CAPITULUM 3

Et cum iam ventillavi diu esse materiale et corporale ipsius speciei
rei corporalis in medio, quod cum iam teneo secundum veritatem,
5 sequitur tertia veritas, mirabilis vulgo ex ymaginatione falsi; nulli
tamen sapienti sit stupenda. Sed propter magnitudinem occultationis
tante veritatis et propter hanc eliciendam, laboravi evidentius circa
esse materiale et corporale specierum in medio corporali. Dico igitur
precise quod species rerum corporalium miscentur in omni parte
10 medii quando ad invicem concurrunt ille que sunt contrarie et non

---

118 sicut: *om. L*   119–21 et[2] . . . rerum: *mg. (sed ante* et[1] *hab.* rerum) *O*
122 locis: *om. F*   124 sed: et si *B*   127 induci: radii *B* / cum: tamen *B*
128 tantus: *om. B* / philosophus: communicatus *B om. F*   129 fuit: *om. SA*
130 exponitum *S* / ut: nam non *O* / concluditur *O* concludetur *L* / hoc[1]: hec *L*   131 cum:
et etiam *O* / tangunt *FO*   137 proprium: *om. S*
    2 capitulum tertium *O*   3 et[1]: *om. O* / ventillaverim *O* ventilam *S* / et corporale:

for he determines in *De memoria et reminiscentia* that the elderly
have weak memories because of the excessive dryness of their organs,
which are like old rotted wood that cannot easily receive impressions
and figures;[14] however, the young have bad memories because the
organs of memory are too moist, and consequently they do not
retain the species and figures of things. And I add that Avicenna is of
this opinion in many other places, in both his medical works and his
books on natural philosophy. For he says in *De anima*, book i, that
the common sense receives, but does not retain, species, whereas the
imagination retains them, adding that it is one thing to retain and
another to receive—giving, as an example, water, which receives the
impression of a seal but does not retain it.[15] His innumerable words
on this subject could be introduced, but this is unnecessary. And
therefore, since it cannot be maintained that so great a philosopher
would contradict himself or Aristotle, it must be said that the
passage in *De animalibus*, book x, was badly translated and [even]
more poorly interpreted, so that one can derive from it [the notion]
that a corporeal species has spiritual being, especially since his words
do not literally touch upon spiritual being. In addition to all this, it
can be said that Avicenna does not contradict the view here defended
in any respect, since we speak here of a species in relation to a single
inanimate body in which it is situated, whereas he speaks of a species
in relation to soul and to a body animated principally by soul; and
we have nothing to say here concerning this [latter] relationship,
for this matter has its proper place below, and there I will present its
proper interpretation in so far as it seems useful.[16]

PART III

CHAPTER 3

Since I have now discussed at length the material and corporeal
being of the species of a corporeal thing in a medium, from this
(since I now hold for true [the things asserted]) there follows a third
truth, which seems marvellous to the vulgar owing to what they
imagine to be impossible, though no wise man would be astonished.
But because of the widespread ignorance of such an important truth,
and in order to reveal this truth, I have taken very obvious pains
concerning [the question of] material and corporeal being of species
in a corporeal medium. Therefore, I say absolutely that the species
of corporeal things are mixed in any part of the medium when those
species that are contraries and not contingent[1] intersect one another,

om. F   4 cum: tamen *O* quasi *SA*   5 falsa *FO*   6 sit: sic *B* / propter: *om. F*
7 illiciendam *B*

contingentes, et similiter ille que sunt eiusdem speciei; contraria enim
naturaliter miscentur, aut unum vincit super reliquum ut illud corrumpat, et non numerantur simul in eadem materia et subiecto; similiter res eiusdem speciei non simul numerantur in eadem materia et
15 subiecto. Res autem contingentes vocantur que simul se compatiuntur,
ut album et dulce, que nec sunt eiusdem generis nec eiusdem speciei;
et ideo bene numerantur, quia non est natum aliquid unum fieri ex
eis, et sunt simul in eodem subiecto in mixto, loquendo de vera
mixtione ut nunc loquimur.
20   Cum igitur luces omnes sint eiusdem speciei et congregantur a
diversis luminaribus in una parte medii, dico quod fit una lux numero.
Et similiter quando diversi colores eiusdem speciei veniunt ad idem
punctum medii, fiunt una species; et quando contrariorum colorum
species veniunt, fit una mixta ex eis, nisi altera in tantum dominetur
25 quod reliqua corrumpatur a causis generantibus colores. Similiter
quando due species caloris veniunt ad eandem partem medii, fit una
species et unus calor; et quando species calidi et frigidi veniunt ut
una non corrumpat aliam, omnino fit mixtio. Et ita fit in omnibus,
quod probatur per omnia predicta.
30   Dicit enim vulgus quod species, quia habent esse spirituale et non
materiale, ideo non miscentur sed sunt distincte. Cum ergo probatum
sit quod habent esse vere materiale et nullo modo spirituale, quod
excludat esse vere materiale, ideo manifestum est quod debent misceri
vera mixtione, sicut cetere forme materiales. Iterum ipsa generantia
35 species illas, cum ad invicem veniunt in eodem subiecto, miscentur
vera mixtione; sed species sunt similes nomine et diffinitione et
essentia illis a quibus causantur, quare sequuntur naturam et proprietatem illorum. Item nullus de vulgo studentium vult negare quin
effectus completi quando veniunt in eadem parte materie misceantur
40 vere; sed species sunt penitus eiusdem nature, et fiunt hii effectus
quando completur esse specierum; quare prior est naturaliter mixtio
in speciebus quam in effectibus completis.
    Et Ptolomeus tertio *De opticis* dicit expresse quod mixtio specierum
est in aere, et in colorum speciebus et aliis. Item Alhacen in libro

12 reliquum: relicit *F spatium vacuum B* / illud *FSN*: illum *BLO*   13 eadem . . .
subiecto: eodem s. *O*   15 se: *om. B*   16 eiusdem[1]: eius *BL*   17 non: nec *L* /
aliquid: ad *B*   18 mixta *F*   18–20 in[2] . . . eiusdem: ut in mixto cum ergo luces
omnes sint eius *mg. O*   20 sint *OSAN*: sunt *BFL*   22 veniunt: quando v. *O*
23 fuerit *B*   24 fit: sit *B*   25 corrumpetur *O* corrumpitur *F*   26 *ante* caloris
scr. et del. S cadunt / caloris *LS*: coloris *BFO* calorum(?) *A*   27 color *FO* / ut: ita ut *S*
30 enim: *om. O*   31 ideo: *om. O*   32–3 et . . . materiale: *om. F*   33 excludit
B / ideo: tunc *O*   34 item *FOA* / generatia *B* generant a *L*   38 studentium: *om. F* /
quin: quoniam *S*   39 venerint *S*   40 nature: *om. S*   44 specierum *F* /
ante item *mg. add.* *L*[C] item Alhacen libro primo capitulo 5 cito post principium et etiam
forma coloris est semper admixta cum forma luminis et non distincta ab eo visus ergo non

and also those that are of the same kind; for contraries naturally mix, or else one of them prevails over the other and corrupts it, and they are no longer simultaneously numerable things in the same matter and subject; similarly, things of the same kind are not simultaneously numerable in the same matter and subject. However, things that are simultaneously compatible with one another are called 'contingent', such as white and sweet, which are neither of the same genus nor of the same species; and therefore they can easily exist simultaneously as numerable things, since they are not so constituted as to give rise to one thing, and in a mixture (speaking here of a true mixture) they exist simultaneously in the same subject.

Therefore, when [several] lights, all of the same kind,[2] but from different sources, gather in one part of the medium, I say that one light is produced. Similarly, when different colours of the same kind come to one point of the medium, [a colour of] one kind is produced; and when the species of contrary colours come [to one point], they form one mixture, unless one of them should so dominate that the other is corrupted by the causes generating the colours. Similarly, when two species of heat come to one place in the medium, they produce one species and one heat; and when the species of heat and cold come [to one point] in such a way that neither corrupts the other, there is complete mixing of the two. And so it is with all things, as all the foregoing proves.

However, the vulgar say that species, because of their [supposed] spiritual and immaterial being, are not mixed but remain distinct. But since it has been proved that they have truly material being that is in no way spiritual (for this would prevent it from being truly material), it is therefore clear that they must be truly compounded,[3] as other material forms are. Again, when the things generating those species encounter one another in the same subject, they are truly compounded; and because species are similar in name, definition, and essence to the things that cause them, they must share the nature and properties of the latter. Also, not even the ignorant student wishes to deny that when [several] complete effects come to one part of matter, they are truly compounded; but species are of exactly the same nature, and these [complete] effects occur when the being of, the species is completed; therefore, mixture of the species naturally occurs before that of the complete effects.

And Ptolemy says explicitly in his *Optica*, book iii, that there is mixing of species in air, in the species of colour, and in other things.[4]

sentit lumen nisi admixtum cum colore dignus ergo est ut non sit sensus coloris rei vise et luminis quod est in ea nisi ex forma admixta ex lumine et colore veniente ad ipsum ex superficie rei vise / iterum *BL*

45 primo *Perspective*, dans causam quare una res videatur una cum tamen
ad duos oculos veniant species diverse, dicit quod due species que
veniunt ad duos oculos transeunt ad nervum communem, ad quem
continuantur oculi, et supponitur una alii in eadem parte illius nervi
communis, et fit una forma ex eis; et ideo virtus sensitiva que est
50 in illo nervo iudicat de re una quod sit una propter unam formam
quam habet. Ex qua sententia manifestum est quod species miscentur
ad invicem, et fit una ex illis. Plenitudo vero sapientie istorum
duorum philosophorum in libris suis manifestat quod nullum falsum
dicunt. Et ideo ipsi in libris aspectuum sunt de illis auctoribus
55 qui in omnibus sunt recipiendi, sicut habetur ex prologo huius operis,
quia florem philosophie explicant sine falsitate qualibet.

Sed licet hec pars sit omnino vera, tamen habet valde probabiles
contradictiones per auctoritates multorum male intellectas. Et
propter distinctam visus cognitionem, propter quam vulgus studentium
60 estimat quod species omnes sunt distincte in omni parte medii et
quod aliter salvari non potest distincta visus cognitio, propter quod
vulgus trahit auctoritates multorum et magnorum ad suam partem. Sed
hoc non oportet, quia et possunt salvari auctoritates et distincta
visus cognitio, licet in medio fiat vera specierum mixtio earum que
65 nate sunt misceri. Et ideo propter huius ignorantiam clamat vulgus
in contrarium, et doctores vulgi similiter solatium sue imperitie
querentes manifestande per hunc modum.

Dico igitur quod licet species albi et nigri venientes a diversis
agentibus misceantur naturaliter in parte medii, et veniat species
70 mixta ad pupillam, tamen a loco mixtionis primo in medio una illarum
veniet ab ipsa re sensata perpendiculariter super oculum et pupillam;
et alia secundum lineam accidentalem, nec a re sensata veniet perpendiculariter ad visum, sed solum a loco mixtionis. Et ideo una
venit fortis et occultat aliam, sicut maior lux occultat minorem; et
75 occupatur virtus visiva circa fortius immutans et dimittit aliam
speciem. Et in tantum potest esse dominium unius contrarii quod
illius species prevalebit in loco mixtionis primo, ita quod alia omnino
destruatur, et precipue in medio a loco mixtionis ad oculum, ita quod

45 *post* primo *mg. add. L* istud dico capitulo 5 e(!) | videtur *F*   46 species[1]: due s. *O*
48 alii *OSAN*: aliis *BFL* | in *SAN*: ex *O om. BFL*   49 virtus: *mg. O* unus *B*
51 habent *S*   52 vera *S* | sapientie: istius s. *L*   53 in: quam ostendunt in *S* | suis:
om. *O*   55 huius: istius *O*   59 propter[2]: per *B*   60 distincte: *om. F*
62 auctoritates: *om. FL*   63 hoc: *om. O*   63-4 et[2] ... cognitio: ad
distinctam visus cognitionem *O*   65 note *O* | misceri: visui *O* | huiusmodi *S* eius *O*
66 similiter: *om. S* | imperitium *F*   67 manifestando *O*   69 misceantur: *mg. O* |
veniant *O*   70 mixte *O* | a: alio *S* | illa *F*   71 ab ... sensata: *om. S*   72 alia
SA: alie *BFLO*   73 a loco: ad locum *S*   74 veniet *O* | occultat[1]: occulta *F* | sicut:
sic *F* | maior: *ex* melior *corr. B*   75 fortius: corpus *O* | et: *om. B* | dimitat *F* omittat *S*
76 in tantum: iterum *S*   77 ita: *om. S* | alia: a. causa *B*

Also, Alhazen, in his *Perspectiva*, book i, giving the reason why an individual thing appears individual although different species come to the two eyes, says that the two species that come to the two eyes proceed to the common nerve (to which the eyes are joined), and they are superimposed on one another in some part of that common nerve and give rise to one form; and therefore the sensitive power in the common nerve judges one thing to be one because of its single form.[5] From this argument it is evident that species are mixed with one another, and one species is produced from them. And the great wisdom of these two philosophers, [revealed] in their books, assures us that they do not speak falsely. And therefore, in their books on optics they are among the authors who should be trusted on all points, as one can gather from the prologue of this work,[6] since they explain the choicest parts of [that] philosophy without any error.

But although this explanation [of mixing] is entirely true, it contains many apparent contradictions because of the badly understood statements of many [philosophers]. For on the basis of distinct visual perception the ignorant student judges that all species are distinct in all parts of the medium and that distinct visual perception cannot otherwise be explained; and therefore he distorts the statements of many great philosophers so as to support his view. But this is unnecessary, since both the statements [of the philosophers concerning mixing] and distinct visual perception can be saved, despite the fact that in the medium there is a true compounding of the species [responsible for vision] that are suited to such mixing. And because they do not know this, the ignorant claim the contrary, as do their teachers, seeking solace for their ignorance by revealing it in this way.

Therefore, I say that although the species of white and black coming from different agents naturally mix in [some] part of the medium, and the mixed species proceeds to the pupil [of the observer's eye], nevertheless, from the first place of mixing in the medium, one of those species comes [directly] from the perceived thing itself, falling perpendicularly on the eye and the pupil, while the other comes [to the eye] along an accidental line;[7] and the latter comes perpendicularly to the eye not from the perceived object, but only from the place of mixing. Consequently, one of the species arrives with greater strength and conceals the other, as greater light conceals a lesser light; and the visual power is occupied with the species that alters it more strongly and dismisses the other. And one of the contraries can so prevail [over the other] that its species will prevail in the first place of mixing and totally destroy the other, especially in [that part of] the medium between the place of mixing and the eye, so that

antequam ad pupillam veniat convertatur species una in contrarium
80 per actionem naturalem. Et ideo iudicabit visus de re una per speciem
unam, aut ita fortem quod occultabitur reliqua.

Quod vero a loco mixtionis primo veniat una species perpendiculariter super lineam principalem et alia accidentaliter manifestum est
propter situm oculi respectu duorum visibilium diversorum, quantum-
85 cunque propinque ad invicem collocentur. Quamvis enim ad locum
mixtionis veniat species a visibilibus per lineam principalem rectam vel
fractam vel reflexam, tamen ab illo loco planum est quod una species
super lineam principalem alterius non incedit principali multiplicatione
sed accidentali, quoniam linee principales duarum specierum vadunt
90 per vias diversas et ad puncta diversa medii et oculi; et numquam
concurrunt nisi per aliquas reflexiones vel fractiones cogerentur concurrere. Sed linea principalis unius speciei potest bene concurrere cum
linea accidentali alterius a loco mixtionis usque ad eandem partem
oculi; et tunc vel consumetur species accidentalis per principalem
95 vel per eius fortitudinem occultabitur, ut patet in hac lineatione.

Sit AT [fig. 23] oculus, C punctus a quo species venit perpendiculariter ad oculum super lineam CF. Dico quod in puncto G est vera
colorum trium mixtio seu specierum venientium ab ipsis B et C
et D. Sed ab ipso G non est multiplicatio principalis nisi speciei que

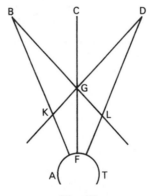

Fig. 23

100 venit ab ipso C; et species principalis sola potest ducere visum in
rei cognitionem; et non accidentalis, ut prius dictum est, nec

83 principalem: perpendicularem *SA*   84 diversorum: contrariorum vel d. *S*
84-5 quantumcunque: *om. B*   85 propinqua *O* / collocantur *O*   86 rectam vel:
om. B   87 tamen: *om. B*   88 principalem: principalis *S*   91 cogantur *S*
94 vel: illis *S*   96 AT *FL*: A *O* AC *S* aut *B*   97 CF: GF *S* / *post* vera *mg. add. O*
mixtio   98 trium mixtio: *om. O*   101 *post* est *add. SA* quia que (*om. A*)
accidentalis / nec: non *SA*

before it reaches the pupil one of the species is converted into the contrary species by natural action. Therefore, sight will judge one thing by means of one species, or else by a species so strong that it conceals the other.

That one species comes perpendicularly along the principal line from the first place of mixing, and the other along an accidental line, is manifest from the position of the eye with respect to two different visible objects, however close together they may be. For although a species comes from each visible object to the place of mixing by a principal line that is rectilinear, refracted, or reflected, nevertheless it is clear that beyond that place one of the species cannot proceed along the principal line of the other by principal [that is, direct] multiplication, but [only] by accidental multiplication, since the principal lines of the two species proceed in different directions and to different points of the medium and the eye; and they never coincide unless they are judged to do so by certain reflections or refractions. But the principal line of one of the species can easily coincide with an accidental line of the other between the place of mixing and a given part of the eye; and then the accidental species will either be consumed by the principal one or be concealed by its strength, as is evident in the following figure.

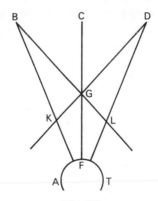

Fig. 23

Let AT [fig. 23] be the eye and C a point from which a species comes perpendicularly to the eye along line CF. I say that at point G there occurs a true compounding of the three colours or species coming from B, C, and D. But from G the only principal multiplication is of the species that comes from C; and only the principal species can lead to visual perception of the object. For an accidental species cannot do this, as was stated above, nor does the latter come

perpendiculariter venit a re ipsa, sed solum a loco mixtionis. Et eodem
modo est in mixtionibus apud K et L. Quoniam igitur a re visa ad unam
partem pupille non venit nisi species una principalis et perpendicularis
105 habens sic duplicem fortitudinem, scilicet ex principalitate et perpendicularitate, propter quas alia consumitur inter locum mixtionis
et partem pupille aut occultatur, oportet quod hec mixtio, licet sit
vera, quod non tamen inducat aliquam confusionem in visu, sed
plenam relinquit distinctionem.

110   Quod igitur auctores varii, ut Alhacen *Libro de aspectibus* et alii
perspectivi, et etiam naturales, ut Seneca et alii in libris naturalibus,
volunt species distingui in medio, intelligendum est hoc modo,
scilicet quod a rebus veniunt species per lineas principales distinctas
usque ad locum mixtionis; et deinde ulterius tendunt per vias
115 diversas et distinctas, loquendo de lineis principalibus, quamvis
accidentales unius cum principalibus alterius coincidant a loco
mixtionis in partibus medii et oculi; et adhuc hec coincidentia
reputatur distinctio eo quod fortitudo principalis multiplicationis
occultat aliam aut corrumpit penitus. Et ideo quod Alhacen in primo
120 libro inducit experimentum ad distinctionem specierum probandam,
scilicet per discursum earum per idem foramen usque ad partes diversas
in corpore obiecto, dicendum quod verum est quod sic est distinctio
ut intendit, quod species a foramine in quo miscentur vadunt per
lineas diversas principales, sicut extra foramen venerunt a rebus per
125 lineas diversas, que terminantur ad puncta diversa in corpore obiecto,
representantia species diversas principales in partibus diversis corporis obiecti; sed tamen in foramine fuit vera mixtio, ut dictum
est, visum nullo modo impediens propter causas dictas; quin distincte
fiat.

130   Et iam iuxta hoc patet quid tenendum est de unitate speciei que
venit a re una vel pluribus. Si enim agens sit unius nature active, ut
lucidum, vel unius coloris vel cuiuslibet alterius proprietatis active,
patet unam esse multiplicationem secundum speciem, nec non et
secundum numerum quantum ad essentiam; nam licet quelibet pars
135 faciat multiplicationem unam spericam, non tamen numerantur in
eadem materia et subiecto, sed cedunt omnes in unam, quia forme

104 perpendiculariter *S*   105 ex . . . et: ex perpendicularitate et *mg. O*
105–6 perpendicularitate: perpendiculariter *B* ex principalitate *O*   106 quam *O*
108 quod: *om. S* / aliam *S*   109 relinquat *O*   110 quod: quoniam *FO* / ut: et *O*
113 scilicet: secundum *S* / quod: *om. O*   116 unius: minus *O* / cum . . . alterius:
om. O   117 adhuc: *om. B*   119 alia *FO* / *post* primo *mg. add. L*[C] capitulo quinque
d(*!*)   123 *post* intendit *add. S* et concludit scilicet *et add. A* concludere scilicet / a:
in *O*   125 diversa: diversas *B*   126 representativa *S*   127 vera: natura *B*
128 visum: unum *B* / quin: quoniam *S*   130 tenendum: terminarum *S*   131 vel:
et *S*   132 vel[1,2]: et *S* / cuiuscunque *F*   133 *post* et *add. L'* quantam ad *et deinde*
add. L[C] unitatem   134 quantum ad: et secundum *L*   135 multiplicationem: *om. B*

perpendicularly from the object itself, but only from the place of mixing. And mixing occurs in the same way at K and L. Therefore, since from the visible object to one part of the pupil comes only one principal and perpendicular species, having a double [source of] strength, namely, its perpendicularity and its status as the principal species (on account of which the other species is consumed between the place of mixing and the part of the pupil, or concealed), consequently this mixing, although a true compounding, cannot introduce any confusion into sight, but allows full discrimination [of the object].

Since various authors, as Alhazen in *De aspectibus* and the other perspectivists, and also natural philosophers, as Seneca and others in books on natural philosophy, think that species remain distinct from one another in the medium, the matter is to be understood in the following way: species come from things by distinct principal lines as far as the place of mixing; and beyond this place they proceed along different and distinct paths; and [it should be emphasized that] I speak here of the principal lines, since beyond the place of mixing the accidental lines of one coincide with the principal lines of another in the parts of the medium and the eye; and yet this coincidence is [mistakenly] taken for distinction, because the strength of the principal multiplication conceals or completely destroys the other. And therefore, as regards Alhazen's description, in book i, of an experiment to prove the distinctness of species, namely, sending them through the same aperture to different parts of the facing body,[8] we answer that it is true, as he maintains, that there is distinction [of species], because the species proceed from the aperture in which they are mixed by different principal lines, just as on the other side of the aperture they come from the objects by different lines and these principal lines terminate on the facing body at different points representing different principal species;[9] and yet in the aperture there is true compounding as was said, but this in no way hinders vision, for the reasons given; on the contrary, vision occurs distinctly.

From all of this it is evident what should be held [as true] concerning the unity of the species coming from one object or from several. For if the agent is of one active nature (for example, lucid) or of one colour or any other active property, it is evident that there is a single multiplication according to species,[10] and it is also numerically single as far as essence is concerned; for although each part produces one spherical multiplication, these multiplications are not [individually] numerable while in the same matter and subject, but all vanish into one, since

136 cedunt: concidunt *O* | *ante* forme *scr. et del. F* sicut

eiusdem nature non numerantur in eadem materia. Si vero sint contrarie nature activa in diversis partibus agentis, ut in pica et scuto vel
aliis, tunc naturaliter miscentur et fit unum per essentiam. Si vero sint
140 contingentes, ut lux et calor in igne, tunc fiunt unum subiecto et sic
unum numero, ut album et dulce in lacte, quia sunt in eodem subiecto
secundum numerum; sed non sunt unum numero in essentia, sicut
nec in specie. Si vero sint diverse res agentes et locis separate, tunc
fit una species hiis tribus modis quando concurrunt ad invicem in
145 eodem loco et subiecto.

Et huic veritati coniuncta est consideratio de continuitate speciei.
Cum enim in superficie tota agentis est una natura activa continua
et medium unum continuum, oportet quod multiplicatio sit continua. Cum vero una natura activa sit in una parte et alia in alia,
150 ut in pica vel scuto vel quomodocunque sit dummodo sint contrarie,
fit continua species et una, sed mixta. Si vero sint contingentes, tunc
nec sunt proprie continue nec contigue multiplicationes, sed diverse
simul existentes. Si vero media et subiecta sint diversa, tunc sunt
species diverse et discontinue propter diversitatem et discontinuita-
155 tem subiectorum et mediorum.

PARS IV
CAPITULUM 1

Habito de generatione speciei et figuratione multiplicationis sue a
loco generationis, insuper existentia speciei multiplicate in medio,
5 nunc considerandum est de eius debilitatione et quibusdam annexis ad
eius debilitationem. Queritur primo an medium ei resistat. Et patet
quod sic per Alhacen et ceteros auctores aspectuum, nam hoc dicunt
expresse. Item sive sit natura elementaris agens sive consequens ad
eam, ut sapor et odor et huiusmodi, sive sit natura celi, necesse est
10 rarefactionem fieri et condensationem, quia nichil generatur in natura
sine istis, quia hee sunt prime passiones materie naturalis ad quas

137 nature: materie *S* | non numerantur: *om. B* | vere *L* | sunt *S*   138 nature:
om. S | vel: et *S*   139 sunt *S*   140 unum . . . et: subiecto u. et (u. et *mg.*) *O* | sic:
om. O   141 quia: que *B*   142 unum: numerum *S*   143 sint *BFL*: sunt *OSA*
147 una: *om. O*   148 continuum: et c. *F* est c. *L om. S*   148-9 et . . . continua:
om. B   150 in scuto *OSA* | quodcunque *O* | *ante* contrarie *scr. et del. S* due
151 sint: *om. F*   152 nec[1] *BFN*: non *LOA* naturaliter nec *S* | proprie: *om. S*
154 in discontinue *L*

forms of the same nature are not [individually] numerable in the same matter. If, on the other hand, there should be contrary active natures in different parts of the agent, as in a pike and shield or other things, then they are naturally mixed and become of one essence. But if there should be contingent natures,[11] such as light and heat in fire, then they share one subject and thus become one in number, as white and sweet in milk, since they are numerically in the same subject; but they are not numerically one in essence, nor in species. Finally, if there should be different agents in different places, then one species is produced in [any of] these three ways when [the species] intersect one another in a single place and subject.

And to this truth we add a consideration of the continuity of species. For since there is one continuous active nature in the whole surface of the agent and one continuous medium, the multiplication [of species] must also be continuous. But when there is one active nature in one part [of the agent] and another active nature in another part, as in a pike or shield or whatever you like, as long as they are contraries, one continuous (though mixed) species is produced. If, however, the natures should be contingent, then the multiplications are not properly continuous or contiguous, but distinct, although existing simultaneously [in the same place]. But if the media and subjects are distinct, then the species are distinct and discontinuous because of the distinctness and discontinuity of their subjects and media.

PART IV
CHAPTER 1

Having treated the generation of a species and the figures according to which it is multiplied from its place of generation, and also the existence of a species multiplied in a medium, we must now consider its weakening and certain related matters. We inquire first whether the medium resists a species. And it is clear from Alhazen and other writers on optics that it does, for they say this explicitly.[1] Moreover, whether that which acts is elemental nature or something consequent to it, as flavour and odour and the like, or celestial nature, there must be rarefaction and condensation, since nothing is generated in nature without them, for these are the first effects of natural matter and are

1 pars quarta huius tractatus habens tria capitula *OF mg. L*   2 capitulum (*om. FL*) primum habet duas conclusiones *OF mg. L*   3 *post* generatione *add. SA* et existentia / *ante* figuratione *add.* S multiplicationis *et add.* A multiplicate et   3–4 a loco: sive *B* 4 insuper . . . multiplicate: *om. SA*   5 debilitate *L*   6 eius: e. vero *BL* debilitatem *L* / queritur: quia *S*   8 sive[1]: si *L* / elementis *B*   9 necesse: *spatium vacuum B* 10 in natura: *om.* S   11 quos *B*

alie sequuntur, ut Aristoteles vult in octavo *Physicorum* et alibi.
Sed rarum naturaliter resistit condensationi et densum rarefactioni;
quare oportet quod omne medium, sive rarum sive densum, resistat.
15 Et Alhacen vult quod rarum habet finem et statum in corporibus
mundi, ita quod rarius possit intelligi esse, licet non sit; et ideo omne
rarum est respective densum, licet non absolute. Et densum natum est
per se resistere, sicut docet Alhacen; et videmus hoc per experimentum
corporum densorum obiectorum speciei lucis et aliorum. Propter
20 quod omne corpus quantumcunque rarum resistit speciei.

Si vero dicatur solum contrarium resistit, et multis speciebus
nichil est contrarium, ut speciei lucis et cuiuslibet celestis, et colori
et sapori et huiusmodi, que sequuntur mixtionem, dicendum est
quod virtuti celesti non est aliquid contrarium absolute secundum
25 suam essentiam; effectui tamen equivoco eius, cuiusmodi est rare-
factio, est aliquid contrarium, et similiter de condensatione et aliis
est aliquid contrarium, et ipsi in quantum est efficiens contrariam
dispositionem in materia. Et sic de colore et aliis que sunt in mixtis,
nam et eodem modo est de eis sicut de celestibus activis, et quod
30 plus est, quia in eis relucet vestigium contrarietatis elementaris,
quia a qualitatibus elementorum contrariis causantur; et licet non sit
in celestibus contrarietas quatuor qualitatum activarum et passivarum,
tamen ibi est contrarietas penes rarum et densum et penes lucidum
et obscurum et huiusmodi, sicut inferius evidentius exponetur.

35 Si dicatur quod materia appetit speciem, quia non est in corruptionem sed in complementum, ut dictum est prius, quare non resistit,
dicendum est quod licet eam appetat, tamen ibi est aliqua transmutatio
modica circa raritatem et densitatem, et densum resistit rarefactioni
et econtrario; que tamen transmutatio recompensatur in melius,
40 propter generationem speciei, per quam quodlibet cuilibet assimilatur
in natura propter salutem partium et totius universi. Sed hec certius
terminabuntur inferius, quando de corruptione specierum agetur.

Deinde accedamus ad debilitationem, et dicendum est quod species
debilitatur magis ac magis in corporibus mundi in quibus multiplicatur,
45 quantum est de natura multiplicationis transeuntis, que manet sub

---

12 sequuntur *FLN*: secuntur *BSA* consecuntur *O*   13 considerationi *S* | calefactioni
F   16 ita . . . rarius: *spatium vacuum B* | rarius *LS*: rarum *O* rarus *F* | omne: *om. B*
18 per²: *om. L*   21 dicat *B*   22 ut: nec *O* non *S* | cuiuslibet celestis *OS*: cuilibet
celesti *BFA* tribus celesti *L*   23 secuntur *S* sequens *F*   25 effectum *BL* | equi-
vocatio *L* | cuius *FS*   26 aliquid: *om. S*   26-7 et¹ . . . contrarium: *mg.* (*sed post
similiter add.* est) *O*   27 aliquid: autem *SA* | quantum: quam *F*   29 *post* sicut
add. S et de consideratione *et scr. et del. A* de condensatione   31 contrariis: *om. F*
contrariis oriuntur et *SA*   32 activa *F*   33 penes²: *om. F*   34 huius *S*
35 quia: quod *S*   38 modica: secundum quod *SA* | et²: ut *F*   38-9 et² . . .
econtrario: *om. S*   39 que: *om. L* | tamen: *om. S* | transmutatio: *mg. O om. S*

followed by others, as Aristotle indicates in *Physics*, book viii, and elsewhere.[2] But the rare naturally resists condensation, while the dense naturally resists rarefaction; therefore every medium, whether rare or dense, must offer resistance. Now Alhazen maintains that the rare has a limit and a fixed degree[3] in mundane bodies, so that it could be understood to be rarer, even if it is not; thus every rare substance is dense relative to something else, although not absolutely. And the dense is naturally suited of itself to resist, as Alhazen teaches; we see this by experience with dense bodies set in the way of the species of light and other things. Therefore, every body, however rare, resists species.

But if it should be claimed that only contraries resist, and many species have no contrary (for example, the species of light and any celestial body, or of colour and flavour and the like, which result from mixing), we reply that there is no absolute contrary to celestial virtue according to its essence; nevertheless, there is a contrary to its equivocal effect, such as rarefaction (and similarly for condensation and other things), and to itself in so far as it produces a contrary disposition in matter. And likewise for colour and other things in mixtures, for it is true of them in the same way as of active celestial things, and more so, since in them a trace of elemental contrariety is reflected, because they were produced by the contrary qualities of the elements; and although the contrariety of the four active and passive qualities does not exist in the heavens, there is nevertheless contrariety according to rare and dense and according to bright and dark and the like, as will be explained more clearly below.[4]

If it should be said that matter desires species, which do not corrupt but perfect it, as was said above,[5] and therefore does not resist them, we reply that although matter desires species, nevertheless it experiences a certain modest transmutation [because of them] in terms of rarity and density, and the dense resists rarefaction, while the rare resists condensation; and for this transmutation it is more than repaid, because the generation of species, by which everything in nature is assimilated to everything else, contributes to the well-being of the universe, both the whole and its parts. But these matters will be more surely determined below, when we treat the corruption of species.[6]

We now turn to the subject of weakening, and it must be said that a species is continuously weakened in the mundane bodies in which it is multiplied, as far as the nature of multiplication passing through [the bodies] is concerned, and this falls under the

42 determinabuntur *OSA*   43 debilitatem *FO*   44 multiplicatur: debilitatur multi-plicatio *S*

ratione speciei. Nam hoc dico propter hoc, quod species aliquando
impeditur transire per medium corporis, et accidit quod illud corpus
natum est recipere speciem continue generatam in eo; unde fortificatur species et fit effectus completus, sicut accidit de luce solis
50 in corpore lune et stellarum; et species ignis fortificatur quando
materia occurrit, ut in combustione magna apparet et quando occur-
runt multum inflammabilia, ut olea et bitumina ardentia sicut napta
et huiusmodi; etiam lana bene sicca aere interposito comburitur et non
aer. Sed nunc loquor de sola specie, et non de effectu completiori
55 qui fit ex congregatione multarum specierum in corpore apto ad eam.
Et hanc debilitationem probamus per sensum, qui minus immutatur a
longe quam prope; item per alias operationes naturales, quoniam
patientia remotiora minus alterantur, ut minus calefit qui ab igne
est remotior, ceteris paribus.
60   Alhacen quidem quarto *Perspective* ponit duas causas huius
debilitationis. Una est distantia ab agente, in qua causa intelligitur
secundum multos expositores quod agens est fortius specie generata
in prima parte spatii; et illa est fortior specie generata in secunda,
et sic ultra. Sed hec causa non sufficit, nam propter debilitatem
65 esse speciei, quia incompletissimum quid est, possunt species prima
et agens producere speciem equalem in materia competenti. Preterea,
quid impediet speciem primam, ut faciat speciem sibi equalem in
medio competenti, cum agens ipsum potest in materia competenti
facere in prima eius parte effectum completum, ut candela una illu-
70 minat et accendit aliam, et comburit lanam et alia levia ei approximata?
Et videmus virtutem adamantis et magnetis fortiorem esse in ferro
distanti quam in aere propinquiori, et tamen transit per aerem ad
ferrum. Et videmus speciem vitri fortiter colorati quando multum
illuminatur apparere fortius in corpore mixto quam in aere propin-
75 quiori. Et tamen sola species et virtus magnetis est in ferro, quia ferrum
manet in natura sua specifica et quantum ad sensum non alteratur;
similiter de specie coloris vitri et de huiusmodi. Quapropter distantia
in quantum huiusmodi non videtur esse causa cum tali expositione.
    Aliam causam assignat Alhacen in eodem loco, scilicet quod a
80 specie ubique exeunt radii accidentales infiniti secundum omnes diametros; propter quam specierum infinitam generationem, debilitatur

49 et: ut *S*   50 lune: solis *F* / fortificatur: f. a longe *SA*   51 occurrit: aptior
concurrit *SA*   52 napta: rapta *L*   53 etiam: *om. F*   54 loquitur *S*
55 qui: et q. *S*   56 debilitatem *O* / qui *OS*: que *FL* quia *B* / minus: unus *B* immutantur
S   58 remotiorum *F* / minus[1]: unus *B*   59 paribus: *om. S*   60 causas: *om. S*
63 spatii: *om. S*   64 ultra: ulterius u. *F* / nam: nec *B* / debilitationem *SA*   65 quia:
quod est *O* / quid *BLA*: quod *OS* quidem *N om. F* / possunt: *correxi ex* potest *BFLOA*
(*om. S*)   66 competenti: completi *B*   67 impedit *O* / equalem: similem *O* / in:
et in *S*   68 cum ... competenti: *om. F*   69 eius: *om. O*   70 ei: sibi *F* /
approximata: *mg. O*ᶜ proximata *O'* permixta *S*   71 esse: *om. F*   72 tamen: *om. S* /

law of species. I say this because sometimes the passage of a species through a corporeal medium is impeded, although that body happens to be suited by nature to receive the species continuously generated in it; wherefore, the species is strengthened and becomes a complete effect, as the light of the sun in the body of the moon and stars; and the species of fire is strengthened when it encounters [inflammable] matter, as we see when a large fire encounters highly inflammable substances, such as oil, pitch, naphtha, and the like; also, very dry, loose wool burns, but not the interspersed air. However, I speak here of a single species [multiplied through a medium] and not of the more complete effect that results from the confluence of many species in a body suited to their coming together. And we prove this weakening by [observing the operation of] the senses, which are less altered at a distance than nearby; also through other natural operations, since more distant recipients are less altered, just as that which is further from fire is less apt to be heated, other things being equal.

Alhazen posits two causes of this weakening in his *Perspectiva,* book iv.[7] One is distance from the agent, according to which it is understood by many expositors that the agent is stronger than the species generated in the first part of the space; and the latter is stronger than the species generated in the second part, and so on. But this is not a sufficient cause, for because of the weakness of the being of species (the most incomplete being there is), the first species and the agent can produce equal species in suitable matter. Furthermore, what would prevent the first species from producing a species equal to itself in a suitable medium, since an agent can produce a complete effect in the first part of suitable matter, as one candle illuminates and ignites another and burns wool and other light things near it? And we see that the power of a lodestone or a magnet is stronger in distant iron than in adjacent air, and yet it passes through the air to the iron. And we see that the species of intensely coloured glass, when strongly illuminated, appears stronger in a mixed body [on which it falls] than in the air through which it first passes. And yet in the iron there is only the species and virtue of the magnet, since the iron retains its specific nature and is not sensibly altered; and similarly for the species of the colour of glass and the like. From this exposition it seems that distance as such is not a cause of weakening.

Alhazen assigns another cause in the same place, namely, that from every part of a species an infinity of accidental rays issues along all diameters; and because of this infinite generation of species, the

ad: et S   76 sua: *om.* O   77 similiter: s. et B s. est S / colorum S   78 non
BSAN: *om.* FLO / cum: tamen B   80 exeant S / infiniti: in priori S   81 infinitam:
om. F

vis generativa secundum incessum principalem ab agente. Sed quando
agens invenit materiam semper aptiorem combustioni, ut ignis in istis
combustibilibus magnis, facit effectum semper completiorem; et tamen
85 ibi est multiplicatio illa accidentalis a qualibet parte ignis secundum
omnes diametros, et non impedit fortitudinem effectus. Ergo si
occurrat in speciei generatione huiusmodi materia, oportet quod fiat
species fortior; et hoc videmus in specie magnetis et specie vitri
et multis aliis.

90   Dicendum tamen quod Alhacen bene dicit secundum intentionem
suam, quia certissimus auctorum est, nec in aliquo fefellit nos in sua
scientia. Sed ipse intendit quod in corporibus mundi que recipiunt
multiplicationem speciei transeuntis, que sunt media pervia et non
retinent speciem, neque propter densitatem ut ibi aggregetur, ut corpus
95 lune respectu speciei lucis, neque propter aptitudinem et convenien-
tiam naturalem, ut in magnete respectu speciei ferri, que convenientia
non est in aere, et sic de multis; in hiis, inquam, corporibus mediis,
oportet quod species lucis et cuiuslibet debilitetur in distantia,
quia a celestibus in inferiora semper ad sensum, vel saltem secundum
100 naturam, augmentatur densitas, et deficit raritas etiam in celis et
in confinio aeris et ignis, licet quantum ad sensum non sit diversitas.
Et quia densum resistit, ideo oportet quod species secunda habet
maiorem resistentiam quam prima, et tertia quam secunda. Et simul
cum hoc est dispersio et debilitatio propter multiplicationes acciden-
105 tales infinitas ab omni parte medii. Sed quia secundum distantiam
maiorem maior crescit resistentia, ideo prevalet causa a parte distantie.
Similiter econtrario quando species ab inferioribus ad celestia pro-
greditur, nam tunc principatur causa secunda Alhacen, scilicet dispersio speciei secundum omnes diametros in omni parte medii, cui
110 debilitationi non potest respondere subtiliatio medii continua a
deorsum in sursum, nam maior est debilitatio quam subtiliatio; et
ideo semper accidit debilitatio maior et maior. Si tamen responderet
subtiliatio debilitationi que est per dispersionem, constat quod fieret
species equalis et non debilitaretur in aliquo, quia esse speciei debile
115 est, et ideo species in omni parte medii posset eam producere.
Similiter non solum secundum sursum et deorsum, sed secundum
alias differentias positionum accidit. Unde quando homo stat in

82 vis: virtus S   83 invenit: habet S   84 combustibilibus FLO^C: combustionibus
O'BS   85 ibi: ubique F / qualibus O   89 et: in B   91 auctorum BLSA:
auctor FON   94 propter: om. O   95 speciei: superficiei S   96 inconvenientia B   97 hiis: h. sibi S   99 a: in S / in: om. BS / sensum vel: mg. F
100 natura S / raritas: mg. O / etiam: et S   102 densis B   103-4 simul
cum: similiter O   104 hic O / et debilitatio: om. F   105 quia: mg. O
106 cressit L / ideo: i. plus B / distantis S   107 econtrario: e converso S
107-8 procreatur S   108 principia S / secundum S   112 respondet S
113 subtili L / per dispersionem: dispersio O   115 possit O   115-17 omni . . .

generative force along the principal line from the agent is weakened. However, when the agent encounters matter progressively more disposed to combustion, as fire in those highly combustible substances, it produces a progressively more complete effect; and although there is that accidental multiplication from each part of the fire along all diameters, this does not prevent a strong effect. Therefore, if such matter should be encountered in the generation of a species, the species would necessarily be strengthened; and we see this in the species of a magnet or of [coloured] glass and many other things.

Nevertheless, it must be acknowledged that Alhazen speaks rightly according to his intention, since he is the most trustworthy of authors and has never deceived us in his science. But he intends that in mundane bodies through which species are multiplied, that is, pervious media that do not retain the species either through density, which would cause them to collect there, as the body of the moon with respect to the species of light, or through natural aptitude and suitability, as in the species of the magnet with respect to iron[8] (which suitability is not present in air), and so of many other things —in these corporeal media, I say, the species of light or anything else must be weakened with distance, since as far as sense can discern (or at least according to nature) density always increases as one proceeds from the heavens to the lower regions, and rarity decreases even in the heavens and at the boundary between air and fire (although the decrease is not apparent to the senses). Because density offers resistance, the second species[9] must encounter greater resistance than the first, and the third than the second. Simultaneous with this are dispersion and weakening through the infinity of accidental multiplications from every part of the medium.[10] But since resistance increases with distance, distance prevails as the cause of weakening. On the other hand, when a species proceeds from lower regions to the heavens, Alhazen's second cause [of weakening] prevails, namely, the dispersion of the species along all diameters to all parts of the medium; and the progressive rarefaction of the medium from bottom to top cannot compensate for this weakening, for the weakening is greater than the rarefaction; and therefore the species becomes progressively weaker.[11] But if rarefaction should exactly compensate for the weakening due to dispersion, then the species would remain equal and would not be at all weakened, for since the being of a species is weak, it follows that a species in any part of the medium could produce a [new and equal] species.

This occurs not only [in multiplication] up and down, but in other directions as well. Thus when a man stands on top of a very high

positionum: *mg. O*   117 differentias: duas *F* / positionis *mg. O*

cacumine montis altissimi et videt per medium aeris ab oriente in occidens et a septentrione in meridiem, oportet quod debilitatio
120 speciei sit propter dispersionem, et magis quam a deorsum in sursum, quia a deorsum in sursum est aliqua subtiliatio continua. Secundum alias positiones non est necesse, sed minor est debilitas quam a sursum in deorsum propter equalitatem raritatis, que non est a sursum in deorsum. Si tamen media in hoc mundo essent sic disposita ut semper
125 esset subtiliatio maior vel equalis debilitationi speciei ex dispersione, tunc non debilitaretur. Sed hoc non est possibile secundum vias contrarias, ut a sursum in deorsum et econtrario; nec est in actu secundum aliquam illarum. Accidentaliter tamen evenit quod speciei occurrat ex distantia corpus magis aptum ad esse speciei, sicut dictum
130 est de magnete et multis; et tunc non debilitatur, sed fortificari potest vel equari.

PARS IV

CAPITULUM 2

Post hoc sciendum de ista multiplicatione an in infinitum apta nata sit fieri, si spatium huius mundi esset infinitum; quod non sic fieret
5 tenendum est, quoniam species debilitatur ex elongatione a sua origine, ut nunc declaratum est, et ideo necesse est ipsam deficere in sui multiplicatione. Quod autem diceretur quod omnis punctus lucis potest se multiplicari secundum omnes diametros, dicendum est quod hoc est falsum absolute loquendo, debet enim hoc artari ad speciem
10 que tantam habet fortitudinem ut possit sibi generare similem, quod non est verum de specie nimis debilitata. Quod vero dicit Aristoteles secundo *De anima*, quod ignis ageret in infinitum si apponeretur combustibile, dicunt quidam quod ibi loquitur de calore igneo in corpore animato, qui ageret indeterminate et indiscrete respectu corporis
15 sustentandi nisi ab anima regularetur et dirigeretur in finem determinatum et certum, ut expedit animato corpori et partibus eius; et ideo infinitum vocat ibi incertum et indeterminatum et ineptum corpori animato.

118 aerem *S*   119 in meridiem: meridie *B*   121 deorsum in sursum: *correxi ex* s. in d. *BFLOS*   122 quam a: quantum ad *O obs. F*   123 in[1]: et *O*   124 mundo: modo *BF*   125 vel: et *S* / ex dispersione: vel dispersioni *O*   126 vias *F*[C]: suas *F'B*   127 in actu: tactu *S*   128 aliquam illarum: alique *S*   130 multis: m. aliis *S* / non: n. inde *O* / fortificari: specificari *F*

2 capitulum secundum *O mg. L*   3 an: si *B* / nata: *mg. O*   4 non: *mg. A*[C]

mountain and looks through the air from east to west and from north to south, there must be weakening of the species owing to dispersion, and more than [in propagation of species] upwards, since in the latter direction there is a certain continuous rarefaction. In other directions [parallel to the ground] this is not the case, but less weakening occurs in those directions than in downward multiplication, because of the equality of density [encountered by the species], which is not present in downward multiplication. However, if media in this world[12] were so disposed that [the strengthening of species owing to] rarefaction was always greater than or equal to the weakening of species owing to dispersion, then there would be no weakening. But this could not occur in each of two contrary directions, such as upwards and downwards; nor is it an actuality in any direction. However, it can occur accidentally that a species encounters, at a distance, a body more suited to the being of species, as was said concerning the magnet and many other things; and then the species is not weakened, but can be strengthened or retain equality of strength.

PART IV
CHAPTER 2

Next it must be ascertained whether, if the world were infinitely large, this multiplication would be suited to proceed to infinity; but this should not be held to occur, since a species is weakened in accordance with elongation from its origin, as has been declared just above, and therefore its multiplication must cease. However, if it should be pointed out that every point of light can multiply itself along all diameters, we reply that, strictly speaking, this claim is false, for it is applicable only to a species that has enough strength to generate another like itself, which is not the case for a species that has been greatly weakened. As for Aristotle's statement in *De anima*, book ii, that fire would proceed to infinity if combustible material were present,[1] some say that he speaks there of fiery heat in an animated body, which would act indeterminately and without discrimination with respect to the body that it is meant to sustain if it were not regulated and directed by the soul to a certain and determined goal, so as to be useful to the animated body and its parts; and therefore by 'infinite' he means uncertain and indeterminate and unsuited to an animated body.

vero *BSA'*   7 multiplicationi *B*   9 debet: oportet *LS* / hoc²: hec *L*   12 ageret: augmentari *F om. O* / in: *om. B* / si: crescit si sibi *O*   13 *ante* igneo *scr. et del. L* combustibili   14 aget *F* agit *O*   15 dirigerentur *S*   16 animam *B*

Sed istud non sufficit, nam si materia magis ac magis inflammabilis
20 continuaretur in spatio infinito, necesse esset quod actio semper iret
continue secundum continuitatem materie. Sed huiusmodi materia
non invenitur respectu multiplicationis speciei, nec posset inveniri,
sicut nec respectu ignis completi generandi. Sed si inveniretur, seu
respectu speciei seu respectu ignis, fieret actio in infinitum. Si tamen
25 contra istud nunc dictum obiciatur quod nulla virtus finita se extendit
ad actionem infinitam, ergo in nulla materia posset species nec ignis
fieri in infinitum, dicendum est quod sicut in divisione continui
ponimus quod potest divisio fieri in infinitum, id est numquam
cessare nec stare ad indivisibile, non tamen quod divisio sit actu
30 infinita, sic est de appositione materie et de generatione speciei
vel ignis quod in infinitum fieret, id est non cessaret, non tamen
quod actio esset actu infinita. Dicendum igitur est quod virtus finita
non se habet simul et semel ad infinitam actionem in actu et inten-
sive, sed potest bene fieri aliqua actio sine fine in tempore, id est
35 continuari, precipue una actio composita et aggregata ex infinitis
sibi invicem succedentibus, ut divisio in infinitum, que ex infinitis
divisionibus causatur, quarum quelibet est in se finita. Et sic est
hic: quelibet actio vel generatio speciei et ignis est finita et in
tempore finito; sed tamen hee possunt succedere sibi invicem
40 in infinitum si materia magis ac magis apta apponeretur in infinitum.
Sed non est possibile quod materia talis inveniatur in hoc mundo,
et ideo speciei multiplicatio stat in actu, sicut et ignis.

Si vero dicatur quod species in parte priori generata est equalis
vel multiplex ad speciem in posteriori parte vel secundum aliquam
45 speciem maioris inequalitatis, ergo secundum considerationem
Aristotelis in septimo *Physicorum*, ubi dicit quod si tota potentia
potest in aliquam operationem, pars poterit in partem, et ita species in
ultima parte posita poterit aliquid spatii alterare, dicendum est quod
hec ratio est nimis violenta in apparentia, et solvi videretur alicui per
50 hoc, quod cum prius ostensum est quod aliquod spatium est generationi speciei determinatum, ut in maiori eo non fiant singule generationes, possunt tamen in minori infinitum. Et ideo concedendum est

19 ac magis: et *S*   20 continuare *F* | infinite *B* | est *O* | erit *O*   23 nec: materia
S | si: non *L spatium vacuum B* | seu: *mg. F om. S*   24 seu: sicut *S* | si: sed *F*
25 nunc: *om. FO* | dictum: *om. O*   26 possit *O* | ante nec *scr. et del. O* nec genus
29 nec: aut *S* | non: nec *FO*   31 in: *om. L* | non² *BSA*: nec *FLO*   33–4 inten-
tione *O*   34 fieri: *om. O scr. et del. F* | id est *LSA*: *om. BFO*   35 continuari:
continue *A ex* continue *corr. S* | infinitis: inferius *B*   36 sibi: similiter *S* | ut: et *B* |
divisio: dicit *F*   37 quarum: qua et *F* | in: per *S*   38 hic: ibi *S* | est: *om. S*
40 in infinitum¹: *om. F* | ac magis: *om. OSA*   41 mundo: modo *B*   44 multiplex:
semper m. *B* | secundum: *om. S*   45 maioris: m. vel minoris *S*   48 aliquid spatii:
mg. O   49 videtur *BF* | per: quod p. *B*   50 *ante* ostensum *scr. et del. S*
contrarium | quod²: per *B*   51 eo: *om. S*   52 in infinitum *O*

But this [response] is insufficient, for if matter of increasing flammability were extended through an infinite space, the action would necessarily extend itself as far as the continuity of the matter allowed. However, matter of this kind is not encountered in the multiplication of a species, nor could it be encountered, either in the multiplication of species or in the complete generation of fire. But if it were encountered, either by a species or by fire, the action would extend to infinity. However, if against this claim it is objected that no finite virtue produces an infinite action and, therefore, that neither species nor fire could extend to infinity in any matter, we reply that, just as in division of a continuum we assume that division can proceed to infinity (that is, without ceasing or reaching an indivisible), although it is not assumed that division is infinite in actuality, so in the presentation of a material medium and the generation of a species or fire [in the medium], the species or fire proceeds to infinity (that is, never ceases), although the action is not infinite in actuality. Therefore, it must be said that a finite virtue cannot, all at once, produce an action infinite both in actuality and intensively, but an action without temporal limit is easily produced (that is, continued), especially a composite action consisting of an infinity of parts succeeding one another, as division to infinity, which is produced by an infinity of divisions, each of which is of itself finite. And so it is in the present case: each action or generation of a species or fire is finite, as is its duration; nevertheless, these can succeed one another infinitely if more and more suitable matter should be provided, extending to infinity. But it is impossible for such matter to be found in this world, and therefore in actuality the multiplication of a species or fire ceases.

But if it should be said that the species generated in the prior part [of a space] is equal to or a multiple[2] of the species in the posterior part [of that space], or [that the two are related] according to some kind [of ratio] of greater inequality,[3] and therefore (according to Aristotle's analysis in *Physics*, book vii, where he says that if the whole power can perform some operation, then the part can perform part of the operation)[4] that the species in the last part [of the space to which multiplication is] supposed [to reach] will be able to produce a [further] alteration of space, we reply that this argument seems too strong, and for some people it would seem to be resolved as follows. Although it was shown above[5] that a species is generated in a certain determined space, so that no individual species can be generated in a greater space, nevertheless there is no lower limit on the size of the space within which generation can occur. Therefore, it is conceded that within

quod infra illam quantitatem determinatam potest species in penultima
parte existens facere sibi simile in ultima, sed numquam extra illam
55 ultimam procedet, neque etiam usque ad terminum illius; et ideo pro
nichilo computatur hec multiplicatio, quia hec quantitas determinata
est valde parva et quasi insensibilis. Per totam igitur hanc quantitatem
in qualibet parte patientis usque ad penultimam potest fieri generatio
speciei; sed species occupans penultimam partem spatii non faciet sibi
60 simile per totam quantitatem ultime partis, sed per partem eius; et
sic numquam transibit species quantitatem ultime partis, sed illa
que est in penultima parte faciet speciem modicam in aliqua parte
ultime partis, et illa species faciet speciem in aliqua parte residui,
et sic ultra. Si vero obiciatur quod tunc in illa parte ultima non
65 cessaret generatio speciei in tempore infinito, responderetur quod
non cessaret si species haberet esse fixum et permanens; sed continue
generatur et corrumpitur, et ideo non continuatur generatio alicuius
speciei in parte illa ultima secundum divisionem partis in infinitum.

Sed ista solutio totius obiectionis videtur esse nimis dura, quia in-
70 dignum nature et tanquam otiosum et frustra videretur actio naturalis
si fieret in tempore infinito in tam parva quantitate spatii quam in
omnibus partibus precedentibus alterat in minimo tempore. Et
ideo potest aliter ad hoc responderi, quod scilicet species in parte
priori est equalis vel in aliqua proportione respectu speciei in parte
75 sequente secundum aliquam specierum maioris inequalitatis; et ideo
nata est secundum illam proportionem alterare aliquid, sed non
oportet quod aliquid medii illius quod prius alteratum est, sed sub-
tilioris et aptioris ad alterandum et quod est sufficiens debilitationi,
quia medium universaliter resistit, sicut Alhacen docet. Sed huius-
80 modi medium maioris aptitudinis et sufficientis debilitationi continuari in infinitum non est possibile; quod si continuaretur, fieret
actio. Si dicatur quod tunc erit hec species otiosa, dicendum est
quod non, quia apta nata est operari, quamvis non operetur et
impediatur, sicut lapis sursum detentus aut pluma per densitatem
85 medii; non enim dicitur res otiosa nisi quando apta nata est operari
et non sit impedita per aliud. Homo enim licet non rideat non dicitur
otiosus in vitium nature, vel licet non semper in actu suscipiat

54 similem *S* / extra: ultra *S*   55 terminum: minimum *S*   56 computetur *O* /
hec[1]: *om. B* / quantitas: contrarietas *S* / determinata: *om. F*   58 in qualibet: quelibet
species in equali *S* / ultimam *B* / potest: partem *F*   58–60 usque . . . partis: *om. SA'*
mg. A[C]   60 similem *mg. A*[C] *om. F*   62 facit *O* / modicam: *om. F*   63 ultime
. . . parte: *om. F* / aliqua *BLA*: alia *OS* / *ante* residui *scr. et del. F* medii   64 obicitur
S   65 responderetur *F*   69 obiectionis: o. istis *S*   70 videntur *B*   71 quam *BSA'*:
mg. F[C] quantum *F'* quantam *LOA*[C]   72 procedentibus: *om. F*   73 ideo: *mg. O*
74 priori est equalis: pori est naturalis *S* / vel: *om. S*   75 sequenti *S* / aliam *S*
79 naturaliter *O*   80 debilitationi *SA*: debilitationis *BFLON*   81 possibile: *om. S*
82 actio: una a. *B* / si: sed *L* / hec: *om. B*   84 impedietur *F* impeditur *S* / detensus

that determined quantity [of space] the species existing in the penultimate part can produce its likeness in the final part, but it will
never proceed beyond that final part, nor even to its extreme boundary; and so this multiplication counts for nothing, since this determined quantity is very small and virtually insensible. Therefore, a
species can be generated through the entire quantity [of space] in
every part of the recipient up to the penultimate [affected] part;
but the species occupying the penultimate part of the space will not
produce its likeness through the whole of the last part, but [only]
through a part of it; and thus a species will never traverse the
[entire] extent of the last part; rather, the species in the penultimate
part will produce a moderate species in a portion of the last part, and
that species will produce a species in a portion of that which remains,
and so on. If it should be objected that in that case the generation of
a species in that last part would not cease in an infinite time, it is
replied that if the species were to have fixed and permanent being it
would not cease; but it is continually generated and corrupted, and
therefore there is no continuous generation of a certain species in
that last part according to infinite division of that part.

But this resolution of the whole objection seems too severe, since
it would seem to be unworthy of nature and, as it were, inefficient
and in vain for a natural action to require an infinite time to take
effect through a space as small as that which, in all preceding parts
[of the multiplication], it altered in the least time. And therefore
there is another response to this objection, namely, that the species
in the prior part [of a space] is equal or in some ratio to the species
in the posterior part, according to some kind [of ratio] of greater
inequality; consequently, it is suited to alter something according
to that ratio, though not necessarily a part of the [same] medium
altered up to that point, but rather something more subtle and
more suited to alteration and compatible with the weakening [of
the species], since all media offer resistance, as Alhazen teaches.[6]
Now it is not possible for such a medium of greater aptitude [to
alteration] and compatability with the weakening [of the species]
to extend infinitely; but if it did, so would the action. If somebody should reply that then this species is otiose, this is denied,
since it is naturally suited to act even when it is impeded and does
not act, as a stone or feather held up by the density of a medium;
for a thing is not called 'otiose' except when it is naturally suited
to act and is not prevented from acting by something else [and
yet does not act]. For a man who fails to laugh or does not always
in actuality accept instruction is not called 'otiose' or said to be in

BL / pluvia *F*   85 apta: *om. F*   86 sit: fit *F* / liceat *L* licit *F*   87 licet: *om. O*

disciplinam. Sed tunc est aliquid otiosum quando, cum teneatur et debeat operari, non operatur; sed non debet operari cum prohibetur
90 a sua operatione, ut lapis non est otiosus quando proicitur sursum vel detinetur, non habens operationem suam; quia enim virtus naturalis est virtus finita, ideo potest ab operatione prohiberi per impediens.

Et iam huic questioni annexum est an quelibet res potest perficere speciem suam per totum medium quodcunque finitum. Et dicendum
95 est quod non, nam res debilis virtutis facit speciem debilem, que invenit resistentiam in medio improportionalem sibi. Medium enim huius mundi a terra usque ad celum ultimum non tantum subtiliatur quantum continue debilitatur species per multiplicationes accidentales infinities infinitas, quoniam in omni puncto lucis fiunt multiplicationes
100 accidentales infinite, sed si aptitudo medii per continuam subtiliationem maiorem et maiorem fieret a terra in celum secundum proportionem debilitationis speciei, bene accideret quod quelibet res suam speciem impleret usque in celum sperice; sed nunc non est ita. Quod si obiciatur quod que est proportio agentis fortis ad speciem
105 fortem in distantia data, eadem est agentis debilis ad speciem debilem in eadem distantia, dicendum est quod si sola ratio distantie consideraretur, verum esset; sed aliud est impediens, scilicet resistentia medii, que impedit speciem debilem citius quam fortem.

Deinde si spatium esset vacuum infra celum, non fieret multipli-
110 catio speciei in eo (et voco vacuum ut philosophi posuerunt, scilicet spatium dimensionatum non habens corpus locatum, possibile tamen recipere corpora locanda secundum eos), quoniam in vacuo dicit Aristoteles nulla est natura, et ideo non competit ei aliqua actio naturalis; sed multiplicatio lucis est huiusmodi. Item nulla forma con-
115 tinere posset partes vacui, quia nullam habet; ergo discrete ab invicem essent in actu; sed partes indimensionate sunt infinite; quare essent infinita actualiter in vacuo, et ideo in medio vacuo minimo essent infinita in actu. Sed non contingit pertransiri infinita, et ideo multiplicatio hec non potest fieri in vacuo aliquo quantumcunque minimo.
120 Quod si dicatur quod in vacuo nulla est resistentia et ideo poterit fieri multiplicatio, patet quod non valet, quia duo exigerentur ad

89 sed: *om. BL* | non[2]: ut *B* | debet: oportet *S*   91 vel: et *S* | detinetur: deter-
minetur *F*   92 virtus: *om. BL*   94 quantumcunque *O*   95 que: quia *L*
98 per: secundum *S*   99 finities *B* | lucis: *om. S*   100 accidentale *L*   102 res:
om. B   103 compleret *O*   104 quod[1]: quoniam *B* | obicitur *S* | quod[2]: *om. O*
105 data: *spatium vacuum B* | eadem: e. enim *S*   106–7 consideraretur *BFL*: consideretur
OSA   107 esset: est *S* | impedientis *B* | scilicet: *om. B*   110 ut: quod *L*
112 dicit: secundum *S*   113 Aristotelem *S*   114 item *OSA*: iterum *BFL*
115 continere posset: contineret *S* | discreti *FL*   116 indimensionate *OANV*: in
dimensionato *FL* indimensionata *B* dimensionate *S*   117 in[2]: *om. F*
117–19 essent . . . minimo: *mg. O*   118 sed: si *B* | pertransiri *BFLN*: pertansire *OSA*

violation of nature. But a thing is otiose when it is obliged and ought to act and yet does not; but it ought not act when it is prevented from acting, as a stone is not otiose when it is projected upwards or detained and does not [on that account] perform its proper action; for since a natural power is finite, it can be prevented from acting by an impediment.

Now to this question is annexed [another]: whether everything can perfect its species through the whole of every finite medium. And it is stated that it cannot, for a thing of weak virtue produces a weak species, and the latter encounters resistance in the medium out of proportion to its weakness. For not only does the medium of this world [extending] from the earth to the final heaven grow subtler as the species [passing through it] is continuously weakened by accidental multiplications infinitely infinite in number (since from every point of light there is an infinity of accidental multiplications), but if the aptitude of the medium should grow from earth to heaven, increasing continuously in subtlety in the same proportion as the weakening of the species, it would certainly happen that everything would send its species spherically as far as the heavens; however, this does not occur. If it should be objected that the ratio of a strong agent to its strong species at a given distance is the same as the ratio of a weak agent to its weak species at the same distance, it is replied that this is true if only the factor of distance is considered; but there is another hindrance, namely, the resistance of the medium, which impedes a weak species more than a strong species.

Next, if the space below the heaven were void, there would be no multiplication of a species in it—I use the term 'void' as philosophers have defined it, namely, dimensioned space containing no body (although according to them it is able to receive body)—since Aristotle says that in a void there is no nature, and therefore it receives no natural action;[7] but the multiplication of light is such a natural action. Also, no form could link the parts of a void, since it has no form; therefore, the parts would be distinct from one another in actuality; but undimensioned parts are infinite in number; thus in a void there would be actual infinities, and so there would be actual infinities [even] in the smallest void. But infinities cannot be traversed, and therefore this multiplication cannot take place in any void, however small.

But if it should be pointed out that there is no resistance in a void and that multiplication should therefore occur, it is evident that this is false, since two conditions are required for the occurrence of

hoc quod fieret multiplicatio, scilicet quod non fuerit ibi resistentia
plena densitatis et quod sit ibi debita dispositio medii respectu
naturalis multiplicationis, que ibi non est, quia in vacuo nulla est
125 proprietas nature, et ideo non est proportionale naturali multiplicationi rei naturalis. Quare nec multo minus in nichil, ut extra celum,
quia non est comparatio alicuius ad nichil nec proportio. Et ideo
stelle et nonum celum et decimum non multiplicant species extra
celum, sive nichil ibi intelligamus sive stulte ymaginemur vacuum
130 (quia Aristoteles vult quarto *Physicorum* et primo *Celi et mundi*
quod non est vacuum extra celum, sed nichil).

PARS IV
CAPITULUM 3

Postea sciendum est quod virtutis multiplicatio est in tempore, sicut
dicit Alhacen secundo *Perspective* et probat per duas rationes. Una
5 est quod omnis alteratio est in tempore, sed alteratur aer in speciei
multiplicatione et receptione. Item in aliquo instanti est lux in
principio spatii vel in medio, non curo, sed in eodem instanti
non est in fine spatii; esset enim in diversis locis simul et semel, quod
non competit creature. Quare in alio instanti est in fine quam in
10 principio vel medio; sed inter quelibet duo instantia cadit tempus
medium. Quare, ut concludit, oportet quod speciei multiplicatio sit
in tempore. Ex septimo vero similiter eiusdem habetur quod citius
pervenit species perpendicularis ad terminum sue multiplicationis
quam species fracta quando veniunt ab eodem agente; sed citius et
15 tardius non sunt nisi in tempore, ut Aristoteles dicit quatuor
Physicorum et sex.
   Item nulla virtus finita agit in instanti, ut habetur ex sex
Physicorum Aristotelis, quia tunc maior virtus ageret in minori quam
instans. Et tunc virtus finita et infinita equarentur in duratione
20 actionis, ut habetur in fine octavi *Physicorum*, quia virtus infinita
agit in instanti; sed speciei est virtus finita. Item que est proportio
puncti ad lineam est instantis ad tempus. Ergo permutatim que est

---

122-4 scilicet . . . multiplicationis: *om. B*   123 plena: *om. SA* / sit: fit *F*
126 quare: quia *S*   128 non: nec *O*   129 ibi: nisi *B*   130 quia: *om. O*
   2 capitulum tertium *O mg. L*   4 et: et hoc *S* / per: *om. B*   6 item: iterum *BL*
8 esset enim: quia e. *B* / et: *om. B*   9 erit *S*   11 species *B*   12 septimo: alio
F / similiter: *om. S* / eius *O* / habetur: h. probatio *F* / quod: idem *S*   13 sue: *om. F*
14 venit *OSA* / agente: accidenti *B*   15 nisi: *om. F*   17 item: iterum *BL* / nulli
B / finita: *mg. L*   18 agent *B* / *post* quam *add. O* instanti et tunc maior virtus ageret in

multiplication, namely that there should be no extreme resistance arising from density and that there should be in that place a proper disposition of the medium with respect to natural multiplication— [the latter of] which [conditions] is not met, since in a void there is no natural property, and therefore it is not proportioned to the natural multiplication of a natural thing. This is all the more true of nothing,[8] as outside the heaven, since there is no comparison and no ratio of something to nothing. Accordingly, the stars and the ninth and tenth heavens[9] do not multiply species outside the heaven, whether we understand nothing to be there or we foolishly imagine a void (since Aristotle maintains in *Physics*, book iv, and *De caelo et mundo*, book i, that there is no void outside the heaven, but nothing).[10]

PART IV
CHAPTER 3

Next it must be known that the multiplication of virtue occupies time, as Alhazen says in *Perspectiva*, book ii, and proves by two arguments.[1] The first is that every alteration occupies time, and in the multiplication and reception of a species air is altered. Also, at a certain instant light is at the beginning or in the middle of a space (it does not matter which), but at that same instant it is not at the end of the space; for if it were, it would be at different places at one and the same time, which is impossible for a created being. Therefore, it is at the end and at the beginning (or in the middle) at different instants; but between any two instants there is an intervening time. And so, as Alhazen concludes, the multiplication of a species must occur in time. Similarly, in book vii of the same work it is maintained that a perpendicular species comes more quickly to the end of its multiplication than does a refracted species when they come from the same agent;[2] but more quickly and more slowly exist only in time, as Aristotle says in *Physics*, books iv and vi.[3]

Furthermore, no finite virtue acts in an instant, as can be gathered from Aristotle's *Physics*, book vi, for if it did, a stronger virtue would act in less than an instant.[4] Moreover, a finite and an infinite virtue would be equal in the duration of their action, as is indicated in *Physics* at the end of book viii,[5] since an infinite virtue acts in an instant; but the virtue of a species is finite. Also, an instant has the same ratio to time as a point to a line. Therefore, by permutation, as

minori quam   19 duratione: *spatium vacuum B*   20 octavi: quatuor *S* / finita *S*
21 *post* finita *mg. add. O* quare non agit in instanti / item: iterum *BL*   22 est¹: et
est *S*

puncti ad instans est linee ad tempus. Sed pertransitus puncti est
in instanti; ergo spatii linearis in tempore. Item prius et posterius
25 in spatio sunt causa prioris et posterioris in translatione spatii
et in duratione, ut habetur in quatuor *Physicorum*. Ergo translatio
speciei secundum prius et posterius spatii habet prius et posterius
in duratione, et ita in tempore. Item multiplicatio speciei non dependet ab alio motu; ponatur ergo quod non sit alius motus. Si ergo
30 huiusmodi non est motus, tunc non est tempus, quia tempus non est
sine motu. Sed instans non est sine tempore, sicut nec punctus sine
linea. Ergo translatio speciei in quantum huiusmodi non erit in
tempore nec in instanti, aut oportet instans posse intelligi sine
tempore, quod esse non potest.

35   Si vero obiciatur quod multi auctores dicunt quod multiplicatio
speciei lucis est subito, ut Averroys et Seneca in *Naturalibus* et
alii, dicendum est quod subito hic sumitur pro tempore insensibili,
et similiter instans in quo dicunt fieri huiusmodi diffusionem. Quod
vero Aristoteles dicit secundo *De anima*, quod in parvo spatio posset
40 nos motus lucis latere, sed in magno, sicut est ab oriente in occidens,
non est hoc possibile, et ita non fiet ab oriente in occidens insensibiliter et imperceptibiliter, sed in tempore perceptibili; dicendum est
quod hoc dicit contra Empedoclem, qui posuit lucem unam et eandem
numero diffundi et ab oriente in occidens esse corpus motum, vel
45 quia posuit lucem esse defluxum corporis, sicut dicit, ut rivulus
defluit a fonte. Sed si esset corpus unum et idem numero sic motum,
non esset possibile quod nos lateret, quia videremus quod fieret
successive ab oriente ad medium celi et ab eo ad occidens, quoniam
mutaret locum sensibiliter. Nunc autem non ponimus lucem esse cor-
50 pus motum; nec ponimus eandem lucem in numero fieri ab oriente in
occidens per omnes partes spatii. Sed ponimus eius generationem fieri
secundum esse debile in parte prima spatii orientis; et ab illa ponimus
aliam lucem fieri in secundam, et sic ultra. Et ideo non apparet nobis
quod fiat ibi successio, tum quia non est corpus sensibile, tum quia
55 non est unum numero. Si etiam esset fluxus corporis, oportet quod
sensibilis esset et in tempore sensibili per partes spatii habentes
sensibilem distantiam.

23 puncti[1]: proportio p. *F* / transitus *O*   24 et spatii *O* / item: iterum *BL*
25 sunt: est *S* / et posterioribus: *om. B*   26 duratione: dictione *B* / *post* duratione
mg. add. O et ita in tempore   27 spatii . . . posterius: *om. B* / habet: item *S*
28 item: iterum *BL*   29 non: mihi *B*   30 huiusmodi: *om. S* h. motus *O* / tunc:
tempus *O* / quia . . . est: non est enim tempus *B* q. tempus non *S*   32 non: nec *BL*
36 subita *S* / Averroim *O*   37 alii: a. dicunt *O* / hic: *om. B*   39 possit *O*
40-1 ab . . . fiet: *mg. O*   43 posuit: ponit *O*   44 et: etiam *O om. S*
46 defluit: deferunt *B* / sed si: si enim *S*   47 nos: non *S* / *ante* fieret *scr. et del. O*
non   49 sensibili *S* / autem: enim *O*   50 motum: *om. F* / fieri: *om. S*
51 eius: ei *B*   53 aliam: alteram *B*   54 tum[1]: *spatium vacuum B*

an instant is to a point, so is time to a line. But the traversal of a point occurs in an instant; therefore, the traversal of a line occurs in time. Furthermore, the prior and posterior [character] of space are the cause of prior and posterior in the traversal of space and in duration, as is maintained in *Physics*, book iv.[6] Therefore, the motion of a species according to prior and posterior [parts] of space entails priority and posteriority in duration, and thus in time. Also, the multiplication of a species does not depend on any other motion [than its own]; let us, therefore, suppose that there is no other motion. Now if there is no such motion, then there is no time, since time does not exist without motion. But there can be no instant without time, just as there can be no point without a line. Therefore, the movement of a species, in so far as these conditions are met, will occur neither in time nor in an instant, unless an instant can be understood to exist without time, which is impossible.

If it should be objected that many authors affirm that the multiplication of the species of light is sudden, as Averroes, and Seneca in his *Natural Questions*, and others,[7] it is replied that 'sudden' here means in an insensible time, as does the 'instant' in which they say such diffusion takes place. As for Aristotle's argument in *De anima*, book ii, that over a small space the motion of light could be concealed from us, but that this is impossible over a great distance, as from east to west, and so light would not pass from east to west insensibly and imperceptibly, but in a perceptible time,[8] we reply that Aristotle says this against Empedocles, who supposed that numerically one and the same light is diffused [from one place to another] and that what is moved from east to west is body, or because Empedocles supposed light to be a flow of body, just as (according to him) a brook flows from a spring. But if it were numerically one and the same body thus moved, [the duration of its motion] could not be concealed from us, since we would see that it moves successively from the east to the middle of the heaven and from there to the west, since it would change place sensibly. However, we no longer judge light to be a transported body; nor do we suppose that numerically the same light passes from east to west through all parts of the [intervening] space. Rather, we suppose its generation to occur according to weak being in the first part of the space, in the east; and we suppose that another light is produced by it in the second part, and so on. And therefore we observe no succession there, both because light is not a sensible body and because it is not numerically one thing. Also, if it were a flow from a body, it would necessarily be sensible and [would move] in a sensible time through parts of space having sensible magnitude.

54–5 corpus ... est: *rep. B* / tum[2] ... est: *om. S*   56 sensibilis: sensibiliter *S* / spatii: *om. F*

Quod vero Aristoteles dicit *Libro de sensu et sensato*, quod de
lumine alia ratio est quam de sono et odore, et loquitur de transla-
60 tione specierum aliorum sensibilium, ut soni et odoris, quam dicit
fieri in tempore, dicendum quod alia ratio est de lumine, quia eius
successio fit in tempore breviori et magis insensibili propter eius
subtilitatem et naturam magis activam; atque sonus fit cum motu aeris
preter successionem proprie delationis; et odor fit cum fumo corporali
65 expirante et cum attractione aeris a naribus, ut Avicenna dicit tertio
De anima. Et ita multiplices motus fiunt circa sonum et odorem, sed
unus solus circa lucem et brevior quam circa illos, propter quod
dicit quod alia ratio est, et non quia fiat in instanti omnino
indivisibili; non enim hoc dicit, sed solum dicit in universali quod
70 de lumine alia ratio est; et iam assignata est ratio quare aliter est in
lumine et in aliis.

Sed quod inducit Iacobus Alkindi fortius est predictis, arguens
quod si in aliquo tempore, licet insensibili, pertransit lux spatium
aliquod parvum, tunc transit duplum illius spatii in duplo temporis
75 et triplum in triplo; et sic in maxima distantia, ut ab oriente ad
occidens, fieret tempus ita multiplex ad primum tempus insensibile
quod hoc tempus multiplicatum esset sensibile. Sed non est; ergo videtur quod lucis generatio sit omnino in indivisibili instanti et non in
tempore. Sed dicendum est quod, propter velocissimam speciei genera-
80 tionem, tempus imperceptibile habet gradus multos in quibus primi
temporis minimi sumatur tempus multiplex, quantum oporteat multiplicationi toti inter oriens et occidens, ita quod ultimum multiplex
sit infra metas sensibilitatis, sicut et primum tempus minimum, licet
magis accedat ad sensibilitatem, remanens tamen semper extra eam.
85 Si vero dicatur quod conceditur, si species corpus esset, quod
pertransiret partes spatii in tempore sensibili; et nunc tot sunt
generationes singule in singulis partibus quot essent replicationes
particulares illius corporis per singulas et easdem partes spatii;
ergo sicut replicationes ille corporis moti fierent in tempore
90 sensibili, sic hee generationes in eisdem partibus spatii; dicendum
est quod hoc est fortius aliis predictis, nam valde videtur esse
simile de huiusmodi multiplicatione per singulas partes et de

58 quod²: et *B*   60 aliarum *F*   62 fit: *om. S*   64 preter *BFSA*: propter
LON / dilatationis *O*   69 et indivisibili *S* / universali: vult *S*   72 predictis: omnibus
p. *S* / arguit *S*   75 in¹: etiam *S* / maxima: materiam *B* / ut: *mg. O*   77 quod . . .
sensibile: *om. F* / sensibilius *O* / sed: *om. S* / est: e ita *O*   77–8 videtur: verum *S*
78 in¹: *om. S* / divisibili *L* / instanti *O*: continenti *LFA om. SBV obs. N* / et non in: vel *S*
81 tempus: *om. F* / multiplicatione *L* multitudini *O*   82 ultimum: ulterius *B*
84 semper *BFNV*: *om. LOSA* / *post* extra *scr. et del. L* per / eam: ipsam *O*   85 quod¹:
q. cum *S* / species: *om. S* / quod²: et *B*   86 pertransit *FO* / sensibili: *om. F*   87 in:
et *B* / partibus: p. spatii *S*   88 corporis: *om. O*   89 mote *B*   90 *post* eisdem

As for Aristotle's claim in *De sensu et sensato*[9] that light is different in character from sound and odour (and he speaks of the transport of the species of the other sensibles, as sound and odour, which transport, he says, takes place in time), we reply that the different character of light is that its succession occurs in a shorter and less sensible time because of its subtlety and more active nature; and in sound there is a motion of the air in addition to the succession of its own propagation,[10] while odour occurs from the exhalation of corporeal vapour combined with the attraction for air exercised by the nostrils, as Avicenna says in *De anima*, book iii.[11] And so in sound and odour there are many motions,[12] but in light only one—and a quicker one than in the others—for which reason Aristotle says that light has a different character, but not that it moves in an altogether indivisible instant; for he does not say the latter, but says only that in general light is different; and we have now identified the particular respect in which light differs from the other [sensibles].

But the argument advanced by Jacob Alkindi is stronger than the foregoing, for he argues that if in a certain time (albeit insensible) light traverses some small space, then it traverses twice the space in twice the time and triple the space in triple the time; and thus in an exceedingly great distance, as from east to west, the time would be such a large multiple of the first insensible time as to be sensible. But it is not sensible; and therefore it seems that the generation of light occurs altogether in an indivisible instant and not in time.[13] We reply that, owing to the exceedingly swift generation of a species, there are many degrees of imperceptible time according to which the composite time is related to the first minimum time, as required for the whole multiplication between east and west, so that the final composite would fall short of sensibility, as does the first minimum time, although the composite time would more closely approach sensibility while always remaining beneath it.

If it should be admitted that if a species were body it would traverse the parts of a space in a sensible time; and according to our position there are as many individual instances of generation in individual parts [of the medium] as there would be particular repetitions of that body through the same individual parts of the space; and therefore, that just as those repetitions of the moved body occupy a sensible time, so must these instances of generation in the same parts of the space; to this it is replied that this argument is stronger than the preceding ones, for multiplication through individual parts [of the medium] seems to resemble closely the traversal of those same

scr. et del. SA temporibus   90–117 dicendum . . . spatio: *om. SA' mg. A*[c]
91 hic *B*   92 huius *B*

translatione illius per easdem. Magis autem movet hec cavillatio: quia tempus duplicari videtur in multiplicatione respectu temporis in
95 translatione; nam inter singulas multiplicationes est quies media propter hoc, quod quelibet pars per ordinem transmutat aliam, et primo permutatur prima pars quam permutet secundam; et sunt actiones divise, quia agentia et patientia sunt distincta et diversa; quare quies erit media inter singulas, et omnis quies est in tempore.
100 Sed in translatione locali continua non intercipitur quies; quare cum multiplicetur tempus in generatione speciei magis quam in translatione corporis, tunc magis erit successio sensibilis in multiplicatione lucis quam si lux esset corpus vel defluxus corporis. Item tertio fortificatur hec obiectio, quia in hac multiplicatione speciei est
105 actio per contrarium propter medii passionem contrariam, ut dictum est; sed in translatione corporis non est actio per contrarium; ergo videtur quod plus de tempore requiritur in speciei generatione quam in corporis translatione. Et dicendum est quod resistentia medii in divisione sua per corpus motum est maior longe quam resistentia medii
110 penes contrarietatem que invenitur in generatione speciei. Nam species est res debilis valde, et ideo debilis est medii alteratio; atque materia multum appetit speciem, sed non appetit mobile, quia omni nisu ei resistit. Et propter has duas causas velocissima est speciei multiplicatio et incomparabilis quantum ad sensum respectu transla-
115 tionis corporalis. Et ideo possunt quietes insensibiles intercipi, ut tamen totum tempus sit insensibile respectu motus localis in tanto spatio. (φ)

PARS V

CAPITULUM 1

Dicto in primis de generatione speciei, et secundo de eius multiplicatione figurata, et tertio de eius existentia in medio, et quarto de
5 debilitatione et eius annexis, nunc quinto dicendum est de eius

93 alius *FL*   95 translatione: transive *F* | est: inest *FO*   96 transmutat: transeat *B* | et: eo quod *O*   97 *ante* prima *scr. et del.* *O* prima pars per ordinem transmutat naturam quod primo permutatur | quam: *om.* *F* | permutet: permutat *O* 98 divise: diverse *B* | diversa: divisa *O*   99 quare: quia *B*   100 continuo *FL* | quare: quia *B*   101 in¹: *om.* *B* | transmutatione *F*   103 *ante* lucis *scr. et del.* *L* speciei / vel defluxus: et reflexus *B*   104 fortificatur: certificatur *B* | hec: *om.* *F* | hanc multiplicationem *B*   106 transmutationem *B*   108 dicendum: aliter *L* | resistentiam *F*   112 quia: quoniam *O*   113 consistit *F*   114 incorporalis *B*

parts by the moved body. Yet even more persuasive is the following sophism: that the time required for multiplication seems to be
twice the time required for traversal; for between individual multiplications there is a moment of rest, because each part in turn alters
another, and the first must be altered before it can alter the second;
and these are separate actions, since the agents and recipients are
distinct and different; therefore rest will intervene between the
separate alterations, and every [moment of] rest occurs in time. But
in the continuous traversal of space rest does not intervene; therefore,
since time is more plentiful in the generation of a species than in the
translation of a body, succession will be more sensible in the multiplication of light than it would be if light were body or a flow from
body. And in a third [argument], this objection is strengthened, since
in this multiplication of a species the action of a contrary is involved,
owing to the contrary disposition of the medium, as was said; but in
the translation of a body there is no action by a contrary; therefore,
it seems that more time is required for the generation of a species
than for the translation of a body. To this we reply that the resistance of a medium to division by a moved body is much greater than
the resistance of a medium resulting from contrariety, which is encountered in the generation of a species. For a species is a very weak
thing, and therefore it produces a weak alteration of the medium;
and matter strongly desires a species, but it does not desire a moving
body, but makes every effort to resist it. And for these two reasons
the multiplication of a species is exceedingly swift and incomparable,
as far as sense is concerned, to the translation of corporeal substance.
Therefore insensible intervals of rest can intervene, while the whole
time nevertheless remains insensible in comparison to that of local
motion over the same space. (φ)

PART V

CHAPTER 1

Having spoken first of the generation of a species, second of its multiplication according to figure, third of its existence in the medium, and
fourth of its weakening and related matters, now, fifth, we must discuss

115 possint *L* / quietas *O*   116 tamen: cum *F* / respectu: qua *B*   117 *post* spatio
mg. add. O tempus enim insensibile potest habere gradus innumerabiles ut dictum est

   1 pars quinta de actione speciei et habit tria capitula *FLO*   2 capitulum (*om. FL*)
primum habet tres conclusiones principales *FLO*   4 figurata: et figura *O* a loco generationis *SA*   4-6 et[1] . . . eius[1]: nunc tertio (5 *A*) dicendum est de eius actione (*om. S*)
et (*om. S*) effectu et (*om. A*) quantum pertinet hic in universali ut sciatur fortitudo et
debilitas actionis et omnis eorum gradus *SA* (*The text replaced by this is, however, also
included in the margin of A in a later hand*)   5 et eius: *spatium vacuum B*

actione secundum omnes gradus eius. Sed actio univoca est eius multiplicatio, ut lux facit lucem; actio vero equivoca est ut quando
species facit aliquid alterius essentie, ut lux facit calorem et alia.
Nunc igitur licet principaliter intendo prosequi equivocam, tamen
10 quod omissum de actione univoca, scilicet quantum ad fortitudinem
et debilitatem, patebit hic, nam eadem est consideratio utrobique;
sed in actione equivoca debet fieri certificatio de hiis, quia principaliter et magis intenta est a natura propter rerum generationem et
corruptionem in hoc mundo.

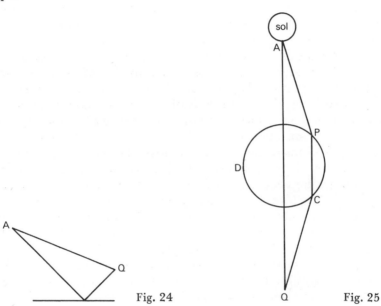

Fig. 24   Q   Fig. 25

15   Et primo considerandum est de proprietate actionis secundum lineas,
deinde secundum figuras; et primo secundum lineas rectas. Quod
autem super eas sit melior actio Aristoteles dicit quinto *Physicorum*.
Et probat illud, dicens natura operatur breviori modo quo potest; sed
linea recta est brevissima omnium linearum ductarum ab eodem puncto
20 ad aliud punctum unum et idem, ut ipse ibidem dicit. Et patet ad
visum, ut si ab A puncto ducatur linea recta ad Q punctum [fig. 24],
erit brevior quam linea reflexa inter illa puncta. Similiter linea
recta est brevior linea fracta, ut AQ linea recta est brevior quam AQ
fracta duplici fractione [fig. 25]. Sit A punctus solis, AQ sit linea

6 omnes: *om. B*   7 facit: f. in esse *L*   8 aliquid: alium *S* effectum alium *A* /
essentie: cause *S*   9 equivocam: actionem e. *S*   10 quod: *om. O* / univoca:
equivoca *B*   12 quia: *om. SA* et *B*   13 *ante* et[1] *add. SA* quoniam hec est
actio principalior   18 brevioribus *S*   20 ibidem: ibi *S*   21 *post* Q *scr.*

all the degrees of its action. Now the multiplication of a species, such as light producing light, is univocal action, whereas its action is equivocal when a species produces something of a different essence, as when light produces heat and other things. Although I intend principally to investigate equivocal action, that which has been omitted concerning univocal action, namely, discussion of its strength and weakness, will be evident here, for the same considerations apply to both cases; but we must be certain about these matters in regard to equivocal action, since it is principally (and more [than univocal

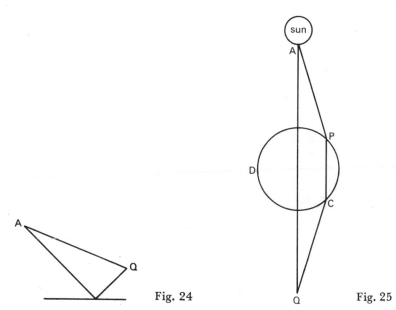

Fig. 24   Fig. 25

action]) intended by nature for the generation and corruption of things in this world.

First we must consider the properties of action according to lines, then according to figures; and first of all according to straight lines. That action along straight lines is better is stated by Aristotle in *Physics*, book v.[1] And he proves this by arguing that nature acts in the shortest way possible; and a straight line is the shortest of all lines drawn from a given point to another given point, as he says in the same place. This is evident to sight, for if a straight line is drawn from point A to point Q [fig. 24], it will be shorter than the reflected line connecting those points. Similarly, a straight line is shorter than a refracted line, as straight line AQ is shorter than doubly-refracted line AQ [fig. 25]. Let A be a point on the sun and AQ a line

et del. F linea recta est brevior quare   23 fracta . . . AQ²: *mg. O*

25 perpendicularis cadens super vas vitreum rotundum quod est D. Primo
frangetur AP radius in superficie vasis, quia est corpus alterius
dyaphanitatis quam aer extra; item cum transit aliam partem vasis
frangetur adhuc in C, quia aer est alterius dyaphanitatis quam vas;
et sic per duplicem fractionem cadet radius fractus in punctum Q.
30 Sed AQ linea perpendicularis non fracta est brevior, ut manifestum est
sensui. Similiter est in una fractione, ut patet in figura [fig. 26]. Nam
in hoc triangulo, AB linea continet cum basi angulos rectos; ergo
ABD angulo opponitur maximum latus per decimam nonam primi
Euclidis. Sed BC et DE latera parallelagrami sunt equalia, nam ex

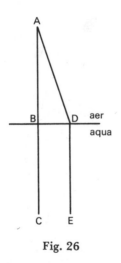

Fig. 26

Fig. 27

35 ypotesi trahantur ad equalitatem. Ergo per conceptionem oportet
quod AE linea sit longior quam AC.
    Similiter patet quod linea recta est brevior quam tortuosa, ut
hic ipsa lineatio ostendit [fig. 27]. Sed tamen non oportet comparari
tortuosam aliis in actione, quia nichil deperit eius actioni propter
40 virtutem anime que speciem dirigit tortuosam; non enim debetur linee
tortuose aliqua multiplicatio secundum se, sed propter animam. Et
ideo non oportet comparari eam ad alias, non enim accidit in corporibus mundi inanimatis. Similiter est brevior quam accidentalis longe
magis, quia linea accidentalis non potest nisi per incurvationem

25 D: C S   26 frangetur: *mg. L^C om. L'* / alterius: *mg. O*   27 item: iterum
BL / vasis: v. in aerem S   28 C: E B   29 cadet: accidet F   32 triangulo: et
in angulo L / angulos rectos: maiorem angulum B   33 ABD: ab D B / decimam nonam:
29 B   34 Euclidis: elementorum E. *LS* elementorum B / parallelagrami: paralelle
longrami S   35 trahuntur F trahatur S / *post* equalitatem *add. SA* per 34 primi
elementorum   36 AE: DE S   38 hic: *om. FO* / comparare S   39 tortuosum

perpendicularly incident on round glass container D. Ray AP will first be refracted at the surface of the container, since the latter is a body differing in transparency from the surrounding air; it is again refracted when it passes through the other side of the container at C, since the transparency of the air [again] differs from that of the container; and so by a double refraction the refracted ray reaches point Q. But the perpendicular, unrefracted line AQ is shorter, as is evident to sense. The same is true in the case of a single refraction, as is evident in the figure [fig. 26]. For in this triangle, line AB forms right angles with the base; therefore the largest side is opposite angle

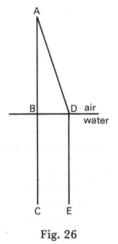

Fig. 26

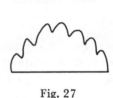

Fig. 27

ABD, by Euclid, i. 19.[2] But BC and DE, the sides of a parallelogram,[3] are equal, for by hypothesis they are drawn so as to be equal. Therefore, it follows that line AE is longer than line AC.

It is also evident that a straight line is shorter than a twisting line, as this drawing [fig. 27] shows.[4] Nevertheless, the action of a twisting line need not be compared with that of the others, since none of its action is lost, because of the [sustenance provided by the] power of the soul, which directs the species in its twisting course;[5] for a given multiplication achieves a twisting path not according to itself, but because of the soul. And therefore it need not be compared to the others, since it does not occur in inanimate bodies of the world. A straight line is also shorter than an accidental line to a much greater degree, since an accidental line cannot come from one end of

FO / in actione: fractione *B* / actioni *OAN*: actionem *BFLS*   41 aliqua: alia *S* /
animatum *B*   42 eam: eque *B*

45 fractionis aut reflexionis venire a termino uno linee recte principalis
ad terminum alium, hoc modo [fig. 28].

Quapropter cum natura eligit rectam lineam nisi impediatur fortius,
aget per species venientes super lineas rectas; quanto enim patiens
magis approprinquat agenti, tanto plus recipit de eius virtute; et
50 quanto species minus recedit a sua origine, tanto fortior est. Ceterum,
linea recta est uniformis et equalis; sed in omnibus aliis est
difformitas et diversitas et quedam inequalitas. Sed melius est equale
inequali, ut dicit Boetius in sua *Practica geometrie*, et natura
operatur semper meliori modo. Et dicitur *Libro de causis* quod omnis
55 virtus unita est fortioris operationis; sed diversitas et difformitas
contrariantur unitati et unitioni et uniformitati. Quapropter cum

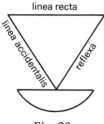

linea recta

linea accidentalis

reflexa

Fig. 28

secundum lineam rectam fit uniformitas virtutis in suo decursu,
precipue cum Aristoteles ostendit quinto *Methaphysice* quod linea
recta magis est una quia magis continua et non habet angulum, alie
60 habent angulum, quoquomodo manifestum est quod fortior est virtus
veniens super rectam lineam quam super alias.

Et hoc est intelligendum per se loquendo, non per accidens, quia
per accidens potest fieri maior actio et per reflexionem et fractionem,
eo quod multe virtutes et species possunt congregari per reflexionem
65 et fractionem, que non possunt aggregari per rectum incessum, sicut
satis patebit in sequentibus. Et propter hoc possunt radii infiniti
congregari in quolibet puncto aeris per reflexionem factam a superficie terre et aque et corporum densorum inferiorum, quoniam fiunt
infinite reflexiones; et per has accidit intersectio radiorum infinitorum
70 in quolibet puncto medii; et ideo est generatio caloris, que non
generaretur per radios incidentes; et hoc magis manifestabitur post.
Sed de linea accidentali est universaliter tenendum quod est debilior

47 lineam: *om.* O   48 venientes: *om.* S / super: per L / rectas: *om.* LS
52 equali F   56 uniformitati: *om.* S   57 fit: sit *BF* / decursum F   58 quinto:
quique S   59 est continua S / angulos S   60 angulum: *om.* S / quoquomodo:
quodammodo B ergo O   61 lineam: *om.* F / quam: quantum L   63 actio: *mg.* L
64 species: s. agentes S   65 quem S / aggregari: *om.* F   65-7 per . . . congregari:
p. rectum incessum et propter hoc possunt c. radii *mg.* O *et deinde in textu habet* infiniti

the straight principal line to the other without being bent back [to it] by refraction or reflection, in this way [see fig. 28].[6]

Therefore, since nature chooses straight lines unless forcefully prevented from doing so, it will act through species coming along straight lines; for in so far as the recipient is closer to the agent, to that extent it receives more of the agent's virtue; and a species is stronger the less it recedes from its origin. Besides, a straight line is uniform and even, whereas all other lines exhibit non-uniformity and diversity and a certain unevenness. Now the equal is better than the unequal, as Boethius says in his *Practica geometriae*,[7] and nature always acts in the better way. And it is stated in the *Liber de causis* that every united virtue acts more forcefully;[8] but diversity

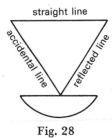

straight line

accidental line

reflected line

Fig. 28

and non-uniformity are contrary to unity and unification and uniformity. Therefore, since uniformity of virtue belongs to the straight course, especially since Aristotle shows in *Metaphysics*, book v, that a straight line is more united since it is more continuous and has no angle,[9] whereas the others have an angle, it is evident in all ways that virtue coming along a straight line is stronger than virtue proceeding along any other line.

And this is to be understood [of rectilinear propagation] *per se*, not *per accidens*, for accidentally there can be a greater action by reflection or refraction, because by reflection or refraction many virtues and species can be gathered together, as they cannot be by rectilinear propagation, and this will be sufficiently evident below.[10] Therefore, an infinity of rays can be gathered together at any point in the air by reflection from the surface of the earth and water and dense terrestrial bodies, since reflections are infinitely produced; and the result is the intersection of an infinity of rays at every point of the medium; and therefore heat is generated, as it is not by [directly] incident rays; and this will be clearer below.[11] But it is universally admitted that an accidental line is the weakest of all,

69 et accidit *O* / *ante* intersectio *scr. et del.* S reflexio / inferiorum *O*   70 qui *O*
71 generaretur: generatur *FO* / manifestabitur: manifestum est *S*

omnibus propter hoc, quod ab agente non venit, sed a specie; et est
species speciei, ut prius dictum est. Et ideo de ea non est amplius
75 dicendum respectu aliarum.

Sed linea recta aut cadit ad angulos equales aut inequales; sed
fortior est actio ad angulos equales, quia equale melius est, ut
dictum est. Et similiter virtus magis uniformiter venit et non tantum
diversificatur in angulis equalibus sicut in angulis inequalibus, et
80 virtus uniformis est maioris operationis. Et illa que ad angulos
inequales cadit est de necessitate longior, ut patet tam in casu super
lineam rectam quam circularem, quia AF linea [fig. 29] cadens ad

Fig. 29

Fig. 30

angulos equales super lineam rectam est brevior AQ linea per decimam
nonam primi Euclidis. Si enim AFQ angulus est equalis angulo sibi
85 conterminali, tunc rectus est per diffinitionem, et ideo per tricesimam
secundam primi AFQ angulus est maximus in triangulo; ergo ei
opponitur maximum latus, quod est propositum.

Similiter quando cadit super lineam circuli (AQ [fig. 30] vero
facit angulos equales sed obtusos), quod patet si ducatur linea
90 contingens circulum in puncto P, ut expositum est in quarta parte
huius tractatus, si proprie velimus loqui. Item AQ est brevior quam
AP, sicut patet per octavam tertii *Elementorum*, quia perficit diametrum circuli. Si vero virtus veniat ad angulos equales rectos, melior
est operatio quam ad equales obtusos. Aristoteles autem secundo
95 *Celi et mundi* dicit quod grave descendit ad angulos rectos, et hoc
dicit Alhacen primo *Aspectuum*; et eadem ratio est de omni actione
nature quantum possibile est. Et Averroys dicit super secundum *Celi*

73-4 et est species: *mg. O*   74 species: *om. S*   76 aut²: vel *SA* / sed²: non
(vero *A*) ad equales *SA*   77 actio: *spatium vacuum B̃* / ad . . . equales: quem ad
inequales *S*   79 sicut . . . inequalibus: *om. F*   80 que: *om. L*   88 vero *BL*:
non *FOSAN*   89 dicatur *B*   91 item *BN*: cum *FO* sed *SA* si etiam *L'* i. etiam *L^C* /

because it does not come [directly] from the agent, but from a species; and it is the species of a species, as was said above.[12] And there is no more to be said by way of comparing this [accidental] line with the others.

Now a straight line is incident either at equal angles or at unequal angles;[13] but action at equal angles is stronger, since the equal is the better, as has been said. Similarly, virtue comes with greater uniformity and less diversity at equal angles than at unequal angles, and uniform power acts more strongly. Also, a line incident at unequal angles is necessarily longer, as is evident in incidence on either a

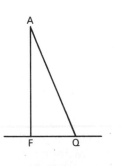

Fig. 29

Fig. 30

straight or a circular line, since line AF [fig. 29] falling on to a straight line perpendicularly is shorter than line AQ, by Euclid, i. 19.[14] For if angle AFQ is equal to the coterminal angle,[15] then it is a right angle by definition, and therefore by [Euclid,] i. 32, angle AFQ is the largest in the triangle;[16] therefore, the longest side is opposite it, which was to be proved.

The same is true when the line is incident on the circumference of a circle (where AQ [fig. 30] forms equal but, strictly speaking, obtuse angles), as is evident if a line is drawn tangent to the circle at point P, as we have explained in the fourth part of this treatise.[17] Also, AQ is shorter than AP, as is evident by *Elements*, iii. 8, since it is an extension of the diameter of the circle.[18] But if virtue comes at equal right angles, its action is better than at equal obtuse angles. Moreover, Aristotle says in *De caelo et mundo*, book ii, that a heavy body descends at right angles, and Alhazen says the same thing in *De aspectibus*, book i;[19] and the same is true of every natural action in so far as possible.[20] And Averroes says, [in commenting] on *De*

quam: quod *F*   92 per: *om. S* / elementorum: Euclidis *FO*   97 Averroim *O*

et mundi quod sol magis calefacit nos circa solstitium estivale quam ante, quia eius radii magis accedunt ad rectitudinem; et hoc patet
100 per dicta. Et etiam magis dispergitur et diversificatur virtus in angulos obtusos equales quam in rectos, propter hoc quod angulus ille obtusus est compositus ex recto et acuto, et ideo non est tanta uniformitas nec unitas nec regularis congregatio et unitio virtutis in angulis obtusis equalibus sicut in rectis. Sed omnis virtus unita
105 et non dispersa nec diversificata est maioris operationis. Atque cum rectum sit index sui et obliqui, secundum Aristotelem, oportet quod sit nobilius et melius, et super ipsum magis eliget natura operari.

PARS V
CAPITULUM 2

Ceterum, linearum quedam dicitur cadere perpendiculariter, quedam non. Sed secundum auctores aspectuum incessus perpendicularium est
5 fortissimus, et ideo natura eligit super illas operari; et hoc patet de omni genere perpendicularium, sive cadant super lineas sive super superficies et corpora. Quando vero cadunt super lineas, tunc si cadant super rectas, manifestum est per diffinitionem quod cadunt ad angulos equales, et quod breviores sunt aliis, et quod habent maiorem
10 uniformitatem. Et ideo, ex hiis tribus causis, virtus fortior venit super eas, quia etiam cadunt ad angulos rectos, et rectitudo etiam angulorum ex sua proprietate melior est obliquitate, et ideo augmentat adhuc fortitudinem actionis.

Similiter quando cadit super convexitatem circuli habet fortitudinis
15 causas plures, sed non tot sicut quando cadit super rectam. Colligitur enim eius fortitudo ex brevitate linee, et ex uniformitate virtutis (in quantum uterque angulus est obtusus), et ex equalitate; linea enim perpendicularis super circulum, ut ostensum est quarta parte huius tractatus, est que super eius circumferentiam cadit ad angulos
20 equales et obtusos; linea vero non perpendicularis cadit ad angulos inequales et obliquos, quorum unus obtusus et alius acutus. Et patet ex octava tertii Euclidis quod linea perpendicularis brevior est, quoniam illa perficit diametrum circuli. Quando vero comparatur linea perpendicularis ad superficies vel ad corpora, in idem redit,

---

100 predicta *FO* / spargitur *S*   103 aggregatio *O*   106 sui et: s. et s. *S*
107 super: ideo s. *SA* / eligit *S* / natura *LSA*: naturam *O* materia *B om.* F
    2 capitulum secundum *O* tertia conclusio *mg.* L   3 dicuntur *OS* dicitur eadem *B*
4 sed: *om. O*   5 illas: ipsos *F*   6 generatione *F* / cadunt *F* / super[2] *BLO: om. FSA*
8 cadant: cadunt *FO*   9 quod[1]: *om. O*   11 etiam[2]: *om. O*   12 *post*

caelo et mundo, that the sun gives us more heat near the summer solstice than before, since [at that time] its rays more closely approach
perpendicularity;[21] and this is evident from what we have said. Also,
virtue is more dispersed and diversified [when incident] at equal
obtuse angles than at right angles, because the obtuse angle is a composite of a right angle and an acute angle, and consequently there is
not as much uniformity or unity or regular convergence and uniting
of virtue in equal obtuse angles as in [equal] right angles. But every
united, undispersed, and undiversified virtue acts more strongly. And
since rectitude is the measure both of itself and of obliquity, according to Aristotle,[22] it must be nobler and better, and nature prefers
to act according to it.

PART V

CHAPTER 2

To continue, it is said that some lines are incident perpendicularly,
some nonperpendicularly. But according to the authors of books on
optics, the incidence of perpendiculars is strongest, and therefore
nature chooses to act along such lines;[1] and it is evident that this is
true of every kind of perpendicular, whether incident upon lines or
upon surfaces and bodies. When incident upon lines, if upon striaght
lines, it is clear by definition that they are incident at equal angles,
that they are shorter than the others, and that they have greater
uniformity. And therefore, owing to these three causes, stronger
virtue comes along such lines—also because they fall at right angles
and rectitude of angles is, because of its special character, better than
obliquity, and therefore it further augments strength of action.

Similarly, when a line is incident on the convexity of a circle[2]
there are several causes of strength, but not as many as when it is
incident on a straight line. For its strength arises from the brevity of
the line, and from the uniformity of the virtue (inasmuch as both
angles are obtuse), and from equality; for a line perpendicular to a
circle is that which is incident on its circumference at equal obtuse
angles, as was shown in the fourth part of this treatise;[3] and a nonperpendicular line is incident at unequal oblique angles, one of which
is obtuse and the other acute. And it is evident from Euclid, iii. 8, that
the perpendicular line is shorter, because it is the extension of the diameter of the circle.[4] Now if we compare a line perpendicular to surfaces
with a line perpendicular to bodies, they come to the same thing, since

proprietate *add. SA* in eo quod / ideo: *om. S*   15 *post* rectam *mg. add. O* lineam
16 uniformitate: *om. B*   17 qualitate *B*   19 circumferentia *B*   22 octava:
similiter *B* quatuor *S* / tertii: *om. B*   23 quando: quoniam *B*   24 superficiem *S*

25 quia corpora non recipiunt nisi mediantibus superficiebus. Perpendicularis autem super superficiem planam est proprie que est brevior
omnibus lineis rectis ab eodem puncto exeuntibus cum illa perpendiculari ad superficiem planam, ut ex quarta parte huius tractatus
manifestum est. Et nichilominus constituit angulos rectos cum omni-
30 bus lineis rectis exeuntibus ad eodem puncto cum ea in superficie
plana. Et continet angulos rectos cum linea que est differentia communis sue superficiei et superficiei plane ad quam terminatur, sicut
prius declaratum est. Et ideo multipliciter patet per predicta quod
hanc eligit natura in sua actione.

35   Perpendicularis vero super corpus spericum convexum est proprie,
sicut ostensum est in quarta parte, que brevior est omnibus lineis
ductis ab eodem puncto extra speram ad superficiem spere. Et licet
hoc secundum rationem spere, sicut nec in plano non inveniat angulum;
tamen cum omnibus lineis contingentibus circulum circumdantem
40 speram facit angulos rectos; et cum linea que est communis differentia
sue superficiei et superficiei plane tangentis speram continet angulos
rectos; et cum circulis super idem punctum revolutis in superficie
spere facit angulos equales, licet obtusos. Ex quibus omnibus patet
per predicta quod natura eligit operari super lineam hanc magis quam
45 super aliam.

Sed cum perpendicularis super concavitatem circuli sit que per
centrum transit et cadit ad equales angulos super illam concavitatem,
hec non facit ita bonam operationem sicut alie perpendiculares, quia
longior est quam multe perpendiculares, ut patet ex septima et octava
50 tertii Euclidis. Similiter cum perpendicularis super spere concavitatem
sit illa que transit per centrum ad angulos equales super communem
differentiam sue superficiei et superficiei plane contingentis concavitatem spere; similiter que continet angulos equales cum omnibus
circulis super idem punctum transeuntibus ad quod perpendicularis
55 terminatur; oportet quod sit longior aliis per septimam et octavam
tertii Euclidis, et ideo non oportet quod species incidens super
huiusmodi perpendiculares faciat ita fortem actionem sicut alie
perpendiculares super convexitatem spere. Et per iam dicta de spera,
patet de columpna rotunda et pyramide.

Species autem veniens super lineas alias habet comparationem in

26 quod *S*   29 et: et hec *SA*   31 *post* plana *mg. add. O* ad quam terminantur
31–2 communis: corporis *S spatium vacuum B*   32 et superficiei: *mg. O*   33 per
predicta: *om. F*   35 super corpus: *rep. F*   36 sicut: ut *S*   38 nec: videtur *O*
40 speram: *om. F*   41 et superficiei: *om. O*   42 *post* rectos *scr. et del. O* et cum
linea que est communis differentia sue superficiei et superficiei plane tangentis speram continet angulos rectos   44 quod: quid *O*   47 *post* angulos *scr. et del. O* super linee
concavitatem circuli sit que per centrum transit et cadit ad equales *et deinde add.* angulos /
illam: linee *O*   48 ita: in *B*   48–9 quia ... perpendiculares: *mg. O*

bodies are recipients only through surfaces. However, properly speaking, it is the perpendicular to a plane surface that is shorter than all other straight lines issuing to the plane surface from the same point as the perpendicular, as is clear from the fourth part of this treatise.[5] Nevertheless, it forms right angles with all straight lines lying in the plane surface and passing through the same point [of the surface] as it does. And right angles are contained between the line of intersection of its surface[6] and the surface of the plane at which it is terminated, as was explained above.[7] Therefore, it is multi-fariously evident from the foregoing that nature chooses this line for its action.

The perpendicular to a spherically convex body is, properly speaking, shorter than all other lines drawn to the surface of the sphere from the same point outside the sphere, as was shown in part 4 [of this treatise].[8] And although we are here concerned with spheres, as in the case of a plane surface no angle [strictly speaking] is formed;[9] nevertheless, right angles are formed with all lines tangent to the [great] circles passing around the sphere [through the point of inci-dence of the perpendicular];[10] and it forms right angles with the line of intersection of its surface and the plane surface tangent to the sphere [at the point of incidence]; and it forms equal, but obtuse, angles with the [great] circles drawn around the sphere through that same point. From all of this it is evident, by the aforesaid, that nature chooses to act along this line in preference to all others.

But since the perpendicular to the concavity of a circle[11] is the line passing through the centre of the circle and incident at equal angles on that concavity, this does not produce as strong an action as do other perpendiculars, since it is longer than many perpendicu-lars, as is clear from Euclid, iii. 7-8.[12] Similarly, since the perpendi-cular to the concavity of the sphere is the line that passes through the centre and forms equal angles with the intersection of its surface and the plane surface tangent to the concavity of the sphere [at the point of incidence of the perpendicular]—and it is also the line that forms equal angles with all circles passing through the point where the perpendicular is terminated—therefore, it must be longer than other [perpendiculars] by Euclid, iii. 7-8, and consequently species incident along such perpendiculars do not produce as strong an action as [species incident along] the perpendiculars to the con-vexity of a sphere. And from what has now been said concerning spheres the facts concerning cylinders and cones are evident.

Species incident along other lines can [also] be compared in

fortitudine. Nam fracta est fortior quam reflexa, quia fracta vadit
in partem incessus recti, licet parum ab eo declinet; reflexio vero
vadit in contrarium recti incessus, et ideo magis debilitat speciem
quam fractio. Sed fractio que est per recessum a perpendiculari, que
65 fractio et perpendicularis exeunt ab eodem puncto, est debilior quam
illa que appropinquat eidem perpendiculari, quoniam perpendicularis
est fortior; et ideo accessus ad eam habet fortitudinem maiorem,
quamvis diverse fractiones accidunt diversimode in planis et spericis
diversum situm habentibus, et secundum quod res in ipsis corporibus
70 habent situm diversum. Nam in corporibus mundi spericis, incipiendo

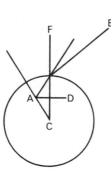

Fig. 31   Fig. 32

a sursum in deorsum, fractio semper vadit declinando ad perpendicularem que ab eodem puncto egreditur cum ea; quod si corpora densiora
essent superius, econtrario modo accideret. Et cum densiora sunt inferiora secundum situm naturalem corporum mundi, planum est quod
75 fractio veniens a re posita inter centrum mundi et superius recedit a
perpendiculari, ut patet in figura [fig. 31]; nam si AD sit res, AB radius
fractus recedit a perpendiculari CF. Et illa que venit a re posita
ultra centrum mundi, si posset facere speciem suam superius in partem
centri, iret ad perpendicularem, ut patet in figura [fig. 32]; nam

61 fracta² *SA* : fractio *O* fortior *BFL*   62 reflexa *SA* | vero: v. non *B*
63 debilitant *S*   64 fractio²: fractam *S* | incessum *F*   64-5 que¹ . . . fractio:
scilicet *S*   65 fracta *B* | et: *om. B*   68 quamvis: que *S* | fractiones: actiones *B*
69 diversum: et d. *FSA* etiam d. *O*   70 *ante* corporibus *scr. et del. S* diversis
73 essent: *om. F* | econtrario: e contra *S* | sint *BO*   75 fractio: f. veniens a re *SA*
76 ut . . . res: si AD sit r. ut patet in figura nam *L* | si AD: *om. B* | AB: AL *B*   76-7 ut

strength. For a refracted species is stronger than a reflected one, since a refracted species proceeds in the [general] direction of the incident path, although diverging a little from it; reflection, on the other hand, proceeds in a direction opposite to the incident path, and therefore it weakens the species more than does refraction. But refraction in which the refracted line recedes from the perpendicular (issuing from the same point) is weaker than refraction in which the refracted line approaches the perpendicular, since the perpendicular is stronger;[13] and therefore approach to it leads to greater strength, although refractions occur differently in plane and spherical bodies having different positions, and according to different positions

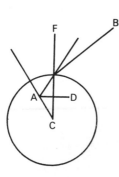

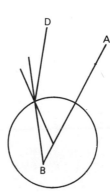

Fig. 31   Fig. 32

of the objects [from which the species emanate] in those bodies. For in proceeding downwards through the spherical bodies of the world, the refracted line always bends towards the perpendicular drawn from the same point as that from which it [the refracted line] proceeds; but if the denser substances were above, refraction would occur in the opposite direction. And since the denser substances are lower, according to the natural place of mundane bodies, it is clear that the refracted ray coming [upwards] from an object[14] situated between the centre and the periphery of the world recedes from the perpendicular, as is evident in the figure [fig. 31]; for if AD is the object, refracted ray AB recedes from perpendicular CF. And the refracted ray coming from an object situated beyond the centre of the world, if it could produce its species upwards in the direction of the centre,[15] would deviate towards the perpendicular,[16] as is evident in the figure [fig. 32]; for

80 BD radius fractus vadit versus perpendicularem AB in corpore subtili,
ut patet in figura. Sed licet in corporibus mundi non sunt huiusmodi
fractiones a rebus positis ultra centrum, aut non bene possibiles
propter densitatem terre, tamen in aliis corporibus spericis positis
in medio, ut sunt vitra et cristalla et vapores sperici, quorum cen-
85 trum non est centrum mundi, et huiusmodi, possibile est fieri ambas
fractiones secundum quod res ponuntur ex una parte centri vel alia.

Sed in planis corporibus quocunque situentur, sursum vel deorsum,
fractio in subtiliori corpore secundo recedit a perpendiculari que
exit ab eodem puncto, ut patet figuranti. Nam posito subtiliori

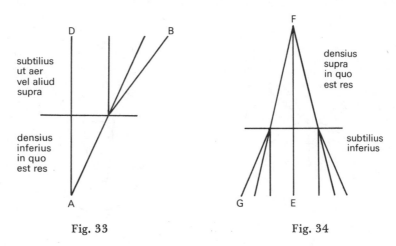

Fig. 33   Fig. 34

90 superius, patet quod radius AB fractus [fig. 33] recedit a perpendiculari AD; et posito inferius, patet FG radium fractum [fig. 34] recedere
a perpendiculari FE.

Reflexio vero que est ad angulos equales illa est fortior ratione
geminationis radii duplicis in eodem loco. Sed quantum est de natura
95 reflexionis, planum est quod magis debilitat, nam omnino vadit contra
incessum naturalem, quem species veniens ab agente nititur tenere
secundum incessum suum rectum. Reflexio vero ad obliquos angulos
maiorem facit actionem quam ad angulos rectos, non solum ex causa

80 BD: *correxi ex* AB *FOS* AD *BL* | AB: AL *B* | subtili: subtiliori *L spatium vacuum B*
80–1 vadit . . . figura: veniens a re posita inter centrum et supra declinat a perpendiculari
EF et DE radius accedit ad ipsum *S* veniens a re posita inter centrum et supra declinat
ad perpendicularem AD cum valet sursum ut patet in figura *A'*   81 sint *S*
82 positis: p. in medio *O*   82–4 ultra . . . medio: *mg. O*   84 et[1]: vel *B om. O* |
cristalla *ANV*: cristallus *FO* cristallina *BLS* | et[2] *OSA*: *om. BFLN*   85 et huiusmodi:
om. S obs. A   86 secundum quod: per quas *S obs. A* | res: *om. F* | vel: et *S*
87 quocunque *BL*: quomodocunque *O* quecunque *F* quomodo *S* quorum centra *NV* |
situerentur *L*   88 secundo: *om. S*   89 exit *OSA*: erit *BFL* | ab: in *B*   90 quod

refracted ray BD deviates towards perpendicular AB in the rarer substance, as is evident in the figure.[17] But although in the bodies of the world there are [in fact] no such refractions from objects placed beyond the centre, or at least they are not easily possible owing to the density of the earth, nevertheless in other spherical bodies placed in the [airy] medium, such as glass and crystal and spherical vapours (the centre of which is not the centre of the world), and the like, it is possible for refraction to occur whichever side of the centre the object is on.

But in plane [transparent] bodies situated any way you like, above

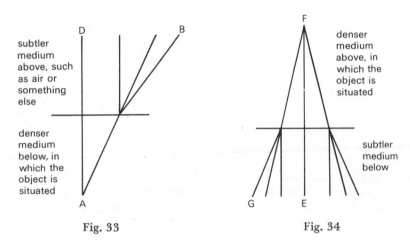

Fig. 33   Fig. 34

or below [the rarer medium], the refracted ray in the second, rarer substance recedes from the perpendicular issuing from the same point, as is evident from the figures. For if the rare substance is positioned above, it is evident that refracted ray AB [fig. 33] recedes from perpendicular AD. And if the rare substance is positioned below, it is evident that refracted ray FG [fig. 34] recedes from perpendicular FE.

Reflection at equal angles is stronger [than refraction], by reason of the doubling of the ray in a given place. However, by reason of the nature of reflection, it is clear that reflection at equal angles produces greater weakness, for it runs altogether contrary to the natural approach, which a species coming from the agent endeavours to retain according to its rectilinear course. But reflection at oblique angles produces greater action than at right angles, not only for the reason

radius: radium *SA* / fractum *S obs. A* / recedere *SA*   91 AD: BD *A* BA *S* / posito:
p. subtiliori *S* / patet: *om. S*   92 *post* FE *add. SA* supra in quo est res   93 ad:
om. O   95 debilitatur *B*   96 quem *OA*: quam *BFLSN* / tendere *S*

dicta, sed ex causa accidentali, quia plures radii possunt congregari
100 per illam que est ad angulos obliquos. Duo enim solum congregantur
in uno loco per reflexionem ad angulos rectos, sed infiniti possunt
congregari per reflexionem ad angulos obliquos, sicut accidit in
quolibet puncto aeris nostri qui sumus inter tropicum cancri et polum
septentrionalem, omnes enim radii solares cadunt semper ad angulos
105 obliquos in hiis regionibus. Reflexio quidem que fit a speculis planis
debilior est quam ab aliis, quia plures radii possunt congregari precipue per concava; et que est quasi ovalis vel anularis figure maxime
congregat radios, ut dictum est prius. Et ideo concava specula plus
comburunt quam plana, et ovalia quam cetera concava.

110   (χ) Sed Euclides docet figurari perspicuum quod comburat ante et
retro. Hoc autem, si fiat per rationem speculi, potest intelligi de
speculis concavis et ovalibus, quia in polo axis inferiori retro fit
combustio, et ante similiter in singulis punctis axis, sicut volumus.
Si vero ad litteram intelligat de combustione ultra speculum, et
115 possibile sit hoc per reflexionem, tunc oportet quod sit quasi anularis
figure, ut ex utraque parte cadant radii, quod est difficilis ymagina-
tionis, nec a me adhuc expertum. Sed certum est quod figurari
potest perspicuum, ut sit concavum ex una parte et convexum ex
alia, habens spissitudinem magnam, quatinus retro fiat combustio per
120 fractionem et ante per reflexionem. Si vero in omnibus hiis combustionibus in axe obiciatur quod combustibile cadet inter solem et
speculum, quare non fieret reflexio nec combustio nec radiorum incidentia, dicendum est quod combustibile non directe apponetur, sed a
latere et cum cautela, quam sciunt experimentatores, non cavillantes
inexperti.

PARS V
CAPITULUM 3

Dicto de varietate actionis penes lineas et angulos, nunc dicendum
est penes figuras. Et licet sperica figura sit propria actioni que est
5 ipsa speciei multiplicatio, tamen fortitudo actionis consideratur

102 reflexiones *S*   106 ab: *om. O* / congregari: et *S*   107 per: *om. L* / quasi:
om. F / vel: et *F*   108 congregant *S*   109 *post* ovalia *scr. et del. O* congregatur
110 figurare speculum *O*   110–25 sed . . . inexperti: *om. S*   111 si: quod *O*
112 inferiori *BFLO*: inferioris *NV* inferiore (?) *A* / fit: fiat *A*   114 vero: non *B* /
intelligat *BLA*: intelligit *FO*   115 anulari *F* armillaris *A*   117 adhuc: hoc *A*

[just] given, but on account of an accidental cause, since many rays can be assembled by reflection at oblique angles. For only two rays are brought together in one place by reflection at right angles, but an infinity of rays can be assembled by reflection at oblique angles, as occurs at any point of our air that we choose between the tropic of Cancer and the north pole, for all solar rays always fall at oblique angles in these regions. However, reflection from plane mirrors is weaker than from other mirrors, since it is chiefly by concave mirrors that many rays can be assembled; and a mirror of oval or annular shape assembles rays most of all, as was said above.[18] And therefore a concave mirror produces combustion more strongly than a plane mirror, and an oval mirror than other concave mirrors.

(χ) Euclid teaches how to shape a glass that produces combustion both before and behind.[19] Now if this occurs by means of a mirror, it can be understood of concave oval mirrors, since [in them] combustion occurs 'behind', at the lower pole of the axis, and also 'before', at any individual point of the axis we choose. But if combustion behind the mirror is taken literally, this too is possible by reflection, though the mirror would require a more or less annular shape, so that rays could fall on it from either side—not an easy thing to imagine and not yet tested by me. But it is certain that a glass can be shaped so as to be concave on one side and convex on the other, having great density, so that it produces combustion behind it by refraction and before it by reflection. However, if, in all of these combustions [occurring] along the axis, it is objected that the combustible substance would rest between the sun and the mirror, and therefore that there could be no reflection and no combustion and no incidence of rays, we reply that the combustible substance is not placed directly [on the axis], but to the side and with care, as experimenters know and as quibblers who have not tried it do not.

PART V

CHAPTER 3

Having discussed the diversity of action according to lines and angles, we must now discuss it according to figures. And although a spherical figure is proper to the action involved in the multiplication of species, nevertheless strength of action is considered with regard to

118 perspicuum: spericum *A* / sit: fit *B* fiat *A* / et: etiam *A*   121 in axe: maxime *LA* / cadit *O*   122 speculi *A* / quem *B* / nec¹: vel *O*   123 apponeretur *B*   124 cum: est *A*

  2 capitulum tertium *O*   3 actionis: *om. B*   4 actionis *SA*

penes figuram pyramidalem cuius basis est superficies agentis et
eius conus in parte patientis determinata. Nam per hanc figuram
potest species venire a qualibet parte agentis obiecta patienti ad
singula puncta patientis; quod non accidit in aliqua alia figura,
10   nam radii venientes a singulis partibus agentis congregantur in conum
pyramidis, qui figitur in aliquo puncto patientis. Et quoniam infinite
pyramides tales veniunt ab eadem superficie agentis, quarum omnium
ipsa superficies basis est, ideo ad singula puncta patientis venit
sua pyramis radiosa, ut actio fiat completa. Nam si ab una parte
15   agentis ad unam partem patientis veniat radius, non posset esse nisi
unus, et ille parum ageret; et ideo elegit natura pyramidem, ut in
ea congreget omnes radios qui veniunt a tota superficie agentis, et
multiplicat eas secundum numerum partium patientis.

Sed tunc considerandum est quod pyramis brevior magis operatur
20   quam longior, quia conus brevioris pyramidis distat minus ab agente
(ψ); et ideo minus debilitatur virtus veniens super eam, ex distantia
enim debilitatur virtus; et ideo patiens ad quod conus pyramidis
brevioris pertingit magis alteratur. Item conus pyramidis brevioris
est obtusior, et maiorem angulum continent eius radii, sicut patet
25   ex vicesima prima primi *Elementorum*, ut patet in figura [fig. 35].

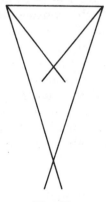

Fig. 35

Cum ergo quatuor anguli circa conum pyramidis brevioris non valent
nisi quatuor rectos, et similiter anguli quatuor circa conum pyramidis
longioris, quia circa punctum unum in superficie non possunt esse

the pyramidal figure whose base is the surface of the agent and whose vertex is a determined part of the recipient. For by means of this figure a species can come from any part of the agent facing the recipient to individual points of the recipient; and this cannot occur by means of any other figure, for rays coming from individual parts of the agent are assembled at the vertex of the pyramid, which is located at some point of the recipient. And since infinitely many such pyramids come from the same surface of the agent, each with that surface as base, it follows that to each point of the recipient comes its own radiant pyramid to complete the action of the agent. For if a ray should come from one part of the agent to one part of the recipient, there would be only one ray, and that would not be sufficiently active; and therefore nature chooses the pyramid, in which all the rays coming from the whole surface of the agent converge; and such pyramids are as numerous as the parts of the recipient.

Next, it is to be noted that a shorter pyramid acts more strongly than a longer pyramid,[1] because the vertex of the shorter pyramid is less distant from the agent (ψ); and therefore the virtue coming by means of it is less weakened, for virtue is weakened by distance; consequently, the recipient reached by the vertex of a shorter pyramid is

Fig. 35

altered more. Also, the vertex of a shorter pyramid is more obtuse, and its rays contain a larger angle, as is evident from *Elements*, i. 21,[2] and from the figure [fig. 35]. Now since the four angles about the vertex of a short pyramid[3] are equivalent to exactly four right angles, and likewise the four angles about the vertex of a longer pyramid, since about one point in a surface there can be

nisi quatuor recti aut valentes eos, oportet quod postquam angulus
30 pyramidis brevioris sit maior angulo pyramidis longioris, quod angulus
contrapositus angulo brevioris pyramidis sit maior angulo contraposito
in longiori, quia anguli contrapositi sunt equales per quintam decimam
primi *Elementorum*. Sed si isti anguli contrapositi circa conum
pyramidis brevioris sunt maiores angulis contrapositis eis consimilibus
35 circa conum pyramidis longioris, oportet quod anguli duo alii contrapositi a lateribus coni pyramidis brevioris sint minores duobus
angulis contrapositis lateraliter circa conum pyramidis longioris,
quia hinc inde non valent quatuor anguli nisi quatuor rectos, et
ideo quatuor anguli circumstantes conum pyramidis brevioris simul
40 sumpti sunt equales quatuor angulis circumstantibus conum pyramidis
longioris simul sumptis; quapropter si duo contrapositi a parte
pyramidis brevioris sunt maiores duobus consimilibus a parte pyramidis longioris, erunt alii duo minores aliis duobus. Sed quanto radii
continent minorem angulum, tanto magis vicinantur; ergo radii omnes
45 qui sunt de corpore pyramidis brevioris continentes angulos cum
radiis eis conterminalibus exeuntibus a cono eius magis vicinantur
et approprinquant quam radii consimiles in longiori pyramide. Sed
vicinia radiorum magis operatur et fortior est; quapropter conus
pyramidis brevioris magis operatur.
50   Si vero arguatur in contrarium, videlicet quod radii infiniti
veniunt ad conum pyramidis longioris sicut brevioris, et cum ille
conus sit angustior, maior est radiorum vicinia et congregatio, quapropter magis intendetur operatio; atque simul cum hoc si dicatur
quod omnes radii pyramidis longioris magis appropinquant incessui
55 perpendicularium exeuntium a terminis basis agentis, quia pyramis
longior includit breviorem, ut patet in figura [fig. 36], et incessus
perpendicularium est fortissimus, et quanto magis fit ei appropinquatio
est maior fortitudo; dicendum est quod hee rationes due procedunt
quantum possunt, sed alie in contrarium sunt fortiores sine compara-
60 tione, precipue prima, et ideo priores prevalent in hac parte. Et
quoniam ostensum est prius quod species pyramidalis non potest
venire a tota medietate corporis sperici, nec a maiore portione, sed
necessario a minore; et exemplificatum est in figura [fig. 37] quomodo

29 *post* eos *add. FLO* ut patet ex corelario 13[e] (12[e] *F licet L*)   31 contraposito:
composito *B*   32 compositi *B* / quintam decimam: 21 *O* 9 *F*   32-3 per . . .
elementorum: *om. SA*   33 elementorum: Euclidis *FO* / contrapositi: *om. B*
33-4 circa . . . consimilibus: circa conum pyramidis brevioris quam anguli contrapositi
eis aut eis consimilibus *mg. O*   34 sint *O*   37 linealiter *O* / longiorum *S* (*S ends
here; variants for A are hereafter supplied in full*)   38 rectos: angulos r. *O*
38-9 nisi . . . anguli: *om. B*   40-1 sunt . . . sumptis: *om. A*   41 compositi *A*
43 erunt: essent *A* / quanto *BA*: quando *L* quanto (*mg.*) quando (*in textu*) *O*   44 vicinantur: *spatium vacuum B*   46 eis conterminalibus: *om. A*   47 longiore *O*
50 videlicet: scilicet *F*   51 cum: *mg. O*   52 sit: fit *B*   60-70 et[2] . . . patiens:

only four right angles or their equivalent, it is necessary, since the angle of the shorter pyramid is greater than the angle of the longer pyramid,[4] that the vertically opposite angle of the shorter pyramid be greater than the vertically opposite angle of the longer pyramid, because angles that are vertically opposite [to each other] are equal by *Elements*, i. 15.[5] But if these vertically opposite angles of the shorter pyramid are greater than the similar vertically opposite angles of the longer pyramid, then the other two vertically opposite angles situated laterally about the vertex of the shorter pyramid must be smaller than the two vertically opposite angles situated laterally about the vertex of the longer pyramid, since in both cases the four angles are equal to exactly four right angles, wherefore the four angles about the vertex of the shorter pyramid, taken together, are equal to the four angles about the vertex of the longer pyramid, taken together; therefore, if two vertically opposite angles of the shorter pyramid are greater than the similar two angles of the longer pyramid, the other two [vertically opposite angles of the shorter pyramid] will be smaller than the other two [vertically opposite angles of the longer pyramid]. Now the smaller the angle between rays, the closer the rays are to each other; therefore, all rays belonging to the body of the shorter pyramid and forming angles with the coterminal rays issuing from its vertex[6] are in closer proximity [to the latter] than are the corresponding rays in the longer pyramid. And proximity of rays produces fuller and stronger action; therefore, the vertex of a shorter pyramid acts more strongly.

But if it should be argued to the contrary, namely, that an infinity of rays comes to the vertex of the longer pyramid, just as to the vertex of the shorter, and that since the former vertex is sharper the proximity and convergence of the rays is greater, so that its action is more intense; and if, at the same time, it should be pointed out that all rays of the longer pyramid more closely approach the path of the perpendiculars issuing from the ends of the base of the agent, since the longer pyramid encloses the shorter, as is evident in the figure [fig. 36], and the path of perpendiculars is the strongest, and the closer the path is to the perpendicular the greater is its strength; it is replied that these two arguments are good as far as they go, but the others to the contrary[7] are incomparably stronger, especially the first, and therefore they prevail in the matter. Also, it was shown above that a pyramidal [or conical] species cannot come from an entire half of the spherical body, nor from the greater portion, but necessarily from the smaller;[8] and the figure [fig. 37] reveals how

om. A   61 quoniam: quandoque *F*   62 venire: *om. B* / torta *B*   63 explica-
tum *B*

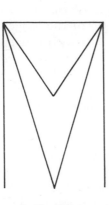

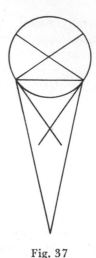

Fig. 36   Fig. 37

pyramides longiores fiunt et breviores, et que est brevissima omnium,
65 quoniam illa cuius latera sunt linee contingentes speram in terminis
diametrorum ductarum a terminis corde intersecantium se, ut patuit
in figura; nunc planum est quod hec magis est activa, propter hoc
quod multipliciter patet ex dictis quod brevitas figurarum et linearum
faciunt vehementem operationem propter propinquitatem agentis ad
70 patiens.

Et non solum est fortis actio in ista pyramide, licet fortior quam
in aliis, sed in omnibus pyramidibus, et non solum illis que cadunt
ultra conum pyramidis dicte infra intersectionem illarum linearum
contingentie que continebant pyramidem predictam. Et hee sunt ille
75 pyramides que includunt dictam pyramidem; et ideo sunt fortioris
actionis quam ille pyramides quarum coni cadunt extra intersectionem
illam et que non continent pyramidem predictam brevissimam, quia
radii qui sunt de compositione istarum pyramidum quarum coni non
includuntur infra dictam intersectionem non possunt a tot partibus
80 portionis agentis venire sicut illi qui sunt de compositione pyramidum
quarum coni cadunt infra dictam intersectionem, ut patet in figura
[fig. 38]. Radii enim in compositione pyramidis BAED veniunt ab
E et A et B et omnibus punctis portionis BAE. Sed radii componentes
pyramidem BAC non possunt venire a tot punctis; nam cum EO linea
85 contingit circulum, non poterit a termino suo, qui est E, alia linea

64 fiunt: sunt *F* / et[1]: *om. O*   64–6 brevissima . . . ductarum: *mg.* (*sed* omnium
in textu ante brevissima) *O*   65 speram *FONV*: speravi *BL*   66 diametrorum *O*:
diametri *BFLNV* / se: *om. L*   67 quod: quia *L*   68 quod[2]: quia *O*   69 comparationem *F* / ad: et *O*   70 patiens: patientis *O*   71 et: et ideo *A*   72 non
O: *om. BFLAN* / solis *BF*   73 ducte *F* / illarum *mg. A*[c] aliarum *A*′   74 continent

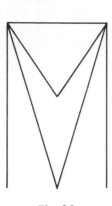

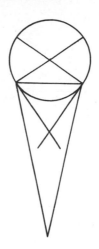

Fig. 36   Fig. 37

longer and shorter pyramids are formed (and [also] the shortest pyramid of all,[9] for its sides are the lines tangent to the sphere at the ends of the diameters drawn from the end of the chord and intersecting one another, as is evident in the figure); from this it is now clear that the shortest pyramid is more active because, as is apparent in many ways from the foregoing, brevity of figures and lines produces a strong action owing to the proximity of agent and recipient.

And strength of action characterizes not only this pyramid (though it is stronger than the others), but all pyramids, and not[10] only those [the vertices of] which fall beyond the vertex of the said [shortest] pyramid beneath the intersection of the lines of tangency that define the aforementioned pyramid. And these are the pyramids that include the said [shortest] pyramid; and therefore their action is stronger than that of pyramids whose vertices fall outside that intersection[11] and which do not contain the aforementioned shortest pyramid, since the rays belonging to those pyramids whose vertices are not situated below the said intersection cannot come from as large a portion of the agent as those belonging to pyramids whose vertices fall below the said intersection, as is evident in the figure [fig. 38]. For the rays belonging to pyramid BAED come from E and A and B and all points of sector BAE. But the rays belonging to pyramid BAC cannot come from as many points;[12] for since line EO is tangent to the circle, no other [straight] line can be drawn from its terminus, E,

O / predictam: est actu fortior *mg. A*^C *om. A'*   77 illam: *om. B* / non: n. illam *B*
78 conum *A*   79 includunt *FA* / infra: *om. L* / ante dictam *scr. et del. A* se
81 *post* figura *add. FO* subscripta *et habet B spatium vacuum*   84 EO: EB *O*
85 E: C *BL*

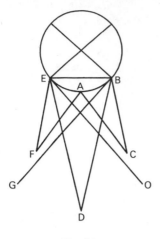

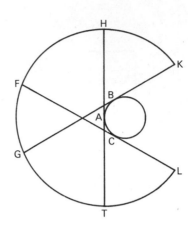

Fig. 38   Fig. 39

duci inter eam et circumferentiam, per decimam quintam tertii
Elementorum; et eadem ratione nulla intercipietur inter BG lineam et
circumferentiam, ut exeat ab ipso B.

Similiter considerandum alio modo quod corpus spericum aliquid
90 obiectum sibi fortius alterat et aliud minus, ut docet Iacobus Alkindi.
Nam corpus luminosum sit ABC [fig. 39]. A puncto igitur A illuminatur totum HT, quia totum illuminatur a puncto quolibet ad quod
possunt duci linee recte; ergo et FG illuminabitur ab ipso B. Item ab
ipso C totum FL illuminatur, ergo et FG; quare a tota portione BAC
95 illuminatur FG. Sed portio FH non potest illuminari nisi a punctis A
et B, per decimam quintam tertii, non enim potest linea duci a C puncto
inter FL lineam et circumferentiam. Similiter GT non illuminatur nisi
ab A et C per rationem consimilem. Sed HK non illuminabitur nisi ab
ipso B solum, quia ab ipso A non duceretur linea recta ultra H, nec
100 a C ultra F, per decimam quintam tertii. Similiter TL non illuminabitur
nisi ab ipso C per consimilem rationem. Quare FG patiens plus
alterabitur quam alia, et hoc est quod demonstrare voluimus.

87 *post* elementorum *mg. add. O* Euclidis / nulla: *mg. L* / intercipitur *O* / inter: ut est *L*
89 considerandum: *mg. O* / aliquid: aliud *O*   90 aliud: aliquid *A*   91 A¹: *om. B*
91-2 A¹ . . . HT: a puncto A illuminatur totum q HT *A'* et illud totum HT *mg. Aᶜ*
92 ad quod: a quo *O*   93 et FG: EFG *O* / ab¹: item ab *A*   93-4 item . . . FG:
totum GK illuminatur ergo FG item ab ipso C totum FL illuminabitur ergo et FG *A*
94 C *N*: G *BO* S *FL* / FL: FB *L* GK *A*   95 illuminatur: *mg. O om. F* / FH: FG *F*
96 per: et B et per *A* / enim: *om. A* / C *Aᶜ*: CG *BFONV* AC *A' S L*   97 FL: FI *B* /
GT: GC *B* / illuminabitur *OA*   98 HK: BK *A*   99 B: H *F* / duceretur *BL*: ducetur

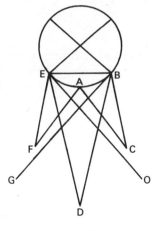

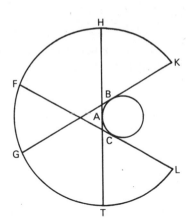

Fig. 38   Fig. 39

between it and the circumference, by *Elements*, iii. 15;[13] and by the same argument no straight line issuing from B can fall between line BG and the circumference.

Similarly, it must be recognized in another way that a spherical body alters some thing facing it more strongly and some other thing less strongly, as Jacob Alkindi teaches.[14] For let ABC [fig. 39][15] be the luminous body. Then the whole of HT is illuminated by point A, since the whole is illuminated by any point to which straight lines can be drawn [from all points of that whole; and thus FG is illuminated by A]. [And the whole of GK is illuminated by point B;] therefore FG is also illuminated by B. Also, the whole of FL is illuminated by C, and therefore also FG. Thus FG is illuminated by the whole sector BAC. But sector FH can be illuminated only by points A and B [among those under consideration], by [Euclid,] iii. 15,[16] for a [straight] line cannot be drawn from point C between FL and the circumference. Similarly, and for the same reason, GT is illuminated only by A and C. And HK will be illuminated only by B, since from A no straight line can be drawn beyond H, nor from C beyond F, by [Euclid,] iii. 15. Similarly, and for the same reason, TL will be illuminated only by C. Therefore, recipient FG will be more altered than any other, and this is what we wished to demonstrate.

OA ducitur *F*   100 a C *OA*: AC *BFL* / TL: TB *F*   101 C: sic *B*   102 alterabitur: illuminabitur *A*′ illuminabitur vel a. *A*^c / quam: quod *A* / voluimus: *F ends here*

PARS VI

CAPITULUM 1

Dicto de generatione speciei et multiplicatione et actione, nunc ergo dicendum est de corruptione. Et patet eam esse corruptibilem, quia
5 est generabilis, omne enim quod generatur natum est corrumpi, sicut Aristoteles testatur et philosophia confitetur. Item nos videmus per experientiam quod huiusmodi species corrumpuntur, ut lumen in aere corrumpitur in nocte, et lux lune corrumpitur in eclipsi, et sic de aliis.

10   Si obiciatur quod huiusmodi speciebus, ut luci et multis aliis, nichil est contrarium, ergo non corrumpuntur, cum omnis corruptio est per contrarium, ut omnes allegant et Aristoteles vult *Libro de morte et vita*; dicendum quod ipse tertio *Celi et mundi* dicit corruptionem duplicem esse: unam per contrarium, aliam per defectum rei
15 debilis in se. Sua igitur auctoritas, quam vulgus sequitur *Libro de morte et vita*, intelligenda est de corruptione que fit ab alio inferente passionem. Species autem propter debilitatem sui esse non habet unde se conservet, et ideo deficit. Atque quia in omnes diametros agit se multiplicando, destruitur et debilitatur in tantum quod
20 deficit ab operatione et tandem ab esse. Ceterum natura patientis specifica completior nata est ad contrarium speciei, si contrarium habeat, vel ad dispositionem contrariam illi que per speciem inducitur, ut natura aeris specifica, que nata est carere rarefactione vel aliqua alia passione quam lux inducit; tandem prevalet super illam disposi-
25 tionem ei contrariam et corrumpit eam. Et sic per consequens species lucis et alterius corrumpitur per accidens per contrarium, etsi non per se.

    Si dicatur quod natura patientis desiderat assimulari agenti per speciem, et quod speciei generatio non est in corruptionem sed in
30 perfectionem et salutem, ut prius suppositum est, ergo natura rei specifica non aget ad eius corruptionem per se nec per accidens, neque ad corruptionem dispositionis naturalis ad ipsam speciem, dicendum quod natura rei patientis est in potentia et appetitu naturali consistens respectu huiusmodi speciei et dispositionis ad ipsam

---

1 incipit pars sexta huius tractatus *O*   2 capitulum primum *O*   3 dicto: *New hand begins in L* | ergo *BANV: om. LO*   4 de *BANV: om. LO*   5 enim: e. genera-bile vel *LO*   8 in[1]: *om. O* | lux *BANV: om. LO* | corrumpitur[2]: *om. A*   10 si: si autem *LO* | ut . . . aliis: *mg. A*[c] *om. A'* | aliis: *om. B*   11 est: et *A* | corrumpuntur *A*: corrumpitur *BLO* | cum: et *A*   12 est: sit *A* | per: *om. B*   13 dicit: *mg. O*   14 esse: omne *B*   15 durabilis *A* | libro: *om. A*   16 intelligendum *B* | que fit *BAV*: qui f. *N* facta *LO*   17 habet: *ex* sed(?) *corr. B*   19 multitudo *B*   21 specifica completior *BA*: s. *LO* c. *NV* | ad: in *A*   23 vel: et *O*   26 et *BLNV*: vel *OA* | etsi non: et *O*   28 per: et p. *L*   29 in[1]: per *O* | corruptione *A*   30 perfectione

PART VI
CHAPTER 1

Having spoken of the generation and multiplication and action of a species, we must now consider its corruption. It is evident that a species is corruptible, since it is generable, for everything that is generated is susceptible to corruption, as Aristotle proves and philosophy acknowledges. Also, we perceive by experience that species are corrupted; for example, light in the air is corrupted at night, and the light of the moon is corrupted during an eclipse, and the like.

If it should be objected that there is no contrary to species such as light (and many others) and therefore that they are not corrupted, since every corruption occurs as a result of the contrary, as everybody agrees and Aristotle maintains in *De morte et vita*;[1] we reply that Aristotle himself says, in *De caelo et mundo*, book iii, that corruption is of two kinds: one as a result of a contrary, the other through the failure in itself of a thing that is weak.[2] Therefore, his opinion in *De morte et vita*, which the vulgar follow, should be understood to be concerned [only] with that corruption which occurs in the former manner, by the intrusion of an effect [from the contrary]. However, a species, owing to the weakness of its being, is unable to preserve itself, and thus dies away. Also, since it acts by multiplying itself along all diameters, it is destroyed and weakened to the point where it cannot act and finally perishes. Moreover, the more complete specific nature of the recipient is suited to the contrary of the species, if it should have a contrary, or to a disposition contrary to that which is introduced by means of the species, as [for example] the specific nature of air, which is disposed to be free from rarefaction or any other effect that light introduces; finally the air prevails over this disposition contrary to itself and corrupts it. And thus, as a consequence, the species of light or something else is corrupted accidentally by its contrary and not *per se*.

If it should be argued that the nature of the recipient wishes to be assimilated to the agent through the species, and that the generation of a species does not induce corruption, but perfection and well-being, as was supposed above,[3] and therefore that the specific nature of a thing does not corrupt the species either accidentally or *per se*, nor the natural disposition towards the species, we reply that the nature of the recipient remains in potentiality and natural appetite towards such a species and such a disposition natural

A / salute *A* / suppositum est *BAN*: supponitur *V* dictum est *LO*   31 per[1]: nec p. *O*
31-2 per[1] . . . dispositionis: *mg. L*   32 naturalis: materialem *B*   33 est: *mg. O*
34 huiusmodi *BLN*: huius *OAV* / et: *om. O* / dispositionis: huius d. *A* ad dispositionem *LO*

35 naturalis. Sed maiorem et perfectiorem potentiam et appetitum habet
ad ea que sunt nature sue specifice; et ideo ea que sunt nature sue
specifice nata est conservare et contraria corrumpere, quantum est
de se. Nec habet de se unde illa conservet, sed indiget alio conser-
vante, ut generante, vel fortitudine ipsorum propria potente conser-
40 vare; et ideo cum nec fortitudo propria nec causa extrinseca sufficit,
natura propria patientis invalescit super omne quod est ei alienum
et perficit se secundum ea que sunt ei propria, quia non habet posse
conservandi alia, licet habeat aptitudinem ad ea. Quoniam igitur res
ita habet potentiam et appetitum speciei aliene ut tamen per se ipsam
45 nec fiat nec conservetur, sed per aliud, ideo cum res sibi ipsi relinquitur redit ad naturam suam propriam integre; et sic per accidens
incidit corruptio speciei. Et concedendum est quod natura propria
rei specifica potest aliquid corrumpere quod appetit secundario et
per actionem et conservationem alterius, sicut est de specie.

PARS VI
CAPITULUM 2

Deinde secundo queritur an in absentia generantis speciem species
recedat. Et non potest dici quod recedat cum generante et transmute-
5 tur de loco in locum secundum mutationem localem generantis; nam
species tunc esset corpus et defluxus corporis, quod Aristoteles negat
secundo *De anima* de luce, et prius improbatur. Et sic necessario
exiret ab agente, et continuaretur cum eius substantia; sed prius
improbatum est hoc. Quapropter alia causa corruptionis eius querenda
10 est in absentia generantis. Et non est alia quam duplex predicta,
scilicet debilitas sui esse et natura propria patientis que prevalet.
Sed tunc quomodo in celestibus in quibus nichil est contrarium, ut
Aristoteles dicit et omnes fatentur, potest natura propria prevalere
ut destruatur species, et maxime completa, sicut est lux lune, que
15 destruitur in eclipsi? Dicendum est quod in celestibus non est contrarietas que est penes quatuor qualitates activas et passivas, que

35 naturalis *A* : naturalem *BLONV* | perfectiorem: per fortiorem *A*   36 nature[1]
sue[1]: n. *O* s. *B*   37 nata: *om. O*   38 habet: h. species *O* | de[2] se[2]: *om. A* |
illa *BANV*: se *LO* | sed indiget: *mg. A* | alio *BANV*: aliquo *LO*   39 ut generante:
om. B | ipsarum *O*   40 cum: *om. L* | sufficienter *L*   41 natura: set n. *O* | ei:
om. A   42 quia *BANV*: quare *LO*   43 licet: neque *O* | habet *LO*   44 ita
A[c]: *om. A′* | aliene: a. nature *L* | ut: cum *LO* | tamen: *om. L* | se *BNV*: *mg. A om. LO*
45 nec[1]: *om. A*   46 integra *O*   47 accidit *O* | et concedendum: considerandi *O* |

to it. Yet the recipient has greater and more perfect potentiality and appetite towards things of its own specific nature; and therefore of itself it is suited to preserve things of its own specific nature and to corrupt its contraries. And of itself the recipient has no power wherewith to preserve those things [not of its own specific nature], but requires some other preserving agent, as something that generates, or strength sufficient for preservation in the things themselves; and therefore, when neither the things' own strength nor an extrinsic cause suffices, the proper nature of the recipient prevails over all that is alien to it and perfects itself according to things proper to it, since it does not have the power of preserving other things, although it does have aptitude towards them. Therefore, since a [recipient] thing's potentiality and appetite towards an alien species are such that the species comes into being and is preserved not by itself, but by another, accordingly, when the thing is left to itself it returns completely to its own nature; and in this way corruption of a species occurs accidentally. And it is conceded that the specific and proper nature of a thing can corrupt something that, secondarily and by the action and preservative power of something else, it desires, such as a species.

PART VI
CHAPTER 2

Second, it is inquired whether a species disappears in the absence of that which generated it. And it cannot be said that it disappears with its generator or that it is moved from place to place with the local motion of that which generated it; for that would be the case only if a species were body or a flow from body, which Aristotle denies concerning light in *De anima*, book ii, and which we disproved above.[1] For thus it would necessarily exit from the agent, and it would be continuous with the substance of the agent; but this was disproved above. Therefore, another cause of its corruption in the absence of its generator must be sought. And this is none other than the twofold cause mentioned above,[2] namely, weakness of its being and the predominance of the recipient's own nature. But then how can the recipient's own nature predominate in the heavens, where there are no contraries, as Aristotle says and all acknowledge,[3] so that the species will be destroyed, even a complete species, such as the light of the moon, which is destroyed during an eclipse? It is replied that in the heavens there is no contrariety as regards the four active and passive

propria: *mg. A*^{C} *om. A'*
  2 capitulum secundum *O*   7 et¹: ut *A*   9 eius: *om. A.*   12 tunc: *om. LO*

sunt calidum, frigidum, humidum, et siccum, talis enim negatur
in celestibus. Sed tamen contrarietas que est inter rarum et densum
et lucidum et tenebrosum et huiusmodi est ibi. Nam una pars lune est
20 alia rarior eo quod macula lune habet plus de densitate substantie
celestis, et luna est densior aliis corporibus celestibus; atque potest
rarefieri per generationem lucis in ea, et iterum redit ad densitatem
naturalem per privationem lucis.

Item si dicatur quod idem facit virtus patris in seminibus quod
25 virtus celi in materia putrefacta, ut Averroys dicit septem, et
naturales et medici confitentur, quod in semine sunt virtutes patris
et remanent in generatione prolis; quapropter possunt species remanere
in absentia generantis eas (et hic in absentia patris, ergo similiter
poterit esse in aliis); dicendum est quod pater et mater sunt eiusdem
30 nature specifice, et ideo species et virtus patris recepta in matre
conservatur per presentiam matris, que sufficit loco patris propter
idemptitatem nature specifice. Si dicatur quod in multis rebus manet,
ut lapis calefactus bene retinet calorem, et calx viva et multa alia,
dicendum quod non solum est ibi species, sed effectus completior; et
35 natura densi bene conservantis speciem cooperatur. Si dicatur quod
luna et stelle sunt corpora multum densa, sicut Averroys docet secundo
Celi et mundi et in *Libro de substantia orbis*, et multiplex probatio
currit super hoc, que non est modo necessaria, et tamen privantur
lumine et eclipsantur plures earum, et omnes possent eclipsari si
40 contingeret eas carere radiis solaribus, sicut est de luna; dicendum
quod non omnis densitas facit ad quamcunque speciem conservandam.
Densitas tamen terrestris multum facit ad conservationem caloris;
siccum enim terrestre est causa caloris, ut dicitur vulgariter, quia
siccum terrestre est combustibile, et causa est quia siccitas exigitur
45 ad aptitudinem caloris, sed ad caliditatem exigitur siccitas cum
densitate elementari, que duo non sunt nisi in materia terrestri.
Propter quod Averroys super quatuor *Celi et mundi* et alibi pluries
vult quod ignis de sua essentia caliditatem non habeat nec in sua
spera, sed aptitudinem solam propter siccitatem, que aptitudo ad
50 actum reducitur quando siccitas iungitur cum densitate terrestri.

17 calidum frigidum: c. et f. *L* caliditas frigiditas *O* | humidum: humiditas *O* | siccum:
siccitas *O* sic *BA*   18 tamen: *om. L*   21 aliis: ceteris *LO*   22 densitatem *BNV*:
condensitatem *A* eius d. *O* huiusmodi d. *L*   24 item: unde *O*   25 virtus: facit v.
LO | petrifacta *A* | Averroys: Avicenna *O* | et: *om. A*   26 naturales *BNV*: philosophi
n. *O* plures n. *F* methaphysice et n. *A* | et medici: *om. NV*   27 genere *B*   28 et:
ut *BA* | hoc *O*   32 remanet *A*   33 alia *LONV*: talia *BA*   34 completus *O*
38 occurrit *A* | modo: *om. A*   39 eorum *O* | possunt *LO*   40 eas *ANV*: ea *BLO* |
solaribus: *mg. A*[c] *om. A'*   43 causa *N*: luna *BA om. VLO* | vulgariter *B*
43-4 causa . . . est[1]: *om. LO*   44 est[1]: e. bene *A*   45 aptitudinem: fortitudinem *O*
47-8 alibi . . . vult: alii plures volunt *O*   48 caliditatem: *om. A* | *post* habeat *mg. add.*
A[c] calorem   50 educitur *A* | cum: *mg. L*

qualities (warmth, cold, humidity, and dryness), for such contrariety
in the heavens is denied. Nevertheless, the heavens do exhibit the
contrariety between rare and dense, between lucid and dark, and the
like. For one part of the moon is rarer than another, since the
blemishes on the moon are characterized by greater density of celestial substance, and the moon [as a whole] is denser than other
celestial bodies; also, it can be rarefied by the generation of light in
it, returning again to its natural density when the light is removed.

Also, if it should be maintained that the virtue of the father produces the same thing in his semen as the virtue of the heavens
produces in putrefied matter (for Averroes says in book vii,[4] and
natural philosophers and physicians agree, that the virtues of the
father are in the semen and that they remain during the generation of
progeny), and therefore that species can remain in the absence of
that which generated them (here in the absence of the father, and
therefore likewise in other cases), we reply that the father and
mother have the same specific nature, and therefore the species and
virtue of the father received in the mother are preserved by the presence of the mother, which suffices in place of the father owing to the
identity of specific nature. If it should be said that species remain
in many things, such as a heated stone (which effectively retains its
heat) and quicklime and many other things, it is replied that not only
is a species present there, but also a more complete effect; and the
nature of the dense, which efficaciously preserves species, co-
operates. If it should be pointed out that the moon and stars are
very dense bodies, as Averroes teaches in [his commentary on]
De caelo et mundo, book ii, and in *De substantia orbis*[5] (and many
proofs deal with this, which need not be presented just now), and
that nevertheless several of them are [at times] deprived of light and
eclipsed, and that all would be eclipsed if solar rays should fail to
reach them, as in the case of the moon, we reply that not every
density contributes to the preservation of every species. However, the
density of terrestrial substance contributes much to the preservation
of warmth; for the dryness of the earth is the cause of warmth, as it
is commonly said, since the dryness of the earth is combustible, and
the reason [for this] is that dryness is required for aptitude towards
warmth; but for [actual] warmth, dryness is required together with
the density of the elements, and these two are found only in terrestrial matter. Wherefore Averroes in [his commentary on] *De caelo
et mundo*, book iv (and many other places) maintains that fire by
its essence and in its sphere has no warmth, but only aptitude for
warmth owing to dryness, which aptitude is brought to actuality
when this dryness is joined with the density of terrestrial substance.[6]

PARS VI
CAPITULUM 3

Deinde tertio considerandum quod cum idem agens iterum redeat
super eandem materiam patientis, facit impressionem seu speciem
5 diversam numero a priore que iam corrupta est, quia actio alia et alia
est numero, et ideo effectus numeratur. Si dicatur quod idem manens
idem semper natum est facere idem, ut Aristoteles dicit secundo *De
generatione*, et ideo eandem faciet actionem et per consequens eundem
effectum, dicendum est quod ipse dicit quinto *Physicorum* quod actio
10 numeratur subiecto, specie, et tempore, et ideo oportet quod in
diversis temporibus actiones faciant diversas. Et propter hoc illa
auctoritas secundi *De generatione* intelligitur de idemptitate in
specie, non in numero. Si dicatur quod tempus non facit actionem nec
aliquid ipsius actionis, unde nullo modo est causa efficiens, sed
15 mensura durationis et quantitas in nullo activa; ergo a diversitate
temporis non erit causa diversitatis actionis, sed ab ipsa potentia
activa que totaliter causat actionem; dicendum est quod actio et
passio et motus sunt successiva, nec educuntur de potentia materie,
quia non sunt res fixe, et ideo non corrumpuntur in eam; et propter
20 hoc omnino deficiunt in se et in nichil. Nam de creaturis fixis et
permanentibus intelligitur quod non cedunt in pure nichil, sed non
de successivis. Sed infinita distantia est inter pure nichil et esse,
quam potentia finita non potest pertransire; et ideo nullum agens
creatum potest suam actionem in idem numero renovare post corrup-
25 tionem, quia omne agens creatum est potentie finite.

Si obiciatur quod tunc in eis que de potentia materie generantur,
cum eadem sit potentia materie et eadem potentia agentis, ergo idem
fiet effectus; quare tunc in eodem aere idem agens, ut sol in singulis
diebus artificialibus, licet nox intercipiatur, faciet eandem speciem
30 in numero que prius corrupta fuit, cum speciei generatio sit de
potentia materie; et dicendum est quod hoc non sequitur, quia ad
effectum hunc non pervenitur nisi per actionem agentis, quam oportet
renovari, ut dictum est, et ideo effectus renovatur. Si vero obiciatur

---

2 capitulum tertium *O*   3 considerandum: consideratur *B* c. est *O*   4 materiam
BNV: naturam *LOA*   5 que: qui *B*   8 faciet *BLNV*: facit *OA* | et² *A^C*: om. *A'*
9 ipse dicit: impeditur quia ex *O* | quod² *LA^C*: om. *BOA'NV*   11 faciat *OA* | hoc:
mg. A^C om. A'   12 secundi: de secundo *BL*   13 tempus: *spatium vacuum B*
16 ab *LA*: sub *BONV*   18 successivam *L* | materie: om. *LO*   19 non²: nec *A*
21 intelligitur: verificatur *O* | *post* cedunt *add. L* in nichil et esse | pure: potentia *A*
21-2 sed . . . nichil: *mg. A^C om. A'*   23 transire *A*   24-5 potest . . . creatum:
mg. A^C om. A'   28 fiet: fit *A* | *post* effectus *add. O* quam econtrario *et add. L* quod
econtrario *et add. B* quam e | quare *AVN*: et *LO om. B* | aere: om. *A*   29 speciem:
diem *O*   30 speciei: eius *O*   31 hoc: om. *A*   32 hunc: tunc *A*

PART VI
CHAPTER 3

Third, it is to be recognized that when the same agent returns [to act] again on the same recipient matter, it produces an impression or species numerically different from the prior, already corrupted, one, for this second action is numerically distinct [from the first], and therefore so is its effect. If it should be argued that what remains the same is always naturally suited to do the same thing, as Aristotle says in *De generatione*, book ii,[1] and therefore should produce the same action and consequently the same effect, we reply that Aristotle himself says in *Physics*, book v,[2] that action is numbered according to subject, kind,[3] and time, and consequently that at different times an agent must produce different actions. Therefore, that statement of *De generatione*, book ii, must be understood of identity in kind but not in number. If it should be stated that time does not produce action or any aspect of action, and therefore that it can in no way be an efficient cause, but [only] the measure of duration and a totally inactive quantity, so that diversity of action will have no cause in diversity of time, but rather in the active potency which is the complete cause of action; it is replied that action, the reception of action, and motion are successive, and they are not brought forth out of the potentiality of matter, since they are not fixed things, and therefore they are not corrupted into the potentiality of matter; consequently they pass away entirely into themsleves or into nothing. Now it is understood of fixed and permanent created things that they do not pass away into pure nothingness, but this is not [true] of successive things. And an infinite distance separates pure nothingness from being, one that cannot be bridged by a finite power; therefore, after corruption, the action of a created agent cannot be renewed as numerically the same action, since every created agent is of finite power.

If it should be objected that then in those things that are generated out of the potentiality of matter the effect will be the same, since the potentiality of the matter and the potency of the agent remain the same; and consequently that in the same air the same agent, as the sun on individual artificial days,[4] despite the fact that night intervenes, would produce a species numerically the same as the one previously corrupted, since the generation of species occurs out of the potentiality of the matter; it is replied that the conclusion does not follow, because this effect is not brought about except by the action of an agent, which must be renewed, as was said, and therefore the effect is [also] renewed. But if it should be objected

quod si species esset immediatus effectus agentis, tunc posset facere
35 eandem numero secundum hanc rationem, quia eadem est potentia
materie et potentia efficientis, similiter et non dependeret ab aliquo
quod cederet in pure nichil, et ita potentia finita posset facere idem
numero; dicendum est quod impossibile est quod species sit effectus
immediatus agentis creati, nec aliquid quod de potentia materie
40 educitur, quia oportet aliquid successivum intercipi, quod de nullo
fit nec in aliquid corrumpitur, et ideo dependet iteratio effectus
ab iteratione actionis, et non potest esse unus numero, sicut nec
actu. Si vero dicatur quod tunc productio actionis et huiusmodi
successivorum erit creatio, et ita agens creatum erit creator, dicen-
45 dum est quod licet ipsa actio, et motus et tempus et passio que
sunt via in effectum, non cedunt in potentiam materie, nec ex ea
producuntur nec ex aliquo, tamen productio istorum non est creatio,
quia creatio non est successivorum secundum quod sumitur in usu,
quia non accipitur nisi respectu permanentium et rerum fixarum in
50 esse de nichilo. Et ideo bene potest successivum produci non ex aliquo
nec de potentia materie, et tamen sua productio non est creatio, nec
ipsum agens est creator, propter hoc quod actus creandi est solum
respectu permanentium producendorum ex nichilo.

   Si dicatur quod archa iam facta resolvatur et iterum coniungantur
55 partes eadem archa erit in numero et eiusdem pretii, ergo agens
finite potentie potest facere idem numero, dicendum est quod
materialia arche sunt eadem numero penitus, sed compositio partium
est alia numero quam prius, et hec compositio est forma arche quam
artifex introducit. Unde quia materia rei artificialis est substantia
60 naturalis, et forma artificialis est accidens et debile quid respectu talis
materie, ideo vulgus materiam talem magis estimat archam quam compositionem. Sed tamen unde artificiatum est, oportet quod constituatur in esse specifico per ipsam compositionem quam ars introducit,
quia ars solum introducit compositionem illam, eo quod ars non facit
65 nisi formam artificialem. Et ideo archa, unde archa est, et hoc est

   34 potest *O*   35 eandem: e. speciem *O* | hanc: eandem *A* | quia: et *B* | eadem:
e. que *B* | potentia: actio *NV*   36 potentia: eadem p. *LO* | efficientis: agentis *LO* |
et²: etiam *O* | dependunt *A*   37 caderet *O* | ita: in *L om. O*   39 *ante* agentis *scr.*
et del. A ipsius   40 educitur *LONV*: producitur *BA*   41 aliquod *L* | iteratio:
om. A   43 actu *BAN*: actus *LO* | vero: *om. L*   43–4 si . . . creator: *om. O*
44 successionis *A*   46 potentia *L* | materie: nature *B*   47 producitur *L*
48 quia . . . est: *om. O* | quia: nam *L*   49 accipitur: a. creatio *O*   52 quod: quia
B | est² *LONV*: dicitur *BA*   53 respectu: r. rerum *BA* | producendarum *BA*
54 quod: q. si *L* | facta: f. si *OA*   55 eiusdem: eadem *B* | pretii: speciei *A* (*et post*
speciei *mg. add. A*ᶜ vel eiusdem p.)   56 quod: *om. O*   57 sed: si *B*
57–8 partium . . . compositio: *om. O*   59 substantia: *om. B*   60 artificialis:

that if the species were an immediate effect of the agent, then it could (by virtue of this) produce numerically the same thing, since the potentiality of the matter and the potency of the agent are the same, and so it would not depend on anything that passes away into pure nothingness, wherefore a finite power could produce numerically the same thing; it is replied that a species could not be the immediate effect of a created agent, nor could anything that is brought forth out of the potentiality of the matter, since something successive, which comes from nothing and is corrupted into nothing, must be interrupted, and therefore the repetition of the effect depends on the repetition of the action, and because the action is not one, the effect cannot be numerically one. But if it should be said that then the production of an action and such successive things would be a creation, and thus the created agent would be a creator, we reply that although the action itself and the motion, time, and reception of influence which lead to the effect do not pass away into the potentiality of the matter, nor are they drawn forth out of it or out of anything else, nevertheless their production is not creation, since 'creation' as commonly employed is not applied to successive things, but only to permanent and fixed things [brought] into being from nothing. And therefore a successive thing can easily be produced, not from something and not out of the potentiality of matter, and yet its production is not creation, nor is the agent a creator, because the act of creation is limited to the production of permanent things out of nothing.

If it should be said that a chest that has been built, and then broken up and its parts reassembled, is numerically the same chest and of the same worth, and therefore that an agent of finite power can reproduce numerically the same thing, we reply that numerically speaking the materials of the chest are exactly the same, but their arrangement [after reconstruction] is numerically different from before, and this arrangement is the form of the chest introduced by the carpenter. Since the matter of an artificial thing is a natural substance, and the form of an artificial thing is an accident and a weak thing by comparison with such matter, the multitude therefore judges such matter, rather than its structure, to be the chest. Nevertheless, inasmuch as it is the product of art, it must be formed in specific being by the structure introduced through art, since art alone introduces that structure because art produces only artificial form. And therefore the chest, inasmuch as it is a chest (that is, inasmuch

accidentalis *NV*   61 magis: *mg. L*   63 quam: *mg. A*^{C} *om. A'*   63–4 introducit . . . ars^1: *mg. L*

unde est res artificialis, dicetur una numero vel plures per unitatem vel numerositatem compositionis et non materie arche.

PARS VI
CAPITULUM 4

Deinde queritur quarto an in aere et huiusmodi dyaphanis, quando continuatur presentia agentis super ea, utrum prima species maneat
5 continue dum agens est presens vel corrumpatur et alia renovetur, ut sic quasi infinities in die artificiali fiat species in eodem aere et corrumpatur per actionem solis. Quod vero quasi infinities corrumpatur et renovetur patet per auctores perspective; nam Alhacen in secundo et alibi determinat quod alteratio dyaphani per huiusmodi
10 species non est fixa nec permanens, sed cito generatur et cito corrumpitur.

Item hoc patet per hoc, quod cum multiplicatio lucis et collectio in eodem loco per modicam fractionem et reflexionem, ut prius exemplificatum est, inducit combustionem sensibilem, tunc longe
15 magis fieret combustio sensibilis si ab ortu solis semper maneret prima species, et intenderetur continue usque ad occasum per continuas multiplicationes, precipue ut hic non esset reflexio nec fractio talis ut in experimentis dictis; et reflexio ac fractio, precipue duplex que accidit in predictis, multum debilitant lucem. Sed a parte solis
20 non est nisi una fractio, et illa est debilis, quia variatio dyaphani in spera celesti et spera ignis non est tanta sicut est cristalli et aeris.

Item in raro est dispersio partium corporalium, et ideo species multum dispergitur et non unitur, et non colliguntur multa in parvo
25 loco, sicut in denso. Quapropter oportet quod sit debilis operationis ad sui generationem; nam sicut omnis virtus unita est fortis operationis, ut dicitur *Libro de causis*, ita omnis virtus dispersa est debilis operationis. Et ideo hec est causa quare non potest diu se conservare in raro quamvis in denso.

66 dicitur *A*   67 vel: et *O* / compositionis: *mg.* A^C comparationis *A'*
2 capitulum quartum *O*   3 quatuor *A*   4 utrum: *om. L*   5 *ante* est *scr.*
et del. A non / vel *LO*: aut *NV* an subito A^C *om. A'* spatium vacuum *B* / renovetur L^C:
removetur *BL'*   6 ut: et OA^C 6–7 ut . . . solis: *mg.* A^C *om. A'*   6 artificiali:
naturali vel a. *NV* a. eadem *LO* / eodem: *om. LO*   7 et: *om. L*   7–8 per . . .
renovetur: et r. quod nova continue generetur *L*   8 removetur *B* / auctores:
actones(*!*) *L*   9 et alibi: libro *O* / determinans *A* / *ante* quod *mg. add.* A^C dicit /
dyaphani: dyafonis non est *A*   10 non est: *om. A*   12 cum *BNV*: si *LO* est *A*
13 prius: *om. A*   14–15 tunc . . . fieret: magis tamen longe fiat(*?*) *A*   16 continue
. . . continuas: *mg.* A^C *om. A'*   17 ut: *om. L*   17–18 talis . . . fractio: *om. O*
19 *post* que *mg. add. O* cum / debilitat *O*   21 spere[1]: spereca(*!*) *L* / tanta: creata *O* / est[2]

as it is the product of art), will be called one or many in number according to the unity or multiplicity of its structure and not the unity or multiplicity of its matter.

PART VI
CHAPTER 4

Fourth, when an agent is continuously present above air and similar transparent substances, it is inquired whether the first species remains continuously as long as the agent is present or is corrupted and replaced by another species, so that during an artificial day through the action of the sun there is a virtually infinite generation and corruption of species in the same [body of] air. That species are corrupted and renewed almost infinitely is evident from authors of works on perspective; for Alhazen, in book ii and elsewhere, determines that alteration of the transparent by such species is not fixed or permanent, but that species are quickly generated and quickly corrupted.[1]

The same thing is also evident as follows: since the multiplication of light and its collection in one place by moderate refraction and reflection produces sensible combustion, as was illustrated above,[2] sensible combustion would be far stronger if the first species produced by the rising of the sun were to endure and to be continuously augmented by continuous [additional] multiplications until sunset, especially since in this case there is no reflection or refraction such as occurs in the said experiments;[3] for reflection and refraction (especially the double refraction that occurs in the aforementioned experiments) greatly weaken light. But between here and the sun there is only one refraction, and that a weak one, since the difference in transparency between the celestial sphere and the sphere of fire is not as great as between crystal and air.

Also, in a rare medium there is dispersion of the corporeal parts, and therefore a species [in that medium] is greatly dispersed and not united, and many species are not assembled in a small place, as they are in a dense medium. Therefore, the action [of such a species] in the generation of itself must be weak; for as every united power is strong in its action, as the *Liber de causis* says,[4] so every dispersed power is weak in its action. And this is why a species cannot preserve itself as long in a rare medium as in a dense medium.

BLV: et *N om. OA*   24 parvo: uno *A*^{C} *om. A'*   25 sit: sicut *A*   26 ad . . .
operationis: *om. LO* | fortioris *NV*   27 *post* operationis *add. O* et ideo *et add.*
LA et / ut . . . causis: in libro de c. dicitur *O* / ita: *om. OA* / omnis *BA*: quod *LO om. NV* |
debilioris *NV*   27-8 ut . . . operationis: *mg. A*   28 operationis: *om. O* | hec: huius
A / causa: c. una *A* / conservare: c. se *B* conservari *NV*

30   Alia causa est quia ab omni puncto aeris lucidi fit multiplicatio lucis secundum omnes diametros; et ideo quando est magna quantitas, sicut accidit in raro, quasi sine comparatione est maior dispersio speciei ab eo quam a denso; et ista multiplicatio infinita inducit debilitationem speciei, precipue cum sit in materia aliena. Et quia
35   sic debilitatur multum per actionem exteriorem, accidit quod non potest se conservare in materia in qua est; et ideo deficit in potentiam materie. Ex hiis de causis potest natura medii dyaphani specifica invalescere super speciem debilitatam, et corrumpitur statim necessario post generationem sine tempore sensibili intercepto. Sed in denso
40   potest diu manere et intendi propter rationes contrarias, ut in luna et stellis dum radiositas solis sit presens eis, quia in parvo loco multum de specie colligitur; et a parva quantitate respectu rari quod tantum haberet de substantia dispersa fit modica dispersio per multiplicationem exteriorem. Et ideo fortificatur semper species et
45   intenditur in tali denso, et non corrumpitur nisi per privationem actionis agentis. Unde luna et stelle semper lucent nisi per eclipsim. Et ideo hec est causa duplex quare densum bene retinet lucem et huiusmodi species, quia bene incorporantur in eo et non sit in raro.
      Si dicatur quod in regionibus sub cancro et alibi est magis
50   combustio aeris, et est ibi mala habitatio nec continua, ut dicit Ptolomeus *Libro de dispositione spere*, quapropter manebunt species et continuabuntur sine corruptione, dicendum est quod non oportet, quia licet corrumpantur quasi infinities ibi in die sicut hic, tamen aer ibi, propter magnam moram solis super capita eorum quasi per
55   quadraginta dies, ut dicit Ptolomeus, propter parvitatem declinationum solis et confusionem equedistantium, recipit dispositionem maiorem ad combustionem quam hic, sicut possumus videre quod propter moram solis magnam accidit in aere nostro quod prope finem octave hore et principium none est maior calor quam in sexta hora,
60   quando magis appropinquat capitibus nostris. Quamvis igitur species corrumpantur successiva, tamen quelibet relinquit ex sua presentia aliquam dispositionem caloris, et sic potest plus et plus calor augmentari propter moram solis super eundem aerem.

33 ea *A* / ista: ita *OA*   34 sit: fit *A*   35 sic: *om. LO*   36 se conservare: conservari *O* / potentiam *BLNV*: potentia *OA*   37 ex: et *A*   38 speciei debilitatam *LA* / corrumpi *O* / necessario: *mg.* A^C *om.* A' 40 luna: *N ends here*   41 sit: fit *L* 42 a: cum *A om. V*   43 fit *AV*: sit *BL* quod sit *O*   44 multitudinem *L* / semper: *obs. O*   45 per: propter *A*   46 semper: *om. A*   48 incorporantur: incorporatur *mg. L* (*correctum ex* in quo operantur) / sit: fit *B*   49 sub cancro: calidis subtiliantur *O spatium vacuum B*   50 aeris: elementaris *O*   53 infinities: in i. *A* / ibi: illic *L om. O*   54 aer: *om. A*   55 quadraginta *BA*: quatuor *LOV*   56 solis: in s. *L* / et *A*: *om. BLVO* / confusionem: *om. O* / equedistantium *OV*: equedistantiam *BLA* / *ante* dispositionem *scr. et del. A* distantiam   57 possumus: *om. LO* / videre: v. hic *A* videmus *O*   59 calor: combustio *mg. O*   60 quando *OL^C*: quoniam *L'* quia *BV* cum

Another cause is that from every point of illuminated air there is multiplication of light along all diameters;[5] and therefore when the medium is of great extent, as in a rare medium, the dispersion of a species in it is almost incomparably greater than in a dense medium;[6] and this infinite multiplication weakens the species, especially when it takes place in an alien substance. And since a species is thus greatly weakened by external action, it is not able to preserve itself in the substance in which it is; and therefore it fades away into the potentiality of the matter. Owing to these causes, the specific nature of the transparent medium can prevail over a weakened species, which is [therefore] necessarily corrupted immediately after its generation, without sensible time intervening. However, in a dense medium it can remain for a long time and be strengthened, for the opposite reasons, as in the moon and stars while the sun irradiates them, since many species are collected in a small place; and from a quantity [of the dense medium] small in comparison to that of a rare medium containing as much substance (spread out), there would be a modest dispersion by external multiplication. Therefore in such a dense medium the species is always strengthened and intensified, and it is corrupted only if deprived of the action of an agent. Thus the moon and stars always shine except during an eclipse. And these two causes explain why a dense body strongly retains light and such species, since they are strongly incorporated in it but not in a rare body.

If it should be argued that in the regions beneath [the tropic of] Cancer and elsewhere there is greater combustion of the air, and [consequently] habitation there is neither good nor continuous, as Ptolemy says in *De dispositione spere*,[7] and therefore that species will [evidently] persist and continue without corruption, we reply that this is not necessarily the case, since although species are corrupted almost infinitely during the day (there as well as here), nevertheless the air there, because of the great delay of the sun over their heads (for almost forty days, as Ptolemy says, because of the minor deviations of the sun and the merging of the parallels),[8] receives a greater disposition towards combustion than here; similarly we can see that in our air there is more heat near the end of the eighth hour and beginning of the ninth than in the sixth hour (when the sun is more nearly overhead), because of the greater duration of the sun's presence.[9] Therefore, although species are successively corrupted, each leaves behind as a result of its presence a certain disposition towards heat, and thus the heat can be more and more augmented owing to the sun remaining over the same air.

tamen sol in sexta hora *A* / magis: *mg. A^C om. A'* / nostris: *om. L*   61 corrumpuntur *B*

Si etiam dicatur quod cum rara non retinent species, sed densa,
65 tunc terra et ligna et lapides et huiusmodi deberent magis habundare
in specie lucis, et per consequens in calore, quam aer, et potest
dici quod huiusmodi densa exterius magis habent de hiis quam aer
et perspicua, ut in partibus exterioribus apparet quando tangimus ea.
Nam lapidem expositum soli magis calidum sentimus quam aerem, et
70 magis est visibilis ex presentia lucis quam aer, quia solum densum
natum est terminare visum. Sed in partibus interioribus densi non
sic est, neque quantum ad visum neque quantum ad tactum, quia
aerem percipimus visu in profundo et calorem eius sentimus, quia de
facili recipit speciem per sui profundum; sed densum non sic, quia
75 difficile recipit propter sui compactionem, licet bene retineat postquam receperit.

64 si: et *A* / etiam: et *L* / quod: *om. O* / retinet *B*   66 aere(?) *A*   66–7 potest
. . . aer: *om. O*   67 quam: quoniam *L* / aer: a. et alia *L*   70 magis: m. etiam *O*
71 exterioribus *O*   72 est: erunt *A* / neque^2 quantum^2: *mg. A^C om. A'* / quia: quoniam
O quando *L*   73 *ante* aerem *scr. et del. L* ad   74 per: pro *O* / profundo *O* / sic:
sit *L*   75 difficulter *O* / *ante* recipit *mg. add. A^C* non / recipit: r. speciem *LO*
76 receperit: recipit *O* / *post* receperit *add. O* explicit tractatus M. Rogeri Bacon de multiplicatione specierum *et scr. et del. L* Licet hoc est itelligendum in istis rebus inferioribus
corporalibus, in rebus vero incorporalibus potest bene species alia compleri in effectum completum sine destructione patientis. Natum est ad huiusmodi effectum de natura sua, ut
stelle et luna nate sunt habere lucem perfectam quem(!) exigit natura sua, licet sol plus
habeat de luce. Et tunc in principio fit species lucis usque ad lunam et stellas, et postea
completur in eis sicut fuit a prima creatione, et sicut post eclipses stellarum accidit; nam
primo debiliter habent lucem, tanquam similem(?) et speciem, et post hoc claram et completam. Cuius signum est quod luna vel in eclipsi rubia est, quia existit in umbra; et quando
est in umbra habet speciem lucis debilem que venit de luce transiunte(!) extra per latera et
fines umbre, sicut postea magis explanabitur. Verumtamen sciendum quod species solis,
que est de natura eius specifica, non potest compleri in luna et stellis, licet in eis fiat, quia
tunc oporteret lunam et stellas fieri solem, quod est impossibile. Lux enim est quantitas
communis solis(!) et stellis et igni, licet magis sit in sole; et ideo potest species lucis compleri
in luna et stellis et non species substantie solis, quia sol et luna et stelle differunt in substantia specifica, sicut posterioribus erit manifestum. Et lux non est de eorum substantia,
sed est accidens commune eis et igni, licet aliqui solebant dicere lucem esse formam substantialem solis et stellarum; sed hoc est falsum *et deinde add. L* explicit tractatus fratris
R. Bacoun de multiplicatione specierum

Also, if it should be said that since rare substances do not retain species while dense substances do, [then] earth and wood and rocks and the like should possess a greater abundance of the species of light (and consequently of heat) than air does, we can reply that such dense substances have more of these species in their exterior parts than do air and transparent substances, as is apparent when we touch their outer surfaces. For rock exposed to the sun feels hotter than air, and it is more visible in the presence of light than is air, since only a dense substance is naturally suited to terminate vision.[10] But this is not true of the interior parts of a dense substance, neither as to sight nor as to touch, since we see into the depths of air and perceive its heat, because it easily receives species in its depths; but this is not so in a dense substance, since the latter is not readily receptive owing to its compactness, although once it receives [a species] it strongly retains [that species].[11]

De speculis comburentibus

[I]

'Ex concavis speculis ad solem positis ignis accenditur.' Hec ultima propositio *Libri de speculis communibus* sic demonstratur ibidem. Esto concavum speculum ABG [fig. 40, p. 276], sol vero EDZ, et sit
5 centrum speculi T; et ab aliquo puncto superficiei solis, utpote D, trahatur linea recta per centrum T usque ad B. Incidat etiam DG radius, et reflectatur ad punctum K in linea TB. Eritque punctum K necessario inter T, quod est centrum speculi, et B punctum, qui est in eius superficie, impossibile enim est quod hic radius reflectatur ad
10 punctum T vel supra. Quod sic demonstratur. Angulus DGI, cum sit angulus minoris portionis circuli, est minor angulo recto per tricesimam tertii *Elementorum*, et ideo minor angulo DGB, cum sit angulus maioris portionis et ita maior recto per eandem. Reflectetur igitur DG radius ex parte DGB anguli. Et quia angulus reflexionis
15 est equalis angulo incidentie et angulus incidentie DGI est minor angulo semicirculi, quia est angulus minoris portionis, erit angulus reflexionis a puncto G minor angulo semicirculi. Non potest igitur DG radius reflecti ad punctum T nec supra, quia si ad punctum T reflecteretur esset angulus reflexionis angulus semicirculi; et si
20 superius quam T reflecteretur esset maior angulo semicirculi, quia esset angulus maioris portionis, quorum utrumque est impossibile, cum angulus incidentie sit angulus minoris portionis et ita necessario minor utroque. Fiet ergo necessario reflexio inter T et B, sitque punctus concursus DG radii reflexi cum linea TB punctus K.
25 Deinde sumatur BA arcus equalis BG arcui, et incidat DA. Erit igitur angulus DAB equalis angulo DGB, quia sunt anguli equalium portionum eiusdem circuli. Reflectetur ergo radius DA, et concurret cum linea TB in puncto K; et patet hoc per iam dictam demonstrationem. Similiter potest ostendi quod omnes radii incidentes ad superficiem
30 speculi et equaliter distantes a puncto B ad idem punctum in linea TB reflectuntur. Tales autem sunt omnes radii cadentes in unam circulationem circa punctum B, cuius ipse B est polus, quia a tota circulatione equedistat.

---

7 *ante* in *scr. et del.* E necessario inter *T*   9 enim: *om.* W   14 DG . . . parte: *om.* W   18 *ante* T¹ *scr. et del.* E D   20 deflecteretur W / semicirculi: *om.* E 22 maioris W   23 fiet: sed W / inter: *om.* W   24 TB punctus: DB in puncto W 26 DAB: ADB *R* ABD *E*   27 concurrunt *E*

'Fire is kindled by concave mirrors that face the sun.' This final proposition of the *Liber de speculis communibus* is there demonstrated as follows.[1] Let there be a concave mirror ABG [fig. 40, p. 277] and the sun EDZ, and let T be the centre [of curvature] of the mirror; and from some point on the surface of the sun, such as D, draw a straight line through the centre T to B. Also let ray DG be incident [on the mirror], and let it be reflected to point K on line TB. Point K will necessarily lie between T, the centre of the mirror, and point B on its surface, for it is impossible that this ray should be reflected to point T or above. This can be demonstrated as follows. Since angle DGI is the angle of a segment of a circle smaller than a semicircle,[2] it is smaller than a right angle by [Euclid's] *Elements*, iii. 30,[3] and therefore smaller than angle DGB, since the latter is the angle of a segment of a circle larger than a semicircle and therefore larger than a right angle by the same [proposition]. Therefore, ray DG is reflected through a portion of angle DGB. And since the angle of reflection is equal to the angle of incidence and the angle of incidence DGI is smaller than the angle of a semicircle (since it is the angle of a segment of a circle smaller than a semicircle), the angle of reflection from point G will be smaller than the angle of a semicircle. Therefore, ray DG cannot be reflected to point T or [any point] above it, since if it were reflected to point T the angle of reflection would be the angle of a semicircle;[4] and if it were reflected [to a point] above T the angle of reflection would be larger than the angle of a semicircle, since it would be the angle of a segment of a circle greater than a semicircle; and each alternative is impossible, since the angle of incidence is the angle of a segment of a circle smaller than a semicircle and therefore necessarily smaller than either [of the aforementioned angles]. Therefore, reflection necessarily occurs [to a point] between T and B; let the point of intersection of reflected ray DG with line TB be point K. Then take arc BA equal to arc BG, and let DA be incident [on the mirror]. Angle DAB will consequently be equal to angle DGB, since they are angles of equal segments of the same circle. Therefore, ray DA will be reflected and intersect line TB at point K; and this is evident by the above demonstration. Similarly, it can be shown that all rays incident on the surface of the mirror and equally distant from point B are reflected to the same point on line TB. Moreover, all such rays are incident on one circle about point B,[5] with B as the pole, since it is equally distant from all points of the circumference.

Quod autem soli radii incidentes ad unam circulationem circa punc-
35 tum B et circa axem TB reflectantur ad unum et eundem punctum,
ita quod radii cadentes in aliis circulationibus ad illum eundem
punctum reflecti non possint, ponendo multiplicationem lucis fieri
a sole secundum modum iam dictum, potest demonstrari ex hoc, quod
omnes radii cadentes inter punctum G et punctum B, quia faciunt
40 maiores angulos incidentie quam sit angulus DGI, quia sunt anguli
maiorum portionum quam sit portio GI, reflectentur inter K et T; et
omnes radii incidentes ad superficiem speculi, inter quorum puncta
terminalia in superficie et punctum B cadit punctus G, quia faciunt
minores angulos incidentie quam sit angulus DGI eo quod sunt anguli
45 minorum portionum quam sit portio GI, reflectentur inter K et B. Et
eodem modo potest demonstrari quod nullius circulationis radii
concurrunt ad eundem punctum ad quem concurrunt radii alterius.
Et quanto propinquius cadunt puncto B altius reflectuntur; quanto
remotius inferius. Et qui in equali distantia a puncto B incidunt ad
50 eundem punctum concurrunt. Iam ergo demonstratum est quod
omnes radii cadentes in unam circulationem circa axem speculi ad
eundem punctum reflectuntur et quod omnes radii cadentes in totam
superficiem reflectuntur super axem que est linea TB, licet ad diversa
puncta. Posito ergo combustibili in axe ubi maior est congregatio
55 luminis, et hoc est in puncto reflexionis maioris circulationis, fiet
combustio validior secundum auctorem huius opinionis. Et hec est
figura [fig. 40].

Iterum aliter demonstratur in eodem libro predicta propositio sic.
Esto speculum concavum ABG [fig. 41, *infra*], sol vero DEZ, et ab
60 aliquo puncto, ut E, per T centrum speculi transeat radius ETB; et ab
aliis, ut D et Z, transeant radii DTG et ZTA; et sic de aliis punctis
totius portionis solis transeant radii per T centrum speculi ad eius
superficiem. Et quia omnes isti radii cadunt ad angulos equales super
superficiem speculi, quia faciunt angulos semicirculorum equalium eo
65 quod transeunt per centrum, ideo quilibet reflectetur in se ipsum.
Omnes ergo concurrunt in centrum. Et intelligit etiam hic commentator quod omnes radii cadentes in totam superficiem speculi transeunt
per centrum et reflectuntur in centrum, quod patet ex verbis suis,
dicit enim concludendo 'omnes radii coincidunt super eos qui per
70 centrum et in centro radios. Radiis ergo calefactis ignis accenditur;

34 quod: quia *W*   36-7 ita . . . punctum: *mg. R*   38 iam: tam *E*
39 intra *W*   · 41 proportionum *R* / T: C *W*   44-5 quam . . . portionum: *om. W*
47 que *E*   48 quanto[1]: quarto *E*   51 circa: *om. W*   51-2 unam . . . in: *om. E*
52 et quod: quia *W*   53 ad: a *W*   54 in axe: *ex* maxime *mg. corr. W*
56 validiorum *W* / hoc *E*   58 iterum: item *W*   59 DEZ: de Z *E*   61 DTG:
DEG *W*   62 ad eius: per *W*   66 concurrunt: reflectuntur *W* / intelligere *RE*
67 quod: quia *W*   68 quod: quia *W* / suis: eius *W*   69 concidunt *W*

That solar rays incident on one circle about point B and axis TB are reflected to one and the same point, so that rays incident on other circles cannot be reflected to that same point (if we assume the multiplication of light to take place from the sun in the aforesaid manner), can be demonstrated from the fact that all rays falling between point G and point B are reflected [to a point] between K and T, since they form angles of incidence [with the mirror] larger than angle DGI because they are the angles of segments [of a circle] larger than segment GI;[6] and that all rays incident on the surface of the mirror [outside G] (point G lying between point B and the periphery of the mirror) are reflected [to a point] between K and B, since they form angles of incidence smaller than angle DGI because they are the angles of segments [of a circle] smaller than GI. And in the same manner it can be demonstrated that rays from no two circles converge to the same point [on the axis]. And as they fall closer to point B they are reflected [to a] higher [point]; as they fall further from point B, [to a] lower [point]. And those incident at an equal distance from point B converge at the same point. It has already been demonstrated that all rays falling on a given circle about the axis of the mirror are reflected to the same point and that all rays falling on the whole surface are reflected on to the axis, line TB, although to different points. Therefore, if a combustible object is placed on the axis at a point of greater confluence of light—that is, at the point of reflection of a larger circle—combustion will take place more vigorously, according to the author of this opinion. And here is the figure [fig. 40].

On the other hand, the foregoing proposition is demonstrated in a different manner in the same book, as follows.[7] Let there be a concave mirror ABG [fig. 41, below] and the sun DEZ, and from some point, such as E, a ray ETB passes through the centre of the mirror; and from other points, such as D and Z, pass rays DTG and ZTA; and so from [all] other points on the entire surface of the sun [facing the mirror] rays pass through the centre of the mirror, T, to its surface. And since all of these rays fall on the surface of the mirror at equal angles,[8] since they form angles of equal semicircles[9] because they pass through the centre, each is therefore reflected back on itself. Therefore, all intersect at the centre. And this commentator understands also that all rays falling on the whole surface of the mirror pass through its centre and are reflected [back] to the centre, and this is evident from his words, for he says in conclusion that 'all rays coincide with those rays that [pass] through the centre and [back] to the centre. Therefore, when [things at the centre are] heated by rays, fire is kindled;

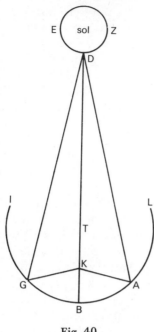

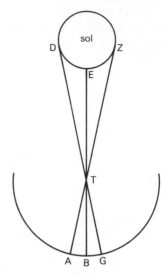

Fig. 40   Fig. 41

quare in eis stupa posita accendetur.' Et hec est figura [fig. 41]. Hoc
etiam est hic intelligendum quod predicta propositio habet intelligi
de speculis concavis spericis.

[II]

Sed quia in prima dictarum demonstrationum duo supponuntur,
scilicet, quod multiplicatio lucis solis fit ab aliquo uno puncto sue
superficiei ad omnia puncta superficiei totius speculi, et quod hec lux
5 dicto modo multiplicata per reflexionem sive per concursum multorum
radiorum, qui concursus accidit per reflexionem a superficie speculi,
sic figurati ut preostensum est, causat combustionem quam videmus
fieri per huiusmodi specula; ideo primo videatur de multiplicatione
radiosa, si taliter fieri possit; deinde, dato quod sic, utrum aliter quam
10 dicto modo possit fieri multiplicatio speciei radiose; tertio, dato
quod possit, que istarum multiplicationum sit principalior et magis
precipua ac fortioris actionis, tam univoce quam equivoce, utpote
illuminationis et calefactionis; quarto, utrum combustio quam videmus

71 quare: quia *W* / eis: eius *E* / accenditur *W* / hec: hoc *E* / hoc: hic *W*   72 hic:
om. W
3 fit: sit *W* / uno: *om. W*   6 radiorum: *om. W*   7 figuratam *E*   8 primum *W*

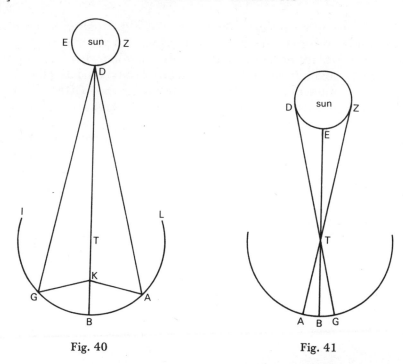

Fig. 40   Fig. 41

wherefore if oakum is placed there it will be ignited.'[10] And here is the figure [fig. 41]. It is to be understood, however, that the foregoing proposition is, applicable [only] to concave spherical mirrors.

[II]

But since in the first of the above demonstrations two things are assumed, namely that the multiplication of light from the sun takes place from any one point on its surface to all points on the surface of the whole mirror, and that this light multiplied in the said manner by reflection or by the convergence of many rays (occurring through reflection from the surface of the mirror, shaped as described above) causes the combustion that we see produced by such mirrors; therefore, it must first be seen whether multiplication by means of rays can occur in such a manner; then, given that it can, whether multiplication of radiant species can occur in any other way; third, given that it can, which of these multiplications is foremost and more important and of stronger action, both univocally and equivocally, namely, in illumination and in heating; fourth, whether the combustion that we see produced by such

fieri per huiusmodi specula concava possit principaliter causari a
15 multiplicatione primo dicta, an potius et efficacius alia via.

De primo ostenditur quod multiplicatio in dicta demonstratione
supposita sit possibilis et actualiter facta sic. Sit sol AB [fig. 42],
et sit punctus multiplicans speciem B, speculum vero CDE; et ducatur FBG contingens corpus solis in puncto B. Arguatur igitur sic:
20 oculus existens in quolibet puncto totius superficiei CDE videt
punctum B, quia a B puncto ad omnia illa puncta possibile est ducere
lineas rectas extra lineam contingentie et corpus solis. Et quia multiplicatio speciei radiose et visio fiunt per lineas rectas in eodem
medio, necesse est quod a B puncto ad omnia illa puncta fiat lucis

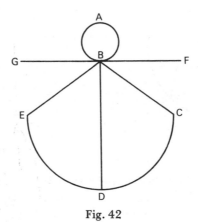

Fig. 42

25 principalis seu primarie multiplicatio, quia visio luminosi non fit
sine luce primaria ab ipso ad oculum multiplicata. Ex quo patet
quod non solum fit multiplicatio lucis ad omnia puncta superficiei
speculi a puncto B, sed ad omnia puncta medii ad que a puncto
B possibile est rectas lineas ducere; et hec sunt omnia puncta medii
30 extra lineam contingentem corpus solis in puncto B una cum omnibus
punctis illius linee contingentis. Nec ad plura puncta medii potest
a B puncto multiplicatio fieri, quia inter lineam contingentie et
circulum vel speram quam contingit non potest duci recta nisi secans
speram vel circulum, sicut patet ex quinta decima tertii *Elementorum.*
35   Ex iam dicta demonstratione statim sequitur aliud, et est secundum,
scilicet quod non solum ab uno puncto superficiei solis, sed ab omni
puncto totius portionis solis, que portio a quolibet puncto superficiei

14 huiusmodi: *om. W*   17 facta: *om. W*   19 FBG: linea FBG *W*   21 a:
ab *E*   23 in: et *E*   24 modo *E* / a B: ab *E*   27 fit: sit *W*   28 ad que:
atque *W*   31 ad plura: *om. E*   32 a B: ab *E*   34 ex: *om. R*   36 puncto:
rep. W

concave mirrors can be caused principally by the first-mentioned [mode of] multiplication, or more powerfully and efficaciously in some other way.

Concerning the first [of these matters], it is shown as follows that the multiplication supposed in the aforementioned demonstration is possible and actual.[1] Let the sun be AB [fig. 42], the point multiplying species B, and the mirror CDE; and draw FBG tangent to the body of the sun at point B. It is then argued that if the eye is situated at any point of the entire surface CDE it sees point B, since it is possible to draw straight lines (outside the line of tangency and the body of the sun) from point B to all those points. And since both

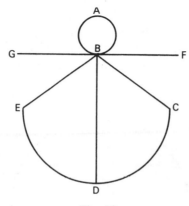

Fig. 42

vision and the multiplication of radiant species occur along straight lines in a single medium, it is necessary that multiplication of the principal or primary light take place from point B to all those points, since vision of a luminous body cannot occur without the multiplication of primary light from that body to the eye. From this it is evident that multiplication of light from point B occurs not only to all points on the surface of the mirror, but to all points in the medium to which straight lines can be drawn from point B; and these are all points of the medium outside the line tangent to the body of the sun at point B, together with all points of that tangent line. Nor can multiplication occur from B to other points of the medium, since a straight line cannot be drawn between the tangent line and the circle or sphere to which it is tangent without intersecting the sphere or circle, as is evident from *Elements*, iii. 15.[2]

From this demonstration another follows at once, and it is the second, namely, that not only from one point on the surface of the sun, but from every point of the entire portion of the sun that can be

speculi potest comprehendi, venit species radiosa ad totam superficiem speculi et ad omnia puncta illius superficiei; nec solum ad
40 hec, sed ad omnia puncta totius medii. Quod sic probatur: designetur sol notis ABCD [fig. 43, *infra*], et ponamus quod sol sit quasi in
centro totius medii in quo potest lux multiplicari, quod medium
designetur litteris EFGH. Et sit speculum MGN ubique in medio. Dato
igitur quolibet puncto speculi, ducantur ab ipso linee contingentes
45 corpus solis, quot possibile est educi; et sit gratia exempli punctus
ille G et linee contingentes GC GD. Patet ergo quod a quolibet puncto
totius portionis CD ad punctum G pervenit radius unus, quippe cum
quilibet punctus totius portionis CD sit visibilis a puncto G; visio
autem non fit sine specie visibili ad visum multiplicata. Et sicut
50 est de G, sic est de omni puncto totius superficiei speculi, immo
etiam totius medii tam sub quam supra secundum omnem differentiam situs et positionis, sicut patet applicando dictam demonstrationem ad omnia puncta data, tam in speculo quam in medio. Et hec
est figura [fig. 43]. Et per hanc figuram superficialem intelligatur

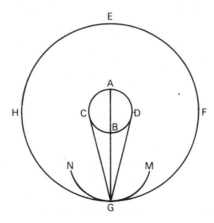

Fig. 43

55 demonstratio in corpore, quoniam eadem est, quod patet secando
corpora per superficies planas.
   Per eandem etiam demonstrationem patet quod ad totam superficiem speculi et ad omnia puncta eius veniunt radii qui, si ducerentur
in profundum corporis solis, transirent per centrum eius; quoniam si
60 corpus solis totum preter eius centrum esset pervium et esset eius

38 *ante* speculi *scr. et del.* R est / speculo E   41 quasi: *om.* R   43 ubicunque W
44 quodlibet R   45 quot: quas W   49 fit: sit W / visibilis RE   52 et: seu W
53 hoc E   57 etiam: *om.* W   59 quoniam: quod W

perceived from any point on the surface of the mirror, comes a radiant species to the whole surface of the mirror and to all points on that surface; and not only to these, but to all points of the entire medium. This can be proved as follows: let the sun be designated by letters ABCD [fig. 43, below], and place it roughly in the centre of the whole medium in which light can be multiplied; and let this medium be designated by letters EFGH. And let there be a mirror MGN anywhere in the medium. Then take any point of the mirror and from it draw lines tangent to the body of the sun, as many as can be drawn; for example, let the point be G and the tangent lines GC and GD. It is evident, therefore, that one ray comes to point G from each point of the whole portion CD, since in fact every point of the whole portion CD is visible from point G; and vision does not occur without multiplication of a visible species to the eye. And what is true of G is true of every point on the entire surface of the mirror, and indeed in the entire medium, both above and below according to every different location and position, as is evident by

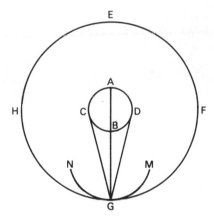

Fig. 43

applying the above demonstration to every point of the mirror and the medium. And this is the figure [fig. 43]. And from this two-dimensional figure one can understand the demonstration in three dimensions, since it is the same thing, as becomes obvious if you cut the [three-dimensional] bodies with plane surfaces.

It is evident from the same demonstration that to the whole sur-face of the mirror and to each of its points come rays which, if they were extended into the interior of the sun, would pass through its centre; since, if the entire body of the sun apart from its centre were

centrum sufficienter densum pro terminatione visus, ab omnibus
punctis speculi posset centrum solis videri, quia inter quelibet duo
puncta in medio pervio potest extendi multiplicatio speciei radiose
super lineam rectam, sicut patet ex prima petitione et ex natura multi-
65 plicationis in eodem medio. Et hoc probamus per effectum sensibilem
in visu. Quare cum inter superficiem solis et superficiem speculi sit
totum medium pervium, necesse est quod ad totam superficiem
speculi veniant radii qui, si ducerentur in profundum solis, transirent
per eius centrum. Et quia omnium radiorum multiplicatorum a super-
70 ficie corporis sperici ad aliquem punctum datum, ille est omnium
brevissimus qui, si duceretur in profundum spere, transiret per centrum, sicut patet per octavam tertii *Elementorum* Euclidis, ut patet in
figura supraposita [fig. 43], radius enim BG est brevissimus omnium
qui a tota portione DC possunt multiplicari ad idem punctum G, est
75 ergo fortioris actionis quam aliquis aliorum, tum quia agens secundum
punctum B propinquius est patienti quam secundum aliquod aliorum
punctorum superficiei a quibus ceteri radii ad punctum G multiplicantur, tum quia totum profundum corporis solis, scilicet AB diameter
solis, correspondet radio BG, omnibus vero aliis radiis ad punctum G
80 terminatis correspondet minus de profundo corporis solis, quia radiis
contingentibus nichil correspondet eo quod si producerentur in
continuum et directum non ingrederentur corpus solis. Et ideo hii
sunt omnibus et singulis aliis debiliores ex hac causa, et etiam ex
alia scilicet ex magna distantia, quia puncta C D contingentie maxime
85 distant a puncto G, et hoc patet per eandem octavam tertii. Et
hoc demonstratur specialiter vicesima secunda propositione *Libri
de visu*, que dicit longior radius ad speram proveniens quasi linea
contingens erit. Ceteri autem, qui sunt inter radios contingentes
et radium brevissimum, sunt tanto fortioris actionis quanto plus
90 brevissimo appropinquant, ex predicta duplici causa, quia scilicet
sunt aliis remotioribus breviores, ut proponit ante dicta octava
tertii, et quia plus de profundo corporis correspondet eis; et ideo
plus de virtute activa est in hiis radiis quam in aliis.

  Ex iam dictis etiam sequitur ulterius, tertium: quod alius modus
95 multiplicationis lucis ab illo quem supposuit prima demonstratio est
principalior et efficacior; quia secundum illam positionem ad unum
punctum speculi non venit nisi unus radius, quia inter duo puncta
solum una linea recta potest extendi, et radius solum multiplicatur

61 densum: *mg.* W / pro terminatione: *correxi ex* per terminatione *RE* penetratione *W*
66 quare: quia *E* / superficiem²: *om.* W   74 a: *om. E* / est: et *E*   75 quam aliquis:
om. W   76 B: G *W om. E*   78 totum: *om.* W   80 minus: *verbum ignotum W*
82 ingredirentur *RE* / hiis *W*   86 libro *W*   87 veniens *W*   91 ponit *W* / octava:
scilicet *W*   92 respondet *W*   94 etiam: *om.* W / quod: quia *W*   98 solum¹:
sola *W*

transparent and its centre were sufficiently dense to terminate sight, the centre of the sun could be seen from all points of the mirror, since between any pair of points in a transparent medium the multi-plication of a radiant species can be extended along a straight line, as is evident from the first assumption [above] and from the nature of multiplication in a single medium. And we prove this by a sensible effect in vision. Therefore, since the entire medium between the surface of the sun and the surface of the mirror is transparent, it is necessary that to the entire surface of the mirror come rays which, if they were admitted to the interior of the sun, would pass through its centre. And since of all the rays multiplied from the surface of a spherical body to a given point, that one is shortest which, if it were admitted to the interior of the sphere, would pass through its centre (as is evident from Euclid's *Elements*, iii. 8,[3] and as can be seen in the figure above [fig. 43], for ray BG is the shortest of all rays that can be multiplied to point G from the whole portion DC), it is therefore stronger in its action than any other—both because at point B the agent is nearer the recipient than at any other point on the surface [of the sun] from which rays are multiplied to point G, and because to ray BG corresponds the entire thickness of the sun (that is, its diameter, AB), whereas to all other rays terminated at point G corre-sponds less thickness of the body of the sun, since for the tangent rays there is no corresponding thickness, because if they were ex-tended directly and continuously they would not enter the body of the sun. And therefore, for this reason, these latter are weaker than any and all others; and also for the other reason, namely, great distance, since points of tangency C and D are at maximum distance from point G, as is evident by the same [proposition] iii. 8. And this is specifically demonstrated in proposition 22 of *Liber de visu*, which says that 'the longest ray coming to a sphere will be the tangent line'.[4] However, the others, which are between the tangent rays and the shortest ray, are stronger in their action in proportion to their approach to the shortest ray for the aforementioned two reasons: because they are shorter than more remote rays, as the aforementioned [proposition] iii. 8 declares, and because a greater thickness of the [solar] body corresponds to them; and therefore there is more active virtue in these rays than in the others.

From the demonstrations already presented there follows another, the third: that another mode of the multiplication of light, different from that supposed by the first demonstration, is more basic and more efficacious; for, according to that [first] supposition, to one point on the mirror comes only one ray, since between two points only one straight line can be drawn, and a ray is multiplied only

super lineam rectam in eodem medio. Sed punctus multiplicans lucem
100 est unus secundum dictam positionem; ergo ab ipso ad unum punctum
speculi non veniet nisi unus radius. Verbi gratia in figura [fig. 44]
ad punctum C non veniet a puncto B nisi radius BC solus. Sed prius
demonstratum est quod ad punctum C veniunt infiniti radii alii,
utpote omnes qui possunt multiplicari a tota portione ABD. Sed
105 infiniti sunt fortiores uno; ceterum unus istorum infinitorum aliorum
a radio BC, ut EC, est fortior et efficacior in agendo quam BC, quia
est eo brevior per octavam tertii *Elementorum*, cum tendat in centrum,
quia etiam plus ⟨habet⟩ de virtute activa radius EC, scilicet tota

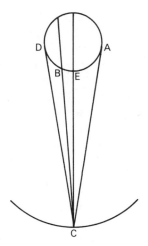

Fig. 44

diameter, quod non accidit in BC. Et quia tales infiniti radii
110 breviores et fortiores incidunt ad superficiem speculi, ut prius
ostensum est (nam ad quodlibet punctum speculi incidit unus radius
a centro solis, et secundum dictam propositionem ad solum unum
punctum speculi incidit radius unus a centro, quia ab uno puncto
superficiei solis non potest duci nisi una linea recta ad centrum, et
115 punctus multiplicans lucem est tantum unus et hoc in superficie
solis, ut ponit hec positio), ideo necesse est lucem multiplicatam
ad speculum secundum dictam positionem esse debilioris actionis
luce aliter multiplicata, dato etiam quod a solo centro solis fieret
multiplicatio. Et superius ostensum fuit quod non solum a centro

102-3 veniet . . . C: *om. W*   105 ceterum: centrum *E* / aliorum: *om. W*
106 ut: ut est *W*   107 elementorum: elementorum Euclidis *W*   108 radius EC
scilicet: *correxi ex* s. radium et *W* radium EC s. *RE*   112 solis: *ex* solus *corr. W*
116 ideo: *om. W*

along a straight line in a single medium. And according to the said view there is only one point multiplying light; therefore from it to one point on the mirror will come only one ray. For example, in the figure [fig. 44] only ray BC comes from point B to point C. But it was previously demonstrated that to point C comes an infinity of other rays, namely, all those that can be multiplied from the entire portion ABD. And an infinity [of rays] is stronger than one; besides, one ray of that infinity of others, for example EC, is able to act more strongly and efficaciously than BC, since it is shorter than BC by *Elements*, iii. 8 (because it extends to the centre), and also because

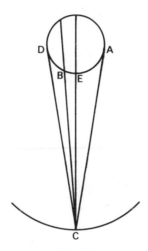

Fig. 44

ray EC has more active virtue, [because it represents a greater thickness of the sun,] namely, the whole diameter, which BC does not. And because such an infinity of shorter and stronger rays is incident on the surface of the mirror, as was shown above—for each point of the mirror receives one ray from the centre of the sun, while according to the stated proposition only one point of the mirror receives a ray from the centre, since from one point on the surface of the sun to its centre only one straight line can be drawn, and according to this view only one point (this on the surface of the sun) multiplies light—therefore, light multiplied to the mirror in the stated manner [light being assumed to emanate from only one point on the sun's surface] must act more weakly than light multiplied in another way (multiplication being assumed to take place only from the centre of the sun). However, it was shown above that multiplication to each point of the mirror does not take

120 fit multiplicatio ad quodlibet punctum speculi; sed etiam a tota
    portione solis, que continet puncta infinita, egrediuntur infiniti
    alii radii. Ideo necesse est quod sine comparatione sit multiplicatio
    quam ponit predicta positio debilior aliis multiplicationibus, que
    iam dicte sunt.

125   Ceterum de numero infinitorum radiorum a tota portione solis ad
    quodlibet punctum speculi incidentium, exclusis omnibus a centro
    solis exeuntibus, sunt infiniti fortiores multiplicati ad omnem punc-
    tum speculi quam sint radii ab unico puncto solis ad quodcunque
    punctum speculi secundum dictam positionem multiplicati, quia sunt
130 breviores illis et plus de profundo solis eis correspondet quam aliis.
    Et hec omnia patent in figura [fig. 45]. Sit enim A centrum solis,

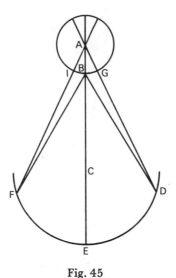

Fig. 45

B punctus in superficie solis multiplicans lucem secundum dictam
positionem, centrum speculi C, et eius superficies DEF. Patet quidem quod ad omnia et singula puncta speculi ad que a puncto B
135 potest duci linea recta potest et ad illa eadem omnia et singula a
    puncto A similiter duci. Et sunt singule harum inter superficiem
    solis et speculum singulis reliquarum breviores, ut patet ex octava
    tertii *Elementorum.* Et ideo sunt fortiores aliis, ut preostensum
    fuit duplici de causa superius expressa, ut DG radius est brevior
140 BD radio et similiter IF est brevior BF. Nec solum pervenit ad D
    radius DG brevior radio DB, sed ab omnibus punctis inter G et B (et

120 fit: sic *W*   125 a . . . portione: ad totam portionem *W*   127 infiniti *W'*:
infinities *mg. W^c*   128 unico: uno *W*   134 ad que: atque *W*
139 fuit: est *W*

place only from the centre; rather, from the whole portion of the sun, which contains an infinity of points, issues an infinity of other rays. Therefore, the multiplication posited by the foregoing view must be incomparably weaker than the other multiplications described.[5]

As for the infinity of rays from the whole portion of the sun incident on each point of the mirror, excluding all those issuing from the centre of the sun, there is an infinity of them multiplied to each point of the mirror, [each one] stronger than the rays from the single point of the sun multiplied to each point of the mirror in the stated manner,[6] since they are shorter than the latter and more thickness of the sun corresponds to them than to the latter. And all these things are evident in the figure [fig. 45]. For let A be the centre of the

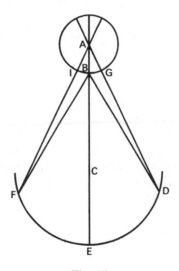

Fig. 45

sun, B the point on the surface of the sun multiplying light in the stated manner, C the centre of [curvature of] the mirror, and DEF its surface. Now it is evident that to each individual point of the mirror to which a straight line can be drawn from point B, a line can similarly be drawn from point A. And lines of the latter sort, [or that portion of them falling] between the surface of the sun and the mirror, are shorter than the others, as is evident from *Elements*, iii. 8. And they are therefore stronger than the others, as was shown above by the two causes there described, for ray DG is shorter than ray BD, and similarly IF than BF. And ray DG is not the only ray coming to D that is shorter than ray DB, for such [shorter] rays come from all points between G and B (and

a totidem citra), que sunt infinita in superficie sperica solis. Et
hoc demonstratur per eandem octava tertii, nam radii brevissimo
propiores sunt ceteris remotioribus breviores, ut in eiusdem octava
145 penultima parte proponitur. Unde ad quodlibet punctum superficiei
speculi, excepto puncto E, perveniunt infiniti radii alii a radiis
transeuntibus per centrum solis, quorum quilibet est brevior radio
ducto a B puncto multiplicationis secundum dictam positionem ad
punctum illud, sicut per eandem octavam pluries repetitam manifeste
150 demonstratur.

Ex quibus omnibus convincitur quod predicta positio insufficiens
est et nimis diminuta, tam ratione multiplicationis quam ratione
combustionis. Ratione quidem multiplicationis deficit nimis, quia
ut preostensum est infinities infiniti radii ad superficiem speculi
155 multiplicantur, de quibus non fit mentio in dicta positione; et tamen
omnes reflectuntur a superficie speculi ad locum combustionis, sicut
fide oculata experimur. Ratione etiam combustionis nimium deficit,
quia ut prius satis diffuse dictum est infinities infiniti fortiores
quam sint radii secundum modum illius positionis multiplicati per-
160 veniunt ad superficiem speculi, qui omnes ad locum combustionis
reflexi in parvum locum congregantur, utpote infra latitudinem unius
denarii, quod fide oculata probamus, ut predictum est. Et patet ex
hoc quod tota lux a superficie speculi paulatim et gradatim coartata
pervenit ad locum combustionis, in quo est maxima coartatio que
165 potest per talem figuram (scilicet spericam) aliqualiter causari,
quoniam ab illo loco et citra et ultra est maior lucis latitudo.

[III]

Quod etiam principalis et precipua multiplicatio lucis fiat a tota
portione solis et non ab aliquo uno puncto potest probari manifeste
per umbras omnium rerum, quoniam umbra cuiuslibet rei minoris sole
5 concurrit in conum pyramidis. Hoc manifeste patet in umbra terre,
cuius conus terminatur ultra speram lune. Quod autem umbra terre
sit pyramidalis figure potest sic demonstrari: quoniam multiplicatio

142 solum *W*   143 brevissimi *R*   144 propinquiores *W* / breviores *W'*: longiores
RE et mg. W^c / eadem *W* / octave *R* igitur *E*   145 penultime *R*   146 speculi:
mg. W   149 octavam: *om. W*   151 convincitur: demonstratur *W* / insufficiens:
ex sufficiens *mg. corr. R*   154 infinities: inferiores *W*   157 ocultata *E*
161 intra *W*   163 a: *om. E*   165 *post* spericam *scr. et del. E* taliter

from equally many points on the other side [of G]), and these are infinitely numerous on the spherical surface of the sun. And this is demonstrated by the same [proposition] iii. 8, for rays nearer the shortest ray are shorter than more remote rays, as is shown in the penultimate part of the eighth [proposition] of the same [book].[7] Thus to each point on the surface of the mirror except point E comes an infinity of rays besides those passing through the centre of the sun, each shorter than the ray drawn to that point from the point of multiplication B in the stated manner, as is manifestly demonstrated by the same often-cited eighth [proposition].

All of this clearly shows that the aforesaid position [which assumes the primary multiplication of light to take place from a single point of the surface of the luminous body] is insufficient and defective, both with respect to multiplication and with respect to combustion. It is defective with respect to multiplication because, as was shown above, the number of rays multiplied to the surface of the mirror is infinitely infinite, concerning which there is no mention in the said position; and all are reflected by the surface of the mirror to the place of combustion, as we know by the testimony of the eyes. It is defective also with respect to combustion because, as was stated quite fully above, rays infinitely infinite in number, stronger than the rays multiplied in the defined manner, reach the surface of the mirror; and, having been reflected to the place of combustion, all of them are gathered in a small place narrower than a denarius; and this we prove by the testimony of the eyes, as was said above. And it is evident from this that all the light from the surface of the mirror is gradually contracted until it reaches the place of combustion, where it has the maximum contraction producible in any way by [a mirror of] such a figure (that is, spherical), for before and behind that point the light occupies a wider space.[8]

[III]

That the principal and most important multiplication of light takes place from the whole portion of the sun and not from any one point can be clearly proved from the shadows of all things, since the shadow of anything smaller than the sun converges to a conical[1] vertex. This is clearly evident in the shadow of the earth, the vertex of which terminates beyond the sphere of the moon. That the shadow of the earth has a conical figure can be demonstrated from the fact that the multiplication of the solar light

166 quoniam . . . citra: *mg. W*

3 uno: *om. W*   6 quod: quoniam *W*   7 figure: *mg. R*

lucis solaris que contiguatur umbre aut fit per lineas equedistantes,
quod esse non potest, quoniam tunc, luna existente in altero nodorum
10 (scilicet capitis vel caude draconis), contingeret ipsam eclipsari
per unum diem naturalem et plus satis, quod est impossibile. Consequentia sic declaratur: umbra terre ex ypotesi continetur lineis
equedistantibus. Ergo diameter umbre in omni loco est equalis diametro terre per tricesimam quartam primi *Elementorum*, ut patet in
15 figura [fig. 46]. Sit AB diameter terre; umbra vero contineatur AC et

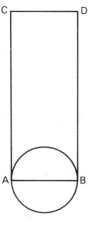

Fig. 46

BD lineis equedistantibus et equalibus. Patet ergo quod CD est equalis
AB per illam tricesimam quartam. Et sic demonstratur ubique. Diameter vero terre continet diametrum lune trigesies nonies et plus, ut
demonstratur in *Almagesti*. Et diameter lune occupat de orbe signorum
20 dimidium gradum et plus, sicut in eodem libro demonstratur. Ergo ex
ypotesi sequitur quod diameter umbre continet diametrum lune trigesies nonies. Ergo centrum corporis lune in pertranseundo diametrum
umbre pertransibit undeviginti gradus et dimidium. Sed tot gradus non
potest transire in die naturali per motum proprium, cum solum
25 transeat tredecim gradus vel parum plus, sicut patet ex *Almagesti*.
Staret ergo in umbra per unum diem et satis amplius. Et sic patet
dicta consequentia.

Si vero umbra non contineatur lineis equedistantibus, tunc necessario continebitur lineis que in aliqua duarum partium ducte, scilicet

9 quoniam: quia *W*   11 naturalem: *om. W*   12 declaratur: probatur *W*
13 umbre: u. ex ypothesi *W*   15 continetur *R*   17 quartam: q. primi *E* / *circa*
ubique *mg. add. R* 33 primi si summitatibus(?) duarum linearum equedistantium equalis
quantitatis alie linee coniungantur utrobique equales et equedistantes erunt   18 diameter *E*   21 umbre: u. terre *W*   25 vel: et *W*   28 continetur *W*

bordering on the shadow must occur either along parallel lines [or along converging lines];[2] but not the former, since, if that were so, when the moon is at one of its nodes (that is, at the head or the tail of the dragon),[3] it would be eclipsed for well over a natural day, which is impossible. This conclusion is proved as follows. Let us hypothesize that the shadow of the earth is contained within parallel lines. The diameter of the shadow is then everywhere equal to the diameter of the earth, by *Elements*, i. 34,[4] as is evident in the figure

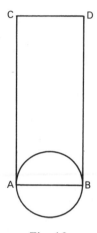

Fig. 46

[fig. 46]. Let AB be the diameter of the earth; the shadow is then contained between the parallel and equal lines AC and BD. It is evident, therefore, that CD is equal to AB by that thirty-fourth [proposition]. And thus it is demonstrated everywhere. Now the diameter of the earth contains the diameter of the moon more than thirty-nine times, as the *Almagest* demonstrates.[5] And the diameter of the moon occupies more than half a degree of the zodiac, as the same book demonstrates.[6] Therefore, by hypothesis, it follows that the diameter of the [earth's] shadow contains the diameter of the moon thirty-nine times. Accordingly, the centre of the lunar body, in passing through the diameter of the shadow, will pass through 19½°. But the moon cannot move that many degrees in a natural day by its proper motion, since it moves only 13° or a little more, as is evident from the *Almagest*.[7] It would thus remain in the shadow for well over a day. And thus the stated conclusion is evident.

But if the shadow is not enclosed within parallel lines, then it must be enclosed within lines which, if extended indefinitely, converge on one side or the other—that is, before or beyond the umbrageous

30 citra umbrosum vel ultra, secundum quantitatem indefinitam concurrent. Si vero concurrunt citra umbrosum, hoc erit necessario vel
in luminoso, utpote si a puncto uno fieret multiplicatio, secundum
quod ponit predicta positio. Et tunc necesse est umbram ultra umbrosum continue dilatari, et accideret ex hoc impossibile satis maius
35 impossibili iam preconcluso ex suppositione equedistantie, sicut
patet in figura exterius [fig. 47]. Et quilibet hoc de facili ymaginatur.

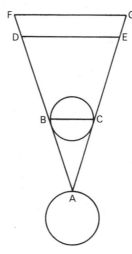

Fig. 47

Sit enim A punctus luminosi a quo lux multiplicetur principaliter,
ut supponit predicta positio. Et sit BC diameter corporis umbrosi
vel opaci. Patet quidem ad sensum quod umbra per continuum
40 discessum ab opaco continue dilatatur. Et hanc experientiam sensibilem confirmat ratio demonstrativa sumpta ex secunda sexti *Elementorum*, quoniam per secundam sexti proportio AB et AD est sicut BC
ad DE, adiuvante permutata proportione. Et per eandem proportio AD
ad AF est sicut DE ad FG, arguendo ut prius ex secunda sexti et per-
45 mutata proportione; vel per solam quartam sexti patet idem, ponendo
BC et DE et FG esse equedistantes, quoniam per vicesimam nonam
primi et quartam sexti arguetur tunc illos triangulos esse similes et
habere latera proportionalia. Sed AB est minor AD et AD minor AF
per conceptionem. Ergo BC erit minor DE et DE minor FG; et hoc
50 est propositum.
    Si vero concursus fiat extra luminosum et retro, utpote si diameter
portionis luminosi a qua fit multiplicatio esset minor diametro

30 umbrosum: *om. W*   31 hec *R*   35 iam: *mg. W* / suppositione:
ex presuppositione *corr. R*   39 vel: seu *W*   40 distensum *R*   51 extra *W*
ultra *RE*

body. If they converge before the umbrageous body, this must be either on the luminous body (multiplication would then take place from a single point, as the aforementioned position posits),[8] [or outside the luminous body]. And then [in the former case], the shadow would necessarily spread out continuously beyond the umbrageous body, and from this would follow impossible consequences even worse than the impossible consequences previously drawn from

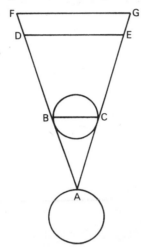

Fig. 47

the supposition of parallclism,[9] as is visibly evident[10] in the figure [fig. 47]. And all of this is easily imagined. For let A be the point of the luminous body from which light is principally multiplied, as the aforementioned position supposes. And let BC be the diameter of the opaque or umbrageous body. It is evident to sense that as the shadow retreats continuously from the opaque body it is continuously spread out. And this sensible experience is confirmed by the demonstrative argument taken from *Elements*, vi. 2,[11] since by that proposition (with the help of a permuted proportion) the ratio of AB to AD is as BC to DE. And by the same [proposition] the ratio of AD to AF is as DE to FG, arguing as before from [*Elements*,] vi. 2, and a permuted proportion; or the same thing is evident from [*Elements*,] vi. 4 alone, if BC, DE, and FG are assumed to be parallel, since it is then argued by i. 29 and vi. 4[12] that those triangles are similar and have proportional sides. But, by assumption, AB is smaller than AD and AD smaller than AF. Therefore, BC will be smaller than DE and DE smaller than FG; and this is what we proposed.

If convergence should occur outside and behind the luminous body —that is, if the diameter of the portion of the luminous body from which multiplication takes place were smaller than the diameter of

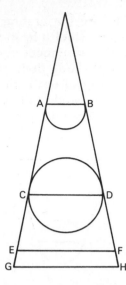

Fig. 48

corporis opaci, sequitur idem inconveniens; et per easdem propositiones demonstratur, et patet extra in figura [fig. 48]. Sit AB corda
55 portionis multiplicantis lucem, CD diameter opaci; arguatur ut prius.

Ex quo igitur umbra non potest contineri lineis equedistantibus
nec lineis concurrentibus in partem corporis luminosi, supponendo
luminosum esse maius, sicut est in proposito, quoniam sol est multo
maior terra. Et per consequens omni opaco super terram erecto necesse
60 est quod sequatur tertium, scilicet umbram contineri lineis concurrentibus ultra opacum et terminatis in conum pyramidis. Hoc autem
non solum potest demonstrari per impossibile, ut iam est demonstratum, sed ostensive sic demonstratur. Sit AB [fig. 49] diameter solis

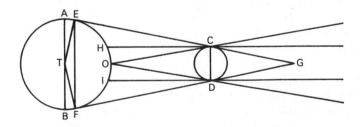

Fig. 49

53–4 propositiones: proportiones *W*   54 et: ut *W*   55 *post* opaci *add. W* et

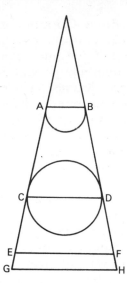

Fig. 48

the opaque body—the same inconvenience would follow; and it is demonstrated by the same propositions. And this is visibly evident[13] in the figure [fig. 48]. Let AB be the chord of the portion multiplying light and CD the diameter of the opaque body; the argument then proceeds as before.

Therefore, the shadow cannot be contained within parallel lines or lines converging in the direction of the luminous body (the assumption being that the luminous body is larger, as in the proposition, since the sun is much larger than the earth). Consequently, for any opaque body raised above the earth the third alternative necessarily follows, namely, that the shadow is contained within lines intersecting beyond the opaque body and terminating in the vertex of a cone. However, this can be demonstrated not only by [the] impossibility [of the alternatives], as has already been done, but also positively, as follows. Let AB [fig. 49] be the diameter of the sun

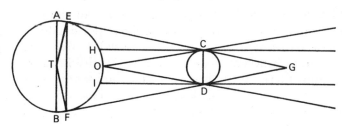

Fig. 49

cetera(?)   56 non: *om. R*   61 termatis *R*   63 sed: s. etiam *W*

et CD diameter opaci; eritque CD minor ex ypotesi, cum ponamus
65 illud luminosum esse solem et opacum terram. Et sit CD equedistans
AB, ducanturque AC et BD due linee contingentes corpus solis in
punctis E et F. Quod autem non possint contingere in punctis A B
patet ex correlario quinte decime tertii et tricesima quarta primi
Elementorum, quia tunc necesse esset EC et FD esse equedistantes,
70 et ita AB et CD equales essent, quod est contra ypotesim et contra
veritatem. Extremi igitur radii qui proveniunt a sole ad puncta C et D
sunt EC et FD, concurrentes in puncto G. Quod autem debeant concurrere probatur per hoc: quod anguli E et F super cordam EF sunt
minores duobus rectis, quia sunt partes duorum rectorum; quod patet
75 per quintam decimam tertii, ducendo a centro T lineas TE et TF
facientes rectos, cum EC et FD contingentibus. Et hii sunt qui
immediate includunt umbram, cum intra eos nichil de luce primaria
possit multiplicari, sicut patet ex quinta decima tertii *Elementorum*.
Omnes autem alii radii qui vel multiplicantur super lineas equedistantes
80 ad puncta C D, ut HC et ID, vel supra lineas ultra C D dilatatas,
ut OC et OD, nichil faciunt ad umbram, cum intra omnes tales sint
alii radii ultra opacum sibi invicem propius adherentes. Intimi autem
omnium sunt radii contingentes corpus solis et corpus opacum, sicut
patet in figura [fig. 49, *supra*]. Et cum hii ultra opacum concurrant,
85 patet umbram in figuram pyramidis coartari. Hec autem omnia exterius
manifeste patent in figura per quintam decimam tertii *Elementorum*,
quia a puncto C vel a puncto D inter CG et DG non potest aliqua
linea recta duci nisi secans arcum CD. Lux autem multiplicatur super
lineas rectas sine sectione vel ingressu sensibili intra opacum, per
90 propositionem antedictam.

[IV]

Quod etiam lux non multiplicetur principaliter ab aliquo uno puncto
solis, sed a tota portione eius, patet manifeste per incidentias radiosas
per angularia foramina transeuntes, que in debita distantia acquirunt
5 figuram omnino similem figure corporis multiplicantis. Quoniam
si luminosum fuerit rotundum penitus, incidentia penitus rotundatur; si vero fuerit novaculatum sive arcuatum, ut accidit in
eclipsi solis, erit incidentia ultra foramina penitus in figura corpori
luminoso conformis. Hoc autem nullo modo esse posset nisi a tota

65 sit: fit *E*   66 BD *W*: D *RE*   71 extimi *E*   72 in ... G: *om. R*
74 rectorum: *mg. R*   75 tertii: t. elementorum *W*   76 EC: ET *W* / FD: FT *W*
77 inter *W*   83 corpus²: *om. W*   85 hoc *E*

and CD the diameter of the opaque body; CD is smaller by hypothesis, since we suppose the luminous body to be the sun and the
opaque body to be the earth. Let CD and AB be parallel, and let the
two lines AC and BD be tangent to the body of the sun at points E
and F. That they cannot be tangent at points A and B is evident from
the corollary to *Elements*, iii. 15, and from *Elements*, i. 34,[14] since
then EC and FD would have to be parallel, and therefore AB and CD
would be equal, which is contrary to the hypothesis and to truth.
Therefore, the outermost rays coming from the sun to points C and
D are EC and FD, which intersect at point G. That they must intersect is proved by the fact that angles E and F on chord EF are
smaller than two right angles, since they are parts of two right angles;
this is evident from [*Elements*,] iii. 15, by drawing lines TE and TF
from the centre, T, perpendicular to tangents EC and FD. And these
are the rays that directly enclose the shadow, since no primary light
can be multiplied inside them, as is evident from *Elements*, iii. 15.
All other rays, multiplied either along parallel lines to points C and
D, as HC and ID, or along lines spreading out beyond C and D, as
OC and OD, contribute nothing to formation of the shadow, since
inside all such rays (beyond the opaque body) are other [pairs of]
rays in closer proximity to one another. However, the innermost rays
are those tangent to the body of the sun and the opaque body, as is
evident in the figure [fig. 49, above]. And since these intersect
beyond the opaque body, it is evident that the shadow narrows in
conical form. And all of these things are perfectly obvious to sense[15]
in the figure, by *Elements*, iii. 15, since no straight line can be drawn
from point C or point D between CG and DG without intersecting
arc CD.[16] And by the aforementioned proposition, light is multiplied
along straight lines that do not intersect or sensibly penetrate the
opaque body.

[IV]

That light is not multiplied principally from one point of the sun,
but from its whole surface, is also clearly evident from incident radiation passing through angular apertures, which in a suitable distance
[beyond the aperture] acquires a shape exactly like that of the multiplying body.[1] For if the luminous body is perfectly round, the incident radiation will be perfectly round; but if the luminous body
is crescent-shaped,[2] as during an eclipse of the sun, the incident
radiation beyond the aperture will conform perfectly to the shape
of the luminous body. But this could by no means be true unless

4 acquirunt: *mg. W*   7 sive arcuatum: *om. W*   9 luminosi *W*

10 portione solis fieret multiplicatio; quoniam illa portio cuius multiplicatio per eclipsim impeditur, deficiente eclipsi, speciem radiosam
sicut cetere multiplicat, et quicquid de incidentia prius a completa
circulatione eclipsis abstulit, lumine portionis eclipsate restituto,
restituitur. Item si ab uno puncto fieret multiplicatio, necesse
15 esset incidentiam figure foraminis penitus conformari; quoniam
lux que est in foramine ab uno puncto multiplicata figuratur secundum figuram foraminis et continue ultra foramen secundum eandem
figuram dilatatur, sicut ymaginatio cuiuslibet manifestat. Nos autem
horum duorum contraria fide probamus oculata, quoniam incidentia
20 ultra foramen in quadam distantia certa continue coartatur, et ab
illo loco ulterius incipit dilatari et in distantia debita in figuram
circularem penitus rotundatur, cuius causa inferius tangetur.

Ceterum, quod a tota portione solis ad omne punctum speculi
veniant radii infiniti probamus fide oculata, quoniam speculo sperico
25 convexo soli opposito videmus oculis a quolibet eius puncto infinitos
radios reflecti, qui non obstantibus radiis incidentibus sensibiliter
oculo presentantur; et videmus per illos totam solis portionem. Nec
potest dici quod illa apparitio sit fantastica, quoniam, posita manu
supra speculum, apparet lux reflexa in manu, et in illa eius parte,
30 scilicet in inferiori, ad quam lux incidens non potest pervenire.
Et hoc accidit ponendo manum in radiis illis visibiliter reflexis, et
solum ibi, quoniam alibi posita manu lux reflexa non apparet in ea.
Quare patet quod illi sunt radii veri et vera lux, non fantastica.

Ex omnibus igitur iam dictis rationibus, tam ostensivis quam ad
35 impossibile, una cum experientiis adiunctis, possumus colligere verum
modum multiplicationis lucis solaris incidentis, exclusa fractione
et reflexione, de quibus non hic sed inferius dicetur. Qui quidem
modus multiplicationis nec erit superfluus nec diminutus, quoniam
omnis multiplicatio excogitabilis et possibilis in hac continetur,
40 et sic non erit hec diminuta; et quia hanc multiplicationem totalem
sine aliqua diminutione et per experientias sensibiles et effectus
experimur, non erit in aliquo superflua. Et sit hec multiplicatio

12 quidquid *W*   20 continue: continentie *W*   23 omnem *R*   27 presenta-
tur *R* / illam *W*   30 scilicet: supra *W*   32 ibi *W*: *om. RE* / quoniam: quia *W*
33 illi: i. radii *W*   34 quam: tam *W*   38 nec[1]: non *W*   39 hoc *W*
41 et[1]: etiam *W* / et[2]: *om. E*

multiplication took place from the whole surface of the sun; for that portion from which multiplication is impeded by the eclipse multiplies radiant species as the rest when the eclipse ceases, and that part of the incident radiation from the complete circle [of the sun] at first lacking because of the eclipse is restored when the light of the eclipsed portion is restored. Furthermore, if multiplication occurred from one point, the incident radiation would necessarily conform exactly to the shape of the aperture; for light multiplied from one point has the shape of the aperture while in the aperture and spreads out continuously beyond the aperture, maintaining the same shape, as anyone's imagination will reveal. However, we declare the contraries of these two claims by visual evidence, since the radiation continuously contracts for a certain distance beyond the aperture, and then begins to spread out and at a suitable distance becomes perfectly circular, the cause of which will be touched upon below.[3]

However, we prove by visual evidence that infinitely many rays come from the whole surface of the sun to each point of the mirror, since when a convex spherical mirror is placed opposite the sun we observe with our eyes that an infinity of rays is reflected from each of its points, and these rays (if not obscured by direct radiation [from the sun]) are clearly perceived by the eye; and by means of them we see the whole surface of the sun. Nor can it be said that this appearance is imagined, since when the hand is placed above the mirror the light can be seen reflected on to the hand, and [only] on to that part of it, namely, its underside, to which direct light cannot reach. And this occurs when the hand is placed in those visibly reflected rays, and only there, since when the hand is placed elsewhere the reflected light does not appear on it. Therefore, it is evident that those rays and that light are not imagined, but real.

From all of the foregoing arguments, both direct and indirect, along with related experiences, we can infer the true mode of multiplication of incident solar light, excluding refraction and reflection, concerning which we will not speak here, but below.[4] And this mode of multiplication is neither superfluous nor defective; for it contains every conceivable and every possible multiplication, and thus it is not defective; and since we experience this entire multiplication without anything lacking, through both effects and sensible experiences, there is nothing superfluous in it. Let us assume that this multiplication

secundum modum dicendum. Sit A [fig. 50] centrum solis, et ymaginemur quod ab ipso A exeant infinite linee per singula puncta totius
45 superficiei singule secundum omnem differentiam situs et positionis,
tam in medio celesti quam elementari, secundum quantitatem indefinitam; vel si diffinire velimus, terminentur hee linee in ultimis et
remotissimis terminis utriusque perspicui. Dico igitur quod super
has lineas multiplicatur lux extra corpus solis in utroque perspicuo.
50 Et hee linee radiose possunt nominari axes, quia omnes transeunt
per centrum solis. Et sunt hii principaliores et efficaciores radii
qui possunt exire a sole, comparando singulos singulis. Nec solum

Fig. 50

super has lineas multiplicatur lux, sed super alias infinitas, quoniam
ad omne punctum quod potest signari in aliqua dictarum linearum
55 extra corpus solis veniunt infiniti radii a tota portione solis que
ab illo puncto potest videri. Et hii omnes radii figuram pyramidis
constituunt. Et extimi radii totius huius pyramidis sunt contingentes corpus solis in circumferentia cuiusdam circuli ex circulis
minoribus spere corporis solis, cuius circuli poli sunt duo puncta
60 in superficie solis que invenit linea ducta a cono pyramidis date
per centrum solis usque ad eius superficiem ulteriorem.
  Et patet quod brevissimus radius totius huius pyramidis inter
superficiem solis et punctum datum est axis huius pyramidis, et est
ille radius qui transit per centrum solis. Et hoc patet ex octava

43 modum: hunc m. W | dicendi W   46 medio: mundo W | elementari: seculari W
47 vollimus R   49 solum W   52 operando W   54 omne: ex omnem corr. R
57 extremi R   60 cono: centro W   63 datum: spatium vacuum W | est²: om. W

occurs in the following manner. Let A [fig. 50] be the centre of the sun, and imagine that from A issue infinitely many lines through individual points of the entire single surface [of the sun] according to every different place and position in both the celestial medium and the region of the elements. And let these lines be indefinite in length; or if we wish to define them, let them be terminated at the final and most remote extremes of both transparent media. I say, therefore, that light is multiplied outside the body of the sun along these lines in both transparent media. And these radiant lines can be called 'axes', since all pass through the centre of the sun. And these are the

Fig. 50

principal and most efficacious rays (comparing rays individually) that can issue from the sun. However, light is multiplied not only along these lines, but also along an infinity of others, since to every point that can be marked on any of the said lines [or axes] outside the body of the sun come rays infinite in number from the whole surface of the sun visible from that point. And all these rays form a conical figure. And the outermost rays of this entire cone are tangent to the body of the sun along the circumference of certain smaller circles [that can be drawn] on the spherical body of the sun;[5] and the poles of each of these smaller circles are the two points on the surface of the sun encountered by the line drawn from the vertex of the given cone through the centre of the sun to its far side.

It is evident that the shortest ray of this whole cone between the surface of the sun and the given point is the axis, and it is the ray that passes through the centre of the sun, as *Elements*, iii. 8,

65 tertii *Elementorum*. Et huic radio brevissimo plus de profundo solis
correspondet, quia tota profunditas secundum diametrum sumpta,
aliis vero radiis huius pyramidis minus de profundo solis correspondet,
quod profundum per cordam diametro minorem designatur. Et
propter hanc duplicem causam dicitur axis huius pyramidis fortior
70 et efficacior in agendo (scilicet illuminando, calefaciendo, et ceteros
effectus equivocos faciendo) quam sint omnes alii radii totius
pyramidis sigillatim accepti. Et de ceteris radiis patet quod quanto
fuerint axi propiores tanto erunt fortiores ex eisdem causis, sicut
patet per eandem octavam tertii. Unde patet radios extimos huius
75 pyramidis esse debilissimos, et aliorum quanto fuerint eis propiores
tanto remotioribus debiliores. Et hec superius patuerunt in figura.
Et sicut dictum est de hac pyramide, ita intelligendum est de omnibus
pyramidibus que possunt in toto illo axe terminari; et sunt infinite,
quia ad quodlibet punctum illius axis terminatur una pyramis (de
80 punctis dico extra corpus solis).

Verumptamen hoc notandum quod ad remotiora puncta a sole venit
plus de lumine quam ad propiora, quia a maiori portione solis multiplicatur, quod patet demonstrative per tricesimam quartam tertii
Elementorum. Nam si a duobus punctis in eadem linea signatis ducan-
85 tur due linee contingentes unum et eundem circulum, patet quod
contingens a remotiori puncto ducta plus occupat de circulo; patet
inquam per octavam tertii *Elementorum* et tricesimam quartam eiusdem. Sit enim circulus ABCD, cuius centrum E [fig. 51, *infra*]; et
ducatur diameter AEB in continuum et directum extra, et signentur in
90 ea extra circulum puncta F G, et ab illis ducantur due contingentes
que sint FC a propiori puncto et GD a remotiori. Dico ergo quod BC
arcus est minor BD arcu, patet enim per dictam tricesimam quartam
quod quadratum FC contingentis est equale superficiei que fit ex FA
in FB; iterum quadratum GD contingentis est equale superficiei que
95 fit ex GA in GB. Et superficies que fit ex GA in GB est maior superficie que fit ex FA in FB, quia ambo latera eius sunt maiora ambobus
alterius, et singula singulis. Per conceptionem hanc omne totum est
maius sua parte; ergo quadratum GD contingentis est maius quadrato
FC per conceptionem; ergo latus FC est minus latere GD; ergo per
100 octavam tertii *Elementorum* punctus D plus distat a puncto B quam
punctus C; arcus igitur BD est maior, quod erat probandum. Et hec

71 sint: *om. W*   72 quando *E*   73 propriores *E*   74 extremos *R*
76 hoc *W* / patuitur *W*   81 hoc notandum: *om. W* / ad: a *E*   85 unum: conum *W*
87 inquam: in qua parte *W*   94 *ante* iterum *add. W* item quadratum GD contingentis est
equale superficiei que fit ex FA in FB / item *W*   95 in²: *ex et corr. E*   96 ambobus:
axibus *W*   97 omne: *om. W*   98 quadrato: quadratis *W*   99 GD: FGD *R*
100 D: G *RE*   101 BD: *correxi ex* BG *WRE* / hoc *E*

makes clear.[6] And a greater thickness of the sun corresponds to this
shortest ray, namely, the whole thickness taken along the diameter;
whereas a smaller thickness of the sun corresponds to the other rays
of this cone, namely, the thickness designated by some chord smaller
than the diameter. For these two reasons the axis of this cone is said
to be stronger and more efficacious in its actions (namely, illuminating, heating, and producing other equivocal effects)[7] than are all
other rays of the entire cone, taken one at a time. As for the other
rays, it is evident that their strength increases with their proximity to
the axis for the same reasons, as is evident by the same [proposition]
iii. 8. It is evident, therefore, that the outermost rays of this cone are
the weakest, and the others are weaker the closer they are to these
outermost rays. And these things were revealed above in the figure.
Now what was said of this cone is true of all cones that can be terminated anywhere on that axis; and they are infinite in number,
since one cone is terminated at each point of that axis—that is, each
point of the axis outside the body of the sun.

However, it is to be noted that more light comes to points remote
from the sun than to closer points, since it is multiplied [to more
remote points] from a larger portion of the sun, which is demonstra-
tively evident by *Elements*, iii. 34. For if from two points marked on
the same line one draws two lines tangent to one and the same circle,
it is evident that the tangent drawn from the more distant point
covers more of the circle; this is evident, I say, by *Elements*, iii. 8
and iii. 34.[8] For let there be circle ABCD with centre E [fig. 51,
below]; and draw diameter AEB, extended continuously and recti-
linearly outside [the circle], and mark on it points F and G outside
the circle, and from them draw the two tangents, FC from the nearer
point and GD from the more remote. I say, therefore, that arc BC
is smaller than arc BD, for it is evident by the aforementioned thirty-
fourth [proposition] that the square of tangent FC is equal to the
surface that results from FA multiplied by FB; on the other hand,
the square of tangent GD is equal to the surface that results from GA
multiplied by GB. And the surface produced by GA times GB is
greater than the surface produced by FA times FB, since both sides
of the former [taken together] are longer than both sides of the
latter [taken together], and the individual sides of the former are
longer than the [corresponding] individual sides of the latter. It is a
common notion that every whole is greater than its part; it is understood, therefore, that the square of tangent GD is greater than the
square of FC; therefore, side FC is smaller than side GD; it follows,
by *Elements*, iii. 8, that point D is further from point B than is point
C; and consequently, arc BD is larger, which was to be proved. And

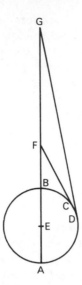

Fig. 51

est figura [fig. 51]. Et quamvis pyramis longior plus habeat de lumine et plures radios quam pyramis brevior, tamen per experientiam scimus quod pyramis brevior est fortioris actionis.

105 Sicut vero dictum est de pyramidibus terminatis ad unum axium solarium, ita omni modo sine aliqua differentia intelligamus de pyramidibus terminatis ad singula puncta omnium aliorum axium. Et per hunc modum ad omne punctum medii vel superficiei speculi vel cuiuscunque alterius corporis existentis in medio veniet una pyramis
110 a tota portione solis, cum quilibet punctus totius medii sit in aliquo dictorum axium solarium. Et patet quod alius modus ab isto modo multiplicationis, sive dicatur fieri super lineas equedistantes sive super lineas ab uno puncto exeuntes, est insufficiens, quia hii modi sunt partiales et accidentales, et continentur omnes in iam dicto
115 modo principali.

[V]

Sed iuxta iam dicta, oportet salvare apparentiam rotunditatis incidentie transeuntis per foramina angularia. Dico ergo quod cum lux non possit multiplicari a sole ad foramen super lineas rectas nisi
5 tribus modis, scilicet super rectas et equedistantes. Et tunc si ita esset, necessario lumen quod sic impleret foramen veniret solum

---

107 *ante* singula *scr. et del.* E unum axium solarium / omni E   114 omnes in iam:
iam o. in W

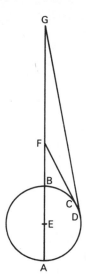

Fig. 51

this is the figure [fig. 51]. And although the longer pyramid has more light and more rays than the shorter pyramid, nevertheless we know by experience that the shorter pyramid acts more strongly.

But what has been said concerning pyramids terminated on one solar axis applies in every way without any difference to pyramids terminated at individual points of all other axes. And thus one pyramid comes from the whole surface of the sun to every point of the medium or the surface of a mirror or any other body situated in the medium, since every point of the entire medium is on one of these solar axes. And it is evident that no other mode of multiplication, whether it is said to occur along parallel lines or along lines issuing from a single point, is sufficient, since these [other] modes are partial and accidental, and all are contained in the already discussed principal mode.

[V]

On the basis of what has been said thus far, it is necessary to explain the appearance of roundness in incident radiation passing through angular apertures.[1] Now I say that light can be multiplied from the sun to the aperture along straight lines in only three ways, [the first of which is] along parallel straight lines.[2] And if this mode were operative, the light that fills the aperture would necessarily come only from

2 iam: *om.* W　　　　　6 lumen: sequeretur *W*

a portione solis figurata secundum figuram foraminis, que portio
esset equalis precise foramini, sicut patet per tricesimam quartam
primi *Elementorum*. Verbi gratia sit foramen triangulare ABC [fig.
10 52], et ab hiis tribus angulis trahantur usque ad solem tres linee

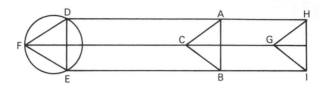

Fig. 52

equedistantes et equales sibi invicem omnes, que sint AD BE CF.
Patet ergo per tricesimam quartam primi predictam quod si inter hec
tria puncta, scilicet D E F, tres linee recte continuarentur, essent
ille tres linee in profundo solis equales tribus lineis terminalibus
15 foraminis, quia applicantur capitibus trium linearum equalium et
equedistantium. Et quia tota multiplicatio secundum dictum modum
intra has tres lineas equedistanter extenditur, necesse esset incidentiam ultra foramen esse in omni loco similem et equalem in
quantitate et figura foramini, sicut patet in triangulo GHI. Quod non
20 videmus, nam lumen prope foramen minus est foramine et longe est
maius.
    Necesse est ergo quod alia via fiat multiplicatio ad foramina.
Hoc autem non potest esse nisi lux multiplicetur super lineas concurrentes, quod potest tribus modis ymaginari: scilicet quod concurrant
25 in luminoso, et hoc vel in eius superficie, utpote si ab uno puncto
superficiei fieret multiplicatio. Et si hoc verum esset, tunc necessario oporteret lumen incidentie ultra foramen statim dilatari et
per continuum discessum magis ac magis; et semper figura lucis
esset similis figure foraminis in omne distantia, cuius contrarium
30 fide probamus oculata. Consequentia declaratur per figuram subiectam
[fig. 53]. Sit enim A punctus multiplicans lucem, BCD foramen
triangulare, et trahantur linee AB AC AD, et ulterius in continuum
et directum usque ad E F G, tractis EF FG GE equedistanter tribus
aliis lateribus foraminis. Et quia tota multiplicatio facta a puncto
35 A continetur inter AE AF AG lineas, necesse est per secundam sexti
EF esse maiorem BC, quia AE est longior AB. Et similiter de aliis
lateribus arguatur. Idem penitus accideret et eodem modo potest

    10 usque: ubilibet *W*   11 que: eque *W*   12 hec: *om. W*   13 scilicet:
om. W / recte: *om. W*   14 tres linee: t. *E* etiam *W*   17 inter *W* / esset: *mg. W*[c]
est *W'*   18–19 in² . . . figura: *mg. W*   19 foramini: *om. W*   33 *post* tractis
interl. add. W lineis   35 secundum *W*

a portion of the sun having the same shape as the aperture; and this portion would be precisely equal to the aperture, as is evident from *Elements*, i. 34.[3] For example, take triangular aperture ABC [fig. 52], and from the three angles draw three equal, parallel lines to the

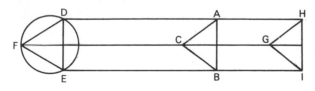

Fig. 52

sun, AD, BE, and CF. It is therefore evident by the aforesaid [proposition] i. 34 that if between these three points, namely, D, E, and F, three straight lines should be drawn, these three lines in the interior of the sun would be equal to the three lines bordering the aperture, since they are applied to the ends of three equal parallel lines. And since the entire multiplication is extended along parallel lines in the aforesaid manner within these three lines, the incident radiation beyond the aperture must be everywhere similar in shape and equal in size to the aperture, as is evident in triangle GHI. But this is not what we observe, since light just beyond the aperture is smaller than the aperture and far from the aperture is larger than the aperture.[4]

Therefore, multiplication to apertures must take place in some other way. However, this requires light to be multiplied along converging lines, which can be imagined in three ways: [first,] lines converging in the luminous body, either on its surface, if multiplication takes place from one point on the surface, [or in its interior].[5] And if the former were the case, then incident light would [begin to] spread out at once beyond the aperture and would continue to spread out more and more; and the light would always be similar in shape to the aperture at every distance, the contrary of which we prove by the testimony of the eyes. This conclusion is revealed by the subjoined figure [fig. 53]. Let A be the point multiplying light and BCD the triangular aperture, and draw lines AB, AC, and AD, extending them directly onwards to E, F, and G; and draw EF, FG, and GE parallel to the three sides of the aperture. Since the entire multiplication occurring from point A is contained between lines AE, AF, and AG, it is necessary, by [*Elements*,] vi. 2,[6] for EF to be greater than BC, since AE is longer than AB. And the same argument applies to the other sides. Precisely the same thing would occur (and the disproof is

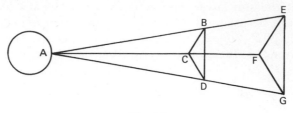

Fig. 53

reprobari, si ponatur quod multiplicatio fiat super lineas concurrentes
in profundo solis vel ultra solem in puncto remotissimo totius cor-
40 poris sui, utpote si poneretur quod multiplicatio fieret ab aliqua
portione cuius diameter esset minor diametro foraminis. Et patet
consequentia omni modo quo prius. Et hec est figura [fig. 54].

Necesse est igitur dare quod fiat super lineas concurrentes versus

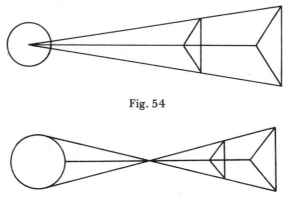

Fig. 54

Fig. 55

partem foraminis, et hoc vel citra foramen vel ultra vel in ipso
45 foramine. Citra fieri non potest, quoniam tunc accideret illud idem
inconveniens quod statim fuit in precedentibus conclusum; et patet
in figura [fig. 55]. Aut igitur fiet super lineas concurrentes in
foramine aut ultra. Et dico quod fit utroque modo, et patebit hoc
per experientias inferius dicendas. Dico ergo quod a triangulo in-
50 scripto maximo circulo totius portionis solis lucem multiplicantis

.

41 minor: coincidens *W*   42 hoc *E*   44 citra: circa *E*   46 fuit: *mg. W*
47 fit *W*

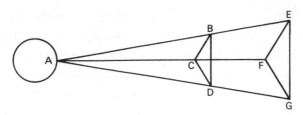

Fig. 53

[therefore] the same) if it should be supposed that multiplication takes place along lines intersecting in the interior of the sun or on its far side at the most distant point of the entire solar body—that is, if it should be supposed that multiplication occurs from some portion [of the sun's surface] the diameter of which is smaller than the diameter of the aperture. And the conclusion is evident exactly as above. And here is the figure [fig. 54].

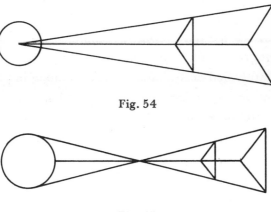

Fig. 54

Fig. 55

It is necessary to maintain, therefore, that multiplication occurs along lines converging in the direction of the aperture— either on the near side of the aperture, on its far side, or within it. Convergence cannot take place on the near side of the aperture, since then the same inconvenience would follow as was recognized at once in the preceding discussion; and this is evident in the figure [fig. 55]. Therefore, multiplication takes place along lines converging either within the aperture or beyond it. And I say that it takes place in both modes, and this will be evident by experiences to be discussed below. I say, therefore, that light is multiplied to the whole aperture from the triangle inscribed in the maximum circle of the whole portion of the sun multiplying light

ad superficiem in qua est foramen angulare multiplicatur lux ad
totum foramen in figura pyramidis triangularis, cuius pyramidis
conus terminatur ultra foramen in distantia proportionali quantitati
foraminis; nam quanto foramen maius fuerit tanto remotius concurrit
55 lux in conum pyramidis, et quanto minus tanto propius. Et quod hoc
sit verum potest probari per effectum, videmus enim lucem ultra
foramen sub figura foraminis in aliqua distantia coangustari, quod
esse non posset nisi predicto modo fieret multiplicatio. Et necesse
est quod illa lux sic coartata quoad aliquam partem eius ultra fora-
60 men in parva distantia concurrat ad punctum unum, sicut patet per
quartam petitionem primi *Elementorum*, quamvis tamen concursum
videre nequeamus, cuius causa est quod non solum ad foramen incidit
lux illius pyramidis sed lux ulterius pyramidis rotunde que venit a
tota portione solis sperica totaliter illuminata omni tempore preter-
65 quam in eclipsi, quoniam tunc novaculatur, et ab illa novaculata
multiplicatur lux. Et huiusmodi pyramidis conus terminatur ad
medium punctum foraminis, et postea ab illo puncto ultra foramen
continue dilatatur. Sed eius dilatatio ultra foramen in parva distantia
percipi non potest, quoniam includitur intra lucem pyramidis tri-
70 angulate predicte, quia angulus huius pyramidis est valde acutus,
propter nimiam distantiam sue basis, scilicet portionis solis a qua venit;
et ideo linee post concursum in parva distantia parum dilatantur.
Quia tamen continue licet paulatim dilatatur hec pyramis a foramine,
et alia continue licet paulatim coangustatur, ideo necesse est dilata-
75 tionem pyramidis rotunde in parva distantia a foramine occultari
a luce pyramidis triangularis, quia in parva distantia a foramine
latior est quam dilatatio pyramidis rotunde; et necesse est etiam
concursum pyramidis triangulate in ulteriori distantia a luce pyramidis
rotunde intersecantis et includentis triangularem penitus occultari,
80 nam in bona distantia ante concursum pyramidis triangularis vincit
ipsam dilatatio pyramidis rotunde.

      61 tamen: t. huius *W*   63 sed . . . pyramidis²: *om. W*   66 huius *W*
73 tamen . . . licet: causa continentie lucis *W* / a foramine: *om. W*   74 continue licet:
continentia lucis *W*

to the plane in which the angular aperture is located, in the shape of a triangular pyramid, the vertex of which is formed beyond the aperture at a distance proportional to the size of the aperture;[7] for as the aperture is greater, the intersection of the light in a pyramidal vertex will be more remote, and as the aperture is smaller, intersection will be closer. That this is true can be proved by a [sensible] effect, for we see that for a certain distance beyond the aperture the light contracts in the shape of the aperture, which could not be unless multiplication occurred in the aforementioned way. And it is necessary for this light, thus contracted to a certain fraction of itself, to converge to one point at a small distance beyond the aperture, as is evident by the fourth postulate of the first book of the *Elements*;[8] however, we are not able to see this convergence because to the aperture falls not only the light of this pyramid, but also the light of the cone that comes from the entire spherical portion of the sun [facing the aperture], which is totally luminous except during an eclipse (since then it is crescent-shaped, and from that crescent light is multiplied). And the vertex of this cone is terminated at the middle point of the aperture and then from that point spreads out continuously beyond the aperture. But its spreading out cannot be perceived close to the aperture, since it is enclosed within the light of the aforementioned triangular pyramid, for the angle of the cone is very acute, because its base (that is, the portion of the sun from which it comes) is extremely far away; and consequently for a small distance beyond the point of intersection the lines [constituting the cone] are not sufficiently spread out [to emerge from the triangular pyramid].[9] Nevertheless, since this cone is continuously, though gradually, spread out beyond the aperture, while the pyramid is continuously, though gradually, narrowed, the spreading of the cone must therefore be concealed for a short distance beyond the aperture by the light of the pyramid, since for a short distance beyond the aperture the latter is wider than the cone; and at a greater distance the convergence of the pyramid must be entirely concealed by the light of the cone intersecting and enclosing the pyramid, for the pyramid, at a considerable distance before its vertex, is overcome by the spreading of the cone.

Et hec omnia manifeste patent in figura [fig. 56]. Sit tota portio
solis sperica sive rotunda multiplicans lucem ad superficiem foraminis
ABC, et triangulus ei inscriptus eisdem litteris equivoce nominetur,
85 et sit foramen triangulare DEF, et ducantur linee AD BE CF concurrentes in puncto G. Deinde a tota rotunditate portionis ducantur
linee a tota portione rotunda ad punctum H, quod est in medio
foraminis, et ulterius in continuum et directum quantumlibet; et
secent radii BH et AH radios AD et BE in punctis I et K. Patet igitur
90 secundum dictam figurationem quod lux pyramidis rotunde usque
ad IK intra triangulam occultatur, et post sectionem IK triangulam
occultat, et quod lux triangula a foramine usque ad IK continue
angustatur in figura triangulari; et ibi est in maxima angustatione

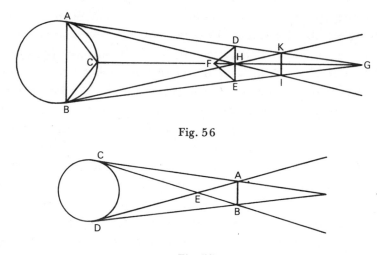

Fig. 56

Fig. 57

visui manifesta, et continue ultra dilatatur in figura rotunda. Et
95 hec omnia sunt penitus convenientia experientie sensibili, quam
comprehendimus oculis manifeste sine aliqua fallacia aut deceptione,
quamvis contra hec sint rationes michi multum difficiles et quarum
solutiones ignoro, que inferius subiungentur.
Ex precedentibus quidem patet quod ad omne punctum medii
100 venit lux a tota portione solis in figura pyramidali, cuius basis est
circulus in superficie solis quem contingunt omnes extime linee dicte
pyramidis. Sit igitur latitudo foraminis designata per lineam AB
[fig. 57], et sit portio solis a qua multiplicatur lux ad totum foramen

91 triangulam[1,2]: triangulum *W*   93 angustatione: triangulatione *W*   97 hoc *W* /
quartum *E*   98 solutionem *W* solis *E*   100 pyramidalis *R* pyramidari *E*
101 quem: quod *WR* / extreme *R*   102 designati *R*

And all of these things are clearly evident in the figure [fig. 56].
Let the whole spherical or round portion of the sun multiplying light
to the plane of the aperture be ABC, let the triangle inscribed in it be
denominated (equivocally) with the same letters, let the triangular
aperture be DEF, and draw lines AD, BE, and CF intersecting at point
G. Then from the entire round surface [facing the aperture] draw
lines to point H, which is in the centre of the aperture,[10] and continuously and directly beyond [that point] as far as you please; rays
BH and AH will intersect rays AD and BE at points I and K. It is thus
evident from the drawing that the light of the cone is concealed within
the triangular pyramid as far as IK, but thereafter conceals the triangular pyramid, and that the triangular light is continuously narrowed

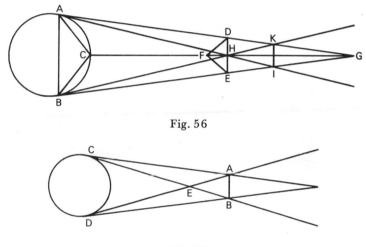

Fig. 56

Fig. 57

from the aperture to IK, in triangular form; and the [composite] light
is there manifest to vision in its maximum narrowness and thereafter
spreads out in a round figure. And all these things are wholly in
agreement with sensible experience, as we manifestly perceive by
means of the eyes without any fallacy or deception—although there
are arguments to the contrary that I find very difficult and the solutions to which I do not know, and these will be introduced below.

From the preceding arguments it is evident that light comes from
the whole portion of the sun to every point of the medium in the
form of a cone whose base is the circle on the surface of the sun to
which all the outermost lines of the cone are tangent. Thus let the
width of the aperture be designated by line AB [fig. 57], and the
portion of the sun from which light is multiplied to the whole

DC. Et ducantur linee DA CA CB DB in continuum et directum.
105 Super has quidem lineas fit multiplicatio lucis, ut prius fuit ostensum. Sed linee AD et BC continue dilatantur ultra foramen, quia concurrunt in puncto E et a concursu ultra fit continua dilatatio. Deberet igitur lux ultra foramen statim dilatari, cuius oppositum videmus ad sensum. Et ex hac experientia quam sensu percipimus
110 potest quis, convertendo dictam argumentationem, destruere ultimum modum multiplicationis. Sic videmus ad sensum lumen ultra foramen coangustari; hoc autem esse non posset si ad quodlibet punctum foraminis terminaretur una pyramis cuius basis esset tota portio solis. Non igitur fit multiplicatio lucis a sole secundum tales pyramides;
115 falsa igitur erit positio, ut videtur, que talem multiplicationem potuit fieri. Consequentia huius ultime argumentationis declaratur per figuram suprapositam [fig. 57].

Item ab uno puncto solis multiplicatur lux ad omnia puncta totius foraminis super lineas rectas, sicut prius fuit demonstratum et
120 certum est. Sed omnes linee recte exeuntes ab uno puncto quanto magis recedunt magis dilatantur; radii ergo venientes ad latera foraminis continue ultra foramen deberent dilatari, et hoc in eadem figura, scilicet foraminis, cuius oppositum sensibiliter percipimus.

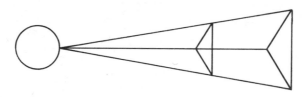

Fig. 58

Figuratio huius patet exterius [fig. 58]. Item super lineas equedis-
125 tantes fit multiplicatio lucis ad foramen, et illa est ubique equalis foramini et eiusdem figure; quod autem super equedistantes fiat multiplicatio superius fuit probatum. Hec omnia ostendunt quod incidentia ultra foramina nullatenus deberet coangustari si verus esset modus multiplicationis ultimo dictus. Et quia angustatio lucis
130 ultra foramen manifeste patet ad oculum, videtur posse concludi convertendo dictas argumentationes quod lux non multiplicetur sicut superius fuit dictum et ostensum. Quid igitur sit hic dicendum

106 continentie *W* / quia: que *W*   ·   107 *ante* continua *scr. et del.* E concursu
108 debet *W*   113 terminarentur *E*   115 falsa: fallatia *E* / ut: et *W* / que:
quidem(?) *W*   116 potuit: ponit *R* posse *W* / consequentia: secundum modum *W* /
declaratur: quod d. *W*   118 iterum *W*   122 continentie *W*   126 super: sunt *E*
128 deberent *W*   129 angustatio: multiplicatio *W*   132 superius: *om. W*

aperture by DC. And draw continuous straight lines DA, CA, CB, and
DB. Multiplication of light occurs along these lines, as was shown
above. But lines AD and BC spread out continuously beyond the
aperture, since they intersect at point E and spread out continuously
beyond that point of intersection. Therefore, light must [begin to]
spread out immediately beyond the aperture, the opposite of which
is evident to sense. And from this sensible experience one can, by
turning the argument around, disprove [this] final mode of multiplication. Thus we see with our eyes that light is narrowed beyond
the aperture; but this could not be true if a cone having the whole
surface of the sun as base were terminated at each point of the
aperture.[11] Therefore, multiplication of light from the sun does
not take place according to such cones; therefore, the position
that such multiplication could occur (which seems true) is false.
The conclusion of this last argument is revealed in the figure above
[fig. 57].

Also, light is multiplied from one point on the sun to every point
of the entire aperture along straight lines, as was demonstrated above
and as is certain. But all straight lines issuing from one point are more
spread out the more they recede [from the point]; therefore, rays

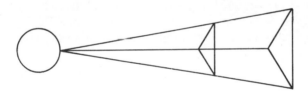

Fig. 58

coming to the sides of the aperture should spread out continuously
beyond the aperture, maintaining the same shape (that of the aperture)
—the opposite of which we sensibly perceive. And this is visibly
evident[12] in the figure [fig. 58]. The multiplication of light to the
aperture also takes place along parallel lines, and this multiplication
is everywhere equal [in size] to the aperture and of the same shape;
that multiplication takes place along parallel lines was proved above.
All these arguments show that the incident radiation should in no
way be narrowed beyond the aperture if the last-mentioned mode of
multiplication[13] were true. And since the narrowing of light beyond
the aperture is manifestly evident to the eyes, it seems possible to
conclude, by turning the foregoing arguments around, that light is
not multiplied as described and established above. I am therefore at a

penitus ignoro, quia quod video ad oculum negare non possum.
Rationes etiam dictum modum multiplicationis probantes michi
135 videntur insolubiles, qualiter enim fieret visio totius portionis solis a
quolibet puncto medii nisi ad punctum illud a tota portione lux
multiplicaretur? Qualiter etiam umbra cuiuslibet rei coangustaretur
nisi sic fieret multiplicatio? Coangustationem vero umbre non solum
ratione sed sensu percipimus, etiam in propinqua distantia. Qualiter
140 etiam potest contradici, quoniam ab uno puncto solis multiplicetur
lux ad omnia puncta medii ad que ab illo puncto possunt duci linee
recte per medium perspicui, excluso omni denso transitum lucis
impediente, cum visio unius puncti solis fiat ab omnibus talibus
punctis medii, sicut sine contradictione quilibet ad sensum experitur?
145 Similiter lucem multiplicari a punctis solis equedistantibus ad puncta
medii equedistantia super lineas equedistantes non videtur rationabi-
liter posse contradici, nisi velit quis dicere visionem posse fieri sine
specie visibilis ad visum multiplicata, quod nullus sapiens ponere
videtur.

150   Credo quod vera causa et completa huius incidentie per foramina,
si esset cognita, induceret cognoscentem in magnam noticiam multiplicationis lucis solis et actionum ad multiplicationem consequentium,
ut illuminationis et calefactionis et ceterarum actionum equivocarum.
Nescio si ea que sequuntur possint habere veritatem; videntur tamen
155 necessario sequi ex hiis que apparent in incidentia. Et est primum
quod unus solus radius lucis veniens ab uno puncto solis ad unum
punctum medii, excluso omni concursu aliorum radiorum ab aliis
punctis totius portionis solis egredientium, non sufficit ad termin-
andum visum vel immutandum (visu dico existente extra radium
160 illum), sicut radius ingrediens per fenestram terminat visum in angulo
domus vel immutat, ad cuius radii singula puncta conterminantur infiniti radii alii a tota portione solis egredientes. Nec mirum, quia visio
radii est visio speciei, et necesse est speciem visibilem multum esse
fortem, quia eius visio fit per speciem debilem, cum sit species speciei,
165 et multiplicatio talium radiorum, per quos fit visio speciei, est
multiplicatio secundaria et accidentalis. Ideo quidem non est mirum
si radius ingrediens per fenestram potest videri, oculo existente
in angulo, quia radius ille est species fortissima, nam ad omne
punctum eius terminantur infiniti radii qui a tota portione solis

133 possunt *R*   139 sensu: et s. *W*   141 ad que: atque *W*   142 omni:
mg. W^C enim *W'*   143 impedientie *E*   145 ad: a *W*   147 *post* sine *mg. add. W*
cum   148 visibili *W* / ad: ad punctum *W* / visum *W'*: visuum *mg. W*^C / nullus: *om. W*
152 multiplicationem: multiplicationum *W*   154 secuntur *E*   155 in: *om. W*
157 omnium *W*   159 immutandum: faciendum *W*   160 ingrediens: *mg. W*
161 *post* domus *mg. add. W*^C quia in introitus / immutatus *W* / ad cuius: *om. W*
165 radiorum: r. est *RE ex* r. est *corr. W* / quam *W*   169 conterminantur *E*

total loss to know what to say, since I cannot deny what I see with my eyes. Moreover, the arguments proving the said mode of multiplication seem to me irrefutable, for how would vision of the whole [facing] surface of the sun from each point of the medium be possible unless light were multiplied to that point from the whole surface? How also would the shadow of anything be narrowed unless multiplication occurred thus? And we perceive this narrowing of the shadow not only by reason but also by sense, and in a small distance [as well as a great]. Also, how can [the said mode of multiplication] be contradicted, since light is multiplied from one point of the sun to every point of the medium to which a straight line can be drawn through a transparent medium (thus excluding dense media that prevent the passage of light), since vision of [any] one point of the sun takes place from all such points of the medium, as sense experience reveals without any contradiction? Similarly, it does not seem possible to contradict by rational means the claim that light is multiplied from points of the sun to equally distant points in the medium along parallel lines, unless somebody wishes to maintain that vision can occur without multiplication of the species of the visible object to the eye, which no wise man seems to suppose.

I believe that if the true and complete cause of [the shape of] this radiation incident through apertures were known, it would lead the knowledgeable person to great understanding of the multiplication of solar light and the actions that result from it, such as illumination, heating, and other equivocal actions. I do not know if the conclusions that are about to follow are true, but they seem to be necessary consequences of the phenomena of incident radiation. And the first is that a single ray of light coming from one point on the sun to one point of the medium, all intersection of other rays issuing from other points of the whole surface of the sun having been excluded, is not sufficient for altering or terminating vision (the eye being situated so that the ray does not reach it directly),[14] whereas sight (located in the corner of a house) is altered or terminated by the radiation entering through a window, at every point of which radiation an infinity of of other rays issuing from the whole surface of the sun is terminated. Nor is this surprising, since vision of a ray is vision of a species, and to be seen a species must be very strong, because vision of it takes place through a weak species, since it is the species of a species, and the multiplication of such rays, through which the species is seen, is a secondary and accidental multiplication.[15] Therefore, it is indeed not surprising that radiation entering through a window can be seen when the eye is situated [off to the side] in a corner, since that ray is a very strong species, for at each of its points an infinity of rays issuing from

170 egrediuntur; et ideo species talis speciei potest esse fortis, et merito
debet speciem principalem tam fortem per speciem eius sensibiliter
apprehendere, precipue cum transit iuxta obscurum et umbram
que est in domo. Et ideo non erit mirum si unus solus radius non
possit videri, exclusa omni conterminatione aliorum, et precipue si
175 ille unus radius sit debilis secundum quod ad ceteros comparatur.
   Et quod hoc sit verum videtur posse confirmari per rationem,
quoniam si unus solus radius et debilis esset sensibiliter visu per-
ceptibilis, tunc sensibiliter aerem illuminaret; propter hoc enim
ita sensibiliter apparet radius ingrediens per fenestram, quia scilicet
180 incomparabiliter excellit illa lux principalis lucem debilem in
obscuro domus existentem. Et si unus radius sensibiliter aerem
illuminaret, tunc sensibiliter aerem calefaceret, quia ad magnam
fortitudinem et excellentiam lucis consequitur magna fortitudo et
excellentia caloris, sicut manifeste patet ex effectu speculorum com-
185 burentium in loco combustionis et alibi; in loco enim combustionis
est maxima lux et claritas, et maximus calor scilicet combustivus
consequitur, in ceteris vero locis secundum intensionem et remissionem
lucis experimur ad sensum intensionem et remissionem caloris. Si
igitur unus radius debilis sensibiliter calefacit, tunc infiniti fortiores
190 in unum punctum congregati infinities fortius calefacerent; ergo
vehementer comburerent. Sed ad omne punctum medii infiniti
congregantur, utpote ab infinitis punctis totius portionis solis
egredientes, qui omnes ad punctum illud conterminantur. Ergo sine
fractione et reflexione, per solos radios incidentes omni tempore
195 et loco sole lucente, comburerentur combustibilia in medio, soli
opposita, cuius oppositum ex sensu patet esse verum. Non ergo
sensibiliter potest unus solus radius et debiles visum sensibiliter
immutare, quoniam hoc dato sequitur dictum inconveniens, ut patet.
   Aliud quod videtur utile ad solutionem dictarum rationum est
200 quod lux fortis occultat debilem, et maior minorem, sicut patet de
luce solis erga lucem stellarum. Nam quamvis lux stellarum veniat ad
oculum, non tamen percipitur propter excellentiam lucis solis in die,
nisi in casu, sicut accidit in puteis quando scilicet radii stellarum
cadunt perpendiculariter super visum existentem in profundo putei,
205 radiis solis principalibus multum a visu remotis. Ex quibus duobus
videtur posse responderi ad predictas rationes. Et gratia huius repetam
rationes contra dictam positionem incidentie una cum positione,

175 ceteros: alios W   183 consequetur W   185 enim: scilicet W
186 scilicet: interl. R   190 in: ad W   191 comburent R / omnem W   192 congregantur: c. radii W   195 comburentur W   196–7 cuius . . . radius: om. W
197 potest E: patet R   198 quoniam hoc: quomodo W / sequetur W / dictum: om. W
200 maior: m. etiam W   206–7 repetam rationes: resumam rationem W
207 dictam positionem: p. W ponem E / positione: positionem W

the whole surface of the sun is terminated; and therefore, the species of such a species can be strong, and the eye should with good reason perceive such a strong principal species through its [secondary] species, especially when it passes through the darkness and shadow in the house. And therefore, it is not surprising that a single ray should be invisible (all mingling with other rays having been excluded), especially if that one ray is weak in comparison to the others.

That this is true seems to be confirmable through reason. For if a single weak ray were sensibly visible, it would sensibly illuminate the air; for the ray passing through the window is sensibly apparent because, as principal light, it is incomparably stronger than the weak light in the dark part of the house. And if one ray should sensibly illuminate the air, then it would sensibly heat the air, since from great strength and excellence of light follow great strength and excellence of heat, as is manifestly evident from the effect of a burning mirror at the point of combustion and from other cases; for light and brightness are maximum at the point of combustion, and maximum heat (that is, combustive heat) follows; and likewise in other places we sensibly experience intension and remission of heat according to the intension and remission of light. Therefore, if one weak ray should sensibly heat [its recipient], then an infinity of stronger rays congregating at one point would heat with infinitely greater strength and therefore produce vehement combustion. But at every point of the medium congregate an infinity of rays, namely, those issuing from the infinity of points of the whole surface of the sun, and all come together at that point [in the medium]. Accordingly, without refraction and reflection, solely by rays incident everywhere whenever the sun is shining, combustible things in a medium opposite the sun would be set on fire—the opposite of which we sensibly perceive to be true. Therefore, a single weak ray cannot sensibly alter sight, since, if it could, the said difficulty would follow, as is evident.

The other [principle] that seems useful for the solution of the said arguments is that strong light conceals weak light, and a greater light conceals a smaller light, as is evident when the light of the sun is compared to the light of the stars. For although the light of the stars comes to the eye, it is not perceived during the day because of the superiority of the solar light—except by accident, as in wells when the stellar rays fall perpendicularly to the eye at the bottom of the well while the principal rays of the sun are far removed from the eye.[16] On the basis of this, we can respond in two ways to the foregoing arguments. And for this purpose, let me repeat the arguments against the said position regarding incident radiation, together with the position itself,

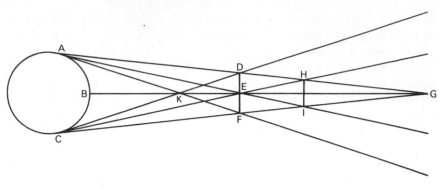

Fig. 59

et subiungam figurationem superius positam [fig. 59]. Sit igitur
ABC portio solis multiplicans lucem ad foramen. Et sit diameter fora-
210 minis DEF, et pyramis luminosa triangula ACG, et pyramis rotunda
terminata ad medium punctum foraminis ACE, que includitur intra
triangulam usque ad puncta sectionum, que sunt H et I, et ab illis
punctis ultra includit triangulam. Unde secundum dictam positionem
apparet lux triangulata usque ad lineam HI et continue coangustata
215 usque ad locum illum, et ab illo loco dilatabitur et rotundabitur.
Sed ratio in contrarium ostendit quod pyramis ACK includet utramque, scilicet triangulam predictam et rotundam, sicut apparet in figura
per eius dilatationem ultra foramen. Sed ex prima suppositione,
si vera sit, patet quod radius CD ultra foramen non poterit visui
220 apparere, tum quia solus nec ad aliquod ·punctum in illo radio ultra
foramen potest alius radius conterminari, sicut patet, tum quia ipse
ad singulos comparatus est omnium debilissimus, ut in precedentibus
fuit ostensum, quia scilicet venit a puncto contactus. Coadiuvat
etiam secunda suppositio, scilicet quod fortitudo lucis pyramidis
225 triangulate ex propinquitate quam habet cum illo radio potest illum
occultare, quia ad singula puncta pyramidis triangulate conterminantur infiniti radii a portione solis venientes. Eadem est ratio in
singulis radiis transeuntibus per singula puncta linee DH, scilicet
quod quia pauci radii conterminantur ad puncta talium radiorum,
230 et precipue in parva distantia ultra foramen, respectu multitudinis
infinitorum radiorum conterminalium in singulis punctis pyramidis
triangule, poterit lux illa excellens reliqua occultare. Et si hec

211 foraminis: *mg. W*   212 triangulum *W*   213 includit: *om. E* | triangulum *W*
214 triangula *W* | coangustatur *W*   215 dilatabitur *W'*: dilabitur *W*^{C} 217 et: *om. E*
220 apparere: *mg. R* | ad: *om. W*   221 illius radiis *W*   224 etiam: et *W* | quod:
mg. W^C que *W'*   225 triangulare *E* | *ante* quam *mg. add. W*^{C} in   225-6 ex . . .
triangulate: *om. R*   226 triangulare *E*   230 in parva: *om. E*   232 hoc *E*

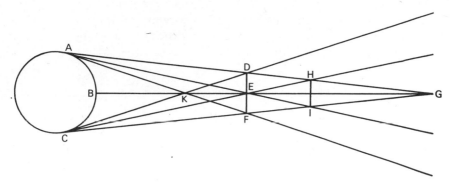

Fig. 59

and let me subjoin the figure given previously [fig. 59].[17] Thus let
ABC be the portion of the sun multiplying light to the aperture.
And let the diameter of the aperture be DEF, the luminous triangular
pyramid ACG, and the cone coming to a vertex at the middle point
of the aperture ACE; and this cone is enclosed within the triangular
pyramid up to the points of intersection H and I, thereafter enclosing
the pyramid.[18] According to this position, therefore, light appears
triangular up to line HI and is continually narrowed as it proceeds
to that place, and thereafter it is spread out and rounded. But in
opposition to this it is argued that pyramid ACK[19] encloses both
of the others (the aforementioned triangular pyramid and cone),
as appears in the figure from the spreading out of ACK beyond the
aperture. But from the first supposition, if true, it is evident that
ray CD will not appear to sight beyond the aperture, both because
no other ray can terminate at any point of that ray beyond the
aperture, as is evident, and because it is weaker than any other
individual ray, as was shown above, since it issues from a point
of tangency [on the sun]. This first supposition is assisted by the
second, namely, that this ray [CD] is concealed by the strength
of the light of the triangular pyramid because of the nearness of
the latter, since infinitely many rays coming from the surface of
the sun are terminated at individual points of the triangular pyramid.
The same argument applies to individual rays passing through individual points of line DH, namely, that since few rays are terminated
at the points of such rays, especially in the space immediately
beyond the aperture, by comparison with the infinite multitude of
rays terminated at individual points of the triangular pyramid,
therefore that superior light [of the triangular pyramid terminating
at G] will be able to conceal the other light [occupying the region
between lines CD and CH and between AF and AI].[20] And if these

vera sunt, patet solutio singularum rationum contra dictam positionem positarum, tam de radiis equedistantibus quam de radiis
235 ab uno puncto multiplicatis.

[VI]

Dicto de multiplicatione lucis incidentis que fit per lineas omnino
rectas, dicendum est de multiplicatione lucis reflexe que fit per
lineas tortuosas compositas ex rectis se tangentibus ad angulum. Et
5 quia intentio est de congregatione lucis reflexe in punctum unum,
que fieri non potest sine debitis figurationibus que nate sunt lucem
congregare, ideo de illis ad presens intendimus facere mentionem.
Certum est autem quod corpora regularia habentia superficies planas
nequeunt per reflexionem lucem congregare. Ad cuius demonstra-
10 tionem preponam unam conclusionem, et eam probabo; et est quod
tota pyramis luminosa que incidit ad quodcunque punctum speculi
plani aut redit totaliter in se ipsam, manente eodem axe, aut redit per
aliam pyramidem cuius conus est punctus incidentie datus et eius axis
est reflexio axis pyramidis incidentis. Sit enim AB [fig. 60] superficies

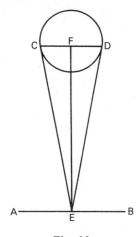

Fig. 60

15 plana, et sit diameter portionis solis multiplicantis lucem ad dictam
superficiem CD. Ex dictis quidem prius planum est quod ad omne
punctum medii vel speculi multiplicatur lux a tota portione solis
in figura pyramidis rotunde. Sit igitur pyramis lucis multiplicata

235 *post* multiplicatis *scr. et del.* E utroque puncto convincent
5 unum: *om.* W   6 lucem: *om.* W   7 congregate E   10 preponam *E:*

things are true, the solution to the individual arguments raised
against the said position is evident, both with regard to parallel rays
and with regard to rays multiplied from one point.

[VI]

Having treated the multiplication of incident light propagated along
perfectly straight lines, we must now discuss the multiplication of
light reflected along a twisting path, composed of straight segments
joined to one another at angles.[1] And since our concern is with the
gathering of reflected light at a single point, which cannot occur
without [mirrors of] the proper shapes, designed for gathering light,
therefore we shall here make mention of these shapes. Now it is
certain that regular bodies having plane surfaces are not able to produce convergence of light by reflection. In order to demonstrate this,
I propose and prove one conclusion: that the entire luminous cone
incident on any point of a plane mirror either returns totally on
itself, with the same axis, or returns along another cone with vertex
at the given point of incidence and, as axis, the reflection of the axis

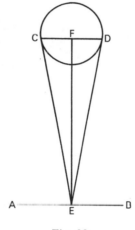

Fig. 60

of the incident cone. Let AB [fig. 60][2] be the plane surface, and let
CD be the diameter of the portion of the sun multiplying light to this
surface. From what has been said it is clear that light from the whole
surface of the sun is multiplied to every point of the medium or
mirror in the form of a cone. Thus let CDE be the cone of light

proponam *R* propono *W*   sit: *Here the margin of R has an anonymous* Notule de
speculis

ad punctum E pyramis CDE, cuius axis sit EF; et sit EF perpendicu-
20 laris tam super solem quam super superficiem speculi. Quia igitur
anguli incidentie et reflexionis sunt equales, patet quod radius EF,
scilicet axis pyramidis, in se ipsum reflectetur, quia est perpendicularis
ad superficiem speculi ex ypotesi. Et quia angulus CEF est equalis
angulo DEF per quartam primi *Elementorum*, cum EC et ED linee
25 sint equales, ut patet ex correlario tricesime quarte tertii *Elementorum*,
et similiter CF et DF equales per correlarium prime tertii, et ideo
angulus CEA erit equalis angulo DEB per conceptionem, quia sunt
residua equalium, scilicet angulorum rectorum, demptis equalibus,
scilicet angulis CEF et DEF, et ideo per legem reflexionis reflec-
30 tetur radius DE in radium CE et econtrario. Et similiter ostendetur
de omnibus radiis totius pyramidis istius, scilicet quod quilibet
reflectitur in sibi oppositum, ita quod tota pyramis in se ipsam
reflectitur.

Incidat iterum ad punctum G pyramis CDG [fig. 61], cuius axis FG
35 cadat oblique super superficiem speculi; et sit angulus FGB equalis

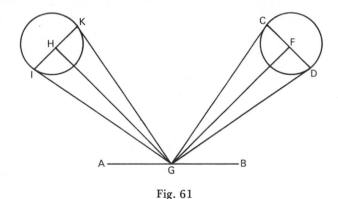

Fig. 61

angulo HGA. Reflectetur igitur radius FG per lineam GH. Et quia
angulus DGB incidentie est minor angulo FGB incidentie per conceptionem, erit ex lege reflexionis angulus IGA sub quo reflectitur
radius DG minor angulo HGA. Radius ergo IG cadet inter HG radium
40 et AG lineam. Et quia CGB angulus incidentie est maior angulo FGB
incidentie, reflectetur radius CG inter GH radium reflexum et FG
radium incidentem; reflectatur ergo per radium KG. Et quia angulus
incidentie CG est tanto maior angulo incidentie FG quanto angulus
incidentie DG est minor eodem, quia anguli CGF et DGF sunt equales,

19 CDE *R*: CBE *W* ECD *E*   26 et²: *om. W*   30 *post* DE *add. E* E   31 quid-
libet *R*   32 sibi: suum *E*   34 incidit *W*   35 cadit *W*   36 radius: angulus *W*
40 CGB: CDB *W*   42 reflectetur *W*   43–4 FG ... incidentie: *om. W*

multiplied to point E, and let EF be its axis; and let EF be perpendicular both to the sun and to the surface of the mirror. Therefore,
since the angles of incidence and reflection are equal, it is evident
that ray EF, the axis of the cone, is reflected back on itself, because
by hypothesis it is perpendicular to the surface of the mirror. And
since angle CEF is equal to DEF by *Elements*, i. 4, because lines
EC and ED are equal, as is evident from the corollary of *Elements*,
iii. 34, and similarly CF and DF are equal by the corollary of proposition iii. 1,[3] therefore it is understood that angle CEA is equal
to angle DEB, since they are residues of equal right angles from
which equals (angles CEF and DEF) have been subtracted, and
therefore by the law of reflection ray DE is reflected into ray CE
and vice versa. Similarly, it is shown that every ray of that entire
cone is reflected into its opposite, so that the whole cone is reflected
back on itself.

Again, let cone CDG [fig. 61] be incident on point G, and let its
axis, FG, fall obliquely to the surface of the mirror; and let angle

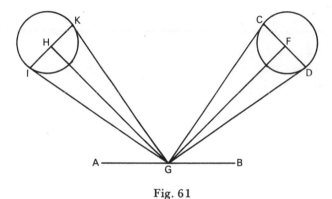

Fig. 61

FGB equal angle HGA. Ray FG will therefore be reflected along
line GH. And since, by common understanding, angle of incidence
DGB is smaller than angle of incidence FGB, angle IGA under
which ray DG is reflected will be smaller than angle HGA by the
law of reflection. Therefore, ray IG will fall between ray HG and
line AG. And since angle of incidence CGB is larger than angle
of incidence FGB, ray CG will be reflected between reflected ray
GH and incident ray FG; therefore, let it be reflected along ray
KG. And since the angle of incident ray CG [angle CGB] exceeds
the angle of incident ray FG [angle FGB] by as much as the angle
of incident ray FG [angle FGB] exceeds the angle of incident ray
DG [angle DGB], because angles CGF and DGF are equal (as was

45 ut prius probatum fuit, quia radii CG et DG equaliter distant a
radio FG, ideo necesse est reflexiones illorum radiorum, scilicet
KG et IG, equaliter distare a reflexione HG, que est reflexio axis,
propter equalitatem angulorum incidentie et reflexionis.

Ex hac ergo demonstratione patet quod pyramis que incidit ad
50 quodcunque punctum speculi plani aut redit in se ipsam, sicut patuit
in prima figuratione, aut redit per aliam pyramidem cuius conus est
punctus incidentie datus et eius axis est reflexio axis pyramidis
incidentis. Quod si ita est in planis, similiter erit in spericis,
columnaribus, et pyramidalibus, et aliis hiis annexis (cuiusmodi
55 sunt specula habentia superficies mukefi, et similiter additas et
diminutas), et hoc sive hec omnia fuerint concava vel convexa,
quoniam in hiis omnibus attenditur equalitas angulorum incidentie
et reflexionis per superficies planas contingentes huiusmodi specula
in punctis incidentie, sicut patet per auctores perspective et simi-
60 liter per auctores librorum de speculis, tam communibus quam
comburentibus. Et hoc est valde utile ad sequentia.

Ceterum quiddam aliud ad sequentia perutile dignum est hic
annecti: et est quantitas anguli pyramidis incidentis (et similiter
reflexe, quoniam eadem est), ut per hoc sciatur quantitas basis in
65 omni distantia a cono quam volumus. Ymaginemur igitur quod superficies speculi transeat super centrum terre, cum non sit in hoc error
sensibilis, sicut patet per Ptolomeum, quia semidiameter terre est
insensibilis quantitatis erga semidiametrum spere solis, sicut patet
per proportiones umbrarum ad gnomones erectos super orizontem et
70 per multas alias vias. Ymaginemur igitur quod quilibet punctus
speculi ad quod incidit pyramis luminosa sit centrum cuiusdam circuli,
cuius circumferentia transeat per centrum solis. Et quia diameter
solis subtenditur tantum 32 minutis unius gradus dicti circuli, sicut
ostendit Ptolomeus in *Almagesti*, necesse est conum pyramidis
75 cuiuslibet luminose (vel angulum illius pyramidis) solum valere 32
minuta unius gradus, secundum quod quatuor anguli recti circa
centrum circuli valent 360 gradus. Si igitur describatur circulus
hic inferius in quadam superficie plana cuius semidiameter sit
quantelibet quantitatis, et dividatur unus gradus sue circumferentie
80 in minuta, et a centro dicti circuli exeant due linee includentes
32 minuta dicte circumferentie, cui arcui scilicet 32 minutis
subtendatur corda, patet quod illa erit diameter basis pyramidis

45 fuit: est *W*   50 aut: *om. W* / in: ad *W*   52 est . . . axis²: *om. W*   54 hiis:
mg. W   55 mukesi *W*   57 attenditur *W*: accenditur *RE*   58 per: quia
W / planas: planam contingere *W* / huius *E*   59 patet: *om. W*   61 comburentibus *R*: obturentibus *E* concurrentibus *W*   62 quiddam *E*: quidam *R* quidem(?) *W*
64 hec(?) *E*   69 portiones *W*   81 cui arcui: quibus *W*

proved above, since rays CG and DG are equally distant from ray
FG), therefore the reflections of those rays (namely, KG and IG)
must be equally distant from reflected ray HG (the reflection of the
axis), because of the equality of the angles of incidence and reflection.

It is evident from this demonstration that the cone falling to some
point of a plane mirror either returns on itself, as was evident in the
first drawing, or returns along another cone having its apex at the
given point of incidence [on the mirror] and its axis along the reflection of the axis of the incident cone. But if this is true in plane
mirrors, it is similarly true in spherical, cylindrical, and conical
mirrors, and in others related to these (such as mirrors having a parabolic[4] surface or some similarly augmented or diminished surface),
whether concave or convex, since in all of them the equality of
angles of incidence and reflection holds for the plane surfaces
tangent to the mirrors at the points of incidence, as is evident from
the authors [of works] on perspective and also from the authors of
books on mirrors, whether common or burning.[5] And this will be
very useful for that which follows.

Another thing very useful for what follows is also properly added
here: and it is the size of the angle of the incident cone (and also of
the reflected one, since they are the same), so that by this one can
know the size of the base at any selected distance from the vertex.
Let us imagine, therefore, that the surface of a mirror passes above
the centre of the earth, since this will introduce no sensible error
[as compared to having it pass through the centre], as is evident from
Ptolemy,[6] because the radius of the earth is of insensible magnitude
by comparison with the radius of the sphere of the sun, and this is
evident from the ratios of shadows to gnomons erected upon the
horizon and from many other things. Thus let us imagine that some
point of the mirror on which a luminous cone is incident is the
centre of a certain circle, the circumference of which passes through
the centre of the sun. And since the diameter of the sun subtends
only thirty-two minutes of a degree of the said circle, as Ptolemy
shows in the *Almagest*,[7] the vertex of any luminous cone (or the
angle of that cone) can have a value of only thirty-two minutes of a
degree, according to the understanding that four right angles about
the centre of a circle equal 360 degrees. If, therefore, here in the
sublunary region a circle of whatever radius you wish is drawn
on a certain plane surface, and one degree on its circumference
is divided into minutes, and from the centre of this circle issue
two lines containing thirty-two minutes of the said circumference
between them, and the chord of this arc of thirty-two minutes is
drawn, it is evident that it will be the diameter of the base of the cone

incidentis ad punctum speculi datum, vel pyramidis reflexe in eadem
distantia ab illo puncto incidentie speculi, quia hec pyramis parva
85 est similis maiori eo quod earum axes sunt suis basibus proportionales.
Sit enim ABC [fig. 62] pyramis magna incidens, et sit diameter sue
basis AB et eius axis CD. Et sit pyramis parva CEG, cuius basis EG
et eius axis CF; et sit hec pyramis parva reflexa pyramis magne, quod
accidit quando CD cadit perpendiculariter super speculum, sicut
90 prius fuit ostensum. Et ponamus EG equedistantem AB. Patet igitur
per secundam sexti *Elementorum* quod triangulus CEG est similis
triangulo CAB. Item per eandem triangulus CEF similis triangulo CAD.

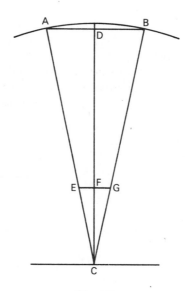

Fig. 62

Ergo proportio CF ad FE est sicut CD ad DA. Similiter ostenditur
quod proportio CF ad FG est sicut CD ad DB. Ergo per quintum
95 librum sequitur ex coniuncta proportionalitate quod CF ad EG sicut
CD ad AB. Patet igitur propositum. Similiterque ostenditur idem si
pyramis incidens non reflectatur in se ipsam, quoniam angulus
pyramidis incidentis est necessario equalis angulo pyramidis reflexe,
quia anguli incidentie et reflexionis sunt equales.
100   Resecando ergo de pyramide incidente equale reflexe, arguitur
ut iam demonstratum est, et solum considero hic de pyramide reflexa

    86 sue: *om. W*   88 CF: *correxi ex* EF *WRE* / sit: fit *W* / hic *W* / pyramis[1]: *ex*
pyramidis *corr. W* / parva . . . pyramis[2]: *om. W*   92 triangulo[2]: angulo *E*   93 CF:
EF *W* / DA: CA *W* / ostendetur *RE*   95 ex: *om. W*   96 similiter *W* / ostendetur
RE / idem: per i. *W*   101 consideritur *W* / hoc *W*

incident at the given point on the mirror (or of the reflected cone at
the same distance from that point of incidence on the mirror, since
this small cone[8] is similar to the larger because their axes are in [the
same] proportion to their bases). Let ABC [fig. 62] be the large
incident cone, and let AB be the diameter of its base and CD its
axis. And let CEG be the small cone, with base EG and axis CF; and
let this small cone be the reflection of the large one, produced when
CD falls perpendicularly on the mirror, as was shown above. And
let us suppose that EG is parallel to AB. It is therefore evident by
Elements, vi. 2,[9] that triangle CEG is similar to triangle CAB. By the

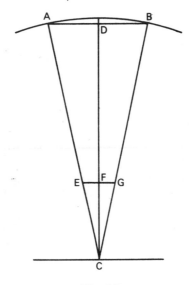

Fig. 62

same reasoning triangle CEF is similar to triangle CAD. Therefore,
the ratio of CF to FE is equal to the ratio of CD to DA. It is shown
similarly that the ratio of CF to FG is equal to the ratio of CD to
DB. Therefore, by [*Elements*,] book v,[10] it follows from the conjoined proportionality that CF is to EG as CD to AB. That which
was proposed is thus evident. And the same thing is shown in the
same way if the incident cone is not reflected back on itself,[11] since
the angle of the incident cone is necessarily equal to the angle of the
reflected cone because the angles of incidence and reflection are
equal.

    To cut short the discussion of an incident cone equal to a reflected
cone, [I note that] one argues as in the demonstrations already presented, and I will here discuss only the cone reflected to the point

usque ad locum combustionis per reflexionem a speculis comburentibus. Et gratia exempli, si combustio distet a superficie speculi per 12
pedes, erit diameter lucis in loco combustionis 9 pars unius pedis
105 cum 36^a eiusdem, sive 5 36te, quod idem est, sicut patet per tabulas
de corda et arcu, quia proportio corde sexte partis circuli (scilicet
60 graduum, cum sit equalis semidiametro eiusdem per penultimam
quarti, et ita sit 60 gradus prout diameter est 120) ad cordam 32
minutorum (et est corda arcus qui subtenditur angulo pyramidis lucis
110 tam incidentis quam reflexe, que corda est 32 minuta et 18 secunda,
sicut per tabulas de corda et arcu patet, evidenter sumendo 50 tertia
pro uno secundo)—proportio inquam prime corde ad secundam est
sicut proportio 12 pedum ad 5 36as unius pedis, sicut per algoristicam
computationem in fractionibus patet manifeste. Et sic patet propositum.

[VII]

Et quia iam demonstratum est quod tota pyramis reflexa sequitur
radium axis reflexum, quia etiam axes sunt omnium fortissimi, ut
prius dictum est, ideo loquamur solum de axibus egredientibus a
5 centro solis et incidentibus ad superficies speculorum, quia ad
congregationem axium in puncto uno consequitur congregatio
omnium aliorum radiorum, in circuitu illius puncti in parvo loco
coartata, ut prius est demonstratum. Et quia in tam parvo loco
infinite pyramides luminose singule a tota portione solis venientes
10 congregantur, necesse est ibi validam fieri combustionem. Dico ergo
quod axes solis quos voco radios, exeuntes a centro solis incidentes
ad superficiem speculi plani, nullatenus possunt congregari per
reflexionem ab eius superficie, sed magis dilatantur post reflexionem
a superficie quam coartantur; secundum veritatem dico, quamvis
15 secundum apparentiam videantur in se ipsos reflecti, quia lux reflexa
a speculis planis est equalis superficiei plane reflectenti secundum
apparentiam sensibilem, quamvis debeat potius post reflexionem
maiorari, cuius apparentie causa tangetur inferius.
   Quod autem hec ita se habeant sic potest demonstrari. Sit circulus
20 ABCD [fig. 63] vice speculi plani rotundi, cuius centrum E. Et
intelligamus ipsum opponi soli, ita quod radius veniens a centro

105 sive: vel *W*   107 sit: fit *E*   108 graduum *W*   113 36as: 36^a *RE*
  3 etiam: et *W*   6 uno: *om. W* / sequitur *W*   7 aliorum: illorum a. *W*
14 coartentur *W* / dico: *om. W*   20 ABCD: ABC *W*

of combustion by a burning mirror. For example, if [the place of] combustion should be twelve feet from the surface of the mirror, the diameter of the light in the place of combustion will be one-ninth plus one thirty-sixth of a foot (or five thirty-sixths, which is the same thing), as is evident from tables of chords and arcs, since the ratio of the chord of the sixth part of a circle (namely, sixty degrees, since it is equal to the radius of the circle by the penultimate proposition of [*Elements*,] book iv,[12] and so must be sixty degrees, just as the diameter is 120) to the chord of [an arc of] thirty-two minutes (that is, the chord of the arc that subtends the angle of the cone of light, incident as well as reflected, and this chord is thirty-two minutes and eighteen seconds, as is apparent from tables of chords and arcs, evidently taking fifty thirds for one second)[13]— the ratio, I say, of the first chord to the second is as the ratio of twelve feet to five thirty-sixths of one foot,[14] as is manifestly evident by algoristic calculation with fractions. And thus what was proposed is evident.

[VII]

And since it has been demonstrated that the entire reflected cone follows the reflected axial ray, and also since the axes are the strongest of all rays, as was said above, let us therefore speak only of the axes issuing from the centre of the sun and incident on the surfaces of mirrors, since the convergence of the axes in one point is accompanied by the convergence of all the other rays, squeezed into a small space in the vicinity of that point, as was demonstrated above.[1] And since an infinity of individual luminous cones coming from the whole surface of the sun is gathered in such a small space, vigorous combustion must occur there. Therefore, I say that the axes of the sun, which I call rays, issuing from the centre of the sun and incident on the surface of a plane mirror, can in no way be gathered together by reflection from its surface, but are more spread out than contracted after reflection from the surface; I speak [here] according to the truth of the matter, although according to appearance they seem to be reflected back on themselves, just as light reflected from plane mirrors appears equal [in width] to the plane reflecting surface, although it must in fact be enlarged after reflection. The cause of this appearance will be touched upon below.[2]

That these things are so can be demonstrated as follows. Let circle ABCD [fig. 63] represent a round flat mirror with centre at E. And let us suppose it to be opposite the sun, so that a ray coming from the

Fig. 63

solis (qui sit FE, dato quod F sit centrum solis) ad centrum speculi
plani, scilicet E, sit perpendicularis ad totam eius superficiem.
Tunc ergo patet quod omnes radii cadentes in unam circumferentiam
25 circa E a puncto F cadunt ad angulos equales. Patet inquam in figura
per quartam primi et per diffinitionem linee perpendicularis ad
superficiem. Et quia omnes anguli incidentie versus centrum sunt
acuti, ideo reflexio fiet extra radios incidentes, quia ex parte
angulorum obtusorum redeunt radii per reflexionem. Sequitur ergo
30 dilatatio, sicut quilibet potest de facili ymaginari. Causa tamen
quare non apparet dilatatio, sed equalitas reflexionis ad incidentiam,
est quia axes in tanta distantia concurrunt, utpote que est inter
solem et terram, quod videntur ad sensum equedistantes et ideo
videntur redire in se ipsos; et hoc est quod facit reflexionem apparere
35 equalem incidentie. Et ideo si ponamus axes solis equedistantes
nullus accidet ex hoc error sensibilis, sicut patet per effectum iam
dictum; sed cogimur per ipsum effectum hoc ponere si volumus
apparentia salvare. Cogimur inquam ipsos secundum apparentiam
ponere equedistantes, quamvis secundum veritatem sint concurrentes.
40 Et hec est causa quare auctor *Libri de speculis comburentibus* ponit
multiplicationem fieri super equedistantes, quoniam si axes incidentes
sunt equedistantes ad sensum, sequitur, secundum quod ipse demon-
strat, quod omnes qui cadunt in superficie speculi figurati prout ipse

22 qui: quidem *W* / FE dato: secundum data *W* / centrum[1]: *om. E.*   25 F: *om. W*
30 causa: eam *W*   31 quare: quia *W*   36 ullus *R* / error: *R contains a marginal
gloss about here*   37 sed: s. quod *W* / effectum: est tantum *W*   40 hoc *E* /
liber *W* / comburentibus: *om. W*   42 sint *RE*

Fig. 63

centre of the sun (let F be the centre of the sun and FE the ray) to the centre E of the plane mirror is perpendicular to its whole surface.[3] It is evident, then, that all rays falling from point F on to one circumference about E fall at equal angles. This is evident, I say, in the figure by [*Elements*,] i. 4,[4] and the definition of a line perpendicular to a surface. And since all angles of incidence near the centre are acute,[5] reflection will take place outside the incident rays, since rays return by reflection in the direction of the obtuse angles. Thus the result is spreading out [of the radiation], as anybody can easily visualize. The reason why we do not observe this spreading, but perceive equality of the incident and reflected radiation, is that the axes[6] converge[7] over such a great distance (namely, that which separates the sun from the earth) that they appear parallel to sense and thus seem to return on themselves; and this is why the reflected radiation appears equal [in width] to the incident radiation. And therefore, if we posit parallel solar axes, no sensible error results, as is evident from the effect already mentioned; indeed, we are compelled by the effect itself to posit this [parallelism] if we wish to save the appearances. We are compelled, I say, to assume the axes to be parallel according to appearance, although according to truth they are convergent. And this is why the author of the *Liber de speculis, comburentibus* assumes multiplication to take place along parallel lines, since if the incident axes are parallel according to sense, it follows, from that which he demonstrates, that all axes incident on the surface of a mirror shaped as he

docet figurari concurrent in punctum unum, ad minus secundum
45 apparentiam. Et ideo omnes pyramides circa concursum axium in
parvo loco coangustate necessario visui apparebunt.

Et quia iam dictum est quod axes solares nequeunt per reflexionem
a speculis planis congregari in punctum unum, immo omnes sunt post
incidentiam secundum sensum equedistantes, aut secundum veritatem
50 magis dilatate quam incidentes, ideo sequitur de spericis, et primo
de convexis. Dico ergo quod axes solares incidentes ad superficiem
convexam speculi sperici nequeunt per reflexionem a tali superficie
in punctum unum congregari, nec super lineas equedistantes redire,
sed magis disgregantur post reflexionem quanto magis a superficie
55 recedunt. Et omnes axes solis cadentes in unam circulationem circa
axem speculi equaliter disgregantur; et qui propinquiores fuerint
axi speculi disgregantur minus, qui vero remotiores plus, sicut patet
in figura [fig. 64]. Et currit demonstratio super hoc.

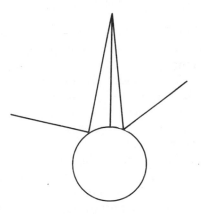

Fig. 64

De concavo sperico patet ex prehabitis quod omnes axes solares
60 cadentes in unam circulationem circa axem reflectuntur ad punctum
unum; et cadentes in aliam ad aliud. Hoc enim demonstratum est
prius, ubi ponebatur multiplicatio fieri ab uno puncto. Et si multiplicatio axium sit super equedistantes secundum sensum, sicut dictum
est, sequitur illud idem, sicut potest demonstrari de facili. Sed con-
65 gregatio radiorum incidentium ad minimum circulum circa axem que
remotior est a superficie speculi omnibus aliis non potest excedere

44 concurrunt *W*   54 *post* sed *interl. add.* *W*^c tanto   56 propiores *R*
58 hec *W*   62 ubi: ut *R*   64 sed: s. cum *W*

describes converge at one point, at least according to appearance.[8]
And therefore, all cones necessarily appear to the eye to be
compressed into a small region about the intersection of the axes.

And since it has already been stated that solar axes cannot be
gathered to one point by reflection from plane mirrors (although
after incidence all are sensibly parallel, but according to truth are
more spread out than the incident rays), we must now consider
spherical mirrors, and first convex spherical mirrors. I say, therefore,
that solar axes incident on the surface of a convex spherical mirror
cannot be gathered into one point by reflection from such a surface;
nor do they return along parallel lines, but after reflection are more
spread out the further they recede from the reflecting surface. And
all solar axes falling on one circle about the axis of the mirror are
equally spread out; and those closer to the axis of the mirror are
spread out less, while the more remote are spread out more, as is

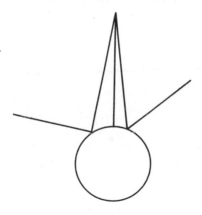

Fig. 64

evident in the figure [fig. 64].[9] And the demonstration proceeds in
this manner.

As for concave spherical mirrors, it is evident from the foregoing
that all solar axes incident on one circle about the axis [of the
mirror] are reflected to one point; and those incident on another
circle are reflected to another point. This was demonstrated above,
where it was supposed that multiplication takes place from a single
point.[10] And if axial multiplication should be along sensibly parallel
lines, as was stated, the same result would follow, as can easily be
demonstrated. But the [point of] convergence of rays incident on the
least possible circle about the axis [of the mirror], which converge
at a point further from the surface of the mirror than do any others,

medietatem semidiametri spere cuius speculum est portio. Et hoc similiter potest faciliter demonstrari. Et hec duo demonstrata sunt in primis duobus foliis, que facta fuerunt ante cedulas; ideo ad
70 presens supersedeo.

Similiter quoque potest demonstrari quod axes solares cadentes in unam circulationem circa axem pyramidis rotunde concave congregantur in locum unum, et qui cadunt in aliam in locum alium, sicut accidit in spericis. Et potest fieri combustio per huiusmodi specula ante
75 vel retro secundum quod placuerit figuranti. Potest etiam fieri unum speculum ex diversis portionibus pyramidum quod comburet ante et retro. Et hec omnia faciliter possunt demonstrari. Sed quia omnes hee congregationes predicte sunt partiales et fiunt in diversis punctis, ideo de hiis supersedendum ad presens. De pyramidali convexo
80 patet quod disgregat et non congregat. De columnari tam concavo quam convexo etiam patet quod neque disgregat neque congregat, sed reflectit per equedistantiam, secundum quod lux equedistanter incidit. Et in hiis omnibus intelligo quod axis speculi convertitur ad axem solis.

[VIII]

Sed presens intentio est de superficie que·reflectit omnes axes solis incidentes ad eam totam in punctum unum, et hec est superficies concava corporis mukefi, secundum quod demonstratur in *Libro de*
5 *speculis comburentibus.* Cuius compositio sic invenitur. Tornetur quedam pyramis rotunda, et quanto maior fuerit tanto melior. Deinde dividatur in duas medietates superficie transeunte per caput eius et per centrum sue basis. Et patet quod communis sectio superficiei plane et pyramidis est quidam triangulus qui totus est intra pyra-
10 midem; et linee terminales illius trianguli due sunt in superficie curva pyramidis, et tertia est diameter sue basis. Et sit exempli gratia ABC [fig. 65] talis triangulus, cuius latus AB sit diameter basis pyramidis, et due linee AC et BC concurrant in capite pyramidis. Et ponamus gratia exempli quod angulus pyramidis sit rectus; erit
15 ergo angulus ACB rectus. Deinde protrahamus quandam lineam equedistantem lateri AC vel lateri BC, non est vis cui, et hoc a quocunque puncto AB linee, et sit gratia exempli a puncto D quod sit centrum basis pyramidis, et sit illa equedistans DE. Secetur igitur altera

68 faciliter: de facili *R* / hic: *E*   69 facte *R* / ante: quando *W*   73 aliam:
alium *W*   76 combureret *E*   81 neque congregat: *om. W*

cannot be further from the mirror than half the radius of the sphere
of which the mirror is a portion.[11] And this too can easily be demonstrated. And these two conclusions are demonstrated in the first two
leaves [of this treatise], which were written before the little slips;[12]
therefore, I now pass over them.

It can be demonstrated similarly that the solar axes falling on one
circle about the axis of a concave conical mirror are gathered in one
place, and those that fall on another circle in another place, as in
spherical mirrors.[13] And the [point of] combustion in such a mirror
can be moved forwards or backwards at the will of the fabricator.
Also, a mirror can be made from portions of different cones to produce
combustion before or behind.[14] And all these things can be easily
demonstrated. But since all of the aforementioned gatherings [of rays]
are partial and occur at different points, we will omit further discussion of them for the present. Regarding convex conical mirrors, it is
evident that they disperse rather than gather rays. Regarding cylindrical mirrors, both concave and convex, it is evident that they neither
disperse nor gather rays, but reflect them along parallel lines, if the
light is incident along parallel lines.[15] And in all of these cases I understand the axis of the mirror to coincide with the axis of the sun.

[VIII]

But our present concern is with that surface which reflects all axes
of the sun incident on the whole mirror to a single point [of focus],
and this is the concave surface of a paraboloidal body, as the *Liber
de speculis comburentibus* demonstrates.[1] The construction of such
a surface proceeds as follows. Have a certain cone turned [on a
lathe], the larger the better. Then divide it into halves by means of
a [plane] surface passing through its vertex and the centre of its base.
It is evident that the common intersection of the plane surface and
the cone is a certain triangle, entirely within the cone; and two sides
of this triangle lie in the curved [lateral] surface of the cone, and the
third is the diameter of its base. For example, let ABC [fig. 65] be
such a triangle, and let side AB be the diameter of the base of the
cone, and let the two lines AC and BC intersect at the vertex of the
cone. And let us suppose, for example, that the angle of the cone is a
right angle; therefore, ACB will be a right angle. Then draw a line
parallel to side AC or side BC (it does not matter which) from any
point of line AB; let it be, for instance, from point D, which is the
centre of the base of the cone, and let that parallel line be DE. Thus

2 intensio *E*　　　3 hoc *E*　　　4 mukesi *W*　　　5 positio *W*　　　8 communis:
omnis *W*　　　13 basis: *rep. RE*　　　15 ACB: ABC *W*　　　18 altera: alia *W*

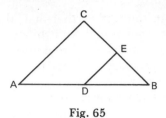

Fig. 65

medietas pyramidis super lineam DE, ita quod superficies secans
20 stet orthogonaliter super superficiem ABC trianguli. Et ad hoc
facilius faciendum, trahatur a puncto D linea perpendicularis ad
lineam AB, et sit illa perpendicularis in basi pyramidis, que non
potest hic in plano figurari. Superficies igitur transiens super illas
duas lineas secat superficiem ABC orthogonaliter quod intendimus.
25 Communis igitur sectio huius plane superficiei secàntis et medietatis
pyramidis secte est sectio mukefi; et continetur duabus lineis rectis
et una tortuosa, que nec est circularis nec recta nec composita ex
rectis. Et est huiusmodi sectio talis figure quasi [fig. 66]. Et una
duarum rectarum, scilicet DE, que fuit in superficie trianguli prime
30 sectionis pyramidis, vocatur axis húius sectionis. Dico ergo quod

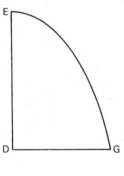

Fig. 66

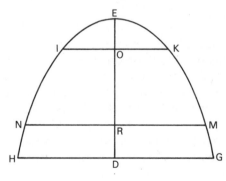

Fig. 67

si super axem DE fixam circumvoluantur due linee, scilicet DG
recta et EG tortuosa, provenit corpus concavum concavitate mukefi
intenta. Et si illud corpus secaretur per superficiem planam transeuntem per punctum capitis, quod est E, et per centrum basis, quod est
35 D, proveniret superficies quasi talis [fig. 67].
Inventa ergo sectione DEG, statuatur ex alia parte axis DE

19 pyramidis: *mg. R*   20 super: *om. E*   21 faciendum: intelligendum *W'*
alias f. *mg. W^C* / perpendiculariter *W*   23 in plano: plane *W*   26 pyramidis: *mg.*
W^C om. W' / mukesi *W*   30 ergo: *om. W*   32 mukesi *W*

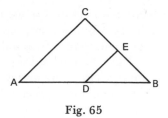

Fig. 65

the half of the cone will be cut along line DE, in such a way that the
cutting surface is perpendicular to the surface of the triangle, ABC.
And to achieve this end easily, draw from point D a line perpendicular to line AB, and let this perpendicular (which cannot be represented here in a plane surface)[2] lie in the base of the cone. Therefore,
the surface passing through those two lines cuts surface ABC perpendicularly, as we intend. Therefore, the common intersection of
this plane cutting surface and the half pyramid that is cut is a
parabola; and it is contained within two straight lines and an irregular
line that is neither circular nor straight nor composed of straight
segments. And such an intersection is of approximately this shape
[fig. 66].[3] And one of the two straight lines—namely, DE, which

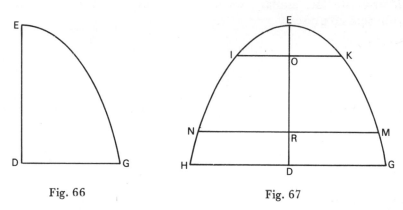

Fig. 66   Fig. 67

was in the surface of the triangle produced by the first cutting
of the cone—is called the axis of this section. I say, then, that
if axis DE remains fixed and the two lines, straight line DG and
irregular line EG, are rotated about it, a concave body of the intended parabolic curvature is produced. And if that body should
be cut by a plane surface passing through the vertex (point E) and
the centre of the base (point D), a surface such as this [fig. 67][4]
would be produced.

Having thus defined section DEG, let a similar section be drawn on

consimilis sectio; et proveniet superficies quasi HEGD [fig. 67, *supra*]. Habita ergo tali superficie, si velimus componere speculum quod sit secundum figuram ovi, abscindemus circa conum E quandam por-
40 tionem, sicut portionem EIK, et tornabimus corpus concavum ita quod IEK linea possit ubique eius concavitati adherere sine medio. Quod sic fiet. Circulabimus in ligno spisso ad spissitudinem OE et amplius circulum, cuius diameter sit equalis IK linee. Et faciemus quandam regulam tortam, que sit equalis IE et omnino similis. Et
45 tornabimus illud lignum super centrum circuli descripti in eo quous-que regula IE possit undique in concavitate coaptari sine medio aliquo usque ad conum. Et concavitas que provenit erit concavitas quesita. Si vero velimus facere speculum anulare, sumemus quandam portionem ex parte HG, sicut est HGMN; et sit MN equedistans HG. Faciemus
50 ergo sic. Sumemus lignum spissum ad spissitudinem linee DR vel amplius. Et describemus in una extremitate eius alium circulum, cuius diameter sit equalis linee MN. Et tornabimus hoc lignum super duo centra duorum circulorum iam dictorum usquoque regula facta sicut HN linea possit coaptari undique in eius concavitate. Et quidem
55 totum quod est inter duos circulos de ligno debet eici. Et concavitas que provenit est concavitas inventa. Hoc etiam notandum quod ovale comburit ante se, anulare retro. De distantia combustionis nichil certum scio ad presens.

    Explicit.

40 tornabitur *W*   41 IEK: ICK *W* / sine: quasi s. *W*   43 equalis: e. se *R*
45 lignum super: supra *W*   47 provenerit *W*   48 sumemus: servemus *W*
50 sumemus: s. ergo *R*   54 quidem: quod *RE*   56 ovale: urinale *W*
57 distantia: d. vero *W*   59 explicit: *mg. E* e. tractatus fratris Rogeri Bacone ordinis fratrum minorum de multiplicatione lucis *W*

the other side of axis DE; there will [thus] be formed a surface
such as HEGD [fig. 67, above]. Having produced this surface, if we
wish to construct an oviform mirror,[5] we must remove from the
vertex E a certain portion, such as EIK, and turn a hollow body [on
a lathe] in such a way that line IEK can everywhere make perfect
contact with its concavity. This is done as follows. We draw a circle
of diameter IK on a thick piece of wood, thicker than OE. And we
construct a certain curved template equal to IE and with its exact
shape. Then we turn that piece of wood [on a lathe] about the centre
of the circle drawn on it until template IE fits into its concavity
everywhere without gaps up to the vertex. And the concavity thus
produced will be of the desired shape.[6] But if we wish to construct
an annular mirror, we take a certain portion near HG, such as
HGMN; and let MN be parallel to HG. We then proceed as follows.
We take a thick piece of wood, as thick as (or thicker than) line DR.
And we draw another circle on one of its ends, equal in diameter to
line MN.[7] And we turn this wood about the centres of the two aforementioned circles until a template in the shape of line HN can fit
everywhere into its concavity. And all the wood between the two
circles should be removed. And the concavity that results is the concavity defined [above]. It must also be noted that the oval mirror
produces combustion in front of itself, the annular mirror behind.[8]
Concerning the exact location of the point of combustion, I have no
certain knowledge at present.[9]

Here ends [the treatise].

Appendix

MSS *S* and *A* add the following passages to *De multiplicatione specierum*; the first of them (*a*) appears also in MSS *M* and *P*. I judge these additions to represent Bacon's own revisions of the treatise (see the Introduction, p. xxx). Additions of fewer than twenty words, as well as deletions, are recorded in the apparatus criticus and do not appear here.

a (PROLOGUE)

Postquam[1] habitum est de principiis rerum naturalium communibus, que sunt materia et forma et privatio potentie passive et active, que omnia sunt ordinata ad productionem rerum naturalium et sunt a parte
5 principii materialis, nunc dicendum est de hiis que ordine naturali sequuntur. Ad productionem vero rerum naturalium de potentia materie patientis, primo incurrit influentia agentis in hanc materiam, ut de potentia talis materie effectus naturales producantur. Et ideo oportet scire actionem agentis et modum agendi in materiam antequam
10 sciamus ipsam productionem sive generationem rei de potentia materie per virtutem agentis. Virtus enim activa agentis transmutat materiam naturalem et assimilat eam sibi, ut per hanc assimilationem faciat effectus completos, univocos vel equivocos. Univocus effectus est qui nomine et diffinitione concordat cum agente, ut homo generatus
15 cum homine generante, et lux generata cum generante. Equivocus effectus est qui non communicat in nomine cum agente nec diffinitione, ut lux generat calorem et calor putrefactionem, et sic de infinitis. Nisi igitur sciatur hec actio agentis in materiam naturalem, quam vocamus influentiam agentis in materiam patientem, nichil poterimus
20 scire de effectuum productione.

Et ideo immediate post predicta oportet tractari hanc influentiam. Circa vero eam plene intelligendam et distincte, oportet ordinari decem capitula principalia, quorum aliqua habebunt aliqua capitula eis subalternata propter veritatum multitudinem que in uno particulari
25 capitulo non possunt concludi. Quoniam primo oportet eam considerari in corporalibus agentibus et patientibus; secundo in spiritualibus, ad invicem et respectu corporalium. In corporalibus vero primo

2 communibus: *om. A* / qui *S*   3 potentie . . . active *M'*: ad potentia passiva et activa *M*^C / que: rep. *S*   6 sequuntur *MP*: secuntur *S* consequuntur *A*   8 ideo *AP*: primo *M* immo *S*   9 scire *MP*: sciri *SA* / agendi *M*^C: agentis *M'SA* patientis *P* 15 lux . . . generante: *om. A* / equivocus: *om. S*   17 infinitis: imperitis *S* 18 quam: *ex* quas *corr. M*   19 *ante* materiam *scr. et del. A* potentiam   27 respectu: idem *S*

oportet sciri quomodo vocetur hec influentia et quid sit; secundo que
res possunt sic influere et agere; tertio de modo generali faciendi
30 huiusmodi influentiam in patiens ab agente; quarto de natura et
proprietate patientium et recipientium huiusmodi influentiam ab
agentibus eis proportionalibus; quinto a quibus agentibus et in
quibus patientibus potest hec influentia compleri in effectus similes
agentibus suis nomine et diffinitione; sexto de modo multiplicandi
35 hanc influentiam in corporibus ab agente et a loco sue generationis
prime secundum modos linearum et angulorum et figurarum in quibus
fiunt multiplicationes naturales; septimo est de modis spiritualibus
essendi huiusmodi influentiarum in rebus in quibus multiplicate
sunt; octavo est de actione et alteratione naturali in corporibus
40 mundi fienda per has influentias, cum plena investigatione totius
fortitudinis et debilitatis et omnium graduum istius actionis
secundum omnem varietatem eius, penes lineas rectas, fractas, et
reflexas et penes angulos rectos et obliquos et penes figuras et
spericas et pyramidales et alias in quibus actio nature pulcris modis
45 variatur; nono de corruptione istarum influentiarum; et tunc decimo
de hac influentia ut tangit spirituales substantias.

Et quia auctoritas in omnibus 'plurimum valet', secundum Tullium
primo *De questionibus*,[2] et Plinius in prologo *Naturalium*[3] arbi-
tratur 'benignum et ingenui pudoris plenum fateri per quos profici-
50 mus', et nimis presumptuosum est aliquem sibi ascribere aliorum
labores, cum sufficiat priores auctores fideliter exponere, et que
desunt apud eos complere secundum cuiuslibet posterioris potestatem,
eo quod 'nichil est perfectum in humanis inventionibus';[4] atque sic
furtive rapientes auctoritatem alienam, merito cadere debent ab
55 auctoritatis dignitate, ut eis non credatur, postquam non dignantur
auctorum titulis dignis que scribunt confirmare. Ideo quos in hiis
que dicam circa influentiam agentis sequi volo prenotare dignum
duco, sicut in aliis feci partibus et capitulis et faciam in sequentibus et maxime propter difficultates maiores pluribus aliis et
60 negligentiam vulgi studentium circa ea que pertinent ad hanc influentiam, et quia hec pars pulcrior est omnibus partibus philosophie
speculative et melior aliis multis. Sunt autem illi quorum sententiis

28 quid: que *A* / sit *APM*^C: scit *M'* fit *S*   29–30 faciendi huiusmodi: efficiendi h.
A h. et f. (et *scr. et del. M*) *MS*   30 in *APM*^C: et *S* in *M'* / ab *M*^C: sub *M'*   32 proportionalibus *M*^C: proportionibus *M'*   34 suis: scilicet *A*   35 hanc: huiusmodi *A*
36 primo *A*   37 multiplicationes *M*^C: multit *M'*   38 influentias *MS*   40 per
. . . influentias: *om. A* propter has i. *S* / cum: est *S*   43 angulos . . . figuras: f. rectas *M*
45 et tunc: *om. M*   46 hac: *om. A* / ut *M*^C: ubi *M'*   47 in: et *S*   49 benignum:
correxi ex benignitati *A* beg¹niuñ *S om. M* / ingenui *M'*: ingenii *M*^C*A* ingenii vel *S* / plenum:
plurimum *S*   49–50 profecimus *A*   50 aliquam *M* / sibi: ei *S*   51 qui *S*
55 auctoris *S* / ut eis: vocis *S* / non¹: *interl. M*^C   56 titulus *S*   57 que: *om. M* /
dicam: *mg. M*^C dicendis *M'* *om. A*

oportet nos principaliter, uti auctores aspectuum sive visuum, et consimiles eis, ut auctores speculorum comburentium et pyramidum
65 et omnium figurationum dignarum. Unde Ptolomeus in *Libris de opticis sive aspectibus* est principaliter imitandus, quia hic dedit omnes radices aspectuum cum ramis qui sunt de necessitate perspective. Alii omnes exposuerunt eum, et addiderunt ea que sunt de bene esse seu de bonitate artis et pulcritudine, inter quos longe precipuus
70 est aliis Alhacen *De aspectibus*; deinde Iacobus Alkindi in *Libro de aspectibus*, et auctor *Libri de speculis*, per que fiat visus reflexus, et Euclides *De aspectibus*, et similiter idem *De speculis*, et Tideus *De aspectibus*, et auctor *Libri de speculis comburentibus*, et Euclides *De libris elementorum*, et Theodosius *De speris*, et Apollonius *De*
75 *pyramidibus*, quorum sententias in tertia parte huius operis pertractabo, ut michi videbitur expedire. Et plures propter prolixitatem nominum istorum non tangentur, precipue ubi ratio evidenter concludit intentum, ut ubi concordat vulgus philosophantium, quamvis sepius ut videtur michi expedire ipsos auctores, et loca
80 suorum librorum nominabo.

Quia vero non habemus in latino libros Aristotelis et Avicenne et Averroys et Alpharabii de ista influentia, scilicet libros eorum de aspectibus, ideo que hic recitari habent non possunt principaliter verificari per vias Aristotelis, Avicenne, et Averroys; oportet uti
85 sententiis istorum in naturalibus libris, quia in libris istorum qui ad manus nostras venerunt cause istius influentie non dantur sufficienter, nec pro maiori parte. Quamvis enim perspectiva non referat intentionem suam nisi ad visum, tamen eadem principia et eedem radices universales que determinantur ab auctoribus visuum et
90 aspectuum possunt et debent applicari respectu aliorum sensuum; et non solum respectu sensus, sed respectu totius materie mundialis alterande per species et virtutes agentium quorumcunque. Et ideo tota nature actio et rerum generatio naturalium capiunt suas radices et principia a predictis auctoribus aspectuum; et hii non certificant
95 aliquid nisi per libros Euclidis et Theodosii et huiusmodi, propter

63 visuum: *om. A*   64 eius *A*   65 dignare *S* / de: *om. S*   66 est: sibi *S* / hic: *om. SA* / dedit *M'*: dividit *mg. M^C*   67 omnes: *om. A*   69 et pulcritudine: *om. S* / longe: legere *S*   70 in libro: *om. M*   71 *ante* auctor *add. M' (sed del. M^C)* de idem de speculis et Trocus de aspectibus / auctor *om. M*   72 similiter: super *S om. M* / Tideus: Trocus *M*   72–3 et¹ ... de²: *mg. add. M^C*   75 sententias *AM^C*: sententiis *M'S*   77 tanguntur *M* / evidenter: precipue *scr. et del. M*   78 intentum: i. suum *S* / philosophantium *S*: probantium *MA*   79 videtur michi: videbit *A*   80 nominabo: *om. A*   81 in latino: *om. S*   82–4 scilicet ... Averroys: *om. A*   83 que: *mg. M^C om. M'*   84 *post* uti *scr. et del. M* eorum   86 *post* manus *scr. et del. M* istorum / pervenerunt *M*   88 eedem: cetere *M*   89 universales: *om. A*   90 aliorum: illorum(?) *A*   91 materie: m. alterantis *M'* m. alterabilis *M^C* / *post* mundialis *interl. add. M^C* vel *M* uno *S*   92 quorumcunque *AM^C*: quocunque *SM'* / ideo: primo *M*   93 tota: *om. M*   95 Theodosum *S* / huius *S*

quod philosophans in scientia naturali et rerum naturalium generatione secundum libros Aristotelis, Avicenne, et Averroys, et Senece non poterit hoc, ut oportet scire, nisi sciat uti sententiis auctorum predictorum. Non tamen convenit ut hic descendam ad ea que sunt
100 propria visui, a quibus autonomatice nominatur perspectiva et scientia aspectuum, sed solum debent hic tangi que sunt communia cum agenti naturali, et in quodcunque fiat actio, sive in visum sive in alios sensus sive in totam mundi materiam. Et quamvis in hac parte auctores aspectuum prevaleant libris Aristotelis, Avicenne,
105 et Averroys, et huiusmodi in latinum translatis, tamen maxime usque ad sextum capitulum multum communicat naturalis cum perspectivo in causarum assignatione.

Sed hec quinque capitula prima paucas habent veritates nec principales circa hanc influentiam, sed introductorias tantum ad ea
110 que principaliter requiruntur, ut patet ex serie tractatus. Scire enim debet philosophans in rebus naturalibus cognoscendis quod naturalis philosophus duo considerat, in quibus stat pondus et potestas naturalis philosophie, scilicet motum secundum formam et motum secundum locum rectum et circularem. Sed motus secundum
115 formam, qui comprehendit generationem et corruptionem, alterationem, et augmentum et diminutionem, non potest intelligi nec manifestari sine multis, quorum unum est influentia agentium naturalium, qui faciunt hos motus per suas influentias. Hec enim influentia non potest sciri causaliter nisi per auctores aspectuum, cum adiutorio
120 Euclidis, Theodosii, et Apollonii, et huiusmodi, ut pars presens manifeste docebit; sicut nec motus secundum locum rectus sine libris ponderum sciri potest, nec circularis sine astrologia, quia ille motus adducit universalia generantia, que sunt stelle, ad singulas partes habitationis prout expedit mundo. Motus etiam mixtionis element-
125 orum et humorum in generatione rerum naturalium secundum gradus et proportiones varias, ut exigitur in rerum generatione mixtarum, non potest sciri sine potestate scientiarum, quarum est omnia genera proportionum considerare et harum rationem dare. Et huiusmodi sunt libri elementorum et libri de proportionibus et

96 quod: *interl.* M^C *om.* S / scientia: philosophia A 98 hec SA 99 convenit: occurrit M / ad M^C: ab M' / que sunt: *ex* quesitio *mg. corr.* M / sint S 100 quibus: *om.* S / denominatur A 101 scientie M / sunt: *mg.* M^C *om.* M' / communia: natura M' universalia *mg.* M^C 102 agenti: omni a. M agente A / et: *scr. et del.* M 103 mundi: *om.* A 110 ex: in M 112 constat S 113 motus A / secundum: et M 115 qui: *om.* A 116–17 manifestari SP: demonstrari A monstrari *mg.* M^C increari(?) M' 117 influendi S 118 qui $M'SP$: que M^CA 120 et huiusmodi: *om.* M 121 manifeste: *scr. et del.* M / secundum locum: sed locus S / rectus M^C: recta M' 122 circularis APM^C: circulariter SM' / sine M^C: nec M' 123 stelle: celi et s. *mg.* M^C 124 etiam M^C: et M' 126 portiones S 127 scientiarum: sententiarum MS / est M^C: enim M' 129 huius S / libri²: liber A

130 arismetica, non solum speculativa sed etiam practica, ex quibus
Iacobus Alkindi suam scientiam utilem in *Libro de gradibus* extraxit;
similiter de generantibus ipsis universalibus, que sunt celi et stelle,
non solum astrologia, sed eius practica astronomia necessarie sunt;
de geometria non solum speculativa, sed magis practica, certum
135 est quod effectus naturales satis egent eis, sicut accidit in fabrica-
tione speculorum comburentium et figuratione perspicuorum et
multorum instrumentorum in quibus ostendantur et per que fiant
miracula operationum nature, ut explanabitur inferius.

Et ideo volens scire generationem universalem rerum naturalium
140 non potest proficere nisi per mathematicas practicas et speculativas,
et scientias aspectuum et ponderum, sicut desiderans scire in particulari generationem harum rerum non potest scire aliquid dignum
sine alkimia et agricultura philosophica et scientia experimentali,
eo quod, ut patuit in prima parte huius operis et in prima specie
145 qualitatis in qua scientie distinguuntur, alkimiste determinant de
omnibus rebus inanimatis in particulari ab elementis ad partes
animalium et plantarum inclusive, et agricultura philosophica
determinat in propria disciplina omnes varietates naturarum et
proprietatum in plantis et animalibus; secundum quod Aristoteles in
150 quinque voluminibus explicavit naturas et proprietates animalium,
et in multis libris ea que ad plantas pertinent explicaverunt ipse,
et alii philosophi qui in libris naturalibus quorum est in universali
de illis determinare non possunt nec debent coartari, sicut nec ea
que de rebus inanimatis scienda sunt, et que alkimiste explicant in
155 particulari.

Scientia autem experimentalis docet certificari omnes conclusiones naturalis philosophie per experientiam, quod non potest
naturalis philosophia tradita in libris Aristotelis apud latinos vulgatis, nisi circa sua principia, quoniam per argumenta concludit
160 conclusiones ex principiis, sed non invenit eas per experientiam;
et ideo certificare non potest sine hac scientia. Quapropter non
est mirandum si circa beatificationem intelligentie agentium
naturalium volo procedere per scientias aspectuum et alias practicas,
quoniam naturaliter philosophans in libris naturalibus quibus vulgus

130 sed M^C: quia M' | etiam *AP*: *om. MS*   131 sententiam *M* | in libro: *om. A*
133 astrologia: a. speculativa *A* | eius: etiam *A* | astronomia: *om. A* | necessario *M*
135 eis: *om. A*   136 et¹: *interl. M^C* in *M'*   137 ostenduntur *A*   140 et
speculativas: *om. M*   143 alkimia *AP*: album *MS* | philosophico *S*   144 operationis
S | prima²: *om. S*   145 alkimiste *A*: album *MS* | determinat *M*   146 *post* elementis
mg. add. A usque   148 omnes: communes *M*   149 in¹: et *M*   150 quinque
MP: quinto *S* 50 *A*   151 eas *A* | plateas *S* | ipse: i. album *M*   152 qui *M'*: que
M^C | *ante* libris *scr. et del. S* aliis   154 alkimiste: aliter *M* | explicantur *MS*
156 experimentalis: particularis *A*   157 per experientiam: *om. A*   162 intelligentie: *om. A*   164 quoniam: quando *A*

165 utitur latinorum nudus est sine aliis scientiis, nec potest multum
nisi per viam narrationis et argumenta dialectica et per effectus
et causas remotas procedere, et multum in universali per omnia. Iam
enim patuit in precedentibus quod philosophia naturalis communiter
et large sumpta habet novem scientias principales, quarum una et
170 vilior est illa qua latini utuntur in libris Aristotelis et Avicenne
et Averroys. Communia enim hec sunt et leviter explicata in libris
eorum qui apud latinos sunt, quorum intentionem cum causarum
assignatione conabor ut potero assignare.

β (I. 1. 29)

175 Equivocat enim ad similitudinem rei, de qua loquimur, et ad speciem
que dicitur relative respectu generis; que species est unum de
universalibus, ut homo est species animalis. Et ideo cavendum est
in sequentibus quando fit intentio de una et quando de altera.

γ (I. 1. 98)

180 Et ideo si agens producit effectum difformem, ut lux colorem, oportet
quod prius producat effectum uniformem. Quod si dicitur quod hoc
est verum, sed hic effectus non est species de qua dictum est, nec
primus omnino effectus sed secundus, ita quod ponantur tres gradus
vel pluries; ut ignis primo faciat speciem et virtutem suam in lignis,
185 deinde per eam educat iterum ignem de potentia materie, tres faciat
exsiccationem et alia consequentia, ut lux solis primo faciat in hiis
inferioribus speciem suam et virtutem, deinde lucem, tres calorem,
quatuor exsiccationem, quinque putrefactionem, sex mortem in
rebus animatis, et sic de aliis agentibus, secundum quod ordinata
190 sunt ad plures vel pauciores operationes; sed hoc stare non potest,
quia si secundus effectus est similis agenti, multo magis primus et
immediatior, postquam agens assimilat patiens quantum potest,
quoniam magis potest in primo effectu quam in secundo, sicut in
secundo magis quam in tertio.

195   δ (I. 1. 222)

Ex quibus apparet erroris evacuatio qui ponit speciem non esse idem
in natura specifica cum agente, et quod non sit individuum aliud

165 nudus: mundus *S*   166 rationis *M* / dialectica: *om. M*   170 illa: i. que
est *MS*   171 Averroys: aliorum *M*   175 equivocat: vocatur *S*   177 homo:
om. A   181 producat: *om. S* / quod² ... quod³: et *A*   184 ut: ita ut *A*
185 eam: *om. A* / inducat *S* / materie: *om. S* / tres: et *A*   192 patiens: prima *S*
197 non: *om. A*

eiusdem speciei specificissime, dicendo quod species albedinis non
est alia albedo. Sed nescio quid aliud figmentum multis erroribus
200 et variis singulorum confectum. Dicendum est enim quod species
albedinis est albedo, licet incompleta et potest compleri. Sed dum
est incompleta vocatur species albedinis, quando vero completa
vocatur albedo. Et tamen secundum veritatem in principio est albedo,
et potest dici et vocari albedo; sicut filius hominis dum est incom-
205 pletus vocatur puer, postea cum ad etatem venerit virilem plene
sortitur nomen hominis. Et tamen in pueritia est verus homo, et
potest sic dici et vocari, licet usualiter appropriamus ei nomen
puer.

ε (I. 3. 90)

210 Et arguitur etiam ad hoc quod nulla forma preter animam movet
materiam cuius est actus. Sed hec virtus movet profundum patientis;
ergo non est forma educta de potentia patientis, hec enim virtus
transmutat ipsum patiens per totum. Et ideo non videtur esse forma
eius cuius non sit anima.

ζ (I. 3. 146)

Quod autem ad hoc idem obicitur solvendum est, quod virtus non
movet materiam cuius est actus et forma, sed aliam ei coniunctam, ut
virtus facta in prima parte patientis non movet illam partem nec transmutat in aliquo, sed perficit ut forma et actus. Movet tamen partem
220 secundam ipsius patientis et generat sibi simile in ea, educendo de
potentia materie illius secunde partis speciem et virtutem ei similem.
Et illa iam educta de potentia secunde partis non movet illam secundam cuius est actus, sed tertiam, educendo in ea similem speciem
de potentia materie illius tertie partis, et sic ulterius. Et hec est
225 sententia Aristotelis, ut explanabitur inferius suo loco. Unde ex
falsa ymaginatione provenit hec cavillatio, sicut alia.

η (I. 4. 73)

Si dicatur quod grave potest esse tam parve quantitatis quod non
descendet et leve quod non ascendet, concedendum est hoc in motu
230 locali propter corpus prohibens et non cedens. Sed non est sic in
actione speciei, quia hec est propria et prima operatio rei active,

200 est enim: *om. A*   201 licet: l. est *A*   202 completa: completur *S*
207 appropriamus: competat *A*   208 pueri *A*   210 et . . . quod: item *A*
216 solvendum est: dicendum *A*   220 similem *A*   226 venit *A*   230-1 in
actione: *om. S*

et ideo ab illa non potest privari, nec potest esse otiosa. Sed motus localis est operatio secunda, propter quod ab illa privari potest, non solum in motu locali, sed in alieno.

235   θ (I. 4. 76)

. . . quo ad gravitatem potentem in motu sursum vel deorsum, vel quantum ad sensum de ea, sicut et in aliis rebus numquam tamen absolute et simpliciter; vel dicendum quod terra vel aliud grave non habet speciem vel actionem terre nisi in quantitate debita. Sed 240 intelligendum est . . .

                             ι (I. 4. 115)

Si vero obicitur illud quod inferius tangetur et quod tactum est, quod si tota potentia agit totam actionem et medietas aget medietatem, patet quod de medietate diversa est intelligendum et non de partibus 245 in toto. Unde totum sine divisione partium agat totam actionem in toto tempore, et pars non agit partem actionis in parte temporis. Et respectu unius agentis talis actio est minima; et tempus illud minimum, quod agens tante virtutis non potest minorem actionem facere in minori tempore, quamvis agens maioris virtutis possit facere 250 maiorem actionem in illo tempore et in minori tempore; similiter et equalem, secundum quod agens est maioris vel minoris virtutis.

                             κ (I. 4. 117)

. . . nec minus, in quo terminetur; et sic stet actio dummodo illud minus sit in quo toto et non dividatur ab eo.

255   λ (I. 4. 126)

Et quoniam actio est determinata, ideo oportet quod sit super quantitatem quam totam et non minus alterabit, quia partem aliam non potest alterare et sufficit ad eius alterationem. Et ideo actio sua non stat nec terminatur in minori; nec igitur ad plus se extendit; 260 nec ad minus limitabitur; et ideo in minori non sistet dummodo illud minus in suo toto remaneat. Et tamen non est indivisibile secundum quantitatem, ut punctus, quia tale imperceptibile non movetur, ut

233 operatio: actio S   234 motu locali: *correxi ex* loco mobili S loco mobilis A
236 ponentem S   237 ad sensum: habendum est S / *post* ea *scr. et del.* A numquam
tamen   242 si . . . tactum: *om.* S   244 *post* diversa *mg. add.* A ab alia
245 agat: *om.* A   246 tempore: t. agit A   247 temporis A   249 posset S
251 maioris: maiorum S   256 determinata: d. et certa A   257 aliam non: aliquam
A   258 sua: tota A

probatur sex *Physicorum*, omne enim mobile est divisibile. Sed unus tamen existens in toto non contingit sumere, ut sit completum
265 subiectum actionis totius. Sed si illa pars in quam totam potest agere in minimo tempore dividatur in medietate, et sit una medietas obiecta per se agenti, aliqui volunt quod non possit esse subiectum actionis. Sed videtur quod agens potest illud alterare, quoniam illud idem alteravit in toto et plus. Et sic semper unus potest accipi, dummodo
270 dividatur pars a toto alterando; sed in toto alterabit partem in parte temporis, sicut in toto tempore totum.

μ (I. 4. 219)

Et si dicatur quod si maior virtus potest aliquam quantitatem quantamcunque alterare, tunc minor virtus debeat minorem quantitatem
275 alterare, dicendum quod non sequitur, quia omnis virtus activa agit per approximationem et requirit utraque patientis extrema sibi coniungi quam possibile est; et ideo virtus magna tam parvam quantitatem patientis requirit sicut parva. Sed sequitur quod virtus magna potest intensiorem speciem facere in eadem quantitate patientis
280 quam virtus parva; et ideo solum sequitur quod ⟨minor⟩ virtus faciet minorem actionem, sed tamen in eadem parte eiusdem quantitatis.

ν (II. 1. 9)

Deinceps[5] oportet ingredi magis sententias certificatas auctorum de visibilibus et aspectibus et mathematicis quibusdam, quoniam purus
285 naturalis non potest multum in hiis quantum tamen explicabitur, et satis patebit scienti libros aspectuum et mathematicas quid est naturale purum et quid de aliis scientiis est necessarium admixtum. Sed hec pars habet sex veritates seu conclusiones. Prima est quod secundum lineam profunditatis in agente oportet poni aliquam
290 partem primam, quia minorem non contingit dare que faciat speciem in patiente quam aliqua pars determinata et certa agit in actuali operatione.

Et approximatio est precipua conditio requisita ad actionem, ut prius tactum est, quia quando maior est approximatio tanto melior

263 divisibile: dissimile(?) S   265 *ante* sed *mg. add.* A[C] sed solum erit subiectum partis actionis   266 medietate: medietates A   267 quod: q. sicut A / potest S
269–71 potest . . . totum: *om.* A   273 maior: tota A / quantitatem: partem A
273–4 quantamcunque: mortalem S   275 quod: *om.* S   276 extrema: exemplificatio S / sibi: ei S   280 parvam S / faciet: *correxi ex* faciens SA   283 deinceps: et in d. S / sententias: ad s. S / auctorum: Aristoteles A   284 visibus S / mathematicis: in animalibus S   285 in: ut A / tamen: non potest A   286 mathematicus S / quod A
287 quod A / necessario S   288 sed: et S / pars: conclusio S   289 aliam A
290 faciat: non f. A   291 certa: circa A   293 approximatio est: approximatione A
294 quando: quibus A

295 est actio. Ergo oportet poni aliquam partem agentis ita parvam quod
non contingit dari minorem, quod si dicatur quod agens in hac
influentia sit quantitas determinata agentis ita quod in minori non
possit agere, dicendum quod in minori potest agere aliam actionem;
unde respectu actionis oportet partem agentis esse indivisibilem.
300 Quare si detur minor, illa est que queritur, quoniam illa faciet
actionem. Si ergo in actione actuali alia pars determinata et
approximata quantum possibilis est operatur et agit, oportet quod sit
certe quantitatis et minime, ita quod in minori secundum lineam
profundi non contingit sumi pro actione naturali. Et ita erit indi-
305 visibilis quantitate respectu actionis. Item si non, tunc signetur
minor, et dividatur illa pars in duas medietates in C puncto. Et sit
AC prima pars prope patientem et CB alia pars interior et a patiente
remotior. Sic ACB prima pars est AC; quod alterabit constat primam
partem patientis, quoniam ei coniungitur. Sed inter CB et primam
310 partem patientis est totum AC, et AC non potest alterari ab ipso
CB. Quare virtus ipsius B non penetrabit A ad primam partem
patientis, nam B non alterabit aliquid de patiente. Item si totum
non agit primo et per se, sed dividatur actio secundum divisionem
quantitatis illius quod agit, ut AC faciat suam actionem ei debitam
315 et CB suam et distinctam secundum quod hee partes sunt distincte,
tunc ostendo quod CB nullo modo agit in illud patiens in quod AC
agit, quod scilicet patiens coniungitur AC a parte AC, quoniam
Aristoteles determinat septem *Physicorum* quod omnino oportet
quod agens et patiens non habeant medium, sed simul sunt secundum
320 suas superficies. Sed CB pars nullo modo habet superficiem coniunctam patienti, dico, quoniam interventa[?] extremitate ei coniungitur;
sed intercipitur AC, quod est corpus habens dimensionem separantem
CB a nominato patiente. Quapropter CB non aget in illud patiens si
ponamus talem divisionem ipsius AB. Cum enim ponimus AB et non
325 minus eo facere actionem in illud patiens, possumus salvare verbum
Aristotelis septem *Physicorum*, quia hec totum quod est AB superficiem suam coniunctam habet ipsi patienti sine medio; et ideo illud
potest esse quod primo et per se agit, quo non contingit sumere minus
in quantitate quod agat. Primo ergo relinquitur quod pars agentis que

296 quod[1]: non q. *S* / agens: ad a. *A*   296–7 hac influentia: hanc materiam *A*
297 sit: non exigitur *S*   298 dicendum: nam tunc d. *S* / aliquam *A*   301 si: cum *S*
302 proximata *A*   306 duas: d *A*   307 proprie *S*   308 sic: *om. A* / ACB:
ACH *S*   309 primam: propriam *S*   312 nam: natura *S* / non alterabit: *om. S*
314 suam: sibi *A* / ei: *om. A*   315 distinctam: distantiam *A*   316 CB: *mg. A* /
patiens: p. scilicet *A* / quod: tota *A*   317 coniungit *A* / a: si *A* / AC[2]: A *A*
319 habent *A*   320 suas: duas *A* / pars: *om. S*   321 patienti: paucitati *A* / interventa: *correxi ex* inventa *S* invenitur *A*   322–3 separantem . . . quapropter: *om. A*
324 talem: idem *A* / AB[2]: AD *S*   325 possumus salvare: salvat *S*   327 illud: *om. S*
328 contingit: contra *S*

330 alterabit primam partem patientis erit indivisibilis penes profundum
quantum ad actionem; et hoc vult Averroys super primum *Physicorum*
et septimo et secundo *Celi et mundi* et multis locis. Quod si dicatur
illud Aristoteles quod tactum est septimo *Physicorum* in fine, quod
si aliqua virtus alterat aliquod mobile in aliquo tempore, medietas
335 illius virtutis mobile ei proportionale alterabit tantum in tanto
tempore, dicendum quod hec divisio virtutis non est intelligenda
secundum quantitatem omnino, sed secundum partitionem potestatis
et nature active, secundum quod communiter loquimur non solum in
quantis sed in rebus spiritualibus de maiori virtute et minori. Et
340 ideo non oportet quod Aristoteles loquitur de divisione agentis
secundum quantitatem eius, sed secundum virtutem et potestatem
activam. Potest etiam ad hoc addi quod potest eius sermo verificari
adhuc de agente secundum quantitatem, secundum quod est divisibile,
non solum absolute sed respectu actionis; et hoc est secundum eius
345 latitudinem et longitudinem, non secundum eius profunditatem,
secundum enim longum et latum agens magnum sicut parvum ipsi
patienti potest coniungi, sed non secundum profundum; et non est
differentia in parvo et minori, quoniam semper minus et minus agens
potest coniungi ipsi patienti secundum longum et latum; et utraque
350 pars agentis potest tangere partem patientis ei proportionalem, sed
secundum viam profundi non sunt hec possibilia. Et ideo oportet quod
una pars minima et indivisibilis, non absolute sed respectu actionis,
faciat operationem, ita quod tota illa pars agit. Unde licet illa pars
⟨alterabit⟩ hanc partem et sic corpus et quantum, tamen tota aget
355 totam actionem in toto tempore.

Quod autem posset dici quod cum actio prima habeat divisionem,
ergo et pars agens prima habebit divisionem, quia actio non potest
habere divisionem nisi ab agente; dicendum quod actio ab agenti
habet divisionem et perceptibilitatem, que perceptibilitas consistit
360 in intentione et remissione. Sed hec divisio non est penes divisionem
quantitativam primi agentis, sed habeat quantitatem et sic corpus
sicut pars corporis est corpus. Sed hec divisio actionis et temporis
causetur a finitate virtutis, propter quod Aristoteles probat sex
Physicorum quod nulla virtus finita agit in instanti, et in octo

330 individualitas *A*   332 secundo: 23 *S*   337 secundum²: *om. S*
338 quod: sed q. *A*   340 locuntur(?) *S*   342 sermo: secundo *S*   344 est:
non *A*   345 non: sed *A* / eius: *om. S*   348 minori quoniam: minora quin *A* /
agens: a. acceptum *S*   349 possit *A*   350 *post* agentis *add. S* seu cuicunque pars
agentis partis / potest . . . patientis: *om. A*   353 *ante* agit *scr. et del. S* minima
353 agit . . . pars: *om. A*   356 cum: *ex* est *mg. corr. A* / habeat: et tunc h. *S* /
divisionem: d. et temporis primum *A*   358 divisionem: *om. A*   360 in: et *S*
362 *post* temporis *scr. et del. S* plus   363 causatur *S*   364 instanti: *correxi ex*
subiecti (*vel* stanti) *SA*

365 *Physicorum* similiter. Omnis autem virtus finita habet quandam perceptibilitatem per quam actio eius habet partem et partem; sed non
est hec perceptibilitas virtutis penes quantitatem, eo quod omnis
creatura habet eam et tam substantia spiritualis quam corporalis,
de qua perceptibilitate oportet suo loco in hoc tractatu requiri,
370 nec est amplius hoc querendum de illa. Item actio et passio sunt in
patiente sicut in subiecto, ut Aristoteles docet tertio *Physicorum*
et secundo *De anima*, propter quod actio partem habet et partem
secundum perceptibilitatem patientis, loquendo de perceptibilitate
actionis quantitativa secundum eius causam, quam perceptibilitatem
375 habet ratione sui subiecti necessario; et ideo non habet eam a partibus agentis, et ideo nullo modo perceptibilitatem recipit propter
partes agentis quantitativas.

Si vero dicatur quod in rebus animatis exigitur augmentum propter
infinitionem[?] quantitatis actionis ad actionem debitam sue speciei,
380 quia aliqua quantitatas certa exigitur in omni actione, ita quod in
minori esse non potest, tunc omnia indigerent augmento sicut animata;
dicendum quod hec quantitas, de qua hic loquor, est ita parva, cum
sit minima saltem secundum sensum, quod natura non denegat eam
alicui rei naturali que debeat agere, et ideo non oportet poni aug-
385 mentum. Sed in animatis oportet poni virtutem augmentativam, et
requiritur augmentum, ut per aliquod corporale adveniens convertendum in rem inanimatam virtus illa augmentativa duceret illam rem ad
debitam quantitatem in qua possit operari per actionem generationis
secundum propagationem. Et ideo hec est necessitas quare quantitas
390 que requiritur est magna, propter magnitudinem actionis que etiam
est alterius generis, quoniam secundum propagationem ad quam
diversa organa diversarum quantitatum exiguntur nec potest istorum
instrumentorum nec totius generandi debita quantitas haberi per
generationem rei animate. Sed illa de qua hic loquor potest haberi in
395 generatione cuiuslibet rei ut haberetur, cum sit minima secundum
sensum et secundum naturam respectu actionis naturalis; et ideo non
requiritur augmentum, sed sufficit sola generatio. Si vero adhuc
obicitur quod prima pars agentis, cum habeat quantitatem sub esse
naturali et forma naturali ubique, potest dividi in partes habentes
400 formas naturales, sed nulla forma naturalis otiosa est, quia nichil est
otiosum in fundamento nature, ut dicit Averroys super secundum
Methaphysice, quare partes prime partis erunt active et nate agere

365 physicorum similiter: dicit *A*   369 in: *om. A*   376 nullo . . . recipit: non
r. aliquo modo perceptibilitatem *A*   379 infinitionem: infectionem *A* / actionis: *om. A*
381 indigent *S*   384 qua *A*   385 ponere *S*   388 pro actione *S*
392 istorum: horum *S*   393 generandi: generationis *A*   395 cuiuslibet: eius *A* /
habetur *S* / minima: quantum m. *A*   398 sub: s^e *A*   399 naturali²: naturalis *A* /
habentis *S*   402-4 et . . . active: *om. S*

et alterare que apta est; dicendum quod illa forma in parte partis
active non esset otiosa, sed faceret illud ad quod apta nata est,
405 scilicet perficeret materiam illius partis, sed non ageret extra ad
generationem sui similis, quia non est apta nata agere sub tali
quantitate. Si vero dicatur quod tunc si transierit superficies rei
agentis per extremitates illius partis active, ut in sole reliquum
solis esset superfluum, et tantum ageret illa pars quantum totus
410 sol modo postquam sola illa pars prima est activa, et ita erit de
omni agente, et tunc parvus ignis sicut magnus equaliter calefaceret
nos; dicendum quod magna latitudo et magna longitudo agentis
exiguntur ad magnam actionem. Sed hee non possunt utique habere
sine magna rei profunditate. Et ideo, cum agens naturale natum est
415 undique agere, indiget magnitudine dimensionum ex omni parte; et
ideo profunditas magna hoc modo requiritur ad hoc, ut fiat undique
actio magna equaliter; quia licet interior pars ultra primam partem
activam non debet illi parti prime, tamen ex eius victoria vigoratur
et comfortatur in esse et continuatur, quia vicinia et approximatio
420 partium in toto facit multum ad salutem partium et totius; et quia
esse prime partis vigoratur per alias et intenditur, oportet quod actio
intendatur et fortificetur ex vicinia illarum, propter quod non
sunt otiose nec sequuntur cetera in communia entia.

Et nunc considerandum est similiter quod prima pars patientis
425 alteranda debet esse minima et indivisibilis secundum sensum et
secundum naturam respectu actionis in quantum est in via profundi,
licet in se sit quanta et divisibilis. Si enim prima pars agentis activa
est minima et indivisibilis secundum viam profundi, erit pars patientis prima ei proportionalis. Et patet hoc per approximationem,
430 que requiritur in alteratione, quia in minori parte maior est
approximatio, et videretur aliqua et quod sit divisibilis. Sit igitur
ACB, et dividatur in C. Constat quod pars agentis activa alterat
primam partem; sed prima alterata potest sufficienter alterare secundam, sicut secunda tertiam, et ulterius, ut oportet poni in huiusmodi
435 alteratione quare pars agentis non agit in secundam partem, scilicet
in CB, sed tantum in AC; ergo AB non fuit pars alterandi, sed AC;
et sic ulterius convenit arguere si AC detur prima pars alteranda,
si enim sit divisibilis sequitur quod eius medietas et non tota
alterabitur ab agente. Et ita prima pars patientis, licet sit divisibilis

404 nata: *om.* A   406 generationem: productionem A / nata: *om.* A
407 transierunt S   413 exigunt S / sed: si A / utique: undique S   418 illi:
ad naturali(?) S / parte A / vigoratur: figuratur A   419 conformatur A
421 vigoratur: figuratur A   426 in[1]: *om.* S / profundi: quantum A   427 si:
om. A   429–30 ei . . . maior: *om.* A   431 proximatio A / videtur S
432 ACB: actio A / in: prima A   434 sicut: sic A   436 AC[1]: hac S
438 sequatur S

440 quantitate, tamen est indivisibilis respectu passionis naturalis,
ita quod minus eo non est subiectum actionis et passionis; et totum
illud alteratur in toto tempore et in qualibet parte temporis; et
illud integrum recipit totam alterationem in toto tempore et partem
alterationis in parte temporis, sicut dictum est de actione tota et
445 parte, et de toto tempore et parte temporis respectu totius partis
prime agentis. Et hoc vult Averroys precise super septimo *Physicorum*
et alibi. Quod si dicatur nullum indivisibile moveri, ostendit Aristoteles sexto *Physicorum* multis modis, et loquitur de indivisibili
secundum quantitatem eius est punctus, ut patet. Sed non pono hic
450 hanc partem primam agentis esse sine quantitate, sed habere quantitatem, et tamen tota recipit totam alterationem et partem eius; itaque
una pars non recipit unam partem alterationis et alia aliam. Quod
vero in secunda conclusione dicit Aristoteles quod parte quiescente
quiescit totum, seu quod non movetur totum, et ideo pars cuiuslibet
455 mobilis primo movetur, ita quod nullum divisibile primo movetur
sed pars; dicendum quod in quantum divisibile est tale mobile, hoc
non supponit in demonstratione dominus, quod quia omne mobile
divisibile est, et una parte non mota non movetur totum, ideo totum
non movetur primo sed pars, et ideo oportet ut illud quod movetur
460 per totum sue partis moveatur. Sed divisio mobilis est in alteratione,
que divisio hic requiritur, que non est nisi secundum viam longi-
tudinis et latitudinis, non secundum profunditatem, propter approximationem que requiritur, ut tactum est de agente. Et ideo quod
in fine septimi dicitur, quod si totum mobile alteratur ab aliqua
465 virtute secundum aliquam alterationem ab aliquo tempore, tunc
medium mobile potest alterari in eodem tempore a medietate potentie
secundum equalem alterationem; dicendum quod verum est quod
mobile alterabile divisibile dicitur respectu alterationis; sed hoc solum
est secundum longum et latum, non secundum profundum, propter
470 causas dictas, que non requiruntur in motu locali nec augmento et
diminutione, sed solum in alteratione et generatione et corruptione,
quia non fiunt nisi per omnimodam approximationem agentis et
patientis ad invicem quantum natura potest facere.

    Deinde considerandum est quod prima pars patientis transmutata
475 transmutat secundam et secunda tertiam et sic ulterius. Et hoc dicit
Aristoteles septimo *Physicorum*, capitulo de alteratione, et primo

440 tamen: tunc *S*   440–2 respectu . . . toto: *om. S*   447 divisibile *A* /
ostendit: dicit *A*   449 qualitatem *A* / eius: cuius *A*   450 sed . . . quantitatem:
om. A   451 itaque: in quod *S*   453 conclusione: c. septimi *A*   454 quod: *mg. A*
457 supponitur *A* / in: etiam *A*   460 divisive *S*   462 profunditatis *S*
463 quod: *om. A*   465 ab: in *A*   466 eodem: toto *A*   469 latum: rarum *A*
470 nec: nature *S*   471 diminutionem *S*   474 deinde: quanto *A*ᶜ *om. A*'
475 sic: similiter *S*

De generatione, capitulo de actione, et secundo *De sompno et vigilia*; et Averroys similiter septimo et alibi. Et hoc oportet, quoniam non coniungitur secunde parte nec aliis; et ideo non alterabit eas, sed
480 prima pars patientis iam alterata habet unde potest alterare secundam cui coniungitur. Quapropter illam alterabit secundam, quoniam in naturaliter agente non requiritur nisi quod possit agere et quod coniungatur sine media quantitate, sicut Aristoteles determinat nono *Methaphysice* et septimo *Physicorum* et primo *De generatione*.
485 Et oportet quod pars secunda sit minima, sicut prima et tertia similiter, et sic de aliis, ita quod currat alteratio semper super partes equales alterantes se continue, quoniam eedem rationes sunt ad probandum quod pars secunda sit minima, et quod prima, et sic de tertia et aliis; oportet enim approximationem fieri equalem in omni-
490 bus, et etiam multo fortius debet secunda esse parva quam prima, quia species in prima parte est debilior quam forma in prima parte agentis; et ideo minus est activa, et ad minorem effectum artatur, propter quod in minorem patientem operatur, vel in equali specie speciem debiliorem. Sed minus in quantitate non potest dari propter
495 rationes superiores; et ideo hec alteratio semper erit per equales partes patientis.

Et propter hoc sequitur alia conclusio ex ista, scilicet quod species semper debilitatur et minus assimilatur agenti. Et hoc ostendit Alhacen quatuor *De aspectibus* dupliciter: unus modus est propter
500 distantiam ab agente; et magis ei assimilatur, et ideo plus habet de essentia specifica agentis quam secunda; et eadem ratione habebit illa plus de illa essentia quam tertia, et sic ulterius. Et huius causa trahitur ex predictis a principio, quia species non est effectus completus agentis. Sed incompletus etiam minus habet
505 de natura specifica quam agens, et ideo effectus suus erit debilior, propter quod debilior est species secunda quam prima, et tertia quam secunda. Ideo secundum Alhacen est dispersio maior in secunda specie quam in prima, et tertia quam secunda, et sic ulterius; quam a quolibet incessus principalis ipsius exeunt multiplicationes
510 accidentales infinities, propter quas vis generativa speciei in linea principali minoratur conscientie, et ideo species generata semper debilior fit in incessu particulari secundum successionem partium. Sed de hac multiplicatione accidentali patebit in sequentibus.

478 hoc: *om.* S | *post* quoniam *mg. add.* A agens   479 aliis: alteri A   480 *post* alterata *mg. add.* A in actu   481 illa S   485 secunda: *om.* A   486 super: *mg.* A   488 sit: si A   491 forma: *om.* A   492 artatur: alteratur A
494 debiliore A   495 ideo: *om.* A | per: propter A   496 patientis: *om.* A
499–500 aspectibus ... ei: *om.* S   502 plus de illa: *om.* A | quam: quod A
503 huiusmodi S   504 incompletus: completus A   505 ideo: uno S | erit: et e. A   507–13 maior ... sequentibus: *om.* A

ξ (II. 2. 11)

515   . . . per se vel per accidens; et ideo super curvam et non rectam
omnino superfluit. Si vero obstet ei corpus, hoc erit valde densum
nec permittet speciem transire quantum ad iudicium visus vel alterius
sensus, de quo non est intentio, ut expositum est prima parte huius
tractatus. Quando sibi hoc contingit, vocabitur reflexio, ut ita
520   dictum est. Quando vero non occurrit obstaculum impediens transitum
sensibilem ipsius speciei, sed tamen medium aliud a priori et diverse
dyaphanitatis seu prospicuitatis seu raritatis, inveniat species non
perpendiculariter super corpus secundum, tunc species non tenet
in secundo corpore incessum suum directum, sed declinat ab incessu
525   recto a dextris vel a sinistris. Et tunc vocatur a modernis fractio
speciei et linea fracta, ut prima parte manifestum est. Sed notandum
quod . . .

o (II. 2. 70)

. . . sic; unde species veniens ab agente B quando venit ad superficiem
530   aque non incedit usque C, sed usque D, et ideo frangitur; . . .

π (II. 4. 158)

Et ideo reputant speram aeris et ignis tanquam unam; quantum ad
incessum speciei velut non habeant superficies distinctas, sed unam
superficiem.

535   ρ (II. 4. 168)

. . . propter unitatem superficiei spere ignis et aeris. Et huic con-
sentit Aristoteles primo *Metheororum*, ubi vult unam superficiem
confundi in ambabus speris, quamvis velit *Libro celi et mundi* tertio
quod superficies aeris sequitur superficiem aque et non superficiem
540   ignis, et quod aer sit gravis in sua spera et non levis. Sed hoc suam
habeant solutionem in loco proprio. Nunc in tantum teneatur quod
non est tanta diversitas spere aeris et ignis que sufficiat ad fractionem, quoniam, sive superficies utriusque sit una sive non, non
est ibi dyaphanitas diversa, sed eadem subtilitas secundum succes-
545   sionem ordinata, sicut in partibus aeris diversis vel in partibus ignis
diversis. Et ideo non potest esse fractio in eorum confinio, una

515–27 per[1] . . . quod: *scr. et del.* A   516 superfluit: *om.* A   517 nec: vel S
518 non: nunc A / huiusmodi S   520 currit A   521 sed: licet A
522 prospicuitatis: *correxi ex* prosperitatis AS   523 perpendit A / secundum: sed A
524 incessum: et i. A   525 vocatur: vat A   529 unde: quarta A   530 incedit:
intendit S   532 quantum: quam(?) A' quas A[C]   541 *ante* loco *scr. et del.* S suo
544 ibi: *om.* S

enim conditionum necessariarum ad fractionem est notabilis diversitas dyaphanitatis, ut sepe tactum est.

σ (II. 6. 126)

550 Quoniam[6] circa punctum unum in eadem superficie non sunt nisi duo recti anguli, sed eandem partem et radius debet semper redire ad angulum equalem angulo incidentie; quapropter redebit super illos angulos eosdem ad quos incidebat radius incidentie et non in eodem loco, et fiunt unus.

555

τ (II. 7. 102)

. . . tanquam radii incidentie et reflexionis essent in eorum superficiebus; sed non est ita, nam solum stat in eorum circumferentiis eo quod radii incidentie et reflexionis cadunt in superficiebus colurorum; . . .

560

υ (III. 2. 87)

Nec est mirum, cum proprietates figurarum sint valde diverse, quod enim optime sonat in una pessime in alia sonat multotiens. Et interpretes non errantes debent scire plene linguas ex quibus et in quas transferunt, et nichilominus ipsas scientias que transferunt, que
565 non acciderunt adhuc in aliquo interprete latino. Et ideo infiniti sunt errores translati pro veritatibus, ut expositum est in prologo huius tractatus. Et si vulgus hoc percipit in multis, sicut et sapientes experti, debemus accedere quod sapientes alia possent erronea invenire in quibus vulgus non potest, quia vulgus habet debilem
570 intellectum in conclusionibus et in principiis propriis, eo quod in hiis fere omnibus discordat a sapientibus probatis, licet in communibus principiis, que sunt conceptiones, tamen concordant, quia 'has quisque probat auditas', ut dicit Boetius in suis *Ebdomadibus*.[7]

φ (IV. 3. 117)

575 Dicendum[8] quod non sequitur, nam lux, si esset corpus, constat quod non esset corpus grave nec leve, sed magis vel celeste vel commune celestibus et igne, quia ignis lucet. Sed celeste corpus non est natum penetrare medium per divisionem partium spatii, nec corpus quod esset commune celo et alii, quia illud non repugnat nature celesti.

547 *ante* notabilis *scr. et del.* S necessaria   556 earum S   563 ex: in A
565 accidunt A   568 aliqua A / possunt S   571-2 communis A   572 tamen:
cum A   576-7 vel[2] . . . celeste: *om.* A   578 *ante* corpus *add.* A lux vel non
transiret medium   579 illum A

580 Et ideo lux vel non transiret medium vel in maximo tempore
pertransiret, et similiter medium sensibile; propter quod non oportet
quod iste generationes lucis in partibus medii comparentur succes-
sioni lucis si esset corpus vel defluxus a corpore, nam quelibet
alteratio certissime fit aliter; actio enim speciei quelibet est velocis-
585 sima, et ideo ex omnibus potest universaliter insensibilis fieri,
quamvis in tempore.

χ (V. 2. 110)

Sed quando per instrumentum congregantur radii tam ante quam
retro, tunc est actio duplex quod instrumentum figuratur a parte
590 ante ad modum speculi concavi, et ex parte post habet magnam
spissitudinem ad modum speculi convexi, ut a priori parte sit reflexio
et a posteriori fiat fractio.

ψ (V. 3. 21)

. . . et quoniam ostensum est prius quod species pyramidis non potest
595 venire a tota medietate corporis sperici nec a maiori portione, sed
necessario a minore. Et exemplificatum est in figura quomodo
pyramides breviores fiunt et longiores et que sunt brevissima omnium,
quoniam illa cuius latera sunt linee contingentes speram in terminis
diametrorum ductarum a terminis corde intersecantium se, ut patuit
600 in figura. Nunc planum est quod hec magis est activa propter hoc
quod multipliciter patet ex dictis quod brevitas figurarum et
linearum faciunt[!] vehementem operationem propter propinquitatem agentis ad patiens ab agente; . . .

580 lux: *om. A*   581 pertransiret: *ex* transiret *corr. A* / similiter: supra *A*
583 si: sicut *A*   584 certissime: *om. A*   588 radii: *om. A*   590 magnam:
magnitudinem *A*   594 et . . . pyramidis: *om. S*   597 sunt: *om. A*
599 ductorum *A*   600 quod hec: *om. A*   601 quod^2: et *A*

Notes to the translation

DE MULTIPLICATIONE SPECIERUM

[*Part* 1, *chap.* 1]

1. Greek letters mark the location of major additions (20 words or more) to the text in MSS *S* and *A*. These additions, by which the revised version of *DMS* is distinguished from the original version, will be found not in the variant readings, but in the Appendix at the end of the treatises. See the Introduction, pp. xxx–xxxi, lxxxi.

2. MSS *S* and *A* revise this passage to read: '. . . according to name, specific cause, and essence'. Small variations of this sort between versions 1 and 2 of *DMS* are recorded only in the variant readings.

3. *DMS* contains a number of passages, such as this, which reveal that Bacon conceived it as part of a larger work; for a good study of this question, see Nascimento, pp. 19–38. Nascimento argues (pp. 27, 31) that part III of the larger work is Bacon's *Communia naturalium* and identifies (p. 276) the passage here cited as II. 2. 4, *OHI* II. 80. 11–13.

4. That is, as Bacon intends to show, the eliciting an action out of the potentiality of the recipient. This is a major theme of *DMS*; see below, I. 3; also the Introduction, pp. lviii–lx.

5. The contrast that Bacon is endeavouring to bring out is that between, on the one hand, stimulating the natural powers of the recipient in such a way as to elicit action *from* the recipient and, on the other, imparting an action *to* the recipient from an external source.

6. On the four species of quality, see Aristotle, *Categories*, 8, $8^b 25$ ff. See also R. F. O'Neill, 'Quality', *New Catholic Encyclopedia*, xii. 2. Cf. below, I. 6. 216–17.

7. I. 2. 8–29.

8. From the Greek *eidōlon*, that is, 'image' or 'replica'. On the history of the use of this term in optical contexts, see Lindberg, *Theories of Vision*, pp. 2–3.

9. Porphyry discusses five predicables, one of which is species, in his *Isagoge*. See Porphyry the Phoenician, *Isagoge*, trans. Edward W. Warren (Toronto, 1975), 27, 34–41. Note that in the revised version of *DMS* (Appendix, β), Bacon elaborates on the two senses of the term 'species'—that is, species as the similitude of a thing and the species that stands in contrast to genus—and urges his reader to observe carefully which usage is intended in any particular discussion. On medieval usage of the term 'species', see Pierre Michaud-Quantin, *Études sur le vocabulaire philosophique du moyen âge* (Rome, 1970), 113–50; on optical usage, see Lindberg, *Theories of Vision*, pp. 98, 112–14; also the Introduction, pp. liv–lvi.

10. The distinction between *lux* and *lumen* appears to have reached the West through the translation of Avicenna's *De anima*; see Lindberg, *Science in the Middle Ages*, p. 356. Those who followed Avicenna's distinction employed the former term to denote the luminous property of fiery or self-luminous objects, the latter to signify its effect (or species) in the surrounding medium. However, many medieval scholars ignored the distinction or employed it haphazardly, and Bacon, as the sequel shows, classifies himself among the latter. When, in my judgement, Bacon wishes to observe the distinction, as he clearly does here, I convey that by leaving the terms untranslated; however, when it appears to me

that he employs *lux* and *lumen* interchangeably (see, for example, I. 1. 210–12), I translate both of them by the term 'light'.

11. *Avicenna Latinus: Liber de anima seu sextus de naturalibus, I–II–III*, ed. S. Van Riet (Louvain/Leiden, 1972), 170–2.

12. Aristotle, *De anima*, ii. 5–6; iii. 4, 429^{a}15–29.

13. Alhazen, *De aspectibus*, i. 18, p. 9 and *passim*. On Alhazen's use of the term 'form', see Lindberg, *Theories of Vision*, pp. 78–80. The name 'Alhazen' is spelled either 'Alhacen' (this most commonly) or 'Halacen' or 'Alphacen' in the manuscripts of *DMS*, never 'Alhazen'. Indeed, in the manuscripts of Alhazen's *De aspectibus* itself, the nearly universal spelling is 'Alhacen'—'Alhazen' being found only once. Nevertheless, because 'Alhazen' has (since Risner's edition of 1572) become standard, I have employed it in my translation.

14. I. 1. 31–2, 37–41.

15. The English term most commonly employed by scholars to translate the Latin *patiens* is the cognate 'patient'—thus the Aristotelian distinction between agent and patient. However, in my judgement 'patient' is overburdened with its more usual modern connotations of forebearance or illness, and in this translation I have usually preferred (but with a few exceptions) the word 'recipient'.

16. Aristotle, *De anima*, ii. 12, 424^{a}17–20.

17. The etymological character of Bacon's argument is lost in translation. It must be noted, therefore, that the Latin verb *patior*, here translated 'undergo', is cognate with the noun *passio*.

18. Below, I. 1. 304–6; IV. 1. 35–6.

19. Aristotle, *De generatione et corruptione*, i. 7, 323^{b}30 ff.; ii. 8, 334^{b}22 ff. Cf. *Physics*, iii. 3.

20. To be numerically the same is to be one and the same individual. To be numerically different is to be sufficiently distinct to be separately numerable.

21. In *Categories*, 1, 1^{b}25 ff., Aristotle defines ten classes or categories (or predicaments) of predicates, also usually considered the ten categories of being. Bacon's point is that the species of fire must (along with fire itself) belong to the category of substance; because if it did not, it would have to belong to one of the nine categories of accidents; but the latter is impossible, since there is no criterion for determining to which of these nine categories it would belong.

22. The text of this sentence (after the semicolon) is either defective or highly elliptical. However, Bacon's meaning is made apparent in British Library, MS Royal 7.F.VIII, ff. 7^v–8^r, where (in a reworking of the opening portions of *DMS*) Bacon substitutes (for the text beginning 'sed nec potest esse . . .') the following: 'Ergo erunt in eodem predicamento cum igne, sed non in alio genere, ut patet, nec alia specie, quia tunc species ignis esset de natura aeris vel aque vel terre, quod dici non potest; ergo species rei erit in eandem specie specialissima cum ipsa.'

23. Note that the expression 'species of fire' is here used in two different senses; see above, I. 1 n. 9.

24. Bacon may have in mind the following passage from Ptolemy's *Optica*: 'Ex his itaque que preposuimus, uidemus unumquodque lucidorum et colorum per passionem que fit in uisu; cetera uero que sequenter uidenter, uidemus per accidentia que illi accidunt. Passio quidem que in uisu fit, est illuminatio aut coloratio . . .' (p. 22, lines 17 ff.). On Ptolemy's doctrine of light and colour, see Albert Lejeune, *Euclide et Ptolémée, deux stades de l'optique géométrique grecque* (Louvain, 1948), 22–31.

25. Aristotle, *De anima*, ii. 7, 418^{b}27-9. Cf. *Opus maius* (Bridges), pt. V. 1, dist. 10, chap. 2, vol. ii. 77.

26. Bacon here distinguishes between the two senses of 'species'—species as similitude, and species as the subdivision of genus; see n. 9, above.

27. Below, I. 6. 189-204.

28. Below, I. 6. 45-188, especially lines 98-173.

29. I. 1. 23 ff.

30. Literally, 'lower'.

31. That is, in the celestial realm.

32. Bacon's use of the term *lux* here reveals that he intends no distinction between *lux* and *lumen*, despite his decision, earlier in the sentence, to use first the one and then the other; for if he wishes to distinguish the two terms, the appropriate one to employ here would be *lumen*.

33. This is a reference to secondary or accidental radiation; see below, II. 2. 116-41. Cf. *Opus maius* (Bridges), pt. V. 2, dist. 3, chap. 2, vol. ii. 104-5. The redness of the light signifies its weakness.

34. Cf. *Communia naturalium*, *OHI* iv. 397-401.

35. Below, I. 6. 45 ff. See also above, I. 1. 159 ff.

36. Probably iii, 440^{b}13-18, where Aristotle argues that compound or mixed colours result from the compounding or mixing of differently-coloured bodies.

37. My translation ignores the term *ideo*, which appears to serve no function, and which Bacon himself omits from version 2.

38. I. 5. Bacon never, in fact, gets around to spiritual recipients; see Nascimento, pp. 19-21.

39. *De anima*, ii. 5, 417^{b}2-3.

40. *De aspectibus*, i. 1, p. 1.

41. Probably *Physics*, vii. 3, 248^{a}6 ff.; cf. vii. 2, 244^{b}10 ff. It is not certain whether Bacon intends this to be a direct quotation or a paraphrase, but I judge it to be the latter on the grounds that he repeats the same phrases in I. 2. 63-4.

[*Part* 1, *chap.* 2]

1. Aristotle, *De anima*, ii. 6, 418^{a}11-16; see also ii. 5. Cf. above, I. 1. 45-6. A proper sensible is the object of a specific sense, specially suited to act on that sense, and concerning which no perceptual error is possible. Colour is the proper sensible of sight.

2. Here Bacon refers to the species of sound, the existence of which he seemed to deny above, lines 8-9. For clarification, see Bacon's *Opus maius* (Bridges), pt. V. 1, dist. 8, chap. 2, vol. ii. 56-7. Bacon, *Liber de sensu et sensato*, *OHI* xiv. 128-34.

3. A visible species generates another visible species, but one sound does not generate another; rather, all sounds are produced by the vibrating parts of the sounding body.

4. See *Metaphysics*, vii. 10 and vii. 17.

5. I am unable to locate the cited passage.

6. Bacon probably has in mind *Metaphysics*, v. 30.

7. Perhaps iii. 2; cf. vii. 6, 1031^{b}7-22.

8. See above, I. 1 n. 41. Bacon here omits the word *naturale*.

9. For Bacon's own definition of the common sense, see his *Opus maius* (Bridges), pt. V. 1, dist. 1, chap. 2, vol. ii. 4-5. Its functions, he notes, are to serve as sources for the specific senses, to judge regarding particular sensibles

(for example, to note diversity between sensibles), to judge the operations of the specific senses (to recognize that sight is seeing), and to receive species coming from the specific senses and reach a judgement concerning them.

10. *Physics*, vii. 2.

11. On the cogitative and estimative faculties, see Bacon's *Opus maius* (Bridges), pt. V. 1, dist. 1, chap. 4, vol. ii. 7-9.

12. Cf. *Opus maius* (Bridges), pt. V. 1, dist. 1, chaps. 2-5, vol. ii. 4-11.

13. *De sensu et sensato*, 4, $441^b 12$-16.

14. *De generatione et corruptione*, i. 7, ii. 4; *De caelo*, ii. 3.

15. Aristotle had defined this fallacy in *Sophistici elenchi*, 5.

16. *Categories*, 5, $3^b 24$; *Physics*, v. 2, $225^b 10$, $226^a 23$-30; *Metaphysics*, xi. 12, $1068^a 11$; xiv. 1, $1087^b 2$.

17. On the identity of Sortes and Socrates, see Heinz Pflaum, 'Sortes, Plato, Cicero: Satirisches Gedicht des dreizehnten Jahrhunderts', *Speculum*, 6 (1931), 499-501.

18. See n. 16, above.

19. I find no such claim in *De generatione et corruptione*. See *Categories*, 5, $3^b 24$, $4^a 12$; *Metaphysics*, iv. 2, $1004^b 30$.

20. *Physics*, i. 5-7.

21. Possibly *De anima*, i. 1, $403^a 2$-18.

22. The MSS could equally well be read *substantiam*, and Bridges so reads them; however, the context seems to require *subiectum*.

23. vii. 8, $1033^b 12$-18.

24. *OHI* ii. 59.

25. In *Opus maius* (Bridges), pt. V. 1, dist. 7, chap. 2, vol. ii. 49, Bacon treats the ability of the eye to see itself in a mirror as proof that a species issues from the eye; for an analysis of the argument, see Lindberg, *Theories of Vision*, pp. 114-15. On the visual power as a source of species, see also *Opus maius* (Bridges), pt. V. 1, dist. 7, chap. 4, vol. ii. 52-3.

26. On this controversy, see Lindberg, *Theories of Vision, passim*. The principal opponent of extramission from the eye had been Alhazen, to whose work Bacon is here directly responding; see ibid., chap. 4.

27. *De generatione animalium*, v. 1, $781^a 1$-2, $781^b 2$-13. In fact, Aristotle at this point did not maintain the extramission theory attributed to him by Bacon, but only seemed to, as a result of a mistranslation by Michael Scot; see S. D. Wingate, *The Mediaeval Latin Versions of the Aristotelian Scientific Corpus, with Special Reference to the Biological Works* (London, 1931), 78.

28. Axel Anthon Björnbo and Sebastian Vogl (edd.), 'Alkindi, Tideus und Pseudo-Euklid. Drei optische Werke', *Abhandlungen zur Geschichte der mathematischen Wissenschaften*, 26. 3 (1912), 75, where Tideus argues: 'It would be impossible for the observer to apprehend the locations of things and their sizes if the power of sight did not extend to the visible object. And similarly, sight would not know the size of an object if its power did not surround the object on all sides.'

29. For a full account of Ptolemy's theory of vision, see Lejeune, *Euclide et Ptolémée*; for a brief account, see Lindberg, *Theories of Vision*, pp. 15-17.

30. *Opus maius* (Bridges), pt. V. 1, dist. 7, chaps. 2-4, vol. ii. 49-53; cf. Lindberg, *Theories of Vision*, pp. 114-16. See also below, I. 2. 234-38; I. 5. 66-71, 124-26; II. 10. 94-106.

31. See above, I. 2 n. 27. Avicenna discusses vision in *De natura animalium*, xii. 11, in Avicenna, *Opera* (Venice, 1508), ff. 49^{r-v}; no extramission theory of

vision is here presented, but reference is made to visual spirit descending from the brain to the eyes. For a full analysis of Avicenna's theory of vision, see Lindberg, *Theories of Vision*, pp. 43-52.

32. That is, the changes produced by an outside agent. *Passiones* must be translated into its cognate, 'passions', since Bacon does not make clear what kinds of change he has in mind.

33. Cf. *Opus maius* (Bridges), pt. V. 1, dist. 10, chap. 2, vol. ii. 76-9.

34. See *Meteorologica*, iv. 1, $378^b 27$ ff.; iv. 2, $380^a 8$; iv. 5, $382^a 1-2^b 9$; iv. 8, $384^b 24$ ff. Cf. *De anima*, ii. 1, $412^a 10$. On Bacon's doctrine of matter as passive potency, see Crowley, pp. 91-110.

35. *De generatione et corruptione*, ii. 9 and elsewhere.

36. Bacon inserts these clarifying words in the revised version; see the apparatus criticus.

37. I. 2. 138 ff.

38. The twenty common sensibles (common in that they can be perceived by at least two senses) are listed in *Opus maius* (Bridges) pt. V. 1, dist. 3, chap. 1, vol. ii. 5-6: 'remotio, situs, corporeitas, figura, magnitudo, continuatio, discretio vel separatio, numerus, motus, quies, asperitas, lenitas, diaphaneitas, spissitudo, umbra, obscuritas, pulchritudo, turpitudo, item similitudo et diversitas in omnibus hiis.' Bacon's source for these is Alhazen, *De aspectibus*, ii. 15, p. 34. Aristotle's discussion of the common sensibles appears in *De anima*, ii. 6, $418^a 18-19$; *De sensu et sensato*, 4, $442^b 4-17$.

39. Ptolemy, *Optica*, pp. 12-14.

40. *De aspectibus*, ii. 15-39, pp. 34-55; iv. 2, p. 102.

41. *De aspectibus*, ii. 16, pp. 34-5. On these aspects of Alhazen's theory of visual perception, see Graziella Federici Vescovini, *Studi sulla prospettiva medievale* (Turin, 1965), 113-32; Hans Bauer, *Die Psychologie Alhazens* (*BGPM* 10. 5) (Münster, 1911), 39-71; Lindberg, *Theories of Vision*, pp. 80-5.

42. Or, 'the eye'.

43. Tideus, *De aspectibus*, in Björnbo and Vogl, 'Drei optische Werke', pp. 74-5.

44. Bacon is here following Alhazen, *De aspectibus*, i. 1, p. 1. For an analysis of Alhazen's argument, see Lindberg, *Theories of Vision*, pp. 61-3.

45. Bacon does not mean to suggest that the dense body (if of itself it were suited to produce a species) would be seen if the intervening body were opaque, but rather if there were no intervening body at all.

46. Cf. Bacon, *Opus maius* (Bridges), pt. V. 1, dist. 10, chap. 2, vol. ii. 77; above, I. 1. 140-6.

47. That is, the common sensibles and the properties subordinate to them; see n. 38, above.

48. Cf. *Opus maius* (Bridges), pt. V. 1, dist. 10, chap. 2, vol. ii. p. 78.

49. See Bacon, *Opus maius* (Bridges), pt. V. 1, dist. 1, chaps. 2-5, vol. ii. 4-12; dist. 10, chap. 1, vol. ii. 74-6.

50. Below vi. 4. 39-48; *Opus maius* (Bridges), pt. IV. 1, chap. 1, vol. i. 128-9.

51. See Alhazen, *De aspectibus*, i. 31, p. 18; i. 41-2, pp. 25-6.

52. The hollow of the common nerve is not the retina, as Bridges argues, *Opus maius*, vol. ii. 428 n. 2. The common nerve is the junction of the two optic nerves, one from each eye, in the optic chiasma; the hollow is simply the interior. It had been argued by Alhazen (*De aspectibus*, ii. 16, pp. 34-5) that there the forms coming from the two eyes are united and perceived by the

ultimate sentient power; on the post-ocular aspects of visual perception, see Lindberg, *Theories of Vision*, pp. 80–5. Cf. Bacon, *Opus maius* (Bridges), pt. V. 1, dist. 2, chap. 1, vol. ii. 14–15; dist. 5, chaps. 2–3, vol. ii. 32–4.

53. The anterior glacial humour is the crystalline lens. Bacon here defines the pupil as the combined crystalline lens and vitreous humour (anterior and interior glacial humours); cf. *Opus maius* (Bridges), pt. V. 1, dist. 2, chap. 3, vol. ii. 18.

54. Cf. *De aspectibus*, ii. 32, pp. 48–9.

55. Cf. *Opus maius* (Bridges), pt. V. 1, dist. 10, chap. 2, vol. ii. 78. For a fuller account of Bacon's theory of vision, see Lindberg, *Theories of Vision*, pp. 109–12.

56. That is, Alhazen. On Alhazen's theory of vision, see Lindberg, *Theories of Vision*, pp. 71–80.

57. Context seems to require that Bacon's *renovatio* or *renovare* be translated 'generation' or 'to generate'; nevertheless, in I. 2. 171–2, Bacon appears to distinguish between *generatio* and *renovatio*. For other instances of the terms *renovatio* and *renovare* in this treatise, see I. 1. 155; I. 2. 49–51; I. 5. 75, 108; III. 1. 72–4, 79, 92–100, 107–8, 113; III. 2. 67; VI. 3. 24, 33; VI. 4. 8. A possible Baconian source for these terms is Avicenna, *De anima_I–II–III*, ed. Van Riet, pp. 181–2.

58. That is, although the particular senses and the common sense are only representative sensitive powers, they have become the sole proprietors of the name 'sense'.

59. I. 2. 73–92.

60. *De aspectibus*, II. 67–8, pp. 69–70.

61. *Communis naturalium*, *OHI* ii. 103–4.

[*Part* I, *chap.* 3]

1. Bacon is attempting to refute the view that a species is something that actually departs from (or is emitted by) an agent and flows into the recipient— a view that had been expressed by the ancient atomists and was known in the Middle Ages through Aristotle's refutation of it (see Lindberg, *Theories of Vision*, pp. 2–3). If there were such an emission, Bacon argues, it would be either of substance or of accident, and the emission of either one would entail the corruption of the agent. Since incorruptibles, such as spiritual and celestial substances, produce species, it is apparent that the emission theory is false. Bacon expresses similar views in *Questiones super librum de causis*, *OHI* xii. 40.

2. I. 1. 118–20.

3. *De anima*, ii. 4, 415^a26–$^b2$.

4. Cf. *Communia naturalium*, *OHI* ii. 19.

5. Note the addition to the text in MSS *A* and *S* (see apparatus criticus).

6. *De anima*, ii. 12, 424^a19; cf. iii. 12, 435^a2–10.

7. Bacon's point in the final third of this paragraph is that a species and an impression are alike in that both affect the surface of the recipient; they are different in that the species also affects the interior.

8. That is, by exclusion of all the alternatives but one.

9. On the *dator formarum*, an idea of Avicenna, see Crowley, p. 103.

10. For Bacon's doctrine of active and passive potentiality, see ibid., pp. 91– 110; D. E. Sharp, *Franciscan Philosophy at Oxford in the Thirteenth Century* (Oxford, 1930), 14–17, 121–3; the Introduction, above, p. lix.

11. *Simul* usually denotes conjunction in time. However, if one examines

Bacon's entire argument, it becomes clear that he has in mind conjunction in both space and time; hence my translation.

12. *Physics*, vii. 1, 242^b23-7; vii. 2, 244^b2-5^b1; perhaps *Metaphysics*, ix. 5, 1048^a5-7; *De generatione et corruptione*, i. 6, 322^b21-9.

13. I. 1. 176-7.

14. The conclusion of this paragraph is that a species is not merely the instrument of the agent, sent forth to produce the agent's intended effect; rather, the species is itself the agent's first and univocal effect. From this it follows that the species is not a virtue sent from agent to recipient (see just above on the emission theory), but is brought forth out of the potentiality of the recipient matter.

15. I. 1. 80-98.

16. VI. 1. 3-49. See also III. 1. 96-100; IV. 2. 64-7; VI. 4. 7-11.

17. Even the first small part of the recipient touched by the active virtue of the agent has an interior. And as Bacon's subsequent argument makes clear, the virtue does not touch merely the surface of this first small part, but its entirety: agents act not on surfaces, but on volumes.

18. That is, a source of change.

19. Bacon here alludes to a prior controversy. It is unclear whom he is quoting.

[*Part* I, *chap.* 4]

1. I interpret the propagation of which Bacon speaks to be biological.

2. *Physics*, iii. 1, 201^a20-4; *De generatione et corruptione*, i. 7, 324^b6.

3. The resistance of matter to being moved was commonly regarded as the 'cause' of time in motion; that is, in the absence of resistance, the speed of motion would be infinite, and no time would be required to traverse a space.

4. Probably *De caelo*, i. 3, 270^a12-35; but cf. i. 7, 275^b5-7.

5. The point is that a corrupting agent may not be regarded as a recipient by virtue of meeting resistance; the agent becomes a recipient only as it is itself altered.

6. *Metaphysica*, ii. 1, in *Aristotelis opera cum Averrois commentariis*, viii (Venice, 1562), f. 28K. Bacon's statement closely paraphrases that of Averroes.

7. Literally, 'a movable body proportional to it'—that is, having the same proportion to the first movable body as the second power has to the first power, hence a movable body of half the size. See Aristotle, *Physics*, vii. 5. 250^a4 ff.

8. i. 4, 187^b19, 187^b35.

9. This is Anaxagoras' doctrine of homeomereia, concerning which see G. S. Kirk and J. E. Raven (edd.), *The Presocratic Philosophers* (Cambridge, 1957), 386-8. Bacon knew the doctrine through Aristotle's attacks on Anaxagoras in *Physics* i. 4.

10. That is, it will not be a point.

11. On the distinction between transforming sense (so as to bring about sensation) and merely altering sense, see the following paragraph.

12. *De sensu et sensato*, 7, 449^a22-30.

13. I do not find the claim in Averroes' *De celo*, bk. ii, but Bacon may possibly have had in mind one of the following passages from that work: *Aristotelis opera cum Averrois commentariis*, v (Venice, 1562), ff. 151K, 160D-E, 160M-161B, 162E, 170C.

14. *Physics*, iii. 6, 206^a16-18; iii. 7, 207^b15-16.

15. The distinction is between mathematical quantity and quantity as it exists in natural or material things.

16. That is, parts having a different depth within the agent.

17. These words are given in MSS *A* and *S*.

18. I. 3. 3 ff.

19. As opposed to what God might decide to achieve by miraculous means.

20. *Almagest*, V. 16, trans. Karl Manitius, *Handbuch der astronomie*, i (Leipzig, 1912), 313. Ptolemy maintains that the ratio between the terrestrial and lunar diameters is 39¼ : 1.

21. *Physics*, vii. 5, 250^{a}1-9. Aristotle does not say precisely what Bacon attributes to him.

22. Aristotle distinguished four kinds of motion or change: local motion (or change of place), alteration (qualitative change), augmentation and diminution (growth and decrease), and generation and corruption.

23. Aristotle, *Physics*, vii. 1, 242^{a}7 ff.

24. Note the addition to the text in MSS *A* and *S* (see apparatus criticus).

25. Note the further addition to the text in MSS *A* and *S*. Note, moreover, that in this case the additional claim is obviously false. Is this merely a Baconian slip, or is it evidence that some of the additions and corrections found in MSS *A* and *S* emanate from somebody with a less sure command of Aristotelian physics than that possessed by Bacon?

26. Aristotle, *De generatione et corruptione*, ii. 10, 336^{a}27-8.

[*Part* I, *chap.* 5]

1. See v. 28, 1024^{b}8-9.

2. I find no such denial in *De generatione et corruptione*. Cf. *Meteorologica*, i. 2-3; *De caelo*, i. 3.

3. Probably a reference to *Communia naturalium*, *OHI* ii. 14-16, 69-72. Cf. above, I. 2. 125-33; below, I. 6. 65-8, 80-5.

4. Literally, 'the motion of the sun along an oblique circle'; however, such a translation obscures the twofold nature of the cause.

5. Cf. *Communia naturalium*, *OHI* ii. 23.

6. Averroes, *De celo*, ii. 3, chap. 1, in *Aristotelis opera cum Averrois commentariis*, v, 131F-I.

7. *Opus maius* (Bridges), pt. IV. 4, chap. 1, vol. i. 129-30. Cf. below, II. 6. 103 ff.

8. *Metaphysics*, viii. 1, 1042^{a}33-^{b}7.

9. *Meteorologica*, i. 8, 345^{b}9.

10. *De caelo*, i. 10. Cf. ii. 1.

11. *De anima*, ii. 5, 417^{b}15-17. For a medieval Latin version of this passage, see *Averrois Cordubensis Commentarium magnum in Aristotelis De anima libros*, ed. F. Stuart Crawford (Cambridge, Mass., 1953), 217: '. . . alteratio est duplex, transmutatio scilicet ad dispositiones non esse, et transmutatio ad habitum et naturam.'

12. I. 5. 16 ff.

13. Or visual power.

14. See the references in I. 2 n. 30.

15. iii. 5, 430^{a}18-19.

16. *Proportio* often has the connotation of just or due proportion, hence equality or uniformity.

17. *Metaphysics,* x. 10, 1058^{b}28.

18. Perhaps *Meteorologica,* i. 2.

19. Cf. *Physics,* iii. 1, 201^{a}19-27; iii. 2, 207^{a}2-12; *De generatione et corruptione,* i. 6-7; *De caelo,* i. 10.

20. *De anima I-II-III,* ed. Van Riet, p. 223; cf. Lindberg, *Theories of Vision,* p. 48.

[*Part* I, *chap.* 6]

1. See *Communia naturalium, OHI* iv. 349-55; *Opus maius* (Bridges), pt. IV. 4, chap. 10, vol. i. 152-7.

2. *De generatione et corruptione,* ii. 10, 336^{a}13-^{b}24. On the climes and geographical regions of the earth, see Lynn Thorndike, *The Sphere of Sacrobosco and Its Commentators* (Chicago, 1949), 16-18, 138-40.

3. *Meteorologica,* i. 3, 340^{a}10-14, 340^{a}24-^{b}3. *De generatione et corruptione,* ii. 4, 331^{a}13-16.

4. *De anima,* ii. 4, 416^{a}16. See below, IV. 2. 11-18.

5. Or perfection.

6. However, as Bacon makes clear just below, these species are not brought to completion or perfection in full and complete effects similar to the agent in name and definition.

7. I. 5. 13-15.

8. Bacon means that *quite apart from* privation, the power of generating effects is missing, and the aptitude alone is present.

9. More literally, the virtues of the two are 'out of all proportion'.

10. Bacon's point is that some things now required for the sake of mankind will, at the end of this world, cease to exist; from this one must infer that they owe their existence to God's recognition of their utility for man. To proceed, as in the final clause of this sentence, to the admission that there are other things also made for mankind's benefit (these things, apparently, not destined for annihilation at the end of this world) only confuses the issue and weakens the point, for it seems clear of these things (since they will continue to exist even when there are no men to benefit) that their existence is not contingent on their utility. There is no contradiction, of course, in maintaining that two such classes of things exist, but the argument is expressed in such a way as to obscure the point.

11. That is, like created spiritual and celestial substances.

12. Avicenna, *Sufficientia,* i. 7, in Avicenna, *Opera* (Venice, 1508), f. 17^{v}b.

13. Note that I am here following the reading of MS *O,* against the others. Were one to accept the majority reading (*in aliis* instead of *aliis*), this phrase would have to be translated 'which is nobler [when situated] in other things' or 'which is nobler [when situated] in [the spheres of] the other elements'. Although it is possible that the latter wording represents Bacon's intention, its failure to complete the comparison (nobler than what?) speaks against it. Moreover, the greater nobility of fire (than the other elements) is not a function of location. In any case, Bacon's general point is clear: fire, when located in its proper sphere, does not convert everything else into fire (a complete effect), but merely produces its species (an incomplete effect).

14. Averroes, *Commentarium magnum in De anima libros,* ed. Crawford, p. 308. 54-5. For amplification of Bacon's views on this subject, see his *Communia naturalium, OHI* iii. 200-6.

15. Above, I. 6. 36-7.
16. Aristotle, *Meteorologica*, i. 3, 340^{b}4 ff.; *De generatione et corruptione*, ii. 10.
17. Bacon probably means 'ignited'.
18. I. 1. 37-41, 134-9; I. 3. 172-202.
19. On odour see *Opus maius* (Bridges), pt. V. 1, dist. 8, chap. 2, vol. ii. 57; dist. 9, chap. 4, vol. ii. 73.
20. I. 2. 8 ff.
21. On the four species of quality, see above, I. 1 n. 6.

[Part II, chap. 1]

1. Not part IV of *DMS*. Perhaps part *IV* of the larger work to which *DMS* was conceived to belong, or some other part of *DMS*. Equivocal action is touched upon in *DMS* I. 1. 174 ff.; V. 1. 7 ff. On Bacon's references to 'part IV', see the Introduction, above, p. xxxi.
2. *Physics*, vii. 2, 244^{b}2-5^{b}1; *De generatione et corruptione*, i. 6, 322^{b}21 ff.; and probably *De somniis*, 2, 459^{a}25-8 (where it is claimed that the objects of sense perception produce perception in the sense organ even after their departure).
3. In the chain of causation being described, one part transmuting the next, all parts reach equally far into the recipient to produce their effect because of their basic equality and the uniformity of nature.
4. It is clear from the argument following that 'infinite' denotes an infinity of directions of radiation, rather than radiation to infinite distance or radiation infinite in power.
5. This passage on the spherical multiplication of light is a virtual paraphrase of a passage in Robert Grosseteste's *De lineis, angulis, et figuris*; see my translation in Grant, *Source Book*, pp. 387-8. See also below, II. 8. 3-25.
6. *De generatione et corruptione*, ii. 5, 333^{a}9-11.
7. The purpose of this sentence seems to be to redefine 'agent', as a quasi-point source from which radiation proceeds in all directions.
8. II. 2. 98-115. See also *Opus maius* (Bridges), pt. IV. 2, chap. 2, vol. i. 117.
9. Ptolemy, *Optica*, ii. 65, p. 46; iii. 14, p. 95; see also Lejeune, *Euclide et Ptolémée*, pp. 37-41. Alhazen, *De aspectibus*, i. 17, p. 9; i. 28-9, p. 17.
10. II. 2. 36-97. See also *Opus maius* (Bridges), pt. IV. 2, chap. 2, vol. i. pp. 112-15.
11. *De aspectibus*, props. 1-6, pp. 4-9. For an analysis of these propositions, see Lindberg, *Theories of Vision*, p. 20.
12. *De aspectibus*, iv. 16, p. 112.
13. *De aspectibus*, prop. 11, p. 13.
14. Ibid., p. 14. Cf. Lindberg, *Theories of Vision*, pp. 24-5.
15. *De aspectibus*, pp. 13-14: 'Quod autem longitudine et latitudine et profunditate caret, non sentitur visu.'

[Part II, chap. 2]

1. On the difference between accidental multiplication and the principal multiplication, see below, II. 2. 116-41.
2. My translation includes a negative not found in the Latin text, because my term 'conditions' represents the negation of Bacon's term *modis*. That is, where

one of his 'modes' is the presence of an obstacle, my corresponding 'condition' is the absence of any obstacle.

3. I take *remote* in MS *O* to be a late correction. Nevertheless, this correction is clearly required, and I would have made it if *O* had not.

4. This is not true. For a possible explanation of Bacon's error, see *Opus maius* (Bridges), ii. 461 n. 1.

5. It was customary in medieval Latin optical treatises to use *dyaphanum* and *dyaphonum* interchangeably; Bacon here protests against the practice on etymological grounds.

6. *De anima*, ii. 7, 419^{a}13-15. What the passage means is that if there is an actually lucid or transparent medium between object and observer, the colour of the object is able to move it so as to affect sight; see Lindberg, *Theories of Vision*, p. 8.

7. Book i of the *Meteorologica*, as we have it in the Greek text, contains no such claim.

8. That is, the medium consists of two different substances meeting at an interface, but its two parts agree in what we would call 'optical density'.

9. II. 4. 143 ff.

10. That is, on their interface.

11. II. 2. 89-90.

12. See below, II. 4. 32, 93, 105, 162-3, where Ptolemy and Alhazen are quoted.

13. The other three are rectilinear, refracted, and reflected. On the twisting path, see Bacon, *Opus maius* (Bridges), pt. IV. 2, chap. 2, vol. i. 117; Lindberg, *Theories of Vision*, pp. 83, 126.

14. II. 2. 4-11.

15. ii. 10, 656^{a}30; cf. *De sensu*, 2, 438^{b}30-9^{a}3.

16. Aristotle, *De iuventute et senectute, De vita et morte*, 3, 469^{a}10-16. Avicenna, *De natura animalium*, xii. 10, in Avicenna, *Opera* (Venice, 1508), f. 49^r. See also Avicenna, *De anima*, in *Avicenna Latinus: Liber de anima seu sextus de naturalibus, IV-V*, ed. S. Van Riet (Louvain/Leiden, 1968), 176-81.

17. *De aspectibus*, ii. 3, p. 26; ii. 6, pp. 26-7. However, Alhazen has the twisting nerves proceeding to the brain rather than the heart.

18. On the history of this claim, see Aydin M. Sayili, 'The "Observation Well" ', *Actes du VIIe Congrès international d'histoire des sciences* (Jerusalem, 1953), 542-50; Lindberg, *Pecham and Optics*, p. 85. For early references to the phenomenon, see Aristotle, *De generatione animalium*, v. 1, 790^{b}20; Galen, *On the Usefulness of the Parts of the Body*, trans. Margaret T. May (Ithaca, 1968), 473. See also below, *DSC* V. 201-4.

19. Cf. *Opus maius* (Bridges), pt. IV. 4, chap. 3, vol. i. 132 ff.

[*Part* II, *chap.* 3]

1. That is, the concave or convex side of a curved line.

2. Not part IV of *DMS*; perhaps part *IV* of the larger treatise of which *DMS* was conceived to form a section, or part IV of the *Opus maius* (ed. Bridges, pt. IV. 3, chaps. 1-3, vol. i. 119-27). See also *Communia naturalium, OHI* ii. 46; and below, V. 1. 76-107; V. 2. 18-19, 28, 36. See also above, II. 1 n. 1.

3. The angle formed between the diameter and the adjoining arc of a semi-circle, judged by medieval mathematicians to be less than a right angle.

4. If a line divides a circle into unequal portions, it forms 'unequal oblique angles' with the immediately adjoining arcs.

5. Or conical. I will generally use the term 'pyramidal' because Bacon is sometimes ambiguous about the precise shape of the base. The terms 'pyramid' and 'pyramidal', then, will denote the figure formed when radiation passes between an apex and a base of any shape.

6. Bacon's 'columnar' figures may, but need not, have a circular cross-section. Thus some are cylinders, and some are not.

7. On reflection from oval and annular surfaces see below, II. 7. 3 ff.; II. 7 n. 16.

8. That is, the refracted ray passes between the rectilinear extension of the incident ray and the normal to the refracting interface.

9. A clear reference to Robert Grosseteste. See his *De iride*, trans. David Lindberg in Edward Grant, *Source Book*, p. 390.

10. Ptolemy's quantitative data on refraction have been skilfully analysed by Albert Lejeune, *Recherches sur la catoptrique grecque* (Brussels, 1957), 153–66; or see his *Optica*, pp. 223–37. On Alhazen, see *De aspectibus*, vii. 10–12, pp. 243–7.

11. *De aspectibus*, vii. 8, p. 240.

12. Ptolemy, *Optica*, v. 9, p. 228; v. 13–17, pp. 230–3. Alhazen, *De aspectibus*, vii. 8, pp. 240–2.

13. Ptolemy, *Optica*, v. 7–21, pp. 227–37. Alhazen, *De aspectibus*, vii. 2–7, pp. 231–40. For a translation of Alhazen's description of an instrument for investigating refraction, see Grant, *Source Book*, pp. 420–2.

14. For the next few paragraphs I closely follow my earlier translation in Grant, *Source Book*, pp. 430–2, but with some improvements. For a full analysis of medieval theories of the cause of refraction, see David C. Lindberg, 'The Cause of Refraction in Medieval Optics', *British Journal for the History of Science*, 4 (1968–9), 23–38.

15. Note that Bacon began this sentence talking about the descent of a species, but became so occupied with his illustrative example (the descent of a stone) that he ended by talking exclusively about the latter.

16. *De aspectibus*, vii. 16, p. 252. In asserting that transparency does not proceed to infinity, Bacon means, I believe, that transparency never becomes infinite in degree. Cf. below IV. 1. 15–16.

17. That is, slower motion.

18. This is the theory of geometrical resistance. For another example of the same theory, see Grant, *Source Book*, p. 334.

19. The argument of this paragraph is exceedingly difficult; for an analysis, see Lindberg, 'Cause of Refraction', pp. 26–8, 31.

20. In preceding paragraphs Bacon has argued that perpendicular incidence is stronger than oblique incidence on an interface, a claim justified by various mechanical analogies. Here (without seeming to notice that he has shifted ground) he maintains that perpendicular traversal of a medium is stronger than oblique traversal of the same medium; resistance within a medium is less in a direction perpendicular to its surface than in other directions. For a fuller analysis of the matter, see Lindberg, 'Cause of Refraction', pp. 26–7, 31.

21. Note Bacon's animistic terminology—for which John Pecham would rebuke him; see Lindberg, *Pecham and Optics*, p. 91.

22. Here we see the fundamental principle employed by Bacon in his explanation of refraction. Species choose a direction in the second medium that will most nearly maintain uniformity of strength or action. Consequently, a species passing from a less dense to a more dense medium deviates towards the

perpendicular, where the greater ease of traversal (by comparison with traversal along more oblique paths) compensates for the greater resistance of the medium; a species entering a less dense medium chooses a more resistant path for the same reason.

23. Similar analyses of refraction in a sphere or urinal are to be found in Pseudo-Euclid, *De speculis*, pp. 105-6; Robert Grosseteste, *De natura locorum*, in *Die philosophischen Werke des Robert Grosseteste*, ed. Ludwig Baur (*BGPM* 9) (Münster, 1912), p. 71; A. C. Crombie, *Robert Grosseteste and the Origins of Experimental Science 1100-1700* (Oxford, 1953), 122-3; Bacon, *Opus maius* (Bridges), pt. IV. 2, chap. 2, vol. i. 113-14; Lindberg, *Pecham and Optics*, pp. 229-31; Theodoric of Freiberg, *De iride et radialibus impressionibus*, ed. Joseph Würschmidt (*BGPM* 12. 5-6) (Münster, 1914), 121-3. See also Eilhard Wiedemann, 'Ueber das Sehen durch eine Kugel bei den Arabern', *Annalen der Physik und Chemie*, NS 39 (1890), 565-76.

[*Part* II, *chap.* 4]

1. Above, II. 2. 36-52.

2. See the quotations from Ptolemy and Alhazen, following.

3. Ptolemy, *Optica*, p. 237. Below, II. 4. 143-70.

4. The additional words inserted at this point in MSS *A* and *S* belong to the Ptolemaic text.

5. The reading of MS *S*, *horizontem*, is also the reading of Lejeune's edition of the Ptolemaic text.

6. On this phenomenon, see Lindberg, *Pecham and Optics*, pp. 153-5; Euclid, *Optica*, Prop. 6, in *L'Optique et la Catoptrique*, trans. Paul ver Eecke (Paris, 1959), 4-5; Alhazen, *De aspectibus*, vii. 15, pp. 251-2; vii. 52, pp. 278-9.

7. That is, stars that are always above the horizon.

8. Ptolemy, *Optica*, pp. 237-8. The passage has been translated from Govi's edition by Morris R. Cohen and I. E. Drabkin, *A Source Book in Greek Science* (Cambridge, Mass., 1958), 281. It is interesting to note that in lines 32 and 44, where the Ptolemaic text reads *visibilis radii*, Bacon omits the term *visibilis*— an expression of his commitment to vision by luminous, rather than visual, rays.

9. On Bacon's expansion of the meaning of 'colure', see below, II. 7 n. 11.

10. This is a reference to Thābit ibn Qurra's explanation of the precession of the equinoxes (the theory of trepidation). See Francis S. Benjamin, Jr., and G. J. Toomer (edd.), *Campanus of Novara and Medieval Planetary Theory* (Madison, Wis., 1971), 378-9; Francis J. Carmody (ed.), *The Astronomical Works of Thabit B. Qurra* (Berkeley/Los Angeles, 1960), 84 ff. For other medieval discussions of Thābit's theory, see Robert Grosseteste, *De sphera*, in *Phil. Werke*, ed. Baur, pp. 25-6; John Pecham, *Tractatus de sphera*, in Bruce R. MacLaren, 'A Critical Edition and Translation, with Commentary, of John Pecham's *Tractatus de Sphera*', Ph.D. dissertation (University of Wisconsin, 1978), 227-8. Cf. Bacon, *Communia naturalium*, *OHI* iv. 454-6.

11. This position is attributed to Albategni (that is, al-Battānī) by Thābit ibn Qurra; see Carmody, *Astronomical Works*, p. 104.

12. Here and at two points later in the quotation, I translate *preservet* as 'observe'. That this is the proper translation is clear from the context. It is interesting that in his edition of Alhazen's *De aspectibus* (1572), Friedrich Risner substituted *observet* for *preservet*; see Brugge, Stadsbibliotheek, MS 512, 101ʳ, for the original reading of *preservet*.

13. This and the other parenthetical expressions in the quotation represent Bacon's explanatory additions.

14. Bacon's parenthetical clarification is required because of the ambiguity of the term *reflexe*, which could mean either 'by reflection' or 'by a broken ray'. Bacon's quotation at this point is faithful to the text of Alhazen's *De aspectibus* found in MS Brugge 512, f. 101ʳ; however, Risner substituted the term *refracte* in the 1572 edition, thus achieving the same clarification as Bacon offered with his parenthetical remark.

15. On the expression *equator diei* see Thorndike, *Sphere of Sacrobosco*, p. 123.

16. Where the MSS of *DMS* read *recto* both the Risner edition and the Brugge MS read *recte*. My translation, as well as my text, reflects the latter reading.

17. Alhazen, *De aspectibus*, vii. 15, p. 251.

18. Ibid., pp. 251-2.

19. The canons are instructions for use of the tables.

20. It would be easy to misinterpret this passage. We must not assume that Bacon (or some predecessor) calculated lunar altitudes theoretically, measured them observationally, noticed a discrepancy, and concluded that the cause of the discrepancy must be atmospheric refraction of lunar radiation. The argument (which, it should be noticed, Bacon admits to having borrowed from Alhazen) is rather that since atmospheric refraction is known to occur (for it is predicted by basic cosmology and the principles of optics), there must consequently exist a discrepancy between observed and theoretically calculated lunar altitudes. No astronomical measurements or calculations underlie the claim—nor is it clear that if they had been made they would have supported it.

21. Ptolemy, *Optica*, pp. 240-1; Alhazen, *De aspectibus*, vii. 16, p. 252.

22. That is, the inside of the heaven and the outside of the sphere of fire.

23. Below, V. 2. 70-92; *Opus maius* (Bridges), pt. V. 3, dist. 2, chap. 1, vol. ii. 146-8. On the phenomenon of enlargement of celestial bodies near the horizon, see Ptolemy, *Optica*, pp. 115-16; Cohen and Drabkin, *Source Book*, p. 283; Alhazen, *De aspectibus*, vii. 51-4, pp. 278-80; *Opus maius* (Bridges), pt. V. 2, dist. 3, chap. 6, vol. ii. 116-17; Witelo, *Perspectiva*, in *Opticae thesaurus*, ed. Friedrich Risner (Basel, 1572), x. 5, pp. 448-9; Lindberg, *Pecham and Optics*, pp. 153, 254 (nn. 175-7).

24. The parenthetical remark is Bacon's.

25. Alhazen, *De aspectibus*, vii. 51, p. 278. Later in the century John Pecham suggested the possibility that a ray of light would undergo gradual curvature in a medium of gradually changing density; see Lindberg, *Pecham and Optics*, iii. 2, p. 213.

26. The Tropic of Cancer represents the most northerly position of the sun and planets. Therefore, planetary species incident north of the Tropic of Cancer cannot be directed towards the centre of the earth.

27. The inhabited region of the earth was variously divided into seven or eight climes, beginning at or near the equator and proceeding towards the north pole; see Thorndike, *Sphere of Sacrobosco*, pp. 138-40.

28. The Latin term (*tropica*) is puzzling in two respects. First, the medieval term was usually masculine in gender (*tropicus, -i*), as it is elsewhere in this paragraph; nevertheless, here the manuscripts are unanimous in giving a neuter form, perhaps treating it as an adjective modifying an understood neuter substantive. Second, Bacon could not have intended a plural, for although species directed

towards the centre of the earth from stars outside the Tropic of Cancer pass through the climes (which begin north of the equator), such species from stars outside the Tropic of Capricorn do not.

[*Part* II, *chap.* 5]

1. *Alibi*: note the variants. My choice of *alibi* was influenced somewhat by the parallel terminology in III. 2. 33, and IV. 1. 12.

2. Boethius, *The Consolation of Philosophy*, trans. Richard Green (Indianapolis, 1962), iii. prose 8, p. 55. Lynceus was one of the Argonauts, celebrated for his keen sight. Note that Bacon concludes that walls are penetrated by the species both of visible objects and of the eye. Cf. *Opus maius* (Bridges), pt. IV. 2, chap. 2, vol. i. 114.

3. *De generatione et corruptione*, ii. 2, 330^{a}11-12.

4. *Commentarium Magnum in De anima libros*, ed. Crawford, pp. 254-5 (at 419^{b}33-20^{a}2).

5. *Optica*, p. 20. 3-4.

6. *De aspectibus*, iv. 17, p. 112. Bacon closely paraphrases Alhazen.

7. 'Perspective' was the mathematical tradition in optics. See Lindberg, *Theories of Vision*, p. 104.

8. According to the theory under attack, the incident ray generates a form in the mirror, which gives rise to its own species; thus the incident and reflected rays represent independent processes of radiation.

9. For similar arguments, see Bacon, *Opus maius* (Bridges), pt. VI, chap. 7, vol. ii. 186-7; Avicenna, *De anima I–II–III*, ed. Van Riet, pp. 217-19; Albertus Magnus, *Liber de sensu et sensato*, 6, in *Opera omnia*, ed. Augustus Borgnet, ix (Paris, 1890), 12; Lindberg, *Pecham and Optics*, pp. 47-8, 169-71.

10. Although Bacon does not go into the matter, the requirement of immobility of the object and the mirror apparently arises from the belief that (in the theory under discussion) the form is fixed in the mirror only as long as the object is present before the mirror; that is, the fixation of forms is momentary rather than permanent.

11. Bacon knows that in plane mirrors the image is situated as far behind the mirror as the object is before the mirror. See *Opus maius* (Bridges), pt. V. 3, dist. 1, chap. 3, vol. ii. 135-6. That this was standard medieval knowledge is revealed by the work of John Pecham; see Lindberg, *Pecham and Optics*, pp. 171-5, and the associated notes.

12. On the multiplication of images in a broken mirror, see Bacon, *Opus maius* (Bridges), pt. V. 3, dist. 1, chap. 6, vol. ii. 144-6; Lindberg, *Pecham and Optics*, pp. 177-9.

[*Part* II, *chap.* 6]

1. Edited by J. L. Heiberg and E. Wiedemann, 'Ibn al Haitams Schrift über parabolische Hohlspiegel', *Bibliotheca Mathematica* (Ser. 3), 10 (1909-10), 220. The manuscripts of *DMS* are unanimous in reading *radius conversus* in line 9. However, some Latin manuscripts of *De speculis comburentibus* (the quoted work) expand this to read *radius incidens et radius conversus*, which makes considerably more sense and must be judged the proper reading (see Heiberg and Wiedemann's text and apparatus criticus for details). If the translation were adjusted to take this improved reading into account, it would read

'. . . intersection of the plane containing the two straight lines (the incident ray and the reflected ray) and the plane surface of the mirror . . . ' However, I have permitted my translation to reflect the defective text as Bacon had it, because he proceeds to deal with the difficulty himself—noting that the author of *De speculis comburentibus* denoted two rays (the incident and reflected) by a single expression (*radius conversus*), and excusing him on the grounds that 'they form one whole line'. The author of *De speculis comburentibus*, unknown to Bacon, was Alhazen.

2. *Optica*, p. 88. 17–19.

3. That is, perpendicularly.

4. Ptolemy, *Optica*, p. 88; Alhazen, *De aspectibus* (identical with the work Bacon here calls *Perspectiva*), iv. 10, p. 108; Alkindi, *De aspectibus*, props. 17–18, pp. 29–31.

5. Ptolemy, *Optica*, pp. 91–4; Alhazen, *De aspectibus*, iv. 7–9, pp. 104–8.

6. The convex mirror is probably cylindrical; it is erected with its axis perpendicular to the base of the instrument, and it is so positioned that reflection takes place at the exact centre of the instrument.

7. That is, the plane in which the incident and reflected rays lie.

8. Interior and exterior, that is, to the substance of the mirror. Angle D includes angle E, as one can infer from the argument and as Bacon says explicitly below; that is, C and D are supplementary. The words in the diagram are supplied only by MSS *A* and *S*.

9. Note the attempt at clarification in MSS *A* and *S* (see apparatus criticus).

10. Alkindi, *De aspectibus*, prop. 17, p. 30.

11. The work to which Bacon refers is not the genuine Euclidean *De speculis*, but a Pseudo-Euclidean work of the same title. For the cited passage, see the edition by Björnbo and Vogl, p. 100.

12. Euclid, *Elements* (Heath), iii. 16, vol. ii. 37–9. Angles of tangency (also known as horn angles) were regarded as true angles; on their history, see Heath's commentary to his translation, i. 177–82; ii. 39–42.

13. This is a quotation from the medieval translation of the genuine Euclidean *De speculis* (see n. 11, above). There is no printed text of this version, but see, for example, Paris, Bibliothèque Nationale, Fonds Latin, MS 7366, f. 87^r.

14. See definition 3.

15. Since no definition of *De speculis* deals directly with this, the reference may be to Euclid's *Elements*. The entire proof is a close paraphrase of the parallel section in *De speculis*.

16. II. 5. 55–109.

17. *Opus maius* (Bridges), pt. IV. 4, chap. 1, vol. i. 129–30; pt. V. 3, dist. 1, chap. 2, vol. ii. 133.

[*Part* II, *chap.* 7]

1. Heiberg and Wiedemann, 'Ibn al Haitams Schrift über parabolische Hohlspiegel', pp. 218–19.

2. That is, on the circle formed by intersection of the oval and a plane perpendicular to its axis—in short, the locus of points at a given distance from the vertex of the oval. The claim is true only if the rays in question issue from a single point, as Bacon makes clear below, II. 7. 31.

3. The statement is true, provided the rays have a common origin. It is

made no truer and no more informative by the addition of the final nine words of the sentence (counted in either the Latin text or the English translation).

4. Above, II. 4. 47 ff.

5. Rays reflected from the circumference of the smallest circle converge at a point on the axis between the illuminating source and the reflecting circumference, whereas rays reflected from the circumference of a larger circle can converge at a point of the axis beyond the reflecting circumference. This is apparent in fig. 14. Bacon's use of the terms 'higher' and 'lower' reveals that he conceives the mirror to be facing upward.

6. Bacon goes through all of this because his figure (fig. 14) will represent reflection along a single great circle—that is, along a vertical cross-section of the mirror, through its centre.

7. This cannot be true if, as Bacon maintained previously, all rays originated from the centre of the sun. That Bacon truly intended the point in question to be the end of the diameter is clear from subsequent references and his claim that rays issuing from it to the edges of the hemispherical mirror converge at the other end of the diameter, B. Apparently, then, Bacon forgot one of the initial conditions of the problem, or was misled by the lack of suitable scale in his diagram. All manuscript diagrams place point A a little more than a diameter from B, but I have corrected this feature on the basis of the clear and unambiguous statements found in the text.

8. This is a reference to the angles on the opposite sides of any given ray in the diagram. A ray that forms a smaller obtuse angle and a larger acute angle is more nearly perpendicular to the surface of the mirror.

9. The 'smaller and larger portions of a circle' are the two arcs of a circle marked off by a chord other than the diameter. Thus the 'angle of the smaller portion of a circle' is the angle bounded by the chord and the smaller of the two arcs. In the present case the 'smaller portion of the circle' is the $90°$ arc (not drawn in the figure) corresponding to chord AQ.

10. My translation corrects a slightly garbled Latin text, which reads (literally) 'the lower extremity of the pole and axis of the sphere'.

11. According to general medieval astronomical usage, there are only two colures—the two great circles passing through the poles and either the solstices or the equinoxes. Bacon, however, expands the meaning of the term to cover all great circles passing through the poles of a sphere. Note in the Latin text of this sentence that *axis* is construed to be feminine (*eandem axem*); despite Bridges, this is the reading of every manuscript I have examined.

12. In the Greek text, book i of Theodosius has only twenty-three propositions, and this quotation is not to be found in any of them. However, it does follow from Definition 5. See *Theodosius Tripolites Sphaerica*, ed. J. L. Heiberg, in *Abhandlungen der Gesellschaft der Wissenschaften zu Göttingen*, Phil.-hist. Klasse, NS 19. 3 (Berlin, 1927), 2–3.

13. What Bacon is trying to say is that reflection actually occurs in the colures (since the plane of the colure contains both the incident and reflected ray, and so forth). The circles in question merely represent the locus of points from which incident rays arranged symmetrically about the axis are reflected; they have mathematical (and perhaps pedagogical) significance, but no physical significance.

14. Euclid, *De speculis*, prop. 32; see Paris, Bibliothèque Nationale, Fonds Latin, MS 7366, f. 90^r. This same quotation serves as the opening line of Bacon's *DSC*.

15. Heiberg and Wiedemann, 'Ibn at Haitams Schrift über parabolische Hohlspiegel', p. 229. 25-9.

16. Bacon's frequent references to annular mirrors can be understood by noting that Alhazen described such mirrors (annular segments of oval or paraboloidal mirrors) in *De speculis comburentibus*; see ibid., pp. 216, 229.

17. No burning mirror meets this condition, nor had Alhazen, whom Bacon is attempting to follow, made such a claim. See my English translation of substantial sections of *De speculis comburentibus* in Grant, *Source Book*, pp. 413-17.

18. In the mirrors Bacon is describing, the colures lose their circularity, but the parallels do not.

19. This is the Pseudo-Euclidean *De speculis*, p. 105. In this proposition it is maintained, surprisingly, that the point of combustion can be located behind the mirror. Such a feat can, in fact, be achieved only by use of an annular mirror.

20. V. 2. 110-17.

[*Part* II, *chap.* 8]

1. II. 1. 25 ff.

2. See *Communia naturalium*, OHI iv. 342-4; *Opus maius* (Bridges), pt. IV. 4, chap. 10, vol. i. 152-7; *Opus tertium*, in *Opera* (Brewer), pp. 135-8. For similar arguments in other authors, see Robert Grosseteste, *On Light*, trans. Clare C. Riedl (Milwaukee, 1942), p. 10; Grosseteste, *De lineis*, trans. Lindberg in Grant, *Source Book*, pp. 387-8; Lindberg, *Pecham and Optics*, pp. 42, 71, 73, 79, 83, 244.

3. If the aperture is small, the image conforms to the shape of the source, and is round only if the source is round. For an analysis of medieval theories of radiation through small apertures, see David C. Lindberg, 'The Theory of Pinhole Images from Antiquity to the Thirteenth Century', *Archive for History of Exact Sciences*, 5 (1968), 154-76; id., 'A Reconsideration of Roger Bacon's Theory of Pinhole Images', ibid. 6 (1970), 214-23; and id., 'The Theory of Pinhole Images in the Fourteenth Century', ibid. 6 (1970), 299-325. See also Bacon's much fuller discussion of the problem in *DSC* V.

4. *Elements* (Heath), i. 26 and i. 4, vol. i. 301-3, 247-8.

5. The figure furnished by Bridges is found only in MS *O* (a relatively late manuscript) and must be regarded as an improvement on Bacon rather than the original Bacon. My fig. 15, taken from other manuscripts, represents the original.

6. Bacon is arguing here that the rounding of the image is not simply a matter of ray geometry; rather, he maintains, there are physical causes that enable some rays to achieve their natural rounded form more readily than others.

7. It would seem to follow that the claim made in the middle of the paragraph—that at a distance behind the aperture equal to that of the agent before the aperture the radiation and the agent are of the same size—cannot hold for solar rays both at noon and in the morning. If there is any genuine phenomenon corresponding to Bacon's alleged differences between solar radiation passing through the aperture in the morning and at noon, it would have to be associated with brightness; that is, there is a penumbral region that could be variously interpreted as illumination or shadow, perhaps as a function of the intensity of the radiation.

8. As Bacon makes clear later in the paragraph, he has a *round* pyramid in mind—hence a cone.

9. Actually, proposition 9 of Pseudo-Euclid, *De speculis*, p. 102.

10. For a brief analysis of this Pseudo-Euclidean proposition, see Lindberg, 'Pinhole Images from Antiquity to the Thirteenth Century', p. 160. When Bacon assigns the cause to 'the intersection of rays' he is asserting that the explanation is found in ray geometry—the rectilinear propagation and intersection of radiation passing through the aperture. For similar terminology in John Pecham, see Lindberg, *Pecham and Optics*, pp. 67-79.

11. 'Direct rays' are those that have not yet experienced intersection. To understand what Bacon is driving at, see *DSC* V. 205 ff., below, and the accompanying figure (fig. 59). 'Intersecting rays' are those that converge at K and perhaps E. 'Direct rays' are those directed towards G or beyond.

12. When preparing an edition of John Pecham's *Perspectiva communis* some years ago, I was puzzled by a passage in which he seemed to assume that one could draw figures of various shapes within the sun and proceed as though radiation issued from them alone; see Lindberg, *Pecham and Optics*, pp. 67-71, 244 (notes 18-19). It now seems clear that Pecham based that discussion (at least in part) on the present passage in *DMS*.

13. II. 10. 3-19; V. 3. 3-18. See also *Opus maius* (Bridges), pt. IV. 2, chap. 3, vol. i. 118-19.

[*Part* II, *chap.* 9]

1. Al-Kindī, *De aspectibus*, pp. 19-20; see also pp. 4-7, 21-2. Al-Kindī is clearly Bacon's principal source for this discussion of shadows.

2. Ibid., p. 21.

3. I. 2. 30-9, 163-79, 211-19.

4. 'Perspectivists' were practitioners of the mathematical tradition in optics. See above, II. 5 n. 7; Lindberg, *Theories of Vision*, pp. 104, 251 (n. 1).

5. Bacon has in mind a pyramid with a round base—that is, a cone—but I nevertheless employ 'pyramid' as the generic term.

6. *Elements* (Heath), i. 19, vol. i. 284-6. On this subject, see *Opus maius* (Bridges), pt. IV. 3, chap. 2, vol. i. 123-4; Lindberg, *Pecham and Optics*, pp. 75-7.

7. *Elements* (Heath), iii. 8, vol. ii. pp. 17-21. The lines to which Bacon refers do not appear in the figure. His point is simply that if all the rays of the pyramid are extended backwards through the sphere, the central one penetrates a greater depth of the spherical agent than any other.

8. In fact, proposition 11 of Pseudo-Euclid's *De speculis*, pp. 103-4. This proposition is analysed in detail in Lindberg, 'Pinhole Images from Antiquity to the Thirteenth Century', pp. 161-2.

9. A curious assumption, since in fig. 17 Bacon reveals his understanding of the principle that illumination comes from all parts of the illuminating body.

[*Part* II, *chap.* 10]

1. The title *De visu* (or *De visibus*) almost always denotes the medieval Graeco-Latin translation of Euclid's *Optica*. On this and the other translations see David C. Lindberg, *A Catalogue of Medieval and Renaissance Optical Manuscripts* (Toronto, 1975), 46-55; Wilfred R. Theisen, 'The Medieval Tradition of

Euclid's *Optics'*, Ph.D. dissertation (University of Wisconsin, 1972), 11–17; Theisen, '*Liber de visu*: The Greco-Latin Translation of Euclid's *Optics'*, *Mediaeval Studies*, 41 (1979), 52–4. Theisen edits *De visu* in the latter publication, edits and translates it in the former; for prop. 24 see pp. 78-9, 211 in the former, p. 76 in the latter.

2. The correct proposition number is iii. 16 in *Elements* (Heath), ii. 37–43.

3. This sentence is potentially confusing. Bacon has hitherto been discussing the pyramids of radiation issuing from stellar bodies (which he takes to be larger than the earth) and the angles formed between the diameter of the stellar body and rays issuing from the ends of the diameter along (or inside of) the line of tangency. Bacon presumably had the same thing in mind when he began the present sentence, except that the subject was now the radiation issuing from the ends of the the stellar diameter *outside* the line of tangency. However, when he attempts to illustrate the point from stellar radiation incident on the earth, Bacon notices that the rays have the required relationship not to the stellar diameter, but to the terrestrial diameter. He therefore abruptly switches perspective, and in the final clause of the sentence he is speaking not of radiation issuing from the ends of the stellar diameter, but of radiation incident on the ends of the terrestrial diameter.

4. The two diameters that Bacon has in mind are illustrated in fig. 20.

5. The intended proposition is probably iii. 16 in *Elements* (Heath), ii. 37–43.

6. V. 3. 19-88. Cf. *Opus maius* (Bridges), pt. IV. 3, chap. 2, vol. i. 123-4.

7. *De aspectibus*, props. 13-14, pp. 23-5. Bacon's figure (fig. 21) is taken from al-Kindī.

8. Proposition iii. 16 of *Elements* (Heath) must be intended.

9. Props. 2-3 of the *De crepusculis* of Abhomadi Malfegeyr (Ibn Muʿādh), printed with Alhazen's *De aspectibus* by Risner (Basel, 1572), 284-5.

10. *Opus maius* (Bridges), pt. V. 1, dist. 7, chap. 4, vol. ii. 52-3.

11. *De visu*, ed. Theisen, 'Medieval Tradition', p. 211; '*Liber de visu*', p. 76.

[*Part* III, *chap.* 1]

1. See Avicenna, *De anima I–II–III*, ed. Van Riet, pp. 177-83.

2. Possibly iii. 3, 998^a13-14; or iii. 5, where Aristotle inquires whether numbers, bodies, points, and planes are all substances. Cf. *De anima*, ii. 7, 418^b17-18.

3. *Physics*, iv. 8, 216^a23 ff. On medieval discussions of void space, see Edward Grant, *Much Ado About Nothing: Theories of Space and Vacuum from the Middle Ages to the Scientific Revolution* (Cambridge, 1981).

4. I. 2. 170; I. 3. 55-9.

5. Bacon has in mind the tree of Porphyry, according to which body is the second genus beneath substance. See Porphyry, *Isagoge*, trans. Warren, pp. 35-6. See also the discussion accompanying Eleonore Stump's translation of Boethius' *De topicis differentiis* (Ithaca, 1978), 237-46. Cf. Avicenna, *De anima I–II–III*, ed. Van Riet, pp. 181-2.

6. Cf. Avicenna, *De anima I–II–III*, ed. Van Riet, pp. 181-2.

7. On Bacon's use of the term *renovare* see above, I. 2 n. 57.

8. Some MSS read *renovet*, others *removet*. Neither term seems perfectly appropriate, but the sense of the sentence is clear.

9. I believe Bacon has in mind the creation of a moving shadow by the

motion of (for example) the moon and sun with respect to each other or the sun with respect to the earth.

10. That is, once the species has been generated in the medium, the agent is no longer required, but only more medium in which the species can continue to reproduce itself.

11. *De anima*, ii. 7, 418^{b}14–16.

12. Ibid. 418^{b}18–20.

13. Ibid. 418^{b}24–6.

14. Aristotle, *Categories*, 8, 9^{a}28–10^{a}10. In E. M. Edghill's translation of the *Categories* (*The Works of Aristotle*, edd. J. A. Smith and David Ross, i), these are called 'affective qualities'.

15. Aristotle, *Topics*, v. 5, 134^{b}29.

16. Aristotle deals with 'example' in a number of places, including *Rhetoric*, ii. 20, and *Prior Analytics*, ii. 24. Although it is by no means clear that it was available to Bacon, the Pseudo-Aristotelian *De rhetorica ad Alexandrum*, 8, 1429^{a}21–7, bears some resemblance to the passage quoted here.

17. On the nature of the stars, see *De caelo*, ii. 7, 289^{a}11–35.

18. *Paraphrasis in de sensu*, in *Aristotelis opera cum Averrois commentariis*, vi. 2 (Venice, 1562), f. 14F. See also Averroes, *De celo*, ii. 3, chap. 1, and iv. 3, chap. 3, in ibid. v, ff. 127B–C, 259H–I. Cf. Bacon, *Liber de sensu et sensato*, *OHI* xiv. 31–3.

19. II. 2. 30–2; cf. VI. 2. 47–50; *Opus maius* (Bridges), pt. IV. 4, chap. 1, vol. i. 128–9; pt. V. 1, dist. 9, chap. 1, vol. ii. 64–5.

[*Part* III, *chap.* 2]

1. This was the position of Averroes; see Lindberg, *Science in the Middle Ages*, pp. 357–8.

2. I. 1.

3. *De anima*, iii. 5, 430^{a}18–19. No such claim is to be found in *Metaphysics*, iv.

4. I have been unable to locate the cited passages in Avicenna and Averroes.

5. *Liber de causis*, 23, in *Die pseudo-aristotelische Schrift Ueber das reine Gute bekannt under dem Namen Liber de causis*, ed. Otto Bardenhewer (Freiburg i. B., 1882), 184–5; Boethius, *Consolation of Philosophy*, trans. Green, v, Poem 4 and Prose 5, pp. 112–14.

6. I. 3. 50–166.

7. Bacon never gets to this subject; see Nascimento, pp. 19–21.

8. I. 2. 138–79.

9. See n. 7, above.

10. *Averrois Cordubensis Compendia librorum Aristotelis qui Parva naturalia vocatur*, ed. A. L. Shields (Cambridge, Mass., 1949), 31–2, 193^{ra}45–8; *Epitome of Parva Naturalia*, trans. Harry Blumberg (Cambridge, Mass., 1961), 15–16; *Commentarium magnum in De anima libros*, ed. Crawford, p. 277.

11. *De anima*, ii. 5, 416^{b}32 ff.; ii. 7, 418^{b}8–27, 419^{a}25–30.

12. I. 3. 172–207.

13. Avicenna, *De natura animalium*, xii. 7, in *Opera* (Venice, 1508), f. 46^v.

14. *De memoria et reminiscentia*, 1, 450^{b}7–12.

15. *De anima I–II–III*, ed. van Riet, pp. 87–8. 19–27.

16. See III. 2 n. 7.

[*Part* III, *chap.* 3]

1. Bacon defines this term just below.

2. Or 'species'. In the Latin this paragraph is confusing because of the use of 'species' in two different senses.

3. On the thirteenth-century usage of *vera mixtio* see *A Latin-English Dictionary of St. Thomas Aquinas*, ed. Roy J. Deferrari (Boston, 1960), 655.

4. *Optica*, probably ii. 108, pp. 66–7, or iii. 63–4, pp. 118–19. Bacon usually refers to this work as *De aspectibus*, but either title is perfectly appropriate. Bacon's reference to the 'mixing of species in air' is clear enough, but I am uncertain what he means by the 'mixing of species . . . in the species of colour'. Perhaps this should be read 'mixing . . . in the species of colour' or 'mixing . . . in the varieties of colour'.

5. *De aspectibus*, i. 27, pp. 16–17.

6. A clear reference to the prologue added to *DMS* in MSS *A, S, M*, and *P*; see the Appendix, *a*. 62–70. It is noteworthy that although all manuscripts contain this passage, only a few contain the prologue to which it refers. On Alhazen's reliability see also below, IV. 1. 90–1.

7. On accidental lines see above, II. 2. 116–41.

8. *De aspectibus*, i. 29, p. 17.

9. My translation omits a redundant phrase.

10. Species as the subdivision of genus.

11. For the definition of 'contingent nature' see III. 3. 15–16.

[*Part* IV, *chap.* 1]

1. Alhazen, *De aspectibus*, vii. 8, pp. 240–1.

2. *Physics*, viii. 7, 260^b9–14.

3. My translation of *statum* is influenced by my understanding of an earlier passage, above, II. 3. 113–15, and n. 16.

4. VI. 2. 12–23.

5. I. 3. 17–19; I. 5. 38–60.

6. VI. 1. 28 ff.

7. *De aspectibus*, iv. 5, pp. 103–4.

8. My translation of this phrase represents what Bacon intended to say, rather than what the manuscripts actually have him saying. Cf. above, IV. 1. 75.

9. That is, the species in the second part of the medium. This entire argument is based on the assumption that the species in question are being propagated downward, from the heavens towards the earth.

10. Bacon means 'from every part of the principal ray'; but these parts, of course, are found in every part of the medium.

11. My translation assumes that Bacon did not mean that the rate of weakening increases, as his words might seem to indicate, but simply that weakening continues.

12. Some manuscripts have the reading *modo* rather than *mundo*; the sense of the sentence is approximately the same in either case.

[*Part* IV, *chap.* 2]

1. ii. 4, 416^a16.

2. In terms of strength.

3. A ratio of greater inequality between A and B is one in which $A > B$.

There are various types of ratio of greater inequality, each with its own name. The simplest is a multiple ratio, in which A is an integral multiple of B; the others are superparticular, superpartient, multiple superparticular, and multiple superpartient; for further discussion of the denomination of ratios, see Michael S. Mahoney, 'Mathematics', in Lindberg, *Science in the Middle Ages*, p. 164. The argument here is that the strength of the species in the prior part of any space is equal to or greater than that in the posterior part—and, if greater, then greater according to some such ratio of greater inequality.

4. vii. 5, 250^a1–$^b9$.

5. I. 4. 116 ff.

6. *De aspectibus*, vii. 8, pp. 240–2.

7. Perhaps *Physics*, iv. 7, 213^b32, 214^a12; iv. 8, 215^a10–11.

8. Bacon here distinguishes between void and nothing—void being 'dimensioned space containing no body', while nothing is simply nothing.

9. On the various heavens, see Edward Grant, 'Cosmology', in Lindberg, *Science in the Middle Ages*, pp. 275–80.

10. *Physics*, iv. 5, 212^b16–18; iv. 6–9; *De caelo*, i. 9, 279^a12–17.

[*Part* IV, *chap.* 3]

1. *De aspectibus*, ii. 21, pp. 37–8. On the speed of light, see David C. Lindberg, 'Medieval Latin Theories of the Speed of Light', in René Taton (preface), *Roemer et la vitesse de la lumière* (Paris, 1978), 45–72. Bacon also treats the speed of propagation of light or species in the *Opus maius* (Bridges), pt. V. 1, dist. 9, chap. 3, vol. ii. 68–71; see my translation in Grant, *Source Book*, pp. 396–7.

2. *De aspectibus*, vii. 8, p. 241.

3. iv. 10, 218^b14–18; iv. 14, 222^b30–3^a15; vi. 8, 238^b29–31.

4. *Physics*, vi. 7, 237^b23–5. This and the following argument are repeated almost verbatim in the *Opus maius* (Bridges), pt. V. 1, dist. 9, chap. 3, vol. ii. 69–70.

5. viii. 10, 266^a12–$^b25$.

6. iv. 11, 219^a13–21.

7. Averroes, *Commentarium magnum in De anima libros*, ed. Crawford, p. 237; Seneca, *Natural Questions*, ii. 8, in *Physical Science in the Time of Nero, being a Translation of the Quaestiones Naturales of Seneca*, trans. John Clarke (London, 1910), pp. 58–9.

8. *De anima*, ii. 7, 418^b24–6.

9. *De sensu et sensato*, 6, 446^b28.

10. On sound, see also above, I. 2. 8 ff.; *Opus maius* (Bridges), pt. V. 1, dist. 9, chap. 4, vol. ii. 72–3; *Opus tertium*, in *Opera* (Brewer), p. 230.

11. I do not believe that anything in book iii is germane, but see *De anima I-II-III*, ed. van Riet, ii. 4, p. 149. See also Bacon's own account in *Opus maius*, cited in the preceding note; also Aristotle, *De sensu et sensato*, 5, 448^a22; and *De anima*, ii. 9.

12. Alternatively: 'And in sound and odour there are so many motions . . . '

13. Al-Kindī, *De aspectibus*, pp. 25–7.

[*Part* V, *chap.* 1]

1. Probably v. 4, 228^b15–229^a2, although if this is the passage Bacon has in mind, he has misunderstood it.

2. *Elements* (Heath), i. 19, vol. i. 284-6.

3. It is a mistake to suppose that the refracted line will ever be perpendicular to the refracting interface (and thus parallel to the cathetus). Moreover, Bacon himself recognized this in other places: see, for example, above, II. 3. 39 ff.; *Opus maius* (Bridges), pt. V. 3, dist. 2, chaps. 1-4, vol. ii. 146-55.

4. The figure is found only in MSS *A* and *S*. A twisting line consists of many different curves.

5. As Bacon explained above (II. 2. 98-115), the tortuous path is found only in animated substances—to be specific, the spirits filling the nerves.

6. Bridges reproduces a figure from MS *O*, f. 376^r. I follow MSS *F*, *L*, *S*, and *A*.

7. Two different texts circulated during the Middle Ages as the *Geometria* of Boethius. Only one of them has been edited, and it does not appear to contain the claim in question; see Menso Folkerts, '*Boethius' Geometrie II: Ein mathematisches Lehrbuch des Mittelalters* (Wiesbaden, 1970). On the two Boethius texts see Mahoney, 'Mathematics', in Lindberg, *Science in the Middle Ages*, p. 171 n. 17.

8. *Liber de causis*, 16, ed. Bardenhewer, p. 179.

9. v. 6, 1016^{a}12-13.

10. V. 2. 93-109. Cf. *Opus maius* (Bridges), pt. IV. 2, chap. 2, vol. i. 115-16.

11. See references in the preceding note.

12. II. 2. 116-41. Cf. *Opus maius* (Bridges), pt. IV. 2, chap. 2, vol. i. 117.

13. That is, at right angles or obliquely.

14. *Elements* (Heath), i. 19, vol. i. 284-6.

15. The supplement of AFQ, formed on the other side of line AF.

16. *Elements* (Heath), i. 32, vol. i. 316-22. If AFQ is a right angle, it is equal to the sum of the remaining two angles.

17. See above, II. 1 n. 1; II. 3 n. 2.

18. *Elements* (Heath), iii. 8, vol. ii. 17-21.

19. Aristotle, *De caelo*, ii. 14, 296^{b}18-21. Alhazen, *De aspectibus*, i. 20, p. 13.

20. That is, unless there is some obstruction.

21. ii. 3, chap. 1, in *Aristotelis opera cum Averrois commentariis*, v, f. 126G.

22. *De caelo*, i. 4, 271^{a}13-14.

[*Part* V, *chap.* 2]

1. Alhazen, *De aspectibus*, vii. 8, pp. 240-2. See also Bacon, *Opus maius* (Bridges), pt. IV. 3, chap. 1, vol. i. 120-1; Lindberg, *Pecham and Optics*, pp. 38, 49-50, 91-3, 99, 121, 159, 161, 213; Lindberg, *Theories of Vision*, pp. 74-5, 109, 190, 243 (n. 85).

2. That is, on the outside of a circle or on a convex curve.

3. Not Part IV of *DMS*; perhaps Part IV of the larger treatise of which *DMS* was conceived to form a section; or Part IV of the *Opus maius* (Bridges), pt. IV. 3, chap. 1, vol. i. 120-1. See above, II. 1 n. 1; II. 3 n. 2.

4. *Elements* (Heath), iii. 8, vol. ii. 17-21.

5. See above, V. 2 n. 3.

6. That is, any surface containing it.

7. II. 3. 6-38; II. 6. 3 ff.

8. See above, V. 2. n. 3.

9. That is, strictly speaking, angles are not formed between lines and surfaces, but between lines and other lines.

10. A stricter rendering of the text would be 'all lines tangent to the [great] circle. . . .' However, there is only one tangent line to a single great circle at a particular point. Bacon's use of the plural ('lines') suggests, therefore, that he had in mind the many great circles passing through that point.

11. That is, incident on a circle from the inside.

12. *Elements* (Heath), iii. 7-8, vol. ii. 14-20. This argument may appear somewhat bizarre, for it would seem clear that the strength of action along a perpendicular should depend on the length of the perpendicular, without reference to the shape of the recipient. What Bacon is attempting to point out, however imperfectly, is that a concave surface tends to retreat from the source of action and, therefore, that the perpendicular to a concave surface is apt to be longer than the perpendicular to a plane or convex surface. Consequently, there is a disadvantage associated with action along a perpendicular to a concave surface.

13. Cf. above, II. 3. 132-68.

14. Note that this phrase is a clarifying addition found only in MSS *S* and *A*.

15. A practical impossibility, owing to the presence of the earth at the centre, as Bacon proceeds to explain.

16. This claim is true only if the perpendicular is that drawn from the point where the species originates, rather than the perpendicular at the point of refraction. When passing from a dense to a rare medium, the refracted species diverges from the latter perpendicular no matter where the object is located.

17. Note that my reading 'BD' corrects the manuscript readings. The text is perhaps corrupt at this point; at any rate, MSS *S* and *A* seem to contain an attempt at clarification or correction.

18. II. 7. 106-42. Bacon's fullest treatment of this subject is in *DSC*, especially Parts I, VII, and VIII; see also *Opus maius* (Bridges), pt. IV. 2, chap. 2, vol. i. 115-16.

19. Pseudo-Euclid, *De speculis*, p. 105. On this proposition, see above, II. 7. n. 19. See also *DSC* VIII. 56-7.

[*Part* V, *chap.* 3]

1. Cf. the parallel discussion in *Opus maius* (Bridges), pt. IV. 3, chap. 2, vol. i. 123-4.

2. Euclid, *Elements* (Heath), i. 21, vol. i. 289-92.

3. To create the four angles one must extend the sides of the pyramid beyond the vertex, as in fig. 35. Note that 'triangle', the reading of the majority of the manuscripts, is corrected to 'pyramid' in manuscripts *S* and *A*.

4. The angle at the vertex, within the pyramid.

5. Euclid, *Elements* (Heath), i. 15, vol. i. 277-9.

6. Bacon is considering the proximity of rays AB and ΛC in fig. 68, one belonging to the pyramid ('belonging to the body of the . . . pyramid'), the other being the extension of the equivalent ray from the other side of the pyramid ('the coterminal ray issuing from its vertex'). These rays, he points out, are closer in a shorter pyramid, other things being equal.

Fig. 68

7. Presented in the preceding paragraph.

8. II. 10. 8-30.

9. That is, the shortest pyramid issuing from a given sector of the sphere.

10. The negative appears only in MS *O*, among those collated, and it is not clear whether it expresses Bacon's true intention. Without the negative, the sentence contains an obvious contradiction (strength is found in *all* pyramids, but *only those* which meet a certain condition). With insertion of the negative, we find Bacon affirming the strength of all pyramids, and not only the special category of pyramids having their vertex between the tangent lines issuing from the luminous sphere (pyramid BED in fig. 38). The difficulty with the latter interpretation is that the main point of the paragraph is to affirm that pyramids whose vertices fall between the tangent lines (such as BED) are stronger than pyramids whose vertices fall outside the tangent lines (such as ABC), and it is not Bacon's custom to begin a paragraph by undercutting or compromising its main point. I think we must opt for inclusion of the negative, but we should recognize that the text (or the original Baconian argument) may be defective at this point.

11. Such as ABC, in fig. 38.

12. The argument would be more persuasive if pyramid BAC were to contain all of the radiation from the agent that can reach point C—that is, if AC and BC were tangent to the circle. It would then turn out, of course, that the quantity of radiation reaching C depends solely on the distance of C from the agent and not at all on its lateral shift outside tangents EO and BG.

13. Prop. 16 in *Elements* (Heath), ii. 37-9.

14. *De aspectibus*, prop. 14, pp. 23-5. The demonstration that follows is taken from al-Kindī. Cf. Lindberg, *Theories of Vision*, pp. 26-30.

15. MSS *F*, *L*, and *A* contain this figure, and all distort it. Distortion is least in *L* (f. 44^r), where curve KHFGTL is moderately oblong. In *A* and *F*, this curve is highly oblong, indeed almost rectangular. An examination of al-Kindī's *De aspectibus*, from which Bacon takes this argument, makes the proper shape of the curve perfectly clear.

16. See above, n. 13.

[*Part* VI, *chap.* 1]

1. Probably *De longitudine et brevitate vitae*, 3, 465^{b}4-10. But see also *De iuventute et senectute, De vita et morte*, 5, 469^{b}21-70^{a}4.

2. *De caelo*, iii. 6, 305^{a}10-11.

3. I. 3. 17-19; I. 5. 38-60; IV. 1. 35-42.

[*Part* VI, *chap.* 2]

1. *De anima*, ii. 7, 418^{b}14-16. Above, I. 3.

2. VI. 1. 14 ff.

3. I know of no Aristotelian passage where the claim is explicitly made, but it can be inferred from the following passages: *De caelo*, i. 3, 270^{b}13-16; i. 4, 270^{b}31-2; i. 10; *Physics*, viii. 7-8; *Meteorologica*, i. 2, 339^{a}12-13; *De mundo*, 2, 391^{b}17-20, 392^{a}5-9; *Metaphysics*, xii. 6, 1072^{a}21-3; xii. 7, 1072^{b}4-7.

4. Probably a reference to Averroes' commentary on Aristotle's *Metaphysics*, vii. 2, chap. 10, in *Aristotelis opera cum Averrois commentariis*, viii, f. 180-1. On semen and its role in generation, see also Averroes, *Paraphrasis in libros de*

generatione animalium, i. 20, in ibid. vi, ff. 65-6. For an elaboration of Bacon's views on generation, see *Communia naturalium*, *OHI* iii. 279-81.

5. *De caelo*, ii. 3, chap. 1, in *Aristotelis opera cum Averrois commentariis*, v, f. 125F-I; *De substantia orbis*, ii, in ibid. ix, f. 7K-M.

6. Despite considerable searching, I do not find such a claim in Averroes' commentary on *De caelo*, book iv.

[*Part* VI, *chap.* 3]

1. *De generatione et corruptione*, ii. 10, 336^{a}27-8.
2. *Physics*, v. 4, 227^{b}22-9^{a}7.
3. Aristotle identifies three kinds of change in *Physics*, v. 1-2, 225^{b}8-6^{b}18.
4. An artificial day is the time during which the sun is actually above the horizon.

[*Part* VI, *chap.* 4]

1. Alhazen, *De aspectibus*, ii. 21, pp. 37-8; i. 28-30, pp. 17-18.
2. II. 3. 169-97; II. 7. 106-42. See also *DSC*.
3. The argument is that if species were to persist and be augmented by additional species, we would observe stronger combustion by *direct radiation* from the sun than in fact we can produce by use of the burning glass or burning mirror.
4. *Liber de causis*, 16, ed. Bardenhewer, p. 179.
5. Bacon is referring to secondary or accidental radiation; on this, see above, II. 2. 116-41.
6. Apparently Bacon conceives dense media (such as glass) to be of much smaller extent than rare media (such as air). I do not believe that Bacon would have been prepared to argue that dispersion through secondary radiation is greater in a rare medium than in a dense medium of the same dimensions.
7. There is no genuine Ptolemaic work by this title, and I have been unable to identify the work to which Bacon refers. For another reference to the same work, see *Un fragment inédit de l'Opus tertium de Roger Bacon*, ed. Pierre Duhem (Quaracchi, 1909), 152. For Ptolemy's remarks on climate, see *Almagest*, ii. 6. Cf. Thorndike, *Sphere of Sacrobosco*, pp. 138-40, 317-18, 337-8.
8. The 'parallels' in question are the sun's diurnal arcs. Under the Tropic of Cancer, the sun is directly overhead at the summer solstice and varies only slightly from that position for some time before and after the solstice (forty days in all, according to Bacon). This means that the diurnal arcs, the paths traversed by the sun on a given day, are so closely packed as to be virtually indistinguishable. I render *declinatio* as 'deviation' to make clear that Bacon is not employing the term in its technical astronomical sense.
9. The sixth hour is noon. Bacon is arguing that at the eighth or ninth hour the sun, although of lower altitude than at noon, has been heating the air for a longer period than has the noon sun; consequently, the cumulative heating effect is greater at that time than at noon.
10. That is, to terminate rays issuing from the eye and hence to produce the act of sight. Bacon's use of the visual ray theory is probably metaphorical here, although it is conceivable that he is simply referring to the visual rays which, in his theory, play a secondary role. On Bacon's theory of vision, see Lindberg, *Theories of Vision*, pp. 107-16.

11. Bridges here appends an additional paragraph, found only in MS *L* and there marked (by the word *va . . . cat*) for deletion. However, Bridges mistakenly combined the first two letters (*'va'*) of *vacat* with the opening word of the appended paragraph (*licet*) to yield the word *videlicet*. I judge the paragraph to be a non-Baconian gloss and relegate it to the apparatus criticus.

DE SPECULIS COMBURENTIBUS

[*Part* I]

1. This treatise, which had a wide medieval circulation under the title *De speculis* or *Liber de speculis*, is generally regarded as a late Greek recension of a genuine Euclidean work. For an edition of the Greek text, see J. L. Heiberg and H. Menge (edd.), *Euclidis Opera omnia*, vii (Leipzig, 1895), 286–342; for a French translation of the Greek text, see Euclide, *L'Optique et la Catoptrique*, trans. Ver Eecke, pp. 99–123. There is no edition of the medieval Latin text of this work; for a list of fifty-two Latin manuscripts, see Lindberg, *Catalogue of Optical Manuscripts*, pp. 47–50. The enunciation of this final proposition of *De speculis*, in the medieval version, is 'Ex concavis speculis ad solem positis ignis accenditur.' Bacon took figs. 40 and 41 directly from *De speculis*.

2. A 'segment of a circle smaller than a semicircle' is the smaller of the two arcs formed when a chord divides a circle unequally. DGI, the 'angle of a segment of a circle smaller than a semicircle', is the angle formed between that smaller arc and the chord.

3. iii. 31 in *Elements* (Heath), ii. 61–5.

4. Any line passing from a point on the mirror to T, its centre, is a radius of the circle; the angle it forms with the surface of the mirror must therefore be the angle of a semicircle.

5. That is, a circle passing through points A and G, in a plane perpendicular to axis DB.

6. Bacon here mis-speaks himself. Angle DGI is not the angle of segment GI of the circle, just as angle DGB is not the angle of segment GB of the circle. What he means to say is that 'they form angles of incidence [with the mirror] larger than angle DGI because they are the angles of segments [of a circle] larger than the segment associated with angle DGI.' A similar correction is required in the clause that follows.

7. The same final proposition of *De speculis*, to which reference has already been made.

8. That is, perpendicularly.

9. Given a modern understanding of the angles formed when a radius intersects its arc, there would be no need to establish that the semicircles in question are equal in size; whether equal or not, the radius forms right angles with the tangent to the arc (or arcs) at the point of intersection. However, medieval mathematicians judged the angle formed between a radius and its arc to be less than a right angle, its precise size being a function of the curvature of the arc. The equality of the semicircles is therefore essential information.

10. The quoted text from Euclid's *De speculis* reads as follows: 'omnes ergo

coincidunt ab omnibus punctis super eos qui per centrum et in centro radios. Eis ergo radiis calefactis accenditur ignis; quare in eis stupa posita accendetur' (Oxford, MS Corpus Christi College 283 [12th-13th century], f. 168^v). Cf. the similar claim in *DMS* II. 7. 109-10.

[*Part* II]

1. On modes of multiplication, see also *DMS* II. 1 and II. 8-10; *Opus maius* (Bridges), pt. IV. 2, chap. 3, and IV. 3, chaps. 1-3, vol. i. pp. 117-27.

2. *Elements* (Heath), iii. 16, ii. 37-43.

3. *Elements* (Heath), iii. 8, vol. ii. 17-21.

4. Actually, prop. 25; see Theisen, '*Liber de visu*', pp. 76-7. On *De visu*, see above, *DMS* II. 10 n. 1.

5. If this paragraph is confusing, the reason is probably that for most modern readers its conclusion is too obvious to require such lengthy discussion. Bacon's point is simply that multiplication of light from a single point of the luminous body cannot be the primary mode of multiplication, because other modes of multiplication are stronger. For further analysis, see the Introduction, above, pp. lxxi-lxxii.

6. The manner described in the second paragraph of this section.

7. *Elements* (Heath), iii. 8, vol. ii. 19.

8. Bacon recognizes that a spherical mirror cannot focus radiation perfectly.

[*Part* III]

1. Literally, 'pyramidal'. However, it seems clear in this case that Bacon has in mind an umbrageous (or shadow-casting) body of spherical shape and hence a pyramid with a circular base.

2. Bacon does not get around to the second half of the disjunction until the next paragraph. Meanwhile, the bracketed expression is required for syntactical clarity.

3. On lunar nodes, see Thorndike, *Sphere of Sacrobosco*, pp. 141-2. On medieval terminology for describing the nodes (head and tail of the dragon), see Benjamin and Toomer, *Campanus of Novara*, pp. 379-80.

4. *Elements* (Heath), i. 34, vol. i. 323-6; also i. 33, ibid. 322-3.

5. $39\frac{1}{4}$ times: *Almagest*, v. 16, in *Handbuch der Astronomie*, trans. Manitius, i. 313.

6. Ibid. v. 14, trans. Manitius, i. 309.

7. Ibid. iv. 3, trans. Manitius, i. 203.

8. II. 16 ff.

9. That is, the shadow through which the moon must pass during its eclipse would be even wider. See the preceding paragraph.

10. This is a free translation of Bacon's phrase, 'sicut patet in figura exterius'. The term *exterius* refers to that which is accessible to the exterior senses—in this case the sense of vision. Similar phraseology is employed in *DSC* III. 54, 85-6; V. 124.

11. *Elements* (Heath), vi. 2, vol. ii. 194-5.

12. *Elements* (Heath), i. 29 and vi. 4, vol. i. 311-12; vol. ii. 200-2.

13. See III n. 10.

14. The relevant propositions are iii. 16 (here and throughout this paragraph, wherever reference is made to iii. 15) and i. 33, *Elements* (Heath), vol. ii. 37-9; vol. i. 322-3.

15. See III n. 10.

16. Earlier in this demonstration, Bacon identified CD as the diameter of the opaque body. He now treats CD as the chord of the segment of arc visible from point G.

[*Part* IV]

1. Bacon deals more fully with radiation through apertures below, part V.

2. Literally, shaped like a razor or bow. The term *novacula* was commonly used to designate the crescent of the moon, or the crescent of the sun during an eclipse.

3. V. 55 ff.

4. Only reflection is discussed below, VI-VII. On refraction, see *DMS* II. 3; *Opus maius* (Bridges), pt. IV. 2, chap. 2, vol. i. 111-14; V. 3, dist. 2, chaps. 1-4, vol. ii. 146-59.

5. These circles do not appear in the figure. Moreover, the cones shown in the figure are not the ones to which Bacon here refers, since the outermost rays of the cones in the figure are not tangent to the body of the sun. It is possible, of course, that the figure, as it appears in the manuscripts, has been corrupted.

6. *Elements* (Heath), iii. 8, vol. ii. 17-21.

7. On equivocal effects see *DMS* I. 1. 176 ff.

8. Euclid, *Elements* (Heath), iii. 8 and iii. 36, vol. ii. 17-19, 73-5.

[*Part* V]

1. For an analysis of the medieval theory of radiation through apertures, including this section of *DSC*, see Lindberg, 'Pinhole Images from Antiquity to the Thirteenth Century'; 'Reconsideration of Bacon's Theory of Pinhole Images'; and 'Pinhole Images in the Fourteenth Century'. See also *DMS* II. 8. 26 ff.

2. The other two modes, treated in subsequent paragraphs, are along converging and diverging lines.

3. *Elements* (Heath), i. 34, vol. i. 323-6.

4. See also below, V. 56-7, 108-12, 129-33. This alleged narrowing of radiation immediately beyond the aperture plays an important role in Bacon's theory of radiation through apertures, for no mode of radiation that fails to account for it can be judged adequate or efficacious. Bacon here uses it to disconfirm the possibility that radiation proceeds from the sun along parallel lines. On the possibility of such an 'observation', see Lindberg, 'Reconsideration of Bacon's Theory', p. 216 n. 11.

5. These two alternatives, together, constitute the first mode of multiplication along converging lines. As Bacon proceeds, he soon gets into subcategories and never clearly identifies the other two modes. However, they are probably convergence outside the luminous body in the direction of the aperture (which Bacon discusses in the next paragraph) and convergence outside the luminous body in the direction opposite to the aperture (which Bacon forgets to mention explicitly, although the arguments applicable to convergence in the body of the sun are applicable to it as well).

6. Bacon's claim is not demonstrated in *Elements*, vi. 2, although such a demonstration could easily be based on the figure associated with that proposition. See *Elements* (Heath), vol. ii. 194-5. See also below VI n. 9.

7. Bacon has in mind the light issuing from triangle ABC (fig. 56, below)

and converging at G. Light is of course multiplied by portions of the sun outside of triangle ABC, but this light is excluded from consideration under the mode of propagation here being discussed. It is dealt with later, lines 62 ff.

8. Postulate 5 in *Elements* (Heath), vol. i. 155, but the fourth postulate in certain medieval translations; see 'The Translation of the *Elements* of Euclid from the Arabic into Latin by Hermann of Carinthia(?)', ed. H. L. L. Busard, *Janus*, 54 (1967), 11.

9. The argument is simply that between H and KI (fig. 56, below) the rays of cone ABCH have not yet spread sufficiently to fall outside the rays of the triangular pyramid ABCG.

10. Fig. 56 places H at the edge of the aperture, but this merely reflects the inability of Bacon or the copyists to handle problems of perspective.

11. There is a small gap in the argument here. Bacon seems to have been leading up to the conclusion that the observed narrowing of the composite light immediately beyond the aperture is incompatible with the mode of radiation represented by cone CDE. Instead, he concludes that the observations rule out radiation 'terminated at each point of the aperture'—that is, the infinity of cones coming to a vertex within the aperture in plane AB. The missing piece of reasoning is that the collection of cones coming to a vertex at each point of the aperture has the same outer boundaries as cone CDE; therefore, the two modes of radiation come to the same thing, and what discredits the one discredits the other.

12. See above, III n. 10.

13. It is not perfectly clear whether Bacon has in mind the mode of multiplication illustrated in fig. 57, that illustrated in fig. 58, or multiplication along parallel lines. All have been recently discussed, and all seem incompatible with the narrowing of light immediately beyond the aperture.

14. This is a long way of saying that a solitary ray of light viewed from the side (that is, a ray that does not itself enter the observer's eye) is imperceptible. The reason for this fact, Bacon goes on to point out, is that the secondary radiation issuing from a solitary ray of light is too weak to stimulate the power of vision. By contrast, a ray of light entering a house through a window is easily visible because it is composite; at its every point terminate an infinite number of rays issuing from the other points on the surface of the sun. Therefore, such a ray is sufficiently strong for secondary light generated by it to affect the power of sight. For additional analysis, see Lindberg, 'Reconsideration of Bacon's Theory', pp. 218-19.

15. On secondary or accidental multiplication, see *DMS* II. 2. 116-41.

16. On the possibility of stellar observations from a well or pit, see the references in *DMS* II. 2 n. 18.

17. Fig. 59 combines features of figs. 56 and 57.

18. Thus far the argument ignores the radiation coming to a vertex at K. Bacon will take it into account in the objections to follow.

19. This will be a cone before passage through the aperture, a triangular pyramid thereafter.

20. It is plausible to argue that rays AF and CD are invisible because solitary (that is, because they are not intersected and reinforced by any other solar rays). However, the argument becomes less plausible when extended to radiation lying between CD and CH and between AF and AI, for rays in this region are not solitary. What Bacon is doing, of course, is comparing the intensity of light within the penumbral region of the shadow cast by the sides of the aperture to

the fully illuminated region of the medium, and arguing that light within the penumbra is totally invisible. Bacon admits his reservations about this theory, but seems to have felt that, despite its weaknesses, it was the only theory capable of accounting for the 'observed' narrowing of the radiation immediately beyond the aperture. It is a way of reconciling the teachings of reason (that rays are multiplied in all the modes originally considered) with the teachings of sense (that the radiation narrows beyond the aperture). For further discussion, see Lindberg, 'Reconsideration of Bacon's Theory', pp. 219–20.

[*Part* VI]

1. Bacon gets immediately sidetracked and does not discuss multiplication along a twisting path. On this subject, however, see *DMS* II. 2. 98–115; II. 3. 3–18; V. 1. 37–43; *Opus maius* (Bridges), pt. IV. 2, chap. 3, vol. i. 117. But note that in none of these passages does Bacon suggest that the twisting path of radiation is a composite of straight segments; indeed, in the passage from the *Opus maius* he seems expressly to deny such an interpretation. Rather, what Bacon here refers to as the 'twisting' path resembles what he elsewhere calls 'accidental multiplication'; on the latter, see *DMS* II. 2. 116–41.

2. This figure and the next are found only in Oxford, MS Ashmole 440 (ff. 16^v, 17^r), a sixteenth-century copy of the treatise, probably in John Dee's hand. They are probably Dee's own reconstructions.

3. The following propositions in *Elements* (Heath): I. 4, vol. i. 247–8; perhaps iii. 25, vol. ii. 54–5; and iii. 1, vol. ii. 6–7.

4. The Latin term, *mukefi*, is a transliteration of the Arabic word meaning parabolic. It was frequently misspelled *mukesi*.

5. See, for example, Alhazen, *De aspectibus*, iv. 12, pp. 109–10.

6. *Almagest*, i. 6, in *Handbuch der astronomie*, trans. Manitius, i. 15–16.

7. Ibid. v. 14, vol. i. 305–9, where the diameter of the sun is said to subtend an arc of 31$'$ 20$''$.

8. Identified just below.

9. This is the second time Bacon has attributed to *Elements*, vi. 2, a demonstration not found there, but easily based on the figure given in that proposition; see above, V n. 6.

10. Bacon's conclusion (that if CF/FE = CD/DA and CF/FG = CD/DB, then CF/EG = CD/AB) follows that of *Elements* (Heath), v. 24, vol. ii. 183.

11. That is, if axis DC of the incident cone should be obliquely incident on the reflecting surface. A figure illustrating this special case is included in Oxford, MS Ashmole 440, 18^v.

12. *Elements* (Heath), iv. 15, vol. ii. 109.

13. Apparently, when Bacon calculated the chord of an arc of 32$'$ he obtained the result 32$'$ 17$''$ 50$'''$, which (taking 50$'''$ for 1$''$) he rounded to 32$'$ 18$''$. However, if he used Ptolemy's table of arcs and chords in *Almagest*, i, Bacon should in fact have calculated the chord at 33$'$ 30$''$ 40$'''$.

14. Bacon sets up the following proportionality:

$$\frac{\text{chord of } 60^\circ}{\text{chord of } 32'} = \frac{\text{distance of place of combustion from point of reflection}}{\text{diameter of light at place of combustion}},$$

the right-hand denominator being what Bacon wishes to determine. To understand Bacon's procedure, we must look first at the left-hand ratio. Since the chord of 60° equals the radius of the circle, this becomes the ratio of the radius

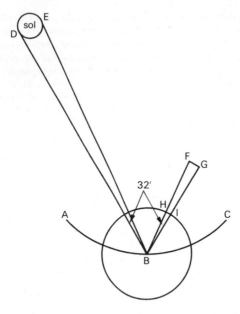

Fig. 69

of an arbitrary circle to the chord of an arc of 32′ on that circle. We can
construct such a circle about the point of reflection on the mirror, as in fig. 69,
where ABC is a burning mirror, which reflects a cone of light DEB, issuing from
the sun, into cone BFG; FG is the place of combustion, and Bacon wishes to
calculate its width. Since the disc of the sun occupies an arc of 32′, this is the
angle at the vertex of both the incident cone and the reflected cone. The left-
hand ratio, then, is simply that between the radius of the arbitrary circle and the
chord of arc HI, that is, between BI and HI. Now, in setting this equal to the
right-hand ratio, Bacon merely affirms that BI is to HI as BG (equals 12 ft.) to
FG. So far this is perfectly correct, but when Bacon calculates FG at 5/36 ft.,
he errs. I am unable to perceive the source of his error, but his 5/36 (= 0.13888)
contrasts with the correct value of 0.10767.

[*Part* VII]

1. VI. 100–15.
2. In the next paragraph.
3. Bacon expresses this poorly. He means that the mirror is perpendicular to
axis EF and hence to the cone of light as a whole. The manuscripts draw chord
AB. However, this confuses the diagram, since rays FA and FB represent an
entire cone of rays incident on the entire circumference ABCE, and I do not
believe it represents Bacon's intention; I have therefore omitted the chord from
my drawing.
4. *Elements* (Heath), vol. i. 247.
5. All rays except the axis are obliquely incident, thus forming (as medieval
scholars viewed the matter) one obtuse and one acute angle with the reflecting

surface; however, the angle of incidence is the smaller of these, and therefore the acute one. Angles of incidence 'near the centre' are to be distinguished, not from angles of incidence near the periphery, but from the angle of incidence *at* the centre—that is, the angle of incidence of the central axis, FE.

6. To understand Bacon's terminology here, one must remember that all rays represented in fig. 63 are themselves the central axes of cones having the surface of the sun as base and a point on the mirror as vertex. These axes, considered as a group, form the cone that we observe in fig. 63.

7. Since all axes emanate from the centre of the sun, they must diverge as they proceed from the sun to the mirror; they converge if traced backwards from the mirror to the sun.

8. Heiberg and Wiedemann, 'Ibn al Haitams Schrift über parabolische Hohl-spiegel', pp. 227-8; Grant, *Source Book*, pp. 416-17.

9. This figure is found only in MS *E*, p. 86, and perhaps in MS *W*, f. 112^v (I express doubt because the figure is misplaced in the latter manuscript and differs in a number of respects).

10. I. 29-54.

11. Bacon understands that rays closest to the axis come to a focus at a point midway between the mirror surface and its centre of curvature, and that all other rays come to a focus at points on the axis closer to the mirror surface. This is in contrast to his remarks above (I. 34-57), where he distributes the points of focus over the axis from the mirror surface all the way to the centre of curvature. It is true, of course, that in the earlier discussion Bacon was attempting to follow the reasoning of the final proposition of Euclid's *De speculis* and had not yet introduced the assumption of parallel (or sensibly parallel) solar axes.

12. In fact, only the first of the two is demonstrated; see above, n. 10. The 'little slips' (*cedule*) were probably small leaves or cards on which supplementary material (perhaps intended for inclusion in subsequent copies) was placed. For other examples of this usage of the term, see Robert Grosseteste, *Commentarius in VIII libros physicorum Aristotelis*, ed. Richard C. Dales (Boulder, 1963), p. xi n. 19; *Joannis Duns Scoti Opera omnia*, ed. Charles Balić, i (Vatican City, 1950), 172*-3*. In the absence of the autograph copy of *DSC*, there is no way of determining what was contained on these *cedule*. The main point is nevertheless clear—namely, that the matter has been treated above and can therefore be passed over here.

13. Bacon's principal source on conical mirrors was undoubtedly Alhazen, *De aspectibus*, pp. 119-23, 156-61, 185-8, 209-14, 229-30.

14. If Bacon means literally 'behind' the mirror, then the mirror in question must be annular, for only such mirrors produce combustion behind (that is, further from the sun than) themselves; see below, VIII. 57; *DMS* V. 2. 114-17. However, Bacon uses the same expression figuratively in *DMS* V. 2. 110-13, to denote a point of combustion close to, but nevertheless before, a non-annular mirror.

15. On cylindrical mirrors, see Alhazen, *De aspectibus*, pp. 116-19, 124, 153-6, 183-5, 205-9, 225-9.

[*Part* VIII]

1. Bacon's discussion of paraboloidal burning mirrors must depend principally on this treatise, whose author (apparently unknown to Bacon) was

Alhazen. An edition of the Latin text and a German translation of the Arabic text appear in Heiberg and Wiedemann, 'Ibn al Hait̲ams Schrift über parabolische Hohlspiegel'. However, Bacon's exposition does not closely parallel Alhazen's.

2. Bacon cannot represent this perpendicular to line AB because it is also perpendicular to the plane of his drawing.

3. In the manuscripts, this curve is simply a quarter of a circle, but I think we must give Bacon the benefit of the doubt and make it parabolic. See the following note.

4. This curve is not parabolic in the manuscript diagrams, but sharply pointed. Although it is impossible to determine precisely how Bacon would have drawn the curve, he would surely have been able to draw something roughly parabolic, and I therefore do the same on his behalf. That is, I take the crude drawings in the manuscripts to be corrupted versions of his original. One can see what may be an example of a similar process of corruption in manuscript copies of Alhazen's *De speculis comburentibus*, Bacon's principal source for this discussion. There, in most manuscripts, we see 'parabolas' every bit as crude as Bacon's; however, one of the earliest extant manuscripts (Vatican, MS Ottobonian Lat. 1850, f. 9^v [13th century]; cf. also Vatican, MS Urbinas Lat. 296, f. 229^{r-v} [14th century]) contains figures that actually look like parabolas. As for the hypothesis that Bacon's original drawing might have been a crude pointed figure owing to the influence of a manuscript of Alhazen's *De speculis comburentibus* containing already corrupted figures, this is surely a possibility, but I discount it because it requires us to conclude either that Bacon did not know what a parabola looked like or that he was too timid to correct his sources.

5. Bacon refers to the mirror as 'oviform' simply to signify that it is closed or cupped, like the end of an egg, and thus to distinguish it from an annular (or ring-shaped) mirror. Each of these mirrors is formed from a segment of the parabola, the 'oviform' mirror from segment IEK (fig. 67) at the vertex, the annular mirror from segment HGMN somewhat removed from the vertex. In choosing this terminology, Bacon was influenced by Alhazen's *De speculis comburentibus* (ed. Heiberg and Wiedemann, p. 229). However, where the Latin translation of this treatise, to which Bacon had access, refers to an 'oviform' mirror, the Arabic original (ibid. 216) refers to a mirror shaped like half an egg, which makes the matter somewhat clearer.

6. Bacon has certainly described how to produce the required shape, but producing it in wood is no way to obtain a mirror. Alhazen's *De speculis comburentibus* instructs the reader to turn the mirror in steel.

7. Apparently, there is also to be a circle on the opposite face of the piece of wood, equal in diameter to line HG. Bacon forgets that the circle drawn above was associated not with the annular mirror, but with the oviform mirror.

8. This is the advantage of an annular mirror, which justifies the attention devoted to it—namely, that if segment HGMN is outside the focus of the parabola, the point of combustion will be situated behind the mirror. On annular mirrors, see *DMS* II. 7. 120–1; V. 2. 110–17.

9. I take this statement to apply to both oviform and annular mirrors. It is, in any case, a surprising statement, since Alhazen's *De speculis comburentibus*, to which Bacon clearly had access, gives quite an adequate account of the location of the point of combustion (specifying its distance from the vertex to be one-quarter of the latus rectum of the parabola); see the edition of Heiberg and Wiedemann, pp. 229–31. Either Bacon must have been depending on a defective copy of the treatise, or he must have found its explanation incomprehensible.

APPENDIX

1. This prologue has been edited from the Milan and London MSS by Ferdinand M. Delorme, 'Le prologue de Roger Bacon à son traité De influentiis agentium', *Antonianum*, 18 (1943), 81–90. My text, based on two additional MSS, differs in many particulars from his.

2. Cicero, *Tusculan Disputations*, i. 12. 26.

3. Pliny, *Natural History*, Praef. 21.

4. Priscian, *Institutiones grammaticae*, ed. Martin Hertz, i (Leipzig, 1855), 2. 13–14; I owe this reference to Delorme, 'Le prologue de Roger Bacon', p. 85.

5. In *A*, a later hand marks virtually this entire insertion for deletion. In terms of content, it surely does not belong where it is found in *S* and *A*. It treats the same material as I. 4 and should probably be regarded as a revised or alternative version of that.

6. This addition to the text is immediately preceded in *S* and *A* by a repetition of II. 6. 3–30 ('Deinde . . . reflexo'). Judged by its subject matter, the addition would be more fittingly placed at II. 6. 30.

7. Boethius, *Quomodo substantiae* (*De hebdomadibus*), in J.-P. Migne (ed.), *Patrologia Latina*, lxiv (Paris, 1847), 1311. The Boethian text in this version reads 'quam quisque probat auditam'.

8. Note that this passage replaces IV. 3. 90–117 ('dicendum . . . spatio').

Bibliography

Abhomadi Malfegeyr, *De crepusculis*, in Friedrich Risner (ed.), *Opticae thesaurus Alhazeni Arabis libri septem* . . . , Basel, 1572. Reprint, with an introduction by David C. Lindberg, New York, 1972.

Abū ʿAbd Allāh Muḥammad ibn Muʿādh, *see* Abhomadi Malfegeyr.

Albertus Magnus, *Opera omnia*, ed. A. Borgnet. 38 volumes. Paris, 1890-9.

Alhazen, 'Abhandlung über das Licht von Ibn al-Haitam', trans. J. Baarmann, *Zeitschrift der deutschen morgenländischen Gesellschaft*, 36 (1882), 195-237.

—— *De aspectibus*, in Friedrich Risner (ed.), *Opticae thesaurus Alhazeni Arabis libri septem* . . . , Basel, 1572. Reprint, with an introduction by David C. Lindberg, New York, 1972.

—— 'Le "Discours de la lumière" d'Ibn al-Haytham (Alhazen): Traduction française critique', trans. Roshdi Rashed, *Revue d'histoire des sciences et de leurs applications*, 21 (1968), 197-224.

—— *Perspectiva, see De aspectibus.*

—— 'Ibn al Haitams Schrift über parabolische Hohlspiegel', edd. and trans. J. L. Heiberg and Eilhard Wiedemann, *Bibliotheca Mathematica* (Ser. 3), 10 (1909-10), 201-37.

—— *De speculis comburentibus, see preceding item.*

Alkindi, *see* Kindī, al-

Alverny, M.-Th. d', 'Notes sur les traductions médiévales d'Avicenne', *Archives d'histoire doctrinale et littéraire du moyen âge*, 19 (1952), 337-58.

Anawati, Georges C., *Études de philosophie musulmane*. Paris, 1974.

(Anonymous), *Liber de causis*, ed. Otto Bardenhewer, *Die pseudo-aristotelische Schrift Ueber das reine Gute, bekannt unter dem Namen Liber de causis*. Freiburg i. B., 1882.

Aristotle. *Aristotle with an English Translation* (Loeb Classical Library). 22 volumes. London, 1926-70.

—— *Aristotelis opera cum Averrois commentariis*. 12 volumes. Venice, 1562-74.

—— *The Works of Aristotle Translated into English*, edd. J. A. Smith and David Ross. 12 volumes. Oxford, 1908-52.

Armstrong, A. H., *The Architecture of the Intelligible Universe in the Philosophy of Plotinus*. Cambridge, 1940.

—— (ed.), *The Cambridge History of Later Greek and Early Medieval Philosophy*. Cambridge, 1970.

Augustine, *Opera omnia*, in J.-P. Migne (ed.), *Patrologiae cursus completus, series Latina*, xxxii-xlvi. 11 volumes. Paris, 1841-2.

—— *The Trinity*, trans. Stephen McKenna. Washington, 1963.

Averroes, *Commentarium magnum in Aristotelis De anima libros*, ed. F. Stuart Crawford. Cambridge, Mass., 1953.

—— *Compendia librorum Aristotelis qui Parva naturalia vocatur*, ed. A. L. Shields. Cambridge, Mass., 1949.

—— *Epitome of Parva Naturalia*, trans. Harry Blumberg. Cambridge, Mass., 1949.

Avicebron, *Fons vitae*, ed. Clemens Baeumker (*Beiträge zur Geschichte der Philosophie des Mittelalters*, 1. 2-4). Münster, 1895.

—— *The Fountain of Life (Fons vitae)*, abridged edn., trans. Harry E. Wedeck. New York, 1962.

Avicenna, *Avicenna Latinus: Liber de anima seu sextus de naturalibus I-II-III*, ed. S. Van Riet. Louvain/Leiden, 1972.

Avicenna, *Avicenne perhypatetici philosophi: ac medicorum facile primi opera in lucem redacta: ac nuper quantum ars niti potuit per canonicos emendata. Logyca, Sufficientia, De celo et mundo, De anima, De animalibus, De intelligentiis, Alpharabius de intelligentiis, Philosophia prima.* Venice, 1508. Reprint, Frankfurt a. M., 1961.

Bacon, Roger, *Compendium studii theologiae*, ed. Hastings Rashdall. Aberdeen, 1911.

— *Un fragment inédit de l'Opus tertium de Roger Bacon*, ed. Pierre Duhem. Quaracchi, 1909.

— *Opera hactenus inedita*, edd. Robert Steele and Ferdinand M. Delorme. 16 fascicules. Oxford, 1905–40.

— *Opera quaedam hactenus inedita*, ed. J. S. Brewer. London, 1859. Reprint, London, 1965.

— *Fratris Rogeri Bacon, Ordinis Minorum, Opus Majus ad Clementum quartum*, ed. Samuel Jebb. London, 1733. Reprint, with corrections, Venice, 1750.

— *The Opus Majus of Roger Bacon*, ed. John Henry Bridges. 2 volumes. Oxford, 1897.

— *The Opus Majus of Roger Bacon*, ed. John Henry Bridges. 3 volumes. London, 1900. Reprint, Frankfurt a. M., 1964.

— *The Opus Majus of Roger Bacon*, trans. Robert B. Burke. 2 volumes. Philadelphia, 1928. Reprint, New York, 1962.

— *Part of the Opus Tertium of Roger Bacon, including a fragment now printed for the first time*, ed. A. G. Little (British Society of Franciscan Studies, 4). Aberdeen, 1912.

— *Rogerii Bacconis Perspectiva*, ed. I. Combach. Frankfurt, 1614.

— *Rogerii Bacconis Specula mathematica*, ed. I. Combach. Frankfurt, 1614.

Badawī, ʿAbdurraḥmān, *Histoire de la philosophie en Islam*. 2 volumes. Paris, 1972.

— *La transmission de la philosophie grecque au monde arabe*. Paris, 1968.

Bauemker, Clemens, *Witelo, ein Philosoph und Naturforscher des XIII. Jahrhunderts* (*Beiträge zur Geschichte der Philosophie des Mittelalters*, 3. 2). Münster, 1908.

Bardenhewer, Otto, *see* (Anonymous), *Liber de causis.*

Basil of Caesarea, *Hexaemeron*, in Philip Schaff and Henry Wace (edd.), *A Select Library of Nicene and Post-Nicene Fathers of the Christian Church* (2nd Ser.), viii. New York, 1895.

Bauer, Hans, *Die Psychologie Alhazens* (*Beiträge zur Geschichte der Philosophie des Mittelalters*, 10. 5). Münster, 1911.

Baur, Ludwig, 'Der Einfluss des Robert Grosseteste auf die wissenschaftliche Richtung des Roger Bacon', in A. G. Little (ed.), *Roger Bacon Essays*, pp. 33–54. Oxford, 1914.

— *Die Philosophie des Robert Grosseteste* (*Beiträge zur Geschichte der Philosophie des Mittelalters*, 18. 4–6). Münster, 1917.

Beierwaltes, Werner, 'Die Metaphysik des Lichtes in der Philosophie Plotins', *Zeitschrift für philosophische Forschung*, 15 (1961), 334–62.

Benjamin, Francis S., Jr. and Toomer, G. J. (edd.), *Campanus of Novara and Medieval Planetary Theory*. Madison, Wis., 1971.

Björnbo, Axel Anthon and Vogl, Sebastian (edd.), 'Alkindi, Tideus und Pseudo-Euklid. Drei optische Werke', *Abhandlungen zur Geschichte der mathematischen Wissenschaften*, 26. 3 (1912), 1–176.

Blumenberg, Hans, 'Licht als Metapher der Wahrheit im Vorfeld der philoso-

phischen Begriffsbildung', *Studium Generale*, 10 (1957), 432–47.

Boethius, Anicius Manlius Severinus, *The Consolation of Philosophy*, trans. Richard Green. Indianapolis, 1962.

— *De topicis differentiis*, trans. Eleonore Stump. Ithaca, 1978.

Bonaventura, St. *Bonaventure's De reductione artium ad theologiam: A Commentary with an Introduction and Translation*, ed. Sister Emma Thérèse Healy (Works of St. Bonaventure, edd. Philotheus Boehner and M. Frances Laughlin, i). St. Bonaventure, N.Y., 1955.

Bouyges, Maurice, S. J., 'Roger Bacon, a-t-il lu des livres arabes?', *Archives d'histoire doctrinale et littéraire du moyen âge*, 5 (1930), 311–15.

Bréhier, Émile, *The Philosophy of Plotinus*, trans. Joseph Thomas. Chicago, 1958.

Bremer, Dieter, 'Hinweise zum griechischen Ursprung und zur europäischen Geschichte der Lichtmetaphysik', *Archiv für Begriffsgeschichte*, 17 (1973), 7–22.

— 'Licht als universales Darstellungsmedium: Materialen und Bibliographie', *Archiv für Begriffsgeschichte*, 18 (1974), 185–206.

Bultmann, Rudolf, 'Zur Geschichte der Lichtsymbolik im Altertum', *Philologus*, 97 (1948), 1–36.

Callus, Daniel A., 'Robert Grosseteste as Scholar', in id. (ed.), *Robert Grosseteste, Scholar and Bishop*, pp. 1–69. Oxford, 1955.

— (ed.), *Robert Grosseteste, Scholar and Bishop*. Oxford, 1955.

Campanus of Novara, *see* Benjamin and Toomer.

Carmody, Francis J. (ed.), *The Astronomical Works of Thabit B. Qurra*. Berkeley/Los Angeles, 1960.

Carton, Raoul, *L'expérience mystique de l'illumination intérieure chez Roger Bacon* (Études de philosophie médiévale, 3). Paris, 1924.

— *L'expérience physique chez Roger Bacon: Contribution à l'étude de la méthode et de la science expérimentales au XIIIᵉ siècle* (Études de philosophie médiévale, 2). Paris, 1924.

— *La synthèse doctrinale de Roger Bacon* (Études de philosophie médiévale, 5). Paris, 1924.

Charles, Émile, *Roger Bacon, sa vie, ses ouvrages, ses doctrines*. Paris, 1861.

Clulee, Nicholas H., 'Astrology, Magic, and Optics: Facets of John Dee's Early Natural Philosophy', *Renaissance Quarterly*, 30 (1977), 632–80.

Cohen, Morris R. and Drabkin, I. E. (edd.), *A Source Book in Greek Science*. Cambridge, Mass., 1958.

Crombie, A. C., *Robert Grosseteste and the Origins of Experimental Science 1100–1700*. Oxford, 1953. Reprint, Oxford, 1962.

— and North, J. D., 'Bacon, Roger', *Dictionary of Scientific Biography*, i. 377–85. New York, 1970.

Crowley, Theodore, O.F.M., *Roger Bacon: The Problem of the Soul in His Philosophical Commentaries*. Louvain/Dublin, 1950.

Dales, Richard C., 'Robert Grosseteste's Scientific Works', *Isis*, 52 (1961), 381–402.

— 'Robert Grosseteste's Views on Astrology', *Mediaeval Studies*, 29 (1967), 357–63.

Daniel, E. Randolph, 'Roger Bacon and the *De seminibus scripturarum*', *Mediaeval Studies*, 34 (1972), 462–7.

Delorme, Ferdinand M., 'Le prologue de Roger Bacon à son traité De influentiis agentium', *Antonianum*, 18 (1943), 81–90.

Easton, Stewart, *Roger Bacon and His Search for a Universal Science*. Oxford, 1952.

Eastwood, Bruce S., 'Grosseteste's "Quantitative" Law of Refraction: A Chapter in the History of Non-Experimental Science', *Journal of the History of Ideas*, 28 (1967), 403-14.

— 'Mediaeval Empiricism: The Case of Grosseteste's Optics', *Speculum*, 43 (1968), 306-21.

— 'Metaphysical Derivations of a Law of Refraction: Damianos and Grosseteste', *Archive for History of Exact Sciences*, 6 (1970), 224-36.

— 'Uses of Geometry in Medieval Optics', *Actes du XIIe Congrès international d'histoire des sciences, Paris 1968*, 3A, pp. 51-5.

Euclid, *The Elements*, trans. Sir Thomas Heath, 2nd edn. 3 volumes. Cambridge, 1926.

— *Opera omnia*, edd. J. L. Heiberg and H. Menge. 9 volumes. Leipzig, 1883-1916.

— 'The Optics of Euclid', trans. H. E. Burton, *Journal of the Optical Society of America*, 35 (1945), 357-72.

— *L'Optique et la Catoptrique*, trans. Paul Ver Eecke. Paris, 1959.

— *see* Theisen, Wilfred R.

Fakhry, Majid, *A History of Islamic Philosophy*. New York, 1970.

Fellermeier, Jakob, 'Die Illuminationstheorie bei Augustinus und Bonaventura und die aprioristische Begründung der Erkenntnis durch Kant', *Philosophisches Jahrbuch*, 60 (1950), 296-305.

Ferguson, A. S., 'Plato's Simile of Light', *Classical Quarterly*, 15 (1921), 131-52; 16 (1922), 15-28.

— 'Plato's Simile of Light Again', *Classical Quarterly* 28 (1934), 190-210.

Fisher, N. W. and Unguru, Sabetai, 'Experimental Science and Mathematics in Roger Bacon's Thought', *Traditio*, 27 (1971), 353-78.

Frankowska, Małgorzata, *Scientia as Interpreted by Roger Bacon*. Warsaw, 1971.

Galen, *On the Usefulness of the Parts of the Body*, trans. Margaret T. May. 2 volumes. Ithaca, 1968.

Gasquet, F. A., 'An Unpublished Fragment of a Work by Roger Bacon', *English Historical Review*, 12 (1897), 494-517.

Gilson, Étienne, *The Christian Philosophy of Saint Augustine*, trans. L. M. Lynch. New York, 1960.

— *History of Christian Philosophy in the Middle Ages*. New York, 1955.

— *La philosophie de Saint Bonvaenture*, 3rd edn. Paris, 1953.

Grant, Edward, *Much Ado about Nothing: Theories of Space and Vacuum from the Middle Ages to the Scientific Revolution*. Cambridge, 1981.

— (ed.), *A Source Book in Medieval Science*. Cambridge, Mass., 1974.

Grosseteste, Robert, *On Light*, trans. Clare C. Riedl. Milwaukee, 1942.

— *Die philosophischen Werke des Robert Grosseteste*, ed. Ludwig Baur (*Beiträge zur Geschichte der Philosophie des Mittelalters*, 9). Münster, 1912.

— 'Robert Grosseteste on Refraction Phenomena', trans. Bruce S. Eastwood, *American Journal of Physics*, 38 (1970), 196-9.

Hackett, Jeremiah M. G., 'The Attitude of Roger Bacon to the *Scientia* of Albertus Magnus', in James A. Weisheipl, O.P. (ed.), *Albertus Magnus and the Sciences: Commemorative Essays 1980*, pp. 53-72. Toronto, 1980.

Hamilton, Gertrude K., 'Three Worlds of Light: The Philosophy of Light in Marsilio Ficino, Thomas Vaughan, and Henry Vaughan'. Ph.D. dissertation, University of Rochester, 1974.

Hauréau, B., *De la philosophie scolastique*. Paris, 1850.

Healy, Sister Emma Thérèse, *see* Bonaventura.

Hedwig, Klaus, 'Forschungsübersicht: Arbeiten zur scholastischen Lichtspekulation. Allegorie–Metaphysik–Optik', *Philosophisches Jahrbuch*, 84 (1977), 102–26.

— 'Neuere Arbeiten zur mittelalterlichen Lichttheorie', *Zeitschrift für philosophische Forschung*, 33 (1979), 602–15.

— *Sphaera Lucis: Studien zur Intelligibilität des Seienden im Kontext der mittelalterlichen Lichtspekulation* (*Beiträge zur Geschichte der Philosophie und Theologie des Mittelalters*, NS 18). Münster, 1980.

Hempel, Johannes, 'Die Lichtsymbolik im alten Testament', *Studium Generale*, 13 (1960), 352–68.

Hoffmans, Hadelin, 'La genèse des sensations d'après Roger Bacon', *Revue néoscolastique de philosophie*, 15 (1908), 474–98.

— 'L'intuition mystique et la science', *Revue néo-scolastique de philosophie*, 16 (1909), 370–97.

— 'La sensibilité et les modes de la connaissance sensible d'après Roger Bacon', *Revue néo-scolastique de philosophie*, 16 (1909), 32–46.

— 'La synthèse doctrinale de Roger Bacon', *Archiv für Geschichte der Philosophie*, 20 (1907), 208–13.

Hudeczek, Methodius, O.P., 'De lumine et coloribus [according to Albertus Magnus]', *Angelicum*, 21 (1944), 112–38.

Hunt, R. W., 'The Library of Robert Grosseteste', in Daniel A. Callus (ed.), *Robert Grosseteste, Scholar and Bishop*, pp. 121–45. Oxford, 1955.

Husik, Isaac, *A History of Mediaeval Jewish Philosophy*. New York, 1916.

Ibn al-Haytham, *see* Alhazen.

Ibn Muʿādh, *see* Abhomadi Malfegeyr.

Ibn Rushd, *see* Averroes.

Ibn Sīnā, *see* Avicenna.

Jolivet, R., 'La doctrine augustinienne de l'illumination', *Revue de philosophie*, NS 1 (1930), 382–502.

Jourdain, Charles, *Excursions historiques et philosophiques à travers le moyen âge*. Paris, 1888.

Kindī, Abū Yūsuf Yaʿqūb ibn Isḥāq al-, *De aspectibus*, edd. Axel Anthon Björnbo and Sebastian Vogl, in 'Alkindi, Tideus und Pseudo-Euklid. Drei optische Werke', *Abhandlungen zur Geschichte der mathematischen Wissenschaften*, 26. 3 (1912), 3–70.

— *De radiis*. 'Al-Kindi, De radiis', edd. M.-Th. d'Alverny and F. Hudry, *Archives d'histoire doctrinale et littéraire du moyen âge*, 41 (1974), 139–260.

— *Propagations of Ray: The Oldest Arabic Manuscript about Optics (Burning Mirror), from Yaʿkub ibn Ishaq al-Kindi*, trans. Mohamed Yahia Haschmi. Aleppo. 1967.

Kirk, G. S. and Raven, J. E. (edd.), *The Presocratic Philosophers*. Cambridge, 1957.

Klein, Franz-Norbert, *Die Lichtterminologie bei Philon von Alexandrien und in den hermetischen Schriften*. Leiden, 1962.

Koch, Josef, 'Über die Lichtsymbolik im Bereich der Philosophie und der Mystik des Mittelalters', *Studium Generale*, 13 (1960), 653–70.

Körner, F., 'Abstraktion oder Illumination? Das ontologische Problem der augustinischen Sinneserkenntnis', *Recherches Augustiniennes*, 2 (1962), 81–109.

Laistner, M. L. W., *Thought and Letters in Western Europe, A.D. 500-900*, rev. edn. London, 1957.

Lejeune, Albert, *Euclide et Ptolémée. Deux stades de l'optique géométrique grecque* (Université de Louvain, Recueil de travaux d'histoire et de philologie (Ser. 3), 31). Louvain, 1948.

— *Recherches sur la catoptrique grecque* (Académie royale de Belgique, Classe de lettres et des sciences morales et politiques, Mémoires, 2. 2). Brussels, 1957.

Lindberg, David C., 'Alhazen's Theory of Vision and Its Reception in the West', *Isis*, 58 (1967), 321-41.

— 'Alkindi's Critique of Euclid's Theory of Vision', *Isis*, 62 (1971), 469-89.

— *A Catalogue of Medieval and Renaissance Optical Manuscripts* (Subsidia Mediaevalia, 4). Toronto, 1975.

— 'The Cause of Refraction in Medieval Optics', *British Journal for the History of Science*, 4 (1968-9), 23-38.

— (ed. and trans.), *John Pecham and the Science of Optics: Perspectiva communis*. Madison, Wis., 1970.

— 'Lines of Influence in Thirteenth-Century Optics: Bacon, Witelo, and Pecham', *Speculum*, 46 (1971), 66-83.

— 'Medieval Latin Theories of the Speed of Light', in René Taton (preface), *Roemer et la vitesse de la lumière*, pp. 45-72. Paris, 1978.

— 'On the Applicability of Mathematics to Nature: Roger Bacon and His Predecessors', *British Journal for the History of Science*, 15 (1982), 3-25.

— 'Optics and Theories of Vision', *Dictionary of the Middle Ages* [forthcoming].

— 'A Reconsideration of Roger Bacon's Theory of Pinhole Images', *Archive for History of Exact Sciences*, 6 (1970), 214-23.

— 'Roger Bacon's Theory of the Rainbow: Progress or Regress?', *Isis*, 57 (1966), 235-48.

— (ed.), *Science in the Middle Ages*. Chicago, 1978.

— 'The Science of Optics', in id. (ed.), *Science in the Middle Ages*, pp. 338-68. Chicago, 1978.

— *Theories of Vision from al-Kindī to Kepler*. Chicago, 1976.

— 'The Theory of Pinhole Images from Antiquity to the Thirteenth Century', *Archive for History of Exact Sciences*, 5 (1968), 154-76.

— 'The Theory of Pinhole Images in the Fourteenth Century', *Archive for History of Exact Sciences*, 6 (1970), 299-325.

— 'The Transmission of Greek and Arabic Learning to the West', in id. (ed.), *Science in the Middle Ages*, pp. 52-90. Chicago, 1978.

Little, A. G., 'Introduction on Roger Bacon's Life and Works', in id. (ed.), *Roger Bacon Essays*, pp. 1-31. Oxford, 1914.

— 'Roger Bacon', *Proceedings of the British Academy*, 14 (1928), 265-96.

— (ed.), *Roger Bacon Essays*. Oxford, 1914.

— 'Roger Bacon's Works', in id. (ed.), *Roger Bacon Essays*, pp. 375-426. Oxford, 1914.

— *Studies in English Franciscan History*. Manchester, 1917.

Lynch, Lawrence E., 'The Doctrine of Divine Ideas and Illumination in Robert Grosseteste, Bishop of Lincoln', *Mediaeval Studies*, 3 (1941), 161-73.

MacLaren, Bruce R., 'A Critical Edition and Translation, with Commentary, of John Pecham's *Tractatus de Sphera*'. Ph.D. dissertation, University of Wisconsin, 1978.

Maier, Anneliese, 'Das Problem der "Species sensibiles in medio" und die neue Naturphilosophie des 14. Jahrhunderts', *Freiburger Zeitschrift für Philosophie und Theologie*, 10 (1963), 3–32. Reprint, in Anneliese Maier, *Ausgehendes Mittelalter: Gesammelte Aufsätze zur Geistesgeschichte des 14. Jahrhunderts*, ii. 419–51, Rome, 1967.

Markus, R. A., 'Augustine: Reason and Illumination', in A. H. Armstrong (ed.)., *The Cambridge History of Later Greek and Early Medieval Philosophy*, pp. 362–73. Cambridge, 1970.

— ' "Imago" and "Similitudo" in Augustine', *Revue des études augustiniennes*, 10 (1964), 125–43.

Marshall, Peter, 'Nicole Oresme on the Nature, Reflection, and Speed of Light', *Isis*, 72 (1981), 357–74.

McCarthy, Edward R., 'Medieval Light Theory and Optics and Duns Scotus' Treatment of Light in D. 13 of Book II of His Commentary on the Sentences'. Ph.D. dissertation, City University of New York, 1976.

McKeon, Charles K., *A Study of the Summa philosophiae of the Pseudo-Grosseteste*. New York, 1948.

Meyer, Gilles, O.F.M., 'En quel sens peut-on parler de "méthode scientifique" chez Roger Bacon?', *Bulletin de littérature ecclésiastique*, 53 (1952), 3–25, 77–98.

Michaud-Quantin, Pierre, *Études sur le vocabulaire philosophique du moyen âge*. Rome, 1970.

Migne, J.-P. (ed.), *Patrologiae cursus completus, series Latina*. 221 volumes. Paris, 1844–64.

Molland, A. G., 'John Dumbleton and the Status of Geometrical Optics', *Actes du XIIIᵉ Congrès international d'histoire des sciences, Moscou, 18–24 août 1971*, 3–4, pp. 125–30. Moscow, 1974.

— 'Roger Bacon as Magician', *Traditio*, 30 (1974), 445–60.

— 'Roger Bacon: Magic and the Multiplication of Species', *Paideia* [forthcoming].

Moorman, John, *A History of the Franciscan Order from its Origins to the Year 1517*. Oxford, 1968.

Morewedge, Parviz, 'The Logic of Emanationism and Ṣūfism in the Philosophy of Ibn Sīnā (Avicenna)', *Journal of the American Oriental Society*, 91 (1971), 467–76; 92 (1972), 1–18.

Mugler, Charles, *Dictionnaire historique de la terminologie optique des grecs: Douze siècles de dialogues avec lumière*. Paris, 1964.

— 'Sur l'histoire de quelques définitions de la géométrie grecque et les rapports entre la géométrie et l'optique', *L'antiquité classique*, 26 (1957), 331–45.

Munk, S., *Mélanges de philosophie juive et arabe*. Paris, 1859.

Murphy, N. R., 'The "Simile of Light" in Plato's *Republic*', *Classical Quarterly*, 26 (1932), 93–102; 28 (1934), 211–13.

Nascimento, Carlos Arthur Ribeiro do, 'Une théorie des opérations naturelles fondée sur l'optique: le *De multiplicatione specierum* de Roger Bacon'. Ph.D. dissertation, Université de Montréal, 1975.

North, J. D., *see* Crombie, A. C.

Notopoulos, James A., 'The Symbolism of the Sun and Light in the Republic of Plato', *Classical Philology*, 39 (1944), 163–72.

O'Neill, R. F., 'Quality', *New Catholic Encyclopedia*, xii. 2–5. New York, 1967.

Paravicini Bagliani, Agostino, 'Witelo et la science optique à la cour pontificale de Viterbe (1277)', *Mélanges de l'école française de Rome (moyen âge-temps modernes)*, 87 (1975), 425–53.

Pecham, John, *Tractatus de perspectiva*, ed. David C. Lindberg (Franciscan Institute Publications, Text Series, 16). St. Bonaventure, N.Y., 1972.

Philo Judaeus, *Philo with an English Translation*, trans. F. H. Colson and G. H. Whitaker. 10 volumes. London, 1929–62.

— *Works*, trans. C. D. Yonge. 4 volumes. London, 1954–5.

Picavet, François, 'La place de Roger Bacon parmi les philosophes du XIIIe siècle', in A. G. Little (ed.), *Roger Bacon Essays*, pp. 55–88. Oxford, 1914.

Pinborg, Jan, 'Roger Bacon on Signs: A Newly Recovered Part of the Opus Maius', *Miscellanea Mediaevalia*, 13 (1981), 403–12.

Plato. *The Republic of Plato*, trans. Francis M. Cornford. London, 1941.

Plotinus, *The Enneads*, trans. Stephen MacKenna, 2nd edn. rev. by B. S. Page. London, 1956.

— *Plotinus with an English Translation*, trans. A. H. Armstrong. 3 volumes. London, 1966–7.

Porphyry the Phoenician, *Isagoge*, trans. Edward W. Warren. Toronto, 1975.

Proclus, *The Elements of Theology*, ed. and trans. E. R. Dodds, 2nd edn. Oxford, 1963.

— *Théologie platonicienne*, edd. H. D. Saffrey and L. G. Westerink. 3 volumes. Paris, 1968–78.

Pseudo-Aristotle, *see* (Anonymous).

Pseudo-Dionysius. *Dionysius the Areopagite On the Divine Names and the Mystical Theology*, trans. C. E. Rolt. New York, 1920.

— *The Works of Dionysius the Areopagite*, trans. John Parker. 2 volumes. London, 1897–9.

Pseudo-Euclid, *De speculis*, edd. Axel Anthon Björnbo and Sebastian Vogl, in 'Alkindi, Tideus und Pseudo-Euklid. Drei optische Werke', *Abhandlungen zur Geschichte der mathematischen Wissenschaften*, 26. 3 (1912), 97–119.

Ptolemy, *Handbuch der astronomie*, trans. Karl Manitius. 2 volumes. Leipzig, 1912–13.

— *L'Optique de Claude Ptolémée dans la version latine d'après l'arabe de l'émir Eugène de Sicile*, ed. Albert Lejeune (Université de Louvain, Recueil de travaux d'histoire et de philologie (Ser. 4), 8). Louvain, 1956.

Quentin, Albrecht, *Naturkenntnisse und Naturanschauungen bei Wilhelm von Auvergne* (Arbor scientiarum: Beiträge zur Wissenschaftsgeschichte (Ser. A), 5). Hildesheim, 1976.

Rashed, Roshdi, 'Optique géométrique et doctrine optique chez Ibn Al Haytham', *Archive for History of Exact Sciences*, 6 (1970), 271–98.

Rosen, Edward, 'Did Roger Bacon Invent Eyeglasses?', *Archives internationales d'histoire des sciences*, 7 (1954), 3–15.

Sabra, A. I., 'The Authorship of the *Liber de crepusculis*, an Eleventh-Century Work on Atmospheric Refraction', *Isis*, 58 (1967), 77–85.

— 'Sensation and Inference in Alhazen's Theory of Visual Perception', in Peter Machamer and Robert G. Turnbull (edd.), *Studies in Perception: Interrelations in the History and Philosophy of Science*, pp. 160–85. Columbus, Ohio, 1978.

Sage, Athanase, 'La dialectique de l'illumination', *Recherches Augustiniennes*, 2 (1962), 111–23.

Saint-Pierre, Bernard, 'La physique de la vision dans l'antiquité: Contribution à l'établissement des sources anciennes de l'optique médiévale'. Ph.D. dissertation, Université de Montréal, 1972.

Sandys, J. E., 'Roger Bacon', *Proceedings of the British Academy*, 6 (1913–14), 371–88.

Sayili, Aydin M., 'The "Observation Well" ', in *Actes du VIIe Congrès international d'histoire des sciences*, pp. 542–50. Jerusalem, 1953.

Seneca, Lucius Annaeus. *Physical Science in the Time of Nero, being a translation of the Quaestiones Naturales of Seneca*, trans. John Clarke. London, 1910.

Sharp, D. E., *Franciscan Philosophy at Oxford in the Thirteenth Century*. Oxford, 1930.

Smith, A. Mark, 'Getting the Big Picture in Thirteenth-Century Perspectivist Optics', *Isis*, 72 (1981), 568–89.

— 'Saving the Appearances of the Appearances: The Foundations of Classical Geometrical Optics', *Archive for History of Exact Sciences*, 24 (1981), 73–100.

— 'Witelo on the Principles of Reflection: A Critical Edition and English Translation, with Notes and Commentary, of Book V of Witelo's *Perspectiva*'. Ph.D. dissertation, University of Wisconsin, 1976.

Simson, Otto von, *The Gothic Cathedral: Origins of Gothic Architecture and the Medieval Concept of Order*. New York, 1956.

Steele, Robert, 'Roger Bacon and the State of Science in the Thirteenth Century', in Charles Singer (ed.), *Studies in the History and Method of Science*, ii. 121–50. Oxford, 1921.

— 'Roger Bacon as Professor: A Student's Notes', *Isis*, 20 (1933), 53–71.

Steenberghen, Fernand van, *Aristotle in the West*, trans. Leonard Johnston. Louvain, 1955.

Steinschneider, Moritz, *Die europäischen Übersetzungen aus dem Arabischen bis Mitte des 17. Jahrhunderts*. Graz, 1956.

Stump, Eleonore, *see* Boethius.

Tachau, Katherine H., 'Vision and Certitude in the Age of Ockham'. Ph.D. dissertation, University of Wisconsin, 1981.

Tarrant, Dorothy, 'Greek Metaphors of Light', *Classical Quarterly*, 54 (1960), 181–7.

Thābit ibn Qurra, *see* Carmody, Francis J.

Theisen, Wilfred R. '*Liber de visu*: The Greco-Latin Translation of Euclid's *Optics*', *Mediaeval Studies*, 41 (1979), 44–105.

— 'The Medieval Tradition of Euclid's *Optics*'. Ph.D. dissertation, University of Wisconsin, 1972.

Theodoric of Freiberg, *De iride et radialibus impressionibus*, ed. Joseph Würschmidt (*Beiträge zur Geschichte der Philosophie des Mittelalters*, 12. 5–6). Münster, 1914.

Theodosius of Bithynia, *Sphaerica*, ed. J. L. Heiberg (*Abhandlungen der Gesellschaft der Wissenschaften zu Göttingen*, Phil.-hist. Klasse, NS 19. 3). Berlin, 1927.

Thonnard, François-Joseph, 'La notion de lumière en philosophie augustinienne', *Recherches Augustiniennes*, 2 (1962), 125–75.

Thorndike, Lynn, *A History of Magic and Experimental Science*. 8 volumes. New York, 1923–56.

— 'Roger Bacon and Experimental Method in the Middle Ages', *The Philosophical Review*, 23 (1914), 271–98.

— (ed. and trans.), *The Sphere of Sacrobosco and Its Commentators*. Chicago, 1949.

— 'The True Roger Bacon', *American Historical Review*, 21 (1915–16), 237–57, 468–80.

Tideus, *De speculis*, in 'Alkindi, Tideus und Pseudo-Euklid. Drei optische Werke', edd. Axel Anthon Björnbo and Sebastian Vogl, *Abhandlungen zur Geschichte der mathematischen Wissenschaften*, 26. 3 (1912), 73–94.

Turbayne, Colin M., 'Grosseteste and an Ancient Optical Principle', *Isis*, 50 (1959), 467–72.

Unguru, Sabetai, *see* Fisher, N. W. *and* Witelo.

Vandewalle, Charles Borromée, O.F.M., *Roger Bacon dans l'histoire de la philologie*. Paris, 1929.

Vescovini, Graziella Federici, *Studi sulla prospettiva medievale*. Turin, 1965.

Vogl, Sebastian, 'Roger Bacons Lehre von der sinnlichen Species und vom Sehvorgange', in A. G. Little (ed.), *Roger Bacon Essays*, pp. 205–27. Oxford, 1914.

Wallace, William A., O.P., *Causality and Scientific Explanation*, i: *Medieval and Early Classical Science*. Ann Arbor, 1972.

Wallis, R. T., *Neoplatonism*. London, 1972.

Wedel, Theodore O., *The Mediaeval Attitude Toward Astrology*. New Haven, 1920.

Weisheipl, James A., O.P., 'Albertus Magnus and the Oxford Platonists', *Proceedings of the American Catholic Philosophical Association*, 32 (1958), 124–39.

— (ed.), *Albertus Magnus and the Sciences: Commemorative Essays 1980*. Toronto, 1980.

Wiedemann, Eilhard, 'Roger Bacon und seine Verdienste um die Optik', in A. G. Little (ed.), *Roger Bacon Essays*, pp. 185–203. Oxford, 1914.

— 'Ueber das Sehen durch eine Kugel bei den Arabern', *Annalen der Physik und Chemie*, NS 39 (1890), 565–76.

Wingate, S. D., *The Mediaeval Latin Versions of the Aristotelian Scientific Corpus, with Special Reference to the Biological Works*. London, 1931.

Witelo, *Perspectiva*, in Friedrich Risner (ed.), *Opticae thesaurus Alhazeni Arabis libri septem . . . Item Vitellonis Thuringopoloni libri X*. Basel, 1572. Reprint, with an introduction by David C. Lindberg, New York, 1972.

— *Witelonis Perspectivae liber primus: Book I of Witelo's Perspectiva*, ed. Sabetai Unguru (Studia Copernicana, 15). Wrocław, 1977.

Würschmidt, J. 'Roger Bacons Art des wissenschaftlichen Arbeitens, dargestellt nach seiner Schrift *De speculis*', in A. G. Little (ed.), *Roger Bacon Essays*, pp. 229–39. Oxford, 1914.

Index of Manuscripts

General Index

Abhomadi Malfegeyr, *De crepusculis*, xxxiv, 175
Accident, 23–5, 33, 43, 89
Accidental multiplication, *see* Radiation, secondary
Action, according to lines, angles, and figures, 229–53, 285–7, 301–5
  strength of, lxx–lxxi, 229–53, 277, 285–7, 301–5
Active potentiality, 47
Adam Marsh, xviii
Aeschylus, xxxv
Agent, action of, as a whole, 67, 355–6
  as recipient, 57–9
  celestial, 45, 67, 71–3, 77, 83
  mode of action of, lx–lxi, lxvi, 45–69, 77–91, 345
  size of, lx, 57, 63, 67, 353–6
  spiritual, 45, 83–5
Agriculture, 349
Albategni, xxxiv, 123
Alchemy, 349
Alexander of Hales, xvii
Alhazen, xxxiv, lxx, 33, 95, 99, 109, 123, 127, 129, 137, 205, 207, 211, 217, 366
  De aspectibus (Perspectiva), xxxiii, xlix, 5, 21, 35, 39, 43, 107, 111, 113, 121, 125, 133, 139, 199, 203, 209, 221, 235, 265, 347, 359
  De speculis comburentibus, xxxiii, xxxv, 137, 147, 155, 333, 337, 347
Alkindi, *see* Kindī, al-
Alpharabius, *see* Fārābī, al-
Alteration, 25, 65, 71–5, 221, 348
Anaxagoras, 59, 61
Angel, 179
Anonymous, *Notule de speculis*, lxxix
Antichrist, xxiv
Apollonius, 348
  De pyramidibus, xxiv, 347
Aries, 123
Aristotle, xxxiii–xxxiv, xlviii–xlix, liv, lvi, lxvi–lxviii, 25–7, 35, 47, 53, 61, 63, 193, 219, 237, 347–51
  Categories, 29
  De anima, xvii, 5, 7, 11, 19, 29, 45, 47, 73, 75, 81, 97, 193, 213, 223, 257, 356
  De animalibus, xvii, 33, 103, 195

De caelo et mundo, xvii, 61, 73, 187, 221, 235, 255, 360
De generatione et corruptione, xvii, 29, 33, 49, 59, 71, 77, 79, 91, 93, 131, 261, 359
De memoria et reminiscentia, 195
De morte et vita, 255
De sensu et sensato, xvii, 17, 27, 61, 225
De somno et vigilia, 91, 359
Metaphysics, xvii, 23, 31, 49, 71, 73, 75, 179, 233, 359
Meteorology, 33, 73, 77, 79, 97, 360
Physics, xvii, 21, 25, 29, 49, 57, 59, 61, 65, 67, 69, 77, 91, 179, 207, 215, 221, 223, 229, 261, 353–6, 358–9
Topics, 185–7
See also Pseudo-Aristotle
Arithmetic, 349
Armillary sphere, 123
Armstrong, A. H., xxxix
Artificial day, 261, 265, 391
Astrology, xliv–xlv, 348–9
Astronomy, 349
Atomists, lxvi
Augmentation and diminution, 37, 179, 348
Augustine of Hippo, St., xxxiii, xxxix–xlii, xlviii–xlix, liv
  De trinitate, lv
Avendauth, xlviii
Averroes, xxxiii–xxxiv, lxvii, 23, 33, 61, 189, 193, 223, 259, 347–8, 350, 359
  De anima, lxvii, 87, 131, 193
  De caelo et mundo, 73, 235–7, 259, 355
  De sensu et sensato, lxvii, 193
  De substantia orbis, 259
  Metaphysics, 59, 356
  Physics, 355, 358
Avicebron, xxxv
  Fons vitae, xlvi–xlix, liv
Avicenna, xxxiii–xxxiv, xlvi, lxvii, 33, 103, 189, 193, 195, 347–8, 350
  De anima, 5, 77, 195, 225, 365
  De animalibus, 33, 193
  Metaphysics, xlix, 85
  Physics, 87
  Shifā, xlviii

Bacon, and mathematical science, vii, xx
  apocalyptic views of, xxiv